14371

ALL ABOUT
BETTE

Her Life from A to Z

RANDALL RIESE

CB
CONTEMPORARY
BOOKS
CHICAGO

Library of Congress Cataloging-in-Publication Data

Riese, Randall.
    All about Bette : her life from A–Z / Randall Riese.
       p.   cm.
    Includes bibliographical references.
    ISBN 0-8092-4111-0
    1. Davis, Bette, 1908–   .   2. Motion picture actors and actresses—United
States—Biography.   I. Title.
    PN2287.D32R44   1993
    791.43′028′092—dc20
    [B]   93-27871
                                                CIP

Some of the material in this book was culled from the Warner Brothers Archives at the University of Southern California. The material is copyrighted by Warner Brothers and is reprinted herein with permission.

Published by Contemporary Books, Inc.
Two Prudential Plaza, Chicago, Illinois 60601-6790
Manufactured in the United States of America
International Standard Book Number: 0-8092-4111-0
10   9   8   7   6   5   4   3   2   1

To Mark Goins and Neal Hitchens

"Margo is a great star. Margo is a true star.
She never was nor will be anything more or anything less."

Addison DeWitt, *All About Eve*

CONTENTS

ACKNOWLEDGMENTS

Given the magnitude and duration of Bette Davis's career, the development of this work was an arduous but ultimately rewarding undertaking. For their various contributions, I would like to thank the following:

The Academy of Motion Picture Arts and Sciences
Leith Adams, Warner Brothers Archives, USC
Clark Allen
Gene Allen, Society of Motion Picture Art Directors
Lindsay Anderson
Jack Artenstein
Charles Bowden
Larry Cohen
Frank Corsaro
Norman Corwin
Nancy Crossman
Matt de Haven
Christopher Esposito
Christopher Frith, Lincoln Center for the Performing Arts
Mark Goins
Gordon Hessler
Neal Hitchens
Peter Hoffman
Gerilee Hundt
Waris Hussein
Aaron Kass
Irwin Kass
Linda Laucella
Paula Lawrence
Joan Lorring
The Margaret Herrick Library
Christopher Nickens
Judith Noack, Warner Brothers
Marvin Paige
Harvey Plotnick
Cyndy Raucci
Billy Roy
Irving Schneider
Irving Sudrow
Lise Wood

INTRODUCTION

The image is eternal. The hips swinging, one hand affixed to one hip while the other arm swings from the elbow, this way, then that. She struts or sashays across a room, depending on her mood, like a drag queen in heat. She then freezes in a stance, high-heeled feet planted apart. She raises her cigarette, puts it to her lips, fixes someone somewhere with a drop-dead stare, and then blows. And, oh, yes, the eyes are popped. "Fasten your seat belts," she says, spitting the words out like sharp, pointed daggers of diction. "It's going to be a bumpy night!"

She made a hundred films, give or take, some among the best Hollywood has ever produced (*The Little Foxes, All About Eve*), some among the most beloved of all time in the hearts of filmgoers (*Dark Victory, Now, Voyager*). Arguably, no other actor in the history of the American cinema has produced a more impressive portfolio of films than she or played a wider diversity of roles. She played bitches and prostitutes and virgins and queens and mothers from the Bronx with equal aplomb. And, oh, what glorious lines she has spoken, punctuated with her husky, staccato delivery and fervent puffs on her ever-present cigarette. "I'd love to kiss you, but I just washed my hair"; "Oh, Jerry, don't let's ask for the moon—when we have the stars"; and, of course, "What a dump."

She was Margo Channing. She was Charlotte Vale. She was Mildred Rogers. She was Julie Marsden. She was Baby Jane Hudson. And she was Elizabeth I—twice.

This massive volume, which represents three years of research, is a reaffirming compendium of her unparalleled career. She was—is—and will always be Bette Davis. "Bette Davis"—the name alone connotes *star*. In an age when the term seems to apply to anyone on the latest Aaron Spelling television show about teenage angst, Bette Davis recalls to mind what a *star* really is. She was brilliant, and, yes, she was "difficult." She was loved by audiences and loathed by directors. She would amend that, of course, to read "by *bad* directors." But it was her temperament, in part, that gave her her dynamic, that set her apart. On the very first film she ever made, a scene called for Bette to diaper a baby. Upon reading the script, Bette insisted on knowing the *sex* of the baby. "What the hell difference does it make?" the astonished director shot back at her. For Bette, it made a difference. It always would. There has never been, nor is there ever likely to be, another one like her. And this book is *All About Bette*.

A

NORMA ABERNETHY

Norma Abernethy was, for years, a proverbial pain in Bette Davis's side. Since at least October 1979, Abernethy made persistent phone calls and wrote long and urgent letters to Bette, claiming to be her daughter. According to Bette, Abernethy threatened to report their mother-daughter relationship to the press unless she was in some way compensated. The situation escalated to a point that, according to court documents, "on or about July 27, 1980" Abernethy showed up at Bette's West Hollywood apartment and proceeded to knock loudly on the door, demanding entrance. Bette subsequently filed a restraining order against Abernethy, saying, "Ms. Abernethy is a pathetic individual and I of course ignored the letters and did nothing to encourage her attempts to contact me. Unfortunately, I cannot ignore the situation any longer. . . ." Still, Abernethy continued to pursue Bette through 1984, at which point she suddenly stopped, much to Bette's great relief. Abernethy's claim that Bette Davis was her mother has never been substantiated.

ABORTIONS

Bette had at least two, and perhaps more, abortions while married to Ham Nelson in the 1930s. They were performed, reportedly, at the urging of her mother and husband, when her career was just burgeoning. Bette had another abortion after her divorce from Nelson, during the 1940 shooting of *The Letter*. As for her political and religious views on abortion rights, Bette told *Playboy* in 1982, "I believe abortion is better than having 10,000,000 children you can't support. . . . the Catholic church's big argument being that you're killing a human being. Perfect nonsense! Ridiculous, this murder thing. There is no child involved if you get an abortion at one month. . . . There are many great women who were just never meant to be mothers, that's all."

THE ACADEMY OF MOTION PICTURE ARTS AND SCIENCES

On November 7, 1941, while she was shooting *In This Our Life* (which she was miserable making, by the way) for John Huston, Bette Davis became the first woman ever elected president of the Academy of Motion Picture Arts and Sciences. The previous evening she had received a phone call from academy executive Jimmy Johnston, who gave her the news. Bette had been nominated to the post by Darryl Zanuck, for whom she had worked in the early 1930s, and was voted in by the academy's board of governors, which included David O. Selznick, Walter Wanger, Frank Capra, and Rosalind Russell. Bette succeeded Wanger, who was then demoted to first vice president. From the set Bette proclaimed, "Naturally, it's a great honor. But it was so completely unanticipated that I hardly know what to say."

Bette almost immediately ruffled the film academy's feathers. It seems that there was some talk that year among the board members that the group *not* hold its annual Academy Awards dinner because of the ongoing war in Europe. Bette had another idea. She proposed that the awards go on as scheduled but that they take place in a large theater (at the time the awards dinner was still an intimate affair usually held in a hotel banquet room) and that the public (*the public!*) be invited to attend at an admission cost of $25 each, with proceeds going to the British War Relief.

The board of governors was aghast. On December 17, 1941, the board announced that the awards dinner would not take place that year. As *The Hollywood Reporter* noted, "Bejeweled stars with trailing ermine, and all the hothouse trappings that are traditional for that internationally renowned night is [sic] being sloughed off in view of existing war conditions."

Ten days later, citing poor health and overwork, and despite a clichéd warning from Zanuck ("If you resign, you'll never work in this town again"), Bette announced her resignation as president. The academy's public stance was that she had not been prepared to handle the onslaught of responsibilities that went with the prestigious title. She was promptly replaced by her predecessor, Walter Wanger.

On January 30, 1942, after a barrage of public outcry over the cancellation of the awards dinner, the academy announced that it was reinstating the ceremony as previously scheduled. And two years later the academy moved the awards proceedings to Grauman's Chinese Theater in Hollywood. As often happened in her life and career, Bette Davis had the last and deciding word.

Over the years other celebrity presidents of the academy have included Douglas Fairbanks, Gregory Peck, and Karl Malden.

ACTING

Actors are divided into two definite groups: those who have the ability, like Claude Rains, to transfer themselves into a character, and those who don't. Among the stars who are transference actors are Helen Hayes, Paul Muni, Jimmy Cagney, Spencer Tracy, Judith Anderson, Ralph Richardson, Robert Newton, John Gielgud, Alec Guinness, and Celia Johnson. Among the newer American actors there are three who possess the magic quality of transference— Marlon Brando, Julie Harris and Kim Stanley.

On the other hand, the nontransference actors are equally important to Hollywood—perhaps even more so because their box office appeal is the backbone of the industry. This group consists of terribly attractive people who play themselves. Joan Crawford is the prime wonderful example of this group. Others are Gary Cooper, Clark Gable and Marilyn Monroe.

Bette Davis, Collier's, *December 9, 1955*

I think acting should look as if we were working a *little*. I think we should be a bit larger than life—a little bit theatrical. [And] you must love the actual sweat more than the lights and the glamour. This you must love the most.

Bette Davis

As a teenage girl in New England, Bette Davis had no aspirations to become an actress. Rather, she fancied herself a dancer flying across the stage in costumes of flowing chiffon. It was only after seeing a performance of *The Wild Duck* with Blanche Yurka and Peg Entwistle that she redirected her considerable ambition toward acting. She wanted art, but she also wanted fame.

In later years, when asked for advice on technique, as she frequently was, Bette would tell aspiring actors that developing concentration—the ability not to be distracted by anything or anyone—was of the greatest importance to an actor. One of her techniques, learned from George Arliss, was to memorize an entire script. Film acting is commonly shot out of sequence, and Bette felt it essential that actors keep every scene being shot in its proper context. As for acting schools, Bette recommended them only for the basic teachings: how to walk, how to talk, how to project. She believed far more in experience. Stock companies, she would tout, were the greatest foundation for an actor's career. She was particularly disdainful of actors who attained sudden "stardom" via a television series, without having paid their dues, without having learned or mastered the craft. "Nothing can teach you to act," Bette was fond of saying, "like acting."

THE ACTORS STUDIO

Bette was never a member of Lee Strasberg's famed Actors Studio, nor was she a proponent of The Method. In a 1959 interview Bette acknowledged, "I am afraid that I am not a particular fan of The Method. The way I see it, the principal function of the actor is to 'give a show' to the audience. There is certainly no point in everyone having the time of their realistic little lives in a film if they are boring the pants off the customers." She would also quip that anyone who wanted to see reality could simply stand on a neighborhood street corner—for free. But, she conceded, "I am willing to admit that The Method has produced some fine artists who have given exciting performances. It's just not for me."

Shortly after making that statement, Bette was cast in the Broadway-bound production of Tennessee Williams's *The Night of the Iguana* in which both her director and her leading man were proponents and practitioners of The Method. The play was a horrendous experience for Bette (detailed later in these pages), further tainting her impression of the Actors Studio.

Shortly before her death in 1989, Bette told a reporter, with her distinctly clipped delivery, "I don't draw upon any-thing for *my* performance. That is what *they* teach at the Act-ors Stu-di-o. They tell you to think of a be-loved pet that di-ed. Oh, no, no, no! I just played the char-ac-ter! I didn't *have* to get back to my child-hood for gui-dance!"

ADVERTISEMENTS

As was typical in the twenties and thirties, Bette's image was used without her consent to promote various, sometimes innocuous products tied to the opening of her latest stage play or picture. Probably the earliest print ads she appeared in were for Hanan's Shoes and Hosiery in Rochester, New York. At the time Bette was the ingenue with George Cukor's stock company, the Temple Players. One ad read, "You probably wouldn't recognize Miss Bette Davis, star of the Temple Players, from her nether limbs. . . . As you see, she prefers Hanan's brown suede tie-Oxford with a lizard trim." During her years at Warners, she was no better served. One typical ad, for Quaker Puffed Rice, featured a photograph of Bette with the accompanying copy, "Breakfast fit for a queen of the screen."

In later years, after the courts stepped in and declared the practice of using an unconsenting star's image to promote a product illegal, Bette was far more discriminating in her endorsements. Still, she was not above occasionally hawking such products as Jim Beam liquor (in an ad with Robert Wagner) and Max Factor cosmetics.

THE AFRICAN QUEEN

On April 22, 1947, top Warners producer Henry Blanke wrote in a letter to Bette that he had just finished reading a script called *The African Queen*.

Adapted from the novel by C. S. Forester, the script featured the challenging role of a prim, repressed missionary, which Blanke thought would be a good change of pace for Bette. Blanke, who had produced numerous pictures for Bette, was so enthused about the script that he enclosed with his letter a copy of it for Bette to read with the instruction "Please let me know what you think of it."

She loved it. She was also excited about the prospect of working with James Mason, with whom Blanke wanted to pair her. In fact Bette Davis would most likely have made *The African Queen* in 1947, if not for one factor. On May 1, 1947, she gave birth to a baby girl, Barbara Davis Sherry. She still might have done the film if it had not required location work and considerable physical exertion. And so she turned it down, or rather placed it on hold.

Before and after her departure from Warner in 1949, Bette actively sought the role. But by that time the woman whom Bette considered her primary acting rival, Katharine Hepburn, was also interested in it.

The African Queen (1951) was produced by Sam Spiegel, directed by John Huston, and written by James Agee. In addition to Hepburn, who received a Best Actress Oscar nomination for her performance, the film starred Humphrey Bogart (Best Actor Oscar winner), Robert Morley, Peter Bull, and Theodore Bikel.

THE AGENTS

"I've had most of them from time to time."
Bette Davis on agents

The following is an alphabetical list of just some of the agents who, over the years, represented Bette Davis:

Martin Baum	Leland Hayward	Arthur Lyons	Lew Wasserman
David Begelman	Paul Kohner	Marion Rosenberg	Corlyn Wood*
Michael Black	Robert Lantz	Myron Selznick*	Vernon Wood*
Jane Broder	Mike Levee	William Shiffrin	
Kurt Frings	Lester Linsk*	Jules Stein	

*business manager/agent

BRIAN AHERNE

Aherne costarred as the blond and bearded Maximillian opposite Bette's Carlota in the 1939 historical picture *Juarez* (for which he was awarded a Best Supporting Actor Oscar nomination). Aherne later performed opposite Bette in a radio broadcast of *Elizabeth the Queen*. Still, there was no love lost between the two, with Bette contemptuous of what she perceived to be Aherne's physical vanity, a trait she disliked in women and despised in men. In later years she would frequently relate an incident that happened on the set of *Juarez*. Bette complimented Aherne on the blond beard he had donned for the film. Thinking that Bette was sarcastically criticizing his prebeard appearance, Aherne retorted that she should retain the black wig that she wore for the role of Carlota.

Brian Aherne (1902–1986) appeared in numerous films beginning with the silent *The Eleventh Commandment* (1924) and ending with *Rosie!* (1967). In between were such films as *The Constant Nymph* (1934), *My Sister Eileen* (1942), and *I Confess* (1953). His performance in *Juarez* is generally regarded as the best of his career.

CHARLES AINSLEY

Bette's amorous suitor in Rochester, New York, circa the fall and winter of 1929. The relationship was serious enough for young Ainsley to propose marriage to Bette, who, at the time, was the ingenue in the Cukor-Kondolf Repertory Company. By the time Bette opened with *The Earth Between* off Broadway, the two were engaged to be married. However, during a tour of Ibsen's *The Wild Duck* a short time later, Bette received a letter in her backstage dressing room breaking off their engagement. Marriage to an actress, it seems, was apparently unacceptable to her prospective in-laws.

ROBERT ALDRICH

Director who almost single-handedly revived Bette's film career (and pocketbook) in the 1960s. Aldrich produced and directed Bette in *What Ever Happened to Baby Jane?* (1962) and *Hush . . . Hush, Sweet Charlotte* (1964).

Robert Aldrich (1918–1983) directed films including *The Big Knife* (also produced, 1955), *The Dirty Dozen* (1967), *The Killing of Sister George* (also produced, 1968), and *The Longest Yard* (1974).

> "These ladies [Davis and Crawford] are pros. They were polite to each other but the tension was terrific. Most of the time I felt like an umpire at the World Series."
>
> *Robert Aldrich*

> I was fond of Robert, . . . but he had strange lapses of taste. I thought the scene in *Charlotte* in which the head bounces down the stairs was a bit much.
>
> *Bette Davis*

"ALFRED HITCHCOCK PRESENTS"

Bette Davis starred in "Out There, Darkness," a 1959 episode of the durable television suspense series "Alfred Hitchcock Presents." The show was directed and photographed by Bette's old friends Paul Henreid and Ernest Haller, respectively.

ALL ABOUT EVE ★★★★

20th Century–Fox
1950   138 minutes   bw
Directed by: Joseph L. Mankiewicz
Produced by: Darryl F. Zanuck
Screenplay by: Joseph L. Mankiewicz, based on a story by Mary Orr
Cinematography by: Milton Krasner

Cast: Bette Davis, Anne Baxter, George Sanders, Celeste Holm, Gary Merrill, Hugh Marlowe, Thelma Ritter, Marilyn Monroe, Gregory Ratoff, Barbara Bates, Walter Hampden, Randy Stuart, Craig Hill, Leland Harris, Claude Stroud, Eugene Borden, Steve Geray, Bess Flowers, Stanley Orr

One of the most devastatingly venomous, witty, and literate scripts in cinema history in the hands and mouth of one of the powerhouse performers of all time is the primary and considerable appeal of Joseph L. Mankiewicz's *All About Eve*. The picture is simultaneously a true and savage comic indictment

of the theater and those who people its front and back stages; a morality tale about the choices we make to get the things that we want; and a grand old will-they-or-won't-they romance on a par with the best of them. *All About Eve* goes for it all and concedes nothing. It's a cocksure, high-risk venture that defies one of Hollywood's primary tenets: it's all talk (but, oh what *talk!*) and very little action. And it succeeds on its own terms. It's a brilliant picture.

In retrospect, the casting of Bette Davis as Margo Channing seems a prerequisite, a foregone conclusion. Has an actor ever been more suited to a particular role? Bette Davis was perfect for Margo Channing the way Marlon Brando was for Stanley Kowalski; the way Vivien Leigh was for Scarlett O'Hara; the way Yul Brynner was for the King of Siam.

It's incredible, then, that the casting of Davis in *All About Eve* was an

afterthought and a desperate compromise. The character was reportedly inspired by English stage actress Peg Woffington, though Tallulah Bankhead made abstract claims at the time that it was *she* who inspired Margo. Darryl Zanuck's first choice for the part of Margo was Marlene Dietrich. Mankiewicz, however, strenuously objected, and the two eventually agreed on Claudette Colbert for the part. Colbert was enthusiastic about the project and had, in fact, signed for the role. However, she first had to complete her assignment in a drama about life in a Japanese prison camp called *Three Came Home*. The picture called for Colbert to enact a rape scene in which she was required to fight off a prison guard, the would-be rapist. During their struggle Claudette ruptured a disk in her back, which put her in traction.

Mankiewicz held out for Colbert. He sent flowers and notes to her hospital room and inquired about her daily progress. He delayed the shooting as long as he could. Finally a decision had to be made. One of the primary shooting locations for the film was to be the Curran Theatre in San Francisco. Zanuck had booked the theater for April 1950 for the only two weeks that it was available. It had been paid for in advance and was the only available theater that met the various needs of the production. So, if they couldn't get another theater, they'd have to get another actress. Forty years later Colbert was still lamenting over what could have been and how missing out on *Eve* had impacted the course of her career. "It was one of the worst times in my life and the worst thing that happened in my career. Awful! Awful! I was no longer young—I was forty-seven—and people thought that because I was not able to work in that marvelous picture I was sick."

If Zanuck and Mankiewicz were going to find another Margo, they were going to have to find her *fast*. Furthermore, they had to find an actress who could not only play the part but also fit into the meticulously assembled cast of actors, all of whom had already been signed. The actress would not only have to be compatible with Anne Baxter, cast as Eve after it was decided that Jeanne Crain could not be bitchy enough; she would also have to be believable as Bill Sampson's lover. The role called for Margo to be eight years older than Bill. Gary Merrill, signed to play 32-year-old Bill, was 36. They needed an actress who was, or could play, 40. British stage actress Gertrude Lawrence was considered. She had the talent and the theatricality, but she wasn't a movie *name*, had never had an impact on the screen, and, most damaging of all, was too old. It is ironic that for this tale about, in large part, the insecurity of an aging actress, an actress would not be hired to play her because she was too old. Lawrence was 52 at the time and would die two years later.

Next they considered Ingrid Bergman, who, at 35, was a little young for the part but could be made up to look older. The problem was that, two years before, Bergman had been more or less exiled from Hollywood because of her illicit romance with Roberto Rossellini, and she was not ready to return. It would take six more years for Bergman to return to Hollywood, and when she did, with *Anastasia*, she would be forgiven for her so-called sins and be rewarded with an Oscar.

Bette Davis, who was then at RKO finishing up *The Story of a Divorce* (retitled *Payment on Demand* before its release), was feeling a little desperate and more than a little vulnerable. Less than a year before, she had made a dramatic departure, after 18 years of steady employment, from the studio that had fathered and nurtured her talents. She was now on her own, and while the proverbial wolves were not exactly snapping at her ankle-strapped heels, she was not unaware of the talk around town that her career, glorious as it had been once, was dead. Her last few films for Warners had been a far cry (commercially and artistically) from her previous successes, and her temperament, acceptable while she was churning out such box office hits as *Dark Victory* (1939), *The Old Maid* (1939), and *Now, Voyager* (1942), was no longer to be tolerated. The consensus in Hollywood at the time was simply that Bette Davis was no longer worth it.

Zanuck, who had been the head of development at Warners in the early 1930s, had been responsible, in large part, for Bette's early successes with the studio. He was certainly aware of her talent but had left the studio in 1934 to form 20th Century–Fox just before Bette obtained acclaim with *Of Human Bondage* and several years before she attained stardom with *Jezebel*. Still, he had a direct confrontation with her temperament in 1941 when she resigned

as president of the Academy of Motion Picture Arts and Sciences, of which he
was a board member.

And so it was with trepidation that, in April 1950, Zanuck made the
phone call. He telephoned Bette, then in her last five days on *Divorce*, and
told her that he was sending her a script to read. He also warned her that, if
she liked the script and wanted to do the picture, she would have to start
shooting in 10 days. Bette read the script and immediately called Zanuck,
who promptly arranged for a conference between Bette and Mankiewicz,
whose main concern was that Bette look believable with, yet a few years older
than, Merrill. Actually, Bette, at 42, was the perfect age for the part. As she
would later say with her characteristic Yankee candor, "That was the wonderful thing about the part. I didn't have to worry about my looks. If you have
to be concerned about your appearance, acting goes out the window. Margo
Channing was past 40; so was I. I was supposed to look the way I did." Still
concerned, Mankiewicz ordered a photo session to see how this Margo
Channing and Bill Sampson combination would photograph together. It
was the first time Bette Davis and Gary Merrill had met. Within days after
the resulting photographs were delivered to Mankiewicz, Bette joined Celeste
Holm, Hugh Marlowe, Merrill, and others aboard Darryl Zanuck's private
plane destined for San Francisco.

Before shooting commenced, Mankiewicz called his friend Eddie Goulding (who had directed Bette in several films) for advice. "Dear *boy*," Goulding consoled, "have you gone mad? This woman will destroy you; she will
grind you down to a fine powder and blow you away." And, "She will come
up on the set with a large yellow pad and sharp pencils. She will write. And
having written, she will direct." What Goulding was not taking into consideration, however, was that, unlike the pictures he had directed her in, Bette
needed this picture more than it needed her. Furthermore, she was perceptive
enough to recognize from the script that the project was far superior to 99
percent of the stuff she had done at Warners and thus would not have to fight
for its quality. On *All About Eve*, Bette Davis would be on her best behavior,
for these and other reasons.

> Funny business, a woman's career. The things you drop on your way
> up the ladder so you can move faster. You forget you'll need them
> again when you get back to being a woman. That's one career all
> females have in common, whether we like it or not: being a woman.
> Sooner or later we've got to work at it, no matter how many other
> careers we've had or wanted. And, in the last analysis, nothing is any
> good unless you can look up just before dinner or turn around in
> bed—and there he is. Without that, you're not a woman. You're
> something with a French provincial office, or a, a book full of
> clippings. But you're not a woman.
> *Margo Channing*, All About Eve *by Joseph L. Mankiewicz*

In rehearsing her first scene with Gary Merrill, Bette took out a cigarette
and instinctively waited for him to light it. It was a typical power play that

Bette frequently employed with her leading men. However, Merrill calmly and firmly refused the bait. Insulted, Bette turned to her director for allegiance. "Shouldn't he light it?" she asked Mankiewicz. With Eddie Goulding's words of warning shifting through his head, Mankiewicz braced himself for the onslaught. And then Merrill stated, flatly, "Bill Sampson would never light this dame's cigarettes." Mankiewicz, caught in the shark-infested middle, nevertheless boldly proclaimed, "You know, Bette, he's right." Even Bette had to concede, though certainly not verbally, that Merrill was indeed right. And, if such things can be traced to one single moment, it was in that moment that Bette Davis fell in love with Gary Merrill.

Fox had purchased the rights to Mary Orr's magazine story "The Wisdom of Eve" for $1,250. Interestingly, Orr herself was the prototype for the part of Karen Richards, played in the picture by Celeste Holm. For his screenplay Mankiewicz originated the characters of Addison de Witt (which he originally intended for Jose Ferrer), Bill Sampson, Max Fabian, Phoebe, Birdie Coonan, and Miss Caswell. Character actress Thelma Ritter, cast as the cynical, sharp-tongued Birdie, was Mankiewicz's only original choice actually to make it into the picture.

For the part of Miss Caswell, the blond and well-bosomed graduate of the Copacabana School of Dramatic Art, Zanuck balked at the mention of Marilyn Monroe. Sheree North, among others, was interviewed for the part. Johnny Hyde, however, a powerful agent at William Morris, pulled out all the stops for MM, and she was eventually signed for a mere $500 a week. "He haunted my office," Mankiewicz would later recall.

Columnist Harrison Carroll visited the set one day in May and watched the shooting of a scene that called for Bette to indulge in chocolate candy. Mankiewicz halted the shooting when Bette made a peculiar face. "What's wrong?" asked Mankiewicz. "I'm sorry," said Bette. "I didn't mean to, but I *loathe* eating chocolates in the morning." Carroll visited with Bette after the scene was shot and was surprised to find her in husky voice. He asked her if she was doing a takeoff on Tallulah Bankhead. "That 'throaty' voice," Bette replied, "is because I suffered a broken blood vessel in my larynx [from screaming matches with her soon-to-be-ex-husband, William Grant Sherry] and we couldn't wait to start the picture. I had intended to go into a lower register for the role . . . but I hadn't intended it to be quite as hoarse as this. The chief fear now is that my voice will improve before the picture is finished. If it does, Joe Mankiewicz says we will start the day off each morning with a screaming scene." The voice would serve Bette (and Margo) well in the picture.

Brilliant as it is, upon close examination of the film, the one flaw seems to be in the casting. It would have made sense for Anne Baxter's Eve to model herself on the physically similar Claudette Colbert/Margo. It makes sense at the end of the picture for Barbara Bates's Phoebe to model herself on the physically similar Anne Baxter's Eve. It does *not*, however, make sense for Baxter's Eve to model herself on Margo Channing as played by Bette Davis—

they simply have nothing, other than drive, in common. Still, Bette's performance is so definitive that if anyone seems miscast, it is Anne Baxter, as good as she is.

As Margo Channing, Bette Davis never makes a false move. She is both the grande dame actress and Mother Earth. Her Margo starts out as a monster in cold cream who eventually works her way toward becoming a woman. At Margo's party for Bill Sampson, Bette downs one martini and then, as the tempo of the music prophetically changes, downs another. She sashays over to the staircase, clutches the railing, and spins around. Then, as she delivers what may well be her most famous movie line, "Fasten your seat belts; it's going to be a bumpy night," you're aware that you're watching *movie magic*. Moreover, you're aware that you're watching one of the great actresses in full command of her considerable technique and at the pinnacle of her powers.

After seeing the picture and while basking in its acclaim, Bette sent Joe Mankiewicz a wire. Tersely worded, it read, "Thanks, Joe, for raising me from the dead." As for working with Bette, Mankiewicz would later extol, "Barring grand opera, I can think of nothing beyond her range. She's intelligent, instinctive, vital, sensitive—and, above all, a superbly equipped professional actress who does her job responsibly and honestly. To this day I regret deeply that I hadn't worked with her before *Eve*—and that I haven't since."

"ALL STAR REVUE"

Bette Davis gave her first live television performance on a variety show starring Jimmy Durante called "All Star Revue." It was not an impressive debut. *Variety* reported on April 21, 1952:

> Video's newest convert was Bette Davis, and it might be recorded that she broke in reading a commercial—'I'll take two cans of Pet Milk.' Miss Davis was used otherwise in one large scene running close to fifteen minutes. That her coming-out in the channel set was not too auspicious can be traced to an apparent nervousness (people, not cameras) and a lack of sufficient elasticity to 'unbend.' She was no Traubel or Truman, but she outgloried Swanson.

"All Star Revue" aired on NBC from October 1950 to April 1953.

ALL THIS, AND HEAVEN TOO ★★★

Warner Brothers
1940   143 minutes   bw
Directed by: Anatole Litvak
Produced by: Jack Warner and Hal Wallis, in association with David Lewis
Screenplay by: Casey Robinson, based on the novel by Rachel Field
Cinematography by : Ernest Haller
Cast: Bette Davis, Charles Boyer, Jeffrey Lynn, Barbara O'Neil, Virginia

Weidler, Helen Westley, Walter Hampden, Henry Daniell, Harry Davenport, George Coulouris, Montagu Love, Janet Beecher, June Lockhart, Ann Todd, Richard Nichols, Fritz Leiber, Ian Keith, Sibyl Harris, Mary Anderson, Edward Fielding, Ann Gillis, Peggy Stewart, Victor Killan, Mrs. Gardner Crane

When Margaret Mitchell's *Gone with the Wind* was finally toppled from the national fiction bestseller lists, it was replaced by another sweeping historical romance (complete with a suffering heroine), Rachel Field's *All This, and Heaven Too*. Warner Brothers purchased the film rights for Bette in an agreement dated November 30, 1938. Field initially requested $100,000 for the rights (*GWTW* had gone to David O. Selznick for a mere $50,000) but eventually settled for $52,500. Earlier that year the stature of Bette Davis had grown considerably at the studio with the box office success of two pictures from the historical-romance-with-suffering-heroine genre, *Jezebel* and *The Sisters*. In the 1930s, Warners was nothing if not consistent.

The film was to be Warners' answer to *GWTW*. Jack Warner, taking the association to an extreme, even issued a memo to his studio employees stating that all references to the picture should be made with the title *"ATAHT,"* just as industry insiders were referring to *Gone With the Wind* as *"GWTW."* Warner, with Hall Wallis, would supervise this film himself and later take a rare producer's credit (as opposed to his standard "executive in charge of production" credit) for it.

No expense was to be spared, and the studio summoned its brightest talents. Orry-Kelly was to do the costumes. Carl Jules Weyl was to design the period settings. Much was made of the fact that 67 interior sets were to be built for this picture, surpassing the 53 that had been built for *GWTW*. The picture was budgeted at $1,075,000, one of Warners' most expensive productions of the period.

Ernie Haller, Bette's favorite cameraman, was initially assigned to shoot the picture. However, before it went into production Jack Warner replaced Haller with Tony Gaudio. Irate, Bette wrote Warner a letter demanding that Haller be reinstated. He was. Interestingly, though, and indicative of just how important this picture was to the studio, both Gaudio and Sol Polito, two of the best cinematographers on the lot, assisted Haller at various times during the production. The only thing spared on this film was Technicolor. It was thought that, because of the somber nature of the drama, black and white would be more appropriate.

Anatole Litvak, then 38, who had just successfully directed Bette in *The Sisters*, was signed to direct. The studio's top writer, Casey Robinson, was signed to adapt the book and write the screenplay. The story, set in Paris in 1847, involved a governess, Henriette Deluzy-Desportes (modeled on Rachel Field's real-life great-aunt) in love with the miserably married duc de Praslin. When Duchesse de Praslin is murdered, Henriette is arrested as an accomplice.

Bette was not particularly pleased with the script or her role. It was the kind of role that Olivia de Havilland, then Warners' number-two actress, played. In fact anyone viewing the film would find it easy to picture de Havilland in the role. Nonetheless, Bette was well aware of the film's prestige, and she signed for the part.

Laurence Olivier was seriously considered for the role of the duc de Praslin. Others mentioned were Ronald Colman, Melvyn Douglas, Leslie Howard, and Fredric March. At one point it looked as though Bette's perennial costar (and recent lover) George Brent would be cast in the part. But at the time Jack Warner intended to duplicate David O. Selznick's *GWTW* decision to cast four big names in the leading parts. Brent, though one of Warners' more affable and steady leading men, was never a star of the stature of, say, Gable. Unable to find such an actor on his own lot, Jack Warner went searching outside of his studio gates and came back with Charles Boyer.

Bette was thrilled. During her seven-year rise to stardom at Warner Brothers, she had never really been teamed with the leading men of the day. She had played with Spencer Tracy and Henry Fonda before they became stars. She had played with George Arliss but was more like his granddaughter than his lover. She had played with Jimmy Cagney, Paul Muni, and Edward G. Robinson, but they were more character actors than leading men. She had played with Leslie Howard, but he too was never a star of the stature of Gable. Probably the closest she came to playing opposite a top leading man with box office draw was when she played with Errol Flynn, first in *The Sisters* and then in *The Private Lives of Elizabeth and Essex*, the latter of which would be released in December 1939. But Bette despised Flynn. Yes, he was a star, she would concede, but he was a star, in her view, without talent. Boyer was another matter altogether.

For the third starring role, the duchess, Litvak wanted to cast his wife, Miriam Hopkins. "The duchess de Praslin," Litvak said at the time, "is a heartless and venomous bitch. Miriam will be perfect." However, by the time the picture went into production the marriage between Litvak and Hopkins had dissolved, and unable to attract Judith Anderson, Tallulah Bankhead, Rosalind Russell, or Greer Garson to the secondary role, Warner abandoned the idea of a four-star marquee. But he was not ready to abandon the idea of associating his picture with *GWTW* in any way that he could. After testing Mary Astor and Gale Sondergaard for the part of the duchess, Warner signed Barbara O'Neil. Even though she was only 30 years old at the time, O'Neil had just completed her role as Scarlett O'Hara's mother in *GWTW* when she was signed to play the duchess. It was a decision that Bette was particularly disturbed about. And with good reason. The part as written called for a dowdy, unattractive woman. O'Neil was much too young and much too attractive for the part. Bette protested that if the duchess was presented as a beautiful young woman, the audience would find it more difficult to accept the duke's discontent. She was right.

Incidentally, a young actress got her start on this film. For the small role of Isabelle, one of the de Praslin children, Hal Wallis wanted to cast Mary

Anderson (who had, by the way, also been in *GWTW*). Litvak, however, had his eye on 15-year-old June Lockhart. Anderson was tested and retested and was eventually cast in a lesser role. Memos were passed back and forth. Other girls were tested and retested. Lockhart was tested and retested—again and again. More memos passed. Lockhart (who would in later years gain television fame with "Lassie" and "Lost in Space") was eventually cast, but the time-consuming, expensive process undergone to cast one inconsequential juvenile part was indicative of Hollywood excess.

Allotted 42 shooting days, *All This, and Heaven Too* started principal photography on February 8, 1940. At the time, *Gone With the Wind* was still doing blockbuster business in the nation's theaters. In fact, throughout its production *ATAHT* would be haunted by the Selznick picture.

On *The Sisters* (particularly because she had been directed by Willie Wyler on her previous picture), Bette had been initially unaccustomed to, and displeased with, Anatole Litvak's style of direction. Typically, he methodically orchestrated each camera move and, in Bette's view, let the positioning of the camera dictate the shooting. On-the-set inspiration and spontaneity were not in his repertoire. Nonetheless, Bette, recently divorced from Ham Nelson, was attracted to Litvak the man, if not the director, and the two became engaged in a short but tempestuous affair.

Meanwhile, Bette was also attracted to Boyer. Each respected the other's talents, and they got along quite well during the production. But at the time Boyer was having problems in his personal life and was generally miserable on the set. As Litvak later observed, "Charles was a happy fellow in the other pictures we made [together], but in *All This, and Heaven Too* he was surely the least contented man with whom I've ever worked."

Despite her qualms about Litvak's directorial style, Bette, who would celebrate her 32nd birthday with an on-the-set party, was uncharacteristically without temperament during the production. Furthermore, she was uncharacteristically *present*. Bette missed a mere two days of work due to "illness." Still, she was as staunch as ever about the interpretation of her character. She insisted on playing Henriette as an emotionally repressed woman, without surface warmth or sentiment. Hal Wallis balked. "Davis is going overboard again," he wrote to Litvak after watching the rushes, "on her precise manner of speaking. Everything was going along nicely for a while, and then in the prison cell the other day, the scene with Jeffrey Lynn, she went right back into the old fault, and I notice now that in the theater box, she does the same thing in dialogue with Boyer. . . . Hold her down and [have her] underplay. . . . Otherwise, you are going to have a studied, cold performance." Wallis was particularly concerned that if Henriette was going to elicit love from the children, as she did in the book and in the script, Bette was going to have to warm up and lighten her performance. He was right. Today the film seems to be marred in scenes by Bette's curiously staid interpretation.

There was one tragedy during the shooting. Sibyl Harris, who was playing the part of Mlle. Maillard, was stricken with cancer and had to have surgery during the shooting.

All This, and Heaven Too completed principal photography on April 20, 1940. Upon seeing a cut of the picture, novelist Rachel Field, who had been befriended by Bette during the production, wrote a letter to Jack Warner dated May 15. It read, in part, "When *All This, and Heaven Too* was bought for motion pictures I received many dire warnings that once my book reached the screen I might not recognize the story or the characters I had written. . . . But your adapting of this material has been a revelation to me of what sympathetic handling of a book can be." Warner shrewdly incorporated the letter into his marketing campaign for the picture. The ads prominently displayed the cover of the book and, of course, resembled those for *Gone With the Wind*. Having seen her book translated faithfully to the screen, Rachel Field died a short time later.

The picture was released at 143 minutes, far too long compared with most films of the day, but shorter than *GWTW*, which ran for 220 minutes. And although it received highly favorable reviews and would go on to be nominated for a Best Picture Oscar, it was not the *GWTW*-like blockbuster success that Jack Warner had wanted. Years later Anatole Litvak analyzed its comparative failure to Boyer biographer Larry Swindell:

> "The picture was overproduced. You couldn't see the actors for the candelabra, and the whole thing became a victory for matter over mind. Bette Davis was the world's most expensively costumed governess. I'll tell you what was wrong with the picture. *Gone With the Wind* was wrong with it. If it hadn't been for the one picture, the other might have been managed nicely on a more modest scale."

GERETTE ALLEGRA

For much of her life Bette had a secretary/companion/personal assistant on her payroll. Her need for this help was even more pronounced during her later years, particularly after her stroke in 1983. From 1985 to 1987 the job was filled by a young woman named Gerette Allegra. Upon applying for the job, she was greeted at the door by the departing assistant, who warned her, "Don't do this job!" Allegra was paid a salary of $500 a week, and all of her living expenses were absorbed by Bette. Her duties included acting as Bette's liaison with the staff of the hotel in which they lived, with the outside world in general, and with her fans in particular.

In December 1991, Allegra appeared on "The Joan Rivers Show." She had much to say about her famous former employer:

> Well, the first week or so she treated me basically like I was a servant. There was no rapport. . . . One day I was bringing her a glass of wine. She was sitting in her king-sized bed, all propped up. And I said, "Why do you look so sad? You know, you always look so sad." And she goes, "You have no i-de-ah the pain that I am going through right now. You have no i-de-ah!" And I said, "Well, I do. I really do.

I'm in a lot of pain, too. My dad just left my mother for a woman my age, and I understand pain. I do know what you're going through." And she went, "My God! You *do!*" And she jumped off the bed and she ran out and got me a glass of wine, pushed me on the other side [of the bed], picked my feet up, handed me the glass of wine, and said, "Oh, my poor de-ah!" And she said, "We shall *dine* together to-night!"

She was very, very sharp. One day we were walking out the limousine into the hotel we lived in, and there were these little Madonna-wannabes all dressed up. And one of them goes, "Oh, look, there is Bette Davis!" [Then] another girl says, "That can't be Bette Davis, she's *dead!*" We heard her very clearly. And [Bette] turned her head and said, *"I am not!"*

She could be crazy, but that made her interesting. I don't think she was mean. She was tough. But I didn't find her mean-spirited. I mean she was a little nutty. The waiters would come to serve us dinner, and she'd be like, "Don't perform, just serve me. I am not going to give you a role." It was just her way. Underneath there was a real caring person.

CLARK ALLEN

Clark Allen is a guitarist and singer who accompanied Bette Davis in her national tour of the stage presentation *The World of Carl Sandburg* from October 1959 to October 1960. Early in the tour it became apparent to Allen that his musical skill was not his only attribute that attracted Bette.

In a recent interview for this book Allen related, for the first time in print, his experiences on the *Sandburg* road tour, during which the marriage between Bette Davis and Gary Merrill was irrevocably severed.

"Everyone thought I was her paramour, her 'young thing.' Norman Corwin [the director] and everyone else was saying, 'God, I wish I could have some of *that*,' referring to Bette. But they were a little older than I was. I was 32, and she was only 52, but I thought she was an old bat. The truth was that I was a loving, faithful husband, and I just didn't want to get myself in trouble. I knew my place. I was low man on the totem pole. . . .

"I got to know her very well because all day long, all those months, I was riding with her in the car [on the tour, mainly one-night stands in small towns, most of the company traveled via chartered bus, but Bette insisted that Clark, not Merrill, accompany her in the chauffeur-driven car], and then in the evenings I would talk to her over dinner. After the show we'd go to parties together. I was with her at all of the places that Gary should have been, and I felt miserable about it.

"She did everything but grab me. After the shows I'd sit by her bed, and she'd talk about her beautiful breasts in this transparent nightgown. . . . I remember thinking, 'God, here I am at 2:00 in the morning with *Bette Davis*, and I'm sweating blood.' . . . She did everything but say 'f—k me,' because she had enough taste not to do that. I never said, 'No, I'm not going to have sex with you,' but it came just about to that.

"She was promising me records; she was promising me a career. Naturally, she never came through with any of her promises. She must have been mad at me because I was rejecting her."

AMERICAN CINEMA AWARDS

On January 6, 1989, in a ceremony at the Beverly Hilton Hotel, Bette was honored with an American Cinema Award for lifetime achievement. She attended the function and accepted her award, but not without a touch of drama. At one point during the evening Bette passed out and was carried into a private room by a security guard. Someone rushed to the podium and called over the microphone, "If there's a doctor in the house, would he please come to the front of the ballroom." Bette, however, made a sudden recovery and was able to accept her award as scheduled.

Among the celebrities present on Bette's behalf were her former costars Ernest Borgnine, Mike Connors, Joseph Cotten, Frances Dee, Jane Greer, Paul Henreid, Robert Hutton, Joan Leslie, Betty Lynn, Karl Malden, Dennis Morgan, Janis Paige, Robert Stack, Lionel Stander, Robert Wagner, and Teresa Wright. Clint Eastwood led the praises by proclaiming, "Of all the women on the screen, she was the most powerful." Kim Carnes sang her hit song "Bette Davis Eyes" to Bette, who then stood and toasted the singer. It

was Gregory Peck who presented the award to Bette, and after a showing of her film clips he succinctly observed, "Well, boys and girls, *that's* how it's done."

AMERICAN FILM INSTITUTE

"I suppose . . . they decided, 'Let's give it to a dame.' "
Bette Davis, upon receiving her AFI award

Bette was presented with the prestigious Life Achievement Award by the American Film Institute in March 1977. She was the first female recipient of the award, which had previously been bestowed on John Ford, James Cagney, Orson Welles, and William Wyler.

George Stevens, Jr., director of the AFI, said of Bette at the time, "She was one of the first women in motion pictures to shape her own career by vigorously using the power her talent brought her. She remains a bright example to the many women associated with the American Film Institute who are today shaping their own careers behind the camera."

The awards ceremony was coordinated by Harry Stanfield and hosted by Jane Fonda. Present to pay homage to Bette were Olivia de Havilland, Peter Falk, Geraldine Fitzgerald, Henry Fonda, Lee Grant, Paul Henreid, Celeste Holm, Joseph Mankiewicz, Liza Minnelli, Cicely Tyson, Robert Wagner, Natalie Wood, and William Wyler. Sitting with Bette at her table were Wagner, de Havilland, and Mankiewicz.

The ceremony was taped for a CBS television special, "The American Film Institute Salute to Bette Davis," that aired on March 21, 1977. It is currently available on home video as "The American Film Institute Life Achievement Awards: Bette Davis."

AMERICAN THEATRE ARTS

In late 1982 Bette was presented with the American Theatre Arts Lifetime Achievement Award. The ceremony was held at the Century Plaza Hotel in Century City and was hosted by Jean Stapleton.

Those present to pay tribute to Bette included Jimmy Stewart, Lucille Ball, Robert Wagner, Janis Paige, Karl Malden, and Stefanie Powers. Burt Reynolds and Ronald Reagan sent messages on videotape. The latter, then president, said, "I felt honored to be on the same set with this great actress." The ceremony included various performances, the highlight of which was a ballet dancer who, on point, impersonated Bette Davis smoking a cigarette.

In concluding her acceptance speech, Bette delivered her by-then-standard finale at appearances such as this: "Ah'd love ta kiss yuh, but Ah just wash-ed mah hay-er!"

ERNEST ANDERSON

The best thing about the 1942 picture *In This Our Life* was its attempt to portray a young black man without the racist stereotypes then usually seen in films. The story is about Parry Clay, who earnestly seeks a profession and is wrongly blamed for Bette Davis's crime because of his color. The role was given, at Bette's behest, to a studio maintenance man, Ernest Anderson. The Warner Brothers publicity department later contended that Anderson had been so inspired by his role that he decided to complete his education and get a teacher's degree so that "he can help raise the educational level of his race."

Ernest Anderson went on to appear in several other films, including, also at Bette's behest, *What Ever Happened to Baby Jane?* (1962).

LINDSAY ANDERSON

In one of her autobiographies, *The Lonely Life*, Bette referred to Lindsay Anderson, who directed her in the 1987 film *The Whales of August*, as "very opinionated," "disagreeable," and "macho." In an interview for this book Anderson discussed the troubled shooting of *Whales*, detailed later in these pages. On Bette Davis, Anderson reflected: "I must add that, in spite of all difficulties of temperament, Bette was respected by everyone for her past and her ability. It was really a pity that she felt the need to be spurred on by aggression and by finding members of the unit to whom she could be nasty. As I told her, she wasted her time and her energy by fighting unnecessary battles. But then perhaps those battles were exactly what she needed to give her dynamic."

Born in 1923, Lindsay Anderson has directed other films, including *This Sporting Life* (1963), *If . . .* (1969), and *O, Lucky Man!* (1973).

"THE ANDY WILLIAMS SHOW"

On December 20, 1962, to promote her then recently released *What Ever Happened to Baby Jane?*, Bette participated in one of the oddest adventures of her varied career. On the variety television series "The Andy Williams Show" she *sang* a rock number called "What Ever Happened to Baby Jane?" and another song, "Just Turn Me Loose on Broadway," from the 1952 musical revue *Two's Company*. She also joined Andy and the New Christy Minstrels in a medley of folk songs!

ANN-MARGRET

Ann-Margret was 19 years old when she made her film debut as Bette Davis's daughter in *Pocketful of Miracles* (1961). During filming Davis counseled and consoled the young novice. Twenty-eight years later Ann-Margret was the first person chosen by Bette to serve as a presenter at the April 1989 Film Society of Lincoln Center's award ceremony in Bette's honor. To participate in the event, Ann-Margret interrupted her engagement at Caesar's Palace in Las Vegas, flew to New York, presented a speech at the ceremony, and flew back to Las Vegas to resume her scheduled run.

Although she received a Golden Globe award as one of the most promising stars of the year for her performance in *Pocketful*, it was *Bye Bye Birdie*, released two years later, that made Ann-Margret a star. She has since appeared in numerous films, including *Carnal Knowledge* (1971) and *Tommy* (1975), both of which earned her Oscar nominations. Her superlative television work includes the films "Who Will Love My Children?" (1983), "A Streetcar Named Desire" (1984), and "The Two Mrs. Grenvilles" (1987), all of which garnered her Best Actress Emmy nominations.

> "[*Pocketful of Miracles*] was Ann-Margret's first film, and she proved to be a very good actress and most certainly terrific to work with."
>
> *Bette Davis*

THE ANNIVERSARY ★★
Seven Arts–Hammer Productions
Released by 20th Century–Fox
1968   95 minutes   Technicolor
Directed by: Roy Ward Baker
Produced by: Jimmy Sangster
Screenplay by: Jimmy Sangster, from the play by Bill MacIlwraith
Cinematography by: Harry Waxman
Cast: Bette Davis, Jack Hedley, Sheila Hancock, James Cossins, Elaine
    Taylor, Christian Roberts, Timothy Bateson, Arnold Diamond

After their horror outing with 1965's *The Nanny*, producer Jimmy Sangster approached Bette with another demonic tale. This one, adapted from the black comedy by Bill MacIlwraith that had been a hit on the British stage, would feature Bette as the mother to end all mothers—sort of a gothic blend of *Fatal Attraction* and *Mommie Dearest*. And while she saw possibilities in the script, she loathed the genre. She hated being the grande dame of the macabre, which, with *What Ever Happened to Baby Jane?* (1962), *Hush . . . Hush, Sweet Charlotte* (1964), and *The Nanny* (1965), is what she was reduced to in the 1960s. After nearly 40 years in Hollywood, when she was generally regarded as one of the finest actresses in the history of the cinema, she had become typecast in the perverse. The other scripts, the good ones, simply stopped coming. Ironically, having fled Warner Brothers for England in 1936 in self-defense against the trash that she was being forced to make, she now found herself returning to England to shoot, of all things, *The Anniversary*.

Initially Bette had rejected the script. Then, when that proverbial "something else around the corner" never showed, she reconsidered. Trying to make the best of the situation, Bette contented herself with viewing the one-eyed monster of a mother, Mrs. Taggart, as an older Martha from *Who's Afraid of Virginia Woolf?*, a role she had sought and lost two years earlier.

She had made peace with the role. Not so of her director. *The Anniversary* commenced shooting on May 1, 1967, at Associated British Studios in London. Within 10 days Bette had succeeded in having Alvin Rakoff removed from the film. The official announcement proffered that tired and transparent cliché "creative differences." The truth was that Bette was miserable making the movie and had made up her mind that the director, whose experience had been primarily in television, was a talentless rake. As she would say later, "Mr. Rakoff didn't have the first fundamental knowledge of making a motion picture."

Shooting reconvened on Monday, May 15, with Roy Baker in Rakoff's place. Unlike his predecessor, Baker had known Bette for years, and there was little question of compatibility. There were, however, onlookers who speculated that Bette wanted Baker hired because with him she could dominate the proceedings. It was not an empty charge. Over the years Bette was often accused of choosing to work with directors whose decisions she could override. In this case, though, Bette herself would say, "No, he *definitely* directed it. Oh, I did a little—behind the scenes."

The Anniversary completed shooting on July 14, 1967. It was previewed in London on January 11, 1968, and received fair to poor notices. Because of its cold reception, American audiences had little or no opportunity to see it. And that's a pity, because it's worth the price of admission just to see the scene in which Bette, as Mrs. Taggart, tells her son's fiancée to sit elsewhere because her body odor is offensive, or the scene in which Bette leaves her glass eye on the covers of another woman's bed, or, in general, Bette Davis wearing an eyepatch and ultra-short bangs that looked perfectly ridiculous. *The Anniversary* is not a good film, but it does provoke interesting commentary about how the industry treats, or mistreats, its monumental talents.

ANOTHER MAN'S POISON ★ ½

Eros Productions
Released by United Artists
1952   89 minutes   bw
Directed by: Irving Rapper
Produced by: Douglas Fairbanks, Jr., and Daniel Angel
Screenplay by: Val Guest, from the play by Leslie Sands
Cinematography by: Robert Krasker
Cast: Bette Davis, Gary Merrill, Emlyn Williams, Anthony Steel, Barbara
    Murray, Reginald Beckwith, Edna Morris

Another Man's Poison was one of the biggest mistakes of Bette Davis's career. Douglas Fairbanks, Jr., with whom Bette had made a horrid film in 1934 called *Parachute Jumper*, would later say that he had cast Bette in *Poison* out of friendship, despite the fact that she was labeled, at the time, "box office poison." This, of course, was untrue.

In March 1951, Bette was on top of the world and, more important, back atop the Hollywood heap. *All About Eve*, which had resurrected her career, had been nominated for an unprecedented *14* Oscars, including one for Bette as best actress. The awards ceremony was to be held on March 29, and Bette, with some stiff competition from Gloria Swanson for her performance in *Sunset Boulevard*, was the favorite to win. Another film, *Payment on Demand*, made before *Eve* but not released until February 1951, had opened to critical approval. The question, of course, was what Bette would do for a follow-up.

With the phone once again ringing, Bette found herself refusing offer after offer. One that she turned down was the film version of the William Inge play *Come Back, Little Sheba*.

Instead she opted to go to England to do the film version of Leslie Sands's play *Deadlock*, initially intended for Barbara Stanwyck, who backed out at the last minute due to personal problems. The script had Bette as adulterous mystery writer Janet Frobisher, who poisons her husband and later inadvertently kills herself when she is given a glass of the tainted wine. Thus the melodramatic potboiler was predicated on an accident—an easy, lazy way out that is always too hit-or-miss and leaves the audience feeling cheated.

Why would Bette choose such trash, especially given worthy alternatives like the Inge play? At the time, she was quoted as saying, "I've always wanted to play in a suspense picture as they're made in England, with that quiet effectiveness which the British singularly seem to possess."

Unfortunately, the film was neither quiet nor effective nor particularly suspenseful. And if Bette had in fact wanted to make a British film, why would she choose to make one directed by Irving Rapper, a quintessential Hollywood director if there ever was one?

It's quite possible that Bette, flushed with her regained success, thought she could do no wrong—even with a script so obviously inferior. She does overact all over the place, perhaps in an attempt to compensate for the material. (Even Irving Rapper would later refer to it as a "lousy, less-than-B picture.")

Or perhaps she was simply blinded by love. One of the conditions that Bette imposed before signing to do the picture was that Gary Merrill be cast as her leading man. Another was that all of their travel and lodging accommodations, including those for daughter B.D. and her nurse, were to be first class. After all, if the film turned out to be a stinker, at least she and her groom of eight months would get a good (and free) honeymoon out of the deal.

GEORGE ARLISS

There were a few benefactors in the early career of Bette Davis but perhaps none more significant than George Arliss. He was to have a profound impact on her life and career.

In the late 1920s George Arliss (born George Augustus Andrews in 1868) was a respected stage actor known for his particularly fine diction. Bette first met Arliss when he appeared as a guest lecturer at a drama school in New York at which young Bette was a student. At the time, he counseled her, "Learn the right speech, but never overdo it. American actresses talk the way they *think* the English speak. The important thing is to get the sectionalism out of your voice—so that people can't tell whether you're from the North, East, South, West, or Brooklyn." Bette worked with diligence to extract from her voice any trace of her New England heritage. The advice was to serve her well in later years, which would require her to affect southern, British, even Bronx accents.

In 1929, at the age of 61, Arliss was lured back to Hollywood (he had previously made a few silent pictures) for the film *Disraeli*. His performance would win him the Best Actor Oscar and make him a star. By 1932, with the pictures *The Green Goddess* (for which he was nominated for an Oscar that competed *against* his nominated performance in *Disraeli*, (1930), *Old English* (1930), *Millionaire* (1931), and *Alexander Hamilton* (1931), Arliss was the biggest and most revered name on the Warner Brothers lot.

In mid-September 1931, the proverbial ax fell on the film career of Bette Davis, as the option on her contract was dropped by Universal. She had made six pictures since her arrival in Hollywood nine months before, and none of them had showed her to much advantage. For the next few weeks Bette, with the emotional support of her mother, waited for the telephone to ring. Finally, Bette and her mother were in the process of packing for a return trip to New York when the phone rang and the voice at the other end said with precise diction: "Yes, this is Mr. George Arliss, and I would like to speak to Miss Bette Davis."

Bette met with Arliss that afternoon in his office at Warners. She sat across the desk from him and reminded him of their previous meeting. He told her about his new picture, *The Man Who Played God*. He asked her a few questions about her career. He stared at her for a few minutes. "You look very young, my dear," said the 63-year-old actor to the 23-year-old actress. And then he sent her to the casting and wardrobe departments.

With the endorsement from Arliss, Warner Brothers signed Bette Davis to the picture with a standard player's contract. Arliss was known as something of a mentor to young actresses, his most famous protégée at the time being Jeanne Eagels. So when Arliss handpicked Bette Davis to be his new discovery, the Warners publicity department proclaimed, "Arliss Aid Paves Way to Stardom for Bette Davis."

In April 1933, after completing *The Working Man*, another picture with Bette, Arliss walked out on Warner Brothers and joined Darryl Zanuck in forming 20th Century Pictures, later known as 20th Century-Fox.

Still, his association with and kindness to Bette Davis continued. During the aftermath of her unsuccessful court action against Warner Brothers in 1936 that left her career in seeming shambles, Arliss went to visit Bette in her London hotel room. Knowing she was seriously considering appealing the court's decision, Arliss advised, "Bette, you must go home and do anything they ask for one year. You must accept the fact you have lost. It's difficult to handle defeat, but you can take it." She had been, until then, inconsolable. She would listen to no one. But she listened to Arliss. Years later she reflected on her decision: "He was so right: defeat *was* tough. I got into New York Harbor all alone, not a soul met me. Before, the studio had always sent a publicity man and a car. . . . [And] I smiled for one full year. Had I fought them, my career would have ended."

George Arliss, for a second time, had rescued the screen career of Bette Davis. And while his performance have been all but forgotten, his kindness to Davis has not. In retrospect it is quite conceivable that, without George Arliss, movie audiences would never have had the Bette Davis they eventually came to know and love.

George Arliss died in 1946, but he did live to see the astounding success of the scared young girl he had cast in *The Man Who Played God*.

> I think that only two or three times in my experience have I ever got from an actor at rehearsal something beyond what I realized was in the part. Bette Davis proved to be one of those exceptions. . . . When we rehearsed she startled me; the nice little part became a deep and vivid creation, and I felt rather humbled that this young girl had been able to discover and portray something that my imagination had failed to conceive. . . . I am not in the least surprised that Bette Davis is now the most important star on the screen.
>
> *George Arliss, 1940*

THE ARMY BALL

On June 11, 1983, 10 days before secretly checking into New York Hospital because of cancer, Bette Davis was awarded the Distinguished Civilian Service Medal by the United States government for her patriotic service during World War II, particularly for her foundation and organization of the

Hollywood Canteen. The award was presented to Bette at the Army Ball, a ceremony held at the Beverly Hilton Hotel, by a representative of the secretary of defense. The event was produced by Roy Thorsen.

It was to be one of the highlights of her life. Bette was picked up at her West Hollywood home by a marine in full-dress uniform who escorted her, via Rolls-Royce, to the ceremony. As the car pulled up to the hotel entrance, Bette was greeted with military pomp and pageantry. A full orchestra began to play to announce her arrival as the uniformed servicemen stood erect in salute and a red carpet was laid out at her feet. Later, inside the hotel ballroom, Bette was congratulated by many familiar faces who had been volunteers at the Hollywood Canteen 40 years before: Gloria de Haven, Mrs. John Ford, Paul Henreid, Bob Hope, Van Johnson, Joan Leslie, Virginia Mayo, Roddy McDowall, Margaret O'Brien, Martha Raye, and Jane Withers among others. Then, upon presentation of the award, the government official declared, "This is a medal for meritorious service from 1941 to the present, for contributing to the morale and well-being of millions of servicemen and women. This is the Distinguished Civilian Service Medal, the Defense Department's highest civilian award. This was the unanimous decision of all branches of the armed forces—the Army, Navy, Marines and Air Corps."

"AS SUMMERS DIE"

"As Summers Die" was a 1986 made-for-television movie directed by Jean-Claude Tramont and adapted by Jeff Andrus and Ed Namzug from the novel by Winston Groom.

The telefilm, shot on location in Richmond, Virginia, in November 1985, starred Bette Davis, Scott Glenn, and Jamie Lee Curtis. The plot had Glenn as a small-town lawyer and Bette as his unlikely ally. The cast also included John Randolph, Ron O'Neal, Beah Richards, Richard Venture, Paul Roebling, Penny Fuller, Bruce McGill, C. C. H. Pounder, John McIntire, Tammy Baldwin, and Nadia Gray Brown.

MARY ASTOR

Mary Astor (Lucille Langehanke, 1906–1987) first met Bette Davis at the Lakeside Country Club in L.A., circa 1936. Bette aggressively marched up to Astor's table and introduced herself. Bette told Astor that she had just seen *Dodsworth* and that Astor's performance in the film was one of the best she had ever seen.

Five years later, when Eddie Goulding was casting *The Great Lie*, Bette suggested that Astor, whose career was then in decline, be given the second female lead of the piano-playing bitch. During the making of the picture, Astor was surprised to learn that, contrary to the reputation that had preceded her, Bette Davis was accommodating and nurturing and, in fact, was instrumental in having Astor's part expanded. After its release, critics credited Astor with stealing *The Great Lie* from Bette Davis. "People have said,"

Astor wrote in her autobiography, "that I 'stole' the picture from Bette Davis, but that is sheer nonsense. She handed it to me on a silver platter. Bette has always had the wisdom, rare in this business, to know that a star cannot stand alone; she appears to much better advantage if the supporting actors are good." Astor was so good, in fact, that she was awarded an Oscar as the year's best supporting actress. Upon receiving her statuette, Astor thanked two people, Tchaikovsky (for the music she simulated playing in the picture) and Bette Davis.

Years later Mary Astor appeared with Bette in *Hush . . . Hush, Sweet Charlotte* (1964). Her silent pictures include *The Beggar Maid* (1921), *Beau Brummel* (1924), and *Don Juan* (1926); her numerous sound pictures include *Red Dust* (1932), *The Maltese Falcon* (1941), *The Palm Beach Story* (1942), *Meet Me in St. Louis* (1944), and *Little Women* (1949).

THE ATTORNEYS

Over the years, as is common for public figures, Bette Davis was occasionally in need of an attorney. The following is an alphabetical list of her legal representatives:

Paul Angelillo	Martin Gang	Irving Levine	Harold Schiff*
Murray Chotiner	Jerry Giesler	Raoul Magana	David Tannenbaum
Oscar R. Cummins	Tom Hammond*	B. S. McKinney	Sidney W. Wernick
Dudley R. Furse	William Jowitt	Manuel Ruiz	

*business manager/attorney

"I wouldn't be an actress today. I think I'd be a lawyer, like my father. And I'd be a damn good one, too."

Bette Davis, 1983

THE AWARDS

"Greedy, greedy. Can't have too many awards. I've gotten just about every award there is to get. . . . It's an awesome thing, getting these awards. But sometimes you think you get them just because you're still alive."

Bette Davis, 1989

"My blood, sweat and tears."
Bette Davis, as she would frequently refer to her innumerable awards

For Bette (A Selective List)
Academy Award Nominations

Dangerous (1935)*	*Now, Voyager* (1942)
Jezebel (1938)*	*Mr. Skeffington* (1944)
Dark Victory (1939)	*All About Eve* (1950)
The Letter (1940)	*The Star* (1952)
The Little Foxes (1941)	*What Ever Happened to Baby Jane?* (1962)

*Best Actress Oscar winner

Emmy Award Nominations

"Recall," honorary miniature Emmy (1963)*

"Strangers: The Story of a Mother and Daughter" (1979), Outstanding Actress in a
  Limited Series or Special*

"Little Gloria . . . Happy at Last" (1982), Outstanding Supporting Actress in a
  Limited Series or Special

*Emmy winner

Golden Globe Awards

Honorary award "for her accomplishments in four fields of show business" (1952)

Cecil B. DeMille Award for Lifetime Achievement (1973)

New York Film Critics Awards

Best Actress runner-up, *Dark Victory* (1939)

Best Actress, *All About Eve* (1950)

National Board of Review Awards

Best Acting, *Dark Victory* and *The Old Maid* (1939)

Best Acting, *The Little Foxes* (1941)

Others

Best Actress, *Marked Woman* and *Kid Galahad*, Venice Film Festival (1937)

Woman of the Year, *Redbook* magazine (1939)

Queen of the Movies, *Life* magazine and the *New York Daily News* (1940)

Best Actress, Nationwide Press (1940)

Most Distinguished Actress of the Year, the New York City Federation of Women's
  Clubs (1941)

Most Popular Actress in South America (1941)

Golden Apple Award, Most Cooperative Actress, Hollywood Women's Press Club
  (1941)

Favorite All-Time Star, *Screen Guide* magazine (1945)
Favorite Actress, Screen Guild (1946)
The War Department's Award for Meritorious Service (1946)
Worst Actress, *Beyond the Forest* (1949), San Francisco Drama Critics Council
Best Actress, *All About Eve* (1950), San Francisco Drama Critics Council
Best Actress, *All About Eve*, Cannes Film Festival (1951)
Actress of the Year, *All About Eve* (1950), *Look* magazine
Most Popular Actress, *All About Eve* (1950), *Photoplay* magazine Gold Medal Award
Best Actress, *All About Eve* (1950), French film industry
Italy Silver Ribbon (1951–1952)
Top Movie Actress of the Year, *The Star* (1952), *Woman's Home Companion* magazine
Woman of the Year (in film), *Los Angeles Times* (1962)
Best Actress, *What Ever Happened to Baby Jane?* (1962), *Photoplay* magazine Gold Medal Award
Golden Apple Award, Most Cooperative Actress, Hollywood Women's Press Club (1963)
Sarah Siddons Award (1973)
Best Supporting Actress winner, *Burnt Offerings* (1976), Academy of Science Fiction, Fantasy and Horror Films
Life Achievement Award, the American Film Institute (1977)
Mothers of the Year, *Woman's Day* magazine (1980)
Life Achievement Award, American Theatre Arts (1982)
Film Advisory Board Award, Lifetime Achievement (1982)
The Valentino Award (1982)
The Golden Reel Trophy, National Film Society (1982)
Best Actress, "A Piano for Mrs. Cimino," the Monte Carlo Award (1983)
The Crystal Award, Women in Film (1983)
The Distinguished Civilian Service Medal, the United States government (1983)
Special Award, the César, French film industry (1985)
The Kennedy Center Lifetime Achievement Award (1987)
Life Achievement Award, France's Légion d'Honneur, Deauville Film Festival (1987)
Life Achievement Award, Campione d'Italia Merit of Achievement (1988)
Life Achievement Award, the American Cinema Awards (1989)
Film Society of Lincoln Center Lifetime Achievement Award (1989)
Life Achievement Award, the Donostia Lifetime Achievement Award, San Sebastian Film Festival (1989)

For the Movies (A Selective List)

Jezebel (1938)
Best Supporting Actress Oscar winner, Fay Bainter
Best Picture Oscar nomination
Best Cinematography Oscar nomination, Ernest Haller
Best Musical Score Oscar nomination, Max Steiner

Eighth Best Picture of the Year, National Board of Review

Special award, Best Ensemble Acting, Venice Film Festival

Dark Victory (1939)
Best Picture Oscar nomination
Best Original Score Oscar nomination, Max Steiner

Fourth Best Picture of the Year, *New York Times*

Juarez (1939)
Best Supporting Actor Oscar nomination, Brian Aherne
Best Cinematography Oscar nomination, Tony Gaudio

Fifth Best Picture of the Year, *New York Times*

The Private Lives of Elizabeth and Essex (1939)
Best Cinematography Oscar nomination, Sol Polito and W. Howard Greene
Best Art Direction Oscar nomination, Anton Grot
Best Sound Oscar nomination
Best Musical Score Oscar nomination, Erich Wolfgang Korngold
Best Special Effects Oscar nomination

All This, and Heaven Too (1940)
Best Picture Oscar nomination
Best Supporting Actress Oscar nomination, Barbara O'Neil
Best Cinematography Oscar nomination, Ernest Haller

The Letter (1940)
Best Picture Oscar nomination
Best Director Oscar nomination, William Wyler
Best Supporting Actor Oscar nomination, James Stephenson
Best Cinematography Oscar nomination, Tony Gaudio
Best Original Score Oscar nomination, Max Steiner
Best Editing Oscar nomination, Warren Low

The Great Lie (1941)
Best Supporting Actress Oscar winner, Mary Astor

The Little Foxes (1941)
Best Picture Oscar nomination
Best Director Oscar nomination, William Wyler
Best Supporting Actress Oscar nomination, Patricia Collinge
Best Supporting Actress Oscar nomination, Teresa Wright
Best Screenplay Oscar nomination, Lillian Hellman
Best Art Direction Oscar nomination, Stephen Goosson
Best Scoring (Drama) Oscar nomination, Meredith Willson
Best Editing Oscar nomination, Daniel Mandell

Third Best Picture of the Year, National Board of Review

Now, Voyager (1942)
Best Scoring (Drama) Oscar winner, Max Steiner

Best Supporting Actress Oscar nomination, Gladys Cooper

Watch on the Rhine (1943)
Best Actor Oscar winner, Paul Lukas

Best Picture Oscar nomination
Best Supporting Actress Oscar nomination, Lucile Watson
Best Screenplay Oscar nomination, Lillian Hellman and Dashiell Hammett

Best Picture, New York Film Critics
Best Actor, Paul Lukas, New York Film Critics
Second Best Picture of the Year, National Board of Review
Best Actor, Paul Lukas, National Board of Review

One of the Ten Best Films of the Year, *New York Times*

Golden Globe winner, Best Actor, Paul Lukas

Mr. Skeffington (1944)
Best Supporting Actor Oscar nomination, Claude Rains

One of the Worst Films of the Year, *Harvard Lampoon*

Hollywood Canteen (1944)
Best Sound Oscar nomination
Best Song Oscar nomination, "Sweet Dreams Sweetheart"
Best Scoring (Musical) Oscar nomination, Ray Heindorf

One of the Worst Films of the Year, *Harvard Lampoon*

The Corn Is Green (1945)
Best Supporting Actor Oscar nomination, John Dall
Best Supporting Actress Oscar nomination, Joan Lorring

A Stolen Life (1946)
Best Special Effects Oscar nomination

Beyond the Forest (1949)
Second Worst Picture of the Year, San Francisco Drama Critics Council

All About Eve (1950)
Best Picture Oscar winner
Best Director Oscar winner, Joseph L. Mankiewicz
Best Supporting Actor Oscar winner, George Sanders
Best Screenplay Oscar winner, Joseph L. Mankiewicz
Best Sound Oscar winner
Best Costume Design Oscar winner, Edith Head and Charles LeMaire

Best Actress Oscar nomination, Anne Baxter
Best Supporting Actress Oscar nomination, Celeste Holm
Best Supporting Actress Oscar nomination, Thelma Ritter
Best Cinematography Oscar nomination, Milton Krasner
Best Art Direction Oscar nomination, Lyle Wheeler and George Davis
Best Editing Oscar nomination, Barbara McLean
Best Scoring (Drama) Oscar nomination, Alfred Newman

Best Director, Joseph L. Mankiewicz, Directors Guild of America

Best Writing in an American Comedy, Joseph L. Mankiewicz, Writers Guild of America

Best Picture, New York Film Critics
Best Director, Joseph L. Mankiewicz, New York Film Critics

Second Best Picture of the Year, National Board of Review

One of the Ten Best Films of the Year, *Time* magazine

Best Picture, San Francisco Drama Critics Council

Best Film, the British Film Academy

Special Jury Prize, Cannes Film Festival (1951)

Golden Globe winner, Best Screenplay, Joseph L. Mankiewicz

The Virgin Queen (1955)
Best Costume Design Oscar nomination, Charles LeMaire and Mary Wills

The Catered Affair (1956)
Seventh Best Picture of the Year, National Board of Review
Best Supporting Actress, Debbie Reynolds, National Board of Review

Pocketful of Miracles (1961)
Best Supporting Actor Oscar nomination, Peter Falk
Best Costume Design Oscar nomination, Edith Head and Walter Plunkett
Best Song Oscar nomination, "Pocketful of Miracles"

Golden Globe winner, Best Actor in a Musical or Comedy, Glenn Ford

Golden Globe winner, Most Promising Newcomer, Female, Ann-Margret

What Ever Happened to Baby Jane? (1962)
Best Costume Design Oscar winner, Norma Koch

Best Supporting Actor Oscar nomination, Victor Buono
Best Cinematography Oscar nomination, Ernest Haller
Best Sound Oscar nomination

The Empty Canvas (1964)
Special David di Donatello Award, Italy, Catherine Spaak

Where Love Has Gone (1964)
Best Song Oscar nomination, "Where Love Has Gone"

Hush . . . Hush, Sweet Charlotte (1964)
Best Supporting Actress Oscar nomination, Agnes Moorehead
Best Cinematography Oscar nomination, Joseph Biroc
Best Art Direction Oscar nomination, William Glasgow
Best Costume Design Oscar nomination, Norma Koch
Best Editing Oscar nomination, Michael Luciano
Best Song Oscar nomination, "Hush . . . Hush, Sweet Charlotte"
Best Original Musical Score Oscar nomination, Frank DeVol

Golden Globe winner, Best Supporting Actress, Agnes Moorehead

Burnt Offerings (1976)
Best Picture nomination, Academy of Science Fiction, Fantasy and Horror Films

Death on the Nile (1978)
Best Costume Design Oscar winner, Anthony Powell

The Whales of August (1987)
Best Supporting Actress Oscar nomination, Ann Sothern
Best Actress, Lillian Gish, National Board of Review

B

LAUREN BACALL

> "What I went through shouldn't happen to a dog. After they [the producers at Universal] bring me out here, they kinda looked at me. I didn't fit their accepted form of beauty. I had about as much sex appeal, they said, as Slim Summerville. That was 1930. They had a phobia for making everyone absolutely alike. But it's all getting much better now. Take Lauren Bacall. Now she's rather strange. But they aren't changing her—for once they know that her strangeness is what makes her interesting to people."
>
> *Bette Davis, 1945*

Bette Davis was the childhood idol of Lauren Bacall. So, when Bacall (born Betty Jean Perske in 1924) shot to prominence on the Warners lot in 1944 with *To Have and Have Not* (during which she met and fell in love with Humphrey Bogart), she was overwhelmed by being on the same lot with Bette. Later, while Bette was at a hotel in New York, Bacall summoned her nerve and arranged for a meeting. However, legend has it, Bacall fainted upon the introduction. On another occasion, during the run of *Applause* at the Palace Theatre in New York, Bette showed up at one of the performances. "I almost died," Bacall later related. "God, the creator of Margo Channing in *All About Eve*, the definitive performance. My childhood idol was in the audience watching me play *her* part!" After the show, Bette knocked on Bacall's dressing room door. Their meeting was strained, brief. Bacall was the fumbling fan; Bette, the reserved star.

BAD SISTER ★★

Universal
1931   71 minutes   bw
Directed by: Hobart Henley
Produced by: Carl Laemmle, Jr.
Screenplay by: Raymond L. Schrock and Tom Reed, based on the play by Booth Tarkington
Cinematography by: Karl Freund
Cast: Conrad Nagel, Sidney Fox, Bette Davis, Zasu Pitts, Slim Summerville, Charles Winninger, Emma Dunn, Humphrey Bogart, Bert Roach, David Durand

Bad Sister was the first picture of Bette Davis's career. (Actually, *Seed* started principal photography two weeks *before Bad Sister* but was released afterward.) It was not an auspicious beginning.

Bad Sister was based on Booth Tarkington's play *The Flirt*, which had been previously filmed by Bluebird in 1916 and by Universal in 1922, both as silents. When it went into preproduction in early January 1931, it was being called *The Flirt*, and Bette, signed by the studio just a couple of weeks before, was being considered for the leading role. The title was eventually changed to *Gambling Daughters* and then to *Bad Sister*, and the lead was given to Sidney Fox. Bette had to content herself with the lesser role of Laura Madison, the *good* sister. Considering that Bette would attain stardom and acclaim with a series of villainous antiheroine roles, the casting was ironic.

With a budget of $252,000, *Bad Sister* started principal photography on January 26, 1931, just over a month after Bette arrived in Hollywood. It shot for 21 days and completed production on February 21. Indicative of the economic style of the day, it was released to audiences a mere month later to reviews that were tepid at best. Following is the *Variety* review, which gave the picture one of its better notices. It is the first film review that makes mention of the name *Bette Davis*.

> Tailored for family and child draw, with which classes it should be popular. Too slow in action and tamely produced to have any appeal for sophisticates. . . . Universal changed the title several times before hitting upon *Bad Sister*. It might just as well have been called *Spoiled Girl*. There isn't a suggestive touch in the entire reelage, except a moment's flash of repentance in a hotel room. . . . Sidney Fox is restricted to this small town big idea girl and as such is pleasing. Bette Davis holds much promise in her handling of Laura, sweet, simple and the very essence of repression. Story has very few highlights.

LUCILLE BALL

When Bette learned in the early 1970s that Lucille Ball was preparing to star in a screen version of *Mame*, she had herself submitted for the role of Vera Charles, Mame Dennis's bawdy, brassy best friend. Bette and Lucy had never worked together before, despite having been acting school classmates many years earlier. But Lucy, who called the shots on *Mame*, nixed the idea of costarring with Bette. The entire production was designed to showcase Lucy, and she wanted nothing or, more precisely, no one to detract from that goal. And so Bea Arthur, who was far less known then than she is now, was cast in the part. And while the notion of Bette and Lucy together ranks among the classic what-could-have-beens, the film was an unequivocal failure, and it might have been to Bette's advantage that she didn't get the part.

Years later, when Bette was flying from Los Angeles to Washington, D.C., for the Kennedy Center honors tribute, Lucille Ball, who was being similarly honored, was on the same plane. Robert Osborne, columnist for *The Hollywood Reporter*, was Bette's companion on the trip. He later recounted an incident that took place between the two indomitable legends. As he and Bette boarded the plane, they passed by Lucy, Angela Lansbury, Diahann Carroll, Vic Damone, and a few other luminaries. "Bette got on and said, '*Well*, if this plane crashes, I wonder *who* is going to get top billing?' And Lucille Ball said, 'Bette, it'd be you. No question, it'd be you!' "

KAYE BALLARD

In 1960, while in San Francisco touring with *The World of Carl Sandburg*, Bette attended a performance of Kaye Ballard's cabaret act at the Hungry i. That night, thrilled that Bette Davis was in her audience, Ballard nervously announced from the stage, "I want to do a bit about a movie star, but I want to assure Miss Davis that it is *not* about her." Bette shot back from her seat, to the delight of the audience, "*Do* the bit, and we'll dis-cuss it la-tah!"

ANNE BANCROFT

It was Bette's career-long dream to become the first actress to win three Best Actress Oscars. Her last real chance to accomplish this was in 1962, when she was nominated for her performance in *What Ever Happened to Baby Jane?* Bette would later ruefully acknowledge, "I was *positive* I would get it. So was everybody in town. I almost dropped dead when I didn't win." Who *did* win? Anne Bancroft, for reprising on film her stage portrayal of Annie Sullivan in *The Miracle Worker*. Bette would later concede that she thought Bancroft's performance had been "brilliant," but she couldn't resist adding, "I have a theory that someone who has played a play on Broadway for three years and then puts it on the screen has a definite advantage. I think it's more difficult to start from scratch and create a character for a film."

On April 8, 1963, the night of the awards ceremony, Anne Bancroft was starring in *Mother Courage*, then in its first few weeks on Broadway at the Martin Beck Theatre. She decided not to attend the Oscar ceremony, held that year in Santa Monica, California. Her husband, Mel Brooks, later related, "I didn't think she had a chance in the world, and I told her so. We felt that with [Katharine] Hepburn and Davis in it, that Hollywood would salute them for thirty years. . . . that Bancroft was a theatre personality and that Hollywood would honor its own."

TALLULAH BANKHEAD

In 1934, the year that Bette Davis would garner the first great acclaim of her career with *Of Human Bondage*, Tallulah Bankhead was flailing across the stage as Judith Traherne in the Broadway flop *Dark Victory*. Five years later, with the film version of the same play and in the same part, Bette Davis would receive some of the most overwhelming reviews of her career. There lies the basis for the "feud" between Bette Davis and Tallulah Bankhead.

During the early through mid-1930s, Bankhead (1902–1968) rejected some of the screen parts that Davis would go on to play, deeming them unworthy of her stature. *Satan Met a Lady* was one such picture. In later years Bankhead was bypassed in favor of Davis for roles that she *did* want. Further, she lost parts to Davis that she had originated on the stage. It was Bankhead who was initially cast in the stage production of *Jezebel* (she would later walk out and be replaced by Miriam Hopkins), and it was Bankhead who originated the role of Regina Giddens on Broadway in *The Little Foxes*. Bette's public stance was that she was one of Bankhead's great admirers. "I'm kind of a second-fiddle Tallulah Bankhead," said Bette with uncharacteristic modesty. "I've always felt that the things I did after she did she should have done anyway. I do think that particularly about *The Little Foxes*. No one else should ever have played it. I'm an enormous admirer of Miss Bankhead professionally. She's an extremely talented woman."

But while her talent was generally regaled in Hollywood, it was thought that her persona was too strong for the camera and that her personal life was too troublesome to contend with. She was entertaining to observe—from a distance. As one socialite put it, "Tallulah is always skating on thin ice. Everyone wants to be there when it breaks." As for any kind of feud between herself and Bankhead, Davis would always deny it. "The only time I came face to face with Miss Bankhead on nonamicable terms," said Bette in a story she was fond of relating, "was when she sidled up to me at the bar at a party in Jack Warner's house. She leaned on her elbows on the bar and said, 'Dahling, you've played almost all the parts on the screen that I've played on the stage. And, dahling, I've played them all so much better!' I said, 'I certainly agree with you.' And I did—and do. She looked at me curiously, moved away, and I never saw her again that evening." As for Bankhead, when asked if it bothered her that Bette had played her roles, she quipped, bemused, "It bothered Bette Davis, who was most generous and divine about it and was terribly upset. She said that no one but I should have played in *The Little Foxes*."

When *All About Eve* was in production in mid-1950, the rumors started that Bette was modeling her portrayal of the aging stage actress on Bankhead. The origin of the rumors lay in the hand and pen of a reporter who visited the set and proceeded to write that Bette had affected a deep, gravelly, Bankheadlike voice for the picture. Bette contended that the voice change was the result of screaming matches with her ex-husband William Grant Sherry. Bankhead was not convinced. Later, upon the film's release, with all of its attendant acclaim, much was made of the theory that the character of Margo Channing was actually based on Bankhead. When asked if she had seen Bette in the film, Tallulah snapped with characteristic wit, "Yes. Every morning when I brush my teeth." When asked for a response, Bette replied, "There was no intentional imitation of anyone. I feel that in this picture I played myself more than in any part I ever played in the past ten years. Maybe Miss Bankhead and I are alike, you see. That could happen."

Bankhead was still unconvinced and played the comparison for all (and more than) it was worth. At the time, she had a radio program. Whenever the subject of *All About Eve* arose, which seemed to be often, Bankhead would refer to the picture instead as *"All About Me."*

Despite several pictures, including *Tarnished Lady* (1931), *Lifeboat* (for which she should have won an Oscar nomination, the same year Bette got her seventh nomination, for *Mr. Skeffington*, 1944), and *Frantic* (1965), the motion picture screen was never able to capture the extravagance and explosive theatrics that were Tallulah Bankhead.

VILMA BANKY

Born Vilma Lonchit in 1902, Vilma Banky was a non-English-speaking silent screen star. While still a struggling actress in New York in the late 1920s, Bette Davis entered a Vilma Banky look-alike contest. With her mother Ruthie's assistance, Bette made herself up to resemble Banky and then showed up at the Astor Hotel with dreams of winning first prize and being flown to Hollywood, followed of course by impending stardom. She lost. Bette stalked out of the hotel, certain that the contest had been a setup.

"THE BARBARA WALTERS SPECIAL"

Bette Davis was interviewed on "The Barbara Walters Special" that aired on ABC on March 30, 1987. Also interviewed on that show were Elizabeth Taylor and Debra Winger. Said Bette on the show, "I see a lot of me in Debra Winger." She also offered her idea of a good marriage: "Communication, separate bedrooms, and separate bathrooms." And her view on stardom: "Unless you're called very, very difficult in Hollywood, you're nobody at all."

Barbara Walters seemed to struggle in her interview with Bette, who gave mostly perfunctory responses. Walters later related, "I made a big mistake with her. The second hour, I realized what the mistake was. I wanted to talk about her career, and she wanted to talk about her book. We don't usually just plug the book or movie. So the first hour, I asked her all about her films—I've seen every Bette Davis movie—and she was unresponsive. The second hour we got the book over with, and everything else was heaven. It taught me a lesson: get the reason *they* want to talk over with first."

RICHARD BARTHELMESS

By the time he costarred in *Cabin in the Cotton* (1932), the career of silent screen star Richard Barthelmess had diminished to mostly second-rate pictures. And although she was fond of Barthelmess, Bette was disdainful of his tendency to reserve his talent for his close-ups. Barthelmess, meanwhile, was more than a little uncomfortable with his young costar. "There was a lot of passion in her, and it was impossible not to sense it. . . . a lot of electricity that had not yet found its outlet. In a way it was rather disconcerting—yes, I admit it, frightening. . . . She was so exciting and seductive that she would have aroused a wooden Indian."

Richard Barthelmess (1895–1963) appeared in numerous silent pictures, including *Camille* (1917), *Broken Blossoms* (1919), *Tol'able David* (1921), *The Enchanted Cottage* (1924), and *The Patent Leather Kid* (1927). His talking pictures include supporting parts in *Only Angels Have Wings* (1939), *The Man Who Talked Too Much* (1940), and *The Spoilers* (1942).

PAMELA BASCOMB

In 1938 Pamela Bascomb was a 13-year-old girl with a talent for singing. She was discovered by Harmon Nelson, Jr., a musician and the husband of Bette Davis. On March 3, 1938, the Nelsons transplanted young Pamela from her modest home in Pomona, California, to the grandeur of their life in Coldwater Canyon. Said Nelson of his young protégée, whom he viewed as another Deanna Durbin (then a big star), "She has a lovely coloratura soprano voice of operatic caliber. The amazing thing is that she can [also] sing hot tunes. I feel that Pamela has great possibilities. She is at present working with a singing teacher, and I think that in a few weeks we will launch her on her film career. We are both tremendously fond of her." Bette added, "I'm not going to *adopt* her, but I hope I'll be able to 'mother' her. She has no parents and has been living with an aunt. She has exceptional talent—both in music and dancing, and we hope some day she'll be a great screen and stage star." A week after Pamela (whose name they changed inexplicably to Pam Caveness) moved in with them, Bette stated, a little uncertainly, "Silly as it may seem to say that I am going to 'mother' a girl of that age, I am going to do the best I can."

Later that year, Bette and Nelson were divorced. Bette, sensing a potential public relations fiasco, hushed the matter concerning the custody of Pamela Caveness, fka Bascomb. Presumably she was returned to her aunt in Pomona. Certainly the career imagined for her by Nelson and Bette never materialized.

ANNE BAXTER

As the cunning, venomous Eve Harrington in *All About Eve* (1950), Anne Baxter received critical acclaim and was touted for an Oscar nomination. However, there was some controversy over whether she should be nominated in the best actress or the best supporting actress category. Because she had already received a Best Supporting Actress Oscar a few years before for *The Razor's Edge* (1946), Baxter campaigned to be nominated in the Best Actress category. Subsequently, when the nominations were announced, Baxter was indeed cited on the best actress list. However, she was pitted head-to-head with her *Eve* costar, Bette Davis. With unusually strong competition that year from contenders Gloria Swanson (*Sunset Boulevard*) and Judy Holliday (*Born Yesterday*), Baxter and Davis canceled each other out, and Holliday was named the surprise winner.

Years later, shortly before her death in 1985, Baxter confided to an interviewer, "I've decided recently [that] I was wrong. I *should* have accepted another supporting Oscar and Bette would have undoubtedly gotten hers." Upon being told of Baxter's late confession, Bette replied, simply, "Yeah, she should have."

Anne Baxter and Bette Davis crossed paths more than 30 years after *All About Eve* with the ABC television drama "Hotel." Bette signed to star in the series and appeared in the show's September 1983 premiere. However, due to the stroke that she suffered in July 1983, the writers were forced to send her character, Laura Trent, on an extended trip. Management of the hotel was then assumed by Laura's sister-in-law, Victoria Cabot, played by Anne Baxter. Baxter remained on the hit series until her own sickness and death in 1985.

Born in 1923, Anne Baxter made her film debut with the 1940 picture *Twenty Mule Team*. Her numerous other films include *The Magnificent Ambersons* (1942), *Angel on My Shoulder* (1946), and *The Ten Commandments* (1956).

B. D. INC.

"If something isn't done right, you've got to do it yourself." This could have been the life credo of Bette Davis, and it was with this incentive that, in 1943, while still the top female movie star in the world, Bette Davis formed her own production company. She dubbed it B. D. Inc. Her intention was to produce and star in the pictures of her choice, which she would then release under the aegis of Warner Brothers. The contract gave B. D. Inc. the first $125,000 of the net profits on a picture it produced, with Warners getting the next $232,000. Any additional profits were to be split, with 65 percent going to the studio and 35 percent to B. D. Inc. Sitting on the company's board of directors were Jules Stein, Bette Davis, Dudley Furse, and Lew Wasserman. Bette would receive 80 percent of the company's profits; Stein got 10 percent; Furse got 5 percent; and Bette's mother, Ruthie, got the remaining 5 percent.

As for Jack Warner, he was more than glad—and not a little shrewd—to grant Bette her own production company. After all, if it was *her* money that was being spent, and *her* budget that had to be met, perhaps she would be a little less extravagant in her costly striving for perfection.

The contract between B. D. Inc. and Warner Brothers was signed on June 10, 1943, but did not go into effect until May 15, 1944, following the completion of *Mr. Skeffington*. It called for the company to produce five pictures before the expiration of the contract on February 21, 1949. By May 15, 1944, Warners had to submit to the new company at least two stories for consideration as its first picture. Bette had already approved *A Stolen Life* as the initial venture, provided that the studio could acquire all of the necessary rights.

However, the concept of Bette Davis as producer looked better on paper than in reality, and B. D. Inc. was dissolved on August 27, 1947, after delivering a single picture, *A Stolen Life* (1946), and shortly after Bette gave birth to her daughter, whom she ironically dubbed B.D.

B. DALTON BOOKSTORE

On February 13, 1988, bookstore manager Sheldon MacArthur made an industry coup by getting Bette Davis to appear at his store, B. Dalton Bookstore on Hollywood Boulevard, to sign copies of her book *This 'N That*, then just released in paperback.

For 15 minutes Bette posed for photographs for the press. Then the thousands of fans who had lined the sidewalk for hours were allowed into the store to buy copies of the book, to see *that* face and hear *that* voice, and to brush up against a legend. Bette, dressed all in black with a wide-brimmed hat and a sequined heart over her left breast, exchanged pleasantries with her fans, signed copies of her book, and smoked incessantly.

BEAUTY

"Those were the days when the movie girls were all too damned flamboyant. Chromium blondes, clothes consisting mainly of feathers, white fox, sequins. . . . And here was I, guiltless of so much as a lipstick. I had never used a lipstick in my life, except on the stage. I had never been to a hairdresser's. My eyebrows were as God had made them. I wore my hair long, a nice neat bun at the nape of my neck. I smiled a crooked little smile because I was still remembering the brace recently removed from my teeth. There wasn't an artificial thing about me. I looked like Alice wandering about Wonderland!"
Bette Davis to Gladys Hall on her
appearance when she arrived in Hollywood

"A woman doesn't have to be 21 and wear sweaters and bobby sox to have appeal. If a woman keeps her figure, her complexion, and a

youthful outlook on life, she can be considerably more glamorous at
38 than at 21. Why, when I was 21, I must have had about as much
sex appeal as a beetle! I simply didn't know the meaning of style and
poise. Those are things that have to be learned."

Bette, circa 1945

"Any of the times that I looked good, or even pretty, it was thanks to
a great cameraman. My career was never based on beauty."

Bette Davis, 1989

Despite early Warner Brothers press reports that generously referred to her as
a "beautiful blond," Bette Davis was never really a beauty and was only an
artificial blond. Decidedly, as dictated by the standards of her day, she was
attractive at best. Bette herself was ambivalent about her looks. On one hand
she was fond of publicly (and truthfully) stating that she had made it on
talent and not beauty. On the other hand, despite claiming disinterest in her

looks, she secretly resented actresses more beautiful than she.

She also had a penchant, over the years, for selecting roles that deliberately obliterated her natural attractiveness, flaunting what she considered to be her lack of vanity. But this conscious decision on her part was made only *after* she attempted and failed at a complete glamorous makeover. In *Ex-Lady* (1933) and *Fashions of 1934* (1934), Bette donned a platinum wig and a pound of makeup and was barely recognizable. Neither film did anything for her career.

It was not until she resorted to looking haggard and slatternly in *Of Human Bondage* (1934) that Bette made a breakthrough in pictures. It was a lesson that she never forgot. After all, if she could not compete with other actresses in the looks department, she would compete with them by having the audacity *not* to look attractive. So, it wasn't so much that Bette Davis was uninterested in her looks; it was that she shrewdly used them, or the lack of them, to her maximum advantage.

Still, in later pictures, particularly in *Dark Victory* (1939) and *Now, Voyager* (1942), there are moments when she looks positively exquisite. Years later, as she approached 80, Bette was asked what came to her mind when she rescreened her old pictures. "My God!" she gasped, "how could I have ever looked so *beautiful?*"

> "I always massage my face with cold cream, while sitting in a hot bath softened with bath oil."
>
> *a beauty tip by Bette Davis*

CONSTANCE BENNETT

One of Bette's favorite actresses when she arrived in Hollywood in late 1930 was Constance Bennett. It is not surprising, then, that Bette, in her early blond period, attempted to resemble Bennett. Fan magazines even hyped Bette as "the next Constance Bennett." By 1940, with her career in decline, Bennett was up for the part of Sandra, the second female lead, in *The Great Lie*. In fact Bennett wanted the part so much that she campaigned for the role. On October 16 she stooped to sending a telegram to Warners executive Hal Wallis saying, "I'm *dying* to do Sandra in *January Heights* [which it was being called at the time]. How about it? It's about time we got together anyway and I'm sure this would be a home run. Do please let me do it." Unfortunately for Bennett, she was right about the part (it would win a Best Supporting Actress Oscar for Mary Astor) but was deemed the wrong actress to play it.

RICHARD BENNETT

The star of the 1930 Broadway play *Solid South*. Upon being introduced to the young actress cast as his granddaughter, Bennett testily queried, "Are you another of these young *ham* actresses?" The actress retorted by slapping Bennett across the face, much to his admiration. The actress was Bette Davis.

Richard Bennett (1873–1944) was a popular American stage star and the father of Barbara, Constance, and Joan Bennett. He also appeared in a few pictures, including *Arrowsmith* (1932), *If I Had a Million* (1932), and *The Magnificent Ambersons* (1942).

> "She is like my daughters, Constance and Joan, a blending of them, but she is without their limitations."
>
> *Richard Bennett on Bette Davis*

ALVAH BESSIE

Ever since seeing her in *Of Human Bondage* in 1934, novelist and screenwriter Alvah Bessie had harbored something of a crush on Bette Davis. So, when he found himself working at the same studio as Bette in 1943, he approached her in the Warners dining room and presented her with copies of novels that he had written. The two later had lunch, during which Bette told him that she liked one of the novels and would consider starring in a screen version of it, if only he would change the ending. Bessie, to Bette's frustration and yet begrudging admiration, refused.

In 1949 Alvah Bessie was blacklisted as one of the infamous Hollywood Ten. When asked by the House Un-American Activities Committee, "Mr. Bessie, are you now or have you ever been a member of the Communist Party?" Bessie replied, "Unless it has been changed since yesterday in our country, we have a secret ballot; and I do not believe this committee has any more right to inquire into my political affiliations than I believe an election official has the right to go into a voting booth and examine the ballot which has been marked by the voter. General Eisenhower himself has refused to reveal his political affiliations, and what is good enough for General Eisenhower is good enough for me."

Bessie was exiled from Hollywood and condemned to serve time in prison. Upon his release, he worked for a time as a publicity man. Later he spent seven years as the stage manager and lighting man at the Hungry i nightclub in San Francisco. It was there, in April 1960, that Bessie once again met up with Bette Davis. Bette was in town starring in the stage production *The World of Carl Sandburg*. Bessie invited Bette to see a performance by Kaye Ballard, who was then performing at the Hungry i. Bette accepted and ventured backstage. Upon finding Bessie at his lighting board, she demanded, *"What* the hell're you doing *here*, Ahl-vah?!"

Bessie then took his fiancée, Sylviane, to meet Bette backstage following a performance of *Carl Sandburg*. Upon being introduced, Sylviane, a good many years younger than Bette, made the classic mistake of gushing to Bette how she had been a big fan of hers ever since she was a little girl. Bette did a quick head-to-toe scan of Sylviane, turned away from her, and said to Bessie, "Ahl-vah, what're you doing these days aside from working in *that* sewer?" It is unclear whether Bette was referring to the theater.

Alvah Bessie (1904–1985) wrote, among others, the pictures *The Very Thought of You* (1944), *Hotel Berlin* (1945), and *Objective Burma* (Best Original Story Oscar nomination, 1945).

"BETTE DAVIS EYES"

"Bette Davis Eyes," sung by Kim Carnes and written by Jackie DeShannon and Donna Weiss, was the number-one song in the country for an astounding *nine weeks* in 1981, making it one of the biggest pop hits of all time. Bette herself was thrilled with the popularity of the song, which first appeared on the *Billboard* chart on April 11, 1981, particularly because it gave her grandson an indication of the extent of her fame.

BETTE DAVIS IN PERSON AND ON FILM

On February 11, 1973, Bette was honored in New York in a stage series featuring film footage titled "Legendary Ladies of the Movies." From that appearance emerged a one-woman show produced by John Springer (who also produced the "Legendary Ladies" series) dubbed *Bette Davis in Person and on Film: A History of the Career of Bette Davis.* The show featured excerpted footage from Bette's pictures, after which Bette would strut on stage smoking a cigarette. She would then cross the stage, scan the room, put out her cigarette, and announce, "What a dump!"—much to the delight of her audiences. This was followed by a question-and-answer session between Bette and her fans. The show opened in Denver on March 11, 1974 and over the next few years toured 26 states, Australia, and England. For Bette one of the highlights of the tour was her triumphant reception at the Palladium in London. Another was the celebration of her 66th birthday on April 5, 1974, onstage at Symphony Hall in her hometown, Boston. In later years Bette would refer to that evening as a "love-in." In the audience that night was her son, Michael Merrill, along with numerous other relatives and hometown friends and acquaintances.

THE BETTE DAVIS MEMORIAL TRIBUTE

On November 2, 1989, shortly after her death, a tribute in honor of Bette Davis was held at Burbank Studios, on Warner Brothers soundstage 18, the same stage where she had made, among other pictures, *Now, Voyager* (1942). The event, themed "I Wish You Love," was organized by Bette's assistant, Kathryn Sermak, with the guidance of director George Schaefer.

David Hartman hosted the tribute. Behind the podium at which he stood was a giant screen that reflected images of Bette from her greatest pictures. Speeches were delivered by James Woods and Angela Lansbury, among others. President George Bush sent a telegram. Approximately 400 invited guests showed up to pay their respects, among them Ann-Margret, Kim Carnes, Clint Eastwood, Julius Epstein, Glenn Ford, Linda Gray, Roddy McDowall, Vincent Price, Vincent Sherman, and Robert Wagner.

> "Buckle your seat belts; it's going to be a bumpy eternity."
> *James Woods*

"THE BETTE DAVIS SHOW"

Thirty-minute pilot, aka "Decorator," for an ABC comedy series that starred Bette as an interior decorator, designing her way in and out of the lives of her clients. The show was created by Cy Howard, produced by Tom McDermott, and directed by Dick Kinon. Ed Begley costarred with Bette in the pilot episode. The show was produced in mid-November 1964 and was delivered at the end of January 1965. A few weeks later the executive brass at ABC announced that the pilot would not be picked up for the new season.

BEVERAGES

Bette Davis was fond of drinking scotch—sometimes with water, sometimes on the rocks. She was also a fanatical drinker of coffee, which she would consume with numerous heaped spoonfuls of sugar. Another daily ritual was Carnation Instant Breakfast drink.

"She would start off being very funny and sweet, then, as she drank, she'd become witty and sharp, and her comments about our Hollywood friends would be very biting—savage but true."
Paul Henreid, on Bette Davis and alcohol

"Don't you hate people who drink white wine? I mean, my de-ah, every alcoholic in town is getting falling-down drunk on white wine. They think they aren't drunks because they only drink wine. Never, never trust *any-one* who asks for white wine."
Bette Davis

BEYOND THE FOREST ★★
Warner Brothers
1949   96 minutes   bw
Directed by: King Vidor
Produced by: Henry Blanke
Screenplay by: Lenore Coffee, based on the novel by Stuart Engstrand
Cinematography by: Robert Burks
Cast: Bette Davis, Joseph Cotten, David Brian, Ruth Roman, Minor
    Watson, Dona Drake, Regis Toomey, Sarah Selby, Mary Servoss,
    Frances Charles, Harry Tyler, Ralph Littlefield, Creighton Hale, Joel
    Allen, Ann Doran

In June 1943, Bette Davis signed a contract with Warner Brothers in which she agreed to make 14 pictures in five years. Several contracts later, after delivering only six pictures, Bette signed a new contract with the studio on January 27, 1949. It called for her to make a scant four pictures over four years. Aware of her recent relative inactivity (and all too aware of her declining box office allure), Bette was anxious to get back to work. Furthermore, by this point her third marriage, to William Grant Sherry, had all but collapsed, and she was anxious to get away from him. Her anxiety and haste and marital difficulties may have colored her story sense and objectivity about her own capabilities as an actress.

On April 23, 1948, Warners paid $5,000 for the film rights to the Stuart Engstrand novel. Later the studio picked up the option with another $20,000. The script was then assigned to Lenore Coffee, who had previously worked on *The Great Lie* (1941). Coffee proceeded to develop the screenplay, with an uncredited assist from Harriet Frank, Jr. The intention was to create what was then called a "woman's picture," sort of a darker variation of Flaubert's *Madame Bovary*, which was then being filmed over at MGM with Jennifer Jones.

Set in the lumber town of Loyalton, Wisconsin, *Beyond the Forest* has Bette's Rosa Moline miserable and married to the nice (and only) doctor in town, Lewis Moline (Joseph Cotten). Despite having the finest house in town, which is kept by a maid, Rosa loathes life in Loyalton, has an affair with big-city playboy Neil Latimer (David Brian), and dreams of a more glamorous life in Chicago. A train from Chicago passes through Loyalton twice a day, and Rosa regularly sashays through the town to watch the train come and go as she hums the tune "Chicago, Chicago, that toddlin' town . . ." under her breath. The train, in fact, is an integral part of the picture.

The film is prefaced with the rationalization "This is the story of evil. Evil is headstrong—puffed up. For our soul's sake, it is salutary for us to view it in all its naked ugliness once in a while. . . ."

The evil in this case, of course, is Rosa. When her husband the doctor tells her with pride that he has just saved a woman's life, she squawks back, "I wouldn't brag. The only man to envy in this town is the undertaker. He does people a real favor—[he] carries them *out!*" She wants to run off with Latimer, but her problem is exacerbated when she learns that she is pregnant with her husband's child. Then her husband's friend Moose (Minor Watson) learns of her plans and threatens to tell her husband. The following morning the group goes out on a deer-hunting expedition, and Rosa "accidentally" shoots and kills not deer but poor Moose. She is exonerated by the court but still has the problem of the impending child. Determined, Rosa flings herself down a ravine and presumably rids herself of the baby. Unfortunately for her, she also gets quite sick. In *Dark Victory*, Bette elegantly ascended a staircase to her death; in *Beyond the Forest* she ungraciously descends a staircase, then pitifully stumbles through town and to her death in a desperate attempt to catch the train to toddlin' Chicago.

In 1948, while contemplating future projects, Bette told an interviewer, "I like *Beyond the Forest*. I think it's a wonderful story, but Warners will never have the nerve to make it." Bette considered the story on the edge, daring, particularly the self-induced abortion sequence (the Breen Office would later insist that the scene be cut). She also saw in the role ample opportunity to showcase her pyrotechnic histrionics, something that she had not done in her past two pictures—*June Bride*, a comedy, and *Winter Meeting*, a rather somber drama.

Bette was not the only actress to like and see possibilities in the script. Joan Crawford, who had surpassed Bette's recent efforts for the studio, also vied for it. But the truth is that both Crawford and Davis, 43 and 41 respectively, were far too old for the part. The role called for Rosa Moline to be the most desirable woman in town. Why else would her husband tolerate her as he did? Why else would Neil Latimer, certainly used to the beauties of Chicago, be enamored of her? Rosa is an impatient, fidgety woman meant, presumably, to be in her 20s. Certainly she would not have waited until she was 40 to get out of Loyalton. She would have gone to Chicago many years before.

Bette, aware of this, tries to dress younger, act younger. Vidor is also aware of the problem. He populates his town of Loyalton with aging, unattractive women in an effort to make Rosa more appealing. It's a transparent and unsuccessful effort. Bette is unbelievable and a little embarrassing in her peasant tops and flouncy skirts. She's a bit overweight, and it appears at times that her bosom has been accentuated. And the dark wig she wears throughout the picture looks like something somebody picked up at a thrift shop at Halloween. It is interesting to note here that Bette's favorite cinematographer, Ernie Haller, was not on this picture. They had had a fight during the production of *Winter Meeting* the year before, and Haller vowed never again to work on a Davis picture. Subsequently Robert Burks, who had never before photographed Bette and was not familiar with her particular needs, was given the assignment. Suffice it to say that Bette never looked worse (except when she was meant to) on the screen. At times she looks as if she is attempting to impersonate Jennifer Jones in *Duel in the Sun* (1946), which, by the way, Vidor also directed.

Bette did the usual wardrobe and makeup tests with Vidor on May 10, 1949, and more on May 20. Edith Head had been borrowed from Paramount at the considerable expense of $5,000 to do Bette's costumes. In this case it was money most unwisely spent.

Still, on Tuesday, May 24, *Beyond the Forest*, which a few weeks before was titled *Rosa Moline*, commenced principal photography with a good deal of optimism. Bette had not made a picture for eight months and was eager to get back to work. Meanwhile, the studio brass assumed that she would be well rested and in good spirits and that the picture would have an uncomplicated shoot. Bette planned to finish shooting by July 1 so that she could go back east to her farm and avoid the summer heat wave in southern California.

On that first day of shooting, Bette arrived on the set and astonished most of those present with her appearance. She wore a long (and, again, ill-advised) black wig and a calico dress that sold off the racks for $8.90. Bette explained her choice of hairstyle by quipping, "Most of history's bad girls had dark tresses"—which is precisely why Vidor should have stepped in here, for the wig is too obvious. Bette had tested wearing black and red wigs. She should have opted for her own natural color. She didn't, after all, need a black wig to play a villainess in *Of Human Bondage* (1934) or *Jezebel* (1938).

Joseph Cotten did not report to the set as scheduled because his wife, Leonore, was having surgery at St. John's Hospital in Santa Monica at the time. Cotten almost didn't do the picture and, in retrospect, should not have. For the audience to have any interest or sympathy in Rosa's plight to get out of Loyalton, it must first be established that she had something to get away from. Yet in *Beyond the Forest*, Joe Cotten's small-town doctor who fishes is every man's idol and every woman's ideal. It's not that we don't believe Rosa's desire to get out of Loyalton; it's that we think that she's a fool for so desperately wanting to get away from Joe Cotten. In later years, Bette would express that she had wished Eugene Pallette, a fat, then-60-year-old character actor, had played the part. On this point she was not wrong.

Early in the shooting Bette had a line that was to become one of her most famous. As Rosa Moline she glances across the home that her husband has bought for her and announces, "What a dump." Surprisingly, the line is delivered without the punch and punctuation that Davis impersonators (and Davis herself) have since made famous.

The company left for location shooting in Lake Tahoe on Wednesday, June 8. Bette drove to the location with her husband, Sherry, in an effort to salvage their marriage and left their two-year-old daughter at home with her nanny. Bette was miserable on all accounts. As she later told a reporter, she was awakened every morning at 5:30 to, in her words, "shiver in the cold dawn. . . . by noon, I'm panting for breath from scrambling over rocks, getting in and out of canoes, and trying to look pretty for the cameras. Then I eat a catered lunch, with flies and gnats and oversized ants for company."

On Friday, June 17, the company returned to the Burbank soundstage, and trouble brewed on the set. As Vidor would later recount, "[She was] one of the screen's top actresses who probably couldn't help conjuring up a reputation of being difficult to handle. I got along with her fine in the film until one morning I corrected the manner in which she was hurling a small bottle of medicine. I tried to show her the way I felt it should be done which would give more strength to her action. She resented my directions."

By this time Bette was well aware that she had made a mistake with her third marriage *and* with *Beyond the Forest*. She was also aware of how unattractive she looked on camera and what that might do to her career. Her work had always been a refuge from her private life, but now neither offered solace. She lashed out—primarily at King Vidor for making such a picture and Jack Warner for putting her in it. In fact, it was Bette herself who had accepted this picture when she had rejected so many others.

On July 6, 1949, Bette did not report to the set. Rumors abounded; some claimed she was pregnant with her second child, and others contended that she had contracted pneumonia. More insightful reports commented that Bette was simply unhappy with the production. Meanwhile, angry telephone calls were exchanged, lawyers were summoned, and telegrams flew in and out of Burbank. With Bette's continued absence, *Beyond the Forest* was forced to shut down production, and all proverbial hell broke loose. Vidor later explained, "Unbeknownst to me [she] went to the head of the studio and told them that unless I was taken off the picture she would not appear for work the next day. When the executives told her that they were pleased with my work and that I would not be taken off the film she countered with the fact that she would come to work the next day only if they would cancel her contract."

Bette was probably simply playing her tired trump card with the studio. Several times over her 18 years with the studio, when things got particularly combative, Bette had threatened to walk out on her contract, but then everything would be smoothed over by Jack Warner. By July 1949, however, Bette Davis's box office appeal had seemingly diminished, and Warner was more than ready to write off the most expensive star on his lot. Bette had overestimated her importance to the studio, and Warner was going to make her pay for it.

On July 14 Bette returned to the lot, and work on *Beyond the Forest* resumed. Vidor was not told that she had demanded his removal until the last day of shooting, for fear that it would affect their ability to complete the picture. At the wrap party, as Vidor later related, Bette approached him and said that she would love to work with him again on any project that he deemed suitable for her. "Such," Vidor said later, "are the problems of filmmaking and of working with Miss Bette Davis." He would also relate to Joe Cotten, among others, that the picture had been the worst experience of his entire career.

On August 4, the second to last day of shooting, Bette announced to the press that *Beyond the Forest* would be her final picture for Warner Brothers. She claimed that the parting was amicable and that she merely wanted to be free to make other pictures for other studios. That was partly true.

On the set on the final night of principal photography were just Bette, the director, and the camera crew. The scene being shot had Rosa Moline, alone and friendless, dying on a desolate street. As Bette told a reporter a couple of days later, "It was so cold and lonely on the back lot I almost felt sorry for myself until the ironic humor of the thing got me."

Irony struck again in the late morning of August 9, when Bette returned to the studio to do an hour of postrecording dialogue and had to redub the line "I've *got* to get out of here. Let me out of *here*." Bette could not help laughing.

The Hollywood Reporter could not help speculating on September 28, 1949: "Warners suddenly decided to shoot *Beyond the Forest* out for fast release in two weeks. Can't figure whether they have a big hit—or, they wanna forget the whole Bette Davis thing fast." It was the latter, of course, that was true, and upon its release *Beyond the Forest* was branded with the worst reviews of Bette Davis's career. As Hedda Hopper succinctly stated, "If Bette had deliberately set out to wreck her career, she couldn't have picked a more appropriate vehicle."

Meanwhile, the Legion of Decency pinned its infamous "condemned" classification on the film, and in the succeeding weeks Warner received a flurry of postcards that read, "I, as a Catholic, protest the showing of the immoral picture, *Beyond the Forest*." The Church had some success in preventing the film from being shown in some theaters around the country, but it was the bad word of mouth that really condemned the picture at the box office. Warner Brothers attempted to battle back with a titillating marketing campaign: "She's a Midnight Girl in a 9 o'clock Town!" "Nobody's as Good as Bette When She's Bad!" More accurate, of course, would have been "Nobody's as Good as Bette When She's Bad—in a Good Picture!"

Actually, in retrospect *Beyond the Forest* is not quite as bad as it was originally made out to be. It is even entertaining (albeit in a camp kind of way) at times. And one has to admire Bette's audacity (if not intelligence) in playing a role so obviously miscast and a character so utterly devoid of redeeming qualities. Bette, it seems, was lambasted by the press not just for her performance but also for her defection from Warner Brothers. In the past Bette had had the power of the studio to protect her from the press. Beginning with the release of *Beyond the Forest*, she did not. And all those in the press who had been waiting for years to take a shot at her finally had their chance. They took it with a vengeance.

THE BIG SHAKEDOWN ★½

Warner Brothers

1934   64 minutes   bw

Directed by: John Francis Dillon

Produced by: Samuel Bischoff

Screenplay by: Niven Busch and Rian James, based on a story by Samuel Engel

Cinematography by: Sid Hickox

Cast: Charles Farrell, Bette Davis, Ricardo Cortez, Allen Jenkins, Glenda Farrell, Henry O'Neill, Philip Faversham, Robert Emmett O'Connor, John Wray, George Pat Collins, Adrian Morris, Dewey Robinson, Samuel S. Hinds, Matt Briggs, William B. Davidson, Earl Foxe, Frederick Burton, Ben Hendricks, George Cooper, Sidney Miller, Oscar Apfel

Routine action programmer that illustrates, if nothing else, that Warner Brothers did not have a clue about what to do with Bette Davis. Here she is Norma Frank, the good, pregnant, and suffering wife of Jimmy Morrell (Charles Farrell), a pharmacist who unwittingly gets caught up in a counterfeit medication racket schemed up by Nick Barnes (Ricardo Cortez). Norma eventually loses her baby in the hospital after she is administered the worthless medication, and Barnes ends up paying for his sins by taking a swim in a vat of acid.

Based on Sam Engels's story "Cut Rate," the picture went into preproduction under the title *The Shakedown*. Universal, however, sent word over to Warners that it had a picture with the same name. So some studio wag, who apparently subscribed to the notion "the bigger the better," thought up the alternative title, *The Big Shakedown*.

Initially the studio had wanted Robert Young for the part of the naive pharmacist. Young, however, backed out at the last minute to make a picture at RKO with Ann Harding. So Charles Farrell was signed for the picture for the lump sum of $17,500. Bette was paid a weekly salary and would earn about $1,500 for the entire picture. The picture was budgeted at $176,000 and was allotted 18 shooting days. It started shooting on August 28, 1933, and finished on September 18.

Upon viewing a cut of the picture, Hal Wallis, then head of the studio's production, sent it back for additional retakes in late October. Director John Francis Dillon, however, was ailing (he would pass away in the next few months), so Wallis assigned cameraman Brick Enright to shoot the retakes. Wallis ended up being displeased with Enright's work—and so did the critics. *The Big Shakedown* opened to poor reviews in February 1934.

BIRTH

Ruth Elizabeth Davis was born to Ruth Favor Davis and Harlow Morrell Davis in Lowell, Massachusetts, on April 5, 1908.

ARTHUR BLAKE

One of the first female impersonators to include a Bette Davis routine in his show. Bette saw Blake's impersonation of her at the Trocadero nightclub in Los Angeles, during a break from the shooting of *Deception* (1946). The following day she entertained the cast and crew by impersonating Blake impersonating her.

Still, she was less than pleased when Blake opened at Larry Potter's Supper Club shortly after the dismal release of *Winter Meeting* in 1948. Blake launched into his Davis routine by spouting, "I'm *so* ner-vous! You'd be toooo, if you had read the reviews for *Winter Meeting*!"

Years later, reflecting on those who had impersonated her, Bette would credit Arthur Blake as being the first and, in her view, the most brilliant.

HENRY BLANKE

Warner Brothers producer Henry Blanke, "Heinz" to those who knew him, made enormous contributions to the career of Bette Davis. Blanke functioned as "supervisor" (read: producer) on the pictures *Bureau of Missing Persons* (1933), *Fashions of 1934* (1934), *Fog Over Frisco* (1934), *The Girl from Tenth Avenue* (1935), *The Petrified Forest* (1936), and *Satan Met a Lady* (1936). As *The Life of Emile Zola* (Best Picture Oscar winner, 1937), *The Adventures of* named *associate producers*, who functioned under the auspices of executive producer Hal Wallis. In effect, however, associate producers like Blanke still did the same work: produce. Under the credit *associate producer*, Blanke produced *Jezebel* (because it was running considerably behind schedule, Blanke also worked as a second-unit director on the picture, 1938), *Juarez* (1939), *The Old Maid* (1939), and *The Great Lie* (1941).

When Hal Wallis left to pursue independent production, the studio regrouped again and its associate producers were finally credited with the appropriate title *producers*. With this credit Blanke produced the 1943 picture *Old Acquaintance*.

After Wallis's departure, Henry Blanke's stature at the studio grew. In April 1945 he signed a 15-year deal with Warners starting him at $3,500 a week, guaranteeing his assignment to only the expensive A productions, and giving him complete control over his pictures, at least until the first preview. His first project under this new agreement was the 1946 production *Deception*. Blanke's subsequent pictures included *Winter Meeting* (1948), *June Bride* (1948), and *Beyond the Forest* (1949).

The non-Davis pictures in the career of Henry Blanke (1901–1981) include *The Story of Louis Pasteur* (Best Picture Oscar nomination, 1936), the power structure at Warners changed, the studio's supervisors were re-*Robin Hood* (Best Picture Oscar nomination, 1938), *The Maltese Falcon* (Best

Picture Oscar nomination for Hal Wallis, 1941), *The Treasure of the Sierra Madre* (Best Picture Oscar nomination, 1948), *The Fountainhead* (1949), and *The Nun's Story* (Best Picture Oscar nomination, 1959).

> "A producer of infinite taste, an understanding man, whatever the problems."
>
> *Bette Davis on Henry Blanke, 1974*

JOAN BLONDELL

In the late 1920s Rosebud Blondell attended the Robert Milton–John Murray Anderson School of the Theatre in New York. One of her classmates was Bette Davis. Together they appeared in a school production of *Their Anniversary*. In Hollywood a few years later, Blondell, by then renamed Joan, found herself costarring with Bette in a picture called *Three on a Match* (1932). Bette was a little miffed that Blondell had the better part, the interest of their director, and a salary of $100 more a week. Further, at that point in their careers it was Joan Blondell and not Bette Davis for whom Warner Brothers had high hopes. Within two years Bette would replace Blondell in the Cagney picture *Jimmy the Gent* (1934), and at the top of the Warner roster of most promising actresses.

Joan Blondell made her picture debut in 1930 with *Sinner's Holiday*. Her subsequent pictures were numerous, but none elevated her to true stardom.

HUMPHREY BOGART

Despite the fact that they started out in pictures together and would later wage similar battles at Warner Brothers, Bette Davis and Humphrey Bogart tolerated, rather than befriended, each other. Bogart disdained what he considered to be Bette's pretensions of acting greatness; and although she was by no means prudish, she found Bogart crass. Worse, she regarded him as an inferior talent—a personality rather than an actor.

Still, they appeared in several pictures together: *Bad Sister* (Bette's film debut, 1931), *Three on a Match* (with Bogart a gangster even then, 1932), and *The Petrified Forest* (1936). In the last, in which he reprised his stage role of Duke Mantee, Bogart gave his first breakthrough performance on the screen. He was not under contract to Warners at the time and was paid the relatively paltry sum of $750 a week (top male stars of the period were earning over $5,000).

Following Bette's unsuccessful strike against and return to Warner Brothers, she and Bogart appeared in two 1937 pictures together, *Marked Woman* and *Kid Galahad*. After viewing dailies of the former, studio executive Hal Wallis issued a memo dated January 12, 1937, to director Lloyd Bacon that read, in part, "Will you tell Bogart to be a little more careful, a little more particular about his appearance? . . . Tell him to wear something conservative, some plainer things and be sure that he looks good when he goes into a scene." In an earlier memo to Bacon, Wallis instructed, "Be sure and have Bogart use makeup throughout the rest of the picture, as his beard

Hall Wallis: "Will you tell Bogart to be . . . a little more particular about his appearance?"

shows up so badly—he looks dirty." It is ironic that the same characteristics that appalled Hal Wallis would contribute to Bogart's eventual popularity.

Bogart also appeared as Bette's lustful Irish stablehand in *Dark Victory* (1939) and was cast opposite Bette in another picture that year, *The Old Maid*. However, after viewing the early footage, the powers that be decided that Bogart was miscast as a romantic lead and promptly replaced him with George Brent. Later, Davis and Bogart both appeared in the all-star Warners Musical, *Thank Your Lucky Stars* (1943).

Although they started their screen careers during the same period, Humphrey Bogart (1899–1957) would have to wait longer than Bette Davis for stardom. For him it came finally, after about *40* films, with *The Maltese Falcon* in 1941. His performance in this and subsequent pictures would establish him as the king of the cool, fast-talking detective-in-trenchcoat genre of the 1940s.

The numerous other pictures of Humphrey Bogart include *Casablanca* (Best Actor Oscar nomination, 1943), *To Have and Have Not* (1944), *The Big Sleep* (1946), *The Treasure of the Sierre Madre* (1948), *The African Queen* (Best Actor Oscar winner, 1951), and *The Caine Mutiny* (Best Actor Oscar nomination, 1954).

THE BOOKS ABOUT BETTE DAVIS

Title	Author	Year
Bette Davis: a Biography	Peter Noble	1948
Bette Davis	Jerry Vermilye	1973
Mother Goddam	Whitney Stine (with Bette Davis)	1974
Bette	Charles Higham	1981
Bette Davis: Her Film and Stage Career	Jeffrey Robinson	1982
Bette Davis: A Biography in Photographs	Christopher Nickens	1985
My Mother's Keeper	B. D. Hyman	1985
Bette Davis: a Celebration	Alexander Walker	1986
Bette & Joan: The Divine Feud	Shaun Considine	1989
Bette Davis: An Intimate Memoir	Roy Mosely	1989
Bette Davis: A Tribute	Roger Baker	1989
The Complete Films of Bette Davis	Gene Ringgold	1990
Fasten Your Seat Belts	Lawrence J. Quirk	1990
"I'd Love to Kiss You . . ."	Whitney Stine	1990
Me and Jezebel: When Bette Davis Came for Dinner—and Stayed	Elizabeth Fuller	1992
Bette Davis: a Biography	Barbara Leaming	1992
More than a Woman	James Spada	1993

THE BOOKS BY BETTE DAVIS

Title	Author	Year
The Lonely Life	Bette Davis	1962
This 'N That	Bette Davis (with Michael Herskowitz)	1987

BORDERTOWN ★★★

Warner Brothers
1935   80 minutes   bw
Directed by: Arthur L. Mayo
Produced by: Robert Lord
Screenplay by: Laird Doyle and Wallace Smith; adaptation by Robert Lord, from the novel by Carroll Graham
Cinematography by: Tony Gaudio
Cast: Paul Muni, Bette Davis, Margaret Lindsay, Eugene Pallette, Robert Barrat, Henry O'Neill, Gavin Gordon, Arthur Stone, Soledad Jiminez, William B. Davidson, Hobart Cavanaugh, Vivian Tobin, Nella Walker, Oscar Apfel, Samuel S. Hinds, Chris Pin Martin, Frank Puglia, Jack Norton

Bordertown was adapted primarily as a vehicle for Paul Muni, who, after his considerable successes in *Scarface* (1932) and *I Am a Fugitive from a Chain Gang* (1932), was on his way to becoming the most important star on the Warners lot. In fact it was Muni himself who initiated the project. In March 1934 he sent the novel by Carroll Graham to Hal Wallis, chief of production. It's easy to understand the attraction the project held for Muni. The controversial story revolved around the central character of Johnny Ramirez, a Mexican lawyer who engages in an adulterous affair with Marie Roark, a prostitute, and degenerates into a murderer.

Muni had no idea that the story would achieve the dubious distinction of being the object of censorship. While Ed Chodorov was drafting the script (novelist Graham having been dismissed after the studio was dissatisfied with what he had come up with) the Catholic Church established the Legion of Decency. In effect a censor, it would recommend to millions of Catholics which movies to see and which to avoid. Of particular concern to the Church were pictures that in any way glorified violence or depicted sexuality.

The legion's proscriptions would change not only the *Bordertown* story but also Warners' house style and, in fact, the entire motion picture industry. In response to the legion, Hollywood panicked and, on July 15, 1934, its self-censoring board, the Production Code Administration (which had been around since 1930 but was generally dismissed), went into renewed effect. From that point forward, before a script could go into production, its studio would have to submit it to the PCA for approval.

The script for *Bordertown* was one of the first to be scrutinized by the revitalized PCA. Upon reviewing the material, the censor informed Jack Warner that "it would be difficult, if not impossible, to produce a picture which would meet the requirements of the Production Code."

In a state of panic, Wallis hired a new writing team headed by Robert Lord. Over the next few weeks Chodorov's script was completely overhauled. Instead of committing murder, Ramirez merely punches out a rival attorney and, disbarred, manages a seedy casino in an equally squalid bordertown. And instead of carrying on an adulterous affair with a prostitute, he spurns the advances of Marie Roark, now the casino owner's wife, who eventually murders her husband in an effort to win Ramirez's love.

Muni, who could and did get just about anything he wanted at the studio (within the PCA's standards), wanted either Carole Lombard or Lupe Velez for the role of Marie. Jack Warner was about to secure Lombard when one of his contract players scored with a breakthrough performance in a loan out to another studio. The picture was *Of Human Bondage*, and the player was Bette Davis. And so it was with Muni's misgivings that Warner signed Bette to play Marie Roark in *Bordertown*.

It took three weeks for the new script to be written, and upon its completion it was resubmitted to the PCA, which this time gave its approval. On August 17, 1934, with a budget of $343,000, *Bordertown* finally went into production.

Bette, coming from a vacation, did not join the *Bordertown* company until two weeks later. Inflated by her experience and success on *Bondage*, Bette was determined to do things her way. One scene called for her to awaken in the middle of the night and rush out onto the street. When the time came to shoot the scene, Bette raised the collective eyebrows of the crew when she walked onto the set with curlers in her hair and no makeup on her face. Director Archie Mayo barked, "You can't appear on the screen—like *that!*" Bette won the battle, retorting, "The hell I can't. This is *exactly* how a woman looks when she gets up in the middle of the night!"

Another scene caused a more significant controversy. After viewing the dailies, Hal Wallis decided that he didn't like the way Mayo was directing Bette. In a September 13 memo Wallis wrote to Mayo: "I don't like the way you played Bette Davis at all in the scene in the construction set. It's about time she's starting to crack, and if she's getting the willies from walking around the house she certainly doesn't show it in this scene. She plays it like Alice in Wonderland. I want you to take this scene over and make it in a more emotional-hysterical way. . . ." Later that day writer Lord issued a counter memo to Wallis in Mayo's defense: "I emphatically disagree with your criticism of the way Miss Davis is played. . . . I think Archie has directed the scene as I, who wrote it, intended it to be directed. . . . and the lady is giving an outstanding performance." Lord further expressed that he had an additional scene to shoot that would display the wanted histrionics and noted that "if we start Miss Davis cracking up and screaming too early, we will have absolutely nothing left for her in the later clinching scenes."

The scene Lord was referring to in particular was the scene in which Marie suffers a mental breakdown in court. When it came time to shoot the sequence, Mayo, sensitive that Wallis wanted and expected hysteria, directed Bette to pull out all the stops and go hair-yanking *insane*, Hollywood style. Bette refused. The scene was shot Bette's way, and after viewing the footage, Wallis allowed it to stand the way it had been shot.

Bordertown completed principal photography on September 28, 1934, and was released in January 1935. And although it was initially intended primarily as a vehicle for Paul Muni, it was Bette Davis who stole the picture and walked off with the reviews. The film was significant to her career because it proved that *Of Human Bondage* was no fluke.

BOSTON, MASSACHUSETTS

Although she was born in Lowell, Massachusetts, Bette spent much of her childhood in the Boston area and frequently referred to Boston as her hometown. In later years Bette would make several triumphant return visits to the city. In 1929, the Ibsen Repertory Company's production of *The Wild Duck* toured the East Coast, including a stop in Boston. Following the performance, the show's star, Blanche Yurka, took Bette by the hand, led her centerstage, and allowed Bette a curtain call by herself, to the ovation of an audience that included family and friends.

Years later, Bette returned to Boston, specifically to Symphony Hall, with her one-woman show, *Bette Davis in Person and on Film*. The performance took place on April 5, 1974, and was a celebration of Bette's 66th birthday.

BOSTON UNIVERSITY

Beginning in 1972 and continuing throughout the years, Bette Davis donated her papers, including an extensive collection of letters, scripts, scrapbooks, and other memorabilia totaling 109,000 items, to Boston University. Today the Bette Davis Collection is housed at the university's Mugar Memorial Library, under the supervision of curator Howard Gotlieb. "It took ten years of courtship to persuade her to let us have the papers," Gotlieb explained. "Miss Davis sent at least half a dozen personal friends to look me over and to see what kind of facility we have." Ask Gotlieb why Bette would select Boston University, besides its obvious appeal of being near her hometown, and he is glib. "I offered her the best curator in the country." Boston University also houses the archives of Edward G. Robinson, Gene Kelly, and Robert Redford.

CHARLES BOWDEN

Producer of the 1961 play *The Night of the Iguana*, Charles Bowden, along with his wife, Paula Lawrence, developed a lasting friendship with Bette Davis. Says Bowden, "I had great respect for Bette Davis as a star and as a woman. I think she was brave. I think she was tough. I think she was hard on everybody and on herself, even more so on herself. She was a valiant woman."

Prior to producing *Iguana*, which would earn him a Best Play Tony nomination, Charles Bowden produced *Fallen Angels*, a revival of *Auntie*

Mame with Sylvia Sidney, Tennessee Williams's *27 Wagons Full of Cotton* with Maureen Stapleton, and *Caligula*.

BOX OFFICE
The following is a list of the top male and female box office stars in the world from 1938 to 1945 (Bette Davis's halcyon years) according to Quigley Publications:

1938: Shirley Temple
  Clark Gable
1939: Shirley Temple
  Mickey Rooney
1940: Bette Davis
  Mickey Rooney
1941: Bette Davis
  Mickey Rooney

1942: Betty Grable
  Abbott and Costello
1943: Betty Grable
  Bob Hope
1944: Betty Grable
  Bing Crosby
1945: Greer Garson
  Bing Crosby

More Bette Davis Box Office Facts
☆ According to the annual *Motion Picture Herald Survey* of the top 10 box office stars, Bette placed sixth in 1939, ninth in 1940, eighth in 1941, and 10th in 1944.
☆ In 1940, Bette and Mickey Rooney were named the Queen and King of the Movies by *Life* magazine and the *New York Daily News*.
☆ *Juarez* was one of the top-grossing pictures of 1939.
☆ *The Old Maid* (1939) was Bette's biggest box office between 1932 and 1940. The film earned $1.5 million in North American rentals* and ranked as the 22nd biggest hit of the 1930s (*Gone With the Wind* was first).
☆ *All This, and Heaven Too* was one of the top-grossing pictures of 1940.
☆ *The Bride Came C.O.D.* was one of the top-grossing pictures of 1941.

☆ *In This Our Life*, *The Man Who Came to Dinner*, and *Now, Voyager* were all among the top-grossing pictures of 1942.

☆ *Thank Your Lucky Stars* was one of the top-grossing pictures of 1943.

☆ *Mr. Skeffington* was one of the top-grossing pictures of 1944.

☆ *Hollywood Canteen* was the biggest Bette Davis–related hit between 1941 and 1950. It earned $4.2 million in North American rentals.

☆ *A Stolen Life* (1946) grossed a respectable $3 million in North American rentals.

☆ *Deception* (1946) cost $2 million to make and grossed only $2.3 million in North American rentals.

☆ *Winter Meeting* (1948) opened at the Warner Theatre in New York and in its first two days earned less than $8,000, the weakest opening for a Bette Davis picture in years. It signaled the beginning of the end of Bette's box office reign.

☆ *June Bride* (1948) grossed a mediocre $1.5 million in North American rentals.

☆ *Beyond the Forest* (1949) grossed a disappointing $1.5 million in North American rentals.

☆ *All About Eve* was the 11th top-grossing film of 1950 with $2.9 million in North American rentals. *Samson and Delilah* was first with $11 million.

☆ *Payment on Demand* grossed a mediocre $1.6 million in North American rentals.

☆ *Phone Call from a Stranger* (1952) grossed an unimpressive $1.35 million in North American rentals.

☆ *The Star* (1952) grossed a very disappointing $1 million in North American rentals.

☆ *John Paul Jones* (1959) grossed a paltry $1 million in North American rentals.

☆ *Pocketful of Miracles* (1961) grossed a respectable $2.5 million in North American rentals.

☆ As reported by *The Hollywood Reporter*, "*What Ever Happened to Baby Jane?* [1962] made film history by amassing through the weekend $1,600,000 in film rental, putting the picture into the profit column in less than two weeks."

  The Film Daily touted in its November 13, 1962, issue, "*Baby Jane* Phenomenon. What appears to be the phenomenon of show business is the $1,245,000 box office gross in a matter of eight days for *What Ever Happened to Baby Jane?* in some 300 theaters around the country."

  The film went on to become one of the biggest hits in Bette's career, grossing a reported $5 million in North American rentals. The low-budget film cost an estimated $900,000.

☆ *The Nanny* (1965) grossed a mediocre $2 million in North American rentals.

☆ *Burnt Offerings* (1976) grossed a disappointing $1.56 million in North American rentals.

☆ *Death on the Nile* (1978) grossed a respectable $8.134 million in North American rentals.

☆ *Return from Witch Mountain* (1978) grossed a fair $7.25 million in North American rentals.

☆ *The Watcher in the Woods* was considered one of the major flops of 1980–1981. Disney studios wrote it off as a $6.7 million loss.

---

*The rental fee is the money the theaters pay the distributor to show the movie; the box office gross is the money the moviegoer pays to the theater to see the movie. Box office grosses are higher than the rental fees in almost all cases. The figures shown here are North American rental fees only. Foreign market rentals usually equal or slightly surpass domestic rentals.

CHARLES BOYER

One of the great romantic leads of his day, Charles Boyer costarred in the 1940 picture *All This, and Heaven Too*. His allure was certainly not lost on Bette Davis, who all but swooned under the gaze of his brown eyes. She also respected his abilities as an actor and would later include him on her short list of favorite costars.

Charles Boyer (1899–1978) appeared in numerous pictures, including *Conquest* (Best Actor Oscar nomination, 1937), *Algiers* (Best Actor Oscar nomination, 1938), *Hold Back the Dawn* (1941), *Gaslight* (Best Actor Oscar nomination, 1944), *Fanny* (1961), *Barefoot in the Park* (1967), and *Lost Horizon* (1973).

MARLON BRANDO

Although she was generally contemptuous of The Method, Bette would call Brando, perhaps its most esteemed practitioner, "remarkably gifted." She would hasten to add, however, that "he transcended the techniques he was taught." At the March 30, 1955, Oscar ceremonies, Bette presented Brando with the best actor award for his performance in *On the Waterfront*. A short time later she would say, "I felt a strange kinship with Marlon. Both of us were nonconformists, battlers, who had refused to allow ourselves to be cast in the artificial Hollywood mold."

> "I wouldn't hire Marlon Brando as a gateman."
> *Jack Warner, 1962*

GEORGE BRANSON

Justice Sir George Branson decided the 1936 British court case between Bette Davis and Warner Brothers. Bette later confessed, "During the case I used to sit staring up at Mr. Judge Branson, trying to hypnotize him with thought transmission to give a judgment in my favor." The bewitchment, however, failed; Branson decided in favor of the studio. While deciding whether or not to appeal, Bette told reporters, "I won't attend the rehearing [which was eventually dropped] because my hypnotism didn't work on the judge the first time. So silly of me, wasn't it? I am not a good hypnotist."

GEORGE BRENT

One of Bette Davis's frequent and favorite (on and off the screen) costars. The two met, virtual newcomers to Hollywood, during the making of the 1932 picture *So Big*. Bette was at once smitten, and she carried the unrequited affection onto the set of their next picture, *The Rich Are Always With Us* (1932). By this time Brent was quite the popular young stud at the Warners stable. He had charm and style and a sense of security, if not exceptional good looks. During the making of *The Rich*, Bette's interest in Brent intensified. He, however, carried on an affair with the picture's star, Ruth Chatterton, whom he married shortly thereafter.

Nonetheless, Jack Warner apparently enjoyed partnering Brent and Davis, two of his most promising players, and he reunited them in a series of pictures, *Housewife* (1934), *Front Page Woman* (1935), and *The Golden Arrow* (1936). The repeated pairings naturally launched the usual rumors, much to

Bette and Brent look glum in an "insipid comedy."

the delight of the Warners publicity department, but the fact was that Brent had little interest in his spirited costar. Besides, he was still married to Chatterton, and Bette was married to Ham Nelson.

By the time they made their next picture together, *Jezebel*, it was obvious that their careers were traveling in opposite directions. He had been reduced to playing the second male lead (Henry Fonda was first), and she was positioned to become the number-one box office attraction in the world. Brent began to view Bette with sudden amorous interest. By the time they went into their next picture, *Dark Victory*, he was divorced from Chatterton, and Bette, on the verge of emotional collapse, had divorced Ham Nelson. She was comforted on the set, and eventually (and finally) in his bed, by George Brent. Their affair lasted for the duration of the picture; then it sparked off and on for a couple of years. Despite her obvious attraction to him, Bette found Brent somewhat vain, a trait she disliked in men. She chastised him for dying his hair and for his participation in men's fashion shows. Reportedly (and rather ridiculously) their split was precipitated when Brent released to the press his list of the 10 most glamorous women in Hollywood: Joan

Blondell, Margaret Cartew (a starlet of the period), Dolores Del Rio, Marlene Dietrich, Irene Dunne, Kay Francis, Greta Garbo, Norma Shearer, Loretta Young, and Joan Crawford. The omission of Bette Davis, was glaring. Bette's vanity was affronted, and she never fully forgave him for it.

Brent had a fairly small part in one of Bette's next pictures (and one of her greatest box office triumphs), *The Old Maid* (1939), was seriously considered for the male lead (but would be discarded in favor of Charles Boyer) in *All This, and Heaven Too* (1940), and was cast as the subordinate male lead in *The Great Lie* (1941). By the time of the last, Bette had married Arthur Farnsworth, Jr. By the time of their next and final picture together, *In This Our Life* (1942), Brent was involved with Ann Sheridan, whom he would later marry.

Decades later Bette, 67, and Brent, 71, had something of a reunion in San Diego, where Bette was touring with her one-woman show, *Bette Davis in Person and on Film*. It was 1975, and the two met in her backstage dressing room. For Bette the meeting was bittersweet. It prompted the realization that she was no longer the Judith Traherne who had gushed to his Dr. Frederick Steele in *Dark Victory*, "Darling, poor fool. Don't you know I'm in love with you?" Still, Bette would later refer to Brent with affection. "Of the men I didn't marry," she reflected, "the dearest was George Brent."

George Brent (born George Brent Nolan, 1904–1979) appeared in numerous other pictures, including *Under Suspicion* (1930), *Miss Pinkerton* (1932), *Forty-Second Street* (1933), *God's Country and the Woman* (in which Bette was supposed to be his costar, 1936), *The Gay Sisters* (1942), *The Affairs of Susan* (1945), *The Spiral Staircase* (1945), and *Lover Come Back* (1946).

THE BRIDE CAME C.O.D. ★

Warner Brothers
1941   92 minutes   bw
Directed by: William Keighley
Produced by: Hal Wallis in association with William Cagney
Screenplay by: Julius J. and Philip G. Epstein, based on a story by
     Kenneth Earl and M. M. Musselman
Cinematography by: Ernest Haller
Cast: James Cagney, Bette Davis, Jack Carson, George Tobias, Eugene
     Pallette, Harry Davenport, Stuart Erwin, William Frawley, Edward
     Brophy, Harry Holman, Chick Chandler, Keith Douglas, Herbert
     Anderson, Creighton Hale, Frank Mayo, DeWolf Hopper, Jack Mower,
     William Newell

After they had both appeared in a series of serious dramatic fare, someone at Warners thought it inspired to pair its two biggest stars, Cagney and Davis, in a comedy. And not a witty, sophisticated comedy at that, but, rather, a pratfall farce dubbed *The Bride Came C.O.D.* The story had been purchased with Cagney in mind on September 17, 1940, for the sum of $7,000.

Those initially considered for the part of heiress Joan Winfield were

Ann Sheridan, Ginger Rogers, Alice Faye, Loretta Young, and Rosalind Russell. A young Rita Hayworth tested for the part on November 28, 1940. Jane Wyatt tested on December 10. At the time there wasn't much thought of Bette in the part. After all, who would have thought she'd accept it? By mid-December, Olivia de Havilland was signed for the picture for a fee of $12,500. Cagney was to be paid $150,000. Then, in a matter of days, Bette reported to Hal Wallis that she was interested in the part. Suddenly de Havilland was out and Davis was in, and the budget was increased to accommodate Bette's salary of nearly $67,000.

Bette with smudges on her face and cacti pricking her derriere.

Shooting started on Monday, January 6, 1941, with Cagney, but without Bette, who was still on her brief honeymoon with Arthur Farnsworth, Jr. Bette arrived on the set on Wednesday, and on Sunday, January 12, the company traveled to Death Valley, California, for location shooting. One of the pivotal scenes in the picture called for Joan Winfield to jump out of a plane and land in a patch of cacti. Bette's stunt double on the picture, Audrey Scott, performed the actual jump, but Bette had to be seen actually landing in the cacti. Bette ended up with 45 cactus needles pricking her derriere. A doctor was called to the set; with tweezers in hand, he extracted the offending (and painful) needles. During the shooting of another scene, Bette was again injured, albeit not as seriously, when Cagney's Steve Collins uses her rear end as a slingshot target.

As usual, Bette considered the location shooting a pain, and the 100-plus-degree climate did little to appease her. Nevertheless, she was on generally good behavior when the company returned to the studio on Wednesday, January 22. Furthermore, she was generally on time, and with just a few exceptions she showed up on the set every day that she was scheduled. Still, the company fell behind.

Late into the production, during the first week of March, producer William Cagney had to be hospitalized for an appendix operation. A few days later, on March 11, principal photography on the picture was completed, 20 days and $50,000 over budget.

Upon its release in July 1941, *The Bride Came C.O.D.* received mixed, tolerant reviews but nonetheless performed well at the box office.

The popularity of the picture was, of course, the novelty draw of Cagney and Davis together and in a comedy. But in addition to the flimsy, farfetched story, the casting of Bette was also the picture's downfall. It would have worked far better with a light comedienne such as Jean Arthur. The character was a 23-year-old madcap heiress. First of all, Bette Davis was always far too forceful and cumbersome to play madcap. Second, at 33 she could not get away with playing a character 10 years younger the way some other actresses could. Bette looks every bit her 33 years in the film. Third, she does not have the timing to play light comedy. Her scenes with Cagney are labored, stodgy. They have no chemistry.

At the time everyone at Warners (and in Hollywood, for that matter) was curious as to why Bette Davis agreed to do *The Bride Came C.O.D.* The answer is obvious and can be explained in two words: Katharine Hepburn. Hepburn, whom Bette viewed as her primary acting rival, had just come off considerable successes (playing heiresses, by the way) in the now-classic madcap comedies *Bringing Up Baby* (1938), *Holiday* (1938), and *The Philadelphia Story* (1940). Bette saw her chance, took it, and flopped in a pile of cacti.

The picture starts out fairly promisingly without Cagney or Davis (look for George Tobias, years later Abner Kravitz on "Bewitched"), but once left to its comic devices, it falls flat. Director Keighley did manage to devise, however, effective individual introductions for his two stars. Bette is shot from the back, talking on a telephone in a nightclub phone booth, as the club spotlight searches for her presence. Cagney is introduced in long shot as a pilot doing aerial stunts. He is then shown in profile kissing his female copilot, the apparent provocation of his aerial excitement. Unfortunately, however, the picture goes downhill from there. Bette would fare far better the following year in the sophisticated comedy *The Man Who Came to Dinner*.

BROADWAY

Bette Davis made her professional stage debut at the Lyceum Theatre in Rochester, New York, in *Broadway*, written by Phil Dunning and George Abbott and produced in 1928 by the Cukor-Kondolf Repertory Company.

Director George Cukor was introduced to Bette Davis via a letter from actor Frank Conroy. Cukor needed a chorus girl for his production of *Broadway*, and Conroy enthused about Bette, then 20 years old. In the show Bette had to wear a negligee and do the Charleston. However, two days after the show opened, Rose Lerner, who played one of the leads, twisted her ankle, and Bette, who had studied the part at her mother's prophetic behest, was assigned the part.

Broadway costarred Robert Strange and ran at the Lyceum for a week.

BROKEN DISHES

When asked, shortly before her death in 1989, what the greatest triumph of her professional career had been, Bette Davis was quick to respond, "The first time I saw my name in lights on Broadway." The date was November 5, 1929, and her name was on the marquee at the Ritz Theatre announcing the opening of *Broken Dishes*.

Broken Dishes was a comedy written by Martin Flavin, produced by Oscar Serlin, and directed by Marion Gering. The play costarred Donald Meek and Eda Heinemann as Bette's parents and featured Ellen Lowe, Etha Dack, Reed Brown, J. Francis-Robertson, Duncan Penwarden, Josef Lazarovici, and Jean Adair.

Prior to its opening on Broadway, *Broken Dishes* held tryouts at Fox's Hempstead Theatre on Long Island on October 18, 1929, then at Fox's Playhouse in Great Neck, and finally at Werba's Brooklyn Theatre on October 21.

Upon its Broadway opening the show received mostly favorable notices, particularly for Bette. It ran for 178 performances.

Bette took a summer break at the Cape Playhouse in Dennis, Massachusetts, then returned to the play for its fall 1930 road tour, which began in Baltimore and went on to Washington, D.C.

Broken Dishes was purchased by Warner Brothers and was made as *Too Young to Marry* (1931) with Loretta Young. It was subsequently remade, twice, as *Love Begins at Twenty* (with Patricia Ellis, 1936), and *Calling All Husbands* (with Lucille Fairbanks, 1940).

ROBIN BROWN

Bette's lifelong friend, whom she met when they were both teenagers in Ogunquit, Maine. Bette was vacationing with her mother at the Sparhawk Hotel, where Robin was working as a waitress. At the time, Robin's name was Marie Simpson, and she was later known as Robin Byron.

In 1929, aspiring young actress Bette moved to Greenwich Village to become a member of the Provincetown Players. She lived for a while in a basement apartment on Eighth Street. Her roommate was Marie, who had by then changed her name to Robin. Later, when Bette and her mother moved into an apartment on East 53rd Street, Robin moved with them.

In later years, after Bette had attained stardom, Robin moved to Los Angeles. For a while she lived with Bette and worked as her secretary.

JANE BRYAN

Bette's protégée. Bette discovered Jane Bryan in the stage play *Green Grow the Lilacs* (on which the Broadway musical *Oklahoma!* would be based). Impressed with Bryan's performance, Bette cajoled the powers that be at Warner Brothers to sign her to a contract and costar her as Bette's younger sister in the 1937 picture *Marked Woman*. Bette then had Bryan cast in her next picture, *Kid Galahad* (1937), followed by *The Sisters* (1938) and as Bette's daughter in *The Old Maid* (1939). The two became good friends, and Bette continued to tout Bryan's talents. In 1939, she rhapsodized to *Silver Screen* magazine:

> "Of anyone in Hollywood now, I'd say Jane Bryan, ten years from now, can be the most important. I first saw Jane in an amateur play here in town, and while it was her first performance she was thoroughly at home. She has all the elements of acting greatness. She has that power instinctively to be 'it.' Jane is just beginning, comparatively, but she is very intelligent and could take advantage of a big chance. Of all the younger girls, Jane, to me, is most liable to develop amazingly."

However, after a few more pictures in Hollywood, and much to her mentor's dismay, Jane Bryan (born Jane O'Brien in 1918) gave up her career to become a housewife. A short time later, Bette married Arthur Farnsworth, Jr., in a ceremony held at the Arizona ranch home Bryan shared with her husband, Justin Dart.

BUNNY O'HARE ★ ½

American International Pictures
1971   92 minutes   Movielab color
Directed by: Gerd Oswald
Produced by: Gerd Oswald and Norman T. Herman
Screenplay by: Stanley Z. Cherry and Coslough Johnson, from a story by
    Stanley Z. Cherry
Cinematography by: Loyal Griggs, John Stephens
Cast: Bette Davis, Ernest Borgnine, Jack Cassidy, Joan Delaney, Jay
    Robinson, John Astin, Reva Rose

On April 14, 1970, American International Pictures (AIP) announced that it had secured Bette Davis to appear in its new picture, which had gone through a series of title changes: *Bunny and Claude*, *Betty and Claude*, and then, to favor Bette, *Bunny*. Shooting was scheduled to start on July 1, 1970. However, producers Norman T. Herman and Gerd Oswald had difficulty casting the male lead, and the production was postponed. In mid-July, Ernest Borgnine became attached to the project, and the title was changed to *Bunny and Billy* (the original title of the story by Stanley Z. Cherry) to accommodate him; shooting was scheduled for late August. However, the production continued to have starting jitters, apparently due to a lack of

financing, and shooting was rescheduled for September 28. Meanwhile, on September 14, and presumably to placate the impatient Bette, the title was changed again, this time to *Bunny O'Hare*, which it was to remain.

Production, however, did not start until November. *Bunny O'Hare*, a rather offbeat tale about a couple on the other side of middle age who dress as hippies, rob banks, and use a motorcycle as their getaway vehicle, was shot primarily in Albuquerque, New Mexico. Bette, who had an aversion to location shooting on principle, loathed the desert heat and the interminable amount of time she spent on the back of a motorcycle, clinging to Ernie Borgnine's thickened middle. It was an unhappy production that required the services of two cinematographers and pitted the director against the executive producers, James H. Nicholson and Samuel Z. Arkoff. Oswald was attempting to shoot a picture of comic social commentary. Nicholson and Arkoff wanted less commentary and more exploitation.

After Oswald delivered his first cut to AIP, Nicholson and Arkoff took over the film. They ordered that additional footage be shot in Hollywood, featuring the characters played by John Astin and Reva Rose. These scenes may have been written and/or directed by Astin, who subsequently received a "creative consultant" credit on the screen.

Bunny O'Hare was previewed in Los Angeles on June 24, 1971. Outraged, on August 23, 1971, Bette filed suit against AIP in the New York Supreme Court. She sought $3.3 million in alleged damages to her stature and reputation, mental anguish, and loss of income. She charged that AIP had altered the final footage and that it was no longer the script that she had approved. She called the revised film a "tastelessly and inartistically assembled production."

Meanwhile, director Oswald lent Bette her support, publicly stating, "I am 100 percent with Bette Davis in her suit. I feel that they mutilated the picture completely after I had turned in my final cut. They made a different film from that we had conceived."

Nevertheless, Bette's lawsuit was settled out of court, and the AIP version of *Bunny O'Hare* was released in October 1971 to mixed, mostly poor reviews.

BUREAU OF MISSING PERSONS ★★
Warner Brothers
1933   73 minutes   bw
Directed by: Roy Del Ruth
Produced by: Henry Blanke
Screenplay by: Robert Presnell, based on the book by Captain John H.
     Ayers and Carol Bird
Cinematography by: Barney McGill
Cast: Pat O'Brien, Lewis Stone, Bette Davis, Ruth Donnelly, Gordon
     Westcott, Glenda Farrell, Allen Jenkins, Hugh Herbert, Alan Dinehart,
     Marjorie Gateson, Tad Alexander, Noel Francis, Wallis Clark, Adrian
     Morris, Clay Clement, Henry Kolker, Harry Beresford, George
     Chandler

In June 1933 Warner Brothers purchased the rights to the novel *Missing Men* by Captain John H. Ayers and Carol Bird for the sum of $5,000. The studio also acquired the rights to an original story by Robert Presnell and decided to combine the two elements in a picture to be called *Bureau of Missing Persons.* Presnell sold the rights to his story for a single dollar, but he was given the assignment of writing the screenplay, for which he was paid considerably more.

The part of Norma Phillips, a wife who enlists the support of the missing persons' bureau to find her husband, was initially slated by the studio for Ann Dvorak. However, because of a scheduling conflict Bette was cast in the picture at the last minute.

Bureau of Missing Persons started shooting on June 19, 1933. Bette joined the company a week later. In typical, economical Warners style, Roy Del Ruth shot the picture fast and without frills. Still, Hal Wallis, in his new assignment as the studio's chief of production, was pleased and sent Del Ruth daily memos complimenting him on his "swell" results. Bette completed her work on *Missing Persons* on July 10, and the film closed production on the following day.

When the picture was in preproduction, Pat O'Brien and Lewis Stone had been top billed. However, by the time the film was released in September 1933, and given her rising stature, Bette Davis had jumped, in some advertisements, from third to first billing.

After seeing a rough cut of the picture, Hal Wallis sent Jack Warner a memo dated July 19, 1933, encouraging Warner to pick up the option on Pat

O'Brien's contract. He also lauded the film to his boss as "colossal, sensational, and stupendous." In retrospect, Wallis's enthusiasm can be attributed to job inexperience and insecurity.

Despite a marketing campaign that featured such exploitative copy as "42 More Persons Will Vanish While You Watch This Thrilling Picture!" and "What *Really* Happens to 'Lost Women,' " *Bureau of Missing Persons* received generally only fair reviews.

BURIAL

Bette Davis is buried in a mausoleum at Forest Lawn Cemetery overlooking Burbank, California. In the mid-1970s Bette quipped to interviewer Rex Reed, "It's the final irony. From where I'll be buried, you can look right down and spit on Warner Brothers!"

> She did it the hard way.
> *Bette Davis's epitaph*

BURNT OFFERINGS ★
United Artists/P.E.A. Films, Inc.
1976   115 minutes   DeLuxe Color
Directed by: Dan Curtis
Produced by: Dan Curtis
Screenplay by: William F. Nolan and Dan Curtis, from a novel by Robert
    Marasco
Cinematography by: Jacques Marquette, Steve Larner
Cast: Karen Black, Oliver Reed, Bette Davis, Burgess Meredith, Eileen
    Heckart, Lee H. Montgomery, Dub Taylor, Joseph Riley, Todd
    Turquand, Orin Cannon, Jim Myers, Anthony James

Producer Lawrence Turman (*The Graduate*, 1967) had the rights to the novel by Robert Marasco in 1969. He also had a script by Marasco and a commitment from director Bob Fosse, who had recently made his film directorial debut with *Sweet Charity*. Even with this package, Turman was unable to secure financing for the picture, which was then the story of a young couple who rent a beach house for the summer and participate in the destruction of a neighboring family. The project was subsequently shelved.

Fast forward to the late summer of 1975. *Burnt Offerings*, adapted from the novel by Marasco, but with a script by Dan Curtis and William F. Nolan and a budget of $2 million, started shooting in Oakland, California, on August 4. Unfortunately, however, the shooting script had evolved into nearly two hours of silliness about a living, breathing house of horror. A young couple (Karen Black and Oliver Reed), their son (Lee Montgomery), and an accompanying aunt (Bette) rent a summer home with the stipulation that they take care of the owner's old mother, who lives, unseen, in the upstairs bedroom.

Dan Curtis described his film at the time as "an intimate story. Its action is confined to one house and I don't want anything else to intrude. The story opens with the family in their city apartment [a scene which was eventually cut], but once they drive onto the Dunsmuir House grounds I want the feeling that they are driving into the past and that nothing else exists except this confined, totally isolated world." Curtis went on to say that he searched the country for a house that would serve his purposes and have the impact that Manderlay had in *Rebecca*, that Tara had in *Gone With the Wind*. What he eventually found was the Dunsmuir House, in the city of Oakland. However, Curtis's intention of creating a character out of the house was never realized. And the technique of shooting in soft focus to create an eerie, otherworldly effect is far too obvious. We know that we're *supposed* to be afraid, but we keep waiting for something to fear as the final credits role.

Meanwhile, the shooting was not a happy experience. First of all, production shut down for a week and left a pall thereafter due to the suicide of the director's daughter. Second, Bette had little affection or respect for Karen Black and Oliver Reed. She reprimanded the former for showing up pregnant on the set (Curtis rescheduled his shooting sequence and shot Black's swimsuit scenes first), for wearing makeup that didn't match in different shots of the same scene, and for not knowing her lines. She criticized Reed for his liberal consumption of alcohol and for repeatedly showing up on the set with a hangover. He had lost a good deal of weight prior to shooting the film, which he openly attributed to "a diet of white wine and tequila." Midway through the shooting a columnist reported in Hollywood, "The relationship between Bette Davis and Oliver Reed is amusing their co-workers. . . . For some inexplicable reason Reed seems in awe of Bette and the Britisher isn't a boy to 'awe' easily. In the past he has had some very uncomplimentary comments to make on his costars, including Glenda Jackson." The columnist went on to report that Reed and Bette had been slipping notes under each other's hotel room door. What the columnist failed to report, however, was that the notes were decidedly not of the fan letter variety and that it was not awe but contempt that Reed felt for Bette.

At one point Bette hosted a cocktail party in her suite. After Reed failed to make an appearance, which Bette took as a deliberate slap at her ego, Bette collected all the leftover food and beverages and dumped them outside of Reed's hotel room door.

Bette also railed against what she perceived to be the television mentality of the production. Consequently, she felt compelled to tell everyone on the set how to do his or her job, and she stood with smug satisfaction when the original cameraman was fired after the dailies turned out too dark. And certainly producer/director/writer Dan Curtis (who would later have a major success with the television miniseries "War and Remembrance") was not above Bette's reproach. At that point in his career Curtis was still best known for his work on the television series "Dark Shadows" 10 years before, and nothing he did on *Burnt Offerings* proved to Bette that he was ready or equipped for motion pictures. As she related at the time to Rex Reed, "I feel like I've spent the past six weeks in jail. I brought my own coffee pot and my own picture frames from Connecticut to remind me of home, but I can't wait to get out of here! I hate locations. You work six days a week from 6:00 A.M. to 6:00 P.M. and it costs a fortune in food, hotel rooms, and transportation bills. The conditions are horrible, the money is tight and everything is total chaos. . . . I said I'd never make another horror film after *Baby Jane*, and here I am in the biggest horror of them all!"

What Bette was most dissatisfied with, however, was her role, Aunt Elizabeth, which allowed her to do nothing but shake her head in disgust, which she was able to do without contrived motivation. She would later acknowledge that the only reason she took the part was that she had been bored. One scene called for Bette to passively watch as Oliver Reed tries to drown his young son in the swimming pool. No doubt Bette had to restrain herself from jumping into the pool, disposing of Reed ("Fasten your life preserver; it's going to be a bumpy swim!"), saving the boy, and walking off with the picture. We would all have been better off if she had.

C

CABIN IN THE COTTON ★★½

Warner Brothers
1932   79 minutes   bw
Directed by: Michael Curtiz
Produced by: Hal Wallis
Screenplay by: Paul Green, based on the novel by Harry Harrison Kroll
Cinematography by: Barney McGill
Cast: Richard Barthelmess, Bette Davis, Dorothy Jordan, Henry B.
    Walthall, Berton Churchill, Walter Percival, Hardie Albright, David
    Landau, Tully Marshall, William LeMaire, Edmund Breese, Clarence
    Muse, Russell Simpson, John Marston, Erville Anderson, Dorothy
    Peterson, Snow Flake, Harry Cording

Warner Brothers purchased the rights to the novel by Harry Harrison Kroll, author, and Ray Long and Richard R. Smith, publishers, in November 1931 for the sum of $12,500. It was intended to be a vehicle for Richard Barthelmess, a former silent screen star whose career was waning. Little did anyone know then that the picture would be stolen by a hitherto nondescript contract player, Bette Davis. It would also introduce audiences to Bette as a new kind of picture heroine, a character that she could have later patented: a good-bad girl who just can't help it.

   Curiously, director Mike Curtiz objected to Bette's being cast in the

"A new kind of temptress."

73

picture. He didn't think that she projected the sex appeal necessary for the part of Madge Norwood, the seductive cotton planter's daughter who coos, "I'd love to kiss you, but I just washed my hair." Darryl Zanuck, the studio's chief of production, disagreed, and after viewing footage from her previous pictures, so did star Barthelmess. The two overrode Curtiz's veto, and Bette was cast in the part.

Bette was paid $1,400 for her performance, a minor scandal when compared to Barthelmess's salary of $125,000. With an estimated budget of $309,278 and an allotted 27 shooting days, *Cabin in the Cotton* started principal photography on May 9, 1932. Bette, coming off a vacation after completing *The Dark Horse,* joined the company on Tuesday, May 17.

Curtiz, still smarting over Zanuck's casting override, sought revenge by unleashing a verbal assault on Bette. Years later Barthelmess related to Lawrence J. Quirk, "Mike Curtiz was a mean one. I was the star of the film so I could walk away. . . . but Bette was a contract player and had to put up with him." Not only did she put up with Curtiz; she frequently returned the verbal volley, not an unremarkable response from a young, unheralded actress. At one point Curtiz punished Bette by having her play a difficult love scene *alone.* Instead of playing opposite Barthelmess (or even a stand-in), Bette had to exercise her feminine wiles to a camera and kiss empty space. Meanwhile, although she liked him personally, Bette was also having a difficult time with Barthelmess, whose technique it was to give nothing in long and medium shots, reserving his talent for his close-ups. Barthelmess empathized with his young costar but was intimidated by her sheer ambition and burgeoning sexuality. His discomfort shows clearly on the screen. When Bette, positively provocative, looks down at Barthelmess's crotch and delivers the line "I'll be seeing you. We're going to dance the Peckerwood Wiggle, or whatever it's called," Barthelmess looks as though he's going to swallow his tongue.

Bette completed her work on *Cabin in the Cotton* on June 9, 1932, and the picture wrapped production four days later. The picture was released in late September with a marketing campaign that clearly reflected Bette's rising status at the studio: "Meet a new kind of temptress!" the ads teased. "Flaming as Southern Suns, Bewitching as Plantation Moons, She'll Teach You a New Kind of Love—in a New Kind of Dramatic Hit—Barthelmess' Greatest!"

Viewing the picture today makes it plain that Barthelmess, with his heavy silent-screen makeup, and not Bette, is out of place. Worse, he looks out of *era.* As for Bette, she has moments, like the scene in which she undresses in a closet while Barthelmess fidgets nearby, that are astonishing.

The subsequent reviews for the picture were mixed, with Bette receiving mostly favorable, though hardly enthusiastic, reviews. *Cabin in the Cotton* was clearly a herald of Bette's talent and an indication of the type of role to which she was best suited. It would, however, take most reviewers, and Hollywood at large, two more years to recognize her unique gifts.

"The Female Cagney" with the real thing.

JAMES CAGNEY

Early in her career Bette was referred to by some on the Warners lot as "the female Cagney." They both possessed forceful personalities, on and off the screen, and both had a distinctive machine-gun way of delivering a line. Cagney and Davis made two pictures together, both deplorable: *Jimmy the Gent* (1934) and *The Bride Came C.O.D.* (1941).

It was Jimmy Cagney, in part, who inspired Bette to launch her infamous 1936 strike against Warner Brothers. Just a few months before her walkout, Cagney won a substantial settlement against the studio.

Cagney had his breakthrough picture at Warners in April 1931 with the release of *Public Enemy*. At the time, Cagney had been signed to a long-term contract that paid him $400 a week. After the enormous success of the picture, Cagney approached the studio with demands for another contract, but Jack Warner refused. It was to be the first of many battles between Cagney and Warner. In late 1932 Warner finally acquiesced, and Cagney was granted another deal that paid him $3,000 a week. By the time of his 1936 contractual feud Cagney was earning $4,500 a week; Bette at that time was getting $1,600 per week.

Although Cagney and Davis were often compared and forever bonded by their struggles against the brothers Warner, the two never developed a relationship beyond passing, mutual admiration. At one point in the early forties, they even clashed. Cagney was a representative of the Hollywood Victory Committee, which dictated which stars could participate in what events to benefit the war effort; Bette presided over the Hollywood Canteen, which was in need of celebrities on a nightly basis. Cagney called Bette before a meeting and directed her to refer all her future requests for celebrities to the committee. Bette, with typical impatience, refused, arguing that it would be an unnecessary nuisance. The meeting ended with Bette threatening Cagney that unless the committee immediately laid off, she would shut down the canteen. Over the next few days Cagney relented, Bette was allowed to continue her direct contact with celebrities, and the Hollywood Canteen remained open for the duration of the war.

The feud wedged a gap between James Cagney and Bette Davis that was not closed until late 1950, when Cagney sent Bette a gushing fan letter after seeing her performance in *All About Eve*. Still, the two never again appeared together in a picture, a lamentable loss given their seeming combustive compatibility.

James Cagney (1899–1986) appeared in numerous pictures, including *Angels with Dirty Faces* (1938), *Yankee Doodle Dandy* (Best Actor Oscar winner, 1942), *Love Me or Leave Me* (1955), *Mister Roberts* (1955), *One Two Three* (1961), and *Ragtime* (1981).

> "At Warner Brothers, I had a friendly competition with Jimmy
> Cagney. We kept a box score, and when we both left the studio in the
> 1940s we were tied at sixteen suspensions apiece."
>
> *Bette Davis, 1955*

CAMP LOCKETT

During the summer of 1942 Bette took a break from shooting *Watch on the Rhine* and traveled 65 miles south of San Diego to do a USO show at Camp Lockett, California. The show was for a well-known, all-black cavalry regiment, and Bette (with the exception of Dinah Shore) was the only white performer on the bill. She closed her portion of the entertainment with a rendition of "The Star-Spangled Banner."

CANCER

One day in May 1983, 75-year-old Bette Davis was getting dressed when she discovered a lump in her breast. She was familiar with what it was because her sister had had a mastectomy years before. Still, for years Bette had joked that she, a chain-smoker, would never get cancer. Cancer wouldn't *dare*.

In June, she secretly checked into New York Hospital. When the press caught wind of her whereabouts, Bette, always concerned that she be perceived as healthy enough to work, lied, announcing that she was suffering only from "neurological problems." For weeks Bette denied the existence of the cancer. In fact, from her hospital bed she telephoned a columnist from *The Hollywood Reporter* who subsequently wrote:

> Rumors, rumors, rumors have been flying everywhere on the state of
> her health. . . . I spoke with her yesterday and she said, for all the
> town (and all her friends) to hear: "I want to assure everyone, I do
> *not* have cancer and I did *not* have a heart attack. I had a
> neurological problem and that is being taken care of. And that's *it*!"
> Anyone who knows Bette knows she doesn't lie. . . .

As she was rolled into the hospital operating room where her breast would be removed, Bette's first thought, as she later related, was "Thank God it did not happen when I was a young woman with a good body and an active sex life."

"It was a horrid feeling to have a part of your body cut out. . . .
I then prayed that the doctors had caught the cancer in time."

Bette Davis

"The mastectomy was terrible—they had robbed me of something that was mine—but we've heard enough about breasts from Mrs. [Betty] Ford."

Bette Davis

In the summer of 1989 tests showed that the cancer had returned and spread. Bette underwent a new series of radiation treatments at UCLA Medical Center, but again she kept the status of her health a secret from the press and from her friends. In September she packed her bags for an arduous trip to Spain, where she was scheduled to pick up an award. Shortly before leaving, she said to her friend Robert Osborne, "I hope this will prove to the world I'm not dying."

A few weeks later she was dead.

CANNES FILM FESTIVAL

In April 1951 the judges at the Cannes Film Festival awarded *All About Eve* a Special Jury Prize and honored Bette as best actress for her performance as Margo Channing.

Twelve years later, in May 1963, Bette revisited Cannes to promote *What Ever Happened to Baby Jane?*, and although neither she nor the picture won any prizes, Bette's appearance was the undisputed hit of the festival, much to the dismay of Joan Crawford. It seems that Bette used her influence with the film's producers, who dissuaded Crawford from attending. Still, Bette's memories of Cannes would be laced with regret. For it was during that 1963 trip to Cannes that Bette's 16-year-old daughter met Jeremy Hyman, her husband-to-be. It was a marriage of which Bette would strongly disapprove.

In May 1983 Bette had been scheduled to go to Cannes to accept an honorary award as America's finest actress, but she backed out, telling columnist Robert Osborne, "The basic reason is because they said if I didn't come in person, I wouldn't get the award. At least four months ago they asked me to accept, then later when I said I couldn't make the trip, they said they *wouldn't* give me the award. That's the only issue. Just how important *is* the award? How *honest*? Did they really want to honor me, or just have me show up in person? I'm not questioning, not complaining. Nor am I complaining about not going to Cannes. I've been there. It's a rat race."

CAPE ELIZABETH, MAINE

In the 1950s, Bette and Gary Merrill resided in Cape Elizabeth, Maine, a suburb of Portland, in a huge house on the Atlantic Ocean. They had moved there in part so that Bette could recuperate from a 1953 illness and subsequent dental surgery. Bette dubbed the three-story white house that featured huge picture windows overlooking the ocean "Witch-way" (she didn't know which way her career was going; also a humorous reference to Bette's bitch-on-a-broom reputation). Bette later reflected on her arrival in Cape Elizabeth, "I must have shocked my Maine neighbors. Instead of gold lamé and ten servants, they found me running around with a broom."

In Cape Elizabeth, while Merrill commuted to and from New York for television work, Bette went domestic with a vengeance. In addition to being a fanatical housecleaner, Bette attended PTA meetings and worked for the local March of Dimes. She also helped her husband form an amateur hockey team, and during games Bette used to roast and serve hot chestnuts.

FRANK CAPRA

During Bette's heyday at Warner Brothers, Frank Capra also was working at the studio, and their paths often crossed. One day at the Warners cafeteria, Bette spotted Capra and shouted over to him, "When are you going to have something for me?" Capra shot back, "There isn't anything that you *haven't got!*"

Frank Capra and Bette Davis had to wait many years before working together in the 1961 picture *Pocketful of Miracles*. It was to be Capra's final film. The two did not get along very well during the making of the picture; still, Bette appeared as a speaker at the 1982 American Film Institute tribute to Capra.

Producer/director Frank Capra died in 1991 at the age of 94. His legendary career includes the pictures *Lady for a Day* (Best Picture and Best Director Oscar nominations, 1933), *It Happened One Night* (Best Director Oscar winner, 1934), *Mr. Deeds Goes to Town* (Best Director Oscar winner, 1936; Best Picture Oscar nomination), *Lost Horizon* (Best Picture Oscar nomination, 1937), *You Can't Take It with You* (Best Picture and Best Director Oscar winners, 1938), *Mr. Smith Goes to Washington* (Best Picture and Best Director Oscar nominations, 1939), and *It's a Wonderful Life* (Best Picture and Best Director Oscar nominations, 1946).

THE CASE OF THE HOWLING DOG

On June 13, 1934, a Warner Brothers executive sent Bette a telegram commanding her to appear the following day on the set of a picture called *The Case of the Howling Dog*. Bette, after making *Of Human Bondage* at RKO, refused, calling the script inferior to her now proven capabilities. She did not accept the wire sent by the studio, nor did she answer the telephone, which rang incessantly. On June 14 studio executive R. J. Obringer sent a memo to Ralph Lewis, the studio's outside attorney, outlining the situation: "As you know, Bette Davis has been giving us considerable trouble, and appears to have the idea that she has approval of stories, and will work only in those which she selects despite no such provisions in her contract. . . ." Meanwhile,

Bette sent her representative, Mike Levee, to the studio to inform Jack Warner that she would not, under any conditions, appear in the picture. Warner promptly slapped Bette with a suspension without pay and replaced her in the film with Helen Trenholme.

    The Case of the Howling Dog, one of a series of Perry Mason pictures at Warners, was directed by Alan Crosland and starred Warren William. The film, a routine studio programmer, was generally panned upon its release.

During a break from shooting.

THE CATERED AFFAIR ★★★

Metro-Goldwyn-Mayer
1956   93 minutes   bw
Directed by: Richard Brooks
Produced by: Sam Zimbalist
Screenplay by: Gore Vidal, based on the teleplay by Paddy Chayefsky
Cinematography by: John Alton
Cast: Bette Davis, Ernest Borgnine, Debbie Reynolds, Barry Fitzgerald, Rod
    Taylor, Dorothy Stickney, Robert Simon, Madge Kennedy, Carol
    Veazie, Joan Camden, Ray Stricklyn, Jay Adler, Dan Tobin, Paul
    Denton, Augusta Merighi, Sammy Shack, Jack Kenny, Robert
    Stephenson, Mae Clarke

Originally *The Catered Affair* was a television drama that appeared as a segment of "Goodyear TV Playhouse" with Thelma Ritter in the role of Bronx housewife Aggie Hurley. It was adapted into a film after the enormous success of Chayefsky's *Marty* (which made a motion picture star out of Ernest Borgnine) the year before.

Bette would later contend that producer Sam Zimbalist and director Richard Brooks both had to fight MGM executives to have her cast in the picture. In fact it was only Brooks who argued in her behalf. Zimbalist, like Chayefsky, thought Bette was miscast. As written, Aggie Hurley called for simplicity, sincerity, and understatement. As Zimbalist later related to Lawrence J. Quirk, Bette, he felt, "gave the role grand opera, Queen Elizabeth, everything that was wrong for it." But fresh off the success of *The Blackboard Jungle* (1955), Brooks had his way, and Bette was cast.

Certainly it's easy to understand Bette's attraction to the project. If *Marty* could launch Borgnine's career, why couldn't *The Catered Affair* reignite hers? Furthermore, less than a year before, she had played the bejeweled Queen Elizabeth in *The Virgin Queen*, and Bette saw in *The Catered Affair* a chance to dazzle all of Hollywood (whom she felt had forgotten her) with her range and versatility. And finally, the part did not require her to attempt to look attractive for the cameras. After a few years of domesticity in Maine, Bette had obviously put on a few pounds, and her thickened jowls and waistline were perfect for Aggie Hurley. So she threw herself into the part with characteristic abandon. She immersed herself in studying a Bronx accent. She purchased her costumes off the rack of an inexpensive clothing store. She tempered her legendary mannerisms.

The Catered Affair started shooting in Los Angeles in January 1956. The script, adapted by Gore Vidal, was another point of contention between Zimbalist and Chayefsky on one side and Brooks on the other. Zimbalist felt that Vidal was betraying Chayefsky's naturalistic dialogue by inserting effete and bitchy lines that would have been more appropriate in a sequel to *All About Eve* (1950) or *The Star* (1952). Brooks, however, sided with Vidal, and the MGM brass agreed that the Vidal name lent the picture added distinction.

Brooks, meanwhile, was opposed to the casting of Debbie Reynolds as the picture's bride and the Hurleys' daughter. He thought she lacked the talent and seriousness for the part. At the time, Debbie was best known for her musical comedy skills and was engaged in a highly publicized romance with Eddie Fisher. Nonetheless, she was cast in the picture at the insistence of Dore Schary and Ben Thau, the top brass at MGM. During the making of the picture, Brooks frequently mocked Debbie and her beauty contestant/ingenue image by calling her Debbie Dimples or Debbie Darling or Miss Hollywood.

Perhaps recalling that Mike Curtiz and other directors had belittled her in similar fashion when *she* was first starting out, Bette took Reynolds under her wing, comforted her, and offered her advice. Reynolds later recalled in her autobiography:

> You *learn* when you work with Bette Davis. We had a scene together, mother and daughter, where she's cooking fish and talking to me. We

rehearsed that bit for two weeks. Everything had to be timed. Turn on the gas jets on one line. Pick up the spatula on another. Put it down on the third. It had to look very natural. It's very tricky working with props in movies because the different shots have to match. In the end it just looked like the two of us having a conversation. Davis is a perfectionist, and brilliant.

Despite the on-the-set acrimony, Bette was genuinely fond of Ernest Borgnine and expressed delight on the morning of March 21, 1956, after Borgnine had received the Best Actor Oscar for *Marty* the night before. *Marty* also won the Best Picture Oscar, and its resounding success was a boost to the entire *Catered* company.

The Catered Affair was previewed at the Fox Beverly Theatre in Beverly Hills on April 20, 1956. It received generally favorable reviews, but many critics could not see beyond Bette's atypical casting. Some accused her of playing Aggie Hurley as a slumming Queen Elizabeth; others accused her of simply showing off. In retrospect, however, the film offers Bette in one of her most remarkable—least affected, most un-Bette Davis-like—performances. Bette herself would later cite the film as one of the biggest challenges of her career. It was a great disappointment to her that the film did not duplicate *Marty*'s success with the Academy Awards or at the box office.

CENSORSHIP

"Sex cannot be shown honestly on the screen, and any woman's story concerns sex. That is woman's basic problem. Sex shouldn't be shown for sex's sake, but when it's an important part of the movie, and then done with taste, dignity and intelligence [it should be depicted]. That is done in foreign films. After all, sex is life. Why do we try to hide it? Yet censorship allows children to see more killings on the screen. That hurts them more than seeing sex, which they wouldn't understand anyway."

Bette Davis, 1949

"I've just heard that the censors have banned the old woman who lived in a shoe who had so many children she didn't know what to do.' "

Bette Davis, 1949

"We're not in business for children. Let their parents censor for them. As for [female] nudity, there's nothing wrong with it, if it suits the part and she's a beautiful dame. But being naked isn't really very sexy."

Bette Davis, 1965

The Catholic Church officially founded the Legion of Decency on April 11, 1934, to battle via membership boycott what it perceived to be "indecent and immoral pictures." Hollywood's response was to revitalize its own self-censorship board, and, on July 15, 1934, under the directorship of Joe Breen, the new Production Code Administration (PCA) went into effect. Its impact on the industry was astounding. Before scripts were given a production start date, they had to be given the seal of approval by the PCA, also called the Breen Office.

Over the years the PCA forced innumerable revisions on Bette Davis pictures, much to her anger and dismay. But none were affected more than *Bordertown* and *Beyond the Forest*.

Bordertown (1935)

The new PCA (the first one was founded in 1930 but was rendered ineffective) went into effect while the *Bordertown* screenplay was in development. Upon reading the script, Joe Breen rejected it on the grounds that it had "no compensating moral values" and that the character played by Paul Muni was "sympathetic" despite the fact that he lived in adultery with a prostitute and became a murderer. Hal Wallis brought in an entirely new writing team, which totally reworked the script. Muni's character became an attorney whose only real crime was beating up a rival attorney.

Beyond the Forest (1949)

Howard Hawks released *The Outlaw* in 1946 without the approval of the PCA. The picture, which made ample use of Jane Russell's cleavage, was a box office success. Bette Davis wanted Warner Brothers to follow suit with *Beyond the Forest* in 1949. When Jack Warner refused, Bette was furious with him for succumbing to what she viewed as the PCA's outdated and illogical regulations. It was a point of contention that greatly contributed to her displeasure with *Beyond the Forest* and her departure from Warners after 18 years. Even with the changes made to accommodate the PCA, the Legion of Decency pinned its dreaded "condemned" classification on *Beyond the Forest*, calling it a "sordid story" presented in a "morally offensive manner." At the time it was the only major U.S. film on the condemned list. As a result, millions of churchgoers boycotted the picture, and it did disappointing business at the box office. This led industry observers to condemn Bette as "box office poison," a label she disproved a year later with *All Above Eve*.

Now, Voyager (1942)

The PCA vehemently objected to any suggestion that the characters played by Bette and Paul Henreid carried on an adulterous affair. Thus audiences were left wondering how they fell so desperately in love in the first place.

Deception (1946)

The PCA dictated that Bette's character, who shoots and kills Claude Rains, must pay for her crime at the end of the picture. Bette would later contend that this concession ruined the picture.

Winter Meeting (1948)

This turned out to be one of the biggest flops of Bette's career, and she laid blame squarely on the PCA. The story was about a couple who have an affair

without being married. The PCA dictated either that the couple get married or that no suggestion of sex between the two be made.

All About Eve (1950)
Backstage in Margo Channing's dressing room, Eve unravels her tale of woe after which Thelma Ritter, as Birdie, quips, "What a story—everything but the bloodhounds snapping at her ass." At least it did until the PCA stepped in and requested that *ass* be revised to *rear end*.

Storm Center (1956)
Storm Center was only the second film that the Legion of Decency had categorized as a "separate class" since its inception, deeming it "a propaganda film [that] offers a warped, oversimplified and strongly emotional solution to the complex problem of civil liberties in American life." The condemnation played a significant part in the eventual box office failure of the film, which explored the subject of book burning.

The Empty Canvas (1964)
The Legion of Decency branded *The Empty Canvas* with its "condemned" classification for being sexually provocative and for appealing to the "prurient-minded." Consequently, producer Joe Levine had problems running advertisements for the film in daily newspapers across the country, which undoubtedly contributed to its poor box office showing.

ILKA CHASE

Prior to being cast in the 1942 picture *Now, Voyager*, Ilka Chase had appeared on Broadway in *The Women* and had caused a commotion in Hollywood with her autobiographical tell-all book, *Past Imperfect*. On the *Now, Voyager* set an unidentified actress approached Chase and cattily congratulated her on the book. "Who *wrote* it?" she asked, to which Chase retorted, "Darling, I'm so glad you liked it. Who *read* it to you?"

Because of her acid tongue, it was thought by many at the time that Chase and Davis would clash on the set. Actually, however, they got along fairly well.

Ilka Chase (1900–1978) appeared in several other pictures, including *Why Leave Home?* (1929), *The Big Knife* (1955), and *Ocean's Eleven* (1960).

CHATEAU MARMONT HOTEL

Between February 1957 and January 1960 Bette checked into the Chateau Marmont Hotel in West Hollywood no fewer than seven times. During this period Bette frequently left her home in Maine for Hollywood to shoot various television shows. Sometimes she was with Gary Merrill; other times she was alone. It was a rough period in the volatile relationship between Davis and Merrill, and their battles were sometimes waged in their suite or bungalow. These battles, notorious for rattling the elevators and resonating through the lobby, became legendary at the hotel. On one occasion, one of the hotel workers made the mistake of asking her how long she planned to stay at the hotel. "Well," he later related in a huff, "if looks could kill I would've been gone on the spot. Those big eyes of hers got even bigger as she glowered and roared, 'I don't know! And why do you have *the nerve* to ask?' "

On another occasion Bette had been in her suite late one night, watching television and smoking, when she fell asleep on an upholstered chair. Her cigarette fell onto the fabric, and if it had not been for actor Lou Jacobi, a guest in a nearby room who spotted smoke emanating from her window, Bette Davis might have gone up in flames.

On January 7, 1960, Bette checked into the Marmont for one of her last visits. She was in town to shoot an episode of the television series "Wagon Train." On that occasion an electrical short in one of Bette's closets triggered an alarm. Bette, frightened and then irritated, lashed out at anyone who would listen that she was leaving the hotel and would never return.

RUTH CHATTERTON

By the time Bette Davis arrived at Warner Brothers in late 1931, the studio had snatched Ruth Chatterton, then a major star, from Paramount. Chatterton was then earning a whopping salary of $8,000 a week; Davis was getting $300 a week for her work on *The Man Who Played God*.

Chatterton's first picture for Warner Brothers was 1932's *The Rich Are Always With Us*. For Bette it was a thrill and a terror to be on the same set with Chatterton, who, with such pictures as *Madame X* (1929), *The Laughing*

Lady (1929), *Sarah and Son* (1930), and *Unfaithful* (1931), had been one of her favorites. On the first day of shooting Bette marched up to Chatterton and confessed her idolization and fear. Chatterton, to her credit, took Bette under her wing and comforted her.

CHILDREN

> Born. To Bette Davis, 39, high-strung cinemactress, and painter (ex-boxer) William Grant Sherry, 32, her third husband: her first child, a girl, on May Day, which Bette Davis chose for her cesarean section; in Santa Ana, Calif. Name: Barbara Davis Sherry. Weight: 7 lbs.
>
> *Time* magazine, May 5, 1947

Barbara Davis Sherry
Margot Merrill*
Michael Merrill*

---

*adopted

In *Mr. Skeffington*: has any actor done more for the tobacco industry?

CIGARETTES

Has any actor in history done more for the tobacco industry than Bette Davis? In her personal life Bette smoked up to five packs of cigarettes a day and favored Chesterfields, Philip Morris, and, in later years, Vantage. She also carried over her screen tactic of employing a cigarette as a prop and a punctuation mark. In 1937 Bette was approached to endorse and become a spokesperson for Lucky Strike cigarettes. Bette wanted the job; but Jack Warner, who had control over such matters, refused to let her do it.

During her later years Bette was incensed by the onslaught of no-smoking regulations across the nation. "America is no longer a free country," she pronounced while exhaling a great puff of smoke in her listener's face.

Following her stroke in 1983, the only concession Bette was willing to make to doctors was to switch to a low-tar filtered brand. She also claimed she never really inhaled when she smoked. "Instead of inhaling," she would often explain, "I just blow the smoke out of my mouth." Perhaps, but she did so with such style.

> "If I did not smoke a cigarette—they would not know *who* I was!"
>
> *Bette Davis*

CINEMA COLLECTORS

One of the finest stores of its kind in the world, Cinema Collectors (1507 Wilcox Avenue, Los Angeles, California) houses thousands of motion picture photographs and posters, including an impressive collection of Bette Davis–related material.

THE CINEMATOGRAPHERS

> "Our great cameramen, the Ernest Hallers, made us look like we didn't look at all."
>
> *Bette Davis, 1988*

When Bette initiated her 1936 strike against Warner Brothers, one of her demands was having cinematographer approval. She expressed that she was tired of being photographed by men who were incompetent. At that time only three cinematographers met with Bette's approval: Tony Gaudio, Sol Polito, and Ernest Haller.

Cinematographer	Film	Year
John Alton	*The Catered Affair*	1956
George Barnes	*Marked Woman*	1937
Paul Beeson	*The Scapegoat*	1959
Joseph Biroc	*Hush . . . Hush, Sweet Charlotte*	1964
Robert Bronner	*Pocketful of Miracles*	1961
Robert Burks	*Beyond the Forest*	1949
Jack Cardiff	*Death on the Nile*	1978
Charles G. Clarke	*The Virgin Queen*	1955
Arthur Edeson	*Waterloo Bridge*	1931
Arthur Edeson	*The Golden Arrow*	1936
Arthur Edeson	*Satan Met a Lady*	1936
Arthur Edeson	*Thank Your Lucky Stars*	1943
Bryan England	*The Wicked Stepmother*	1989
Mike Fash	*The Whales of August*	1987
Karl Freund	*Bad Sister*	1931
Tony Gaudio	*Ex-Lady*	1933

Cinematographer	Film	Year
Tony Gaudio	*Fog Over Frisco*	1934
Tony Gaudio	*Bordertown*	1935
Tony Gaudio	*Front Page Woman*	1935
Tony Gaudio	*Kid Galahad*	1937
Tony Gaudio	*The Sisters*	1938
Tony Gaudio	*Juarez*	1939
Tony Gaudio	*The Old Maid*	1939
Tony Gaudio	*The Letter*	1940
Tony Gaudio	*The Great Lie*	1941
Tony Gaudio	*The Man Who Came to Dinner*	1942
Roberto Gerardi	*The Empty Canvas*	1964
Henry W. Gerrard	*Of Human Bondage*	1934
Merritt Gerstad	*Watch on the Rhine*	1943
Bert Glennon	*Hollywood Canteen*	1944
W. Howard Greene	*The Private Lives of Elizabeth and Essex*	1939
Loyal Griggs	*Bunny O'Hare*	1971
Burnett Guffey	*Storm Center*	1956
Ernest Haller	*The Rich Are Always With Us*	1932
Ernest Haller	*Dangerous*	1935
Ernest Haller	*That Certain Woman*	1937
Ernest Haller	*Jezebel*	1938
Ernest Haller	*Dark Victory*	1939
Ernest Haller	*All This, and Heaven Too*	1940
Ernest Haller	*The Bride Came C.O.D.*	1941
Ernest Haller	*In This Our Life*	1942
Ernest Haller	*Mr. Skeffington*	1944
Ernest Haller	*A Stolen Life**	1946
Ernest Haller	*Deception*	1946
Ernest Haller	*Winter Meeting*	1948
Ernest Haller	*What Ever Happened to Baby Jane?*	1962
Ernest Haller	*Dead Ringer*	1964
Sid Hickox	*So Big*	1932
Sid Hickox	*The Big Shakedown*	1934
Sid Hickox	*Special Agent*	1935
Alan Hume	*The Watcher in the Woods*	1980
J. Roy Hunt	*Way Back Home*	1932
Michel Kelber	*John Paul Jones*	1959
Robert Krasker	*Another Man's Poison*	1952
Milton Krasner	*All About Eve*	1950
Milton Krasner	*Phone Call from a Stranger*	1952
Steve Larner	*Burnt Offerings*	1976
Ernest Laszlo	*The Star*	1952
Joseph MacDonald	*Where Love Has Gone*	1964
Jacques Marquette	*Burnt Offerings*	1976

Cinematographer	Film	Year
Ted McCord	June Bride	1948
Barney McGill	Cabin in the Cotton	1932
Barney McGill	20,000 Years in Sing Sing	1933
Barney McGill	Bureau of Missing Persons	1933
Hal Mohr	Watch on the Rhine	1943
Ira Morgan	Jimmy the Gent	1934
L. William O'Connell	The Menace	1932
Frank Phillips	Return from Witch Mountain	1978
Sol Polito	The Dark Horse	1932
Sol Polito	Three on a Match	1932
Sol Polito	The Working Man	1933
Sol Polito	The Petrified Forest	1936
Sol Polito	The Private Lives of Elizabeth and Essex	1939
Sol Polito	Now, Voyager	1942
Sol Polito	Old Acquaintance	1943
Sol Polito	The Corn Is Green	1945
Sol Polito	A Stolen Life	1946
William Rees	Fashions of 1934	1934
William Rees	Housewife	1934
Jackson Rose	Seed	1931
Giuseppi Ruzzolini	The Scientific Cardplayer	1972
Allan Siegel	Hell's House	1932
John Stephens	Bunny O'Hare	1971
Gregg Toland	The Little Foxes	1941
Leo Tover	Payment on Demand	1951
James Van Trees	The Man Who Played God	1932
James Van Trees	Parachute Jumper	1933
James Van Trees	The Girl From Tenth Avenue	1935
James Van Trees	It's Love I'm After	1937
Harry Waxman	The Nanny	1965
Harry Waxman	The Anniversary	1968

*uncredited on screen

The Television Cinematographers

Cinematographer	TV Program	Year
Edward R. Brown	"A Piano for Mrs. Cimino"	1982
Charles Correll	"The Dark Secret of Harvest Home"	1978
James Crabe	"The Disappearance of Aimee"	1976
James Crabe	"Strangers: The Story of a Mother and Daughter"	1979
Ernest Day	"As Summers Die"	1986
Jim Dickson	"The Dark Secret of Harvest Home"	1978
Tony Imi	"Little Gloria . . . Happy at Last"	1982
Robert Jessup	"Skyward"	1980

Cinematographer	TV Program	Year
William K. Jurgensen	"White Mama"	1980
William Marguiles	"The Judge and Jake Wyler"	1972
Frank Phillips	"The Dark Secret of Harvest Home"	1978
Tony Richmond	"Madame Sin"	1972
Howard R. Schwartz	"Right of Way"	1983
Lennie South	"Scream, Pretty Peggy"	1973
Brian West	"Murder with Mirrors"	1985

CIVIL RIGHTS

In the late thirties and early forties, Bette was one of the first Hollywood figures to speak out against the stereotypical casting of blacks as servants, clowns, or victims. At the time, Bette made public statements that she would like to see the race cast "normally." She was particulary pleased that her 1942 picture *In This Our Life* was among the first Hollywood films to endow a black character with ambition and intelligence.

As its president in the forties, Bette dictated the rules of conduct for the Hollywood Canteen. One of her most emphatic regulations was that black servicemen were not to be segregated from white servicemen, a controversial stand for the era. Bette would rationalize the rule, with characteristic common sense, by stating that black servicemen were hit with the same bullets as white servicemen and therefore should be treated with equal appreciation.

An incident that happened on the set of *The Corn Is Green* (1945) was particularly telling about Bette's stand on the subjects of equality and prejudice of any kind. Joan Lorring, who costarred in the picture, relates, "There was a young woman who was my stand-in. After some weeks she was replaced, and I had not heard anything about it. When I inquired about it, I found out that this young woman had been sitting outside of Bette's trailer. She was having a conversation with somebody else, and she made some anti-Semitic remarks, which were overheard by Bette Davis in her trailer. That woman was off the set that day and never came back."

In the early sixties, with the civil rights movement exploding all around her, Bette took another controversial stand and one that she may have regretted. While civil rights leaders called for Hollywood to take a leadership role in depicting positive black characters on the screen, Bette, in what appeared to be a contradiction of her earlier stance, wrote an editorial in the industry trade papers basically stating that movies were a business and were not designed to be a "philanthropic" industry. Bette was lambasted for her position by black leaders and by members of Hollywood's vast liberal community.

CLUBS, GUILDS, AND ORGANIZATIONS OF WHICH BETTE DAVIS WAS A MEMBER

The Academy of Motion Picture Arts and Sciences
Actors Equity Association
Americans for Democratic Action (ADA)
American Federation of Television & Radio Artists (AFTRA)

The Cape Players
Christian Association, Cushing Academy
"Coffee-Colored Angels," all-girl football team, Newton High
The Cukor-Kondolf Repertory Company (aka The Temple Players)
Drama Club, Cushing Academy
The Girl Scouts
The Hollywood Canteen
Hollywood Independent Citizens Committee of the Arts, Sciences, and Professions
Hollywood Writers Mobilization for Defense
Ibsen Repertory Company
Portland (Maine) Country Club
The Provincetown Players
Screen Actors Guild
Tailwaggers Foundation
United Negro and Allied Veterans of America

LARRY COHEN

"In all my years, I never heard of a director who never saw rushes, who never listened to me."

Bette Davis

"My attitude is that many people give Bette Davis dinners, many people give Bette Davis awards, but very few give her jobs. I gave her a job."

Larry Cohen

Larry Cohen wrote the 1989 film *The Wicked Stepmother* (which he would also direct) for Bette Davis. However, after the first week of shooting Bette walked off the picture, blaming what she deemed Cohen's deficiencies as a director. *The Wicked Stepmother*, which was completed without her, was to be her final film.

Larry Cohen has directed other films, including *It's Alive* (which he also wrote and produced, 1974), *Q—The Winged Serpent* (which he also wrote, 1982), and *The Stuff* (which he also wrote, 1985). He also wrote the 1976 Brian de Palma film *Carrie*.

CLAUDETTE COLBERT

Bette was offered the female lead in *It Happened One Night* (1934) before it was given to Claudette Colbert, but Jack Warner refused to release Bette to Columbia for the picture. The same year, Bette earned acclaim for her performance in *Of Human Bondage*, and many in the industry felt that she deserved the year's Best Actress Oscar. That award, however, went to Colbert for her performance in *It Happened One Night*.

Years later Colbert was Joseph Mankiewicz's first choice for the role of Margo Channing in *All About Eve*. Colbert signed for the part but later had to withdraw because of a back injury. It was to be the great disappointment of her career. As she later related to columnist Erskine Johnson, "It's like I told Joe Mankiewicz, 'Every time I read the beautiful notices, a knife goes through my heart. It's fate. I had to break my back so that Bette could meet Gary Merrill and get the role of a lifetime.' "

Colbert, who had an odd reputation for bumping into things on the set and also for insisting that only one side of her face be photographed, got her revenge some 35 years later. Bette wanted the part of the elder Mrs. Grenville in the 1986 miniseries "The Two Mrs. Grenvilles." However, Colbert got the part and won an Emmy for her performance.

Claudette Colbert (born Lily Claudette Chauchoin in 1905) has appeared in numerous pictures, including *Cleopatra* (1934), *Imitation of Life* (1934), *Private Worlds* (Best Actress Oscar nomination; she lost to Bette, 1935), *Midnight* (1939), *The Palm Beach Story* (1942), and *Since You Went Away* (Best Actress Oscar nomination, 1944).

COLLECTORS BOOK STORE

Located near Hollywood and Vine (1708 North Vine Street, Los Angeles, California), Collectors Book Store is a haven for film enthusiasts (including fans of Bette Davis), with thousands of books, photographs, posters, and other assorted memorabilia.

JOAN COLLINS

Joan Collins was relatively new to Hollywood when she costarred in the 1955 picture *The Virgin Queen*. Nevertheless, she received little comfort or consolation from Bette Davis, who disliked her from the start. Bette regarded the acting abilities of her young costar with disdain and viewed her as a competitor for the amorous attentions of Richard Todd, who also starred in the picture. Collins later related in her autobiography, "Bette Davis awed me, and I avoided her off the set whenever possible. I had been warned she did not take kindly to young pretty actresses, and she lashed out at me a couple of times. She had a scathing wit and was not known for mincing words, and I thought it best to keep a low profile around her. I was still insecure about my work."

Years later Bette and Joan shared a dressing room backstage at 1983's The Night of a Hundred Stars benefit in New York. That evening Bette was openly contemptuous of Collins, who was then enjoying major television stardom as Alexis Carrington Colby on "Dynasty," as Collins repeatedly arranged her hair and adjusted the dress that she barely had on.

Joan Collins, born in 1933, has appeared in other pictures, including *The Girl in the Red Velvet Swing* (1955), *The Wayward Bus* (1957), and *The Bitch* (1979).

COLORIZATION

It is breaking the heart of many of us. I saw *Dark Victory* with color. All the good taste of my clothes and of the set people, all gone. It just breaks your heart.

Bette Davis, 1989

COMMERCIALS

In March 1933, Bette filmed a promotional spot for General Electric dish-washers. She is seen wearing an apron and loading a dishwasher as she enthuses, "It washes, rinses, and polishes the dishes and silverware . . . [and] it's automatic and self-cleaning, too!" Twenty years later, Bette did a television commercial for Pet milk in which she simply stated, "I'll take two cans of Pet milk." Then, in 1966, Bette shot a commercial for Awake orange drink for General Mills. The spot had her take a sip of the drink after which she exclaimed, "It tastes more like orange juice than orange juice itself." After being criticized for misusing her talents by hawking products on television, Bette rationalized, "I wouldn't sell pills or deodorants. That's unattractive. But this is an innocuous product."

COMMUNISM

Bette Davis was not a Communist, but her liberal leanings made her suspect to many in Washington. The January 15, 1945, edition of *The Daily Worker* heralded, "Bette Davis Joins Sponsors of New Political Action Committee." The accompanying article stated that Bette had joined the recently organized Hollywood Independent Citizens Committee of the Arts, Sciences, and Professions (HICCASP). Later, in July 1946, when the group was being perceived as Communist-dominated, Bette, like other Hollywood notables, resigned. Shortly thereafter, she joined another liberal group, Americans for Democratic Action (ADA), which sought to distance itself from communism.

Although the FBI never conducted a full security investigation on Bette, it did keep a file on her activities. In October 1951 the bureau was considering an investigation into both Bette and husband Gary Merrill. "You are instructed to examine your files to determine if an investigation is warranted concerning the Merrills," a bureau agent was directed. The subsequent examination revealed that Bette had participated in a war bond drive sponsored by the Negro Victory Committee in December 1942. It was also mentioned that *The Daily People's World*, a West Coast Communist newspaper, had printed a photograph of Bette in its March 27, 1943, edition. The photo showed Bette with writers Robert Rossen and Arch Oboler, with a caption stating that the trio was discussing the "Free World Theater" radio program.

Also of alarm to the bureau was that in May 1946 Russian writer Konstantin Simonov had named Charles Chaplin and Bette Davis as "Soviet friends." Simonov stated that both Chaplin and Bette speak "in contempt of the slanderous campaign raised by the reactionary press—particularly the Hearst Press—against the Soviet Union." The bureau further learned that, during a visit to the United States, Simonov visited Bette on the set of *Deception* and then invited her to be a guest aboard his ship, a Soviet war vessel. She accepted.

The Un-American Activities Committee of California reported in 1947 that Bette was a member of the Emergency Committee on KFI, a group formed to protest Los Angeles radio station KFI's decision to discharge six commentators charged with pro-Communist and pro–Soviet Union slanting of their newscasts.

In 1965 the FBI again considered a full investigation of Bette. A letter from an M. A. Jones to a Mr. DeLoach dated November 29, 1965, read in part: "Although we have never investigated Miss Davis, Bufiles reflect that during the 1940s she participated in the activities of the Hollywood Independent Citizens Committee of the Arts, Sciences, and Professions, the Hollywood Writers Mobilization, and the United Negro and Allied Voters of America, all of which have been cited as Communist fronts. . . . In the past, she has been personally acquainted with numerous Communist sympathizers and Party members and over the years has been a close associate and personal friend of [name blacked out]. . . . In 1962, Bette Davis participated in a banquet sponsored by the American Civil Liberties Union which was given for the purpose of encouraging support for a drive to abolish the House Committee on Un-American Activities. . . ."

In later years Bette would acknowledge (though she would *not* provide a name) that she had had a romance with a man, a member of the Communist party, who unsuccessfully tried to recruit her into the party.

Of the McCarthy hearings and subsequent blacklist, Bette said, days before her death in 1989, "It was a disgrace. All of our talented writers were gone. We had no scripts. They were all in prison and not all of them were party members. It was like Hitler, Germany. You could not believe it was America. . . . It was a disastrous thing."

CONNECTING ROOMS ★ ½

L.S.D./Hemdale, England
1972   103 minutes   Technicolor
Directed by: Franklin Gollings
Produced by: Harry Field and Arthur Cooper
Screenplay by: Franklin Gollings, based on the play by Marion Hart
Cinematography by: John Wilcox
Cast: Bette Davis, Michael Redgrave, Alexis Kanner, Kay Walsh, Gabrielle Drake, Leo Genn, Olga Georges-Picot, Richard Wyler, Brian Wilde, John Woodnut, Tony Hughes

Director Anthony Mann had intended to produce *The Cellist* by Marion Hart on a London stage. After Mann's death, John Gielgud expressed interest in staging and starring in the play. When those plans failed to materialize, producer Arthur Cooper acquired the rights to the property and announced his intention to adapt it for the screen.

Bette Davis was first sent the script back in America in 1967. The part called for her to play Wanda, a 50-year-old cellist who lives in a run-down boardinghouse. Her next-door neighbor (played by Michael Redgrave) is a former teacher who lost his job because of his homosexuality. The story, basically, is about their friendship and connection.

With a budget of $1.4 million and a nine-week shooting schedule, *Connecting Rooms* started shooting on February 24, 1969, at Pinewood Studios in London. The subsequent shoot was fairly harmonious, with Davis and Redgrave in a state of mutual admiration. There was a problem, however, with Alexis Kanner, who played Bette's young suitor in the film. After initially approving of his casting, Bette decided that Kanner was wrong for the part and took her case to director Gollings. It was decided, however, that too much footage of Kanner had already been shot, and thus it was too late to have him replaced. Another problem was the obvious friction between Davis and Kay Walsh, who disliked one another from the start. Nonetheless, Gollings managed to keep the two actresses in separate corners for most of the shooting, and the production was completed without major incident.

Despite being produced in 1969, *Connecting Rooms* was not released until 1972, when it was generally panned by the critics.

FRANK CONROY

One of Bette's early mentors, Frank Conroy directed and costarred in *A Midsummer Night's Dream*, staged at the Mariarden School of Dance in July 1925. After observing Bette in this and another production, Conroy took Bette's mother aside and informed her that her daughter was destined for a career as an actress. Later Conroy suggested to George Cukor that Bette be cast in his production of *Broadway*.

Like his young protégée, Frank Conroy (1890–1964) went to Hollywood in 1930. His pictures include *Grand Hotel* (1932), *The Ox-Bow Incident* (1943), and *The Last Mile* (1959).

COOKING

As a schoolgirl in New York, Bette took cooking classes and entered a citywide contest sponsored by the New York Board of Education. Bette made a batch of cookies and won first prize.

In later years, during her marriage to Gary Merrill, Bette further developed her cooking skills and was particularly fond of entertaining guests with such Yankee dishes as Cornish hen and red flannel hash. Bette took great pride in her culinary skills, would not allow anyone to step into her kitchen, and was undoubtedly livid when her daughter B.D. publicly accused her of once heating a frozen dinner that she passed off as her own.

Following her stroke in 1983, Bette was unable to cook for herself, and she went through an arduous process of hiring and firing cooks for her West Hollywood apartment. Director Larry Cohen, who frequently visited Bette during the last year of her life, remembers, "She had a sizable kitchen because she fancied herself a cook—although she had cooks. They were continually being fired and hired and fired. All during the time I knew her, she was always firing her cook and hiring someone else. Nobody could please her in the kitchen. She fancied herself a culinary expert, and no one was up to her standards."

Bette once commented that 35 would-be cooks came—and went. "I would find well-known store-bought cookies," Bette later wrote, "that they claimed to have baked themselves. . . . One cook even went so far as to serve me *Stouffer's* bell peppers with a tomato sauce, which I instantly recognized."

On the set with Billy Roy.

Teacher and pupil.

THE CORN IS GREEN ★★

Warner Brothers
1945   118 minutes   bw
Directed by: Irving Rapper
Produced by: Jack Chertok
Screenplay by: Casey Robinson and Frank Cavett, based on the play by
    Emlyn Williams
Cinematography by: Sol Polito
Cast: Bette Davis, John Dall, Nigel Bruce, Joan Lorring, Rhys Williams,
    Rosalind Ivan, Mildred Dunnock, Arthur Shields, Gwyneth Hughes,
    Billy Roy, Thomas Louden, Leslie Vincent, Robert Regent, Tony Ellis,
    Elliot Dare, Robert Cherry, Gene Ross

The Corn Is Green, an autobiographical play by Emlyn Williams, had been performed to considerable acclaim in England by Dame Sybil Thorndike and on Broadway by Ethel Barrymore. Bette saw Barrymore in the part in New York and later in Chicago. With characteristic audacity, Bette, then 36, believed not only that she could play the 50-year-old spinster, Miss Moffat,

With a miscast John Dall in *The Corn Is Green*.

but also that she could play it better than the revered Barrymore.

The primary problem in preproduction was the casting of Morgan Evans, the male student whom Miss Moffat inspires to greatness. Richard Waring, who played the part on Broadway, was scheduled to reprise his role in the picture (as were Rhys Williams, Gwyneth Hughes, Mildred Dunnock, and Rosalind Ivan). Unfortunately, the timing coincided with Waring's receiving a draft notice. Jack Warner attempted to get a postponement for Waring's induction date, but to no avail, and so a search was conducted for his replacement. Bette's personal choice of costar was Richard Cromwell, whom she arranged to have tested. However, at 34, Cromwell was deemed too old for the part (especially with Bette only two years his senior). John Dall, a newcomer to films, was cast in the part after Warner's wife, Ann, saw him on Broadway in *The Eve of St. Mark* and cajoled her husband into testing him. It would be a major mistake from which the film would never recover.

Not invited to reprise her stage role in the featured part of Bessie Watty was Thelma Schnee. The reason, reportedly, was that she was too old and was deemed not attractive enough by the powers that be. Angela Lansbury was tested for the part, as was contract player Andrea King, whom Jack Warner favored. At one point it was announced that Betty Field had been cast in the part, but such was not to be the case. Cast instead was newcomer Joan Lorring, 18, who had been floundering for a year at MGM. It seems that Bette reviewed the tests of the actresses in contention for the part and had a hand in the selection of Lorring.

Bette underwent extensive makeup and wardrobe tests, typical of all period pictures, and ended up wearing 30 pounds of padding for the part. Joan Lorring recently related, "I know that when she came in to work in her slacks and shirt, she was a slip of a person, and when she came out of her trailer in costume, her shape was altogether different. It didn't *weigh* 30 pounds; it was meant to *represent* 30 pounds. It's lightweight stuff. They were called 'heavenly bodies,' and you put them on just as though they were a jacket."

The Corn Is Green, with Irving Rapper directing, started shooting on June 20, 1944. Bette, having just completed *Hollywood Canteen* and claiming laryngitis, did not report to the set until June 26. Although she was frequently disagreeable (particularly to Rapper) during the film's production, Bette also nurtured both of her nervous young costars. It was one of her characteristic, admirable, and usually unheralded traits.

John Dall, in particular, was terrified of working with Bette, and it unfortunately shows on the screen. As he told a reporter on the set, "Gosh, it's bad enough playing the lead opposite Miss Davis the first time I ever look into a camera. But imagine having to cuss her out besides." Dall's terror of and intimidation by Bette did not serve the film well. Although, after some debate, Bette, Rapper, Chertok, and the writers decided that there should be no sexual tension between the two characters, there is, in fact, no chemistry whatsoever between them on the screen. Dall's playing is awkward and wooden. Still, Bette did what she could to counsel and comfort the young actor. "She was wonderful," he enthused to another reporter. "Every time I played a scene with her, I felt strength coming to me from her. In that scene where I had to tell her off, for instance, in some shots the camera was on me alone. But Bette always stood right behind the camera, facing me, giving the scene the same acting as if she were before the camera."

Bette was equally helpful to Joan Lorring, whose naive shyness appealed to her. "She'd expect you to come to work with your tools. One day I came to the set and I did not have my lines down. I kept going up in two spots of a scene. I was very nervous about it because I knew I didn't know my lines well enough. It was just Bette Davis and me in the scene. We ran through it a couple of times, and I kept going up. In between takes she said to me, informatively and not instructional, 'You know, Joan, every one of us on the set has a special job to do. The men on the lights can't come without their gels because those are their tools. They have to have all their equipment with them. There's no time for anybody to come shorthanded. The carpenters have to come with all of their tools. The grips have to have everything they need. Irving Rapper has to be prepared for what his shots are going to be. And we have to be prepared with everything we need. And our tools are the words. And it's our job to have them so we don't hold anybody up. It costs a lot of money every single minute we're here.' "

Meanwhile, the production lumbered along at a slow pace, in part because Bette insisted that Rapper shoot in continuity. She was also frequently sick and/or demanding vacation time. Bette took Saturday, July 22, through Tuesday, July 25, off. Then, on Saturday, August 5, all hell broke loose when Bette was injured on the set. A heavy arc lamp fell from above and hit her on the head. Fortunately, the padded Miss Moffat wig she was wearing softened the blow and she suffered only a slight concussion. There was speculation at the time, and in years since, that the "accident" had been staged by one of the disgruntled crew members. Bette refused to see the Warner Brothers doctor, opting instead to see her personal physician in Laguna, where she lived at the time. That night Bette showed no ill effects from the injury and attended a party at Warners. Nevertheless, citing the injury, Bette failed to report to work on Monday. She also missed work that Thursday, and from August 18 through August 24 she set the production further behind by taking an unscheduled vacation.

Meanwhile, a furious Jack Warner sent Rapper a memo on August 15, demanding that he speed up the production. "I know you have had a little trouble here and there," Warner wrote, "but I cannot understand why you are eight days behind on a 60-day schedule. . . ."

And so the typically nervous Rapper got even more nervous. There were additional delays in the shooting due to Bette's wig. Initially Bette opted *not* to wear a wig for the picture. However, after a lot of executive deliberation, and after sequences of a wigless Bette had already been shot, the decision was handed down that Bette should indeed wear a wig. Thus all previously shot scenes involving her had to be reshot to accommodate the wig. Also requiring retakes was a scene involving Joan Lorring. After viewing the dailies, Jack Warner decided that he didn't like a dress that Lorring was wearing and insisted that it be changed. Then, of course, there was the difficulty with John Dall. He was never able to overcome his nervousness, and he was also having a problem with the Welsh accent that the part required him to affect. By several accounts Irving Rapper, still being hounded by Warner, lost all patience with Dall. As William Roy, an actor who played one of the boys in the cast, recently related, "Irving just ragged John and made a wreck out of him." At one point, after shooting several takes of a shouting sequence (in combination with Rapper's incessant pressure), poor young Dall lost his voice, and shooting had to be postponed again.

There were a lot of boys and young men in the cast of *Corn*, and as required by law they were accompanied to the set by a guardian, usually their mother. "I remember one day," William Roy recalled, "we were shooting a scene in the schoolroom, and suddenly, in the middle of rehearsal and for no reason at all, Irving began screaming at the mothers, 'I know what all you mothers out there think of me. I've heard all the stories. I'd like to see any of you get up here and direct this goddamned picture!' *Well*, Mildred Dunnock fainted and Nigel Bruce had to carry her out to her dressing room. At times like that, Bette would just turn on her heels and go into her dressing room."

On August 18, Rapper exploded on the set at assistant director Bob Vreeland. The rumor on the set was that Rapper had been jealous of and perturbed by Vreeland ever since Bette confided to Vreeland that she liked him and his work better than she liked Rapper. Certainly Bette regarded Rapper with disdain. She reportedly had little respect for him and had agreed to work with him only because she could run roughshod over him on a set. When asked to describe Rapper's style of direction, Joan Lorring contemplated, then responded, "He wasn't a director who could explain the sense of an *emotion*, the sense of how a character was led to this particular point in life. He was more literal. He might say, 'Curl your hair on your finger as you say this line.' His direction was more technical. That leaves *you* to decide what it is you're doing there, what you're *really* doing. You're not curling your hair on your finger. Bette Davis worked more from the impetus of the character, as the character was written. Irving Rapper wouldn't work that way. I didn't think she much admired him."

According to William Roy, among others, Bette, in effect, codirected *Corn*. "She'd come on the set with her wig, her costume not completely on, and she'd say, 'Well, I think Moffat would walk into this scene and go to the desk and sit down. And then she'd say her line, and then she'd get up and walk over to the window.' And Irving would say, 'OK, let's shoot it.' She could get away with that with him. She had gotten him his first job as a director. She could call the shots, and that's just what she did."

As filming progressed, Bette began to have doubts about her decision to follow in Ethel Barrymore's footsteps. "You know," she confided to a reporter on the set, "I've done many pictures playing roles originally played by other actresses, but there are only two I've had qualms about—this one and *The Little Foxes*. Believe me, I'm not being sweetly humble for publication, but for two years I tried to talk them into getting Barrymore, if they could, for this picture." The fact, however, was that Bette—at that point in her career—had her unofficial pick of properties, and she rejected *Mildred Pierce* to do *The Corn Is Green*. It was a decision she would later regret.

Still, despite all the difficulties during the production, Bette was on relatively good behavior. As the unit manager on the picture reported back to the studio, "I don't think it is worthwhile upsetting her . . . since she is so much better [in temperament] on this picture than she has been on former pictures." Certainly she continued to be kind and accommodating to her young coplayers.

Joan Lorring had a difficult time shooting the seduction scene with John Dall: "I didn't know *how* Bessie was going to have a baby. I had no idea. I didn't even know what 'seduction' meant. I looked it up in the dictionary, and *that* didn't help me." She had even more trouble shooting the final, pivotal scene in which Miss Moffat takes Bessie's baby.

"It came along toward the end of the week," Lorring recalls. "Thursday and Friday were spent doing the master shots and close-ups on that scene. I had been very worried about it because I really didn't feel free to let go [anger] at Bette Davis. And yet that's what the story required Bessie to do. Meanwhile, the pink [memo] slips were coming, and Irving Rapper was being made more and more nervous by these pink slips. It wasn't his fault, really, that he was nervous and not really short-tempered, but tense. It was unmistakable, and it would transmit itself and was felt by everybody. He was being made nervous by the businesspeople. They needed that movie to finish. But this scene couldn't be rushed. That's what the whole movie had been building up to—Miss Moffat having to take this baby. Friday morning, because Bette Davis's close-ups were usually shot in the morning, they did all her close-ups. They finished soon after lunch, and she was finished with that scene. They were leaving all my close-ups for Saturday. Bette Davis had the custom then of leaving as soon as possible on Friday so that she could be in Laguna by Friday evening, and she'd spend the weekend there and come back to work on Monday morning. Bobby Vreeland later told me, 'I went to her after lunch on Friday, in the middle of the afternoon, and I said, "That last shot was your wrap for the day, and we'll see you on Monday." And she said, "No, I'll be here. I'll stay 'til you wrap tonight, and I'll be here tomorrow morning." ' 'Well,' he said, 'Why are you going to do that?' And she said, 'Well, I'll be goddamned if I'm going to leave that girl alone tomorrow!'

"Well, I never heard about that. I only knew that on Saturday morning I came in and the door to her trailer was shut, and they called me for my mark, and I looked up, and there she was, sitting next to the camera. I thought I was going to have to play my close-ups to the script girl—that's how it was done—and I look up, and there's Bette Davis sitting next to the camera. *On a Saturday!* She spent the whole day there with me. And she had on her wig, her Miss Moffat wig. She *was* Miss Moffat. She wasn't going to shortchange me on anything."

On September 13, 1944, two weeks and $50,000 behind, *The Corn Is Green* completed production. Ethel Barrymore was invited to the set to take publicity photographs with Bette Davis. Understandably, she declined. Warners marketed the film by proclaiming, "Only Bette Davis Would Dare Do It!" Industry insiders knew that the line referred to Barrymore; the general filmgoing public thought it suggested salaciousness, which was just what Jack Warner wanted. He also ordered that a glamour photo of Bette wearing a slinky gown be used in the print advertisements. When she saw a copy of the ads, Bette, livid that the integrity of the picture was being compromised and the public deceived, telephoned Jack Warner and demanded that the campaign be revised. It was, and the film eventually proved to be a big disappointment at the box office.

Bette would later comment that she had made a mistake by doing *The Corn Is Green*. At that point in her career, she reflected, the public did not want to see her as a middle-aged schoolteacher. They wanted to see her as a bitch. Perhaps they just wanted to see her in a *good* (well-cast) picture, which *The Corn Is Green* unfortunately is not.

FRANK CORSARO

Directing Bette Davis in the 1961 Broadway production of *The Night of the Iguana* was the worst experience of director Frank Corsaro's entire career. "It was a very unhappy situation," he says 30 years later. "It was really quite horrendous." Of Bette he says, "She was definitely a paranoid lady. There was some [mental] illness going on. This was also a woman who had literally ruled the roost at Warner Brothers for I-don't-know-how-many years, and it was too much to ask her to suddenly take a back seat [with a secondary role]." Bette eventually had Corsaro fired (although he would retain the director's credit) while the play was in out-of-town tryouts in Chicago.

Years after *Iguana*, Corsaro devoted a chapter of his autobiography to his horrendous experience with Bette Davis. His publisher, however, excised the text in fear of a libel suit. Of the censored chapter Corsaro would say, "It was a very clear picture of what it was like to deal with the incredible problems of anyone producing a Broadway play of this caliber." Corsaro was somewhat vindicated when he read about fellow director Joshua Logan's experience with Bette on the 1974 stage musical *Miss Moffat*.

Corsaro recently recalled, "I was working in Washington one day, and at a bookstore I came across a copy of the then-just-published autobiography of Josh Logan. I was very curious. I picked it up, and it practically opened to the chapter on Bette Davis. And I simply stood there and read the chapter, and it was chapter and verse of what I went through. It was almost déjà vu reading it."

Today Frank Corsaro is the artistic director and is on the board of directors of the Actors Studio, of which he has been a member since 1952. He is also a major director of American operas and is the chief adviser of the drama department at Juilliard. His plays include the direction of *The Honeys* with Hume Cronyn and Jessica Tandy; *A Hatful of Rain* with Shelley Winters, Ben Gazzara, and Tony Franciosa; and *The Scarecrow* with Eli Wallach, Patricia Neal, and, in a bit part, the unknown James Dean.

NORMAN CORWIN

Directed the 1959–1960 stage production *The World of Carl Sandburg*. Unlike some of her other stage directors, Bette was fond of Corwin. When he took temporary leave of the show's tour to find a new actor to costar with Bette, she wrote him a note that read, in part, "Norman. . . . I adore you. You are so 'big-Jesus' [a Sandburg quote] talented, so much a human being, there aren't many. You have started me in a new life by giving me my assurance back which, due to uncertainties, we need not go into. I had completely lost. Will miss you like mad. Find us a good man for the show. And don't worry. Your show is too damned right, it would take a real lousy actor to kill it. . . . Will try and do you proud every performance."

COSMETIC SURGERY

In the seventies, while Bette was touring with her one-woman show in

London, one brave lady stood up from the audience and asked if she had had a face-lift. Bette instructed the woman to come down to the stage. When the nervous woman arrived at the stage, Bette knelt down before her, face-to-face, and then demanded, "Don't you think I'd look *better* if I *had* had a face-lift?"

When asked about cosmetic surgery on other occasions, Bette was fond of quipping, "Who the hell would I be kidding?" In fact, however, Bette did have a face-lift in 1978, as a 70th birthday present to herself.

THE COSTARS

The following is a selective alphabetized list:

Brian Aherne	James Davis	Ian Hunter	Oliver Reed
Ann-Margret	Olivia de Havilland	Kim Hunter	Debbie Reynolds
George Arliss	Faye Dunaway	Brian Keith	Edward G. Robinson
Mary Astor	Mildred Dunnock	Hope Lange	Marion Ross
Fay Bainter	Dan Duryea	Angela Lansbury	Gena Rowlands
Carroll Baker	Ann Dvorak	Peter Lawford	George Sanders
Richard Barthelmess	Denholm Elliott	Christopher Lee	William Shatner
Anne Baxter	Leif Erickson	Margaret Leighton	Ann Sheridan
Ed Begley	Douglas Fairbanks, Jr.	Joan Lorring	Maggie Smith
Karen Black	Peter Falk	Paul Lukas	Gale Sondergaard
Joan Blondell	Charles Farrell	Karl Malden	Ann Sothern
Humphrey Bogart	Glenda Farrell	Hugh Marlowe	Robert Stack
Ernest Borgnine	Mia Farrow	Herbert Marshall	Barbara Stanwyck
Charles Boyer	Geraldine Fitzgerald	David McCallum	James Stephenson
Walter Brennan	Errol Flynn	Doug McClure	James Stewart
George Brent	Henry Fonda	Gary Merrill	Barry Sullivan
James Brolin	Dick Foran	John Mills	Richard Todd
Horst Buchholz	Glenn Ford	Marilyn Monroe	Franchot Tone
Victor Buono	Sidney Fox	Robert Montgomery	Spencer Tracy
James Cagney	John Garfield	Agnes Moorehead	Peter Ustinov
Ruth Chatteron	Lillian Gish	Wayne Morris	Joan Van Ark
Lee J. Cobb	Scott Glenn	Paul Muni	Robert Wagner
Charles Coburn	Alec Guinness	Conrad Nagel	Warren William
Joan Collins	Sterling Hayden	David Niven	Natalie Wood
Michael Connors	Helen Hayes	Pat O'Brien	James Woods
Gladys Cooper	Susan Hayward	Patrick O'Neal	Monty Woolley
Ricardo Cortez	Paul Henreid	William Powell	Teresa Wright
Joseph Cotten	Howard Hesseman	Vincent Price	Keenan Wynn
Joan Crawford	Celeste Holm	Claude Rains	Gig Young
Jamie Lee Curtis	Miriam Hopkins	Ronald Reagan	
John Dall	Leslie Howard	Michael Redgrave	

THE COSTUME DESIGNERS

"I suppose I will never be better dressed than I was in *Elizabeth and Essex*. I was the Queen of England. But for heaven's sakes, *who* wants to be well-dressed in the 16th century!"

Bette Davis

Designer	Film	Year
Milo Anderson	*Thank Your Lucky Stars*	1943
Rosemary Burrows	*The Nanny*	1965
Phyllis Dalton	*John Paul Jones*	1959
Fabiani	*The Scientific Cardplayer*	1972
Don Feld	*Dead Ringer*	1964
Phyllis Garr	*Bunny O'Hare*	1971
Edith Head	*June Bride*	1948
Edith Head	*Beyond the Forest*	1949
Edith Head	*All About Eve*	1950
Edith Head	*Pocketful of Miracles*	1961
Edith Head	*Where Love Has Gone*	1964
Elois Jenssen	*Phone Call from a Stranger*	1952
Chuck Keehne	*Return from Witch Mountain*	1978
Orry-Kelly*	*The Man Who Played God*	1932
Norma Koch	*What Ever Happened to Baby Jane?*	1962
Norma Koch	*Hush . . . Hush, Sweet Charlotte*	1964
Bernard Newman	*Deception*	1946
Walter Plunkett	*Of Human Bondage*	1934
Emma Porteous	*The Watcher in the Woods*	1980
Anthony Powell	*Death on the Nile*	1978
Max Ree	*Way Back Home*	1932
Ann Roth	*Burnt Offerings*	1976
Simonetta	*The Empty Canvas*	1964
Emily Sundby	*Return from Witch Mountain*	1978
Julle Welss	*The Whales of August*	1987
Julie Weiss	*The Wicked Stepmother*	1989

*Orry-Kelly was Warner Brothers' premier costume designer for many years. He was responsible for designing the costumes for *all* of Bette Davis's pictures at Warner, beginning in 1932 with *The Man Who Played God* and ending in 1946 with *A Stolen Life*. He was also hired, at Bette's insistence, to do the costumes for the 1941 Goldwyn picture *The Little Foxes*.

Costume Designers for the Stage Plays

Designer	Play	Year
Orry-Kelly	*The World of Carl Sandburg*	1959
Robert Mackintosh	*Miss Moffat*	1974
Noel Taylor	*The Night of the Iguana*	1964
Miles White	*Two's Company*	1952

The Costumes

The two most famous Bette Davis costumes are the red Orry-Kelly ball gown she wore in *Jezebel* and the Edith Head cocktail party ("Fasten your seat

Bette's temper flares
during a wardrobe test.

belts . . .") gown she wore in *All About Eve*. The former was actually bronze-colored (red photographed gray) and cost $850 to make. The latter was a happy accident. Because Bette was rushed into the picture, she did not have adequate time for all the preproduction wardrobe fittings. Subsequently, when it came time to shoot, the dress hung loose around the neckline. Improvising, Bette pulled the gown's neckline over her shoulders, and the dress became a movie costume classic.

Other Bette Davis Costume Facts

☆ Edith Head first designed costumes for Bette Davis for the 1948 picture *June Bride*. Bette was so taken by Head's work that she purchased most of them (at a discounted price, of course) from Warner Brothers for her personal wardrobe.

☆ For the 1948 picture *Winter Meeting*, Bette's costumes were store-bought. She personally selected her wardrobe for the film from the Beverly Hills department store I. Magnin. Upon the picture's release Bette's costumes were generally panned.

☆ Bette liked the costumes designed by Don Feld for the 1964 picture *Dead Ringer*. Following the film's completion, Bette purchased the costumes for her personal wardrobe at a discount of 50 percent.

☆ After she walked off the set of her final film, *The Wicked Stepmother*, in 1989, Bette had the nerve to ask director Larry Cohen if she could have the costumes designed for the film by Julie Weiss. To show that he harbored no hostility, Cohen presented Bette with the costumes (which had cost the production more than $25,000).

JOSEPH COTTEN

Cotten costarred as Bette's whipping post of a husband in the 1949 picture *Beyond the Forest*. The film was Cotten's first Hollywood movie after he had spent eight months in Europe, where he costarred in *Under Capricorn* (1949) for Alfred Hitchcock and *The Third Man* (1949) for Caroll Reed. Years later Cotten (whom Bette was quite fond of) hosted the NBC television documentary "Hollywood and the Stars," which featured an episode about Bette. He also costarred in *Hush . . . Hush, Sweet Charlotte* (1964) and *The Scientific Cardplayer* (1972).

Joseph Cotten, born in 1905, made his film debut in the 1941 classic *Citizen Kane.* His many subsequent pictures include *The Magnificent Ambersons* (1942), *Shadow of a Doubt* (1943), *Gaslight* (1944), *Duel in the Sun* (1946), *Portrait of Jennie* (1948), and *Niagara* (1953).

> I will admit to having stumbled into several trashbins here and there, but never into quite such an important trashbin. After all, I did work with one of the all time great actresses. In spite of the script, we worked well together. I defy anyone not to enjoy acting opposite this woman. She is *all* woman.
>
> *Joseph Cotten on* Beyond the Forest *and Bette Davis*

Vincent Sherman: "Joan called Bette 'a bitch' and Bette referred to Joan as 'a whore'—very often."

JOAN CRAWFORD

1930. Joan Crawford was everything Bette Davis was not: famous, beautiful, glamorous, and anything *but* virginal. She had a way with clothes and a way with men. Conversely, when Bette arrived in Hollywood she was branded: interesting, perhaps, but sexless. Who'd pay to see *her*? Who'd believe that she was the hero's prize at the fade-out? A couple of years later, having proven those skeptics wrong, Bette stepped onto the stage at the Ambassador Hotel to accept a citation as one of the most promising stars of the year, only to be upstaged by the entrance into the room of Joan Crawford, bewigged, bejeweled, and clinging to the arm of her dashing Hollywood prince, Douglas Fairbanks, Jr. It was a spectacular, spotlight-stealing arrival that was fully played by Joan to calculated effect. It was an arrival that should have belonged to *her*, thought Bette, and she never forgot or forgave.

After achieving acclaim, if not stardom, with the 1934 picture *Of Human Bondage*, Bette was signed to appear opposite Franchot Tone in *Dangerous*. At the time, Tone was engaged to Joan, who had since disposed of Fairbanks. During the making of the picture Bette, married to Ham Nelson, was instantly smitten with Tone. But Bette was nothing if not a woman who went after what she wanted, and so she unleashed those magnificent eyes of hers on her defenseless costar, and the two allegedly carried on an affair that lasted the duration of the picture. Upon its completion Crawford retrieved (and married) Tone, and Bette had to content herself with her husband at home and an Oscar, which she would win for *Dangerous*, on her mantelpiece. The Tone affair would establish the course of the fiercely competitive and acrimonious relationship that Crawford and Davis would have over the succeeding 40-plus years. Crawford would get the man, Davis, the acclaim. Each, it seems, wanted what the other had.

By 1940 Bette was the undisputed queen of Warner Brothers, while Joan still reigned, albeit tenuously, at MGM, and they stayed in their respective corners. Thus Bette was none too pleased when Joan showed up on the Warner lot one day during the fall of 1940. Joan was on the lot, Bette learned, to discuss with Hal Wallis the possibility of costarring with Bette in *The Great Lie*. However, after Crawford learned that the role of Sandra was secondary, subordinate to the role to be played by Bette, she declined the picture and returned to MGM. Mary Astor, who would win a Best Supporting Actress Oscar for her performance, was eventually cast in the part.

Crawford's incursion onto the Burbank lot was a harbinger of things to come. When Jack Warner signed Joan Crawford and her suffering-in-mink act to Warner Brothers in June 1943, whispers that it was a calculated attempt to keep the increasingly difficult Davis and her Elizabethan ego in line spread like wildfire. Joan asked for—and got—the star dressing room adjoining Bette's. When Bette returned to the studio one month later, after an extended vacation, Joan courted her favor with flowers and gifts, to no avail. Still, Joan's overt generosity persisted. On one occasion, after Bette was named "favorite all-time actress" by *Screen Guide* magazine, Joan, who had also been in contention for the award, presented Bette with a congratulatory gift: matching handbag and sandals. Bette, as she usually did, ignored the gesture. She wrote it off as cheap and contrived Hollywood sentiment, which she despised, and never more so than when it came from Crawford.

In those days Bette had first choice of all A story properties featuring a major female role. However, when she was presented with James M. Cain's story *Mildred Pierce*, Bette turned it down for three reasons: She considered the story a melodramatic potboiler; she had little interest in working with director Mike Curtiz, who was attached to the project; and she preferred to do the film adaptation of the hit Broadway play *The Corn Is Green*, which she viewed as a far more prestigious production.

The Corn Is Green was released to disappointing box office and less than spectacular reviews in mid-1945. In September of the same year, *Mildred Pierce* opened to big box office and great acclaim (the best of her career) for Crawford. Bette, upstaged at her own studio, was livid. Said Hedda Hopper in her column of January 26, 1946, "Do *not* bring up the name of Joan Crawford in Queen Bette's presence."

And that was *before* the Academy Award nominations were announced. At that point Bette had two Oscars and seven nominations; Joan had no Oscars and no nominations. Thus Joan's nomination as the year's best actress was a blow that sent Bette reeling. After all, *she* had been the only actress in Warner Brothers history to win the coveted Oscar, and the very idea that she was being supplanted by Joan Crawford was appalling. So Bette prayed for a Crawford loss, pinning her hopes on Ingrid Bergman to win for *The Bells of St. Mary's*. Bette attended the ceremonies; Crawford, who would win, did not.

Over the next four years at Warners, as Bette's career seriously slipped, Joan's career enjoyed a considerable revival with pictures such as *Humoresque* (1946), *Possessed* (Best Actress Oscar nomination, 1947), and *Flamingo Road* (1949), all projects that had been rejected by Bette—a fact that drove Bette to frustration. Furthermore, Crawford's name was repeatedly employed by Warner executives in power plays with Bette. When Bette threatened to reject *Winter Meeting* (1948) because of script concessions that were made to appease the censor, producer Henry Blanke informed Bette that if *she* didn't do it, Crawford would. In this case, Bette should have trusted her instincts and let Crawford have it. The film was a failure. Another picture that Crawford wanted that Bette did *not* reject was *Beyond the Forest* (1949). Bette won that particular battle but lost the war. The film was a resounding flop and precipitated the termination of her long, history-making tenure at Warner Brothers.

Years later Curtis Bernhardt, who directed both actresses, compared their talents and temperaments. The following is reprinted from the book *The Celluloid Muse*.

> Compared with Bette Davis, Joan Crawford, whom I subsequently directed in *Possessed,* was as easy to work with as can be. She was naturally a little subdued because she was the studio's second-ranking star, Bette being number one. She threw her handbag at me several times when, having just done a picture with Bette, I called her Bette by mistake.

> The chief difference between Crawford and Davis is that, while Bette is an *actress* through and through, Joan is more a very talented motion picture *star.* That means that, while Joan is just as professional, she is also simpler. Granted, she's not as versatile as Bette. If Bette has an emotional scene, she tackles it completely consciously, and when you say 'cut,' she might ask, 'Do you think that was a little too much this or a little too much that?' But, when

Crawford plays an emotional scene, you have to wait twenty minutes until she comes out of it after you have said 'cut,' because she is still crying or laughing or whatever.

In 1946 there was talk of pairing (pitting?) Davis and Crawford in a picture together. The film was a prison drama entitled *Women Without Men*. The proposition, however, was dismissed as more trouble than it was worth and was later made as *Caged* with Eleanor Parker and Agnes Moorehead. Movie fans would have to wait 16 more years for the extraordinary collaboration of the two movie queens. The picture, of course, was *What Ever Happened to Baby Jane?*, a project that Joan submitted to director Robert Aldrich with the suggestion that it serve as a vehicle for her and Bette. Despite the obvious tension and distance inherent in their relationship, Joan had long admired Bette's talent. On the other hand, while Bette failed to reciprocate the sentiment, she recognized the considerable possibilities in the *Baby Jane* script.

Prior to the shooting Hedda Hopper hosted a cocktail party at her house for the two women. They discussed the film's billing. (Joan willingly conceded top billing to Bette. "She plays the title role. Of course she'd get top billing.") They also talked about the potential for an all-out, fangs-bared feud. ("Us? Never! We're too professional." Right.) Joan deferred to Bette: "This is wonderful for me. *I* usually play the bitches. Now I can sit and watch Bette do it." Talk mixed with alcohol as Bette accepted a glass of Hedda's scotch. Joan, however, produced from her purse a flask of her own 100-proof vodka. "I say if you're going to have a drink," Joan confided to Hedda in a conspiring tone, "have what you want."

During the *Baby Jane* production, reporter Vernon Scott visited the set. His subsequent interviews with the two actresses were telling and, surprisingly, not totally devoid of candor:

Bette: I have admired Joan's performances, but it never entered my mind to work with her. It's interesting casting and I think we have a great curiosity value. We've met in the past, but I wouldn't say we are friends.

Joan and I shouldn't be made to look like Siamese twins. We are two utterly different types of women. There is no way to avoid our differences, so I might as well say, "Yes, working together is murder." I'll keep my fingers crossed.

Joan: I've wanted to work with Bette since 1943. I sent our producer [Robert Aldrich] three scripts for the two of us. . . . I have tremendous respect for Bette as a human being and performer. She's a worker and a prober like I am. She works for the good of the picture, not for herself.

Bette: I'll say one thing. Our producer proved he is a man of stamina and courage. When my cleaning man heard Joan and I were costarring he suggested we shoot the picture in the Coliseum.

The only time that Bette Davis and Joan Crawford competed head-to-head for the Oscar was in 1952, when the former was up for *The Star* and the latter for *Sudden Fear.* Both actresses lost out to Shirley Booth. Ten years later, *What Ever Happened to Baby Jane?* garnered Bette, but not Joan, yet another Best Actress Oscar nomination. Publicly Joan congratulated Bette and wished her luck. Privately, however, she worked to sabotage Bette's chances of becoming the first actress in history to win three Academy Awards. To her friends and associates in the industry, Joan bad-mouthed Bette's performance and personality, despite the fact that she owned a percentage of the picture (and would therefore profit from the box office boost an Oscar win would mean). She also contacted the other four nominees—Anne Bancroft, Katharine Hepburn, Geraldine Page, and Lee Remick—and informed them that she would be more than happy to accept the Oscar on their behalf if they won and were unable to attend. Anne Bancroft accepted the gesture, and when she was pronounced the winner it was Joan Crawford, and not the stunned Bette Davis, who paraded her way to the podium and, in front of the entire movie industry and millions of television viewers, held the coveted Oscar and delivered an acceptance speech.

Once again Joan Crawford had won the war. Hedda Hopper concluded in her column the following day, "I was rooting for Bette. But when it comes to giving or stealing a show, nobody can top Joan Crawford."

Bette had always viewed Joan with disdain, jealousy, and bemusement. Following that night at the Oscars, she seethed with hatred. She had wanted that third Oscar more than anything in her entire career, and it had been single-handedly stolen from her, in her view, by Joan Crawford. Her first act of retaliation was to force Robert Aldrich to have Joan barred from representing *Baby Jane* at the Cannes Film Festival. So, while Bette basked in the spotlight of the French press (her appearance was the overwhelming hit of that year's festival), Joan innocently protested back in Hollywood, "It's as though I was not in the movie at all. And it was I who *begged* Mr. Aldrich to have Bette do this picture with me!" Then, when they were reteamed for the 1964 film *Hush . . . Hush, Sweet Charlotte,* sort of a cousin to *Baby Jane,* Bette virtually terrorized Joan off the set and out of the picture.

In 1973 both actresses were invited to appear—separately, of course—at Town Hall in New York City as part of a series entitled Legendary Ladies of the Movies. When Joan walked onto the stage, she was greeted with a tremendous ovation that caused her to erupt in a great flood of tears. When Bette was greeted with a comparable ovation of her own, she accepted it with theatrical grandeur. Both women were asked what it had been like to work with the other in *Baby Jane.* Bette gave a flippant "No comment"; Joan tried a different diplomatic tack: "Bette and I work differently. Bette screams and I knit. While she screamed, I knitted a scarf that stretched clear to Malibu."

Privately, Bette had plenty to say about Joan Crawford. She ridiculed what she perceived to be Crawford's vanity and pathetic attempts at geriatric glamour; her omnipresent bottle of Pepsi (which was "always half-full of vodka"); her varying sizes of falsies ("She must have a different set for each day of the week. I keep running into them like the Hollywood Hills!"); and her fanatical obsession with cleanliness. Mostly, however, Bette raved about Joan's promiscuity and her lack, in Bette's view, of any real talent. In truth, however, Bette was far less chaste than she wanted anyone to know; and in retrospect Joan (though decidedly not in Bette's class) was a much better actress than most everyone, Bette included, gave her credit for.

In 1977, when Bette was going to become the first woman to be honored with the American Film Institute's Life Achievement Award, Joan fumed with jealousy. Lonely, embittered, and physically ill, 71-year-old Joan was tired of standing in Bette's highly acclaimed shadow. So, as she had some 15 years before, she attempted to sabotage what looked to be a big night for her old rival. She telephoned whatever friends and acquaintances she had left and asked them to boycott the AFI ceremony in which Bette was to be honored. Vincent Sherman, who had directed both actresses, was among those that she called. "She said, 'Please, don't go,' " said Sherman. " 'She's such a bitch!' Joan called Bette 'a bitch,' and Bette referred to Joan as 'a whore'—very often."

On March 21, 1977, the American Film Institute's tribute to Bette Davis aired on national television. Less than two months later, on May 10, Joan Crawford died.

Twelve years later, after her own death, most of Bette's personal memorabilia—letters, scrapbooks, photographs, etc.—was donated to the archives at Boston University. Included in her possessions was a black-and-white photograph of Joan Crawford. It was a typical glamor head shot of Joan in her Hollywood heyday, with one exception: her teeth had been blacked out.

In addition to those already mentioned, Joan Crawford (Lucille le Sueur, 1906–1977) appeared in numerous pictures, including *Pretty Ladies* (1925), *Our Dancing Daughters* (1928), *Grand Hotel* (1932), *Rain* (1932), *Dancing Lady* (1933), *Sadie McKee* (1934), *The Gorgeous Hussy* (1936), *The Women* (1939), *Strange Cargo* (1940), *A Woman's Face* (1941), *Hollywood Canteen* (1944), *Harriet Craig* (1950), *Torch Song* (1953), *Johnny Guitar* (1954), *Female on the Beach* (1955), *Strait Jacket* (1964), *I Saw What You Did* (1965), and *Trog* (1970).

> "Oh, no, I'm not compared with Joan Crawford. It is simply unbelievable to me that we are still talked about as if we were a couple. No two more opposite human beings ever lived, professionally as well as personally."
>
> *Bette Davis*

> "I never go out unless I look like Joan Crawford, the movie star. If you want to see the girl next door, go next door."
>
> *Joan Crawford*

> Bette said that, so far as Joan was concerned, "I don't care if she sleeps around, if she could just act."
>
> *Vincent Sherman*

For myself, I have always felt that Crawford was very much underrated. And Bette? I believe she overrated herself in terms of what she was capable of as an actress. . . . It would be pleasant to imagine that Bette and Joan have now come to an understanding, wherever they are. But I doubt it—fasten your seat belts up there, it's going to be a bumpy eternity!

Liz Smith

JOHN CROMWELL

John Cromwell saw Bette Davis in the 1932 picture *Cabin in the Cotton* and decided that she was the actress he wanted for his Mildred Rogers in the film adaptation of W. Somerset Maugham's *Of Human Bondage*. Cromwell eventually lured Bette away from the contractual clutches of Jack Warner, cast her in the picture, and launched her to stardom.

Over the subsequent years Bette and Cromwell considered reteaming for other projects, including *Anna and the King of Siam* (1946) and *Caged* (1950), but for various reasons they were unable to do so.

John Cromwell (1888–1979) directed numerous other pictures, including *Tom Sawyer* (1931), *Since You Went Away* (1944), *The Enchanted Cottage* (1945), and *The Goddess* (1958).

BOSLEY CROWTHER

Longtime influential critic for the *New York Times* who, over the years, was ambivalent at best when it came to Bette Davis. Still, when Bette walked out on Warners in 1936 in an apparent quest for quality material, Crowther defended her:

> Without taking sides in a controversy of such titanic proportions, it is no more than gallantry to observe that, if Bette Davis had not effectually espoused her own cause against the Warners recently by quitting her job, the federal government eventually would have had to step in and do something about her. After viewing *Satan Met a Lady* . . . all thinking people must acknowledge that a "Bette Davis Reclamation Project" (BDRP) to prevent the waste of this gifted lady's talents would not be a too drastic addition to our various programs for the conservation of natural resources.

GEORGE CUKOR

Director George Cukor fired Bette Davis from the Cukor-Kondolf Repertory Company in 1928, and over the next 50-plus years she never let him forget it. As he once told columnist Sheila Graham, "She keeps telling the story. I find it a great bore."

By the time Bette achieved any semblance of stardom in Hollywood in the early to mid-1930s, Cukor had become a major force in pictures. Their paths, however, did not cross again until David Selznick started casting

Gone With the Wind. Cukor was set to direct the picture, and Bette was one of the candidates for the part of Scarlett O'Hara. In later years Bette frequently cited Cukor's disinterest in her ("He wouldn't even test me!") as the reason she lost out on the part.

Further wedging these two formidable talents was the fact that Cukor had attained considerable success with directing (and befriending) the actress Bette perceived as her primary acting rival, Katharine Hepburn (*A Bill of Divorcement,* 1932; *Sylvia Scarlett,* 1935; *Holiday,* 1938; *The Philadelphia Story,* 1940; *Adam's Rib,* 1949; *Pat and Mike,* 1952).

Cukor also directed Judy Holliday in *Born Yesterday.* The performance won Holliday a surprise 1950 Best Actress Oscar over the favored Bette Davis for her performance in *All About Eve.*

George Cukor (1899–1983) directed numerous other pictures, including *What Price Hollywood?* (1932), *Dinner at Eight* (1933), *Little Women* (Best Director Oscar nomination, 1933), *Camille* (1936), *The Women* (1939), *Gaslight* (1944), *A Star Is Born* (1954), and *My Fair Lady* (Best Director Oscar winner, 1964).

CUKOR-KONDOLF REPERTORY COMPANY

In 1928 Bette Davis was the ingenue of this Rochester, New York, theater company directed by George Cukor and George Kondolf. The company featured weekly guest stars and a regular cast of players that included leading lady Dorothy Burgess, Benny Baker, Sam Blythe, Walter Fohlmer, Wallace Ford, Helen Gilmore, Irma Irving, Rose Lerner, Frank McHugh, Elizabeth Patterson, and Robert Strange.

During Bette's tenure the company staged its plays at the Lyceum Theatre and then at the Temple Theatre (hence its nickname, the Temple Players), both located in Rochester. The plays produced by the Cukor-Kondolf Repertory Company in which Bette appeared are *Broadway, Excess Baggage, Cradle Snatchers, Laff That Off, The Squall, The Man Who Came Back,* and *Yellow.*

During her second season Bette was fired from the company. Over the years Bette often suggested that she had been dismissed because she refused to socialize with other members of the company.

GEORGE CURRIE

Bette's drama teacher at the Robert Milton–John Murray Anderson School of the Theatre made a distinct impression on her. By the time the semester ended, 30 students had dropped out of Currie's class. Bette was among those who remained, and one day she asked him why he seemed to discourage his students from embarking on a theatrical career, when he should have been, in her view, *encouraging* them. Currie responded that students had "enough hope in their soul without some outsider giving them more. Those who are in earnest will bang on in spite of anything I say; the rest automatically eliminate themselves." In later years, when aspiring young actors turned to her for counsel, Bette often employed the reverse psychology that she had learned from her former teacher.

MICHAEL CURTIZ

Curtiz directed a number of pictures that featured Bette Davis: *Cabin in the Cotton* (1932), *20,000 Years in Sing Sing* (1933), *Jimmy the Gent* (1934), *Front Page Woman* (1935); *Kid Galahad* (1937), and *The Private Lives of Elizabeth and Essex* (1939). In addition, when director Lloyd Bacon became ill during the production of *Marked Woman* (1937), Curtiz stepped in and shot some of the scenes.

Perhaps more than any other single director, Michael Curtiz exemplified the Warner Brothers house style of the early through midthirties, with a series of gritty, economical pictures. Certainly he was among the studio's most durable and prolific directors. Nevertheless, in 1932 he saw little potential in the then-unknown Bette Davis and objected to her being cast in *Cabin in the Cotton*. Nor did his opinion of her change much over the years. The disdain was mutual, and when Bette attained power at the studio she opted not to work with him again. She declined the 1945 picture *Mildred Pierce* in large part because Curtiz was assigned as the film's director. It was a mistake and a lesson she learned well. Later Bette actively sought the female lead in *Life with Father* (1947), despite the fact that Curtiz was to be its director. However, she was passed over in favor of Irene Dunne, and Bette carried a heavy grudge against Curtiz until well after his death in 1962.

Michael Curtiz (born Mihaly Kertesz in 1888) directed numerous other pictures, including *Captain Blood* (1935), *The Charge of the Light Brigade* (1936), *The Adventures of Robin Hood* (1938), *Four Daughters* (Best Director Oscar nomination, 1938), *Angels with Dirty Faces* (Best Director Oscar nomination, 1938), *Yankee Doodle Dandy* (Best Director Oscar nomination, 1942), and *Casablanca* (Best Director Oscar winner, 1943).

CUSHING ACADEMY

Bette spent her junior and senior years of high school (1924–1926) at Cushing Academy in Ashburnham, Massachusetts. Her principal was Dr. Hervey Cowell. Bette helped pay for her tuition by working as a waitress in the campus dining room. Still, she overcame the initial embarrassment of catering to her peers and became one of the most popular girls on the coeducational campus. Bette was voted president of the Christian Association, was a member of a sorority, participated in school debates, performed in the junior class play, *Seventeen*, and in her senior year was voted the prettiest girl in her class. She was not, however, considered the best diplomat or policymaker. In her senior year she ran for class president and received a single vote—her own. In her junior year Bette met and was romanced by Ham Nelson, Jr., a senior.

Years later, while shooting *The Great Lie* (1941), Bette addressed Cushing Academy's annual football banquet via long-distance telephone from her Warner Brothers dressing room.

D

DANCE

Bette wore a corduroy jumpsuit to her first high school dance, which she attended unescorted. Her lack of popularity at the dance was humiliating to Bette, and she returned home sobbing. "I'm a wallflower," she wailed to her mother. "I'll be a wallflower all my life!"

Shortly thereafter, Bette took dance instruction at the Mariarden School of Dance in New Hampshire. She initially studied with the Marie Ware Laughton's Outdoor Players, before receiving a scholarship to study with the more prestigious instructor Roshanara. As a member of Roshanara's company, Bette appeared as one of the dancing fairies in *A Midsummer Night's Dream*. She also appeared in a production entitled *The Moth*, in which she donned 18 yards of white Chinese silk.

Later, at the Robert Milton–John Murray Anderson School of the Theatre, Bette took dance instruction from the legendary Martha Graham. In later years Bette would frequently credit Graham for teaching her how to act with her body.

While a member of the Cukor-Kondolf Repertory Company, Bette took Charleston lessons for her role as a chorus girl in *Broadway*. Years later, while living in Maine, she danced the Charleston onstage in a charity benefit performance. She danced the jitterbug in the 1943 picture *Thank Your Lucky Stars*, performed several routines in the 1952 Broadway revue *Two's Company*, and danced the cancan in an episode of the television program "Wagon Train."

DANGEROUS ★★½

Warner Brothers
1935   78 minutes   bw
Directed by: Alfred E. Green
Produced by: Harry Joe Brown
Screenplay by: Laird Doyle
Cinematography by: Ernest Haller
Cast: Bette Davis, Franchot Tone, Margaret Lindsay, Alison Skipworth, John Eldredge, Dick Foran, Walter Walker, Richard Carle, George Irving, Pierre Watkin, Douglas Wood, William B. Davidson, Frank O'Connor, Edward Keane

Dangerous was adapted from an original story by Laird Doyle, who was under long-term contract to Warner Brothers. When it went into preproduction, the picture was called *Hard Luck Dame* in reference to the so-called "jinx" that Joyce Heath, once a great actress, unwittingly casts on the men in her life.

Hal Wallis initially assigned Bob Lord to be the film's producer, but in an April 16, 1935, memo Lord wrote to Wallis that although he thought the script would make a good picture, "this type of story is not for me." Wallis conceded, and Harry Joe Brown was signed to produce.

Upon receiving it, Bette also thought that the picture was not for her. At the time she was fighting Warners for better pictures after her success in RKO's *Of Human Bondage* the year before. Over the succeeding decades Bette continued to berate *Dangerous*, and to her dying day she insisted that the only reason she won an Oscar for it was to compensate her for not having gotten it for *Bondage*. In retrospect, it is difficult to understand her adamant vilification of *Dangerous*. It's not a great picture, but it is not a bad one either. And the part of the has-been actress with gin on her breath and a chip on her shoulder (modeled on stage star Jeanne Eagels, who in 1929, at 35, died from a drug overdose) offered Bette the opportunity to unleash her unparalleled histrionic powers. As Joyce she gets to deliver the Cagneyesque lines "Oh you cheap, petty bookkeeper, you! Every time I think that those soft, sticky hands of yours ever touched me it makes me sick. Sick, do you hear? You're everything that's repulsive to me. Your *wife*! I've never been a wife to you, you poor simpering fool!" Not a particularly endearing heroine, to be sure, but certainly a worthy successor to *Bondage*'s Mildred Rogers.

Wallis persevered, and on August 26, 1935, with a budget of $194,000,

Dangerous started principal photography. A few days later Bette joined the company. The most significant event during the shooting was that Bette, then married to Ham Nelson, fell in love with her leading man, Franchot Tone. They reportedly had an affair that lasted throughout the shooting, which did not preclude Tone from continuing his romance with Joan Crawford. Joan would occasionally show up on the set to take Tone out for lunch. When he returned, it was obvious to a jealous Bette that food and drink had not been the only items on his lunch menu.

Perhaps the biggest controversy surrounding the production was the film's title. After *Hard Luck Dame* it became *Evil Star, The Jinx Woman, Forever Ends at Dawn, Tomorrow Ends*, and *But to Die*. Bette opted for *Evil Star*, and the picture was very nearly called *The Jinx Woman*, but after shooting had been completed on October 16, 1935, Hal Wallis issued the dictum that the picture's final title would be *Dangerous*.

Bette completed shooting with the rest of the company on September 23. The picture actually came in under budget, at around $174,000.

Dangerous was marketed lamely as "A Bolt of Drama That Will Blow the Fuses!" It was rushed through preproduction so that it could capitalize on Tone's escalating popularity via *Mutiny on the Bounty* and was previewed on November 16, 1935, at Warner's Hollywood Theatre to mixed reviews. Bette, however, received almost unanimous raves for her performance.

DARK HORSE ★★½
Warner Brothers
1932   75 minutes   bw
Directed by: Alfred E. Green
Produced by: Ray Griffith
Screenplay by: Joseph Jackson and Wilson Mizner, from a story by Melville
    Grossman, Joseph Jackson, and Courtenay Terrett
Cinematography by: Sol Polito
Cast: Warren William, Bette Davis, Guy Kibbee, Vivienne Osborne, Frank
    McHugh, Sam Hardy, Robert Warwick, Harry Holman, Charles
    Sellon, Robert Emmett O'Connor, Berton Churchill

In the political comedy *Dark Horse*, Bette was assigned the strictly decorative part of Kay Russell, a secretary whose idea of a woman's place in politics was in the boss's bed.

Allotted 24 shooting days, *Dark Horse* started principal photography with Bette on March 14, 1932. Bette completed her assignment on April 9, and the picture wrapped up production four days later.

Released in the election year of 1932, *Dark Horse* was marketed with inane ads that proclaimed, "Democrats are Howling, Republicans are Roaring, the Whole Nation is Joining One Big Party and What a Party! Hilarity Is Just Around the Corner in *Dark Horse!*"

To promote the picture, which was reviewed favorably, Bette and Warren William went on a personal appearance tour that took them to New York.

"THE DARK SECRET OF HARVEST HOME"

Four-hour miniseries of Thomas Tryon's novel that aired on NBC in 1978. The picture was produced by Universal, which was then helmed by Bette's old agent, Lew Wasserman. "The Dark Secret of Harvest Home" was shot on location in Mentor, Ohio, and starred Bette as a witch with a pitchfork in a very strange neighborhood. Compelling as it sounds, the proceedings are disappointingly dull. "The Dark Secret of Harvest Home" was directed by Leo Penn, produced by Jack Laird, and written by Jack Guess and Charles E. Israel from an adaptation by James M. Miller and Jennifer Miller. It co-starred David Ackroyd, (a young) Rosanna Arquette, Rene Auberjonois, John Calvin, Norman Lloyd, Linda Marsh, Michael O'Keefe, Laurie Prange, Lina Raymond, Tracey Gold, Michael Durrell, Stephen Joyce, Joanna Miles, Richard Venture, and the voice of Donald Pleasence. Curiously, the picture required the services of not one but *three* cinematographers: Charles Correll, Frank Phillips, and Jim Dickson.

DARK VICTORY ★★½

Warner Brothers
1939 106 minutes bw
Directed by: Edmund Goulding
Produced by: Hal Wallis in association with David Lewis
Screenplay by: Casey Robinson, based on the play of the same name by
    George Emerson Brewer, Jr., and Bertram Bloch
Cinematography by: Ernest Haller
Cast: Bette Davis, George Brent, Humphrey Bogart, Geraldine Fitzgerald,
    Ronald Reagan, Henry Travers, Cora Witherspoon, Dorothy Peterson,
    Virigina Brissac, Charles Richman, Leonard Mudie, Fay Helm, Lottie
    Williams

Bette Davis's most overrated picture.

Bette: "Is Max Steiner going to play this scene—
or am *I*?"

"Darling, poor fool, don't you
know I'm in love with you?"

As Judith Traherne, Bette received the most exultant reviews of her career.

After she scored a major success with the release of *Jezebel* in early 1938, Jack Warner gave in to her repeated requests to obtain the rights to a failed Broadway play called *Dark Victory*. Warners purchased the rights from Selznick International in an agreement dated June 8, 1938, for the sum of $27,500. Selznick had previously purchased the rights to the play by George Emerson Brewer, Jr., and Bertram Bloch. Ironically, at the 1939 Oscars ceremony, David Selznick's *Gone With the Wind* would be in competition with his former property, *Dark Victory*, as the year's best picture.

Casey Robinson, probably the studio's top scenarist, was assigned to the picture, and he received considerable uncredited assistance from director Edmund Goulding. It was Goulding who added to the story the character of Ann, Judith's best friend. It was an inspired idea, one that alleviated the need for the dying Judith to wallow in self-pity—Ann could do it for her.

Despite the fact that Warners purchased the picture for her, there was some discussion at the studio, about a month before actual production started, of casting another actress as Judith. Bette was in the throes of an emotionally demanding affair with her *Jezebel* director, William Wyler, and was in the process of being divorced by her husband, Harmon Nelson. Furthermore, the making of *Jezebel*, followed by *The Sisters*, had taken its toll, and she was near physical and emotional collapse.

Among the actresses who tested for the part during this period was Gale Page. Also considered was Tallulah Bankhead, who had starred in the unsuccessful 1934 stage version of the same story. Another actress who desperately wanted the part was Barbara Stanwyck. She later reflected, "I really hated missing out on *Dark Victory* because I'd made what I thought was a brilliant campaign to get it. I learned Selznick had bought it, which encouraged me, and I told my agents to do *anything* to get it. They were told flatly that Selznick was preparing it for Merle Oberon. Okay, so I tried. Then a couple of years went by, and the word was that no writer could lick the problems [in adapting the story], and it was on the shelf. Well, that wasn't going to stop this girl. I'd done several 'Lux Radio Theatres,' so I pitched *Dark Victory* as a 'Lux,' and I was set to do it on radio. It was a very successful show. When I heard through the grapevine some time later that Warners was buying it, hallelujah, I had it! Then word got around that Casey Robinson, their top writer, had licked it. Terrific. Then it was announced that Bette Davis would be doing it. Not so terrific."

The casting of the male lead, the part of Dr. Steele, was even less certain. Casey Robinson, with Bette's enthusiastic endorsement, wanted Warners to borrow Spencer Tracy from MGM for the part. Tracy, however, read the script and passed. He was well aware, as were some of the other top actors who were approached, that this was to be Bette's show. Basil Rathbone was tested on August 27, 1938, but the part was awarded to George Brent.

A far less important casting decision was the selection of Judith's two dogs. Goulding had a difficult time finding two dogs who were compatible not only with each other but also with Bette, who would have to interact with them. He solved the problem by hiring Bette's sister's two dogs. One final casting note: for the part of the picture's third male lead, a drunken, sexually ambiguous waste of mankind, Goulding selected Ronald Reagan. For his work in the picture Reagan was paid $1,258, a trifle compared to Bette's $35,000.

Meanwhile, Hal Wallis concerned himself with the look of the picture. Particularly troublesome to Wallis were the hair and makeup of Bette and also of Geraldine Fitzgerald, then a little-known British actress, cast in the part of Ann. "If Bette Davis is going to wear her hair in any unusual manner, I want tests made immediately. I don't want to have to go back and make retakes because of any freak hairdress that she may turn up in the dailies," Wallis wrote in a memo to Goulding on October 7. He added, "I don't like Bette Davis' outfit #9 at all—the gold pantaloons or whatever the hell she is wearing, and that black top piece and that black hat that she has on. It is a weird looking outfit, and I don't like it at all. Don't use it."

Although it doesn't show up on the screen, production files indicate that Warners spent a good deal of time and money conducting medical research, specifically brain tumor research, for the preparation of the picture. There was even an effort to enlist Dr. Sigmund Freud, then in London, as a technical adviser on the picture. Dr. Freud, however, rejected the proposition. Nonetheless, everything from proper technical medical terminology to trivial beauty concerns was addressed in preproduction. One question asked of the Warners research department by writer Robinson was "How long before the hair would grow back to normal hair dress length after it has been shaved for a brain operation?" The reliable research department responded, "from eight months to one year" and noted that "During this period, most female patients wear wigs."

Rehearsals for the picture were held on Saturday, October 8, 1938. On Monday, October 10, with a mere 30 allotted shooting days and a budget of $500,000, *Dark Victory* started principal photography.

The plot of *Dark Victory* concerns the tragedy of a dying young heiress. The news of her plight is withheld from her by her noble best friend and by the doctor whom she is in love with. She discovers the truth, however, when she stumbles onto her file in the doctor's office and reads the words *prognosis negative*. She goes into a fitful mourning but eventually comes to her senses and marries the good doctor. They live happily, but not ever after, as the mysterious brain ailment manifests itself, and Bette makes her grand and classic departure by ascending the great staircase to heaven with Max Steiner's chorus of angels as her accompaniment. Bette hesitated before shooting this final sequence. She started up the stairs, stopped, spun around, and then demanded of Goulding, "Is Max Steiner going to play this scene—or am *I*?" Bette wanted the scene to rely strictly on her skills as an actress, without the dramatic swelling of composer Steiner's orchestra. Goulding assured Bette's actress's ego that the scene was hers and hers alone, so she went ahead and played it. Later, when Goulding did in fact incorporate Steiner's score into the scene, Bette was offended and infuriated.

The production seemed doomed at the outset. Only two days into the shooting Bette, claiming sickness, did not report to the set. Both her health and her mental state improved, however, as the picture progressed—developments that can be seen on the screen. The picture was shot in sequence, and in her early scenes there is an odd, hysterical quality to Bette's playing that is not evident in later scenes. The primary reason for this was George Brent. For seven years Bette had been trying to lure Brent into bed, and during *Dark Victory* she finally succeeded. It's easy to understand Brent's newfound attraction to her. First, at the time *Dark Victory* started shooting Bette was still riding a considerable crest of critical and box office popularity with *Jezebel*. Second, Bette was 30 years old and (with the exception of *Now, Voyager*) at her most beautiful. Third, her emotional instability at the time made her, for once, vulnerable. The combination was irresistible to Brent, and the two engaged in a romance that lasted the duration of the picture and beyond.

As usual when she was in love, Bette was generally agreeable on the set. She also liked the script and trusted her director. Next to William Wyler, Eddie Goulding was the director she most respected. Therefore her characteristic temperament was displayed only a couple of times. One such incident caused a rather ridiculous ruckus with the Warners front office. The scene called for Bette as Judith to wake up in bed in the middle of the night to the sound of a ringing telephone. Bette wanted to play the scene with tousled hair, *sans* makeup. Wallis, who was intent on giving the picture all the glamour and gloss the studio could provide, objected. The scene as it played on the screen was a compromise.

On December 5, 1938, 14 days behind schedule, *Dark Victory* completed principal photography. The picture was released several months later with a pompous and pretentious marketing campaign that heralded, "Deep in the heart of every actress lives the ideal role she longs to play—a role that embodies every talent she possesses. Now such a role has come to Bette Davis. . . . Eight years she has waited to play this role. We sincerely believe it's her greatest screen performance." And "The Greatest Picture of a Woman's Love That the World Has Yet Seen!"

The campaign worked. For her performance in *Dark Victory*, Bette Davis was accorded the most exultant reviews of her entire career. She received a Best Actress Oscar nomination (losing out only to Vivien Leigh's Scarlett O'Hara), and the picture itself received a Best Picture Oscar nomination and was a considerable hit at the box office. In later years Bette would continue to cite *Dark Victory* as one of the two or three best pictures she ever made.

In actuality the picture is a high-gloss soap opera with an uneven performance by Bette and little more. It is obvious, particularly in the early scenes, that Goulding lost control of Bette. She is mannered to the point of being laughable. Also, because we know from the outset that Judith is going to die, the film is too obvious and hence often bores. There is little actual drama. George Brent and Geraldine Fitzgerald brood about Judith's fate and deliver preachy speeches that must have been more effective on the page. There is no real plot to speak of. Girl gets boy; girl gets brain tumor.

Bogart, who plays the role of Judith's horse trainer with an Irish brogue and a creepy kind of sexuality, seems terribly miscast and out of place. As for Reagan, he doesn't do much of anything except guzzle vast quantities of alcohol and generally embarrass himself.

The film, however, has its moments, and predictably they all belong to Bette. When Bette grabs Brent by the lapel and coos, "Darling, poor fool, don't you know I'm in love with you?" it's obvious why the line became an instant movie classic. And the entire final sequence with Bette and Geraldine Fitzgerald planting spring bulbs, then suddenly realizing that "the time" has come, followed by Bette's ascension up the staircase, is played and staged superbly. Bette rehearsed going blind for the scene in a rather unorthodox way. "Driving home at dusk," she confided to a reporter, "I'd pretend it was really daylight and I was going blind and I'd try to look just as far as I could into the darkness." It was a rather simplistic approach, but it works on the screen. This final sequence, in fact, makes the entire picture worth watching. As for the film's title, Bette says at one point to George Brent, "Nothing can hurt us now. What we have can't be destroyed. That's our victory—our victory over the dark." It's that *kind* of picture—the kind they used to call a "woman's picture." Today they call it "The Young and the Restless."

DATES: THE BETTE DAVIS CHRONOLOGY

04-05-08 Birth of Ruth Elizabeth Davis
07-23-25 First professional appearance: a dancing fairy in *A Midsummer Night's Dream*
04-27-28 To Rochester; appears in *Broadway* for one week
03-05-29 *The Earth Between* opens off Broadway
11-05-29 *Broken Dishes* opens on Broadway
10-14-30 *Solid South* opens on Broadway and runs for two weeks; Universal screen test; Bette is summoned to Hollywood
12-08-30 Bette and Ruthie board train in New York, arriving in Hollywood on 12-13-30
01-12-31 *Seed* starts principal photography, finishing on 03-04-31
01-26-31 *Bad Sister* starts principal photography, finishing on 02-21-31
03-30-31 *New York Times* unfavorably reviews Bette's performance in *Bad Sister*
04-18-31 Louella Parsons after seeing *Seed*: "Keep an eye on Bette Davis; that girl has something worth developing"
09-31 Bette's option at Universal is dropped in the middle of the month
11-18-31 Bette signs first Warner Brothers contract; she starts shooting *The Man Who Played God* the following day
05-09-32 *Cabin in the Cotton* starts production; Bette joins the company on 05-17 and finishes on 06-09-32
08-18-32 Bette marries Harmon Nelson, Jr.
02-12-34 Bette starts shooting *Of Human Bondage*, completing work in the beginning of April
06-28-34 *Of Human Bondage* is released; Bette receives rave reviews

08-26-35 *Dangerous* starts shooting without Bette; she joins production on 08-28-35; production finishes on 09-23-35

11-18-35 *Variety* hails *Dangerous*, saying of Bette, "This is perhaps her best achievement"

03-05-36 Bette wins the Oscar for *Dangerous*

06-20-36 Bette is suspended by Warner Brothers

07-02-36 Announcement that Bette has "quit" Warner Brothers

08-03-36 Bette secretly flees Hollywood

09-09-36 Warner Brothers serves injunction against Bette

10-14-36 Bette Davis vs. Warner Brothers: the London trial begins

10-19-36 The case is decided in the studio's favor

10-25-37 *Jezebel* starts shooting with Bette, finishing on 01-17-38

03-08-38 *Variety* and *The Hollywood Reporter* give *Jezebel* and Bette rave notices, with the latter acclaiming the film as the best picture ever made by Warner Brothers

03-28-38 Bette on the cover of *Time* magazine

10-10-38 *Dark Victory* starts shooting with Bette, finishing 12-05-38

11-22-38 Ham Nelson files for divorce, granted on 12-06-38

01-23-39 Bette appears on the cover of *Life*

02-23-39 Bette wins her second Oscar, for *Jezebel*

03-08-39 *The Hollywood Reporter* and *Variety* give Bette and *Dark Victory* rave notices. "Davis [is] magnificent in box office smash," raves *HR*

03-15-39 *The Old Maid* starts production with Bette, finishing on 05-06-39

08-11-39 *The Old Maid* is released in New York to rave reviews

12-31-40 Bette marries Arthur Farnsworth, Jr.

04-14-41 Bette to Goldwyn to shoot *The Little Foxes*; she finishes on 07-03-41

08-13-41 *Variety* gives rave review to *The Little Foxes*

04-07-42 *Now, Voyager* starts shooting, finishing on 06-24-42

08-19-42 *Variety* gives rave review to *Now, Voyager*

10-03-42 Hollywood Canteen opens

08-23-43 Arthur Farnsworth, Jr., falls on Hollywood Boulevard; he dies two days later

05-15-44 B. D. Inc. contract with Warner Brothers goes into effect

11-22-45 Hollywood Canteen closes with a celebration party

11-29-45 Bette marries William Grant Sherry

12-15-46 Bette is excused from Warner Brothers because of her pregnancy

05-01-47 Barbara Davis Sherry is born

09-30-47 B. D. Inc. is dissolved

03-27-48 Hedda Hopper's scathing review of *Winter Meeting* is printed

04-07-48 *The Hollywood Reporter* and *Variety* give *Winter Meeting* poor reviews

05-24-49 *Beyond the Forest* starts shooting with Bette, finishing on 08-05-49

05-26-49 Warner Brothers announces its new four-year contract with Bette

08-04-49 Bette announces to the press that she is ending her long association with Warner Brothers

10-18-49 *The Hollywood Reporter* gives scathing review to Bette and *Beyond the Forest*

10-21-49 Bette files for divorce from William Grant Sherry

10-21-49 *Beyond the Forest* opens in New York and is lambasted

11-10-49 Bette announces reconciliation with Sherry

04-15-50 Bette starts shooting *All About Eve* in San Francisco, finishing at the end of May

07-04-50 Bette receives Mexican divorce decree from Sherry; she returns to L.A. from Mexico

07-28-50 Mexican divorce becomes final; Bette marries Gary Merrill

10-13-50 *All About Eve* premieres in New York to rave reviews

11-06-50 Bette places hand and (high-heeled) footprints in the cement forecourt of Grauman's Chinese Theater

01-06-51 Margot Merrill is born; Bette and Gary adopt her a week later

03-29-51 Bette, nominated for an Oscar for *All About Eve*, loses

01-05-52 Michael Merrill is born; he is adopted a week later by Gary and Bette

10-20-52 On opening night of *Two's Company* in Detroit, Bette collapses during her first number

12-15-52 On opening night on Broadway for *Two's Company*, the show receives mixed reviews

03-11-53 *Two's Company* shuts down

03-16-53 Bette undergoes operation at New York Hospital

02-28-55 Bette returns to Hollywood to prep *The Virgin Queen* and holds press conference at Bel Air Hotel; she starts shooting the picture a few weeks later and finishes in May

10-12-59 *The World of Carl Sandburg* opens in Portland, Maine

03-01-60 *The World of Carl Sandburg* plays in Los Angeles with Merrill back in the cast

05-04-60 Bette files for divorce from Merrill; it is granted on 07-07-60

09-14-60 *The World of Carl Sandburg* opens on Broadway to mixed reviews; it closes on 10-08-60

05-61 Bette makes *Pocketful of Miracles* at Paramount; toward the end of shooting, during the first week of July, her mother, Ruthie, dies

12-28-61 *The Night of the Iguana* opens on Broadway; it receives favorable reviews

04-04-62 Bette leaves *Iguana*

05-09-62 Bette signs *Baby Jane* contract

07-19-62 Bette returns to Warner Brothers for luncheon with J. L. Warner and Joan Crawford

07-23-62 *Baby Jane* starts principal photography, finishing on 09-12-62

09-21-62 Bette takes out a "job wanted" ad in the entertainment trade papers

10-22-62 *Baby Jane* has highly successful preview in New York

02-25-63 Bette receives her 10th Oscar nomination for *What Ever Happened to Baby Jane?*

04-08-63 Bette, up for an Oscar for *Baby Jane*, loses; she also presents the writing awards

03-21-77 "The American Film Institute Salutes Bette Davis" airs on CBS

06-09-83 Mastectomy at New York Hospital

06-18-83 Bette suffers a severe stroke

05-19-85 *My Mother's Keeper* debuts on the national bestseller lists

04-25-88 Bette starts shooting *The Wicked Stepmother*

05-02-88 Bette does not report to the set; she flees to New York; later it is announced that
    she has quit work on the picture
09-22-89 Bette is presented with the Donostia Award for Lifetime Achievement at the San
    Sebastian Film Festival in Spain
10-06-89 Death in Paris

BARBARA DAVIS

Barbara Davis alternately fought and accepted living in the shadow of her
sister. Fame aside, no one who ever met Bette Davis came away without a
vivid impression; Barbara, on the other hand, was instantly forgettable. She
was tragic in her blankness. Even during their childhood in New England,
when they attended the same schools, Bobby, as she was dubbed, always
seemed a step behind. "Why can't you be more like your sister?" was a
question she heard often from teachers who had them both. Even their
mother, Ruthie, favored Bette, and their father—well, their father deserted

That's Bobby Davis, second from the left.

them both. And so it was ordained that Bette was the star and Bobby the
sidekick and accompanist. When Bette was granted a scholarship to study
dance one summer of their teenage years, it was with the stipulation that
Bobby play the piano for the company's daily rehearsals. Bobby, it seemed,
was there to fulfill the seemingly more important needs of her sister and little
more.

When Bobby was struggling in her senior year at Newton High School,
she was left to stay with her uncle Myron and aunt Mildred while Ruthie
escorted Bette to Norwalk, Connecticut, because Bette needed a change of
scenery.

Upon her own graduation from high school, while her sister flirted with the New York theater, Bobby chose to attend the distant Denison University in Granville, Ohio. For Bobby it was an act of rebellion and a major step in establishing her own identity.

But Bobby had neither the strength nor the fortitude of her sister, and when Hollywood called for Bette, Bobby couldn't help following. Over the years her self-image crumbled as she faded farther into Bette's background. She lapsed into moments of hysterics and other moments of sullen depression. Bobby, who had always found solace, if not an identity, in the "three muske-teers" relationship that she had shared with her mother and sister, was particularly disturbed when an outsider intruded upon the trio. Bette's marriage to Harmon Nelson so upset Bobby that it provoked a nervous breakdown. Sensing that it would expedite her recovery, which it did, Ruthie took Bobby to familiar surroundings back east. But from that point forward, Bobby's mental health would be tenuous at best.

Upon her return to Hollywood, Bobby decided on a misguided and unfortunate direction. "Why can't you be more like your sister?" her teachers had asked, and Bobby was now willing to comply. She began to dress like Bette, talk like Bette, wear her hair like Bette. Worst of all, *Of Human Bondage* had been released a few months before to great critical acclaim for Bette, and Bobby deduced with childlike optimism that such widely ap-plauded talent must run in the family. In December 1934 Bobby called a meeting with the press and announced, "I want to be an actress, just like my sister." As a favor to Bette, Bobby was signed to a contract at Warner Brothers. But, as best can be determined, Bette never did more for Bobby in this regard. She never, for instance, got her sister even a small part in one of her pictures, which was certainly something she could have arranged. Privately, Bette snickered at Bobby's ambition; publicly, she opined, "I think it's swell. I mean to help Barbara as much as possible. I think the course for her to adopt is to enter one of our little theaters here [in Hollywood] and let movie offers come to her."

Nothing came. When Bobby finally realized that Bette could not or would not launch her career and that she would have to content herself with the reflected glory of her sister's limelight, Bobby suffered another break-down. This time she underwent extensive psychological testing and rehabil-itation, all paid for, of course, by Bette. Then, following her "recovery," Bobby took another swipe at independence: she ran off and eloped to Ti-juana with a man, Robert Pelgram, her sister disapproved of.

Four years later, while Bette was vacationing in Franconia, New Hamp-shire, after months of arduous and consecutive work, Bobby gave birth to a daughter she named Fay. Shortly afterward, she suffered yet another break-down. While she was institutionalized, her husband and daughter lived with Bette at her home in Glendale, California.

Bobby's marriage to and child by Pelgram were essentially the only things she could call her own. Virtually everything else had been bought and paid for by Bette. Her marriage, however, was not to last. Around the same time that Bette, 37, married William Grant Sherry, 30, Bobby divorced Robert Pelgram. Then, one month after the birth of Bette's daughter (whom she named Barbara at Bobby's insistence), Bobby eloped with a man named David Berry who was, coincidentally, seven years her junior. In lighter times ahead Bette and Bobby referred to themselves as Mrs. Sherry and Mrs. Berry.

And so it continued through the years. When she wasn't well, Bobby was institutionalized (often at Payne Whitney in New York). When she *was* well, Bobby served as Bette's assistant, cook, companion—*servant*. And appalling to outsiders, Bette treated her as such, particularly after the death of Ruthie in 1961. Bette worked hard for a living and was contemptuous of anyone who didn't. Bobby was not her sister as much as she was her dependent. For some who caught a glimpse of them together during the sixties and seventies, their relationship eerily evoked the one shared by Jane and Blanche Hudson in the 1962 picture *What Ever Happened to Baby Jane?* It had everything but the dead rat on the platter and maybe even that.

During the latter part of the seventies, Bette and Bobby had long since separated and were barely speaking. When Bette learned that Bobby was dying of cancer in Phoenix, Arizona, she chose to remain in California. "Let her come and visit me," Bette told her friends. But neither sister visited the other, and Bobby died in 1979.

BETTE DAVIS: AN ORAL BIOGRAPHY

"I can't imagine any guy giving her a tumble."
            Carl Laemmle, Jr., 1931

She told me a very interesting story. She wouldn't name who the actor was, but she was playing opposite this actor. At that time the director did the longshot, then the twoshot, then the close-up of one actor, then the close-up of the other actor. Well, Bette was forced to do all of her close-ups first. Then this actor, who was a major star, would do his close-ups. But he didn't do them with Bette; he did them with a script girl. And when he did his close-ups he would suddenly change the whole interpretation, and so Bette was stuck. This upset her very much. So, as she rose to power, one of the first things she did was to make her director shoot her close-ups last.
                                Gordon Hessler, 1992

"I think Bette Davis would probably have been burned as a witch if she had lived two or three hundred years ago. She gives the curious feeling of being charged with power which can find no ordinary outlet."
                                E. Arnot Robertson, 1935

Nobody but a mother could have loved Bette Davis at the height of her career.
                                Brian Aherne

You see, she was very strict with herself. Her standards for herself were almost beyond reach. She expected herself to know every single thing she was scheduled to know for that day.
                                Joan Lorring, 1991

"It may sound like I'm going overboard when I say it, but Bette Davis is one of the most intelligent women in America. It's generally recognized that she knows as much about the movie business as most anyone you can name. She knows camera angles. She knows story values. She knows how lines should be read. Just the other day during a dramatic scene some people on the set remarked that she had a grim, unpleasant expression and didn't look very pretty. They were all for reshooting the scene but Bette wouldn't permit it. 'How do you expect a woman who just shot a man to look?' she asked sharply. 'Like a ballerina?' "

Pat Clark, still photographer, 1946

If Bette Davis and Joan Crawford come to blows during the promotion of their joint film *What Ever Happened to Baby Jane?*, it is now possible to make book on the probable winner, Bette Davis. Each of these movie queens has a good right cross and left hook, and both are formidable in-fighters. But Bette Davis is the more aggressive. She can take out an opponent with one punch.

Brooks Atkinson, 1962

I heard a wasp stung her. Knowing Bette Davis, I'm surprised she didn't sting back.

columnist Dorothy Manners, 1971

There was nothing you could put over a woman like this that hadn't been done 15 times before. She was a highly intelligent girl, and you couldn't fool her. And if there was something wrong you just had to be very honest with her. She was very suspect of producers.

Gordon Hessler, 1992

Bette Davis has given close to fifty years of great performances on the screen, and yet to my mind none of these compares to the performance she gives offscreen.

Joshua Logan

Bette Davis—who died Friday in Paris at the age of 81—always made the world aware of her presence. And she often made Hollywood quake in that presence. She also changed the course of women in film.

Robert Osborne, 1989

"It's entirely possible that if it hadn't been for Bette Davis, actresses like Meryl Streep wouldn't have a career today."

Olivia de Havilland, 1989

"Such a person has a different standard than we mere mortals. I don't happen to believe that. Mother abuses everyone she comes in contact with—her family, her employees, business people, other actors and actresses."

B. D. Hyman, 1985

To me she is a friend. I will follow her star till kingdom come, and I savor the fact that she is one of my few friends who call me Joseph. She is also the only one who pronounces it with three syllables.

Joseph Cotten

"She was difficult to work with, but there will never be another like her. God bless you, Bette, and mellow out. Don't be ordering everybody around in heaven."

Ann Sothern, 1989

She made bystanders feel guilty as hell for not working as hard as she. She'd let you have it—words flying like balled fists, right between the eyes.

Gary Merrill

You don't carry on a conversation with Bette Davis, you ask a question and then duck.

Louella Parsons

HARLOW DAVIS

Why waste time hating your father when he had a father who had a father?

Bette Davis

Bette never really knew her father, Harlow Morrell Davis. He was 6'2", balding, brooding, and bespectacled. He had graduated from Bates College in Maine, where he had been a champion debater, head of the Athletic Association, and president of his class for four consecutive years. Following his marriage to Ruth Favor in 1907, he entered Harvard Law School. Certainly he was a man whose defenses were difficult to penetrate. He was an atheist, a loner, and something of an introvert. He was anything but demonstrative. Upon his graduation from Harvard he became a patent attorney with the United Shoe Machinery Company of Boston.

By the time Bette was seven, Harlow was fully engaged in an extramarital affair. The relationship was serious enough for him to put his wife,

Ruthie, and their two daughters, on a train bound for Florida for a vacation. He was never to live with them again, divorcing Ruthie a few years later.

Over the years Harlow had little to do with the family he had left behind. After Bette opened off Broadway in *The Earth Between*, he sent her a basket of flowers. To Bette it was a pathetic and empty gesture. One night Harlow appeared in her backstage dressing room after a performance. At the time Bette had the measles, was in no mood for a social call, and treated her father with all the casual disdain she could summon. Future brushes between father and daughter, infrequent as they were, were treated by both with civil formality and little more. Harlow attended Bette's triumphant opening night performance of *The Wild Duck* in her old hometown of Boston. Years later he visited Bette in California and met her husband, Ham. "He's a nice boy," father told daughter, and the two never saw one another again. Harlow lived to see Bette's widely acclaimed performance in *Of Human Bondage* (1934), but he died shortly before she attained true stardom with the release of *Jezebel* in 1938.

Harlow Morrell Davis died of a heart attack at the age of 52. His daughter, Bette, expressed surprise that her father had a heart at all and did not attend his funeral.

> "We were sent to Florida that winter. When we came back, it was all over. There has been endless discussion, innumerable books and articles written about the 'children of divorce.' I can only know how it affected me. It didn't. Not at the time. That it affected all of my later life, there can be no doubt. For had my mother and father remained together I would never have gone on the stage. My father would not have approved. And by the time it would have been necessary for him to forbid it, I would have been beyond rebellion. I would have grown up in New England, gone to college, married, no doubt, settled down and become an outwardly placid and contented housewife and mother, an inwardly frustrated and bitter woman."
>
> *Bette Davis*

> "He was one of the cruelest, most unfatherlike creatures that ever walked this earth. So I don't think I missed having a father. I knew what a louse he was. I always sided with my mother. He was not, incidentally, the man my mother wanted to marry. My grandmother wanted my mother to marry him so she did, but my mother loved someone else. I met the man several times later, and my mother was right."
>
> *Bette Davis*

JAMES DAVIS

James Davis was making minimum wage laying cement for a living when he was signed by MGM in the early forties. However, the studio failed to pick up his option, and he returned to manual labor. Then, when Bette couldn't get Robert Mitchum, Burt Lancaster, or Glenn Ford to play her leading man, a naval hero, in the 1948 picture *Winter Meeting*, she opted to go for an unknown. Taken by his impressive 6'3", 193-pound stature, Bette arranged for James Davis to be tested for the part. Upon signing his Warner Brothers contract (valued at $500 per week), Davis asked Bette whether she wanted his last name to be changed. Bette quipped that the name had served her well and that a theater marquee was large enough to accommodate two Davises.

After the dismal box office and critical failure of *Winter Meeting*, Warners failed to pick up the option on his contract, and James Davis got a job hauling concrete in a wheelbarrow. One writer described Davis's seeming demotion as "a tragedy of Hollywood." Another surmised that the flop of *Winter Meeting* had made Davis unemployable in Hollywood. "Cripes," Davis publicly responded, "I turned down two roles—one because it didn't pay enough money and the other because I didn't like the part."

Later, when RKO was casting *The Story of a Divorce* in early 1950, Bette suggested James Davis. She had him over to dinner at her house and all but guaranteed him that he would get the second male lead in the picture. It has been speculated that the two Davises engaged in something of an affair, but if they did nothing came of it; nor did anything come of the male Davis being cast in *Divorce*, later titled *Payment on Demand*. The part went to Kent Taylor.

James Davis (1915–1981) appeared in pictures including *White Cargo* (1942), *The Romance of Rosy Ridge* (1947), *Cavalry Scout* (1952), *The Last Command* (1954), *Bad Company* (1972), and *The Choirboys* (1977). He is best known, however, for his performance as Jock Ewing on the popular television series "Dallas" (1978–1981).

RUTH DAVIS

"Her mother, frankly, was a pain in the neck, and it's a miracle she didn't sink Bette's career from the outset. She was endlessly and sentimentally fussing over her. She was a weak, silly creature and, despite Miss Davis' loyal demurs then and later, she was the show-biz mother to end all!"

Blanche Yurka to Charles Higham

"She was *not* a stage mother. Ginger Rogers, Greer Garson, Anita Louise—they had *wild* stage mothers!"

Bette Davis, 1983

Ruth Augusta Favor first met Harlow Davis in Ocean Park, Maine, when she was seven. They married on July 1, 1907, when she was 22. After their honeymoon the young couple moved into Ruthie's mother's house on Chester Street in Lowell, Massachusetts. Harlow was accepted by and enrolled in Harvard Law School while Ruthie gave birth to their first child, Ruth Elizabeth, later dubbed Bette.

Ruthie was a fascinating character, colored with contradictions. She was not a terribly attractive woman and tended to be frivolous and doting. And yet, particularly when it came to the well-being of Bette and then Bobby, she was industrious and tenacious. After being jilted by Harlow in 1915, and after concluding that his alimony checks would not provide a sufficient education for her girls, Ruthie decided to get a job. She placed Bette and Bobby in an exclusive boarding school in the Berkshire hills of Massachusetts and then found employment as a governess of three young boys in New York City. She later got a job as a housemother at Miss Bennett's School for Girls in Millbrook, New York.

One of the pivotal events of Bette's young life was when she suffered burns to her face at school. Facing possibly permanent scarring, Bette was sent to her mother in Millbrook. Each night for the next several weeks, Ruthie woke up every hour and applied a lotion to Bette's face. The burns healed, leaving no scars.

Ruthie then enrolled in the Clarence White School of Photography in New York City. Like a few women before her and many since, Ruthie decided to parlay her personal interest into a profession. It wasn't so much feminism; it was survival. She enrolled the girls in a nearby school, and the family lived together for the first time in many years, albeit in a shabby one-room apartment. But, like many mothers with more imagination than money, Ruthie transformed the drab, dilapidated space at 144th Street and Broadway into a home, and her girls never realized the extent of their poverty.

Ruthie then moved her young family to New Jersey, from which she commuted to her job as a photographic retoucher in New York City. However, her daughters quickly tired of life in Jersey, so they picked up again and moved to Newton, Massachusetts, where Ruthie got a job as a photographer.

As she did every year, Ruthie planned a special summer vacation for her girls. One summer Ruthie worked as a housekeeper for a minister so that she and her daughters could spend their vacation in Provincetown on the tip of Cape Cod. Another year she worked as a photographer in Peterborough, New Hampshire, so that both of her girls could attend a nearby theatrical school.

Determined that her daughters receive the best education, the best foundation possible, Ruthie enrolled them at the expensive Cushing Academy, where she too had gone to school. She helped pay for their tuition by arranging to take photographs of Bette's graduating class. In fact, if Bette Davis's ambition to succeed can be traced back to one single moment, it would be the day of her high school graduation in 1926. From the podium where she accepted her diploma, Bette looked down into the crowd and saw Ruthie with clear and admiring eyes. She was wearing a big straw hat, a cheap printed dress, and held a camera in her hands. She had been stricken by some type of poisoning weeks before; her face was blanched, and she was painfully thin. In that one moment Bette vowed to herself: "One day Ruthie will never again have to work." It was a terrific incentive and one that Bette would draw on many times in the succeeding years.

Bette would frequently acknowledge over the years that it had been Ruthie's confidence, not her own, that had sustained her. It was Ruthie who had driven Bette from Newton to New York to audition for Eva Le Gallienne in September 1927. And after Le Gallienne left Bette rejected, dejected, and back in Newton, it was Ruthie who shook her out of her lethargy. First they moved to Norwalk, Connecticut, and when that failed to rouse her slumbering daughter, Ruthie took her by the hand and marched her back to New York to the Robert Milton–John Murray Anderson School of the Theatre. Ruthie, with Bette in trembling tow, strutted into the office of the school's administrator and announced, "My daughter Bette wants to be an actress. I don't have the money to pay for her tuition, but I assure you that eventually I will. Will you accept her?" Then, after Bette was interviewed and accepted (on the installment plan), Ruthie took a job as a housemother in nearby Burlington, New Jersey, to pay for Bette's tuition.

She was a woman of many resources, among them a sixth sense and a gift for fortune-telling that was much respected by both of her daughters. One summer night when Bette was a teenager, Ruthie permitted her to go out on her first unchaperoned date. Any prospect of romance, however, was unceremoniously quashed when one of Bette's other beaux presented himself. His name was Dick Thomas, and he had been sent to the scene by Ruthie to bring Bette home. Ruthie, it seems, had been overcome by a premonition that something terrible was about to happen to Bette. The following morning they learned that after Bette's abrupt departure her date had been killed in an automobile accident.

Years later, as Bette boarded a plane to Rochester, New York, to appear as a chorus girl in a play called *Broadway*, Ruthie instructed her to learn the part of the female lead. Ruthie proceeded to tell her with urgency that the actress playing the lead would have an accident and would have to be replaced. Weeks later Ruthie's prophecy came true and Bette was given the lead in her first professional production.

When Bette was fired from the Cukor-Kondolf Repertory Company several months later, Ruthie was there to curb her despair and steer her in the direction of the Provincetown Players and the off Broadway play *The Earth Between*. And Ruthie was there the morning after the show's opening to share in the glowing reviews accorded her daughter. It was, after all, her victory too.

Then, when Bette contracted the measles after landing the costarring part of Hedvig in Blanche Yurka's production of Ibsen's *The Wild Duck*, Ruthie became her nurse, counsel, and coach. Every night Ruthie sat at Bette's bedside reading and rereading the play aloud, drilling the script into her memory. Bette may have missed Yurka's rehearsals, but Ruthie saw to it that, come opening night, she'd know her lines. Later, during the run, Ruthie also saw to it that Bette had freshly washed and pressed costumes. Bette had the luxury of not having to worry about a thing beyond the performance she gave nightly.

In those early days they came as a package. When Bette arrived in Hollywood at the summoning of Universal, Ruthie was at her side. Over the succeeding years she continued to orchestrate their lives and Bette's career. It was with relentless prodding by Ruthie that Bette finally married Ham

Nelson in 1932. Then, when the newlyweds moved into their new home in West Hollywood, Ruthie (and Bobby) moved into the guest house in the back. Without any apparent opposition, and despite the fact that Bette now had the will of a husband to adjust to, Ruthie continued to organize and control their lives. She walked in and out of the front house at will. When Bette discovered a few months later that she was pregnant, it was Ruthie who determined that an abortion was in order. Husband Ham had little to say about the matter, as was typical when he was confronted with the combined forces of mother and daughter Davis.

Sadly, Ruthie missed the production and premiere of Bette's first great picture triumph, *Of Human Bondage* (1934), but she saw it in New York and telephoned her elation long-distance. And by the time Bette stepped to the podium to receive her first Oscar, for *Dangerous* (1935), Ruthie was back in Hollywood, applauding loudly from the front row. Her job was now done. Her daughter had "arrived," as they say, and Ruthie could now sit back and enjoy everything that Bette's imminent stardom could yield. Over the following years some observed that Ruthie had become the model parent turned spoiled child. She spent well beyond Bette's still limited salary, and to the casual onlooker she was taking advantage of her daughter's success with a vengeance. But few were aware of the inordinate sacrifices that Ruthie had made to secure that success. Certainly she deserved everything she got, or so Bette rationalized.

In November 1945, at the age of 60, Ruth Davis married a man named Robert Woodbury Palmer at the Smoke Tree Ranch in Palm Springs, California. This time it was Bette who stood at *her* side. One week later Bette married William Grant Sherry, whom she had only recently met. It was Bette's most blatantly rebellious act of opposition against her mother. The more strenuously Ruthie disapproved of Sherry, the more convinced Bette was of her love for him. Bette had long since taken control of her own life and career, and if there were any doubts, her marriage to Sherry made the point with an exclamation. The relationship between Ruthie and her new son-in-law was often acrimonious, and tension eventually escalated to the point that Sherry did something Ham Nelson never even thought of doing: he banished Ruthie from the house.

Contrary to Blanche Yurka's statement quoted earlier, Ruth Davis had never been the typical stage mother. Although she provided the inspiration, the ambition, and often the direction of Bette's career, she never intruded by telling Bette how a particular scene should be played. She knew her place, her own particular role, and she played it beautifully. Like most stage mothers, however, Ruthie was herself a frustrated actress. She had studied dramatics as a child in Lowell, Massachusetts, but her dreams were squelched by Yankee practicality and rigid New England mores. And so she abandoned those early aspirations of becoming an actress. Until May of 1949.

In early 1947 Ruthie separated from, and later divorced, Robert Palmer. By the spring of 1949 Bette was consumed with her own failing marriage (and had no patience for Ruthie's *I told you so*s), a declining career, and the raising of her two-year-old daughter, Barbara. After years of activity and purpose, Ruthie finally found herself with time on her hands and no one to console and control but herself. Thus, at the age of 64, she announced her plans to embark on an acting career.

It was a short-lived proposition. Ruthie was to make her professional debut in a summer stock play in Laguna Beach. Instead she met a retired army officer named Captain Otho Budd. The two eloped to Nevada in April 1950. Bette, on the set of *All About Eve*, received a telegram from her mother that read: "Married Captain O. W. Budd in Immanuel Community Church, Las Vegas. We're on our way to Bakersfield and will then return to Laguna." Like her proposed new career, however, Ruthie's marriage was not to last. After months of separation she was granted a divorce on December 11, 1951. Ruthie's physician testified in court that Budd's indifference to her had provoked an extreme nervous condition that required the attention of a doctor.

Ruthie despaired greatly over the downward spiral of Bette's career, which lasted through most of the fifties and beyond, and did not live to see her great comeback with the 1962 picture *What Ever Happened to Baby Jane?* During Christmas of 1960 Ruthie, still living in the Laguna house that Bette had purchased for her, became quite sick. Nonetheless, she was present at Bette's March 1961 opening-night performance of *The World of Carl Sandburg* in Los Angeles. She sat, as she always had, in the front row of the theater. It was to be the last time she would share in one of her daughter's triumphs. On July 1, while Bette was making *Pocketful of Miracles*, Ruth Davis died at the age of 76. On her tombstone Bette had engraved the following tribute:

Ruthie, you will always be in the front row.

OLIVIA DE HAVILLAND

Bette's strange but durable friendship with Olivia de Havilland was laced with conflicting measures of competition and camaraderie. Bette first became fully aware of Olivia, then an unknown, when she was cast in a role that Bette had wanted. The picture was *Anthony Adverse*, and Bette, 27, resented Olivia, who was then 19 and regarded as something of a beauty. With *A Midsummer Night's Dream* (1935) and *Captain Blood* (1935) to her credit, Olivia had quickly joined the group, which included Bette, of the most promising and popular young actresses on the Warner Brothers lot.

The two women were cast together in the 1937 comedy *It's Love I'm After*, in which Leslie Howard was the star. The following year, with the release of *Jezebel*, Bette broke far ahead of the pack of Warners actresses (Olivia included) with her triumphant performance in *Jezebel*, and she never looked back. From that point forward, as long as she remained at Warners, Olivia had to content herself with the number-two slot.

In 1939 Olivia was upset to learn that she had been cast in the tertiary role of Bette's lady-in-waiting in the historical biopic *The Private Lives of Elizabeth and Essex*. At the same time, she was making what was considered the most prestigious picture in Hollywood, David Selznick's *Gone With the Wind*. She knew the role of Melanie was an important one for her, and the shooting of *Elizabeth and Essex* frequently had to be coordinated and rescheduled according to her availability as dictated by the *GWTW* shooting. Exhausted and near mental collapse (in addition to being frustrated by what she perceived to be Warners' misuse of her talents), Olivia was less than personable on the set of *Elizabeth and Essex* and made no friend of Bette Davis, who regarded her at that point as an upstart underling. Bette was no doubt irked that the shooting of *her* picture had to be scheduled to accommodate a supporting player like Olivia. She was also jealous that Olivia was one of the stars of *GWTW*, a privilege Bette bitterly missed.

The two women would not become friends until the shooting of the 1942 picture *In This Our Life*. Reportedly, on the first day of shooting, Bette marched up to Olivia, stopped, stared, and pronounced through a great puff of cigarette smoke, "You are one hell of an actress!"

By that point Bette was secure in her position as queen not only of the Warners lot but all of Hollywood. Olivia, meanwhile, was engaged in a tempestuous and punishing romance with the picture's director, John Huston. She was miserable and in need of a confidante. And so to Bette she let down her defenses, and the two women commiserated. Certainly they had things and men (Howard Hughes, for one) in common. Both were strong actresses who felt mistreated by Warner Brothers and manhandled by the studio system. After her considerable success in *Gone With the Wind*, for which she was nominated for a 1939 Best Supporting Actress Oscar, Olivia was sent by Warners from one piece of garbage to the next. She scored a success (and a 1941 Best Actress Oscar nomination) for *Hold Back the Dawn*, but that was while on loan to Paramount. Certainly Bette, who had been similarly abused by Warners after her RKO loan-out success with *Of Human Bondage*, understood what Olivia was going through. Olivia greatly admired Bette's 1936 court battle against Warners, albeit an officially unsuccessful one, and she discussed with Bette her own plans of one day taking the studio to court.

Furthermore, both women had a sister with whom they had a mostly adversarial relationship—Bette with the mentally unstable Bobby and Olivia with actress Joan Fontaine. In February of 1942, around the same time that *In This Our Life* was released, Olivia was competing for the Best Actress Oscar (for *Hold Back the Dawn*) against Fontaine (for *Suspicion*) and Bette (for *The Little Foxes*). After Fontaine won, Olivia publicly congratulated her sister, but privately she seethed. Years later, when Olivia won an Oscar of her own for *To Each His Own* (1946), she reportedly snubbed Joan backstage. Their feud and estrangement continued through the years and, like Bette's feud with Joan Crawford, became a popular part of Hollywood folklore.

Naturally, as top actresses at the same studio, and later as peers over succeeding decades, Bette and Olivia were frequently competitors for the same parts. Olivia was signed to do the 1941 picture *The Bride Came C.O.D.* opposite Jimmy Cagney until Bette stepped in and announced to the powers that be that the part was hers. Many years later Bette was all but signed for the part of the dowager empress in the 1986 NBC miniseries "Anastasia: The Mystery of Anna" when she suddenly backed out and was replaced by Olivia.

In September 1943, de Havilland filed suit against Warner Brothers to put an end to the open-ended contract that bound nearly all studio players. It was common practice in Hollywood for a studio to punish actors, for myriad reasons, by suspending them. The time spent on suspension would then be tacked on to the end of the actor's contract term. But, in March 1944 the Superior Court of Los Angeles ruled in de Havilland's favor, saying that the studio could no longer suspend a player without pay for an indefinite period of time and then add that period to the end of the player's contract. It was a major victory for all actors and was one of the primary factors in the eventual demise of the studio system. With Warners legally unable to expand the term of her contract, Olivia became a free agent. Within a few years she would enjoy the greatest stardom and critical success of her career with pictures including *Devotion* (1946), *The Dark Mirror* (1946), *To Each His Own* (Best Actress Oscar winner, 1946), *The Snake Pit* (Best Actress Oscar nomination, 1948), and *The Heiress* (Best Actress Oscar winner, 1949).

Despite their bond and mutual respect, Davis and de Havilland did not make another picture together until the sixties, although both made an appearance in the all-star musical *Thank Your Lucky Stars* (1943). It was not until Olivia agreed to replace Joan Crawford in the 1964 macabre melodrama *Hush . . . Hush, Sweet Charlotte* that the two were professionally reunited. Unfortunately, given the two talents involved and their past individual accomplishments, the picture was a rather silly and disappointing effort.

In later years the two actresses saw one another only on occasion. Olivia flew to Los Angeles from Paris to surprise Bette on the Ralph Edwards television program "This Is Your Life." Then, in 1977, Olivia appeared as a presenter on the nationally televised special "The American Film Institute Salutes Bette Davis." However, at the ceremony, Olivia was perceived by some, including Bette, to be promoting herself rather than honoring Bette. Olivia acknowledged to Bette and to the audience, "Bette had the career I wanted to have" and added that she had been a fan of Bette's since she was a child. She further reminded the audience, "All actors want an Academy Award. Bette won two. Later, so did I." And she concluded with "I am thrilled that Bette is the *first* woman to be honored in this way." It seemed to some that in the way she emphasized "first," Olivia was suggesting to the powers that voted that she wanted to be the second woman so honored.

The morning after the tribute, Bette called her friend Roy Moseley and groused, "What do you think of *that*? Olivia saying she remembered watching me as a *kid*! I told you she hated me!"

Still, Davis and de Havilland remained on cordial terms, although when Bette was given the list of names of would-be presenters for the 1989 Film Society of Lincoln Center tribute in her honor, she nixed de Havilland. It wasn't so much that she no longer liked Olivia; she simply had no intention of being upstaged. Upon Bette's death a few months later, Olivia de Havilland released a statement from Paris about her longtime and sometime friend: "What a loss. She was a remarkable person to work with, highly professional, innovative, brilliant and quick. She was very well-disciplined. I thought she had some marvelous personal qualities, and I was very fond of her."

In addition to those heretofore mentioned, Olivia de Havilland (born in 1916) appeared in pictures including *The Adventures of Robin Hood* (1938), *My Cousin Rachel* (1950), *Lady in a Cage* (1964), and *Airport '77* (1977).

DEAD RINGER ★★
Warner Brothers
1964   116 minutes   bw
Directed by: Paul Henreid
Produced by: William H. Wright
Screenplay by: Albert Beich and Oscar Millard, based on a story by Rian James
Cinematography by: Ernest Haller
Cast: Bette Davis, Karl Malden, Peter Lawford, Philip Carey, Jean Hagen, George MacReady, Estelle Winwood, George Chandler, Mario Alcade, Cyril Delevanti, Monika Henreid, Bert Remsen, Charles Watts, Ken Lynch

Melodramatic thriller that took Warner Brothers 20 years and untold dollars to make. Today, just as in 1964 upon the film's release, the question looms: was it worth all that effort?

Rian James concocted his murder story involving twin sisters, then dubbed *Dead Pigeon*, and pitched it to Warner Brothers in 1944. However, at the time, the studio already owned a similar property titled *A Stolen Life*, which, ironically, was being prepared as a vehicle for Bette Davis, and passed on the project. James, unable to sell his story in Hollywood, sold the Spanish-language rights to a production company in Mexico City, which produced and released the film under the title *La Otra* (*The Other*).

After the success of *The Other* in Latin markets, Hollywood began to rethink its position on *Dead Pigeon*. After all, if a film is a success in one language, time period, or setting, then why not in another? To this day this type of thinking is not at all uncommon in Hollywood. It is also quite common (and unfortunate) in Hollywood for a studio head or producer not to recognize whether a script is any good—until another studio head or producer makes a successful picture out of it.

At any rate, on March 4, 1946, and for the sum of $14,000, Rian James sold the English-language film rights of *Dead Pigeon* to Michael Curtiz Productions, which was affiliated at the time with—who else?—Warner Brothers. Meanwhile, the studio was engrossed in the complicated postproduction of *A Stolen Life*, which was being prepared for a May 1946 release. Apparently the similarities in plot between the two projects was no longer a primary concern. After all, if Bette Davis could play twins in *Stolen*, why couldn't Joan Crawford, whom Curtiz had in mind when he purchased the story, do the same in *Pigeon*? It had been, after all, Curtiz who had directed Crawford in her Oscar-winning performance in *Mildred Pierce* only the year before.

Catherine Turney, who had also scripted *A Stolen Life*, was signed to adapt the James story into a workable screenplay. However, upon reading the first 52 pages of her script, Curtiz voiced strong objections to the direction of her work and, after further revisions did not meet with his satisfaction, placed the project on hold to work on, among other things, *Life with Father* with Irene Dunne and William Powell and *Flamingo Road* with Joan Crawford.

By October 1949 Crawford was no longer interested in *Dead Pigeon*, and Bette Davis had departed the studio in a furious puff of cigarette smoke. But Curtiz, along with producer and writer Anthony Veiller, resumed tinkering with the script, then intended as a vehicle for either Loretta Young or Susan Hayward.

However, problems with the script persisted. Curtiz and Veiller could not agree about such fundamental things as whether the film should be made in a period or a modern setting. In November 1949 Veiller submitted another script to the studio, and again Curtiz balked. By this time the disagreements between the two had become so bitter that Veiller went to Jack Warner and pleaded that Curtiz be replaced with another director. Specifically, Veiller wanted Bretaigne Windust for the job. On May 23, 1950, Veiller wrote a memo to Warner that read, in part, "It is his [Windust's] conviction that, with this picture, he can make Pat Neal into a star as important as [Bette] Davis ever was. . . ." But Warner refused to do so (or was legally restricted from doing so by Curtiz's ownership). And thus the project remained in "creative differences" limbo for the next few years.

By 1953, with Curtiz still attached to it, *Dead Pigeon* had been redubbed *Masquerade*. But even a title change was not enough to propel this pigeon into production.

By 1955, Jack Warner was understandably frustrated by the thwarted efforts of his creative team, not to mention the considerable amount of money his studio had poured into the development of this nonsensical story that he had initially rejected 11 years before. And then he came up with an idea to salvage the situation—a brilliant idea, or so he thought: why not just release the Spanish version, *La Otra*, and *dub* it into English? It would be quick and cheap, and promised to recoup the studio's mounting losses on the project.

Enthused, and without first checking with his studio attorneys, Warner assigned editor Rudy Fehr to oversee the dubbing process. It was Fehr who first suggested to studio executive Steve Trilling that the title be changed to *Dead Ringer*. However, no one but Fehr seemed to like the proposed title, and for the time being *La Otra* was retained.

Finally, after a considerable amount of time and work involving editors, musicians, and translators, et al., Jack Warner was informed by his attorneys that maybe this dubbing business wasn't such a good idea—or, rather, not such a *legal* idea. Apparently, even though Warners owned the English-language rights to *Dead Pigeon*, it did not have and could not obtain all of the necessary rights from the producers of *La Otra*. And so, completely exasperated, Jack Warner issued a dictum, and the "dead pigeon" was finally buried. For the next several years the nightmare of *La Otra*, fka *Masquerade*, fka *Dead Pigeon*, left a decidedly bad taste in the mouths of the studio's executives. The entire subject was, as they say in Hollywood, "put to bed."

But it woke up.

After the immense and unexpected success of *What Ever Happened to Baby Jane?* at the end of 1962, Jack Warner picked up the telephone receiver and asked Bette Davis, who had left the lot with a furious spin on her heels almost 15 years before, to come back to work. He had a new project for her. It was called *Dead Pigeon*.

Curtiz was gone. Veiller was gone. What remained were Jack Warner, *that* title, and the basic plot. Edith Phillips reunites with her twin sister, Margaret de Lorca, after a separation of 18 years at the funeral of Margaret's husband, Frank, whom Edith had loved but Margaret had tricked (with a fake pregnancy) into marriage. Margaret, by way of her marriage, is wealthy. Edith is not. When Edith learns, all these years later, of the deception Margaret used to ensnare Frank into marriage, she plots her revenge. Edith

kills Margaret, dons her clothes and makeup (she's a well-groomed, if griev-
ing, widow), moves into her home, and takes her place. All goes well until
Frank's dog, who had loathed Margaret, takes a liking to Edith, arousing the
suspicion of others.

The irony of Bette's return to Warner Brothers was not lost on anybody,
least of all on Bette. This was her triumph. In March 1963, with *Baby Jane*
still provoking terror and ticket sales at the box office, Bette was nominated
for yet another Best Actress Oscar nomination. It was an astounding 10th
nomination for her. And, by all indications, it was going to be the film that
would win her her third Oscar, not to mention the fact that it would, after
several struggling years, make her wealthy again. But perhaps sweetest of all
was to be back at Warner Brothers and to have Jack Warner himself, if not
reduced to begging on his well-trousered knees, at least in a stance of
begrudging salute. And she savored every minute of it.

In March 1963 producer Wright sent to studio executive Steve Trilling a
list of directors who might be suitable to helm the return of Queen Bette.
They included such new talents as John Cassavetes, Sidney Lumet, Arthur
Penn, and Robert Aldrich, the last, of course, Bette's director on *Baby Jane*.
The list also included Bette's old director (*The Sisters*; *All This, and Heaven
Too*) and former lover, Anatole Litvak. At the time, the film industry was
also beginning to acknowledge the potential artistry of television and was
actively recruiting some of its directors. On April 3 Wright sent Trilling an
additional list of television directors, all of whom had come to him highly
recommended. They included Stuart Rosenberg, Robert Altman, and Lamont Johnson. Interestingly, heading the list was Elliott Silverstein, who was
described by Wright's adviser as "extremely brilliant."

A week later, on April 10, Bette attended a script conference at the studio.
She complained that she found a lot of the dialogue in the script shallow and
that the role of Tony (later cast with Peter Lawford) had not been developed
sufficiently. The script had been worked on for 17 years, beginning with
Catherine Turney, and it still, at least in Bette's estimation, was not fit to be
filmed. By the way, neither Turney nor Harold Medford, P. J. Wolfson, nor
any of the others who worked on the script at various stages over the years
would receive screen credit for what eventually became *Dead Ringer*. The end
result was almost completely the work of the most recent writers, Albert Beich
and Oscar Millard.

Also of concern to Bette was the casting of her leading man, Edith's love
interest, Jim Holland. Bette was most anxious that an actor by the name of
James Philbrook be cast. Apparently Bette had seen Philbrook as Loretta
Young's love interest on Young's television show and liked the way he looked
in a pair of pants. The part, however, would later go, at a substantial cost
($75,000), to Karl Malden, fresh off the successes of *Bird Man of Alcatraz*,
Gypsy, and *How the West Was Won*. As for director, Bette's agent, also in
attendance at the meeting, suggested Elliott Silverstein. However, by that
time both Wright and Trilling had requested and seen samples of Silverstein's

work and were unimpressed. Interestingly, despite the highly favorable early word on Silverstein, he never went on to much success in film. His most noteworthy effort was probably the 1965 comedy *Cat Ballou*.

With Silverstein out of the picture, Wright suggested William Conrad, a choice that pleased Bette's agent but left Bette herself skeptical. She was tired of all this talk about television directors. Considering herself something of an expert (after all, she had starred in and produced *A Stolen Life*), Bette contended that an experienced director of features was necessary. Moreover, because of the trick photography involved, she demanded that a highly experienced cinematographer be hired, specifically her old favorite from her halcyon days, Ernie Haller.

In addition to Haller, Bette requested and was granted the services of her *Baby Jane* stand-in, Babs Jones. Also, her regular wardrobe mistress was hired, and to Bette's delight Chuck Hansen, one of her favorite assistant directors from the old days at Warners, was also hired. She was also paid a substantial salary, $100,000 plus 15 percent of the film's net profits.

Of particular importance to Bette, she was also given the right to "consult" on the choice of director. When she was sent a print of *For Men Only* directed by Paul Henreid, who years before had directed Bette in an "Alfred Hitchcock Presents" television show, Bette decided that Henreid was the man she wanted for the job. She took his name and his cause to the studio, but Steven Trilling and other Warners executives were reluctant to give such a major assignment to a man they viewed only as an actor. Bette was adamant, and by the time she was sent a revised script on May 31, 1963, Paul Henreid had been signed on as director.

> "Despite all the roles I've played, work I've done and thrills and honors I've enjoyed, the success of *Dead Ringer* and the reaction to my performance seem as important to me now as was the outcome of my first starring part."
>
> *Bette Davis*

Bette started rehearsals on Friday, June 28, 1963. And on Tuesday, July 2, with a budget, excluding studio overhead, of $882,000 (the entire film would cost less than Elizabeth Taylor's salary at Fox for *Cleopatra*, which was released that year), *Dead Ringer* started principal photography. Ironically, however, Bette's first day back at Warner Brothers did not take place on the lot at all but at a cemetery. Specifically, the Rosedale Cemetery at Washington Boulevard and Normandie Avenue in Los Angeles. Most of the subsequent shooting did not take place at the studio either but at the famous Greystone Mansion on Doheny Boulevard in Beverly Hills. Shooting days were generally long, and Bette, forever the trouper, typically worked from 7:30 A.M. until 6:30 P.M. Monday through Saturday.

A typical Davisism took place early in the shooting. The scene called for Bette to appear as a corpse (the not-so-poor departed Margaret) in the morgue. During a break between shots, Bette's hairdresser rushed to her side to primp her hair into place. Bette snapped out of her comatose state and dismissed the startled hairdresser with a curt "I-am-not a-mooo-vy-stah—I'm-a-*de-ad*-woman!"

Another typical but little-known Davis trait was exemplified by her treatment of Babs Jones. When Bette found out that the studio had hired Jones at a weekly salary of $115 a week, Bette immediately increased the amount to $250 a week—with the difference coming out of Bette's own pocketbook.

Assisting Bette with the tricky nature of the shooting was Connie Cezon, an "acting double" who would "perform" the role of one of the sisters off camera (the back of her head was as close as she got to appearing *on* camera) while Bette would portray the other sister in scenes in which both sisters appeared.

Bette completed shooting on Thursday, August 29, and much to Jack Warner's delight and Paul Henreid's credit, the company finished the following day—on schedule.

Bette promptly packed her bags and went to Europe to make her next film, *The Empty Canvas*. While in Rome, she was sent a letter by Steve Trilling on September 27, 1963, telling her that he, Henreid, Warner, and Wright had viewed the first rough cut of the picture and that it loomed to be a major hit for all concerned. "It comes up to my fondest expectations. We have a real fine picture. . . . and need I add that you have given one of your finest performances."

Dead Ringer was previewed at Warner Brothers on January 14, 1964. It received mixed reviews. Most critics cited the absurdity and implausibility of the script. Some branded the film as an old-fashioned melodrama out of step with contemporary audiences. Some were entertained by the colorful antics of two Bettes. Others merely felt sorry that she had been reduced to antics such as this.

On January 24, after seeing the first published ads for the film, an agitated Bette wired Trilling that she objected to the depiction of a cadaver in the ads and that the photo used in the ads was not from *Dead Ringer* at all. "The curls," Bette pronounced, "are Baby Jane's!"

Dead Ringer was supposed to build on Bette's regained stature following *What Ever Happened to Baby Jane?* Together with her old mentor, Jack Warner, Bette was going to prove that her success in the former picture was no fluke, and in doing so she was going to remind Hollywood how a good picture was made. Instead, for all her ambition, she, along with her old cigarette-trick partner from *Now, Voyager*, succeeded only in making what *Time* magazine called a "trite little thriller." It was hardly worth 20 years of on-and-off script development and hardly a fitting vehicle for Bette Davis.

DEATH

In September 1989, Bette was in San Sebastian, Spain, for a film festival tribute in her honor. With her friend and assistant Kathryn Sermak at her side, Bette participated in the festival's many activities and press conferences

and attended the award presentation ceremony. After the close of the festival, Bette remained in Spain for additional dinners with local dignitaries, press interviews, and a holiday. Suddenly, however, she was stricken with what was thought to be the flu. When she became so weak that she couldn't get out of bed, she was transported via air ambulance to the American Hospital in Paris. It was Tuesday, October 3, 1989.

Still, it was thought that Bette would be fine. She was simply run down with the flu and exhausted after the overload of activities in Spain. Doctors told her that she would probably be able to return to the United States in a couple of days. On Thursday, however, the French doctors informed her that the cancer she had had in 1983 had returned and spread uncontrollably. On Friday, October 6, Bette spoke over the phone to her son, Michael; to her friend and attorney, Harold Schiff; and in person to Kathryn Sermak. She was given morphine to ease the considerable pain, and late that night she died.

The following day Philippe Duprat, an American Hospital spokesperson, issued a terse statement:

> During a trip to Western Europe, the health of Miss Davis deteriorated. She was admitted at the hospital on October 3. She died last night as a consequence of her illness.

According to official records, Bette Davis died of cancer in Paris on October 6, 1989. She was 81 years old.

> "I would hate to pass on after a long, lingering illness. It should be something sudden. And I don't want anyone sending money to any little charity instead of flowers. I want flowers at the service. I want *millions* of flowers. I want it to be ludicrous with flowers. . . . I want everyone to weep. Copiously."

> *Bette Davis, 1987*

Bette as Mrs. Van Schuyler.

DEATH ON THE NILE ★★

EMI; released by Paramount
1978   140 minutes   Technicolor
Directed by: John Guillermin
Produced by: John Bradbourne and Richard Goodwin
Screenplay by: Anthony Shaffer, based on the novel by Agatha Christie
Cinematography by: Jack Cardiff
Cast: Peter Ustinov, Jane Birkin, Lois Chiles, Bette Davis, Mia Farrow, Jon
    Finch, Olivia Hussey, George Kennedy, Angela Lansbury, Simon
    MacCorkindale, David Niven, Maggie Smith, Jack Warden, Harry
    Andrews, I. S. Johar, Sam Wanamaker

In 1962 Agatha Christie's *Murder on the Nile* went into preproduction with
George Sanders toplining. The project, however, was shelved, where it
remained until 1975, when it was announced that Albert Finney would
reprise the role of Hercule Poirot, which he had played in the highly successful 1974 *Murder on the Orient Express*. Finney, however, dropped out of the
project and was replaced by Peter Ustinov.
    The story, based on Christie's 1937 novel, chronicled the further adven-
tures of detective Hercule Poirot. Heiress Lois Chiles snatches good-looking
Simon MacCorkindale from the arms of her good friend Mia Farrow. Newlyweds Chiles and MacCorkindale venture to Egypt on their honeymoon and
are stalked by the jilted Farrow. Most of the subsequent action takes place
aboard a boat dubbed the *Karnak*, which provides the setting for the eventual
murder of Chiles. Naturally, as in *Orient Express*, everyone has a secret
motive for perpetrating the crime, and it is left for Poirot to come to the
detecting rescue.

With a budget of $10 million, *Death on the Nile* started shooting in England without Bette on September 12, 1977. Location shooting in Egypt commenced on October 10, but "The Dark Secret of Harvest Home," a made-for-television movie that Bette was making in Ohio, fell behind schedule, preventing her from arriving on the *Nile* set on the designated date. The picture was by then inexplicably being called *Death on . . .* instead of *Murder on . . .* and was being shot on location in Aswan, Egypt. Director Guillermin was not at all pleased to be kept waiting by Bette and was thus not in terribly good spirits when she finally arrived. His greeting words to her, in fact, were "Well, I see you finally got here." He then made the mistake, shortly thereafter, of telling Bette, "See that you know your lines." This, of course, was taken by Bette as a considerable insult. She had, after all, been memorizing entire scripts for more than 45 years.

Bette was also displeased to be on location. When she learned the picture was going to be shot in Egypt, she demanded of her agent, "What if they start a war while I'm in Egypt?" He retorted, "They wouldn't *dare!*" Later, during a break from shooting, Bette turned to Guillermin and quipped, "Surely you could have built the Nile at the studio?" To a reporter on the set: "It's a long way to come for a film. You've got to realize that for the first twenty years I was in Hollywood I hardly left the soundstage. We didn't go on locations. If they wanted a background for you, they built it. They'd have built the Nile for you and you'd never know it. Nowadays, well, it's all different. Films have become travelogues and actors, stunt men. I mean, look at that deep sea thing they've made [*The Deep*], Jackie Bisset going down to the bottom of the ocean. What's that got to do with acting?"

Bette was not the only member of the cast to loathe the location shooting. The temperature on the boat soared to 130 degrees and was made more unbearable by the elaborate but stunning costumes that would later win an Oscar for their designer, Anthony Powell. Most of the crew worked drenched in sweat and stripped to the waist. Boredom prevailed, as is the case on most sets, and everyone took turns doing arm-flailing, cigarette-waving impersonations of Bette Davis.

Bette would later say that she loved being part of the all-star cast and had particularly nice words to say about David Niven, Peter Ustinov, Maggie Smith, and Angela Lansbury. She was also fond of Mia Farrow, whom she had known since Farrow was a child. She did *not*, however, get along well with Olivia Hussey, who refused to speak to her by the time the location shooting completed on November 9. From Egypt the company returned to Pinewood Studios in England, where the production resumed until its completion on January 17, 1978.

Upon its opening, *Death on the Nile* was met with mixed reviews. Anthony Shaffer's script occasionally crackles with wit, but the film is a predictable bore, directed rather unimaginatively by Guillermin. The picture's best scenes, without question, are those featuring the verbal sparring of Maggie Smith and Bette Davis (with Smith the better of the two), of which there are too few.

DECEPTION ★ ½

Warner Brothers
1945   112 minutes   bw
Directed by: Irving Rapper
Produced by: Henry Blanke
Screenplay by: John Collier and Joseph Than, based on the play by Louis
    Verneuil
Cinematography by: Ernest Haller
Cast: Bette Davis, Paul Henreid, Claude Rains, John Abbott, Benson Fong,
    Richard Walsh, Suzi Crandall, Richard Erdman, Ross Ford, Russell
    Arms, Bess Flowers, Gino Cerrado, Clifton Young, Cyril Delevanti,
    Jane Harker

"You gotta have a gimmick," or so trumpets the famous striptease number
from the hit Broadway musical *Gypsy*. By early 1946, Bette Davis was in need
of a box office hit, and if gimmickry could help get her one, she was certainly
not above attempting it. Thus, for *Deception*, Bette was reunited with Paul
Henreid and Claude Rains, the costars of one of her biggest previous hits,
Now, Voyager. In addition, assigned to direct the picture was her *Now,
Voyager* director, Irving Rapper. Furthermore, instead of reviving the cigarette trick that they had made famous in *Now, Voyager*, Henreid and Davis
devised for *Deception* another gimmick, "the triple kiss." Bette kisses Henreid on his forehead, on the tip of his nose, and finally on his chin. This
gesture apparently was expected to make women swoon and to launch a
forehead-to-nose-to-chin trend all over America. The studio also made much
of the fact that it was the woman who kissed the man. It was this "daring"
on which the hopes of *Deception* rested.

The 1927 play *Monsieur Lamberthier* by Louis Verneuil, upon which
Deception was based, had previously been made as a 1929 Paramount film
called *Jealousy*. Verneuil resold the rights to Warner Brothers for $20,000 in
an agreement dated December 31, 1943. Jack Warner also wanted to call his
picture *Jealousy*, but a 1945 Republic picture bearing the same title precluded
him from doing so. So, on October 29, 1945, Warner changed the title from
Jealousy to *Her Conscience*, but he was not entirely satisfied with that title.
On February 21, 1946, the project became known as *Deception*.

Meanwhile, Hal Wallis resolved his legal disputes with Warner Brothers
and made his final departure from the studio on December 31, 1944. That
left Wallis's protégé, Henry Blanke, in a new position of considerable power,
with *Deception* his first picture under his new Warners contract.

Blanke's first order of business was to have Verneuil's original French
play translated. He then assigned the story to John Collier and Joseph Than,
who proceeded to write the script with an uncredited assist from S. K.
Lauren. The plot of the picture revolves around Bette as a concert pianist
who has for years been having an affair with her musical mentor, Claude
Rains. Suddenly, out of the past, her true love, Paul Henreid, whom she had

given up for dead, arrives on the scene, igniting renewed romance and conflict.

Unable to get Orry-Kelly, Blanke secured Bernard Newman to design Bette's costumes for the picture. Bette showed up at the studio for hair, makeup, and wardrobe tests on April 11, 19, and 22. Three days later, on April 25, 1946, and with a budget of $2 million and a generous 60-day schedule, *Deception* commenced shooting.

Bette, who had taken some piano lessons as a child, learned the proper finger placements on the keyboard and in fact rehearsed Beethoven's *Appassionata*, the number her character was to play in the picture, at some length. Bette even entertained the idea of actually performing the number for the film. Rapper, however, talked her out of it: since audiences wouldn't believe she was actually playing anyway, why bother? Bette relented, and the recording was done instead by professional pianist Shura Cherkassky.

It was to be a troubled production. Rapper was a notoriously slow director, and Bette did little to improve his reputation. On Saturday, May 4, she had a minor car accident, and shooting was halted. The company was forced to shut down until Bette returned to the set on Wednesday. Bette was "sick" on Thursday, May 23, and shooting was halted until her return on Monday, May 27. No shooting was done on Thursday, May 30, in observance of Memorial Day, and on Friday both Bette and Henreid phoned in sick. Henreid returned to work on June 4, and Bette returned the following day. As the production fell behind schedule, studio executive Steve Trilling showed up on the set on a Saturday and told Bette that she would have to increase her working hours. She had been working from 10:00 to 5:00; Trilling told her that she was going to have to work from 9:00 to 6:00. The order set Bette off in a rage of expletives and tears, and to get even with Trilling she feigned another illness on Monday. After various other illnesses and delays, the company shut down on Monday, July 1, because of a strike. Fortunately, however, the strike was brief, and shooting resumed on Wednesday, July 3. However, that day Bette injured her finger on the set and went home. She did not report back to work until Monday, July 8.

On July 15, Claude Rains caused a bit of a ruckus on the set by engaging in a fight with Rapper over, of all things, a cat that was being used in the scene. Rains wanted the cat thrown off the set. Rapper, however, stood by his cat, insisting that the scene be shot as scripted. Rains stalked off the set. Both Bette and Henreid sided with Rains and could not understand Rapper's dogged devotion to this cat. Rains later said, "Never have I been given so much trouble as [the trouble] Petey, a Siamese, handed me in *Deception*. And what made it worse, I was supposed to love the animal. Bette would get her lines off beautifully, with no interference from Petey. But the moment I began some dialogue, the animal would set up a howl, snarl, and spit at me. That cat, I would gladly have dispatched with no pain whatsoever."

Meanwhile, the film proceeded at an exceptionally slow pace. Problematic also were the scenes in which Henreid, anything but a natural musician, appeared playing the cello. Actually, of course, he didn't play at all. Nor did he even attempt the hand placements and finger movements. Instead, two cellists were hidden behind him off camera. One moved the bow while the other provided the proper fingering. It was an elaborate setup that took time to accomplish. Furthermore, Henreid was having difficulty getting along with Rapper. Tensions between them escalated to a point where Blanke had to step in and referee. From then on, for the rest of the shooting, Henreid and Rapper barely spoke to one another.

On Friday, July 19, Bette again failed to report to the set. She showed up for work the following day, much to the relief of the studio, but little actual work was accomplished as Bette spent a good deal of the day crying and was physically unpresentable to go before the cameras. It seems she was having a difficult time at home with her husband, William Grant Sherry. She would later contend that Sherry had been physically abusive. Al Alleborn, unit manager on the production, reported to his superiors that "Bette Davis came in and on arrival looked very bad, continuing to cry throughout the morning and after lunch she looked so bad that it was impossible to shoot closeups or anything with her, so we made a long shot and we had to stop at 3:00, as she could not continue on."

Both Bette and Rains called in sick on Tuesday, July 30, which forced the company to shut down once again. Bette returned to the set on Thursday, but Rains did not. The following day Ernie Haller called in sick, and shooting was halted because Bette refused to work with another cameraman. Rapper, who usually worked with another top Warners lenser, Sol Polito, was perturbed, to say the least, with Bette's insistence on Haller. Interestingly, Polito, who was something of an expert technician, was initially assigned to shoot the picture, and Haller, regarded as a cosmetician, was assigned to another picture. However, when Bette learned that the picture Haller was assigned to was *Humoresque* starring Joan Crawford, Bette, who had first choice in such things, demanded Haller for *Deception*. It wasn't that she didn't like Polito; he had shot some of Bette's best pictures, including *Now, Voyager*. The point was that Crawford may have won the Best Actress Oscar for *Mildred Pierce* a month or so before *Deception* went into production, but at Warner Brothers, Bette Davis still called the shots.

Haller returned to work on Monday, August 5, and Rains finally reported back to the set two days later. However, just when Rapper began to think that he had his company back in gear, Bette called in sick again on Saturday.

Beginning on August 17, Bette was granted a vacation because Rapper was in the process of filming a concert sequence in which her presence was not required. She worked very little throughout the rest of the month. It's interesting to note that it was during this period that Bette's only natural-born child, B.D., was conceived. Bette did not know about the pregnancy until shortly before the picture completed shooting, at which point she started referring to it not as *Deception* but as *Conception*. Paul Henreid later related in his autobiography, "Bette, still married to William Sherry, became pregnant, and in her typical fashion started calling the picture *Conception*. The marriage was in great trouble by then, and Lisl [Henreid's wife] and I thought the pregnancy was an attempt to hold it together; but if so, it was a futile attempt, and during the making of the movie I could see her marriage crumble. To make matters worse, the rumor on the set was that I was really the father of Bette's baby!"

Toward the final days of shooting, Henreid was sick and did not report to the set. However, a more serious problem took the production's attention: the ending itself. With Bette killing Rains, how could she end up with Henreid when the Production Code censor dictated that all movie characters must pay for their sins? As Bette later admitted, "*Deception* was completely ruined by censorship. We tried that last scene, in which I had to confess my crime, ten thousand ways. But it was so phony I never did get it right."

And so, with an ending that no one was entirely satisfied with, *Deception* finally lumbered to its conclusion on Tuesday, September 17, after a whopping 106 shooting days—46 days behind schedule.

Its a pity that the considerable amount of trouble, pain, and effort, not to mention money, that went into *Deception* does not translate to the screen. It's a mediocre, uninvolving melodrama that seems contrived not only in its problematic ending but also in its beginning and middle. Still, upon its release in October 1946, with a marketing campaign that touted, "She Deceived with All Her Cunning so She Could Love with All Her Heart!," *Deception* received generally favorable reviews. Most critics agreed that Claude Rains had walked off with the picture (cat skirmish aside), and Louella Parsons even hailed him as a surefire Oscar candidate. She was wrong. Nor did the revised ending give Bette a hoped-for nomination. In fact, the picture failed to accomplish much of anything. It didn't, after all was said and done, even generate much interest in the touted forehead-to-nose-to-chin triple kiss. The kiss, like the movie, is without passion.

THE DIRECTORS

> "I had one top director—and that's Mr. William Wyler."
> *Bette Davis, 1974*

> "Our great directors are gone. We have some new ones that are all right [but] they aren't Willie Wyler."
> *Bette Davis, 1988*

The Movie Directors

Director	Picture	Year
John Adolfi	*The Man Who Played God*	1932
John Adolfi	*The Working Man*	1933
Robert Aldrich	*What Ever Happened to Baby Jane?*	1962
Robert Aldrich	*Hush . . . Hush, Sweet Charlotte*	1964
Lindsay Anderson	*The Whales of August*	1987
Lloyd Bacon	*Marked Woman*	1937
Roy Ward Baker	*The Anniversary*	1968

Director	Picture	Year
Curtis Bernhardt	*A Stolen Life*	1946
Curtis Bernhardt	*Payment on Demand*	1951
Richard Brooks	*The Catered Affair*	1956
David Butler	*Thank Your Lucky Stars*	1943
Frank Capra	*Pocketful of Miracles*	1961
Larry Cohen	*The Wicked Stepmother*	1989
Luigi Comencini	*The Scientific Cardplayer*	1972
John Cromwell	*Of Human Bondage*	1934
Dan Curtis	*Burnt Offerings*	1976
Michael Curtiz	*Cabin in the Cotton*	1932
Michael Curtiz	*20,000 Years in Sing Sing*	1933
Michael Curtiz	*Jimmy the Gent*	1934
Michael Curtiz	*Front Page Woman*	1935
Michael Curtiz	*Kid Galahad*	1937
Michael Curtiz	*The Private Lives of Elizabeth and Essex*	1939
Damiano Damiani	*The Empty Canvas*	1964
Delmer Daves	*Hollywood Canteen*	1944
William Dieterle	*Fashions of 1934*	1934
William Dieterle	*Fog Over Frisco*	1934
William Dieterle	*Satan Met a Lady*	1936
William Dieterle	*Juarez*	1939
John Francis Dillon	*The Big Shakedown*	1934
Edward Dmytryk	*Where Love Has Gone*	1964
John Farrow	*John Paul Jones*	1959
Robert Florey	*Ex-Lady*	1933
Franklin Gollings	*Connecting Rooms*	1972
Edmund Goulding	*That Certain Woman*	1937
Edmund Goulding	*Dark Victory*	1939
Edmund Goulding	*The Old Maid*	1939
Edmund Goulding	*The Great Lie*	1941
Alfred E. Green	*The Rich Are Always With Us*	1932
Alfred E. Green	*Dark Horse*	1932
Alfred E. Green	*Parachute Jumper*	1933
Alfred E. Green	*Housewife*	1934
Alfred E. Green	*The Girl From Tenth Avenue*	1935
Alfred E. Green	*Dangerous*	1935
Alfred E. Green	*The Golden Arrow*	1936
John Guillermin	*Death on the Nile*	1978
Robert Hamer	*The Scapegoat*	1959
Stuart Heisler	*The Star*	1952
Hobart Henley	*Bad Sister*	1931
Paul Henreid	*Dead Ringer*	1964
Howard Higgin	*Hell's House*	1932
Seth Holt	*The Nanny*	1965
John Hough	*Return from Witch Mountain*	1978

Director	Picture	Year
John Hough	*The Watcher in the Woods*	1980
John Huston	*In This Our Life*	1942
William Keighley	*Special Agent*	1935
William Keighley	*The Bride Came C.O.D.*	1941
William Keighley	*The Man Who Came to Dinner*	1942
Henry Koster	*The Virgin Queen*	1955
Mervyn LeRoy	*Three on a Match*	1932
Anatole Litvak	*The Sisters*	1938
Anatole Litvak	*All This, and Heaven Too*	1940
Joseph L. Mankiewicz	*All About Eve*	1950
Arthur Mayo	*Bordertown*	1935
Arthur Mayo	*The Petrified Forest*	1936
Arthur Mayo	*It's Love I'm After*	1937
Jean Negulesco	*Phone Call from a Stranger*	1952
Roy William Neill	*The Menace*	1932
Gerd Oswald	*Bunny O'Hare*	1971
Irving Rapper	*Now, Voyager*	1942
Irving Rapper	*The Corn Is Green*	1945
Irving Rapper	*Deception*	1946
Irving Rapper	*Another Man's Poison*	1952
William A. Seiter	*Way Back Home*	1932
Vincent Sherman	*Old Acquaintance*	1943
Vincent Sherman	*Mr. Skeffington*	1944
Herman Shumlin	*Watch on the Rhine*	1943
John M. Stahl	*Seed*	1931
Daniel Taradash	*Storm Center*	1956
King Vidor	*Beyond the Forest*	1949
William A. Wellman	*So Big*	1932
James Whale	*Waterloo Bridge*	1931
Bretaigne Windust	*Winter Meeting*	1948
Bretaigne Windust	*June Bride*	1948
William Wyler	*Jezebel*	1938
William Wyler	*The Letter*	1940
William Wyler	*The Little Foxes*	1941

The Stage Directors

Director	Play	Year
Frank Corsaro	*The Night of the Iguana*	1961
Norman Corwin	*The World of Carl Sandburg*	1960
Jules Dassin	*Two's Company*	1952
Marion Gering	*Broken Dishes*	1929
James Light	*The Earth Between*	1929
Joshua Logan	*Miss Moffat*	1974
Rouben Mamoulian	*Solid South*	1930
Jerome Robbins	*Two's Company*	1952

The Television Directors

Director	Program	Year
Fielder Cook	"Family Reunion"	1981
Jackie Cooper	"White Mama"	1980
David Greene	"Madame Sin"	1972
Anthony Harvey	"The Disappearance of Aimee"	1976
Gordon Hessler	"Scream, Pretty Peggy"	1973
Ron Howard	"Skyward"	1980
Waris Hussein	"Little Gloria . . . Happy at Last"	1982
Milton Katselas	"Strangers: The Story of a Mother and Daughter"	1979
Dick Lowry	"Murder with Mirrors"	1985
Leo Penn	"The Dark Secret of Harvest Home"	1978
David Lowell Rich	"The Judge and Jake Wyler"	1972
George Schaefer	"A Piano for Mrs. Cimino"	1982
George Schaefer	"Right of Way"	1983
Jean-Claude Tramont	"As Summers Die"	1986

"THE DISAPPEARANCE OF AIMEE"

During her heyday at Warner Brothers in the forties, Bette pushed to play the part of evangelist Aimee Semple McPherson, but the proposed project was reportedly nixed by the studio censor. Some 30 years later Bette was given the opportunity to play not Sister Aimee but the secondary role of the evangelist's mother. Initially Ann-Margret was going to play Sister Aimee. Bette, who had played Ann-Margret's mother years before in *Pocketful of Miracles* and was fond of her, signed for the part. However, shortly before production was to start, Ann-Margret backed out of the project, and Faye Dunaway was signed to replace her.

Bette was at once unimpressed with the performance and professionalism (or alleged lack thereof) of Dunaway. While the company was suffering in the sweltering summer heat of Denver, which was exacerbated by the discomfort of the heavy period costumes, Dunaway repeatedly kept the company waiting on the set. Bette, to her credit, attempted to maintain the company's spirits. When not signing autographs, she kept everyone enthralled with stories of her days at Warners. At one point she announced, "I think I'll go entertain the troops," and she proceeded to delight the company with her impersonation of Bette Davis impersonators. At another point she performed "I've Written a Letter" from *What Ever Happened to Baby Jane?* for a vast audience of appreciative extras.

It was fortunate for the film that Bette's character was called on to throw frequent disparaging glances in Dunaway's direction, and this she does with aplomb. The rest of the film, however, is mostly mediocre, and Dunaway's performance is frequently cartoonish and over the top.

"The Disappearance of Aimee" was directed by Anthony Harvey, produced by Paul Leaf, written by John McGreevey, and photographed by James Crabe. In addition to Dunaway and Davis, the cast included James Sloyan, James Woods (in one of his earliest roles), John Lehne, Lelia Goldoni,

Severn Darden, William Jordan, Sandy Ward, Barry Brown, Rena Andrews, Lucian Berrier, Paul Felix, Richard Jamison, Liz Jury, Harlan Knudson, Lester Palmer, Jerry Reitmeyer, Dusty Saunders, and Irby Smith. It was produced by Tomorrow Entertainment, and aired on NBC in 1976.

DIVORCES

> "Friendly divorces are bunk! People do not divorce unless they hate each other immensely, unless they are fighting cat and dog, tooth and talon, claw and fang."
>
> *Bette Davis*

> "I have never asked any of my husbands for alimony. I don't believe they should have to pay for the privilege of going to bed with me."
>
> *Bette Davis*

Harmon Nelson, Jr.
Nelson filed for divorce November 22, 1938; it was granted on December 6.

William Grant Sherry
Bette initially filed for divorce against Sherry on October 21, 1949. However, the two reconciled, and Bette had the divorce action postponed. She then resumed the proceedings in April 1950. Bette received a Mexican divorce decree on July 4, 1950, that became final on July 28.

Gary Merrill
After filing and then withdrawing separation papers in 1957, Bette filed for a divorce from Merrill in May 1960. The divorce was granted on July 7.

DONALD DUCK
Bette Davis vs. Joan Crawford, yes. But Bette Davis vs. Donald Duck? It's true. Bette was peeved with Donald because she had been supplanted by him at the 1957 Academy Awards ceremony. It seems that because of time considerations the director of the show cut out presenter Bette's television airtime, after having earlier aired a segment devoted to Donald. Bette fumed off the stage and later told reporters, "My segment was six minutes in length. Unfortunately, that was also the length of Mr. Duck's bit of film, and they chose Donald Duck. You always have to settle for less on TV."

MARGARET DONOVAN
Bette's hairdresser on numerous pictures, including *Satan Met a Lady* (1936), *Marked Woman* (1937), *Kid Galahad* (1937), *That Certain Woman* (1937), *It's Love I'm After* (1937), *The Sisters* (1938), *Dark Victory* (1939), *Juarez* (1939), *The Old Maid* (1939), *The Private Lives of Elizabeth and Essex* (1939), *All This, and Heaven Too* (1940), *The Letter* (1940), *The Great Lie* (1941), *The Bride Came C.O.D.* (1941), *Mr. Skeffington* (1944), and *Deception* (1946). Donovan was also quite friendly with Bette. Her boyfriend was Bette's longtime makeup artist, Perc Westmore.

BESSIE DOWNS

Upon her return home from the hospital after the birth of her daughter in May 1947, Bette hired a live-in nurse named Bessie Downs. However, after only three days on the job, nurse Downs, 64, was abruptly dismissed. Claiming that she had been fired "without just cause," Downs filed a breach of contract lawsuit against Bette in which she sought damages totaling $2,325. Bette, who did not appear in court, contended that Downs failed to feed the baby every three hours as instructed and also did not weigh the baby on a daily basis. The case appeared before Superior Court judge Raymond Thompson in Santa Ana, California, and on January 16, 1948, the jury, composed of eight men and four women, decided that nurse Downs had been unfairly discharged. Bette was ordered to pay Downs the sum of $1,500.

FAYE DUNAWAY

> Without doubt the most impossible co-star I've worked with.
> *Bette Davis on Faye Dunaway*

To be fair to Faye Dunaway, the part of Aimee Semple McPherson was one that Bette Davis had wanted to play for decades. Then, with the 1976 "The Disappearance of Aimee," a made-for-television movie, Bette, 68, found herself playing not Aimee but Aimee's *mother*. It was a slap not only to Bette's actress's ego but also to her female vanity.

With that aside, it was Bette's contention that Faye Dunaway, then 35, was the most unprofessional actress with whom she had ever worked. She chastised Dunaway for her nocturnal habits, which included, according to Bette, sipping champagne all night in the backseat of a chauffeur-driven limousine and then showing up late and hung over on the set the following morning. She also regarded Dunaway's performance with disdain. As a child Bette had seen McPherson in action, and it was her view that Dunaway's performance didn't approach the evangelist's real-life authority and magnetism. Naturally Bette thought she could have played the part more effectively if she had been given the chance. Still, it was Dunaway's behavior that vexed her most. To costar James Woods, Bette prophesied on the set, "In this case, it's really irrelevant because I'm sure she'll be dead within five years either by her own hand or somebody else's." Years later, Woods recalled that at the time she expressed those words, Bette "was eating a kosher dill pickle, and never missed a beat."

Faye Dunaway, born in 1941, has survived far past Bette's five-year prediction. Her pictures include *Hurry Sundown* (1967), *Bonnie and Clyde* (Best Actress Oscar nomination, 1967), *Little Big Man* (1970), *Chinatown* (Best Actress Oscar nomination, 1974), *Network* (Best Actress Oscar winner, 1976), *Mommie Dearest* (1981), and *Barfly* (1987).

"THE DUPONT SHOW WITH JUNE ALLYSON"

Bette starred with Leif Erickson in "Dark Morning," a 1959 episode of the CBS television series "The DuPont Show with June Allyson." Bette portrayed a spinster teacher who defends an 11-year-old girl suspected of murder.

E

JEANNE EAGELS

The stage and film star who was the model for the 1935 picture *Dangerous* starred in the 1929 picture *Jealousy*, later remade with Bette as *Deception* (1946), and also in the original 1929 film version of W. Somerset Maugham's *The Letter*. Eagels collapsed during the making of the picture, and a double had to be used to complete her scenes. A few months later she was dead at the age of 35.

THE EARTH BETWEEN

Off Broadway play by Virgil Geddes that opened at the Provincetown Playhouse in Greenwich Village on March 5, 1929. The play provided Bette with her New York City stage debut and dealt, rather daringly, with the incestuous relationship between a Nebraska farmer, Nat Jennings (Carroll Ashburn), and Floy (Bette), his 16-year-old daughter. Bette had a difficult time grasping the nature of Floy's struggle, and years later she acknowledged that she had had no idea what her character—or, for that matter, the play—was about.

The Earth Between was directed by James Light, produced by Light and M. Eleanor Fitzgerald, and also starred Bill Challee, Jane Burbie, Warren Colston, and Grover Burgess. The show was a hit and was extended to 27 performances. Bette, however, missed the final week of performances after being stricken with the measles.

SHIRLEY EDER

Columnist for the *Detroit Free Press* who, over the years, had a fairly amicable relationship with Bette. On the night of the 1987 Academy Awards, Eder shared a table with Bette at the postawards dinner. She later wrote of the experience:

> An exhausted-looking Bette slowly walked toward us with her secretary, Kathryn, and Kathryn's fiancé. When she had finally settled in, Arlene [Dahl] said warmly, "Hello, Bette." Davis grunted a curt "Hello," as if she didn't know who had greeted her. Trying to help, I whispered to Bette, "That's Arlene Dahl." WELL!!! In that sometimes evil-sounding tone she'd used on screen, Davis turned on me, exclaiming: "Shirley Eder—who made Y-O-U hostess at this table!?! Don't you think I know Arlene Dahl when I see her? I still have my mind, you know!"

THE EMMY AWARDS

Bette received a special miniature Emmy for her performance in the 1963 television drama "Recall." Others who received the special miniature Emmys that year were Veronica Cartwright, Paul Coates, Maury Green, and Dick Gregory.

Bette had to wait for the 1979 drama "Strangers: The Story of a Mother and Daughter" to win a regular Emmy. On that occasion she was named the outstanding lead actress in a limited series or special. A few years later Bette was nominated for an Outstanding Supporting Actress Emmy for her performance in "Little Gloria . . . Happy at Last" (1982).

THE EMPTY CANVAS ★

Italy/France, CC Champion/Concordia
Released by Embassy Pictures
1964   118 minutes   bw
Directed by: Damiano Damiani
Produced by: Carlo Ponti
Screenplay by: Tonino Guerra, Ugo Liberatore, Damiano Damiani, based
    on the novel by Alberto Moravia
Cinematography by: Roberto Gerardi
Cast: Horst Buchholz, Catherine Spaak, Bette Davis, Isa Miranda, Lea
    Padovani, Georges Wilson, Daniela Rocca, Leonida Repaci, Marcella
    Rovena, Daniela Calvino, Renato Moretti, Edorado Nevola, Jole
    Mauro, Mario Lanfranchi

Going into production of *The Empty Canvas*, Bette publicly enthused that she was thrilled to be plunging into the "continental film industry." In fact she privately resented having to go overseas to make a film. She felt snubbed and unappreciated by Hollywood, particularly after the considerable success of *What Ever Happened to Baby Jane?* (1962).

Nonetheless, in September 1963, days after completing *Dead Ringer* at Warner Brothers, Bette traveled to Rome to shoot the film version of the Alberto Moravia novel *La Noia (The Bore)*. The story cast Bette as the wealthy mother of Horst Buchholz, an uninspired artist who broods over an empty canvas. Much to Bette's dismay, he falls in love with a model (Catherine Spaak), who lures him out of his slumber.

When asked why she accepted the part, Bette responded with her usual rationalization: "There are no good parts for women these days." Certainly she should have realized that *The Empty Canvas* offered her nothing more to do other than snarl in mink. Furthermore, she is terribly miscast as the German Buchholz's mother in a picture set in Italy. It's an inconsequential part that Bette attempts to dress up with an atrocious blond wig and an equally appalling (and inexplicable) southern accent.

The picture was shot in and around Italy on location and at the Titanus Appia Studios. From the outset Bette was graphically made aware that movies were made differently in Italy than in Hollywood. "My first day on the set," Bette related to a reporter, "I arrive, and here is this completely naked girl—and I mean *completely* naked—walking around, and the grips and the electricians are ogling her and naturally not getting any work done at all, and I thought I'd taken leave of my senses! Then somebody thinks to introduce me, and the naked lady turns out to be my co-star, Catherine Spaak."

Also on the first day, Bette could not understand why the director, Damiani, would shoot a master shot and then, when he shot the scene at another angle, not even attempt to match the movements from the master shot. Bette was completely befuddled by this type of picture making. She turned to an assistant director on the set beside her and said that the master shot would have to be redone. When he failed to respond to her, Bette at first attributed it to communication problems. Later in the day she learned that this was how they made pictures in Italy. "As the day's shooting progressed, I saw that not only do they not *know* how to match, the whole *concept* of matching to a master shot is foreign to them. I began to realize the kind of trouble I was in. Understandably, I began to have the feeling that I was going to come out *very* badly in the picture."

Meanwhile, Bette was equally distraught over real-life motherhood. Her teenage daughter, B.D., had recently met and fallen in love with the much older Jeremy Hyman, who lived in England. When Bette flew to Italy to make the picture, she was accompanied by B.D. They stopped off in London, and when Bette had to leave for Rome, B.D. pleaded to be allowed to stay in London. Bette, who disapproved of Hyman, refused. In Italy, however, B.D. suffered an attack of appendicitis and insisted that she be operated on at a London hospital. With *The Empty Canvas* already in production, Bette was forced to remain in Italy, but her mind was in London, and she was decidedly in bad temper.

In addition to her ire over the filmmaking technique being employed, Bette was completely frustrated by the language barrier. She wanted to rant and rave, but since she spoke little Italian, she did so in vain. At one point she quipped, "This sounds like the General Assembly of the United Nations during a lunch break!"

Still, she managed to communicate that she hated the costumes that had been designed for her, which she had the producer trash, and instead she had the fashion couturier Simonetta hired. It was a small victory, and Bette continued to be vexed by the Italians' casual style of filmmaking, which, to her horror, relied heavily on improvisation. Furthermore, she was completely contemptuous of Buchholz, the star of the picture, an Actors Studio type of actor who slinked, brooded, and Brandoed about the set.

Bette eventually got her revenge. By the time shooting completed, Damiani and Ponti decided that they didn't like the accent Bette had affected for the part, and they asked her to redub her voice. Offended but sensing an opportunity, Bette responded that she would be pleased to do the redubbing—at a price of $50,000. The picture was released, not surprisingly, with Bette's southern drawl intact.

The production was so miserable for Bette that she vowed never again to make an Italian picture (she broke the vow with the 1972 film *The Scientific Cardplayer*). In fact the only positive thing Bette had to say about *The Empty Canvas* was that she liked the work of the cinematographer, Roberto Gerardi.

Her complaints were not unfounded. *The Empty Canvas* is an empty, pretentious film. Buchholz acts with his cheekbones, and Spaak acts with her braless bosom and swaying hips, which she moves in synchronization with the drumbeat of the soundtrack. She's a nubile thing, but not the new Bardot as she was touted to be at the time. The film is supposed to be charged with sexual tension. In fact it's not charged with anything at all and is in dire need of a jump start that it never gets. The only real conflict in the movie is generated by the viewer, who keeps looking from the screen to his wristwatch, wondering when the whole mess will be over. It doesn't have a shred of decent acting (Bette's performance included), much of a script, or even the bones of a good story.

Fortunately for those involved, the Catholic Legion of Decency branded *The Empty Canvas* with its dreaded "condemned" rating, and upon its release newspapers refused to run advertisements for it. Few people ever saw the movie, and of those who did, few stayed awake.

PEG ENTWISTLE

Shortly after her graduation from high school, Bette attended a performance of Ibsen's *The Wild Duck* in Boston. The play changed Bette's life. She was so impressed by Peg Entwistle's performance as Hedvig that Bette decided that she too wanted to be an actress.

In later years Entwistle moved to Los Angeles with hopes of embarking in a screen career. When she was unable to find work in pictures, Entwistle, despondent, climbed atop the legendary Hollywood sign and leaped to her death.

JULIUS J. AND PHILIP G. EPSTEIN

Screenwriters of the pictures *The Bride Came C.O.D.* (1941) and *The Man Who Came to Dinner* (1942). After winning a Best Screenplay Oscar for the 1943 picture *Casablanca*, the Epsteins were promoted at Warner Brothers to producer status on their next picture (which they also scripted), *Mr. Skeffington* (1944). However, during production they clashed with Bette and director Vincent Sherman, and they disassociated themselves from the picture.

Philip Epstein died in 1952, but Julius, born in 1909, went on to write pictures including *Fanny* (1961), *Any Wednesday* (1966), *Pete 'n Tillie* (1972), and *Reuben Reuben* (Best Adapted Screenplay Oscar nomination, 1983).

ETHAN FROME

There was no picture in her entire career that Bette Davis tried harder to get made than *Ethan Frome*. It proved to be one of the great disappointments of her life that her efforts went for naught.

In the midforties, at Bette's urging, Jack Warner purchased the rights to the 1911 novel by Edith Wharton. The story featured a couple, Ethan and Zenobia Frome, who take a servant girl, Mattie, into their home. Ethan falls in love with Mattie, and the two make a Romeo-and-Juliet-like suicide pact. However, before they can carry out their plans, they are maimed and are placed in Zenobia's care.

The story had been produced as a successful stage play in New York with Raymond Massey, Pauline Lord, and Ruth Gordon.

Bette met with producer Henry Blanke on August 14, 1945, to discuss the project. At that time Bette, who wanted the part of Mattie for herself, desperately wanted Gary Cooper as her Ethan. Years later she would say that Cooper declined the part because he was engaged in making *Sergeant York*. In fact, however, *York* had been made several years before. Cooper simply had little interest in the project, a fact that Bette had a difficult time accepting. With Cooper out of the casting scheme, English actor David Farrar was signed for the part. Mildred Natwick was to play Zenobia, and the picture was to be directed by Curtis Bernhardt, from a screenplay by Helen Deutsch.

The project was, however, put on hold for a variety of reasons: Bette was fully engaged at that point with the launching of her company, B. D. Inc., and in her new role as the producer of *A Stolen Life*; she married William Grant Sherry in November 1945; Warners then slated her to do *Deception* before *Ethan*, and by the time *Deception* completed shooting, Bette learned that she was pregnant.

In 1948, after months of recovering from the birth of her daughter, Bette resumed plans to star in *Ethan Frome*. It was announced that she would follow *June Bride* with *Ethan*. By that time the casting of the picture had changed. Natwick was out, and one possible scenario had Joan Crawford playing Zenobia to Bette's Mattie, with either Humphrey Bogart or Glenn Ford as Ethan.

Both *June Bride* and Bette's previous picture, *Winter Meeting*, proved to be disappointments at the box office, and the talk in Hollywood was that the public had tired of Bette Davis. At age forty, she was beginning to be considered a has-been by some, and the general consensus at Warners was that *Ethan* was too somber a project to reignite Bette's box office appeal and that she was too old to play the part of the servant girl.

As of May of 1949, while she was making *Beyond the Forest*, Bette was still talking about making *Ethan*. In fact one of the reasons Bette stalked out of Warners was that the studio continued to stall the production of *Ethan Frome*.

Warners later sold the rights to the novel to producer Jerry Wald (*Mildred Pierce*) in the early sixties. At that time Bette, in her fifties, had switched her sights from Mattie to Zenobia and wanted Gregory Peck as Ethan, Julie Harris as Mattie, and William Wyler as director. Wald failed to get the project produced, however, and later sold the rights to Columbia Pictures. Indicative of her tenacity, in the midseventies Bette Davis was still promoting herself for *Ethan Frome*. Bette contacted the powers that be at Columbia with the suggested package of either Jimmy Stewart or Henry Fonda as Ethan, Liv Ullman (whom Bette personally called and sent the script to) as Mattie, and Bette as Zenobia.

Of course it was not to be. It was not until 1992, nearly 50 years after Bette Davis initially pursued it, that *Ethan Frome* finally went into production.

Her first starring role.

ETHNICITY
English, French, Welsh.

EX-LADY ★ ½
Warner Brothers
1933   70 minutes   bw
Directed by: Robert Florey
Produced by: Lucien Hubbard
Screenplay by: David Boehm, based on a story by Edith Fitzgerald and
    Robert Riskin
Cinematography by: Tony Gaudio
Cast: Bette Davis, Gene Raymond, Frank McHugh, Monroe Owsley, Claire
    Dodd, Kay Strozzi, Ferdinand Gottschalk, Alphonse Ethier, Bodil
    Rosing

Bette Davis's first starring vehicle.
    Warner Brothers purchased the rights to the story "Ex-Lady" by David
Boehm for $1,500 on December 15, 1932. Two years before, the studio had
purchased the rights to the play *Illicit* by Edith Fitzgerald and Robert Riskin
for the sum of $30,000.

In 1931 Warners turned *Illicit* into a picture starring Barbara Stanwyck. When Darryl Zanuck, the studio's head of production, thought Bette was ready for stardom after seeing her performance in *Cabin in the Cotton*, he ordered *Illicit* to be taken off the shelf and recycled (with a little bit of Boehm's "Ex-Lady") into a vehicle for her.

Zanuck was right in recognizing her potential but wrong in his approach to maximizing her appeal. Zanuck summoned the Warner Brothers arsenal and ordered that Bette be Garboized. Her hair, makeup, and wardrobe were calculated to make her beautiful; she would later complain that it succeeded only in making her invisible.

Ex-Lady started shooting with Bette on Monday, December 12, 1932. It was allotted a mere 17 shooting days. On the second day of shooting, the picture's director, Howard Bretherton, a second-rate director of B pictures, was replaced by the more skilled Robert Florey. The picture completed production on December 31, one day behind schedule.

Warner Brothers promoted the picture by touting Bette as "The Latest Movie Cinderella!" and hailing her appearance as "gorgeous." But Bette's makeover failed to impress either the public or the critics, with the *New York Times* chastising Warners for making such a suggestive, risqué piece of tripe.

A few weeks before the picture's release, Darryl Zanuck resigned from his position at Warner Brothers over a salary dispute. If *Ex-Lady* was any indication, it's quite possible that Bette would have had an entirely different career had Zanuck remained in power. At any rate, after Zanuck's departure Bette was relegated back to costar status with the release of her next picture, *Bureau of Missing Persons* (1933), and her hopes of stardom had to be placed on hold.

THE EYES

They were the basic feature I had to offer the camera. The *only* feature I had to offer the camera.

Bette Davis, 1989

Popeye the Magnificent.
Time *magazine, 1938*

F

DOUGLAS FAIRBANKS, JR.

Douglas Fairbanks, Jr., claimed that he was cast in *Parachute Jumper* (1933) by Jack Warner as punishment for his vocal objection to the studio's reluctance to reinstate employee salaries, which had been cut. "Today," Fairbanks wrote in his 1988 autobiography *Salad Days*, "I have no more idea of the story of *Parachute Jumper* than what anyone may guess from its title. I didn't even appreciate my new young leading lady, fresh from the stage [actually, she had been in Hollywood for two years]. She was not particularly pretty; in fact, I thought her rather plain, but one didn't easily forget her unique personality. We got on well enough, although she thought director Al Green's sense of humor was as infantile as the story we were obliged to act out. She was always conscientious, serious, and seemed devoid of humor of any kind. But then, there was not much to be humorous about. It was a job and she attacked it with integrity. Our careers were to cross a couple of times many years later, but then our only interest was to get the damned thing over with."

Fairbanks, born in 1909, later produced the 1952 picture *Another Man's Poison*. His pictures as an actor include *Morning Glory* (1933), *The Prisoner of Zenda* (1937), and *Gunga Din* (1939).

"FAMILY REUNION"

Produced by Columbia Pictures Television as a four-hour miniseries, "Family Reunion" (1981) was shot on Long Island, New York, and offered Bette, who celebrated her 73rd birthday on the set, the opportunity to act with her 11-year-old grandson, Ashley Hyman.

Based on a story that appeared in *Ladies Home Journal* by Allan Sloane and Joe Spartan, "Family Reunion" featured Bette as a retired schoolteacher who attempts to rediscover her past by organizing a family reunion.

"Family Reunion" was directed by Fielder Cook (who replaced Jackie Cooper, who was initially signed to direct), produced by Lucy Jarvis (with whom Bette did not get along), and written by Sloane. The cast also included John Shea, David Huddleston, Roy Dotrice, David Rounds, Kathryn Walker, Roberts Blossom, Roberta Wallach, Jeff McCracken, Ann Lange, Paul Rudd, Beth Ehlers, Paul Hecht, Charles Brown, Christopher Murray, Rikke Borge, and Julie Garfield.

FAMOUS LINES

Has any actor in screen history delivered lines with more authority than Bette Davis? She often made even ordinary lines memorable, and when given something witty or substantial to say, she articulated it to the hilt.

As Margo Channing, *All About Eve* by Joseph L. Mankiewicz

"Don't fumble for excuses, not here and now with my hair down."

"Funny business, a woman's career. The things you drop on your way up the ladder so you can move faster. You forget you'll need them again when you get back to being a woman."

"Fasten your seat belts—it's going to be a bumpy night."

"I admit I may have seen better days—but I am still not to be had for the price of a cocktail!"

"I detest cheap sentiment."

"Everybody has a heart—except some people."

As Fanny Skeffington, *Mr. Skeffington* by Philip G. and Julius J. Epstein

CLAUDE RAINS: Fanny, a woman is beautiful when she is loved, and only then.

BETTE DAVIS: A woman is beautiful if she has eight hours sleep and goes to the beauty parlor every day.

As Marie Roark, *Bordertown* by Laird Doyle and Wallace Smith

"You're nothing but a barroom bouncer. . . . You'll always be one. If it wasn't for me, you'd still be rolling drunks at the Silver Slipper. I made you rich, I put those swell clothes on your back. Now, just because you got your neck washed, you think you're a gentleman. No one can make you that. You're riffraff, and so am I. You belong to me, and you're going to stay with me because I'm holding on to you. I committed murder to get you!"

"The only fun I get is feeding the gold fish—and they eat only once a day."

As Charlotte, *The Old Maid* by Casey Robinson

To her rival, Miriam Hopkins: "Tonight, she belongs to me. Tonight, I want her to call me mother!"

"I've shocked you. I should keep my kisses for my husband—nice girls do."

"A woman can't wait forever. I wanted children and a home of my own. I couldn't bear to be—an old maid!"

As Regina Giddens, *The Little Foxes* by Lillian Hellman

To her husband, Herbert Marshall: "Ah hope you die. Ah hope you die very soon. I'll be waitin' for you to die."

As Joyce Heath, *Dangerous* by Laird Doyle

To her husband, John Eldredge: "It's going to be your life or mine! If you're killed, I'll be free. If I'm killed, it won't matter any longer. And if we both die—good riddance!"

To her husband, John Eldredge: "Oh, you cheap, petty bookkeeper, you! Every time I think that those soft, sticky hands of yours ever touched me it makes me sick. *Sick*, do you hear! You're everything that's repulsive to me. Your *wife*! I've never been a wife to you—you poor, simpering fool!"

As Leslie Crosby, *The Letter* by Howard Koch

To her husband, Herbert Marshall, about her lover, David Newell: "With all my heart, I still love the man I killed."

As Lynn Mason, *Fashions of 1934* by F. Hugh Herbert, et Al.

As William Powell orders a drink that neither one of them can afford:

> BETTE DAVIS: Are you crazy? Who's going to pay for it?
> WILLIAM POWELL: My dear, they say if you stay at this bar long enough, you'll meet everyone in the world.
> BETTE DAVIS: Do you think I might meet somebody with a sandwich?

As Louise Elliott, *The Sisters* by Milton Krims

To Errol Flynn: "I want you to go in there and write the best fight story you've ever written in your life. Something people will talk about. We can't take chances now—I'm going to have a baby!"

As Mary Donnell, *That Certain Woman* by Edmund Goulding

To Donald Crisp: "For once I have something you can never take away— that's Jack's love for me. You want to take my son away from me? All right. I'll take your son away from you!"

As Julie Marsden, *Jezebel* by Clements Ripley, et Al.
To Henry Fonda: "Marriage, is it? To that washed-out little Yankee thing?"

As Stanley Timberlake, *In This Our Life* by Howard Koch
To her husband, Dennis Morgan: "I hate you. I hate the day I married you. I hate everything about you—you and your righteous airs. Why don't you go back to Roy where you belong. She's just fool enough to have you!"

As Mrs. Taggart, *The Anniversary* by Jimmy Sangster
To one of her sons: "You belong to me. If I could stuff you, I'd put you in the cabinet there, along with my other beautiful possessions."

To one of her sons' girlfriends: "My dear, would you mind sitting somewhere else? Body odor offends me."

As Maggie Patterson, *The Great Lie* by Lenore Coffee
To Mary Astor: "That child is mine. Your part was finished the minute you gave that baby to me. From that day on, I had only one purpose in my life: to make that baby mine—and to forget you ever existed!"

As Kit Marlowe, *Old Acquaintance* by John Van Druten and Lenore Coffee
"There comes a time in every woman's life when the only thing that helps is a glass of champagne."

As Charlotte Hollis, *Hush . . . Hush, Sweet Charlotte* by Henry Farrell and Lukas Heller
To Olivia de Havilland: "What do you think I asked you here for—*company*?!"

As Maggie Cutler, *The Man Who Came to Dinner* by Julius J. and Philip G. Epstein
To Richard Travis: "You're sort of attractive in a corn-fed sort of way. I can imagine some poor girl falling for you if—well, if you threw in a set of dishes."

As Linda Gilman, *June Bride* by Ranald MacDougall
To Robert Montgomery: "Oh, you're incredible, utterly incredible. Perched up on that pinnacle of masculine ego, looking down at poor, defenseless females—and pitying them because they don't have beards."

As Rosa Moline, *Beyond the Forest* by Lenore Coffee
"What a dump."

"If I don't get out of here, I'll just die! Living here is like waiting for the funeral to begin. No, it's like waiting in the coffin for them to carry you out!"

As Charlotte Vale, *Now, Voyager* by Casey Robinson

PAUL HENREID: Why, darling, you are crying.
BETTE DAVIS: Oh, I'm such a fool—such an old fool. These are only tears of gratitude—an old maid's gratitude for the crumbs offered. You see, no one ever called me 'darling' before.

To Paul Henreid: "I see no such fancy has occurred to you. Again, I've been just a big sentimental fool. It's a tendency I have."

To Paul Henreid: "Oh, Jerry, don't let's ask for the moon—when we have the stars."

As Jane Hudson, *What Ever Happened to Baby Jane?* by Lukas Heller

To Joan Crawford: "You didn't eat your din-din."

As Judith Traherne, *Dark Victory* by Casey Robinson

To George Brent: "Darling, poor fool, don't you know I'm in love with you?"

As Mildred Rogers, *Of Human Bondage* by Lester Cohen

To Leslie Howard: "You cad! You dirty swine! I never cared for you, not once! I was always making a fool of you. You bored me stiff. I hated you. It made me sick when I had to let you kiss me. I only did it because you begged me. You hounded me and drove me crazy. And after you kissed me, I always used to wipe my mouth, *wipe my mouth!*"

As Madge Norwood, *Cabin in the Cotton* by Paul Green

"I'd love to kiss you, but I just washed my hair."

ARTHUR FARNSWORTH, JR.

After making a grueling five pictures in a row between June 1938 and July 1939, Bette, physically exhausted and near emotional collapse, fled the soundstages of Burbank to the recuperative solace of her beloved New England. In the course of her travels throughout the Northeast, during which she revisited places from her childhood, Bette discovered a charming town to which she would frequently return over the succeeding decades. It was called Sugar Hill, located in Franconia, New Hampshire. On this particular trip Bette took residence at Peckett's Inn. Soon her attraction to the land was supplanted by her affection for the inn's assistant manager, Arthur Farnsworth, Jr.

Bette had been divorced by her first husband, Harmon Nelson, Jr., less than a year before. She had also recently been engaged in a tempestuous affair with William Wyler and another one with George Brent. In Arthur Farnsworth, son of a Yankee doctor who would eventually inherit a good deal of money, Bette found someone who was the antithesis of the men she knew in Hollywood. Strong, silent, secure, well educated, and without apparent vanity or temperament, he had breeding and good manners. He was not jealous of her success, nor was he particularly impressed by her celebrity. Furthermore, recently divorced from Betty Jane Adeylotte, a Boston socialite and art designer, Arthur Farnsworth, 33, was available.

Bette's sojourn away from Hollywood was to last a remarkable seven months (being away from the industry for that long was considered professional suicide in the Hollywood of the thirties and forties). She spent much of the time scouring the area and its environs in search of a piece of land to buy. With Farney, as she came to call him, at her side, she found and purchased the property, 150 acres of rocky and rolling land, upon which she intended to build her dream house, a retreat to return to in between pictures.

For Bette, her extended stay with Farnsworth in Franconia was an idyllic time, certainly among the happiest of her life. At the age of 31, and for the first time since she went to Hollywood in 1930, Bette was finally able to sit back, rest, enjoy, and reflect on the overwhelming success she had achieved. With *Jezebel*, *The Sisters*, *Dark Victory*, *Juarez*, and *The Old Maid* released, and with *The Private Lives of Elizabeth and Essex* in the can, Bette Davis was at the pinnacle of her career, and the view from atop Sugar Hill was a glorious one. Certainly the setting for romance could not have been more ideal, nor the timing more on cue.

When Bette reluctantly, finally, returned to Hollywood in January 1940, she presented Farney with a plaque that read, "To Arthur Farnsworth, Keeper of Stray Ladies." A short time later, Farney drove to California for a two-week vacation. He stayed with Bette, who, at the time, was making the aptly titled picture *All This, and Heaven Too*. Then, after completing work on the picture, Bette rejoined Farney, spending her summer vacation back in Franconia.

In early January 1941, Bette sent a characteristically succinct telegram to the press: "Arthur Farnsworth and I were married at 8 o'clock Tuesday evening [December 31, 1940] at the ranch of Mr. and Mrs. Justin Dart in Arizona."

It wasn't much of a honeymoon. Within days Bette was in Death Valley, California, for the location shooting of *The Bride Came C.O.D.* That was followed by a picture Bette had been campaigning for a year to get, Sam Goldwyn's *The Little Foxes*, a tumultuous production directed by Bette's former lover William Wyler. Then, because Warner agreed to lend her out to Goldwyn for *Foxes*, Bette had to rush back, with virtually no break, to the Burbank lot to make *The Man Who Came to Dinner*.

She was then scheduled to go right into *In This Our Life* when she received word in October 1941 that Farney, working in Minneapolis as a representative of the Honeywell Corporation, was seriously ill with lobar pneumonia. His condition was so grave that his doctors advised Bette, who was terrified of flying, to make the trip by plane, which she did.

Meanwhile, back in Burbank, everyone involved with *In This Our Life* was on hold, waiting for Bette's return. She, however, remained at her husband's hospital bedside as he gradually began to recover. On October 22 she wired an anxious Hal Wallis at the studio: "Farney not out of danger yet. Doctor thinks by the end of week will know. Feel I must stay here until I know. So sorry to be an inconvenience but would be of no use to you trying to work under those circumstances. He has had a very narrow escape and doctor feels my presence here very important to his recovery." Still, the studio, losing money daily, was anxious for her return. On October 25 Bette wired Jack Warner: "Do not intend to leave until Mr. Farnsworth is completely in no danger of relapse. . . . Why would I stay longer than necessary? I am usually fairly honest about such things." Powerless, Warner pointedly instructed her to *fly* back as soon as possible. With Farney finally out of peril, Bette, irritated by what she perceived to be the studio's insensitivity to her emotional well-being, took a train.

After the completion of *Old Acquaintance* in May 1943, Bette went to Mexico on vacation. Farney went back east to Franconia, prompting speculation that their marriage was in trouble. The rumor was that Bette had been having an affair with a man she met at the Hollywood Canteen. She was also having an affair with her *Old Acquaintance* director, Vincent Sherman. Certainly the volatile production of *Acquaintance*, during which Bette and Miriam Hopkins were engaged in a rather nasty battle of bitchery, took its toll on Bette's marriage. Still, following her holiday in Mexico, Bette joined Farney in New Hampshire in June, and in July the two traveled back to Hollywood together.

On the afternoon of August 23, Farney had lunch with his and Bette's lawyer, Dudley Furse. After lunch, at about 2:30 P.M., Farney was walking down Hollywood Boulevard, back toward his car. At 6249 Hollywood Boulevard, in front of a cigar store, Farney suddenly screamed, fell backward, and crashed to the sidewalk with a thud. According to the cigar store owner, Dave Freedman, "We were standing just inside the entrance of my store and suddenly I heard a terrifying yell. It sounded as though something had suddenly overcome somebody from within and it made my blood curdle. The yell came from a man walking just in our view and as I heard him yell I saw him suddenly fall straight backwards, and land on his head. Blood rushed from his ears and nostrils."

Another eyewitness, Gilbert Wright, added, "I had seen him walk past the store entrance. When he was almost past, he let out a throaty cry and [in] the next moment, he came down on the back of his head just as if he were doing a backflip and hadn't quite made it. I ran to him and it was all I could do to hold him because he was in convulsions. The blood was flowing from his nose and ears."

Bette rushed again to Farney's bedside, but this time, to no avail. Without regaining consciousness, on August 25, 1943, Arthur Farnsworth, Jr., died.

At the subsequent inquest before coroner Frank Nancy, autopsy surgeon

Dr. Homer Keyes dismissed the Hollywood Boulevard fall as the cause of death, stating that it must have been *another* blow that precipitated the fatal damage. Upon questioning, Bette responded with a prepared statement: "When I learned of the autopsy report and was asked if I could remember any recent accident which might account for an earlier brain injury, I recalled a fall that Farney had at Butternut, our New Hampshire home, late in June. He was coming down the stairs in his stockinged feet to answer the telephone when he slipped on the first landing and slid the full length of the stairs. He landed on his back, struck the back of his head and quite severely scraped his back. He suffered the usual lameness for several days but, not being the complaining kind, he said nothing more about it and so I thought no more about it. I realize now that little things that happened since, which I thought nothing of at the time were the result of that fall, all of which have been confirmed by Dr. Moore [Bette and Farney's physician]. At least to find a reason for a seemingly ridiculous accident is a relief and comfort to me."

However, Dr. Keyes was unconvinced by Bette's explanation. He claimed the fracture to Farney's head must have been inflicted less than two weeks prior to his death. "The blood in the fracture," Dr. Keyes wrote in his autopsy report, "was black and coagulated, not merely purple and partially congealed as it would have been if the injury had been received only last Monday. The fracture could have been inflicted as long as two weeks ago, and, conceivably, Farnsworth had been walking around ever since with the condition fructifying until it eventually caused his death."

Authorities suspected for a time that the fatal blow, if not caused by either the Hollywood Boulevard or New Hampshire falls, may have been caused by a blunt instrument, such as a blackjack or the butt of a gun. Possible motivation for the murder of Farnsworth, it was reasoned, was that he may have had, through his work with the Honeywell Corporation, secret war aviation information in his possession.

Dr. Moore, however, disagreed with Keyes's determination and stated that "The previous accident satisfactorily explains Mr. Farnsworth's subsequent fatal fall." The six-man jury agreed with Dr. Moore and concluded that Farney's death was caused by the New Hampshire fall, aggravated by the Hollywood Boulevard fall. "No person was to blame," the jury told a relieved Bette, who showed up at the inquest in mourning clothes.

The investigation into Farney's death was suspended; the rumors, however, persisted. For years speculation has abounded that Bette had actually been with her husband on Hollywood Boulevard and that it was *she* who pushed him to an unintentional death. Vincent Sherman, who directed Bette in her next picture, *Mr. Skeffington*, later claimed that during production of the film Bette had confessed to him that she had inadvertently caused Farney's death. In addition, William Grant Sherry, Farney's successor as Bette's husband, was quoted as saying, "Bette and I were walking across Hollywood Boulevard on our way to her attorney's office. And as we got across the street and near the curb, Bette became very nervous and looked very frightened.

And I asked her what was the matter. And she pointed to the curb and said, 'This is where I pushed Farney and he hit his head on the curb. I thought he was drunk.' " Although quite plausible, this theory, however, would still not explain Dr. Keyes's determination that it had been a *previous* blow to Farnsworth's head that caused his death. Another theory was that Farney had been engaged in an adulterous affair and had been caught in the act by the woman's husband, who, in a jealous rage, delivered the fatal blow. Neither theory has been substantiated, and the ruling of the coroner's inquest has withstood time.

The funeral was held on Saturday, August 28. Bette attended the services at the Church of the Recessional in Forest Lawn with her mother on one arm and Jack Warner on the other. She arrived at the cemetery in a military staff car supplied by Colonel Paul Mantz, a friend of Farney's. Warner Brothers police kept the crowd of fans in control. The 75 people who attended included John Garfield, Perc Westmore, Lucille Farnsworth (Farney's mother), and Dan Farnsworth (his brother). Bette's uncle, Dr. Paul Gordon Favor, a retired Episcopalian minister, conducted the services.

Bette accompanied Farney's body back east and had him buried at their beloved home in Sugar Hill. Later, in June 1945, Farney's family had his body dug up and transported to the family vault in Rutland, Vermont.

In later years Bette was ambiguous about her relationship with Farney. Sometimes she would acknowledge that her love for him had been based more on comfort than on passion. At other times she would dismiss him almost entirely and would attribute their less than harmonious relations to what she claimed was his alcoholism. And then sometimes she reflected that, had he lived, they would have remained happily together as man and wife.

MIA FARROW

Daughter of director John Farrow who, at age 13, during the 1958 shooting of *John Paul Jones* in Spain, befriended B.D., Bette's 11-year-old daughter. Twenty years later Mia costarred with Bette in the Agatha Christie picture *Death on the Nile*. Later, after the publication of B.D.'s scathing book about Bette, *My Mother's Keeper*, Mia wrote a letter to Bette, reprinted in *This 'N That*, that read, in part, "When I was a little girl living in Madrid for the filming of *John Paul Jones*, you took me along with B.D. to Toledo for the day. I have never forgotten your generosity and kindness to me on that trip and as I watched the two of you all day I thought how loving and committed and 'present' you were in B.D.'s life. . . . I'm positive every parent who hears anything about this will feel outrage, too, and profound sympathy." Curiously, however, when Bette was presented with a list of possible participants for the 1989 Film Society of Lincoln Center award, she nixed Farrow.

Mia Farrow (born Maria Farrow, 1945) attained fame with the television series "Peyton Place" (1964–1966). She has starred in films including *Rosemary's Baby* (1968), but is perhaps best known for her relationships with

Frank Sinatra and Woody Allen, the latter producing a series of memorable movies (*A Midsummer Night's Sex Comedy*, 1982; *The Purple Rose of Cairo*, 1985; *Alice*, 1990; et al.).

FASHIONS OF 1934 ★★

Warner Brothers
1934   78 minutes   bw
Directed by: William Dieterle
Produced by: Henry Blanke
Screenplay by: F. Hugh Herbert and Carl Erickson, based on a story by Harry Collins and Warren Duff
Cinematography by: William Rees
Cast: William Powell, Bette Davis, Frank McHugh, Hugh Herbert, Verree Teasdale, Reginald Owen, Henry O'Neill, Philip Reed, Gordon Westcott, Dorothy Burgess, Etienne Giardot, William Burress, Nella Walker, Spencer Charters, George Humbert, Frank Darien, Harry Beresford

Bette and William Powell hustling for ostrich feathers.

Warner Brothers purchased the rights to the story "King of Fashion" by Warren Duff, which was derived from the story "The Dressmaker" by Harry Collins, for $5,000. Warner initially intended to use Duff's title but feared alienating the targeted women's market.

With an estimated budget of $247,000 (of which William Powell was to get $40,000 and Bette $5,000) and 24 allotted shooting days, *Fashions of 1934* started shooting on October 16, 1933.

The film, in essence, had two directors: William Dieterle for the dramatic sequences, Busby Berkeley for the musical numbers. Early in the production Dieterle got into the habit of rewriting scenes on the set or having Hugh Herbert rewrite the film as it was being shot, much to the ire of Hal Wallis, who promptly informed Dieterle that the script was good to begin with, and rewriting of any kind was superfluous and costly. Herbert, it seems, was also working on another Warners script, and Wallis did not want him unduly interrupted.

Berkeley, meanwhile, received mixed signals on the budget. He argued with Wallis over how many sets were to be used in the musical sequences. Having been responsible for the lavish musical sequences in *Forty-Second Street* (1933), *Gold Diggers of 1933* (1933), and *Footlight Parade* (1933), Berkeley naturally wanted bigger, better, and more numerous sets; Wallis, however, balked. One of the picture's big numbers, "Ostrich Feather," was particularly vexing. On October 11, 1933, Warner executive William Koenig sent a memorandum to Berkeley instructing him to minimize the production costs on the sequence. Instead of having a decorative background wall constructed, Koenig suggested using a drape. However, just the day before, Berkeley had received another memo, this one from Wallis (who had been pinching pennies until this point), telling him to pull out "all the stops" for the ostrich number. In fact the only thing that Wallis and Berkeley debated about on this particular sequence was the exact number of dancing girls to be used. Berkeley, of course, wanted more than he was eventually given.

Still, late in the shooting the budget expanded and the production fell behind due to the illness of William Powell.

As for Bette, she was coiffed, costumed, glamorized to the hilt, barely recognizable, and miserable. She resented being cast in a *costume* picture, and she seethed off the set. As she recalled years later, "I played a fashion model in a wig, with my mouth painted almost to my ears. Imagine *me* a model!" Actually, she didn't play a model at all, but a fashion illustrator named Lynn who falls in love with Powell and becomes involved in his crooked scheme to duplicate Paris fashions. She slinks around from scene to scene in a vast and varied number of wigs, mounds of makeup, and a lot of fur. She even affects a different voice for the picture, one that is presumably meant to sound sophisticated.

Bette was granted one small consolation during the making of the picture. One scene called for her to kiss a dog. Bette used her influence and got her real-life dog, Tibby, to play the scene and make his motion picture debut.

Actually, given what she has to work with, Bette plays the part with verve: smart, sassy, and sort of a predecessor to her cool secretary in the 1942 picture *The Man Who Came to Dinner*. Ironically, in *Fashions*, Bette even refers to William Powell as "Sherry," her name for Monty Woolley in *The Man Who Came to Dinner*. Still, effective as Bette is, the picture is all but stolen by Verree Teasdale as the duchess with a less-than-royal past.

Fashions of 1934 was intended by Warner Brothers to duplicate the colossal success of its *Forty-Second Street*, another sprightly musical with attractive women and fashions. When it opened to less than successful box office, there was much consternation at the studio. In a January 27, 1934, memo to Jack Warner, Hal Wallis offered the opinion that the studio had made a mistake in its initial marketing campaign for the film. Wallis denounced the sales department for selling the film with biographical information on Orry-Kelly (the studio's premier designer) instead of selling it as a musical spectacular. Wallis also felt that the studio had made a mistake in changing the title from *King of Fashion* to *Fashions of 1934*.

Immediately the title of the film was revised to include the word *Follies*. At the time, Hollywood film executives were under the curious delusion that a title that included the word *Follies* would automatically and magically translate into box office gold. Thus the film was changed to *Fashion Follies of 1934*. Some confused theater managers marqueed the picture as *Follies and Fashions of 1934*.

The revised ad campaign gushed: "10 Big Stars! 200 Lovely Girls! 60 Gorgeous Models!" And, "Here They Are Again! The Gorgeous Girls of *Forty-Second Street*, *Gold Diggers* and *Footlight Parade*, All Dressed Up in Fans!" Still, despite being gussied up and made over, the picture found little favor at the box office. Later Davis would say of the picture, "There was nothing left of Bette Davis in this film. I had hit the bottom of the barrel."

Today *Fashions of 1934*, aka *Fashion Follies of 1934*, aka *Follies and Fashions of 1934*, is sometimes referred to simply as *Fashions*.

FATHER
Harlow Morrell Davis.

PAUL FAVOR
Because Bette was basically without a father, her uncle, Ruthie's brother, Paul Gordon Favor, was a primary influence in her childhood. Whenever they were between apartments or without money, Bette, Bobby, and Ruthie were guests in his home. Paul Favor was the rector of the Episcopal Church in White Plains, New York. He later became a minister of the Trinity Episcopal Church in New York City. In later years Paul and his family moved to Laguna Beach and lived, for a time, with Ruthie. It was in Laguna that Favor, at the age of 64, passed away. Bette interrupted the shooting of *June Bride* to attend his funeral on June 1, 1948.

FAVORITES
Her Favorite Movies That She Made
Jezebel
Dark Victory
Now, Voyager
All About Eve

Her Favorite Role
Queen Elizabeth (*The Private Lives of Elizabeth and Essex*, *The Virgin Queen*)

Her Favorite Movie That She Was Not In
The Best Years of Our Lives

Her Favorite Movie Line
"I'd love to kiss you, but I just washed my hair," from *Cabin in the Cotton* (1932)

Her Favorite Childhood Actors
Douglas Fairbanks, Sr.
Rudolph Valentino

Her Favorite Actors upon Arrival in Hollywood
George Arliss
John Barrymore
Ruth Chatterton
Greta Garbo

Her Favorite Actors with Whom She Worked
   Note the exclusion of actresses.

George Arliss
Charles Boyer
James Cagney
Claude Rains
Spencer Tracy

Her Favorite Actors with Whom She Never Worked
Judith Anderson   John Gielgud   Laurence Olivier
Marlon Brando   Katharine Hepburn   Ralph Richardson
Greta Garbo   Charles Laughton   Laurette Taylor

Her Favorite Actors in Later Years

Jill Clayburgh Burt Reynolds Meryl Streep
Sally Field   Paul Scofield Debra Winger
Marsha Mason   Sissy Spacek   James Woods
Steve McQueen

Her Favorite Director with Whom She Worked

William Wyler

Her Favorite Director with Whom She Never Worked

Mike Nichols

Her Favorite Writers

F. Scott Fitzgerald
W. Somerset Maugham
Carl Sandburg
Thomas Wolfe

Her Favorite Singers

Judy Garland
Edith Piaf

Her Favorite Fashion Designers

Geoffrey Beene
Edith Head
Orry-Kelly
Patrick Kelly
Nolan Miller
Valentino

Her Favorite Interviewer

David Hartman

Her Favorite Photograph of Herself

with Anwar el-Sadat

FEMINISM

Contrary to popular belief, Bette Davis was not the first or only actress to wield her box office and critical appeal to wrest power in sexist Hollywood or even at Warner Brothers. When Ruth Chatterton signed with the studio, she demanded—and got—story approval and a fat $8,000-a-week salary, things that few of Hollywood's top *male* stars commanded. Ann Dvorak fled Warners—and Hollywood—in protest against being underpaid. Katharine Hepburn battled with RKO, Margaret Sullivan with Universal, and Carole Lombard with Paramount.

Still, Bette was certainly among the handful of actresses who fought for equal rights for women in Hollywood. Furthermore, her screen persona arguably helped precipitate the women's movement. Nonetheless, over the years Bette balked when referred to as a feminist. She was a "strong-minded career woman" and not one of "those women's libbers." She believed in equal pay for equal work, but that's as far as it went. Most women, in her view, were in fact inferior to men in many areas of life, although she would acknowledge that there were some exceptions. Bette considered herself to be one such exception. She would also point out that although she had acquired success on her own terms, she longed for the company of a man. Her biggest disappointment in life was that she hadn't found the right man with whom she could share her life.

> "More than anything else, the emotional qualities of women hold them back. And that's as it should be. The majority of females are emotionally unsuited for politics—or business, for that matter—but there are others who can do the job as well or better than men."
>
> *Bette Davis, 1964*

> "They've sort of given the impression that they don't really need any men in their lives. Well, of course, that's absurd. They're very valuable in our lives."
>
> *Bette Davis on feminists, 1987*

FEUDS

> I do not regret one professional enemy I have made. Any actor who doesn't dare to make an enemy should get out of the business.
>
> *Bette Davis*

Bette Davis's professional "enemies" included, and are in no way limited to, the following:

Frank Corsaro	Faye Dunaway	Joshua Logan
Joan Crawford	Errol Flynn	Jack Warner
George Cukor	Miriam Hopkins	

FILM SOCIETY OF LINCOLN CENTER

On April 24, 1989, Bette was presented with the Film Society of Lincoln Center award for lifetime achievement. The award itself was a stylized film strip set in stainless steel, designed by François D'Allegret. The event was directed by Wendy Keys and produced by Joanne Koch, Tony Impavido, and Keys. The ceremony, held at Avery Fisher Hall in Manhattan, featured speeches by selected presenters, clips from Bette's films, and an appearance by Bette herself. In accepting her award, Bette surveyed the theater, then bellowed, "What a dump!" She closed her speech with "I'd love to kiss you, but I just washed my hair!"

Prior to the ceremony, Bette scrutinized the list of suggested presenters and eliminated several names, including those of Helen Hayes, Lillian Gish, Olivia de Havilland, Mia Farrow, and Ronald Reagan. The last was rejected by Bette because, in her words, "He can't act." Those approved by Bette were James Stewart, Geraldine Fitzgerald, Joseph Mankiewicz, and Ann-Margret.

Previous recipients of the award included Yves Montand, Barbara Stanwyck, Claudette Colbert, Elizabeth Taylor, Alec Guinness, Federico Fellini, John Huston, Alfred Hitchcock, Charles Chaplin, Fred Astaire, and Laurence Olivier. Said Bette at the time, "I waited a very long time and have been disappointed that the Film Society of Lincoln Center had avoided me for so long. I'm really thrilled to be *finally* receiving this award."

GERALDINE FITZGERALD

Actress who arrived in Hollywood to costar in the 1939 picture *Dark Victory*. Forewarned back in England, Fitzgerald fully expected to be antagonized by Bette in a battle for screen favor. Instead she found her more experienced costar to be nurturing and too concerned with the overall good of the picture to engage in petty actress warfare. Their experience on *Dark Victory*, and later on *Watch on the Rhine* (1943), established a friendship and mutual respect that endured for decades, until Bette's death.

Geraldine Fitzgerald, born in 1912, has appeared in pictures including *Turn of the Tide* (1935), *Wuthering Heights* (Best Supporting Actress Oscar nomination, 1939), *The Gay Sisters* (1942), *Wilson* (1944), *Rachel, Rachel* (1968), *Harry and Tonto* (1974), and *Arthur* (1981).

AGNES FLANAGAN

"Bette is, as is well known, a perfectionist. But she's different from most because she's always just and fair about it. She has definite ideas on how she wants her hair dressed, as well as on other things, and she's almost always right. She is considerate, too. Once I had a weekend trip planned when a situation arose in which Bette needed a hairdresser at Laguna Beach for a whole day. I offered to cancel my weekend plans but Bette wouldn't listen to it. She insisted that I go ahead. She went without a hairdresser that day. . . . although she needed one badly."

Agnes Flanagan, 1946

Agnes Flanagan was Bette's hairdresser on the pictures *A Stolen Life* (1946), *Deception* (1946), and *Winter Meeting* (1948). Later she was Marilyn Monroe's longtime hairdresser.

ERROL FLYNN

When Warner Brothers was casting the 1935 picture *Captain Blood*, it was looking for an actor-as-swashbuckling-hero replacement for Douglas Fairbanks. Fredric March, Ronald Colman, and Robert Donat were all considered. But it was Errol Flynn, who had the prerequisite physique, athleticism, and charm, if not the experience, who got the part. The picture, followed in rapid succession by *The Charge of the Light Brigade* (1936) and *The Adventures of Robin Hood* (1938), made him a major star.

Bette Davis resented Flynn from the start. They were cast together in the

In a publicity shot for *The Sisters*, Bette with one of her least favorite costars.

1938 picture *The Sisters*, yet despite the gender implications of the title, Jack Warner deemed that Flynn was to be given top billing. Bette thought Errol Flynn in *The Sisters* a ridiculous notion. The picture was to be Flynn's first dramatic effort, and Bette, contemptuous of his (in her view) lack of talent, did not think that he was up to the task.

Flynn and Davis—or, rather, Davis and Flynn—were paired together again a year later in *The Private Lives of Elizabeth and Essex*. By that time Bette had scored a second Oscar and a considerable box office hit with *Jezebel* and was thus granted billing over Flynn. She was also given the title. Jack Warner initially wanted to dub the picture *The Knight and the Lady*, thus favoring Flynn. Bette balked and insisted on *Elizabeth and Essex* or a variation thereof.

Still, Bette harbored great hostility toward Flynn and his casting in the picture. To play Queen Elizabeth had been one of her dreams. But in those dreams Errol Flynn was *not* her Essex—Laurence Olivier was. She further resented Flynn's quickly attained stature at the studio when it had taken her six years of arduous work in mostly mediocre pictures. That Flynn was making more money than she infuriated her. It's also quite possible that she had something of an unrequited crush on Flynn, who had his choice of practically every woman on the lot. Years later even Bette acknowledged that he was one of the most beautiful male specimens ever to appear on the screen. She would not, however, acknowledge that he had talent as an actor.

Flynn regarded Bette with equal disdain. He respected her talent but, as did others, felt that she overrated herself. Certainly he was not physically attracted to her (particularly in her Elizabethan garb). In fact, according to Flynn, Bette's resentment toward him was partially the result of his spurning her invitation to go out for an after-work cocktail.

The tension between Davis and Flynn on the set of *The Private Lives of Elizabeth and Essex* culminated one day during rehearsal. The scene called for Elizabeth to deliver a royal slap across the face of Essex. However, instead of faking it, as was the custom, or at least softening the impact, a ring-laden Bette laid into Flynn with all the power she could summon. The blow sent Flynn reeling. He almost passed out.

Over the years the two frequently ran into one another at the studio or around town. Once, as Flynn later wrote in his autobiography, "I had the embarrassing moment of going by a table where she was seated, and saying, 'Well, Bette, how are you?' She looked the other way."

Errol Flynn (1909–1959) appeared in numerous other pictures, including *The Prince and the Pauper* (1937), *The Dawn Patrol* (1938), *The Sea Hawk* (1940), *They Died with Their Boots On* (1941), *Gentleman Jim* (1942), *Thank Your Lucky Stars* (1943), *That Forsyte Woman* (1949), and *Too Much Too Soon* (1958).

FOG OVER FRISCO ★★
Warner Brothers
1934   68 minutes   bw
Directed by: William Dieterle
Produced by: Henry Blanke
Screenplay by: Robert N. Lee and Eugene Solow, based on a story by
    George Dyer
Cinematography by: Tony Gaudio
Cast: Bette Davis, Donald Woods, Margaret Lindsay, Lyle Talbot, Arthur

Byron, Hugh Herbert, Douglas Dumbrille, Robert Barrat, Henry
O'Neill, Irving Pichel, Gordon Westcott, Charles C. Wilson, Alan
Hale, William B. Davidson, Douglas Cosgrove, George Chandler,
Harold Minjir, William Demarest

Almost immediately after she would complete work on *Fog Over Frisco*, a
routine thriller adapted from George Dyer's *The Five Fragments* (the rights to
which were purchased for $5,000), Bette was scheduled to go into a project
that she had spent months trying to attain, RKO's *Of Human Bondage*.
Knowing this, she couldn't wait to finish *Frisco*.

Fog Over Frisco cast Bette as Arlene Bradford, daughter of a wealthy
broker. More for the thrill than for the money, Arlene acts as a fence for a
band of international swindlers and soon becomes a target of the San
Francisco underworld.

Titled at various times during the production *The Five Fragments*,
Golden Gate, *The Gentleman from San Francisco*, and *Fog Over San Francisco*, *Fog Over Frisco* started shooting with Bette on January 22, 1934. It was
allotted 24 shooting days. The picture completed production on February 16,
one day ahead of schedule. Bette, however, completed her assignment on
February 9 and within three days was shooting *Bondage* at RKO.

Initially billed third, Bette was promoted to first after Jack Warner heard
the favorable buzz on *Bondage*. The picture, released in June 1934, was
marketed with typical contrived fanfare: "Female Earthquake Rocks Frisco!"
"The Most Amazing Drama That Ever Crashed the Golden Gate!"

FOLLIES

Circa 1974, Bette was in negotiations with MGM to appear in the film
version of the hit 1974 Broadway musical by Harold Prince, *Follies*. At that
time the proposed star-studded movie cast also include Elizabeth Taylor,
Shirley MacLaine, Henry Fonda, Gene Kelly, Debbie Reynolds, and Joan
Crawford. Bette was to deliver the show-stopping tune "I'm Still Here," sung
by Yvonne de Carlo in the stage version. MGM, however, decided not to
finance the extremely expensive project, and *Follies* has yet to be produced
for the screen.

HENRY FONDA

Bette's relationship with Henry Fonda went all the way back to 1925, when
she was 17 and he was 20. Fonda's friend, Hunter Scott, was dating Bette's
sister, Bobby. One weekend Hunter drove Bobby, Henry, Bette (Henry's date),
and Ruth Davis (chaperoning her daughters) in his Packard convertible to
Princeton University to attend a football game. Upon their arrival Hunter
put the Davis women up at the Nassau Inn while he and Henry stayed at the
campus dormitory. Unbeknownst to their dates, the boys engaged in a contest
to see which of them could tally the greatest number of kisses over the course
of the weekend. Fonda recalled, over 50 years later:

Fonda: "I've been close to Bette Davis for thirty-eight years—and I have the cigarette burns to prove it!" The two are shown here in *That Certain Woman*.

Mrs. Davis was a stern New England lady but she knew Hunter well enough, she thought, and she trusted him. So she allowed us to drive them to the stadium. Well, after we parked, Hunter got out with Bobby and left. I was sitting there with [Bette] a girl I didn't even know. . . . I knew I'd never win [the contest] but I didn't want to disgrace myself by not having [even] one point. I sat there thinking, 'I've got to kiss her. I've got to!' She looked at me with those enormous saucer-like eyes and, what the hell. Well, I sort of leaned over and gave her a peck on the lips. Not a real kiss, but what a relief to me. One point. I felt like Casanova.

Henry Fonda, Fonda: My Life

The following morning Henry and Hunter put the Davis women back on the train to Boston. En route, Bette wrote Fonda a letter that read, in part, "I've told my mother about our lovely experience together in the moonlight. She will announce the engagement when we get home." Fonda recalled his anxiety upon receiving the letter, "Holy shit! One kiss and I'm engaged!" He added, "That's how naive I was, and that's what a devil Bette Davis could be at seventeen."

Two years later Fonda was the third assistant stage manager and aspiring actor at the Cape Playhouse in Dennis, Massachusetts. Bette was the theater's usher. When Fonda was cast as the juvenile lead in the company's production of *The Barker*, Bette attended rehearsals daily and developed quite a crush on him. One night Bette, Bobby, and Ruthie entertained Fonda at their nearby cottage with a dinner of steamed clams. Bette attempted to transfix their guest by popping and widening her eyes in amorous overdrive. Fonda, who never reciprocated the attraction, ate his clams and said good night.

Ten years later Fonda and Bette were cast together in the 1937 picture *That Certain Woman*. Neither of them was yet a full-fledged star. Fonda had two years to wait until *Young Mr. Lincoln* (1939) and *The Grapes of Wrath* (Best Actor Oscar nomination, 1940). For Bette, stardom came sooner, with the next picture she and Fonda appeared in together, *Jezebel* (1938).

Henry Fonda agreed to do *Jezebel* on one condition: that he be finished with the picture by December 18, 1937, so that he could fly to New York to be with his wife for the birth of their child. However, the production fell behind schedule, and it appeared for a while that director Wyler would not meet the Fonda deadline. This naturally caused considerable consternation at the studio (Fonda intended to leave whether his work was completed or not). Bette agreed to work with Fonda until all hours every night so that he could make his appointed plane. Complicating the matter, however, were William Wyler and his demands for repeated takes. Somehow, however, when the date arrived, Fonda, his work completed, was at his wife's hospital bedside for the birth of their daughter, Jane.

Henry Fonda and Bette Davis never made another film together, although they came close on several occasions. Fonda did appear, years later, at a Dean Martin roast in honor of Bette. Quipped Fonda, "I've been close to Bette Davis for thirty-eight years—and I have the cigarette burns to prove it!"

Henry Fonda (1905–1982) made his film debut in the 1935 picture *The Farmer Takes a Wife*. In addition to those already mentioned, his subsequent pictures, in one of the most durable careers in cinema history, include *The Lady Eve* (1941), *The Ox-Bow Incident* (1943), *My Darling Clementine* (1946), *Mister Roberts* (1955), *Twelve Angry Men* (1957), *How the West Was Won* (1963), *The Boston Strangler* (1968), *Sometimes a Great Notion* (1971), and *On Golden Pond* (Best Actor Oscar winner, 1981).

JANE FONDA

In the early seventies Jane Fonda was hailed by some as "the next Bette Davis." Pauline Kael wrote in her review of the 1969 picture *They Shoot Horses, Don't They?*: "Jane Fonda stands a good chance of personifying American tensions and dominating our movies in the seventies as Bette Davis did in the thirties." To an extent Fonda fulfilled Kael's prophecy. She also, in 1977, hosted the American Film Institute's tribute to Bette Davis.

LYNN FONTANNE

Fontanne portrayed the title role in Maxwell Anderson's Broadway play *Elizabeth the Queen*, which was adapted as the 1939 picture *The Private Lives of Elizabeth and Essex*. With her husband and acting partner, Alfred Lunt, Lynn Fontanne was a part of perhaps the most legendary stage acting team in history. At one point Bette wanted very much to join the Lunts in a series of radio plays. Jack Warner, however, much to Bette's dismay, refused to allow her to do so.

GLENN FORD

In 1945, while preparing *A Stolen Life* as her first picture as producer, Bette conducted, according to publicity of the day, a "national talent search" for her leading man. Actually she had been turned down by several big-name actors for various reasons and was frustrated by the casting process. She signed Robert Alda for the part, but, after having a chance meeting with Glenn Ford, just out of the marines, she changed her mind. Years later Ford recalled, "I went to lunch at the Warner Brothers commissary. Bette asked me to sit at her table. She looked at me and said, 'Well, maybe you're too young.' Then she said, 'A week from Sunday you are to come to the studio, and wear a tweed coat and smoke a pipe.' She said to a friend, 'That will make him look older' and then told me, 'I want to make a test with you.'"

He wasn't easy to get. At the time, he was still under contract at Columbia, where he had floundered before the war, and he was loaned to Bette at double his usual salary (paid, of course, to Columbia). Furthermore, in exchange for allowing him to do the picture for Bette, the studio insisted that he allow his existing contract to be extended for 20 months. It was a considerable price but one that Ford never regretted. It was, after all, his performance in *A Stolen Life* that led to his being cast in *Gilda*, the picture that made him a name.

During production of *A Stolen Life*, Bette reportedly made amorous advances toward Ford, who politely declined them. He was, at the time, married to dancer Eleanor Powell, who had just given birth to their son. Nonetheless, relations between Bette and Ford remained relatively amicable during the shooting, and when she was considering leading men for *Winter Meeting* two years later, Bette suggested Ford. This time, however, he rejected the part, an act of betrayal in Bette's estimation, which she did not easily forgive.

Years later, when no one in Hollywood, it seemed, wanted to cast Bette in a major picture, Ford phoned her and asked if she would be interested in playing Apple Annie in *Pocketful of Miracles*, a remake of *Lady for a Day*. He was to be the costar and associate producer of the picture, which was to be directed by Frank Capra (as was the original). *Pocketful of Miracles* provided Bette with her first starring role in a big-budget, A-class picture in many years. For this she should have been eternally grateful to Ford. Instead she became furious with him after he made the mistake of telling a reporter that he had cast her in the picture as a favor. With her ego wounded, she shot back to another reporter, "He's a marine—not a star. He'll never be a star! And, he hasn't improved over the years."

Bette Davis had nothing to do with Glenn Ford for many years after that. Then, a few months before her death, she was on the same plane from London to Los Angeles as Ford. When she learned of this, Bette instructed a flight attendant, "Tell Mr. Ford to come sit with me." Ford later related, "It wasn't 'Would he come sit with me?' It was an order, so I obeyed, and I'm glad I did."

Glenn Ford (born Gwyllyn Ford in 1916) appeared in other pictures, including *The Blackboard Jungle* (1955), *The Fastest Gun Alive* (1956), *The Teahouse of the August Moon* (1956), *Dear Heart* (1964), and *Superman* (1978).

"FORD THEATRE"
Dramatic television series that aired on CBS from 1949 to 1951, on NBC from 1952 to 1956, and on ABC from 1956 to 1957. The filmed series was notable for, among other things, presenting the professional debut (in a February 1953 episode entitled "First Born") of the team of Ronald Reagan and Nancy Davis. Bette Davis portrayed Dolley Madison in "Footnote on a Doll," the April 24, 1957, episode of "Ford Theatre." Natalie Schafer costarred.

FOREST LAWN MEMORIAL PARK
Bette, Bobby, and Ruth Davis are buried in the family sarcophagus in the Courts of Remembrance at Forest Lawn Memorial Park. Bette was quite proud of what was to be her final resting place, and for years she conducted tours for family and friends of the large, ornate structure fronted by a statue of Diana. Forest Lawn Memorial Park, located on the Burbank side of the Hollywood Hills, overlooks Warner Brothers, a fact that greatly pleased and amused Bette. Even in death she would reign.

KARL FREUND
The cinematographer who shot Bette's Universal screen test, as well as the 1931 picture *Bad Sister*, convinced Universal to pick up Bette's three-month option with the words "But she has such beautiful eyes!"

Karl Freund (1890–1969), famous as the cinematographer of the 1926 German silent *Metropolis*, shot other pictures, including *Dracula* (1931), *The Good Earth* (Best Cinematography Oscar winner, 1937), and *Key Largo* (1948).

FRIENDS
During her 81 years of life and her 60-year career, Bette Davis, strong-minded, willful, opinionated, and the personification of individuality, made countless thousands of acquaintances but few actual friends. She allowed few

people into her life, and those that she did were expected to meet her own high standard of conduct, which few were able to sustain. To be fair, few wanted to. For in her personal life (particularly as she got older), as in her career, Bette Davis dictated all the shots, and the people around her were usually reduced to supporting and bit players whose primary purpose was in some manner or another, to serve the star.

The following is a selective alphabetical list of Bette Davis's friends. Naturally these friendships varied greatly in intensity and duration.

Ellen Batchelder	Olivia de Havilland	Paul Henreid	Harold Schiff
Dori Brenner	Margaret Donovan	Betty Lynn	Kathryn Sermak
Robin Brown	Liz Fisher	Roddy McDowall	Peggy Shannon
Terry Brown	Geraldine Fitzgerald	Roy Moseley	Whitney Stine
Jane Bryan	John Garfield	Robert Osborne	Robert Taplinger
Grace Brynolson	Ruth Garland	Chuck Pollack	Robert Wagner
Helene Byers	Vik Greenfield	Claude Rains	Perc Westmore
Virginia Conroy	Radie Harris	Violla Rubber	Emlyn Williams

FRONT PAGE WOMAN ★★

Warner Brothers
1935 82 minutes bw
Directed by: Michael Curtiz
Produced by: Samuel Bischoff
Screenplay by: Roy Chanslor, Lillie Hayward, Laird Doyle, based on a
      story by Richard Macaulay
Cinematography by: Tony Gaudio
Cast: Bette Davis, George Brent, June Martel, Dorothy Dare, Joseph
      Grehan, Winifred Shaw, Roscoe Karns, Joseph King, J. Farrell
      MacDonald, J. Carroll Naish, Walter Walker, DeWitt Jennings,
      Huntley Gordon, Adrian Rosley, Georges Renevent, Grace Hale,
      Selmer Jackson, Gordon Westcott

"Women Are Bum Newspaper Men" was an article by Richard Macaulay that appeared in the September 1, 1934, issue of the *Saturday Evening Post*. On September 5, Hal Wallis received a memo from screenwriter Robert Presnell that read, "I just read 'Women Are Bum Newspaper Men.' I think it has a great deal of possibilities for a fast moving newspaper story on the order of *High Nellie*. Of course, like most short stories it will have to be completely rewritten or rebuilt for pictures. But with a good writer this could be done and I think rather successfully. I see it for Glenda Farrell and Pat O'Brien and believe it can be made very cheaply. I do not think it will make a great picture, but I am sure it will make an entertaining one." Three days later Wallis received another memo, this one from screenwriter Roy Chanslor: "I have just read a corking newspaper story in the *Saturday Evening Post* called 'Women Are Bum Newspaper Men' by Richard Macaulay. I think this would make a swell picture." After reading the article himself, Hal Wallis purchased the film rights for $2,000 with the intention of developing it as a vehicle for James Cagney and Glenda Farrell. Such is the way pictures were born in the Hollywood of the thirties and forties.

Despite Wallis's dictum "We want to make this picture for as little money as possible," *nine* writers were brought in to work on the project: Chanslor, Lillie Hayward, and Laird Doyle, each of whom eventually received screen credit; and Jerry Wald, Julius Epstein, Carl Erickson, Abem Finkel, Erwin Gelsey, and Presnell, all of whom did not.

Mike Curtiz was assigned to direct the picture, and he requested the then-standard shooting schedule of 24 days. Wallis responded that he wanted the picture shot in only 18 to 21 days.

Budgeted at $185,000, *Front Page Woman* started shooting on April 18, 1935. The cast was toplined not by Glenda Farrell and James Cagney or Pat O'Brien, but rather by Bette Davis, the studio's rising star, and Donald Woods. To hasten the proceedings Curtiz worked his actors overtime. On April 26 Bette worked from 9:00 in the morning until 10:00 at night; on May 4 from 9:00 A.M. to 9:00 P.M.; and on May 8 from 9:00 A.M. until 3:20 *the next morning*! Bette never forgave Curtiz for overworking her to this degree, and her experience on this picture certainly factored in her strike against the studio the following year.

The rather flimsy prefeminist plot featured Bette as Ellen Garfield, a sob story reporter who falls in love with George Brent, a reporter for a rival paper. She refuses, however, to marry Brent until he at least acknowledges that, conventional wisdom aside, she is indeed a good reporter. Despite such nonsense, the picture received generally favorable reviews upon its release in July 1935. The marketing ads proclaimed, "The Screen's Enchanting Man-hunter Proves That Getting Away With Murder Isn't the Half of What a Gal Has to Do to Become a Front Page Woman." Additional ads had Bette proclaiming, "Men Are to Me What Goiters are to Science . . . A Pain in the Neck!"

FUNERAL

On Thursday morning, October 12, 1989, Bette Davis was laid to rest at Forest Lawn Memorial Park in Burbank, California. The private ceremony and graveside service were restricted to 25 relatives and close friends. The services were conducted by Reverend Robert Bock of the First Christian Church in North Hollywood.

G

GRETA GARBO

There were few actresses whom Bette Davis idolized. Hepburn was one. Garbo, certainly, was another. Despite all of her loud public protests over being cosmetically Garboized for the pictures *Ex-Lady* and *Fashions of 1934*, Bette envied few things more than Garbo's beauty. She was also in awe of Garbo's screen presence. "She is a very, very great actress," Bette once proffered. "She's given performances no on else has even touched. I'd give my left arm to be able to do what she does on the screen. I rate her *Camille* as one of the high spots."

In the mid-1930s Bette rented Garbo's Brentwood house, and although she never became friendly with her, Bette maintained her great admiration for Garbo over the years. In 1982 Bette was still praising Garbo. "Someone like Garbo never won [the Oscar] and should have for *Camille*. . . . She was brilliant, but . . . she made all her money here [in the United States] and she hadn't become a citizen, and everyone resented that very much."

> "I was the biggest imitation of Miss Garbo that ever lived. Oh, ludicrous. I looked perfectly absurd."
> *Bette Davis on her (attempted) Garbo period*

AVA GARDNER

In 1958, while both were in Spain, Ava Gardner approached Bette Davis in the lobby of the Hilton Hotel in Madrid and gushed, "Miss Davis, I'm Ava Gardner and I'm a great fan of yours." Bette stopped, turned, responded, "Of course you are, my dear, of course you are," and then swept out of the room. A few years later Gardner got her revenge when she, not Bette, was cast in the film version of Tennessee Williams's *The Night of the Iguana*, in the part Bette had originated onstage.

JOHN GARFIELD

Early in his Hollywood career John Garfield tested for roles in the pictures *The Sisters* (1938) and *The Private Lives of Elizabeth and Essex* (1939). He got neither part but did receive the admiration of Bette Davis, who commented to a reporter, "From the way John Garfield worked with me in a test, I'll bet he will make his mark faster than any other new actor we have. He knew he was completely wrong, physically, and yet he did all he could. He had a sincerity and a humility that was remarkable."

Garfield *did* get a part in the 1939 picture *Juarez*, and he and Bette became quite friendly, with her championing his talent to the top brass at Warners. Later the two partnered in another venture, the foundation and management of the Hollywood Canteen. And Garfield was not far from Bette's side at the 1943 funeral of her husband, Arthur Farnsworth, Jr. Their friendship reportedly cooled, however, after Garfield costarred with and befriended Joan Crawford on the set of the 1946 picture *Humoresque*.

John Garfield (Julius Garfinkle, 1913–1952) made his film debut in the 1938 picture *Four Daughters*. His subsequent pictures include *The Sea Wolf* (1941), *Thank Your Lucky Stars* (1943), *Hollywood Canteen* (1944), *The Postman Always Rings Twice* (1946), *Body and Soul* (Best Actor Oscar nomination, 1947), and *Gentleman's Agreement* (1947).

TONY GAUDIO

One of Bette's favorite cinematographers, Tony Gaudio shot the pictures *Ex-Lady* (1933), *Fog Over Frisco* (1934), *Bordertown* (1935), *Front Page Woman* (1935), *Kid Galahad* (1937), *It's Love I'm After* (for which he was uncredited, 1937), *The Sisters* (1938), *Juarez* (Best Cinematography Oscar nomination, 1939), *The Old Maid* (1939), *The Letter* (Best Cinematography Oscar nomination, 1940), *The Great Lie* (1941), and *The Man Who Came to Dinner* (1942).

Bette was so fond of Gaudio and his work that while making *The Great Lie* she wrote a letter to Hal Wallis requesting that he be available for all of her pictures. "Would it be possible for me to know you will always plan Tony Gaudio's schedule for me? I could never get this permission for Ernie Haller because directors I had wouldn't work with him. They will with Tony, and he has now worked with me enough that he is doing a wonderful job. I wish you could know the confidence it gives a girl particularly to never worry about her looks. It's so important."

Known early in his career as Gaetano Gaudio (1885–1951), Tony Gaudio's non-Davis-related work includes *The Mark of Zorro* (1920), *Hell's Angels* (Best Cinematography Oscar nomination, 1930), *Anthony Adverse* (Best Cinematography Oscar winner, 1936), *The Life of Emile Zola* (1937), *The Adventures of Robin Hood* (1938), *Corvette K-225* (Best Cinematography Oscar nomination, 1943), *A Song to Remember* (Best Cinematography Oscar nomination, 1945), and *The Red Pony* (1949).

THE GIRL FROM TENTH AVENUE ★★

Warner Brothers
1935   69 minutes   bw
Directed by: Alfred E. Green
Produced by: Henry Blanke
Screenplay by: Charles Kenyon, based on the play by Hubert Henry Davies
Cinematography by: James Van Trees
Cast: Bette Davis, Ian Hunter, Colin Clive, Alison Skipworth, Katherine Alexander, John Eldredge, Philip Reed, Helen Jerome Eddy, Gordon Elliott, Adrian Rosely, Andre Cheron, Edward McWade, Mary Treen, Heinie Conklin

Warner Brothers purchased the rights to the play *Outcast* by Hubert Henry Davies in an agreement dated February 18, 1935. Davies had passed away in 1917, and Warners paid the sum of $5,000 to his estate. The property cast

Bette Davis as Miriam Brady, an upstart young lady from the wrong side of the tracks who fights a high-society dame to hold on to her man.

Under the title *Outcast*, and with a budget of $195,000 and 24 shooting days, the picture went into production on March 7, 1935. Shortly into the shooting, Hal Wallis changed the title to *Men on Her Mind* to better feature Bette, who, with *Of Human Bondage* and *Bordertown* still fresh, was certainly poised for stardom.

According to studio files, on March 23, 1935, producer Henry Blanke informed Wallis that he was disturbed that Katherine Alexander, who played the part of the society woman, was not half as attractive as Bette and that audiences would not be able to understand leading man Ian Hunter's interest in her. In Blanke's view she did not have an ounce of sex appeal, and he suggested that the part be recast despite the additional costs. He went on to propose that Claire Dodd be signed promptly, a suggestion that went quietly unheeded.

Meanwhile, Wallis was still fretting about the picture's title. On March 20 he memoed boss Jack Warner that *Men on Her Mind* was too soft a title. Wallis suggested *Tough Baby*, noting that it would be an appropriate title for a Bette Davis picture. Other suggestions were made and shelved before a consensus was reached on *The Girl from Tenth Avenue*, and it was under that title that the picture closed slightly ahead of schedule on April 1, 1935. Interestingly, considering her later penchant for calling in sick, Bette did not miss a single day of work on this production, putting in a full six days a week every week.

"The Girl from *Bordertown* and *Of Human Bondage* in The First Starring Show All Her Own!" touted the ads for the picture. Actually, it had been in *Ex-Lady*, a full two years before, that Bette had had her first starring role. Facts, however, are of trivial importance when it comes to promoting a movie. Additional ads proclaimed, "The Man-Tamer of *Bordertown* Shows a Society Dame What it Takes to Hold a Man!" and have her daring Katherine Alexander, "You've Got Wealth, Class, Position. But, Sister, I've Got What it Takes. Take Him Away From Me—If You Know How!"

The Girl from Tenth Avenue opened in New York on May 26, 1935, to fair to favorable reviews.

GIRL SCOUTS

As a teenager in New York City, Bette Davis was an ambitious Girl Scout who, in her own words, "would have tripped an old lady in order to pick her up." She excelled as a scout member and became a golden eaglet and patrol leader.

LILLIAN GISH

When she made *The Whales of August*, Lillian Gish was 90 years old and had 105 movies to her credit in a career that spanned *eight* decades. Her costar, Bette Davis, was 78, with more than 80 movies to her credit. Despite the fact that they could have found much to respect in each other, the two actresses did not get along well during the production. Bette, in particular, treated Gish with icy disdain. When someone in the company congratulated Gish on one of her close-ups, Bette quipped, "She ought to know close-ups. Jesus, she was around when they invented them!"

Lillian Gish (born Lillian de Guiche, 1896) started acting at the age of five and became a major star with such silent pictures as *Birth of a Nation* (1915), *Intolerance* (1916), *Broken Blossoms* (1918), and *Way Down East* (1920). Her talking pictures include *Duel in the Sun* (1946) and *The Night of the Hunter* (1955).

> "When I was in films, we pretended to kiss but we didn't. It was considered unsanitary. Now they swallow each other's tonsils. It's disgusting."
>
> *Lillian Gish, 1987*

THE GLASS MENAGERIE

In 1949, while Bette was making *Beyond the Forest* at Warners, the studio was preparing the film version of *The Glass Menagerie*, which had been a major hit on Broadway for playwright Tennessee Williams. Jane Wyman was signed to play the part of the fragile daughter, Laura, but the part of the strident mother, Amanda Wingfield, had yet to be cast. Film rights to the play were owned by powerful agent Charles Feldman, who asked one of his clients, director Irving Rapper, to approach Bette with the idea of doing the film. Enthusiastic about the idea, hoping that *Menagerie* would propel her out of her recent slump, Bette agreed to do a test. However, tension on the set of *Beyond the Forest* escalated and resulted in Bette's breaking her contract and long-standing association with the studio. When Jack Warner found out that Feldman, Rapper, and the film's coproducer, Jerry Wald, wanted Bette to star in *Menagerie*, he stated in no uncertain terms that not only was Bette *not* to be cast in the part; she was also no longer welcome on the lot.

The Glass Menagerie (1950) was produced with Gertrude Lawrence as Amanda Wingfield. Jane Wyman, Kirk Douglas, and Arthur Kennedy co-starred. Irving Rapper directed.

Circa 1966–1967, producer David Susskind announced that he was mounting a television production of the play. Bette informed Susskind that she was interested in playing Amanda, but negotiations with the networks fell through, and Susskind was not able to produce his version on the air until 1973. By then he had secured as his Amanda, much to the embitterment of Bette, Katharine Hepburn.

The Glass Menagerie was again produced as a feature film in 1987 with Joanne Woodward as Amanda. The film was directed by Woodward's husband, Paul Newman.

GOD'S COUNTRY AND THE WOMAN

When Bette refused to show up at Warner Brothers for scheduled wardrobe tests for a picture called *God's Country and the Woman* in June 1936, she was suspended. Jack Warner's insistence that she appear in the film and Bette's defiant refusal to do so culminated in a London courtroom in October that year.

The film, to be shot on location in Longview, Washington, and scripted by James Oliver Curwood, would have cast Bette as Jo Barton, a female lumberjack. Bette referred to the proposed picture at the time as *God's Country and the Idiot Woman*.

With Bette on suspension, studio head Hal Wallis hoped to borrow Merle Oberon for the picture. However, after reading the script Oberon responded in writing that the role was unsuitable.

God's Country and the Woman was eventually filmed with newcomer Beverly Roberts in the role rejected by Davis and Oberon. William Keighley directed; George Brent costarred. The picture was previewed in Hollywood on December 14, 1936, and was met with (to Bette's delight) a dismal reception.

THE GOLDEN ARROW ★ ½

Warner Brothers
1936 68 minutes bw
Directed by: Alfred E. Green
Produced by: Samuel Bischoff
Screenplay by: Charles Kenyon, based on the play by Michael Arlen
Cinematography by: Arthur Edeson
Cast: Bette Davis, George Brent, Eugene Pallette, Dick Foran, Carol
    Hughes, Catherine Doucet, Craig Reynolds, Ivan Lebedeff, G. P.
    Huntley, Jr., Hobart Cavanaugh, Henry O'Neill, Eddie Acuff, Earl
    Foxe, E. E. Clive, Rafael Storm, Sarah Edwards, Bess Flowers, Mary
    Treen, Selmer Jackson

After a string of successes that culminated with *Dangerous* (for which she would win an Oscar), Bette naturally assumed that she would be rewarded with better roles. Instead she was assigned *The Golden Arrow*, an insipid comedy in which the primary ingredient was a series of alternating black eyes for the characters played by Bette and George Brent. Irate at being demoted to properties such as this, Bette would, months later, walk out on her studio contract. In fact she would later state that it was *this* picture that prompted her walkout.

Based on the play *Dream Princess* by British playwright Michael Arlen, which was subsequently published by *Liberty* magazine on September 14, 1935, it was purchased by Warners on October 14, 1935, for $3,500. It was initially intended as a vehicle for Kay Francis, but Francis deemed the script to be tripe and refused to do it. For that Warners suspended her without pay for eight weeks. Unfazed, the studio promptly signed Bette to the part of Daisy, an heiress who has a $30-a-week newspaperman marry her to protect her from a pack of fortune hunters. Warners would tout the property as Bette's "first important *sympathetic* role."

The Golden Arrow started principal photography on January 20, 1936. It was allotted 24 shooting days. Bette joined the company on January 24, and shooting proceeded without much disturbance, despite the company's general discontent with the material. The picture completed shooting on February 25, eight days behind schedule.

The Golden Arrow needed all the help it could get. Marketing ads touted, "Warner Brothers Have the Great Honor to Present the 1935 Academy Award Winner" and "Here She Is! The 1935 Academy Award Winner in Her First Picture Since Winning Filmdom's Highest Honor!" The picture opened to poor to fair reviews in early May 1936. Bette's strike against the studio would commence a couple of weeks later.

THE GOLDEN GLOBE AWARDS

The Golden Globe awards, presented annually by the Hollywood Foreign Press Association, were not initiated until 1943 and thus missed Bette Davis's succession of exemplary performances from 1938 to 1942. Her best chance of winning a Golden Globe was in 1950 for her performance in *All About Eve*. She lost, however, to Gloria Swanson for her work in *Sunset Boulevard*, which also won the Golden Globe as the year's best picture. Bette was again nominated for a Golden Globe in 1962 for her performance in *What Ever Happened to Baby Jane?* However, the award that year was presented to Geraldine Page for *Sweet Bird of Youth*.

Bette *did* receive two honorary Golden Globes. The first occasion was at the February 15, 1953, ceremony held at the Club Del Mar in Los Angeles. The special award commemorated "her accomplishments in four fields of show business during 1952." That year Bette had appeared on various radio programs, on television in "All Star Revue," in movies in *The Star*, and on Broadway in *Two's Company*.

The 1973 Cecil B. DeMille Golden Globe award was presented to Bette in honor of her lifetime achievement. Among those who had preceded her in receiving the award were Jack Warner, Judy Garland, Fred Astaire, John Wayne, Alfred Hitchcock, Bob Hope, Jimmy Stewart, and Joan Crawford.

On January 24, 1986, Bette appeared at the Beverly Hilton Hotel as a presenter on the televised Golden Globe awards. The event marked one of Bette's first public appearances since her mastectomy and stroke in 1983 and was designed to show the world (and the industry in which she worked) that she was still in good shape. However, onlookers were mostly shocked and dismayed by her frail, ravaged, and much changed appearance.

SAMUEL GOLDWYN

It was a talent scout for Samuel Goldwyn who summoned Bette Davis for her first screen test in 1930. However, after viewing the test, Goldwyn dismissed Bette as unsuitable for picture stardom. In later years, never one to relinquish a grudge, Bette constantly reminded Goldwyn and anyone else who would listen of his all too apparent error in judgment. She also paid Goldwyn back when he requested her services for his 1941 picture *The Little Foxes*. Bette later made repeated public claims that she had demanded and received from Goldwyn the extravagant fee of $385,000 to star in the film. In fact she was paid the still substantial sum of $150,000. Furthermore, she drove up costs on the picture, while Goldwyn watched helplessly in horror, with her frequent and lengthy absences from the set.

Years later Goldwyn hosted a dinner party at which *Foxes* director and writer, William Wyler and Lillian Hellman, respectively, were guests. Author A. Scott Berg wrote about the dinner, a timeless and classic tale of Hollywood, movies, and moguls, in his 1989 biography *Goldwyn: A Life*:

> "Everything was going fine," Miss Hellman remembered, until Bette Davis's name came up. "I had her in a very good picture I made," said Goldwyn, *"The Three Little Foxes."* Hellman was more irritated than amused that after all this time, he still had not gotten the name of her play right. "Oh, really, Sam?" she said. "Well, I wrote the play and I wrote the movie."
>
> "Of course you did," Goldwyn snapped back. "Who said you didn't write it? It was a great picture." Trying to recover, he turned to Wyler and asked, "Did you ever see it?" Keeping the lid on *his* temper, Wyler said that he had directed it. "Of course you did," insisted Goldwyn. "Who said you didn't direct it?"

Samuel Goldwyn (1882–1974) got his start as a glove salesman named Sam Goldfish. He ventured into motion pictures by partnering with Jesse Lasky and Cecil B. DeMille to form the Jesse L. Lasky Feature Play Company. Later Goldfish partnered with a man named Edgar Selwyn and was inspired to change his name by combining the first syllable of his name with the last syllable of Selwyn's name; hence Samuel "Goldwyn" was born. In 1924 Goldwyn's production company merged with Metro Pictures. The following year the company was joined by Louis B. Mayer Pictures to form Metro-Goldwyn-Mayer, although Goldwyn himself opted to set up an independent venture, the Samuel Goldwyn Company.

> "I don't care if my pictures don't make a dime, so long as everyone comes to see them."
>
> *Sam Goldwyn*

GONE WITH THE WIND
In her entire six-decade career the single role that Bette Davis coveted more than any other was that of Scarlett O'Hara, Margaret Mitchell's Yankee-killing, drapery-wearing, "fiddle-dee-dee"-exclaiming heroine in *Gone With the Wind*.

Twice Bette had a shot at obtaining the part, and twice she lost. The first time occurred in the summer of 1936, when Jack Warner, attempting to cajole the raging Bette into abandoning her strike against the studio, told her that he had optioned a book for her. *"What* book?" she demanded of her boss. *"Gone with the Wind,"* replied Warner. Bette, unaware of the book at the time, shot back with true Scarlett obstinance, "I'll bet it's a *pip!*" and stormed out of Warner's office.

By the time Bette acquiesced and returned to the studio, months later, *Gone with the Wind* had become the biggest-selling publishing blockbuster in years. Upon reading the novel Bette was instantly seized by what she perceived to be the similarities between herself and Scarlett. "The role could have been written for me!" she insisted to friends who advised her to stand in the lengthy line of Scarlett wannabes. But it did not deter Bette that every actress in Hollywood under the age of 40 who could affect a southern accent and a "fiddle-dee-dee" also wanted the part. Here, finally, was a worthy successor to Mildred Rogers in *Of Human Bondage* (1934). Mildred had brought her acclaim; Scarlett O'Hara, Bette was certain, would surely bring her stardom.

Her hopes, however, were diminished, if not crushed, upon learning that Warners' option on *GWTW* had lapsed and the film rights had been acquired (for a mere $50,000) by David O. Selznick, who announced his intention of conducting a massive national talent search and casting an unknown actress in the part. Bette's chances of playing Scarlett were later resurrected when Selznick was approached by Jack Warner with a package proposition: Warners would distribute the picture with Errol Flynn, Bette, and Olivia de Havilland, all under contract to Warners, as Rhett Butler, Scarlett, and Melanie Hamilton, respectively. When Bette was informed of the possibility, her enthusiasm was undoubtedly tempered by the notion of Flynn as her costar. Bette, like the rest of the country, knew that the only actor who could play Rhett Butler as written was Clark Gable. Still, she probably would have (despite her later ego-inflated claims to the contrary) accepted Flynn as her costar if Selznick had not declined Warners' package deal in favor of a better one offered at Metro.

Selznick wrote in a letter dated September 20, 1938, to columnist Ed Sullivan, "You may inquire why I didn't give up the idea of a new girl and get Bette Davis, for instance. . . . you ought to know that Warner Brothers wouldn't give up Bette Davis for a picture to be released through MGM, even had we wanted Miss Davis in preference to a new personality. Warner Brothers offered me Errol Flynn for Butler and Bette Davis for Scarlett *if* I would release the picture through Warners—and this would have been an easy way out of my dilemma. But the public wanted Gable, and I was determined that the public should have Gable. And Gable it is going to have. . . ."

With Gable secured and George Cukor set to direct, Selznick continued his search for Scarlett. When his national scouting for unknown actresses failed to provide a definitive choice, Selznick reconsidered a select group of Hollywood "names." *Time* magazine argued the case for Bette, saying that she "came close to what the public seemed to want in Scarlett. . . . tempestuous, intense, compact and case-hardened, with diamond dust in her voice, bug eyes lit with a cold blue glitter, and as wide a dramatic range as any cinemactress in the business."

In fact, however, Bette Davis was no longer in the running. She wasn't even given a screen test. It was thought by some that Jack Warner refused to consider loaning her to Metro; some said that it was Gable who objected to her, arguing that she was not beautiful enough to be the subject of such adulation from Rhett Butler, Ashley Wilkes, and half the Confederate army. Bette herself deduced that she was simply disliked by George Cukor, who had fired her years before when she was a member of his Rochester, New York, repertory company. For decades Bette harbored a grudge against Cukor, holding him personally responsible for her missing out on the chance to play Scarlett. As she later related, "Cukor hired me as a green and unknown ingenue. When I felt (years later) that I was a logical contender for the role of Scarlett O'Hara in *Gone With the Wind*, apparently he saw only the groping youngster he had fired in Rochester. I have always felt those weeks as Cukor's ingenue prevented me from getting the role which I wanted very much to play." Ironically, Selznick would later fire Cukor, well into the shooting, and replace him with Victor Fleming, who presumably had no predisposition against Bette or casting her as Scarlett.

Nevertheless, as of November 18, 1938, Selznick had limited his choice of Scarletts to Paulette Goddard, Doris Jordan, Jean Arthur, Katharine Hepburn, and Loretta Young. Three days later he expanded the list to include Joan Bennett. Then, on December 10, while Cukor was shooting the burning of Atlanta sequence, Selznick was introduced on the set to Vivien Leigh. Two days later Selznick's list had been narrowed down to the Scarlett finalists: Goddard, Arthur, Bennett, and Leigh. On January 4, 1939, after seeing her test, which had been shot under Cukor's direction, Selznick cast Vivien Leigh as Scarlett O'Hara.

Back in the fall of 1937, while Selznick was still searching the American South for his Scarlett, Jack Warner decided to produce his own southern-belle-as-heroine-vixen story and rush it into theaters before *Gone With the Wind*. He found the perfect property in *Jezebel*, an unsuccessful play by Owen Davis, Sr., that had been sitting on a Warners shelf for over a year.

Jezebel, starring Bette Davis, started shooting on October 25, 1937. It was previewed in Hollywood to great acclaim on March 7, 1938. The following day David Selznick telephoned Jack Warner and castigated him for plagiarizing *GWTW*, which had yet to go before the cameras. When *Jezebel* became a box office hit (and made a star out of Bette Davis), it was speculated in Hollywood that Warner had shrewdly stolen the thunder that seemingly belonged to Selznick. *Time* magazine suggested that *Jezebel* was as similar to *GWTW* "as chicory is to coffee." In its review of *Jezebel*, the *New York Evening Sun* was more pointed:

Perhaps they had better put off the filming of *Gone With the Wind* for another two years. The Warners, as usual, have sensed a trend and become the first to present a picture which should be a pacemaker for any Old South drama of this or practically any season. A vivid drama, with an ever-mounting suspense. The acting is top-notch. Bette Davis is at her best, sensitive and emotional in the most exacting role of her career.

Selznick needn't have fretted. Upon its release in December 1939, *Gone With the Wind* was accorded unprecedented critical raves and phenomenal box office. It went on to receive eight Oscars (nine including a special award) in 13 nominations, including best picture, best actress (Vivien Leigh), best director (Victor Fleming), best supporting actress (Hattie McDaniel), and best screenplay (Sidney Howard).

Today it is difficult to fathom anyone *but* Vivien Leigh as Scarlett O'Hara. Certainly the image of Bette Davis returning to Tara, scouring the fire-stricken rubble left by the looting Yankees, and pronouncing, "What a dump!" is a farfetched and humorous one that belongs in the front ranks of Hollywood *what-if*s. Still, although she admired the picture and the performance by Leigh, Bette insisted until her death in 1989 that *she* would have made a better Scarlett.

EDMUND GOULDING

Bette Davis and director Edmund Goulding had a love-hate relationship; both recognized and admired the other's talent, but both were disdainful of the other's temperament and technique. Bette was particularly distressed by Goulding's customary practice of personally acting out the parts for the actors to illustrate how he wanted the characters to be played. "Mr. Goulding is a genius moviemaker," Bette conceded, "[but] he was also an extraordinarily difficult man. . . . He *did* find me difficult, because I was very stubborn about the woman I was playing. I didn't think he could play her as well as I did."

William Wyler is generally considered the best director Bette Davis ever worked with, but it was Eddie Goulding who directed Bette in her two biggest box office and critical successes, *Dark Victory* and *The Old Maid*, both released in 1939. He also directed her in the 1937 picture *That Certain Woman* (a remake of his 1929 picture *The Trespasser*) and *The Great Lie* (1941) and was scheduled to direct her in others. *Jezebel* (1938) was initially assigned to Goulding, but he was replaced before production started. He was also slated to direct *The Letter* (1940), a project he personally convinced Warners to buy as a vehicle for Bette, but he was replaced by Wyler on that assignment as well. He was also the initial director assigned to *Now, Voyager* (1942) and in fact wrote early versions of the script before he was replaced by Irving Rapper. *Old Acquaintance* (1943) and *Mr. Skeffington* (1944) were also Goulding pictures until he was replaced on both by Vincent Sherman.

Edmund Goulding (1891–1959) was generally regarded in Hollywood as one of the best directors of "women's pictures." Remarkably, he was never nominated for an Academy Award. His films include *Grand Hotel* (1932),

The Constant Nymph (1943), *The Razor's Edge* (1946), and *We're Not Married* (1952).

MARTHA GRAHAM
While she was a student at the Robert Milton–John Murray Anderson School of the Theatre, Bette was given dance instruction by the legendary dancer/choreographer Martha Graham. Bette would later credit Graham with having taught her how to walk, how to move, how to express emotion with her body. Of her famous former pupil Graham said, "She had control, discipline and electricity. I knew she would be something."

SHEILA GRAHAM
Hollywood gossip columnist with whom Bette feuded. Graham contended that Bette was one of the most difficult stars she ever had to deal with in Hollywood. Bette responded that Graham was a vile woman whose only claim to fame had been to sleep with F. Scott Fitzgerald. A typical Graham column was published after Bette filed for divorce against William Grant Sherry in 1949: "Bette Davis Acts to Rub Out 3rd Marriage," Graham's headline read. The column continued, "Screen tragedienne Bette Davis chalked up another real-life setback late today when she filed suit for divorce here from her artist-husband William Grant Sherry, accusing the muscular one-time masseur of rubbing her the wrong way." Bette, incensed by the careless, flippant tone of the column, had Graham barred from the set of her film *Payment on Demand*.

GRANDCHILDREN
J. Ashley Hyman
Justin Hyman
Cameron Merrill
Matthew Merrill

GRAUMAN'S CHINESE THEATER
Bette placed her hand and footprints in the forecourt of Grauman's Chinese Theater in Hollywood on November 6, 1950, in conjunction with the premiere of *All About Eve*. At the induction ceremony Bette, observing the immortalized legs of Betty Grable, quipped, "It's too bad there's no way to imprint my poached-egg eyes here."

THE GREAT LIE ★★
Warner Brothers
1941   107 minutes   bw
Directed by: Edmund Goulding
Produced by: Hal B. Wallis, in association with Henry Blanke
Screenplay by: Lenore Coffee, based on the novel by Polan Banks
Cinematography by: Tony Gaudio
Cast: Bette Davis, George Brent, Mary Astor, Lucile Watson, Hattie

To Mary Astor: "This picture is going to *stink*!"

McDaniel, Grant Mitchell, Jerome Cowan, Sam McDaniel, Thurston
Hall, Russell Hicks, Charles Trowbridge, Virginia Brissac, Olin
Howland, J. Farrell MacDonald, Doris Lloyd, Addison Richards,
Georgia Caine, Alphonse Martell

Rights to the novel by Polan Banks were purchased by Warner Brothers for $6,000. The studio spent an additional $1,000 to acquire the rights to *Die Grosse Luge*, a novel by Lola Stein of Hamburg, Germany. The latter would go uncredited on the screen.

The Great Lie was almost never made. There was a good deal of dissension at the studio regarding its potential. On January 10, 1939, producer Lou Edelman issued a memo to Hal Wallis stating that he had read the script and, in his opinion, the film should not be made. The same day, Wallis received another memo, this one from producer David Lewis, who also cautioned against making the picture. "This is in no way," Lewis wrote diplomatically, " a criticism of the work done in preparing this version." Lewis further noted that the story seemed to belong to a previous era and that modern audiences required more action and excitement to remain in their seats.

Determined, Hal Wallis had the script revised and relocated the setting from Europe to New York. The genre of the picture changed too, from a romance to a comedy. However, after reading the revision, screenwriter Wolfgang Reinhardt wrote to Wallis and suggested that the comedic approach be tempered in favor of the romance (then referred to as a "woman's angle").

Wallis also vacillated on who was to direct the picture. Henry Blanke pressed the issue and finally demanded to know whether it was to be Curtis Bernhardt or William Dieterle. On February 20, 1940, Blanke received a memo from Jack Warner that stated succinctly, "Let us have it definitely understood that Vincent Sherman will be put on *January Heights* [which it was being called at the time] as the director."

Problems, however, persisted with the script. The initial writer on the project was Richard Sherman, who took an inordinate amount of time to come up with an acceptable draft. Upon reading the script, Vincent Sherman wrote to Blanke on March 1, expressing his dissatisfaction. He complained that he didn't agree with the approach to the material or with the tone of the entire script. He said that although he considered the novel to be "pretty bad literature," it nonetheless contained good movie situations with plenty of sentiment. He objected to the film's tone of light comedy. Like Reinhardt, he saw the film as a serious woman's picture.

Instead of waiting for a response from Blanke and working through the proper channels, Vincent Sherman made a mistake: he went directly to writer Sherman and began to work with him on the script revisions. This so infuriated Wallis that he scribbled a note to Blanke ordering director Sherman not to confer with writer Sherman while the script was still being written. If a director was allowed to confer with a writer while the script was being written, he felt, the entire process would slow down to "a walk."

Upon being informed of Wallis's anger, Vincent Sherman promptly issued a letter apologizing for overstepping his bounds. Still, it was not long before Sherman was taken off the picture and replaced with Eddie Goulding. It was at this point that Warners fashioned the film as a reunion among

Goulding, Bette, and George Brent, the principals involved in the highly successful 1939 picture *Dark Victory*. Meanwhile, Richard Sherman finally finished his rough draft during the second week of April 1940. By late May, Hal Wallis had more or less scrapped the Sherman script. Novelist Polan Banks wanted his shot at writing the script. He had previously sent Wallis a telegram that read, in part, "Remember your promise to me to give me first crack at working on the script of any story you bought from me? Please keep it. . . ." Nevertheless, Wallis took to having meetings with screenwriter Lenore Coffee. Ironically, Coffee's eventual shooting script turned out much like what Vincent Sherman had wanted. The comedy angle was dropped in favor of the woman's angle. The plot concerned Madame Sandra Kovack, a concert pianist who cajoles Peter Van Allen (Brent) to marry her while on a drunken spree, even though he is in love with rich country girl Maggie Patterson (Davis). They spend the first few days of their honeymoon with a bottle between them in bed. Peter then learns that their marriage isn't legal because Sandra's divorce from her previous husband had not yet been finalized. So he goes back to Maggie in sobriety and marries *her*, all to the swelling sounds of Tchaikovsky on the soundtrack.

Casting was an arduous task. Bette Davis was set for the part of Maggie. George Brent was to be her leading man. It was the secondary part of Sandra that was difficult to cast. Hal Wallis wanted an accomplished and big-name actress for the part. He had a time, however, enticing such an actress to take a lead secondary to Bette Davis. Joan Crawford was interested for a period. So was Barbara Stanwyck, but she backed out after reading the first 95 pages of the script. Tallulah Bankhead was also sought, but she sent word back that she was on tour and unavailable. Also interested was Rosalind Russell, who went so far as to have cocktails with Goulding to discuss the part. Finally, however, she could not bring herself to play a supporting role. Others who were considered included Marlene Dietrich, Claudette Colbert, Greer Garson, Olivia de Havilland, Ann Sheridan, Geraldine Fitzgerald, Ida Lupino, Carole Lombard, Loretta Young, Paulette Goddard, Rita Hayworth, and Constance Bennett. The last, savilly aware of the dramatic potential of the role, actively, albeit unsuccessfully, campaigned for the part.

The picture was slated to begin principal photography in October 1940. As of September 21, Sandra had yet to be cast. Wallis wrote a memo to Blanke urging him to have Goulding rush preparation of the picture. He also stressed that it was imperative that the part of Sandra be cast immediately. Blanke, Goulding, and Wallis eventually settled on Mary Astor, whose career was by then in decline and who had been recommended for the part by Ernst Lubitsch. The casting made sense. Astor was something of a pianist and would at least look competent when faced with a keyboard. Later Bette would claim that it was she who had insisted that Astor be given the part. It was, in fact, Bette who telephoned Astor with the news that she had gotten the part.

With an estimated budget of $757,000, the picture, then being called

Women of Today, finally went before the cameras in October as scheduled. A month later it was retitled *Far Horizon,* then *Her Great Lie,* and finally *The Great Lie.*

Bette, coming directly from *The Letter,* in which she had been directed by Wyler, was discontented with Goulding and his penchant for acting out the parts for his actors. Primarily, however, she was displeased with the script. Shooting would frequently be slowed while Bette went off and rewrote her lines. "One morning," Mary Astor related in her autobiography, "Bette said to me in a very peremptory manner, 'Hey, Astor! Let's go talk a minute!' We went to her portable [trailer] and she closed the door and I had the old 'What have I done now?' feeling. She flopped on the couch and said, 'This picture is going to *stink*! It's too incredible for words. . . . You've got to help. You and I, really just us, because I've talked to the writers and to Eddie, and everybody's satisfied but me, so it's up to us to rewrite this piece of junk to make it more interesting. All I do is mewl to George about 'that woman you married when you were drunk . . . please come back to me' and that crap. And that's just soap opera." Bette also raved about the title, claiming that it gave away the plot. She also quipped that the lie referred to in the title was *not* a "great" one at all. She wanted the picture retitled, curiously and to no avail, *Aren't Women Fools?*

Bette did not restrict her comments about the picture to Mary Astor. During a break from shooting she told Harrison Carroll, a columnist for the *Los Angeles Herald Express,* that the picture would not be one of her "important" pictures. After reading Carroll's column the following day, Hal Wallis became enraged and penned a note to Jack Warner telling him that "something must be done" to prevent a recurrence of this type of insubordination. Wallis requested that Warner instruct the publicity department that Bette was to give no further interviews during the production and that all newspaper people were to be barred from the set.

Meanwhile Bette continued to conspire with Astor to rewrite their scenes. It was Bette's contention that the script would be improved if a constant conflict and competition existed between Maggie and Sandra. The two actresses devised a series of bitchy lines and various bits of business that would be evident throughout the film, most particularly in the Arizona sequence, which was actually shot on location in Victorville, California.

While Astor was in fact a skilled pianist, the actual recording of Tchaikovsky's Concerto in E Flat Major was performed by Max Rabinowitsch while Astor appeared before the cameras with a dummy piano. The close-ups of hand and finger placements were performed by concert pianist Norma Boleslavsky. Everything had to be rehearsed repeatedly until every note, every finger placement was in complete synchronization. Matching the close-ups of Boleslavsky with the medium and long shots of Astor was a difficult and tedious task and one that would not be overlooked when the 1941 Best Supporting Actress Oscar was handed out. Upon receiving the award, Mary

Astor stepped up to the podium and thanked two people: Tchaikovsky for his music and Bette Davis for rewriting the script, setting petty competition aside, and improving Astor's part.

Between takes, Bette got along uncommonly well with her costars. George Brent frequently broke the tension on the set by tickling her feet. Off the set he no longer warmed her bed, replaced by Arthur Farnsworth. Bette also got along well with Astor and even invited Astor and her husband, Manuel del Campo, over for dinner at her Glendale home. The day after they shot the scene in which Bette slapped Astor, Astor showed up on the set with severely swollen cheeks. Concerned and guilt-ridden, Bette apologized profusely until Astor unloaded the wads of cotton that she had stuffed into her jaws. Both women broke down in laughter.

Toward the end of the shooting, cinematographer Tony Gaudio fell ill with the flu and was replaced by Ernie Haller. It was with Haller behind the camera that production finally completed on December 25, 1940.

While the picture was in postproduction there was some controversy over George Brent's billing. Initially his name was to be placed alongside Bette's, before the title. Then it was to be placed just below Bette's but still before the title. Finally he was demoted to placement following the title.

The picture was promoted by calling Bette a "pajamas girl" and Mary a "nightgown girl." Upon its release in April 1941, it was accorded mostly mediocre reviews, though reviewers were quick to praise both Astor and Davis for their performances. Astor was particularly singled out for raves, and some critics went so far as to say that she had stolen the picture from Bette.

ALEC GUINNESS

Bette's daughter, B. D. Hyman, attributes the terms "overbearing, egotistical, snotty, and a dreadful actor" to her mother in reference to Alec Guinness. Bette naturally denied making the critical comments, but there can be little doubt that she had little affinity for Guinness during the making of the 1959 picture *The Scapegoat*. Guinness served as co-executive producer of the film, and Bette contended that he had maliciously left most of her part on the cutting room floor.

Biographer Charles Higham quotes Guinness as saying, "Not only did she not trust the director [Robert Hamer], she was suspicious of me. I don't know whether she thought I was going to try to take scenes from her, which wouldn't have been possible anyway, but I was prepared happily and rightly to sit at her feet, as it happened. I was proud to have worked with her and sad that she didn't seem to have enjoyed working with me."

"GUNSMOKE"

In 1966 Bette guest-starred in "The Jailer," an episode of the phenomenally popular television series "Gunsmoke." She portrayed Etta Stone, a mother of four sons who is determined to avenge the hanging murder of her husband.

She totes a shotgun and goes after Marshall Matt Dillon (James Arness) and Miss Kitty (Amanda Blake). Bette enjoyed working on the show and enthused, "I am in awe, absolutely in awe of these people. How they can maintain enthusiasm after twelve years and still work together as a team is marvelous." The episode aired on October 1, 1966.

One of the most successful programs in television history, "Gunsmoke" aired on CBS from September 1955 until September 1975.

"If this wasn't a series I'd get my man. I'd hang him. But, of course, we all know the hero has to be back next week."

Bette Davis, 1966

HAIR

It's hard to think of Bette Davis as just another Hollywood bleached blond posing for the "cheesecake" photos of the early 1930s—but she was. For her first Warner Brothers picture, *The Man Who Played God* (1932), studio makeup man and hairstylist Perc Westmore decided to lighten her naturally brown hair. For her next picture, *The Rich Are Always With Us*, released the same year, Westmore gave her an even blonder look. The lighter hue was well received, and for the first time in her fledgling movie career critics commented favorably on Bette's appearance. Some contended that she resembled Constance Bennett and/or Carole Lombard.

For the 1933 picture *The Working Man* her hair was dyed a reddish hue. The following year, for *Fashions of 1934*, her hair was glamorized, Garboized, and platinum. Bette was displeased with the results and vowed never again to attempt a cheap imitation of Garbo or Harlow. In fact, for the 1936 picture *The Petrified Forest*, Bette conspired with Westmore and without the consent of the studio darkened her hair to her natural color.

> "I'm particularly glad I let my hair go natural before I went to England last summer. English people don't like the bleached blond hair we went for so enthusiastically a while ago in Hollywood. I was thankful a hundred times during my visit to London that my hair was natural."
>
> *Bette Davis, 1937*

> "You just can't imagine what it's like. In the first place, the head must be shaved every morning; it develops a 5 o'clock shadow. And someone must do it for you—you can neither see nor reach to do it yourself. . . . The noise of the electric razor shaving my head was one of the most nerve-wracking experiences of my life. It's like a dentist drilling. And when you let the hair grow out again, it itches. I thought I'd go mad. It was agony, sheer agony."
>
> *Bette Davis, who went bald for the pictures* The Private Lives of Elizabeth and Essex *(1939) and* The Virgin Queen *(1955),*
> Los Angeles Times

> "The malt crystallizes, gives the hair body and makes it look real pretty for the cameras."
>
> *Bette sharing her beauty secret of washing her hair in stale beer,*
> Free Press, *August 31, 1949*

> "I don't see how anybody can make love in a sophisticated coiffure. You'd have to be thinking constantly about your hair, and of course that's *not* what you should be thinking about. . . . I think any girl would admit she can make love better with her hair down. There's something psychological about it, makes her feel more feminine and all that."
>
> *Bette sharing her love and beauty secrets,*
> Hollywood Citizen News, *May 2, 1946*

"I can't possibly imagine making love with a bun on the back of my neck, or with an upswept hairdo. And anyway, I don't think men like it that way. There's something forbidding about a woman with a formal coiffure—it's like making love to your maiden aunt."

Bette on the same subject, 1949

During her later years Bette always wore a wig for public appearances. At one of her one-woman shows in London during the seventies, a bold audience member stood up and called out, "Is that your real hair, Miss Davis?" Taken aback and then quickly recovering, Bette stuck out her chest and convincingly lied. "Yes it is. And these are my real eyes, my real teeth, and my real *tits!*"

The Bette Davis Hairstylists
A selective alphabetical list:

Martha Acker	Ruby Felkner	Gwen Holden	Tillie Starriet
Norman Allison	Agnes Flanagan	Helene King	Dione Taylor
Jean Burke	Betty Glasgow	Nellie Manley	Helen Turpin
Dothea Carlson	Ramon Gow	Emily Moore	Perc Westmore
Olga Collings	Florence Guernsey	Jane Romeyn	Bette Wilson
Linda Cross	Sidney Guilaroff	Peggy Shannon	
Ora Curtis	Virginia Hatfield	Joan Smallwood	
Margaret Donovan	Ethel Hogan	Bobbie Smith	

JAMES HALL
One of 15 Universal actors whom Bette had to kiss for a 1931 screen test. Bette later recounted the event. "When I arrived on the stage, James Hall was waiting. He was one of the big names at the moment because of his appearance in *Hell's Angels*. I was told to sprawl out on a divan for a love scene. . . . Jim approached me and started to read lines. He bent over me and all I could do was lie there while he made impassioned love, ending his speech with a lusty kiss. 'That's fine,' the director said, and as the overhead lights were dimmed he called, 'Who's next?' "

ERNEST HALLER
During Bette Davis's long and legendary tenure at Warner Brothers a handful of men, extraordinary talents all, made immense contributions to her art. Ernest Haller was certainly among them. One of the premier cinematographers of his or any other era, Haller was known within the industry primarily as a glamour photographer rather than an intricate technician. He was much in demand by the leading female stars of the thirties and forties, and he was certainly Bette Davis's favorite cinematographer. Their pictures together are classic examples of cameraman, lighting, and subject in perfect sync and harmony: *The Rich Are Always With Us* (1932), *Dangerous* (1935), *That Certain Woman* (1937), *Jezebel* (Best Cinematography Oscar nomination, 1938), *Dark Victory* (1939), *All This, and Heaven Too* (Best Cinematog-

raphy Oscar nomination, 1940), *The Bride Came C.O.D.* (1941), *In This Our Life* (1942), *Mr. Skeffington* (1944), *Deception* (1946), *Winter Meeting* (1948), *What Ever Happened to Baby Jane?* (Best Cinematography Oscar nomination, 1962), and *Dead Ringer* (1964). In addition, Haller replaced Tony Gaudio in the latter part of production on *The Great Lie* (1941) and Sol Polito for a substantial part of *A Stolen Life* (1946) but did not receive screen credit for either.

Winter Meeting was such a flop for Bette, and so many disparaging comments were made about her physical appearance in it that it caused a rift in her relationship with Haller. She so castigated him for his work that Haller publicly vowed never again to work with Bette. The two would not make amends for many years. They finally reunited for several television programs in the 1950s, including an episode of "Alfred Hitchcock Presents," before rejoining forces for the 1962 success *What Ever Happened to Baby Jane?*

The other pictures of Ernest Haller (1896–1970) include *Gone With the Wind* (Best Cinematography Oscar winner, shared credit, 1939), *Mildred Pierce* (Best Cinematography Oscar nomination, 1945), *The Flame and the Arrow* (Best Cinematography Oscar nomination, 1950), *Rebel Without a Cause* (1955), and *Lilies of the Field* (Best Cinematography Oscar nomination, 1963).

TOM HANKS

After appearing as a presenter at the March 30, 1987, Oscar ceremony, actor Tom Hanks attended the postawards dinner party with a date. He was seated at a table that included Jeff Bridges and his wife, Arlene Dahl and her husband, and columnist Shirley Eder and her husband. While waiting to be served their first course, Hanks and his date left the table to dance, leaving their personal belongings beside their empty plates. While they were dancing, Bette arrived at the table with her companion, Kathryn Sermak. By then dinner had been served, and Bette proceeded to push aside Hank's belongings and devour his dinner. Upon returning to his table, Hanks playfully pronounced, "Someone is sitting in my chair!" Bette, however, refused to acknowledge his presence or the fact that she was sitting in his seat and eating his dinner. Hanks tried again. "Someone is eating my food." Bette continued to ignore him. He decided to make one last effort. "The someone who is sitting in my chair and eating my food is *Bette Davis*, so it's all right with me!" When Bette continued to ignore him, Hanks scooped up his personal belongings and pronounced to his date, laughing, "It's obvious we're no longer welcome at this table," and departed. Bette, meanwhile, continued to eat in oblivion, without so much as a glance at the departing Hanks.

REX HARRISON

Bette badly wanted the role of Anna opposite Rex Harrison's king in the 1946 production of *Anna and the King of Siam*, a part she would lose to Irene Dunne. Later Bette appeared with Harrison, or "Sexy Rexy" as he was dubbed by some, in a radio play entitled "The Small Servant," which was broadcast on the "Hollywood Players" program. About Harrison, Bette would later enthuse that he was one of the most attractive men she had ever met. "I also consider him," she added, "a truly great actor."

PATRICK HASTINGS

Celebrated British trial attorney Sir Patrick Hastings represented Warner Brothers in its 1936 court case against Bette Davis. During the trial Hastings incensed Bette by referring to her as "a naughty young lady" who simply wanted more money. Hastings, reportedly, was the model for Agatha Christie's lawyer in the 1957 Billy Wilder picture *Witness for the Prosecution*.

HELEN HAYES

When they costarred together in "Murder with Mirrors," an Agatha Christie story for television shot in England in 1984, legendary ladies Davis and Hayes became anything but friends. As was characteristic of her, Bette was unwilling to share the screen with an actress who even approached her stature. On the first day of shooting Bette startled Hayes by snapping at her, and things failed to improve from there. Still, upon completing the movie, Bette related to reporters that she had been honored to work with Hayes. Apparently it was Bette's impression that Hayes had also enjoyed the experience. Upon completion of their work together Bette presented Hayes with an antique silver mirror. However, when it came time for her to consider presenters for the 1989 Lincoln Center tribute in her honor, Bette cut Hayes from the list of possibilities. Hayes reciprocated with her 1990 autobiography in which she derided Bette for having been difficult and competitive during the shooting of their only movie together.

Interestingly, it was Helen Hayes and not Bette Davis whom Frank Capra had wanted many years before as his Apple Annie in *Pocketful of Miracles* (1961). It was only after Hayes backed out that second-choice Bette was offered the part.

Helen Hayes, born in 1900 and often referred to as "the First Lady of the American Stage," appeared in pictures including *The Sin of Madelon Claudet* (Best Actress Oscar winner, 1931), *A Farewell to Arms* (1932), *Anastasia* (1956), and *Airport* (Best Supporting Actress Oscar winner, 1970).

SUSAN HAYWARD

Before she costarred with her in the 1964 picture *Where Love Has Gone*, Susan Hayward had several brushes with Bette Davis—none of them particularly pleasant. At the age of 20 Hayward, then an unknown starlet, appeared in a bit as a telephone operator in the 1938 picture *The Sisters*. Hayward envied and admired Bette, who was then on the ascent to stardom. Bette, of course, did not know that Hayward even existed. Seventeen years later Susan Hayward was, with *My Foolish Heart* (1949 Best Actress Oscar nomination), *With a Song in My Heart* (1952 Best Actress Oscar nomination), and *I'll Cry Tomorrow* (1955 Best Actress Oscar nomination), one of the biggest stars and one of the most respected actresses in Hollywood. Bette, conversely, was considered something of a has-been. But it was Hayward who, on the morning of April 26, 1955, attempted suicide by gulping down a handful of sleeping pills. At the time, Bette was working at 20th Century–Fox, the studio where Hayward reigned, making *The Virgin Queen*. On April 29 Hayward was transported from Cedars Sinai Hospital in the studio limousine that had been assigned to Bette during the making of *Queen*. This had been done without Bette's permission or knowledge, and when she learned that she was stranded without transportation, Bette became livid and let everyone at the studio know of her displeasure.

Then, in 1963, Susan Hayward made the mistake of making a movie called *Stolen Hours*, an attempted remake of Bette's classic 1939 picture *Dark Victory*. The film was less than successful, with critics complaining that it paled when compared to the original. Bette was irritated that Hayward would even attempt to compete with her original performance and took delight in the failure of *Stolen Hours*.

Thus by the time they made *Where Love Has Gone* the following year, Davis and Hayward were already at odds, and nothing that transpired on that set rectified their mutual animosity. It didn't help, of course, that Bette played Hayward's mother in the film (despite the fact that she was only 10 years older) or that she secretly wished she had been cast in Hayward's part rather than her own. On the last day of shooting the picture Bette reportedly whipped off her wig and, with one last parting shot ("F—k you!"), threw it in Hayward's face. Hayward would later provoke Bette's wrath again when she would be cast, instead of Bette, in the 1967 picture *Valley of the Dolls*.

Susan Hayward (Edythe Marrener, 1918–1975) made her debut in the 1938 picture *Girls on Probation*. Her subsequent films include *Change of Heart* (1943), *David and Bathsheba* (1951), *I Want to Live!* (1958 Best Actress Oscar winner), *Back Street* (1961), and *The Honey Pot* (1967).

RITA HAYWORTH

Early in her career, before she attained stardom, Rita Hayworth (Margarita Carmen Cansino, 1918–1987) screen-tested for many Warner Brothers pictures in which she would have appeared with Bette Davis. Despite their 10-year age difference, Rita even tested for some of the roles that Bette ended up playing, such as the female lead opposite Jimmy Cagney in *The Bride Came C.O.D.* (1941).

After selling her home in Glendale in the midforties, Bette rented a guest house in Brentwood that was adjacent to a much larger home occupied by Rita. By then, by way of pictures including *Cover Girl* (1944) and *Gilda* (1946), Hayworth was a major box office star, while Bette was just beginning her slip from the top ranks of stardom. Nonetheless, Bette and her recently wed husband, William Grant Sherry, took delight in peering from the windows and watching Rita's comings and goings. Additionally, Bette was having immense difficulty getting a telephone installed. While waiting for the hookup, Bette made her calls from, and had calls directed to, Rita's telephone. As neighbors, they were friendly enough, although Bette could not help feeling jealous when Sherry paid Rita the least bit of attention. One night Bette and Rita attended the same party. As Bette recalled, "Rita was so beautiful I couldn't stand it! Yes, she was *that* beautiful. Rita had a very low-cut dress on. Mine was not. All the men were around Rita and finally, I'd had enough. So I went upstairs, got some scissors, cut my dress down to *here*, and went back downstairs to prove [that] I have two of them too!"

Years later Bette Davis's jealousy of Rita Hayworth intensified after the breakup of her marriage to Gary Merrill in the early 1960s. Instead of collapsing in despair over the divorce, Merrill embarked on a much publicized affair with Hayworth, much to Bette's ire. Bette even attempted to block Merrill's child visitation rights because of his association with *"that woman."*

"Every man I knew had fallen in love with Gilda and wakened with me."

Rita Hayworth

EDITH HEAD

For the 1948 picture *June Bride*, Warner Brothers shelled out $5,000 to borrow the services of costume designer Edith Head. Bette was so pleased with Head's dress designs for the picture that she requested that the studio make replicas of them for her personal wardrobe. Head went on, at Bette's request, to design the costumes for *Beyond the Forest* (1949), *All About Eve* (Best Costume Design Oscar winner, shared credit, 1950), *Pocketful of Miracles* (Best Costume Design Oscar nomination, shared credit, 1961), *Where Love Has Gone* (1964), "Madame Sin" (1972 TVM), and "The Disappearance of Aimee" (1976 TVM). Head's *sketch* of Margo Channing's famous "Fasten your seat belts" gown from *Eve* sold at an auction in April 1990 for $23,100.

Generally regarded as *the* premier motion picture costume designer of all time, Edith Head (1907–1981) made her picture debut with *She Done Him Wrong* in 1933. She would go on to receive Oscar nominations for an unprecedented 18 straight years, from the time the award was initiated in 1948 through 1966.

Edith Head was one of the guests at a 1981 party Bette hosted at her apartment in West Hollywood. Head died shortly afterward, and Bette Davis gave the eulogy at her funeral. "A queen has left us," Bette said to the mourners. In later years she would frequently say in honor of Head, "Hollywood will never have another one like her."

LILLIAN HELLMAN

Playwright from whose works the successful pictures *The Little Foxes* (1941) and *Watch on the Rhine* (1943) were adapted. Hellman also wrote the adapted screenplay for *Foxes* (Best Screenplay Oscar nomination) and was credited with "additional scenes and dialogue" for *Rhine* (Best Screenplay Oscar nomination). For the latter Hellman was paid the then-phenomenal salary of $150,000 *plus* 15 percent of the total gross receipts.

Lillian Hellman (1905–1984) is also responsible for the pictures *These Three* (adapted from *The Children's Hour*, 1936), *The Children's Hour* (1961), *Toys in the Attic* (1963), and *Julia* (1977).

HELL'S HOUSE ★★

Capital Films
1932   72 minutes   bw
Directed by: Howard Higgin
Produced by: Benjamin F. Zeidman
Screenplay by: Paul Gangelin and B. Harrison Orkow, based on a story by
    Howard Higgin
Cinematography by: Allan Siegel
Cast: Pat O'Brien, James "Junior" Durkin, Bette Davis, Junior Coughlin,
    Charles Grapewin, Emma Dunn, James Marcus, Morgan Wallace,
    Wallis Clark, Hooper Atchley

In later years, while grousing about the time and money it took to make a
contemporary picture, Bette contended, "Why, I made a picture with Pat
O'Brien called *Hell's House* that we completed in one week." She would then
take a puff of her omnipresent cigarette and exclaim, "Of course, the picture
looked like the title."

Actually, *Hell's House*, originally called *Juvenile Court*, took 13 days to
make and in fact was not that bad. Bette was probably displeased with it
because Universal loaned her out to the cheapie Capital Films to make it and
because she was incidental to the film's impact. The story focused instead on
Junior Durkin as a young farm boy who goes to the big city after the death
of his mother, innocently gets mixed up with bootlegger Pat O'Brien, and
ends up in a detention home. Bette plays O'Brien's girl, Peggy, who functions
more or less as his conscience. It's not much of a part, but Bette registers and
looks good as a blond.

PAUL HENREID

Paul Henreid attained lasting fame with the 1942 picture *Now, Voyager* in
which he played Jerry Durrance, the suffering married man who falls in love
with Bette Davis aboard a cruise ship and has a particular flair for lighting
cigarettes. Warner Brothers, expecting big things out of Henreid, tried to
rush him through the picture so that he could segue directly into *Casablanca*
(1943), in which he would play Ingrid Bergman's love interest until she is
reunited with Humphrey Bogart in a gin joint known as Rick's.

A few years later Henreid and Bette were reunited, with less successful
results than before, in *Deception* (1946). He had previously turned down
opportunities to costar with her in *Watch on the Rhine* (1943) and *Mr.
Skeffington* (1944).

"There was something about her manner, flirtatious and friendly, flattering and yet honest," Henreid would later say regarding his introduction to
and eventual relationship with his famous costar, "that made you think of
her as an immediate friend. . . . we got along famously. In fact, a very close
friendship started between us, and she has remained a dear, close friend—
and always a very decent human being."

Bette encouraged the rumor that she and Henreid were having an affair. They are shown here in a publicity still for *Now, Voyager*.

There is some speculation that Bette and Henreid had something of an affair. According to Henreid, it was Bette herself who encouraged the rumor. "She would tell our friends, 'I have such a crush on Paul, but he just won't give me the right time. I don't know how I can get an affair going with him.' " At the time, both were married. Nonetheless, they certainly maintained a long friendship. In the 1950s Henreid directed Bette in "Out There, Darkness," an episode of the television series "Alfred Hitchcock Presents." And in 1964 Bette handpicked Henreid to direct her in the feature *Dead Ringer*.

In the early 1970s Henreid appeared on the "This Is Your Life" television tribute to Bette, re-creating the legendary scene in *Voyager* in which he puts two cigarettes in his mouth, lights them both, and presents one to Bette.

Paul Henreid, born Paul Hernried in Austria in 1907, went to Warner Brothers following success in the British pictures *Goodbye, Mr. Chips* (1939) and *Night Train to Munich* (1940). He made his American debut in *Joan of Paris* (1941). His subsequent pictures include *Of Human Bondage* (1946), *A Woman's Devotion* (also directed, 1957), *The Four Horsemen of the Apoca-*

lypse (1962), *The Madwoman of Chaillot* (1969), and *Exorcist II: The Heretic* (1977).

KATHARINE HEPBURN

> "I always wanted to *be* Katharine Hepburn. I've wanted to look like her—to have that marvelous face, not my round, drawn face. Oh! I adore the way she looks. I could kill for the way she looks."
>
> *Bette Davis*

If there was one person in Hollywood that Bette Davis envied more than any other, it was Katharine Hepburn, who in Bette's view had it all: looks, talent . . . Tracy.

Throughout the years some have propagated the idea of Davis and Hepburn as rivals. In fact they admired each other, although they never really knew one another beyond pleasantries exchanged in passing. But Bette wanted few things more than the chance to costar opposite Hepburn. When she won the 1935 Best Actress Oscar for *Dangerous*, Bette openly chastised the voters, saying that Hepburn, nominated for *Alice Adams*, had given the better performance. Around the same time, John Ford was directing Hepburn in the title role of *Mary of Scotland*. It was to Bette's great disappointment that she was not cast opposite Hepburn as Queen Elizabeth, a role she vigorously campaigned for.

For years Bette searched for a vehicle big enough for the two of them. After being cast in Tennessee Williams's 1961 Broadway play *The Night of the Iguana*, Bette was enthusiastic about the possibility of Hepburn's playing the part of Hannah Jelkes, the repressed artist, to her Maxine Faulk. Hepburn, however, eventually turned down the part.

After losing a great deal of weight following her 1983 stroke, Bette quipped, "All my film career I had envied Katharine Hepburn's high cheekbones and narrow face. Now I had them." After the 1985 publication of Bette's daughter's book *My Mother's Keeper*, Hepburn publicly went to Bette's defense, chastising the book as "a disgusting thing to do! What a profound betrayal."

Until the end of her life, Bette continued to hold out hope that she would play opposite Hepburn. "I would give anything," she told a reporter only months before her death, "if a film for both of us could be found. Two Yankee ladies. . . . ah, yes, that would be great."

Another great disappointment for Bette was that Hepburn and not Bette became the first actress to win three Best Actress Academy Awards. "If only I would have won for [*Baby*] *Jane*," Bette lamented in February 1989. "I would have been the first. I would have beaten Ms. Hepburn. But she won the race." Still, there was no one that Bette would rather have lost to.

Born in 1907, Katharine Hepburn made her picture debut in *A Bill of Divorcement* (1932). Her success in that picture was followed promptly by *Christopher Strong* (1933) and *Morning Glory* (Best Actress Oscar winner, 1933). Her subsequent pictures include *Little Women* (1933), *Sylvia Scarlett*

(1935), *Stage Door* (1937), *Bringing Up Baby* (1938), *Holiday* (1938), *The Philadelphia Story* (Best Actress Oscar nomination, 1940), *Woman of the Year* (Best Actress Oscar nomination, 1942), *State of the Union* (1948), *Adam's Rib* (1949), *The African Queen* (Best Actress Oscar nomination, 1951), *Pat and Mike* (1952), *Summertime* (Best Actress Oscar nomination, 1955), *The Rainmaker* (Best Actress Oscar nomination, 1956), *Suddenly, Last Summer* (Best Actress Oscar nomination, 1959), *Long Day's Journey into Night* (Best Actress Oscar nomination—which pitted her against Bette, up for *Baby Jane*—1962), *Guess Who's Coming to Dinner?* (Best Actress Oscar winner, 1967), *The Lion in Winter* (Best Actress Oscar winner, in a tie, 1968), *The Madwoman of Chaillot* (1969), *Rooster Cogburn* (1975), *On Golden Pond* (Best Actress Oscar winner, 1981), and *The Ultimate Solution of Grace Quigley* (1984).

CHARLTON HESTON

Bette was not particularly fond of Charlton Heston, and she detested his politics. According to B. D. Hyman's book *My Mother's Keeper*, Bette regarded Heston as a "lousy" actor and a "pompous ass." Still, she delighted in the sight of Heston sipping wine from her slipper, as he did in homage to her at an industry function in 1987.

GENE HIBBS

A protégé of Perc Westmore, makeup artist Gene Hibbs was introduced to Bette by publicist Rupert Allan circa 1963. For many years thereafter, Hibbs was employed by Bette as her personal makeup man, specializing in "straps," a nonsurgical and temporary form of face-lift that Bette was particularly pleased with. His film credits include *Dead Ringer* (1964), *The Empty Canvas* (1964), and *Hush . . . Hush, Sweet Charlotte* (1964). His television credits include a 1970 episode of "It Takes a Thief" in which Bette guest-starred and "Scream, Pretty Peggy," a 1973 made-for-television movie.

JUDY HOLLIDAY

It was not veteran Gloria Swanson (*Sunset Boulevard*) who stole the 1950 Best Actress Oscar from Bette Davis (for *All About Eve*) as some predicted. It was relative newcomer Judy Holliday who stole not only votes but hearts as well with her performance as Billie Dawn in *Born Yesterday*.

Judy Holliday (Judith Tuvim, 1922–1965) first garnered acclaim with the 1949 picture *Adam's Rib*. Following her success with *Born Yesterday*, her career took a tailspin with lesser, uneven pictures including *It Should Happen to You* (1953), *The Solid Gold Cadillac* (1956), and *Bells Are Ringing* (1960).

HOLLYWOOD, CALIFORNIA

"Look out for yourself—or they'll pee on your grave."
Louis B. Mayer to Mervyn LeRoy on Hollywood

"From the time I arrived they treated me like a poor cousin. They treat you according to your salary scale."

Bette Davis on Hollywood

From the time she arrived in Hollywood via train with her mother, Ruthie, on one arm and her dog, Boojum, in the other, Bette loathed the town. In fact for several years she clung fervently to her vow that she would never own anything in Hollywood that she couldn't pack in a suitcase bound for New England. Even as late as 1946, during the making of *Deception*, Bette was still telling reporters, "My *real* home is Butternut [her home in New Hampshire]. I only work in Hollywood." Perhaps it had something to do with the fact that her arrival on December 13, 1930, was met without fanfare. In fact the Universal Pictures representative who was sent to meet her at the station failed to recognize her. She didn't *look* like an actress, he would later explain in embarrassment. Four years later everyone in Hollywood would know her face and her name.

Despite her discontent, Bette played the Hollywood publicity game, claiming love for her new home in studio-arranged press interviews. She enthused about the plethora of greenery, the blossoming of flowers, the sunshine. She was, after all, used to (and privately longed for) New England winters. "I thought Hollywood was a little town," she said coyly to one reporter, "like Universal City. I like the gaiety everywhere. I like the picturesque informality on the streets. If you appeared in Boston or New York in golf trousers without a hat, the people would be quite shocked! Oh yes, and I like premieres!"

Bette's first rented home in Hollywood was on Alta Loma Terrace in the Hollywood Hills, not far from the Hollywood Bowl. From there she and her mother moved to several other Hollywood-area homes until Bette's 1932 marriage to Ham Nelson. The three of them continued to move in and out of various rented homes until 1935, when they settled into a modest home at 5346 Franklin Avenue in Hollywood. They lived there for several years, until Bette hit it big with *Jezebel* in 1938, at which time they made the customary move to Beverly Hills. Still, it would be several years before Bette would break down and buy a house in the Hollywood area.

Packed suitcase or not, it was not until 1952, after being more or less rejected by the Hollywood upper echelons, that Bette, then Mrs. Gary Merrill, made an unequivocal move back to New England. Upon one of her occasional work visits back to the West Coast, Bette chastised the town and the industry that spawned her. "Hollywood," she announced, "has changed completely. Now it's fear-ridden and unhappy. Hell, they don't even have *stars* there anymore. They have businessmen, all owning land or cattle or their own production companies. When I see people like Burt Lancaster surrounded by lawyers and accountants I want to scream."

Lancaster was not the only one pierced by her barbs. "Television," she groused in 1960, "should have taught this industry how to make something good cheaply. But it didn't. Imagine," she huffed, "taking a whole year to make a movie as Kirk Douglas has with *Spartacus* and Marlon Brando has with *One-Eyed Jacks*. I never heard of such a thing! It's sinful. It's difficult enough just to act without actors taking on the mantles of producers, directors and writers. It has made the directors like little slave boys. When I was working here we made *Jezebel* in six weeks, *Dark Victory* in four. And we got quality. We worked. We prepared. We knew ahead of time what we were doing." Nor were mere moguls spared her wrath; "Hollywood is into its third generation of the same bosses. This doesn't work. They're too tired, too rich and too old. They don't care anymore."

Certainly Bette was deeply hurt by what she perceived to be Hollywood's rejection of her. When she couldn't get work in Hollywood pictures, Gary Merrill, among others, encouraged her to accept work in European films. Bette balked. "I am not going to Europe to make some shitty, little picture," she said with her precise diction. "I, am, a, *star*. I will return to Hollywood when I have a story that pleases me. I will make it on my own terms and in my own good time . . . and, I, do, not, want, to, hear, another, word, about, it."

In 1961, following the demise of her marriage to Merrill, Bette returned to the Hollywood area in search of work. While making *What Ever Happened to Baby Jane?* in 1962, the former top box office attraction told a reporter, "Today, Hollywood is really an all-king kingdom. Most of the queens are gone. Why, in the latest box-office poll, only one actress was listed among the top ten and [she] was in ninth place. It makes one wonder if some of the loss in the popularity of filmgoing might not be attributed to the failure of studios to develop new actresses. I'm glad I collected all the baubles and trinkets of stardom when I did. The newcomers aren't finding it easy."

In 1965, after accepting that her *Baby Jane*-propelled comeback was to be short-lived, Bette returned to her beloved New England, where she would remain for many years. In 1977, attempting yet another comeback in pictures, Bette returned to live in the Hollywood area, where she would remain until her death in 1989.

In her later years Bette reminisced and, despite her struggles with it at the time, bemoaned the loss of the "studio system" of the thirties and forties. This is somewhat ironic, of course, since she was one of the stars who helped to precipitate its demise. Nonetheless, she was fond of recalling how the studio system would allow a "player," as they were then called, constant and repeated exposure in five or six films a year. Not only did this, Bette pointed out, give a player the opportunity to develop his craft; it also gave an audience ample opportunity to discover him. And if that alone didn't do it, the massive studio publicity machinery was there in full force.

In the old days, Bette would explain, actors had "continuity" to their careers. In the 1980s it was not infrequent for a top star to go three or more years without making a movie. Back then that would have been considered professional suicide for a star. Back then, she would lament, scripts were also written for actors. "Today," Bette would say, "they just cast them." She was also appalled at the salaries actors commanded in the eighties and the astronomical budgets that were allotted by the studios. Stars, Bette would say with dripping sarcasm, were ruining the industry by demanding salaries that could have financed an entire picture. Finally, she bemoaned the loss of the old studio moguls, the old Jack Warners, who had once been her nemesis. They, Bette would say in chastising contemporary studio heads who hem and haw about backing a picture, at least had the guts to take chances and the conviction to make the movies they wanted to make.

> "Hollywood's trial by suspense. On the stage, you can go after parts. You can force the hand of Providence a bit. But here, you must wait. You can't hope too much for a role—no matter how much you want it—and you must keep up your morale. It is an ordeal to break into pictures after you've already made a name on the stage. I can walk into any New York agent's office and they know me. Here, I'm right back where I was three years ago, getting my first foothold. But if you can stand the discipline of waiting, and you have what the public wants. . . ."
>
> *Bette Davis, 1931*

THE HOLLYWOOD CANTEEN

Even considering her impressive body of film work, there are those who regard the foundation of the Hollywood Canteen, an entertainment haven for men serving in World War II, as Bette Davis's most impressive achievement.

The canteen was actually the inspiration of John Garfield, who envisioned it as a West Coast version of Jane Cowl's Stage Door Canteen in New York City. Garfield took the idea to Bette while the two were lunching in the Warner Brothers dining room. To her credit Bette, then shooting the antifascist *Watch on the Rhine*, instantly recognized it as a worthwhile venture and proceeded to throw her vast energy and resources behind it.

Located at 1451 Cahuenga Boulevard in a former stable in Hollywood (which was converted with the compliments of the motion picture carpenters' union), the Hollywood Canteen opened its doors on October 3, 1942. Legend has it that, on opening night, the place was so jammed that Bette, elegantly gowned and coiffed, had to climb the back fence and enter through a window to get in. On that night other Hollywood stars paid $50 each for a seat in the bleachers. A sign at the entrance read: "Through these portals pass the most beautiful uniforms in the world."

Bette was made the canteen's chairman of the board of trustees, the president, and a member of the finance committee; John Garfield was the second vice president; and Mervyn LeRoy was the third vice president. Kay Kyser provided the house orchestra, and Mrs. John Ford supervised the kitchen under the auspices of Chef Milani. Jules Stein headed the highly successful finance committee, which obtained initial funding from the premiere and postscreening party of Columbia's *Talk of the Town*, to which guests were charged $25 a couple. Later, massive amounts were accrued from the Warner Brothers pictures *Thank Your Lucky Stars* (1943; from which the performers donated their salaries, including $50,000 from Bette) and *Hollywood Canteen* (1944).

Over the next three years the canteen reportedly hosted more than two million servicemen. Every night, Monday through Saturday, 7:00 P.M. to midnight, two shifts of servicemen were granted entry. Bette and Garfield enlisted the support of 3,500 volunteer dance hostesses, the 42 unions and guilds that comprised the motion picture industry (the musicians' union, most notably), and the services of some of the top stars of the day.

Hormones raged and romances ignited, and the starry-eyed servicemen rubbed shoulders (and sometimes other anatomical parts) with the visiting glitterati. Sometimes the latter stuck with their own kind (Betty Grable was romanced at the canteen by orchestra leader Harry James, Hedy Lamarr by John Loder, and so forth). Most often the celebrities simply graced the room with their presence. One of the outstanding star appearances was made by Marlene Dietrich, who showed up one night and thrilled the crowd with her costume of gold body paint. On other occasions she volunteered her help in the kitchen. Bing Crosby provided another highlight. Accompanied by his four sons, Crosby spent an entire Christmas Eve singing carols to the homesick servicemen.

On any night in which she was unable to obtain a star, Bette herself entertained the men at the canteen because, as she later explained, "there *had* to be a star there every night." Once Bette had Perc Westmore, Warner's cosmetic master, make her up as Groucho Marx, complete with mustache, heavy eyebrows, glasses, and a cigar. On other nights Bette would be slapped in the face with a pie, much to the delight of the servicemen, who derived pleasure from seeing the serious dramatic actress taken down a notch or two. Usually, though, she just talked and/or danced with the men.

At the end of the war, on November 22, 1945, the Hollywood Canteen closed its doors with a celebration. Bette hosted the party, Bob Hope emceed, and Ingrid Bergman performed a skit with Jack Benny. Dinah Shore, Jimmy Stewart, and Hedy Lamarr also entertained on that final night.

Following Bette's death nearly 45 years later, Charlie Leonard of Danville, California, wrote to the "Letters" section of *Time* magazine (November 13, 1989). It was a eulogy Bette would have been proud of:

> The media may have been fooled by Bette Davis but I wasn't. In 1944, during World War II, Miss Davis met five 17-year-old U.S. Marines at the Hollywood Canteen. She took us in hand, sat at our table, served us and never stopped smiling, chatting and caring. "Majestic arrogance"? Hogwash! She was the most beautiful and charming person I have ever met.

HOLLYWOOD CANTEEN ★★

Warner Brothers
1944   123 minutes   bw
Directed by: Delmer Daves
Produced by: Alex Gottlieb
Screenplay by: Delmer Daves
Cinematography by: Bert Glennon
Cast: Joan Leslie, Robert Hutton, Janis Paige, Dane Clark, Richard Erdman, James Flavin, Joan Winfield, Jonathan Hale, Rudolph Friml, Jr., Bill Manning, Larry Thompson, Mell Schubert, Walden Boyle, Steve Richards

With guest stars: The Andrews Sisters, Jack Benny, Joe E. Brown, Eddie Cantor, Kitty Carlisle, Jack Carson, Joan Crawford, Helmut Dantine, Bette Davis, Faye Emerson, Victor Francen, John Garfield, Sydney Greenstreet, Alan Hale, Paul Henreid, Andrea King, Peter Lorre, Ida Lupino, Irene Manning, Nora Martin, Joan McCracken, Dolores Moran, Dennis Morgan, Eleanor Parker, William Prince, Joyce Reynolds, John Ridgely, Roy Rogers and Trigger, S. Z. Sakall, Alexis Smith, Zachary Scott, Barbara Stanwyck, Craig Stevens, Joseph Szigeti, Donald Woods, Jane Wyman, and Tommy Dorsey and His Band, et al.

Warner Brothers ended up paying a whopping $250,000 to the Bette Davis–formed armed services charity, the Hollywood Canteen, for the movie rights to this picture. Based on a true incident, the film tells the story of the one millionth serviceman to visit the Hollywood Canteen, which opened its doors to servicemen during World War II. A September 17, 1943, press account, which inspired the film, rather crudely reported that "three girls last night did what the Japs in New Guinea couldn't do. They made Sergeant Carl W. Bell surrender—and like it."

To replicate the real canteen, Warners went after—and got—an all-star cast. There was some controversy, however. A dispute between Warners and the Screen Actors Guild nearly halted the production. SAG charged that Warners had tried to cut costs on the film by bargaining with the actors to lower their usual rates out of patriotism. Warners filed a suit against SAG for allegedly attempting to sabotage the production. The case was eventually settled out of court. Still, many stars were prevented from appearing in the picture because of SAG regulations. "It was an unfortunate situation," Bette lamented at the time, "since so many of the top stars of Hollywood help make the Canteen a success. Girls like Hedy Lamarr, who is there every week, surely should be in any film done around the place. I'm very sorry they can't be [in the picture]."

Bette started shooting her segments for the picture on June 5, 1944. She finished on June 15, less than two weeks before segueing into *The Corn Is Green*.

HOLLYWOOD HOTEL

In a letter dated July 26, 1937, Bette wrote of her discontent to Jack Warner: "I have worked very hard to become known as a dramatic actress. . . . If the two girls in *Hollywood Hotel* were written well, I could see some point to your request, but one girl (Beatrice) is ridiculous, in that there is no living actress such a fool, and the waitress almost entirely spoils the plot—a dull person. . . . you know that Mr. Berkeley will want me to do some kind of a musical number in the Hollywood Bowl sequence, and I could not even attempt it. This fact will annoy him, and rightfully so. You need a girl trained for this kind of work."

Hollywood Hotel, directed by Busby Berkeley, proceeded without Bette. The picture starred Dick Powell, Rosemary Lane, Lola Lane, and Ted Healy. Featured in a bit part as a radio announcer was Ronald Reagan.

HOLLYWOOD INDEPENDENT CITIZENS COMMITTEE OF THE ARTS, SCIENCES, AND PROFESSIONS

Formerly known as the Hollywood Democratic Committee, this political action committee was regarded by the FBI as "a communist front." Bette was not only a member of the organization but was elected vice chairman on June 7, 1945.

"THE HOLLYWOOD PALACE"

Popular ABC-TV variety series that Bette guest-hosted on February 20, 1965. Bette opened the show by singing a song called "Single." She then appeared with Bert Lahr in "Jealousy," a sketch from her 1952 Broadway revue *Two's Company*. Also appearing on the show were singer Julius LaRosa and comic Jan Murray. Humorously, when announcing the guest host for the following week, Bette said, "Our *horse* next week is Roy Rogers."

THE HOLLYWOOD WOMEN'S PRESS CLUB

In September 1962 Bette made an appearance at a meeting for the Hollywood Women's Press Club, held at the Beverly Hills Hotel. Having just completed *What Ever Happened to Baby Jane?* (but, of course, unaware of its eventual success), she addressed the group: "As to the present, I am no longer a defeated woman. I again have a goal. I again intend to fight to be once more a part of the motion picture industry, in my opinion the greatest medium for the actor. I am hoping for a chance to be a contributor once more; I feel, quite immodestly, I have been in the past. . . . I may fail in my attempts to regain my place in the sun—but I do ask for the chance to prove whether I can or can't."

HOMES

The following is a selective chronological list of the many homes in which Bette Davis lived:

The Childhood Homes (1908-1928)

Address	City/State
22 Chester Street	Lowell, MA
Chestnut Street	Lower Belvedere, MA
Cambridge Street	Winchester, MA
Washington Street	Newton, MA
Crestalban [Boarding] School	Berkshire Hills, MA
West 144th St. and Broadway	New York, NY
N/A	East Orange, NJ
Lewis Terrace	Newton, MA
Cushing Academy [boarding school]	Ashburnham, MA
N/A	Peterborough, NH
Perkins Cove	Ogunquit, ME
Cabot Street	Newton, MA
N/A	Norwalk, CT

The Aspiring New York Actress Homes (1928-1930)

Address	City/State
Robert Milton–John Murray Anderson School of the Theatre boardinghouse on E. 58th St.	New York, NY
N/A	Rochester, NY
8th St. apt.	New York, NY
E. 53rd St. apt.	New York, NY
50th Street apt. between 5th and 6th Ave.	New York, NY

The Hollywood Starlet Homes

Address	City/State	Years
6655 Alta Loma Terrace	Hollywood, CA	1930–1931
2639 N. Canyon Dr.	Beverly Hills, CA	1932
N/A	Toluca Lake, CA	1932
N/A	Zuma Beach, CA	1932
1217 Horn Ave.	West Hollywood, CA	1932–1933
1414 N. Havenhurst Dr.	West Hollywood, CA	1933
1717 San Vicente Blvd.	Los Angeles, CA	1934
906 N. Beverly Dr.	Beverly Hills, CA	1934
5346 Franklin Ave.	Hollywood, CA	1934–1938

The Homes Befitting a Star

Address	City/State	Years
1700 Coldwater Canyon	Beverly Hills, CA	1938
612 N. Rodeo Dr.	Beverly Hills, CA	1938
301 N. Rockingham Rd.	Brentwood, CA	1939
9965 Beverly Grove Dr.	Beverly Hills, CA	1940
*1705 Rancho Ave. "Riverbottom"	Glendale, CA	1940–1945
"Butternut"	Franconia, NH	1941–1957
2739 Laurel Canyon Blvd. (while "Riverbottom" underwent renovations)	Los Angeles, CA	1942
N/A	Brentwood, CA	1945
671 Sleepy Hollow Ln.	Laguna Beach, CA	1945
1991 Ocean Way	Laguna Beach, CA	1946–1952
N/A	Toluca Lake, CA	1949
N/A	Greens Farms, CT	1950
N/A	Malibu, CA	1950
1757 Camino Palmero	Hollywood, CA	1951–1952
Beekman Place penthouse apt.	New York, NY	1952–1953
Homewood Inn	Yarmouth, ME	1953
"Sanborn House"	Windham, ME	1953
"Witch-Way"	Cape Elizabeth, ME	1953–1960
641 N. Bundy Dr.	Brentwood, CA	1957
Emerald Bay Beach Club	Laguna Beach, CA	1957
Hanover Drive	Beverly Hills, CA	1958–59

---

*first home purchased by Bette

N/A	Pacific Palisades, CA	1960
E. 78th St. town house	New York, NY	1960–61
9515 Heather Rd.	Beverly Hills, CA	1962
1100 Stone Canyon Rd. "Honeysuckle Hill"	Bel Air, CA	1962–65
One Crooked Mile "Twin Bridges"	Westport, CT	1965–73
78 River Rd. "My Bailiwick"	Weston, CT	1973–77
1416 N. Havenhurst Dr.	West Hollywood, CA	1977–89

HOMOSEXUALITY

Rumors aside, Bette was anything *but* homosexual or bisexual. In fact she harbored ambivalent feelings about the subject of homosexuality itself and sometimes professed that she didn't understand how anyone could want to be intimate with a person of the same sex. It baffled her. She refused to publicly endorse or support gay causes, and in private life she would sometimes make flippant antigay remarks.

On the other hand, Bette certainly believed in equal rights for all people, regardless of their age, race, religion, or sexual orientation. She was also well aware that a good deal of her enduring popularity came from the gay community. "A more appreciative, artistic group of people for the arts does not exist," Bette was once quoted as saying. "Conceited as it may sound, a great deal of it has to do with their approval of my work. They are knowledgeable and loving of the arts. They make the average male look stupid."

BOB HOPE

Bob Hope and Bette Davis, legends both, never particularly liked one another, despite their shared interest in the war effort. Although the two never appeared together on screen, they did appear together at the Hollywood Canteen and also performed together in a radio play for the "Screen Actors Guild Theatre."

In 1983 Hope made an appearance at the Army Ball at which the Department of Defense honored Bette with the Distinguished Civilian Service Medal for her work 40 years before with the Hollywood Canteen. It was Bette's impression that night that Hope, who was seated at her table, was perturbed by the proceedings. "He did not seem to like it very much," Bette would later say, "that this entire superb evening was all in *my* honor."

Bette on Miriam: "The most thorough-going bitch I've ever worked with."

MIRIAM HOPKINS

Miriam Hopkins was a star player in and the undisputed belle of George Cukor's repertory company in Rochester, New York, circa 1928–1929. At the time, Bette, a struggling and soon-to-be-fired ingenue, wrote in her scrapbook that Miriam was "very good-looking" and "nice to everyone." Hopkins starred in the company's play *Excess Baggage*, among others.

When Warner Brothers purchased the film rights to *Jezebel*, Miriam, who was part owner of the play, signed a waiver dated February 26, 1937, relinquishing her rights. It was her understanding that doing so would allow her to star as Julie Marsden in the picture. However, Bette Davis was cast instead and was subsequently awarded the Best Actress Oscar, while Miriam seethed from the sidelines.

On the first day of shooting *The Old Maid* in March 1939, Miriam showed up on the set, to Bette's horror, wearing an exact replica of the famous gown Bette had worn in *Jezebel*. Words were exchanged, and although the two actresses retreated to their corners, Miriam never let Bette forget that *Jezebel* should have been hers.

During the shooting of *The Old Maid*, when Bette had a particularly difficult speech to deliver, Miriam was known to break in at the most inappropriate moment with something like "Oh, I'm so sorry. One of my buttons came unbuttoned." Bette would of course have to start her speech over from the beginning. She would then accuse Miriam of trying to sabotage her performance. She also claimed that in the scenes calling for the two characters to age Miriam secretly started to apply false eyelashes and makeup to make her appear younger and more attractive than Bette.

When asked, years later, about her strategy in dealing with this particular costar, Bette related, "Miriam was a wonderful actress, but a bitch, the most thorough-going bitch I've ever worked with. . . . I never blew up at her because if you let her get to you, you'd be the loser. . . . But I'd go home and just scream my head off afterward."

The tension escalated on the set of *The Old Maid* and culminated on the day that Bette was to deliver a scripted slap across Miriam's face. On the day of the shoot the set was crammed with spectators who practically salivated in anticipation. Then, when the cameras were set to roll, Bette whacked Miriam on cue. Bette later enthused, "I got in a perfectly timed swat. I can only report that it was an extremely pleasant experience. She spent the rest of the morning weeping just beyond camera range in what I assume was one last attempt to disconcert me."

Bette took another whack at Hopkins by having an affair with her recently estranged husband, director Anatole Litvak, during the making of *All This, and Heaven Too* (1940). Bette never acknowledged that the affair was at least partially provoked by her dislike for Miriam, an effort to make her jealous, but that is likely the case, given that Bette later said that she was not all that fond of Litvak and their affair was brief.

Director Vincent Sherman braved reuniting the two actresses (after the considerable success of *The Old Maid*) in the 1943 picture *Old Acquaintance*. When asked what it had been like to direct the two of them, Sherman quipped, "I didn't direct them. I refereed!"

Shortly before her death in 1989 Bette was asked if time had softened her recollections about and impression of Miriam. Bette answered succinctly, "A total disaster. A bitch. Impossible to get along with."

Miriam Hopkins (1902–1972) made her film debut in 1930 with *Fast and Loose*. Her subsequent pictures include *Dr. Jekyll and Mr. Hyde* (1932), *Trouble in Paradise* (1932), *Becky Sharp* (Best Actress Oscar nomination—she lost to Bette Davis, 1935), *These Three* (1936), *Lady with Red Hair* (1941), *The Heiress* (1949), *Carrie* (1952), *The Children's Hour* (1961), and *The Chase* (1966).

HEDDA HOPPER

Bette Davis is Hollywood's problem child. There's no doubt about it, she'll have to have another Academy Award for her performance in *Dark Victory*, making it three straight. I've never seen anything like it on any screen. She's topped everything she's ever attempted.

Hedda Hopper, March 13, 1939

In the days when hatted female columnists stalked the land of Hollywood and issued dicta from the keys of their typewriters, no hat stood taller than the one worn by Elda Furry, aka Hedda Hopper (1890–1966). Virtually every studio executive, producer, and actor in Hollywood courted Queen Hedda's favor by smooching her royal (and substantial) rump. Bette, who outqueened just about anybody, had a love-hate relationship with Hedda.

One of Hopper's biggest scoops occurred after the birth of Bette's daughter, B.D., in May 1947. Recuperating, Bette was holed up in her Laguna Beach home and was refusing all requests for interviews. Undaunted, Hedda drove up to Bette's house and marched up to the door. She reportedly suspected that Bette's baby daughter had actually been adopted and was determined to discover the truth for herself. Hedda found a startled Bette lying out by the pool. Privately seething at the intrusion, Bette smiled sweetly and granted Hopper an exclusive interview, much to the wrath of Hopper's rival, Louella Parsons. The following week Louella cattily wrote in *her* column that "Since Bette Davis has had so many unwelcome visitors, she has had to have her gate padlocked."

Shortly thereafter, Hedda turned on Bette, publicly attacking her in her column. In her March 27, 1948, column Hedda blasted Bette's performance in *Winter Meeting*—allegedly without having even seen the picture. The following year she trashed Bette's performance in *Beyond the Forest*. Her review was so scathing that she practically called for Bette's resignation from the acting profession. "If Bette had deliberately set out to wreck her career," Hopper wrote, "she couldn't have picked a more appropriate vehicle."

Hedda tried to make amends the following year after the triumphant success of *All About Eve*. "Hollywood wondered," Hedda wrote, "was Bette Davis through? The answer is that a girl like Bette is never through until the last gong has sounded. She's a battler from the word 'go.'. . . For my money, her performance in *All About Eve* topped anything she ever did, including the two pictures that brought her Oscars. To a brilliantly conceived and written part she gave everything that any director could desire. If the job doesn't get her a third Academy Award, I'll miss my guess."

Prior to finding her niche as a columnist, Hedda Hopper worked in Hollywood as an actress. She also made a few postcolumnist screen appearances. Her films include *Don Juan* (1926), *Wings* (1927), *The Man Who Played God* (in which Bette made her Warners debut, 1932), *Alice Adams* (1935), *The Women* (1939), *Sunset Boulevard* (1950), and *The Oscar* (1966).

"HOTEL"

Much was made of Aaron Spelling's having cajoled Bette Davis to star in his new ABC television series "Hotel," which was inspired by Arthur Hailey's bestselling novel of the same name. However, after appearing in the show's pilot and premiere, which aired on September 21, 1983, Bette walked out on the show.

Actually, she had undergone a mastectomy and suffered a stroke and was expected to return when physically able. So Spelling tried to accommodate her by sending her character, Laura Trent, on an extended trip and having the St. Gregory Hotel (actually, San Francisco's Fairmount Hotel) managed in the meantime by Trent's sister-in-law, Victoria Cabot, played by none other than Anne Baxter, Margo Channing's lady-in-waiting in the 1950 picture *All About Eve*.

Spelling continued to send Bette future scripts of the show, hoping to rekindle her interest. Bette, however, denounced the development of the show and quite openly and sarcastically dismissed it as "Brothel." Still, the show proved to be a considerable hit, and Bette did give some thought to returning to it. "If I do bring Miss Trent back," she warned a reporter, "what I'd really like to do is fire everyone in the hotel."

"To this day," Bette's daughter, B. D. Hyman, related to reporter George Christy in 1985, "I cringe thinking that she turned down $100,000 a day to appear in Aaron Spelling's 'Hotel.' . . . Aaron was willing to accommodate her in the event she became tired. Rather than have her work one full day, he was willing to have her work two half days. The role was tailor-made for her, and I did everything but physically shake her, telling her he was giving her the movie-star treatment in the television world, which is rare, and that it was an elegant part in a classy show."

Bette never did return to the show, and it ran successfully through 1988. Anne Baxter died during the 1985–1986 season, and management of the hotel was taken over by Peter McDermott, played by James Brolin. Other "Hotel" cast members included, over the years, Connie Sellecca, Nathan Cook, Shari Belafonte-Harper, Shea Farrell, Michael Spound, Heidi Bohay, Michael Yama, Harry George Phillips, Efrem Zimbalist, Jr., Michelle Phillips, Valerie Landsburg, Susan Walters, and Ty Miller.

> "You know, my illness was fortunate in one area. At the time, I had a four-year contract to star on 'Hotel.' . . . I've never seen so many people getting in and out of bed in my life."
>
> *Bette Davis, 1987*

HOUSEWIFE ★★

Warner Brothers
1934   69 minutes   bw
Directed by: Alfred E. Green
Produced by: Robert Lord
Screenplay by: Manuel Seff and Lillie Hayward, based on an original story by Robert Lord and Lillie Hayward
Cinematography by: William Rees
Cast: George Brent, Bette Davis, Ann Dvorak, John Halliday, Ruth Donnelly, Hobart Cavanaugh, Robert Barrat, Joseph Cawthorn, Phil Regan, Willard Robertson, Ronald Cosbey, Leila Bennett, William B. Davidson, John Hale

Immediately after completing *Of Human Bondage* at RKO, Bette was summoned back to Warner to make this nondescript drama in which she plays Patricia Berkeley, an amorous businesswoman who has an affair with a married man.

Bette objected to the part and at first refused to do the picture. It went into production without her on April 11, 1934, and during the course of the following week Bette was eventually pressured to accept the picture.

The film was generally panned on its release and was considered a substantial blow to Bette's career after the reputation she had attained with *Bondage*. Interestingly, when the film went into production, Bette was billed third behind Ann Dvorak and George Brent. By the time of its release, she was promoted to top billing.

Bette resists the amorous charms of Leslie Howard in *It's Love I'm After*.

LESLIE HOWARD

Costar of the pictures *Of Human Bondage* (1934), *The Petrified Forest* (1936; Howard also starred in and coproduced the preceding Broadway version), and *It's Love I'm After* (1937). At the time of the latter Howard released to the press his list of "The Ten Most Intelligent Women in Hollywood." The list cited, in no particular order, Ruth Chatterton, Elissa Landi (author/actress), Georgia Caine (actress), Dorothy Parker, Jane Murfin (screenwriter), Bess Meredyth (screenwriter), Mary McCall, Jr. (screenwriter), Dorothy Arzner (director), Sheila Graham (columnist), and his sometime costar Bette Davis. Despite the mention, Bette was not especially fond of Howard. She was particularly distressed by his blatant womanizing, which was in complete contrast to his gentlemanly persona on screen.

Born Leslie Stainer, Howard (1890–1943) was a British actor of Hungarian descent, perhaps best remembered for his performance as Ashley Wilkes in *Gone With the Wind* (1939). He made his debut in the 1930 picture *Outward Bound*, and his subsequent credits include *Berkeley Square* (Best Actor Oscar nomination, 1932–1933), *The Scarlet Pimpernel* (1935), *Romeo and Juliet* (1936), *Pygmalion* (also codirected, Best Actor Oscar nomination, 1938), *Intermezzo* (1939), and *The First of the Few* (also directed, 1942).

> "Leslie Howard was definitely a great ladies' man. . . . His wife used to say that the only leading lady he hadn't gone to bed with was Bette Davis."
>
> *Bette Davis, 1982*

RON HOWARD

When Bette learned that Ron Howard, television's Opie from "The Andy Griffith Show," was going to direct (and executive-produce) her in "Skyward," a 1980 made-for-television movie, she was skeptical at best. Her fears were allayed, however, as Bette later wrote, when "Mr. Howard went assuredly ahead directing me, which was exactly the right way to handle my disapproval. It would have been fatal to show any fear of me."

Howard, then 27, was not unaware of her discontent. "I think she was a little nervous at first," he allowed, "about taking direction from a kid. In one of the early scenes, I wanted her to do it in a certain way and, in front of the whole crew, she said, 'No, no, no. It won't work. You're wrong. I'll try it, but it won't work!' She tried it and, then, waving her arms, she told the crew, 'Right, right, right. He was absolutely right. That's the way to do it!' When we finished, she thanked me for not being intimidated by her and said how much actors appreciate direction."

Born in 1953, Ron Howard made his feature directorial debut with *Grand Theft Auto* (1977), which has been followed by pictures including *Night Shift* (1982), *Splash* (1984), *Cocoon* (1985), *Backdraft* (1991), and *Far and Away* (1992).

GORDON HUGHES

Hughes directed Bette's broadcasts on the 1958 radio program "Whispering Streets." "Bette is so easy to work with," he told a reporter at the time. "It's a lot of fun to be with her. I have only one complaint—there's not enough time for the two of us to be together. She comes in once every two or three weeks and tapes her part of the shows. As a performer she is remarkable. She is always entirely prepared, knows all the stories and her narration, and never goofs. She does the whole job in about two and a half hours."

HOWARD HUGHES

Walter Winchell sent movie fans into a flurry of speculation when he announced in 1939 that Bette Davis was about to marry a millionaire. Al-

Bringing out her maternal instinct.

though he didn't name him, the man of much money was none other than Howard Hughes, the tall, lanky, uncommunicative aviator and filmmaker. Hughes had met Bette when he sat at her table at the Tailwaggers Ball in Beverly Hills in 1938. She was married at the time to Ham Nelson, though that did not prevent her from embarking on an affair with Hughes.

The adulterous liaison fizzled when Nelson allegedly bugged a sexual encounter between Bette and Hughes and demanded the sum of $70,000 to keep the tapes out of the hands of the press. Some reports allege that Hughes threatened to silence Nelson with the fists of hired thugs. Instead, however, the money was allegedly paid and the affair terminated.

Bette and Hughes reconciled, at least professionally, on the 1951 picture *Payment on Demand*, which Hughes executive-produced.

> "He brought out something in me that no man ever had before. As I look back, it was kind of—well, not quite but almost, a *maternal* instinct."
>
> *Betty Davis on Howard Hughes*

PETE HUNGATE

In a letter to Jack Warner dated July 24, 1939, Bette, providing a glimpse of her character at its best, wrote the following in support of studio technician Pete Hungate:

> I feel I would like to call your attention to an accident which happened upon the *Elizabeth and Essex* set June 23 or thereabouts. An electrician by name Pete Hungate fell from the catwalk, breaking every bone in his body. In fact, he is completely pulverized and is in

the hospital where I understand he is likely to have to remain for the next eighteen months. This unfortunate incident has been haunting me. . . .

I understand he is to receive $25 a week permanently from the Group Insurance and $15 a week for thirteen weeks only from the Warner Bros. Club of which he is a member. His wife, who at one time was a stock girl at MGM and has played several bit parts, is anxious to get to work again in order to save their home, and somehow I feel sure that by laying the case before you, you might make arrangements to have her placed upon the list of permanent stock girls at our Studio?

Warner apparently responded favorably to Bette's plea, because on July 27, 1939, she wrote again to Warner: "Thank you so very much for your kind letter and I really leave with a feeling of happiness knowing that the Hungates will be taken care of."

HUSH . . . HUSH, SWEET CHARLOTTE ★★½

An Associates and Aldrich Production
Released by 20th Century–Fox
1964   133 minutes   bw
Directed by: Robert Aldrich
Produced by: Robert Aldrich
Screenplay by: Henry Farrell and Lukas Heller, from a story by Henry Farrell
Cinematography by: Joseph Biroc
Cast: Bette Davis, Olivia de Havilland, Joseph Cotten, Agnes Moorehead, Cecil Kellaway, Victor Buono, Mary Astor, Wesley Addy, William Campbell, Bruce Dern, Frank Ferguson, George Kennedy, Dave Willock, John Magna, Percy Helton, Kelly Flynn, Michael Petit, Ellen Corby, Helen Kleeb, Marianne Stewart, Mary Henderson, Lillian Randolph, Geraldine West, William Walker, Idell James, Teddy Buckner and His All-Stars

The shooting of *Hush . . . Hush, Sweet Charlotte* had enough drama in itself for a potentially explosive book, but it will be covered here only in summary.

Set from 1927 to 1964, the plot concerns the efforts of spinster Charlotte Hollis, who fights, shotgun in hand, to protect her family mansion from the hands of the government. She has a hard time holding on to her sanity as well, thanks in large part to the plotting provocation of her cousin Miriam, who, in tandem with Drew, the town's middle-aged stud, intends to wrest control of the estate from Charlotte.

It's an inane plot, really, that was intended to stand in the shadows while showcasing the histrionics of Bette Davis (Charlotte) and Joan Crawford (Miriam). Spurred on by the considerable and unexpected success of *What Ever Happened to Baby Jane?* (1962), Robert Aldrich actively searched for a property to reunite his dynamic duo of camp horror. He commissioned

writer Henry Farrell (original author of *Baby Jane*) to create a suitable vehicle. What he delivered was an (allegedly) original story he titled *What Ever Happened to Cousin Charlotte?* Bette, however, was adamantly opposed to the title and even threatened not to do the picture if it was not changed. In fact, when Aldrich initially approached Bette about doing a follow-up to *Baby Jane*, she had three conditions: in an age when movie sequels were not as commonplace as today, she did not want to do a sequel to or a rip-off of *Baby Jane*; it was not to be called *What Ever Happened to Cousin Charlotte?*; and it was *not* to costar Joan Crawford.

Aldrich agreed that the film would not be a sequel per se, and the title was changed at Bette's behest, with a little prodding from legal representatives of Warner Brothers, who also strenuously objected to its use. But he stood firm on the final condition. He wanted Crawford despite the fact that she had campaigned against Bette's bid for a *Baby Jane* Oscar (and thus against the picture itself) and even accepted the Oscar for Anne Bancroft, the actress who won.

Crawford accepted the reteaming without reservation. She asked for a mere $50,000 fee, plus $5,000 in living expenses and 25 percent of the profits. She also demanded top billing, rationalizing that Bette had gotten top billing on *Baby Jane*. In response to Crawford's demands, Bette consented with three conditions. First, she wanted an increase in her fee, from $160,000 to an even $200,000. Second, she would accept second billing *if* an asterisk explained that the positioning was "in alphabetical order." And finally Bette wrested from Aldrich a verbal promise that she would be an unofficial partner in the creative decisions made on the film. Later, during preproduction, when she felt that Aldrich was not delivering his promise of partnership, Bette threatened to walk out. The succeeding weeks would find Aldrich doing a high-wire act not with tigers snapping at his heels but the perhaps more deadly fangs of two fading movie queens.

During preproduction Henry Farrell walked off the picture after an argument with Aldrich and was replaced by Lukas Heller, *Baby Jane's* screenwriter. Production was to start in April; however, at Crawford's request it was postponed until June so that she could attend a sales convention for Pepsi-Cola in Hawaii.

On May 31, 1964, after two weeks of rehearsal, the company traveled via a beat-up old chartered plane that Aldrich got at a discount to Baton Rouge, Louisiana, for 10 days of location shooting. Bette was on the plane; Joan was not. Joan arrived three days later, fresh from her first-class commercial flight and accompanied by an entourage and a trail of luggage. It was not a very promising omen when no one met her at the airport. It seems that someone (her costar, perhaps?) had misinformed production people about her arrival time. To make matters worse, when Joan arrived at the motel she found her room was not ready and she had to wait out in the lobby, tapping her foot and fuming all the while.

With a budget of $1.3 million, the picture went before the cameras on June 1. For Crawford it would be a troubling shoot. She had to wake up early every morning and travel to the designated location, a decaying local mansion that was an hour's drive from the motel. She had to endure the heat (which would not have been a problem if shooting hadn't been postponed to accommodate her schedule), which she combated with her omnipresent glass of Pepsi (laced with vodka). Worse, she had a sense almost from the start that Bette was trying to sabotage her performance (and her well-being for that matter) and that she was an outcast in the company. One night back at the motel Bette hosted a party to which everyone *but* Joan was invited.

Bette also hinted to Joan that she was having an affair with Aldrich. Certainly they were working close enough together to give Joan that impression, and it was no accident that Joan began to doubt her standing in the company.

Finally, and worst of all, Joan realized that, top billing or not, her role was secondary and she was likely to be overshadowed by Bette as she had been in *Baby Jane*. On June 13, while the rest of the company flew back to Los Angeles via chartered plane, Joan plotted aboard a commercial jet. Upon arrival she promptly checked in at Cedars Sinai Hospital, claiming a sudden illness.

For the next few days Aldrich shot around Crawford as much as he could. Meanwhile, Joan remained in her hospital bed, working on the script and expanding her part. "I am bedded with the script," she told the visiting Hedda Hopper. "It will be a much better movie when I'm recovered." Joan, according to her doctors, was sick with a sore throat that later turned into pneumonia.

His hands tied, Aldrich shut down the production on July 2. Shooting resumed on July 20, but not for long. For the next couple of days Joan left the set before noon, claiming she was too weak to work. Actually she was upset that the revisions she had made in the script had not been implemented. That weekend of July 24 and 25, Aldrich hired a private detective to stake out Joan's Hollywood apartment to record her movements. On Saturday she drove her brown Rolls-Royce through Beverly Hills and managed to give the private detective the proverbial slip. She did not return home that evening.

Joan *did* return to work on Monday, July 27, but she left the set before 1:00 P.M. Furious, Aldrich telephoned Joan's lawyer in New York and threatened either to cancel or to recast the picture. The following day Joan showed up on the set and worked for five hours. The day after that she again complained of fatigue and informed Aldrich that her workdays would have to be shortened further. At that point relations between Crawford and Aldrich became so strained that they refused to speak to one another except through her makeup man, Monte Westmore.

Production shut down again from July 29 to August 3. Meanwhile, the insurance company's doctor examined Joan and determined that she was well enough to work. Joan, however, called her own doctor, who had her rushed back to Cedars Sinai via ambulance. She would remain there for the next 30 days.

On August 4 the production was suspended again. Full pay was given to the cast and crew. Back at Cedars, Joan wore her diamonds with her hospital gown and had her meals catered by Chasen's. Director Vincent Sherman, who had previously directed (and romanced) both Bette and Joan, was summoned to her hospital bed. "I sent some flowers to her," Sherman related, "because I thought she was ill. And she called to thank me and said, 'Why don't you come down and see me? I want to talk to you.' So I went down, and that's when she said, 'I'm not really sick. I just want to get out of the part because,' she said, 'Bette has been influencing the director to cut me down, and I just won't stay in it, and this is the only way I can get out of the picture.' Then she locked the door and invited me to come to bed with her. It threw me for a loop."

Aldrich, in counsel with Bette, decided to recast the part. Vivien Leigh, Loretta Young, and Barbara Stanwyck were approached. All three rejected the part. Olivia de Havilland, at Bette's suggestion, was also approached. She too rejected the part but was a little less emphatic than the others. With Bette's encouragement, Aldrich boarded a plane to Paris on August 20 with a mission to convince Olivia to change her mind—which he would, with the lure of $100,000 plus $1,000 per week in expenses.

Still, the production continued to be plagued. A court ordered Bette to postpone work on *Charlotte* until the court had decided whether she had to return to Paramount to shoot an additional scene for *Where Love Has Gone.*

Meanwhile, upon hearing that she had been replaced in the picture, Joan seethed from her hospital bed. Angry not that she had been replaced but that she had not been informed, she told columnist Radie Harris of *The Hollywood Reporter,* "Aldrich knew where to long distance me all over the world, but he made no effort to alert me that he had signed Olivia. He let me hear it for the first time in the radio release—and, frankly, I think it stinks." The *Chicago Tribune* quoted Bette as saying, "The only thing I will say about Miss Crawford is that, when Olivia replaced her in the film, Crawford said, 'I'm glad for Olivia—she needed the part.' Joan issued these daily releases from her oxygen tent!"

Finally, during the third week of September, with all legal matters resolved, *Hush . . . Hush, Sweet Charlotte* resumed production. At one point during the comparatively harmonious shooting Bette turned to Olivia and said, "Dear, I just saw your dressing room. All those flowers—you'd think you just died!" Olivia responded, "No, dear. I'm just getting ready to go to the hospital." "Dear, God, no!" Bette shrieked in mock horror.

On November 22, 1964, the *Charlotte* company finally shut down—this time for good. Bette was pleased with the results and with herself. The picture was not a sequel to *Baby Jane,* it was not titled *What Ever Happened to Cousin Charlotte?,* and Joan Crawford was *not* her costar. Upon its release, the picture received mixed reviews and did only fair box office. As for Crawford, she mysteriously recovered and checked out of the hospital shortly after learning that she was no longer in the picture.

Such are the wicked games that people in Hollywood sometimes play.

JOHN HUSTON

At William Wyler's request, John Huston was assigned to cowrite the 1938 picture *Jezebel.* He later cowrote *Juarez* (1939) and directed Bette in *In This Our Life* (1942). While making the latter picture, Huston irritated Bette by having an affair with her costar, Olivia de Havilland, whom he tended to favor with the better camera angles. Following his work on *In This Our Life,* Huston interrupted his fledgling career as a director to take up duties as a captain with the U.S. Army Signal Corps.

John Huston (1906–1987), son of Walter Huston and father of Anjelica, made his impressive directorial debut with the 1941 picture *The Maltese Falcon.* His subsequent pictures include *The Treasure of the Sierra Madre* (Best Director and Best Screenplay Oscar winners, 1948), *The Asphalt Jungle* (Best Director and Best Screenplay Oscar nominations, 1950), *The African Queen* (Best Director and Best Screenplay Oscar nominations, 1951), *The Misfits* (1961), *The Night of the Iguana* (1964), and *Prizzi's Honor* (Best Director Oscar nomination, 1985).

Huston and Bette never particularly liked one another, something he reaffirmed in 1964 by casting Ava Gardner in *Iguana* in a part that Bette had wanted and originated on Broadway.

Mommie or Daughter Dearest? *That* is the question.

BARBARA DAVIS HYMAN

Bette Davis is going to have a baby! It will be her first child—and she's absolutely thrilled about it. No, she didn't disclose the date, but she did tell me happily: 'I don't care whether it's a boy or a girl. Either one will be perfect!'

Hedda Hopper, Sept. 26, 1946

"Be a fanny-spanking disciplinarian—until your kids are ten—then they'll turn out all right."

Bette Davis, 1962

What was quite possibly the most devastating personal blow in the entire life of Bette was struck by her daughter with the publication of her 1985 book *My Mother's Keeper.*

Named after Bette's sister Bobby but called B.D. to avoid confusion (not to mention the fact that Bette loathed the nickname Bobby), Barbara Davis Sherry was born via cesarean section at the Santa Ana Community Hospital on May 1, 1947. Bette, then 39, carried her baby girl home to their Laguna Beach home on May 6. A custom-designed nursery was constructed on the second floor and was wired for sound so that B.D.'s cries could be heard in any part of the house.

A few days after Bette's return home, she had a surprise visitor in the snooping person of Hedda Hopper. After recovering from the initial shock of Hopper's audacity, Bette consented to an interview and enthused over the joys of motherhood. "I've wanted her ever since I was 21," reflected Bette. "Now that she's actually here in my arms, I can't believe it's true. Hedda, isn't she a beauty? . . . I've wanted Barbara for so many years, I can't tell you. I used to think it was awful I hadn't had her when I was 21. But now I realize how perfect it is to have her now. I could never have enjoyed my baby then as I can now. When I was that age I was struggling so hard to get somewhere. Now I've got the time and the chance to enjoy her."

In 1948, during the making of *June Bride*, progressive mother Bette was asked by a reporter if B.D., then 13 months, would follow in her mother's high-heeled footsteps. Bette replied, with words she may have regretted later, "Barbara will choose her own kind of life. She may become a stenographer, a musician, or a painter like her father, or just a housewife. But whatever she does it will be of her own choosing. . . . She is already showing a remarkably firm inclination to make up her own mind."

And make up her own mind she did.

In 1962, at the age of 15, B.D., always a headstrong girl, marched into a Los Angeles court and demanded that her name be legally changed from Merrill back to Sherry. Two years before, Bette had divorced Gary Merrill, a man B.D. apparently loathed. She would later say of her onetime adoptive father, "I'm convinced he hates everyone," and "I didn't want any legal ties to that man."

B.D. was raised outside Hollywood in the more proper, in Bette's view, environment of New England. Still, B.D. led what many would consider a charmed life: fine schools, a home overlooking the ocean, her own horse. She was introduced to the renowned entertainment and political figures of the day, including President John F. Kennedy. She struck those to whom she was introduced as attractive if a little tall, intelligent, and remarkably well adjusted. Certainly Bette was pleased with her development. In her 1962 autobiography *The Lonely Life*, Bette wrote of her daughter, "She is utterly trustworthy and responsible. She is a young woman of whom I am proud."

In 1963 B.D. accompanied her mother to the Cannes Film Festival. She frequently, in fact, traveled with her mother. Among other trips, B.D., age four, accompanied Bette to London for the location shooting of *Another Man's Poison*; in later years she accompanied Bette to Spain for the location shooting of *John Paul Jones* (1959) and then back to London, as well as on a tour throughout Europe (in Rome she got to watch William Wyler oversee the chariot race in *Ben Hur*), for the location shooting of *The Scapegoat* (1959). The purpose of the trip to Cannes was to promote *What Ever Happened to Baby Jane?*, a picture in which B.D. had a small part. It was not, however, her film debut; she had appeared, at the age of three, in *Payment on Demand* (1951).

On the promotional tour of *Baby Jane* that culminated in their trip to Cannes, Bette and B.D. delighted movie fans and provided fodder for cynics by appearing in a series of U.S. theaters where they would perform a duet of a jazzed-up version of "I've Written a Letter to Daddy," a song from the picture.

At Cannes, Bette arranged for Jeremy Hyman, 29, cousin of Ken Hyman, executive producer of *Baby Jane*, to escort B.D. to a dinner party. What she hadn't planned on, of course, was that the 16-year-old and the 29-year-old would fall in love. Bette never really forgave either of them.

Following their return to Los Angeles from Cannes, Bette and B.D. repacked their bags and headed to Italy for the location shooting of *The Empty Canvas*. En route, they stopped off in London, where B.D. was reunited with Jeremy. Once there, B.D. insisted that she be allowed to remain in London with Jeremy while Bette worked in Italy. Bette refused. B.D. subsequently accompanied Bette to Italy, but soon thereafter she suffered an attack of appendicitis and insisted that her operation be performed back in London. Bette conceded. After finishing *The Empty Canvas*, Bette rejoined B.D. in London, but by then it was too late. Jeremy would propose marriage; B.D., to Bette's horror, would accept.

Bette had taught her daughter well to make her own decisions, and the lessons came back to haunt her. Bette was appalled not only that B.D. intended to marry at such a young age but also that she had chosen as a mate someone who would, in Bette's view, dominate her. The idea of a daughter of Bette Davis, a woman who had conquered studios and moguls, deferring to *any* man was something that Bette could not live with.

Despite her objections, Bette lent her support and money to the impending wedding. She gave the couple an expensive engagement party at the Bel Air Hotel and footed the bill for their wedding ceremony held in a Beverly Hills church. It was a formal wedding, and Bette allowed B.D. to design her own gown (with a veil of handmade lace from Marseilles), which was then made by Stella of I. Magnin, who also provided the gowns for the attending bridesmaids. Bette also hosted the subsequent reception, with a full orchestra, at the posh Beverly Wilshire Hotel.

The day after the wedding B.D. and Jeremy, sans a honeymoon, flew to New York, where Jeremy had a job with his uncle's Seven Arts production company. It's interesting to note that, just prior to their marriage, Jeremy was abruptly transferred from the Seven Arts office in London to its office in New York. It is quite possible that the move came about at Bette's behest. She had, after all, some influence at Seven Arts, the company that had produced *Baby Jane*, and she was reticent about having her young, albeit now married, daughter leave the country.

After living in New York for a year or so, the Hymans moved to Weston, Connecticut. Shortly thereafter, Bette moved from Los Angeles to Westport, Connecticut, to be closer to her daughter. In 1969 B.D. gave birth to her first child, J. Ashley Hyman. According to Bette, Jeremy had her banned from the hospital.

In the late seventies B.D. appeared on television in an interview for "60 Minutes." During the course of the interview B.D. discussed Bette Davis's abilities and accomplishments as a mother: she credited Bette for bringing up her and her brother in a home away from Hollywood, for teaching them responsibility and good manners, for trusting them to pick out their own friends and date whomever they wanted, for allowing them to make their own judgments and hence their own mistakes, for not being vain and not playing the star role at home, for being honest—"She's painfully honest about everything," B.D. stated—and for being, unlike other movie star mothers, *there* for her kids. B.D. enthused that there were no real disadvantages to being the daughter of Bette Davis and that the only thing negative about her mother was her lack of humor. Shortly after the broadcast of the interview, *Woman's Day* named Bette one of five "Mothers of the Year."

When the Hymans, by then living in Pennsylvania, faced financial distress in 1983, Bette presented them with a substantial sum of money. B.D. responded with a letter that Bette reprinted in her book *This 'N That*. It read, in part, "I will never not be indebted to you for helping us through this frightening time and saving our home. I sincerely hope that our boys will look back at their childhoods in Pennsylvania as fondly as I do my childhood in Maine. . . . I love you very much."

In June 1983 Bette suffered, in devastating tandem, a mastectomy and a stroke. It would not be B.D. at her mother's bedside, however, but a young woman named Kathryn Sermak, Bette's paid assistant. She became something of an adopted daughter to Bette, a relationship that may well have impacted the deterioration of Bette's relationship with B.D.

Still, in 1984, celebrating their 20th wedding anniversary, the Hymans spent 10 days with Bette at her condominium in West Hollywood. Bette threw them an anniversary party and got them a room at the Beverly Hills Hotel to commemorate their wedding night. Later that year, when Bette was in New York en route to London to make "Murder with Mirrors," B.D. drove from Pennsylvania to meet with Bette. It may have been the last time mother and daughter ever saw one another.

> "I've often said to my daughter, 'What are *you* going to write about?'
> and she said, 'Nothing' and I say, 'Thank God.' "
> *Bette Davis, upon the publication of* Mommie Dearest, *1979*

Just before completing "Murder with Mirrors" in London, Bette received a telephone call informing her that B.D. had written a *Mommie Dearest*-like book that was about to be published. Bette was at first shocked, then furious, then crushed. Publicly Bette was more guarded. A month before publication of the book she confided to a reporter, ". . . It can't possibly be a *Mommie Dearest* [type of book] since I have never been a *Mommie Dearest* [type of] mother, and B.D., to my knowledge, is not a liar." Later, after the book's publication, Bette described its impact on her by saying, "It was as catastrophic as the stroke. I'm rather proud that I managed it as well as I have," and "That book was not written by the girl I knew."

JEREMY HYMAN

Bette had numerous objections to Jeremy Hyman as her son-in-law. Besides the tender youth of her daughter, she was greatly perturbed by Jeremy's seemingly dominant nature—it matched, after all, her own. What infuriated Bette the most, perhaps, was that B.D. typically acquiesced, or so it seemed to Bette, to Hyman's every wish. Bette Davis was a woman who took orders from no man. She wanted—and indeed expected—her only daughter to be the same and was disappointed that she was not.

One of Bette's earliest reasons for disliking Hyman was provoked by his and B.D.'s wedding ceremonies. Bette planned an elaborate, old-fashioned church wedding for January 4, 1964. Hyman, however, convinced B.D. to get married a few days earlier in a simple civil ceremony to capitalize on the year-end income tax deductions. Bette was livid with Hyman, not only for sabotaging the wedding she had planned and for reducing the ceremony to a calculated financial decision but also for depriving a mother of the full impact of her daughter's wedding day. Furthermore, she was disturbed by Hyman's decision to bypass the traditional rite of a honeymoon; *her* daughter, Bette insisted, deserved a honeymoon; *her* daughter, Bette proclaimed, deserved *better*.

Still, at the reception following the wedding Bette lifted her glass of Dom Perignon and proposed a toast that essentially said she forgave Hyman for taking her beloved daughter away from her. In the succeeding years, however, Bette would not be able to live up to those words. Privately she resented Hyman and hoped that his marriage would end in "I told you so" disaster and that B.D. would come crawling back, pleading for forgiveness.

Such, however, would not be the case. Jeremy and B.D. Hyman have, as of this writing, been married for 29 years. It is quite possible that Bette's problems with Jeremy Hyman and, in extension, the dissolution of her relationship with her daughter were rooted in envy. B.D., after all, attained—and at the age of sixteen—the one single thing that eluded her mother for a lifetime.

I

ILLNESSES

Despite her pretensions of being the ultimate professional, Bette Davis was not beyond dismissing the show business credo "The show must go on." In fact, over the years Bette frequently caused delays and shutdowns of her various film and stage productions with her various illnesses, some of which were genuine, others feigned. The following is a chronological sampling:

☆ Bette missed the final week of performances of the 1929 off Broadway play *The Earth Between* and some performances of Ibsen's *The Lady from the Sea*, because of an outbreak of the measles.

☆ In October 1932, during the shooting of *Parachute Jumper*, Bette suffered an acute attack of appendicitis. Upon completion of the picture she underwent an appendectomy.

☆ During the 1935 shooting of *Dangerous*, Bette was stricken with ptomaine poisoning.

☆ While shooting *The Sisters* in June 1938, a few months after recovering from bronchitis, Bette was stricken with laryngitis.

☆ During the December 1938 shooting of *Juarez* Bette was sick with pleurisy.

☆ During the June 1939 shooting of *The Private Lives of Elizabeth and Essex*, Bette was again stricken with laryngitis.

☆ While shooting *The Little Foxes* (1941), Bette collapsed on the set. She claimed "physical exhaustion," which shut the picture down. Insurance company doctors, however, later determined that she was perfectly healthy and advised her to return to the set. She did.

☆ On April 21, 1941, just prior to doing a radio broadcast at a station on Vine Street in Hollywood, Bette consumed what she thought was a teaspoon of aromatic spirits of ammonia. Unfortunately, however, the spoon contained old-fashioned household ammonia instead, and a physician was rushed to the station.

☆ Bette reported to the set of *The Corn Is Green*, during the summer of 1944, one week late. She claimed to have had laryngitis. She was ill—or claimed to be ill—several more times during the production.

☆ The 1946 picture *A Stolen Life* was shut down for about four weeks due to Bette's illnesses. She suffered from laryngitis and from a facial laceration.

☆ Because of Bette's various health problems, the 1946 picture *Deception* was shut down several times for numerous days. Bette missed approximately 20 days of work.

☆ During shooting of the 1948 picture *Winter Meeting*, Bette's illnesses were frequent and lengthy. Basically she was sick with a mere cold and a case of indigestion. Still, the production had to shut down for over two weeks to accommodate her recovery. It is likely that she was simply perturbed by the development of the production.

☆ On July 6, 1949, during shooting of *Beyond the Forest*, Bette called in sick. When she did not return to work for several days, rumors circulated that she was pregnant or sick with pneumonia. Hedda Hopper reported that she had a case of tick fever. In fact Bette was simply unhappy with Warners and with the film she was making. She reported back to work on July 14.

☆ The 1952–1953 Broadway production *Two's Company* was forced to shut down due to Bette's diagnosed case of osteomyelitis of the jaw. The subsequent operation was conducted on March 16, 1953.

☆ Bette was granted leave from the 1961 Broadway production of *The Night of the Iguana* because of various illnesses, real or imagined.

☆ The 1974 Broadway-bound musical *Miss Moffat* was shut down due to Bette's various illnesses, real or imagined.

☆ In 1983 Bette was diagnosed with breast cancer. Nine days after her mastectomy she suffered a series of strokes.

IN THIS OUR LIFE ★★½

Warner Brothers
1942   101 minutes   bw
Directed by: John Huston
Produced by: Hal B. Wallis, in association with David Lewis
Screenplay by: Howard Koch, from the novel by Ellen Glasgow
Cinematography by: Ernest Haller
Cast: Bette Davis, Olivia de Havilland, George Brent, Dennis Morgan, Charles Coburn, Frank Craven, Billie Burke, Hattie McDaniel, Lee Patrick, Mary Servoss, Ernest Anderson, William B. Davidson, Edward Fielding, John Hamilton, William Forest, Lee Phelps

Following his considerable critical success with *The Maltese Falcon* (1941), his first picture as a director, John Huston curiously agreed to helm the adaptation of the Ellen Glasgow novel *In This Our Life*. He would later admit that the genre, which was then being referred to as "women's pictures," was not to his liking and that the only reason he accepted the project was that it offered him, he thought, the opportunity to venture into "the big time." It was Bryan Foy who counseled Huston and told him, "You don't really rate as a director until you've worked with the stars and show how you make out with them." Huston, then 35 and cocksure, was up to the challenge. "With *In This Our Life*," he later related, "ambition stepped in. It was laid out on a silver platter—the biggest stars in Warner Brothers all together: Bette Davis, Olivia de Havilland, George Brent, Dennis Morgan, Charles Coburn. I thought, 'Oh, boy, I've arrived!' "

Warner Brothers purchased the rights to the novel for $40,000 in an agreement dated March 1941. The plot revolved around the antics of two sisters with boyish names, Stanley and Roy Timberlake. After Roy marries the handsome Peter Kingsmill (Dennis Morgan), Stanley steals him (just to prove that she can) and then drives him to suicide. To its credit, the story *does* break out of the melodramatic doldrums of the day on two counts. First is the rather daring subplot featuring wealthy Uncle William Fitzroy (wonderfully played by Charles Coburn) and his incestuous lust for Stanley. More significant is its presentation of a black man as someone of substance and intelligence, a rare achievement in the Hollywood of the thirties and forties. The script has Stanley blame a fatal hit-and-run car accident, for which she was responsible, on Parry Clay (Ernest Anderson), a family servant who spends his evenings attending law school. Stanley contends that it was Clay and not her who was driving her car at the time of the accident. Naturally, being white and a member of a prominent family, she is believed and he is not, and

Clay is carted off to prison—until the truth is discovered.

According to an August 19, 1941, Warner Brothers casting sheet, Bette Davis was up for both parts of Stanley and Roy. Also up for the part of Stanley were Ida Lupino, Ann Sheridan, Joan Fontaine, Jean Arthur, Barbara Stanwyck, Joan Crawford, Tallulah Bankhead, Rita Hayworth, and, interestingly, Olivia de Havilland. Considered for the part of Roy, which eventually went to de Havilland, were Greer Garson, Rosalind Russell, Loretta Young, Norma Shearer, and Janet Gaynor.

For Bette it was a choice of doing *In This Our Life* or *The Gay Sisters*. In a memo she wrote to Jack Warner she pleaded, "You know I can never *really* be enthusiastic about *Gay Sisters*. . . . *In This Our Life* is such a terrific thing I think it would be a suitable follow-up to *Little Foxes*. Would be so grateful if you would give *The Gay Sisters* to someone else." Warner agreed, and Bette was cast in *In This Our Life* as Stanley ("a regular little Hitler of a girl" as she described the character she was to play).

In another interesting casting development, the studio ran 25 tests of black actresses for the part of Parry Clay's mother. Finally an exasperated Jack Warner wrote a memo to Hal Wallis saying that he should immediately cease testing actresses for the part and sign Hattie McDaniel, "the greatest," in Warner's words, "colored actress in the world."

Making unexpected and uncredited appearances in the film would be, among others, John Huston's father, Walter, as a bartender in the scene in which Stanley waits impatiently for her beau (George Brent). Also, a shadow seen briefly through a glass door was provided by Huston's friend (and star of *The Maltese Falcon*) Humphrey Bogart.

In This Our Life was scheduled to start shooting on October 13, 1941. Production was, however, abruptly postponed when Bette's husband, Arthur Farnsworth, Jr., was hospitalized in Minneapolis. His condition was so grave at one point that doctors advised that Bette drop whatever she was doing and fly to Minneapolis, which she did. For over a week a flurry of telegrams went back and forth from Minneapolis and Warner Brothers Studios in which Bette reported on Farney's condition and Hal Wallis urged her prompt return. Bette, however, refused to give Wallis a date for her return, saying only that she would be back as soon as Farney's condition permitted it. Meanwhile, *In This Our Life* remained on hold.

Bette returned to Los Angeles on October 30 and reported directly to the studio for wardrobe tests. Upon her return Bette engaged in a fight with Wallis over his desire to change the names of Stanley and Roy to more traditional female names. Bette balked, claiming that it would be an affront to the integrity of the book. She enlisted Huston's support in the matter, and the names Stanley and Roy were retained.

Olivia de Havilland, meanwhile, was having problems of her own. She derided the costumes that Orry-Kelly had designed for her, saying that they were not "unusual" enough. Wallis countered by saying that the reason the costumes didn't look right was that Olivia had gained a considerable amount of weight since her wardrobe tests. Furthermore, she was engaged in a highly volatile relationship with the married John Huston, which left her in emotional shambles.

Meanwhile, great efforts were expended to make Bette look young and attractive for the picture. The part, after all, called for a young and spoiled beauty who had a flock of men at her command. Her mouth was painted in a cupid's bow to suggest youth and petulance. Long artificial eyelashes were glued over her own. Her hair was lightened and coiffed with bangs. And she was dressed in soft, feminine costumes. The cosmetic gimmickry would not, however, be sufficient. One of the primary flaws in the film would be the altogether obvious miscasting of Bette Davis as Stanley Timberlake.

Still, we know we're in for an entertaining (if campy) ride when, at the beginning of the picture, Bette as Stanley turns to Roy's husband and coos, "I adore you, Pe-tah!" It was from this film (although she never actually says the line) that Bette Davis impersonators derived the expression, "Pe-tah, Pe-tah, Pe-tah."

With a budget of $643,000, production finally started on November 1, 1941. On opening day John Huston received a note from Hal Wallis that read, "Best of luck. I know you will repeat [the success of *The Maltese Falcon*]."

Typical of her, Bette showed up for the first day of filming, surveyed the set for the Timberlake home, and proceeded, much to the chagrin of the art director, to redecorate. Still, her spirits were generally agreeable early into the production. She put in two weeks of work before calling in sick on November 15. Not to be outdone, upon learning that Bette was not coming in to work, Olivia de Havilland complained of a sudden illness and was excused to go home. Without either star available, the company was dismissed. They both returned to work two days later.

On one day that Bette had off and Olivia was required to work, the scene to be shot had Olivia as Roy expressing exasperation after reading a letter. When it came time to shoot the scene, Olivia opened up the letter and was surprised to find a note scribbled in Bette's handwriting. "Livvie," it began, "while *you* are working today, *I've* been given the day off. It's a beautiful day. Wish you were here. Bette." Upon reading the letter, Olivia registered, without additional motivation, the required exasperation.

During the month of December a pall fell over the production. On December 7, 1941, Pearl Harbor was bombed by the Japanese and the United States entered World War II. Put into perspective, the picture, for Bette, lost much of its meaning and importance. During the month she frequently called in sick, complaining of a variety of illnesses.

Meanwhile, tension escalated on the set. Both Warner and Wallis accused Huston of favoring de Havilland with camera angles and close-ups. Bette, who had earlier befriended Olivia, was by now disturbed with her and infuriated with Huston. She would later reconcile with de Havilland, but not with Huston, with whom she never worked again.

Hal Wallis, meanwhile, openly chastised Bette and what he labeled her "Hepburn manner of speaking" and suggested that Huston was deliberately encouraging Bette to overact. Numerous retakes were called for, and the production fell well behind schedule. Director Irving Rapper was called in to shoot with a second-unit crew. On December 17 Jack Warner issued a memo to Huston reprimanding him for the small amount of footage he was producing. Warner instructed Huston to double his daily output. By this point, however, Huston was frustrated in his relationship with Olivia, had lost all interest in the picture, and had enlisted in the military. Raoul Walsh was called in to shoot the final retakes, and production closed with Bette on January 8, 1942.

Marketing ads had Bette as Stanley proclaiming "Go Ahead! Kiss Me! . . . Forget You're Married to My Sister!" and "I Can Get Anything I Want . . . Even Your Husband!"

In This Our Life was previewed on February 10, 1942. Hal Wallis was disturbed that many of the preview cards commented unfavorably about Bette's appearance, particularly her new hairstyle and cupid-bow lips. The following day Wallis issued a memo to Perc Westmore, the studio's makeup chief: "In the future, before you change anyone's makeup as radically as you did Davis' in this picture, I would like to be informed of the fact so that we can discuss it carefully, make exhaustive tests, and then determine just how far we want to go."

Years later Bette would acknowledge that she had been too old for the part of Stanley Timberlake and that the script itself had been mediocre. In fact she would cite *In This Our Life* when asked about the worst pictures of her career (a decided overstatement, given some of her other debacles). "It was just an unfortunate film," Bette was quoted as saying, "but a brilliant, brilliant book by Ellen Glasgow. I talked to her about it later. She was horrified by the film."

INJURIES

The following is a selective chronological list of injuries that befell Bette Davis over the years:

☆ In February 1932 Bette was injured in a fire that engulfed her car, which was parked outside of her Toluca Lake, California, home. She was dragged from the flames by her sister, Bobby.

☆ On November 22, 1935, Bette slipped on the wet steps of her studio dressing room and suffered a sprained ankle. She was unable to walk on her left foot for a week, complicating the shooting of *The Petrified Forest*.

☆ During the making of *It's Love I'm After* in the spring of 1937, Bette fell six feet from the stage into the orchestra pit. She suffered only minor injuries.

☆ During a July 1937 vacation in Carpinteria, California, Bette was stricken with sunstroke and subsequently bedridden for four weeks.

☆ During the shooting of *Jezebel* in the latter part of 1937, Bette suffered a charley horse on the set and had to be sidelined.

☆ Shooting a stunt for the 1941 picture *The Bride Came C.O.D.*, Bette accidentally (and painfully) landed in a clump of cacti. A doctor was summoned to extract the cactus needles from her rear end.

☆ During a break from shooting *Mr. Skeffington* (1944), Bette, as was her custom, washed her eyes out with a special rinse. Upon emptying the solution into her eye, however, she unleashed a scream. Her makeup man, Perc Westmore, swiftly applied castor oil to the burning eye. A subsequent examination determined that the solution was not eyewash but acetone. It was rumored at the time that someone (any one of Bette's numerous detractors) had tampered with the eyewash in an act of vengeance. Nonetheless, no investigation resulted and the matter was dropped.

☆ While shooting *The Corn Is Green* during the summer of 1944, Bette was injured when a heavy steel cover from an overhead arc light fell and hit her on the head. Fortunately she was wearing a heavy, well-padded wig, which provided some protection and prevented a concussion. Again, there was speculation that the "accident" might have instead been an act of malice.

☆ On May 4, 1946, during the shooting of *Deception*, Bette was involved in a car accident in which her head broke through the windshield. Luckily, her injuries were not serious, and she missed only four days of work.

☆ On June 15, 1949, while shooting *Beyond the Forest* on location in Lake Tahoe, Bette was injured in a scene that called for her to shoot a porcupine. Bette insisted on doing the actual shooting herself. However, when the director called "Action," the gun recoiled and blackened her right eye.

☆ On June 29, 1957, Bette fell down the basement stairs of her rented home in Brentwood, California. She cracked a vertebra and fractured a finger. Claiming that the injuries prevented her from accepting a leading role in the Broadway play *Look Homeward, Angel*, Bette filed an $85,000 lawsuit against the owners of the house and the real estate agents who represented it. In court Bette contended that when the house had been shown to her, the door leading to the basement was described as the door to a closet. The case was finally decided in June 1960. The trial lasted four days, beginning on June 16. Bette entered court wearing a black-and-white checked dress with a black coat. In court, while awaiting the selection of a jury, Bette did some quick public relations work by complying with a barrage of autograph seekers. While signing the autographs, Bette fidgeted with a gold cigarette lighter and entertained the crowd with her impersonations of other people impersonating her. On June 22, after deliberating for five hours, the jury returned with a verdict in Bette's favor. Judge Carlos M. Teran subsequently awarded Bette the sum of $65,700. As the verdict was read, Bette, seated beside her attorney, Raoul Magana, smiled and openly wept. As she departed from the courtroom, Bette repeatedly struck one of her fists into the palm of her other hand and declared at the top of her voice, "*This*, has, been, a great, blow, for jus-tice!"

☆ During the Glasgow, Scotland, shooting of "Madame Sin," a 1972 made-for-television movie, Bette was stung in a vein by a bee, which caused her arm and upper lip to swell.

☆ Following the devastating back-to-back blows of a mastectomy and a stroke in June 1983, Bette fell and broke her hip. For a time it was thought that she would never be able to walk again. After numerous physical therapy sessions, however, Bette relearned to walk, albeit with a noticeable limp.

"IT TAKES A THIEF"

Bette appeared in "A Touch of Magic," a January 1970 episode of the ABC television series "It Takes a Thief." She portrayed an ill and poverty-stricken woman who had been the world's greatest female jewel thief. Her life is revitalized when Alexander Mundy (Robert Wagner) persuades her to join him in one of his capers. The episode was directed by Gerd Oswald and produced by Jack Arnold.

For Bette the program was particularly satisfying for several reasons. Not only did it star her friend Wagner; for the first time in years she was also lavished with treatment befitting a star. Wagner saw to it that Bette had the star dressing room with her name on the door, fresh flowers on her dressing table, and a car at her disposal. Bette never forgot Wagner's generosity, and the two remained friends for many years thereafter.

IT'S LOVE I'M AFTER ★★½
Warner Brothers
1937   90 minutes   bw
Directed by: Archie Mayo
Produced by: Hal B. Wallis, in association with Harry Joe Brown
Screenplay by: Casey Robinson, based on a story by Maurice Hanline
Cinematography by: James Van Trees
Cast: Bette Davis, Leslie Howard, Olivia de Havilland, Patrick Knowles, Eric Blore, George Barbier, Spring Byington, Bonita Granville, E. E. Clive, Veda Ann Borg, Valerie Bergere, Georgia Caine, Sarah Edwards, Lionel Bellmore, Irving Bacon, Thomas Pogue, Grace Fields, Harvey Clark, Ed Mortimer, Thomas Mills

This generally agreeable attempt at madcap comedy evolved almost solely because Leslie Howard, then a star of some stature, informed the powers that be at Warner Brothers that he wanted to make a comedy. "I think this is a good and fairly trivial comedy," wrote writer/producer Robert Lord to studio executive Walter MacEwen in a memo dated December 15, 1936. "It is not at all important, nor at all inspired. Yet it is possible that Mr. Howard might think it great. . . . Just in passing, why does Mr. Howard want to make a comedy? He is not particularly good at comedy and I do not believe that picture audiences would ever accept him as a comedian."

Still, Howard persisted in his desire to make a comedy, and he deemed the Maurice Hanline story "Gentleman After Midnight" to be a suitable vehicle. The plot cast Howard as Basil Underwood, a matinee idol of the American stage whose romantic exploits with his acting partner, Joyce Arden, are more entertaining off the stage than on.

Initially Howard was enthusiastic about casting Gertrude Lawrence as Joyce Arden. Hal Wallis, however, had reservations about the idea. He did not, frankly, think that stage star Lawrence had the looks to make it in the movies. Subsequently Wallis asked director Archie Mayo to meet personally with Lawrence to see what *he* thought. Mayo met with her for lunch and agreed with Howard that she would be good in the picture. Wallis, however, remained unconvinced. He instructed studio executive Steve Trilling to "keep Lawrence in abeyance." For the next several weeks Gertrude Lawrence was

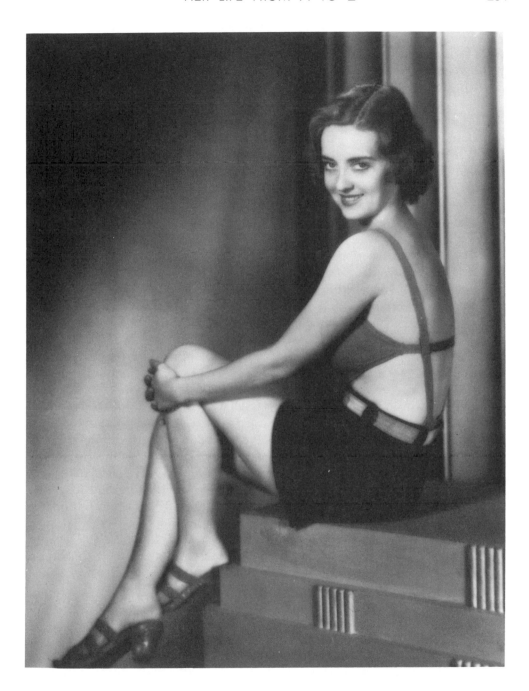

kept in limbo, uncertain whether or not she would be cast in the picture.

Meanwhile, Howard tested with many unknown or little-known actresses for the part. As late as April 7, one week before production was to start, the part of Joyce Arden had yet to be cast. Finally Gertrude Lawrence was eliminated from consideration. On April 5 Wallis sent a memo to Archie Mayo: "Saw English picture made by Lawrence with Miriam Hopkins [and] she photographs brutally. We're all cold on her including [Leslie] Howard." With that settled, Wallis added, "[I] have hopes [for] working [it] out [with Bette] Davis."

Another problem emerged in preproduction. Hal Wallis wanted Howard to wear a mustache for the part. Howard refused, saying that only people with black hair wore mustaches and that it would look awkward on him. On this point Howard prevailed.

While the search for Joyce continued, the screenplay was given added polish. Contributing to Casey Robinson's script were Crane Wilbur and Margaret Levino, although their efforts would go uncredited on the screen.

There was some concern at the studio that there were scenes in the script that resembled scenes from a Deanna Durbin picture at Universal called *That Certain Age*. Also of concern was the title. While in preproduction the picture was called *Gentleman After Midnight*, retaining the title of Maurice Hanline's story. Walter MacEwen in particular objected to the title. He suggested to Jack Warner that the title be changed to *Bachelor of Hearts*. J.L. responded, succinctly, with a memo of his own: "I prefer *Gentleman After Midnight*." Later Warner agreed to change the title to *It's Love I'm After*, which it remained.

The picture started shooting (without a Joyce) on April 14, 1937, with a budget of $467,000 and 36 shooting days. For his work on the picture Leslie Howard would receive $70,000. Olivia de Havilland, cast in the second female lead, would receive $8,615. Gertrude Lawrence would have received $25,000 for the part of Joyce Arden. Nonetheless, upon signing for the part, Bette Davis would receive a mere $2,000 per week, or approximately $6,000 for the entire picture.

Bette joined the company on Saturday, May 15, 1937, 28 days into the shooting. At the time, the production was nearly eight days behind schedule. Shortly after her arrival, cinematographer James Van Trees was taken off the picture and was replaced, at Bette's request, by Tony Gaudio. Nevertheless, it was Van Trees who received sole screen credit.

In early June 1937 the company shot on location at the Jewett Estate in Pasadena, California, and wrapped production on June 9, 12 days behind schedule.

Upon its release the picture received mostly favorable reviews, with most critics enthusing that the comedy was a nice change of pace for the usually somber Leslie Howard.

J

JEZEBEL ★★★

Warner Brothers

1938   104 minutes   bw

Directed by: William Wyler

Produced by: Hal B. Wallis, in association with Henry Blanke

Screenplay by: Clements Ripley, Abem Finkel and John Huston, based on the play by Owen Davis, Sr.

Cinematography by: Ernest Haller

Cast: Bette Davis, Henry Fonda, George Brent, Margaret Lindsay, Donald Crisp, Fay Bainter, Richard Cromwell, Henry O'Neill, Spring Byington, John Litel, Gordon Oliver, Janet Shaw, Theresa Harris, Margaret Early, Irving Pichel, Eddie Anderson, Stymie Beard, Lou Payton

If there was one single picture that made Bette Davis a bona fide box office star, it was *Jezebel*. Curiously, the picture almost never got made. In fact it probably would *not* have been made if not for the phenomenal success of Margaret Mitchell's novel *Gone with the Wind*.

Wyler's celebrated Mardi Gras Comos Ball scene.

As early as February 15, 1935, Warner Brothers executive Walter Mac-Ewen sent a memo to the studio's head of production, Hal Wallis, that read, "Have now read the full play script of *Jezebel* and it is not very good. Nevertheless, there is no denying that it could be improved a great deal in the transference to the screen and that it would provide a good role for Bette Davis [who had recently scored a major success in another studio's picture, *Of Human Bondage*] who could play the spots off the part of a little bitch of an aristocratic Southern girl. She should also look swell in the gowns of the period. . . . " Nevertheless, MacEwen suggested that the project be rejected, not only because it lacked artistic merit but also because the story had no actual hero or heroine whom the audience could root for.

Hal Wallis eventually concurred with MacEwen, and on March 27, 1935, he sent a memo to Jack Warner advising him to back out of the proposed purchase of *Jezebel*. Warner agreed, and the sale of the property was shelved. However, with the blockbuster publishing success of *GWTW*, another morality tale about a southern belle as spoiled bitch, *Jezebel* was revived. Warner agreed in January 1937 to pay Owen Davis, Sr., author of the play, $12,000 for the film rights. Davis, it seems, had been embroiled with the studio in a dispute over another one of his plays. The purchase of *Jezebel* resolved that dispute.

Jezebel opened on Broadway at the Ethel Barrymore Theatre on December 19, 1933. It flopped. The star of the play was Miriam Hopkins. She was also, Warners was disgruntled to learn, part owner of the play, holding 10 percent of all rights. Naturally, when she learned that the play was to be adapted into a motion picture, Miriam wanted the leading role for herself. Apparently Hal Wallis—or Jack Warner himself—assured Miriam that the part would be hers, and on February 26, 1937, she signed a letter of indemnification relinquishing all of her rights to the play.

Warners, however, never considered anyone but Bette Davis for the part of Julie Marsden. Certainly it was a part that Bette wanted fervently. In fact she had seen the play on Broadway with Miriam Hopkins in early 1934 and had suggested that Warners acquire the film rights. By early 1937 Bette, still smarting from her humbling courtroom loss to the studio, was on her best behavior. In January she sent a handwritten note to Jack Warner that enthused, in part, "I am thrilled to death about *Jezebel*. I think it can be as great, if not greater, than *Gone With the Wind*. Thank you for buying it."

Edmund Goulding, who had previously directed Bette in *That Certain Woman* (1937), was initially signed to direct. He was removed from the project after he expressed to Hal Wallis, in a July 1937 memo, "the picture can only tell the story of the triumph of bitchery." Goulding was replaced by Mike Curtiz, who later backed out, to Bette's great relief (Curtiz was among her least favorite directors), to shoot *The Adventures of Robin Hood* instead. Then, on September 6, 1937, Wallis finalized plans to borrow William Wyler (fresh from such successes as *These Three* and *Dodsworth*) from Samuel Goldwyn. Bette was initially apprehensive about the decision. Years before, while still a struggling ingenue, she had been bypassed for a job by Wyler.

For Bette's leading man Hal Wallis wanted Geoffrey Lind. When he proved to be unavailable, Wallis turned to Franchot Tone. On October 6, 1937, Tone appeared to be the leading candidate for the role. Walter Wanger, however, owed a favor to Warners, and the studio decided to collect by obtaining Wanger's client, Henry Fonda, as Bette's costar. By October 15 Fonda was signed for the part of Pres Dillard. George Brent, who had a long-term contract with the studio and whose star was by then descending, was signed for the second male lead. Interestingly, Fay Bainter was signed for the second female lead, Auntie Belle, at the rate of $2,000 per week—about the same amount that Bette would receive for the starring role—an indication of the value that Warners placed on Bette Davis before *Jezebel*.

Meanwhile, the script had problems. The primary problem, of course, was what Walter MacEwen had referred to two years before: how do you make an audience care about and root for a protagonist who is so obviously a bitch who deserves to suffer? It was a problem that the picture, no matter how well done, would never fully overcome.

Of less importance was a scene in the script in which Julie took a trip to Paris. However, the idea of building a Paris set disturbed Hal Wallis's sense of economy, and he ordered that the scene be scrapped. This left a hole in the plot that none of the Warners writers were able to resolve. Wyler consulted with his friend John Huston, who devised a "no Paris" solution for the script. Huston was then hired by the studio, at Wyler's request, to refine the script. Wyler also gave Huston the authority to act in his absence as his representative in meetings with the other writers and producers.

Robert Buckner, another writer on the project, presented another problem. Huston wanted the eventual screen credits to read "Screenplay by Clements Ripley, Abem Finkel, and John Huston, from the play by Owen Davis, Sr."—with no mention of Buckner's contributions. Buckner took his case to the Screenwriter's Guild, which recommended to the studio that he be given an "adaptation by" credit, which he eventually was.

Set against a backdrop of the great yellow fever epidemic that swept Louisiana in 1853 and caused 8,000 deaths, *Jezebel* is foremost the story of the beautiful and beguiling Julie Marsden. Infuriated by her impudence, Pres Dillard breaks off their engagement and leaves town. When he returns, married to a Yankee beauty, Julie responds, "Marriage is it? To that *washed out* little *Yankee* thing?!"

The final draft of the screenplay was approved on October 13, 1937. The picture, budgeted at $783,508, was mounted by the studio as Bette's first true A picture. Ernie Haller was to do the camera work, Orry-Kelly the costumes, Bob Haas the art direction, and Max Steiner the score.

Shooting was scheduled to start on October 18. Due to various delays, however, production didn't commence until October 25. The first scene shot was the interior of Madame Poulard's fitting room, which was shot on Stage 22. Bette was terrified from the outset. She was particularly intimidated by

Wyler. "[For] my first scene in *Jezebel*," Bette later related, "in front of 250 extras, [Wyler] made me do 28 takes until he said, 'Print it.' To say the least, I was in a state of shock and terror of my director."

On Tuesday, November 2, only a week into production, Bette called in sick. Wyler spent the day shooting tests of actors for roles that had yet to be cast. The following day Bette was again absent from the set, and Wyler shot around her. On Thursday she returned to work, but shooting on the picture continued at a crawl. Wyler was constantly behind schedule. By November 16 the picture was already eight days behind. It is surprising, then, particularly given her still relatively lowly stature at the time, that Bette was granted a minivacation November 19–22.

When she returned to work, Wyler's pace remained deliberate, averaging just better than two script pages a day. On November 23 exasperated Warners unit manager Bob Fellows reported back to the front office, "I do not believe," he wrote, "anyone is aware of just how slow Mr. Wyler is." In response Hal Wallis sent a memo to his assistant, Henry Blanke, who was directly supervising the production. "Possibly Wyler likes to see those big numbers on the slate," Wallis said with not a little sarcasm, "and maybe we could arrange to have them start with number 6 on each take; then it wouldn't take so long to get up to 9 or 10."

While filming, Bette suffered two less-than-critical setbacks. The first was a charley horse. A masseur was ordered to the set to tend to her injury, and shooting resumed shortly thereafter. The second, more vexing problem occurred when a particularly irritating pimple popped out on her face. A skin specialist, Dr. Franklyn Ball, was called to the set to administer to the pimple. It was thought that the production could resume without delay, that Wyler could postpone Bette's close-ups, and that he could simply shoot around the pimple in other shots. However, the pesky and persistent pimple remained affixed to her face for a week, and on December 1 Wyler finally sent Bette home. She spent the next five days "recuperating." Thereafter, Bette was particularly concerned, at times even paranoid, about her looks. One night Bette walked into the projection room to view the day's rushes and shouted, "Oh, my, God! No, no, no! I, look, aw-ful!" From that point on, Wyler forbade Bette from watching dailies.

As shooting progressed, the picture fell so far behind schedule that there was considerable angst that Wyler would not finish with Henry Fonda as contracted. In agreeing to do the picture, one of Fonda's demands was that he be finished with his work no later than December 18. He wanted to be at his wife's bedside for the birth of their child. Still, Wyler worked at an alarmingly slow pace. He caused a great furor at the studio when, on December 8, with the picture nearly three weeks behind, he shot *13* takes of George Brent swatting a mosquito.

Tensions between Wyler and Fonda escalated to the point where, on November 4, 1937, Hal Wallis issued a memo to Henry Blanke questioning why Wyler was not content with anything Fonda did until after 10 or 11 takes. The feud between Wyler and Fonda was exacerbated by the fact that both men had been married to and divorced from the same woman, actress Margaret Sullavan.

At one point an infuriated Jack Warner stepped in and threatened to replace Wyler unless he expedited his work on the picture. In retaliation Bette marched into Warner's office and reportedly refused to complete the picture with any other director but Wyler. She had become his champion—and his lover. She was still married to Ham Nelson at the time, but she was overwhelmed by Wyler. She would later cite him as having been the love of her life. She was stunned by his strength and in awe of his talent.

Toward the end of the picture Bette confronts Margaret Lindsay, who played Fonda's wife, and the two actresses argue over who should accompany the fever-stricken Fonda to the quarantined swamps. Bette, in one of her best scenes in the picture, delivers her lines with fervor: "Amy, of course it's your right to go, you're his wife. But are you fit to go? Lovin' him isn't enough. If you gave him all your strength, would it be enough? Do you know the Creole word for fever powder? For food and water? His life and yours will hang on just things like that—and you'll both surely die!"

Wyler was content with Bette's performance in the scene. He was not happy, however, with the work by Lindsay. He shot take after take after merciless take, driving what remained of Lindsay's confidence into the ground. Exasperated, Wyler came up with a creative solution, one that convinced Bette once and for all of his brilliance. Instead of shooting Lindsay in close-up while she delivered her lines (as was scripted and expected), Wyler focused his camera instead on a close-up of the wedding ring on her finger. The scene could not have been more effective no matter how expertly played by Lindsay—or by any other actress for that matter.

Bette was also amazed by the tension that Wyler wrung from the Mardi Gras Comos Ball scene. The scene called for Bette to wear a scarlet gown to the ball when the custom called for all unmarried girls to wear white. It was a deceptively simple scene. Wyler spun his camera in all directions, turning the dance between Bette and Fonda into a thing of torture and horror. The scene became the most famous one from the whole movie and has since become a movie classic.

Wyler's cast, headed by Bette, worked long hours to make up time. Bette would later claim that she worked until midnight every night to keep Wyler from being fired by Warner. This was not true, but it was close. On Tuesday, December 14, Bette and Fonda worked from 1:00 P.M. until 12:20 A.M. The following day Bette worked until 2:20 A.M. and Fonda until 5:00 A.M. But these were exceptions, not the rule, and the overtime had more to do with Fonda's deadline than Wyler's job security. Amusingly, an uproar broke out on the set on the latter day because Donald Crisp's hairpiece couldn't be found.

On Friday, December 17, Henry Fonda finally completed his work and was released by the studio. He boarded a plane out of Los Angeles and was indeed present for the birth of his daughter, Jane. In later years Bette Davis frequently chastised Jane Fonda for having caused so much anxiety and overwork.

By this time the rigorous schedule, combined with the breakup of her marriage to Ham Nelson and the torrid affair with Wyler, had left Bette in emotional shambles. Still, she continued to work. On Monday, December 20, Bette flew into hysterics on the set because Wyler was shooting so much out of continuity that Bette had to snap, at his command, from mood to mood.

Shooting continued through the holidays. Bette worked on Christmas Eve from 10:00 A.M. until 4:00 P.M. The company was given Christmas Day off and reported back to work on Monday, December 30.

On New Year's Eve Bette worked from 9:00 A.M. until 4:20 P.M. On Sunday, January 2, Bette's father's funeral was held in Boston. Bette, who had never been close to Harlow Davis, did not attend. She reported back to the set on Monday. On Thursday, January 6, Bette worked from 9:00 A.M. until 11:05 P.M. To make up time a second unit was called into service, under the direction of Henry Blanke. Still, William Wyler worked at a snail's pace. Hal Wallis flew into a rage on January 7 when it took Wyler *16* takes to shoot a long shot of Bette descending a staircase. "Is he absolutely *daffy*?!" Wallis demanded to know from Blanke.

On Monday, January 10, Bette reported sick, further delaying the picture's much-anticipated close. On Saturday, January 15, she made up for it, working from 9:00 A.M. until 11:50 P.M., and on Monday, January 17, *Jezebel* finally completed production. It had been allotted 42 shooting days and took *70*. The budget had escalated to well over $1 million, a huge sum in the Hollywood of 1938.

In the marketing campaign for *Jezebel* much was made of the fact that Bette wore 16 costumes in the picture, with each one costing over $500. Warners also hyped the film as the greatest cinematic achievement since the advent of talking pictures. About Bette's performance as Julie Marsden the ads said, "Heartless Siren for Whom Men Died!" and "Her Lips Were a Challenge to Every Man . . . Her Heart Beat Only for One!" and "Darling of Dixie . . . Meanest When She's Lovin' Most!" and "The Story of a Woman Who Was Loved When She Should've Been Whipped!" and finally, "Half Angel, Half Siren, All Woman! The Screen's Greatest Actress Comes to You in the Hit Picture of Her Career . . . as the Most Exciting Heroine Who Ever Lived and Loved in Dixie!"

Jezebel was previewed at Warner's Hollywood Theatre on March 7, 1938, to overwhelmingly favorable response. One of the holdouts, however, was David O. Selznick. In Hollywood, *Jezebel* was thought, by Selznick in particular, to be a rip-off of *Gone With the Wind*, which was then still in production. On March 8, Selznick telephoned Jack Warner's secretary and dictated the following letter:

Dear Jack:
Reiterating what I told you last night, I think it would be a very great

pity indeed from your own standpoint, for so distinguished and costly a picture as *Jezebel* should be damned as an imitation by the millions of readers and lovers of *Gone With the Wind*. . . . I am referring to a few specific scenes such as the very well remembered piece of business in which Scarlett pinches her cheeks to give them color. . . .

Nevertheless, reviews for *Jezebel* were enthusiastic. Many reviewers noted that Selznick would have a hard time topping *Jezebel* with his troubled and much prolonged production of *GWTW*. They needn't have worried.

Jezebel also made Bette Davis a star of moneymaking status. The picture started her seven-year reign as the queen of Hollywood. Over the years the picture has retained a reputation as one of Bette Davis's better pictures. Actually, it's often overwrought. Still, it's impeccably filmed, and Bette delivers a fine performance if not one of her best.

JIMMY THE GENT ★ ½

Warner Brothers
1934   67 minutes   bw
Directed by: Michael Curtiz
Produced by: Robert Lord
Screenplay by: Bertram Milhauser, based on a story by Laird Doyle and
    Ray Nazarro
Cinematography by: Ira Morgan
Cast: James Cagney, Bette Davis, Alice White, Allen Jenkins, Arthur Hohl,
    Alan Dinehart, Philip Reed, Hobart Cavanaugh, Mayo Methot, Ralf
    Harolde, Joseph Sawyer, Philip Faversham, Nora Lane, Howard
    Hickman, Jane Darewell, Joseph Crehan, Robert Warwick, Harold
    Entwhistle

Based on an original story, "The Heir Chaser" by Laird Doyle and Ray Nazarro, *Jimmy the Gent* cast Bette as Joan, a decorative secretary in love with crooked Jimmy Cagney. If she seems miscast here, it might be because she was a last-minute replacement for Joan Blondell, who would have been far better suited.

Initially called *The Heir Chaser* and then *Blondes and Bonds*, *Jimmy the Gent* started shooting on November 27, 1933, and finished on December 20. Years later Cagney recalled his experience on the picture:

> My leading lady was Bette Davis, the first time we appeared together.
> She was unhappy doing the picture because she was waiting
> impatiently to go to another studio to do *Of Human Bondage*, which
> was to turn out so well for her. Her unhappiness seeped through to
> the rest of us, and she was a little hard to get along with. But she was
> still a pro and did her job beautifully.

Despite her costar status, reviewers generally didn't comment about Bette, except to note her new coiffure, which was short and parted down the middle.

JOBS
Before stardom Bette Davis held a few jobs, none of them for very long:

☆ Waitress, Mrs. Johnson's Tea Room, Ogunquit, Maine
☆ Waitress, Cushing Academy
☆ Typist for a writer
☆ Theater usher, Cape Playhouse, Dennis, Massachusetts

> "No one swooped tea onto a tea-table with the alacrity I did."
> *Bette Davis*

JOHN PAUL JONES ★★
Samuel Bronston Productions
Distributed by Warner Brothers
1959   126 minutes   Technirama
Directed by: John Farrow
Produced by: Samuel Bronston
Screenplay by: John Farrow and Jesse Lasky, Jr., based on the story by
    Clements Ripley
Cinematography by: Michel Kelber
Cast: Robert Stack, Charles Coburn, Bette Davis, Marisa Pavan, Jean-
    Pierre Aumont, Peter Cushing, Bruce Cabot, Macdonald Carey, Erin
    O'Brien, Tom Brannum, Basil Sydney, Archie Duncan, Thomas
    Gomez, Judson Laire, Bob Cunningham, John Charles Farrow, Eric
    Pohlmann, Pepe Nieto, John Crawford, Patrick Villiers, Frank
    Latimore, Ford Rainey, Bruce Seaton, David Farrar, Susana Canales,
    Jorge Riviere

Warner Brothers had been kicking around the idea of doing a biopic on John
Paul Jones since 1950. Enormous budget projections, however, compelled the
studio to pass on the project, and it was not until producer Samuel Bronston
entered the picture that the production proceeded. In July 1956 Bronston
signed William Dieterle (who had directed Bette years before in another
historical picture, *Juarez*) to direct from a screenplay by Ben Hecht. The
picture was to be shot in the Mediterranean in August 1956.

A lack of financing, however, shut the picture down in preproduction,
and when it finally did go before the cameras (with a budget of $4 million)
in April 1958, it would be in Madrid and Denia, Spain.

Designed to cut costs, Bronston's decision to shoot the picture in Spain
was met with an outcry of protest back in the United States. The American
Federation of Labor Film Council, claiming to represent 24,000 film workers,
protested that it deprived hundreds of Americans of jobs and announced its
decision to take the matter to then president Dwight Eisenhower. Bronston
retorted that shooting the picture in the United States would have cost $10
million and argued that John Paul Jones had lived most of his life in Europe
and not in the United States, as was generally thought. Nonetheless, as

Variety reported on December 17, 1958, "No fewer than 19 litigations are pending in the involved John Paul Jones Productions."

For her guest appearance as Catherine the Great, in which she would be costumed lavishly, Bette was paid the considerable sum of $25,000 (*not* the $50,000 she told the press) for four days and six screen minutes of work. Despite the brevity of her role, Bette's contract called for her to receive star billing equal to that of any other cast member. She also insisted on the credit "And a Special Appearance by Bette Davis as Catherine the Great."

Bette sailed to Spain, with her daughter, B.D., and sister, Bobby, in tow, on the S.S. *Independence* on May 6, 1958. She arrived in Algeciras on May 12, only to discover that her big yellow trunk, which carried not only the white wig and costumes she was to wear in the picture but also her personal wardrobe, had not arrived with her. A great flurry of activity ensued, and another white wig and set of costumes were rushed into production.

Despite its troubles, Warner Brothers envisioned the film as a major blockbuster of historical importance. Following one of its early previews, director John Farrow sent a telegram to studio executive Steve Trilling that read, in part, "Everybody tremendously enthusiastic. Please tell Jack it looks like a big one regards to everybody." Jack Warner responded on March 5, 1959, with a wire of his own: "We equally enthused and warmest congratulations to you. Now that picture finally completed, end result justified the means."

Upon its release, however, the film performed dismally at the box office. Some believed that Robert Stack, cast in the title role, lacked the charisma to carry the picture. Certainly Bette was vocal in this regard. Interestingly, Paul Newman had been the first choice for the role. After some consideration, though, Newman, to Bette's regret, had turned it down.

JUAREZ ★★½

Warner Brothers
1939   132 minutes   bw
Directed by: William Dieterle
Produced by: Hal B. Wallis, in association with Henry Blanke
Screenplay by: John Huston, Aeneas Mackenzie, and Wolfgang Reinhardt,
     based on a play by Franz Werfel and a book by Bertita Harding
Cinematography by: Tony Gaudio
Cast: Paul Muni, Bette Davis, Brian Aherne, Claude Rains, John Garfield,
     Donald Crisp, Joseph Calleia, Gale Sondergaard, Gilbert Roland,
     Henry O'Neill, Pedro de Cordoba, Montagu Love, Harry Davenport,
     Louis Calhern, Walter Kingsford, Georgia Caine, John Miljan,
     Vladimir Sokoloff, Irving Pichel, Gilbert Emory, Monte Blue, Manuel
     Diaz, Hugh Sothern, Mickey Kuhn

Modeled as a Warner Brothers biographical drama along the lines of *The Story of Louis Pasteur* (1936) and *The Life of Emile Zola* (1937), *Juarez* was

based on two primary sources. The first, *The Phantom Crown*, a book by Bertita Harding about Maximilian and his wife Carlota, was purchased by the studio for $5,000. The second, a play by Franz Werfel entitled *Juarez and Maximilian*, sold for $6,000. With the purchase of this second source, the angle of the proposed picture was changed to focus on the revolutionary Benito Juárez, "the Abraham Lincoln of Mexico," as a vehicle for the studio's king of the biopic, Paul Muni.

Initially Muni did not want Bette Davis in the part of the Empress Carlota. Bette had stolen *Bordertown* (1935) from Muni, and he reportedly did not want the competition. Nevertheless, after *Jezebel*, Bette was the top box office star at the studio (while Muni's star was in decline), and Warner Brothers insisted on her participation.

For the role of Maximilian, both Leslie Howard and Fredric March were top contenders. Melvyn Douglas was also considered and tested. The part ultimately went to Brian Aherne, for whom it would be the role of a lifetime, one that would win him a Best Supporting Actor Oscar nomination.

During preproduction an enormous amount of work was conducted by the Warners research department to assure historical accuracy. Whether the filmmakers stuck to those facts is, of course, another matter. As part of the research, a study on the life of Juárez by Jesse J. Dossick was purchased by the studio for $500. Dossick's work and contributions to the picture would go uncredited.

As for the title, Muni did not like the proposed *The Phantom Crown*. When Hal Wallis announced that the title would be changed, public outcry from fans of the Harding book erupted. Wallis wanted the title changed to *Juarez and Maximilian*. A legal matter, however, prevented this. It seems that an independent producer by the name of Miguel Torres had his own picture, entitled *Juarez and Maximilian* (unrelated to the Werfel play), in production. Torres contacted Warner and threatened legal action if the studio proceeded to use the title. So, to avoid a lawsuit, and mostly to appease Muni, Wallis changed the title of the picture to *Juarez*.

Set in 1863, the picture tells what amounts to two stories: that of Benito Juárez, the president of Mexico and the leader in the war against Napoleon III (played by Claude Rains), emperor of France; and that of Empress Carlota, played by Bette (in black wig) to Aherne's Emperor Maximilian. Carlota's tragedy is that she cannot have a baby, information that both her husband and her doctor withhold from her. With Maximilian's impending death by a Mexican firing squad, Carlota goes crazy (with Bette in fine histrionic form) in Napoleon's palace.

Designed as an A picture blockbuster, *Juarez* was budgeted, with studio overhead, at $1.2 million. Of this Muni's salary was an astounding $112,500. Davis would be paid $35,000, and Aherne, enlisted from outside the studio gates, would get $40,000.

The picture went into production on November 17, 1938. Bette, in the throes of her divorce from Ham Nelson, and also still finishing *Dark Victory* for Eddie Goulding, did not join the production until December 12. Production was frequently shut down thereafter due to Muni's various illnesses. Also causing delays was his makeup, about which he was quite particular and which, due to the molding of rubber, was causing him a great deal of irritation.

Bette finished her work on *Juarez* on February 3, 1939, and the picture completed production on February 6, 17 days behind schedule.

Bette later said of the role, "Carlota was one of the least difficult of my recent pictures. It was necessary only to do a faithful living portrait of a woman who has left a vivid and complete record on the pages of almost contemporary history. So much research was given that screenplay by historians, writers and producers that almost all I had to do was don Carlota's lovely gowns, step back in time some 70 years, and read my lines. . . . We had something definite to work from in that picture."

Pleased as she was with the role, Bette was far from content with the final cut of the picture. She was also particularly disturbed by Muni. His ego, she would later charge, virtually ruined the film. "When Mr. Muni reported to the stage," Bette asserted, "he brought some fifty additional pages of script that he demanded be inserted. He had the power to enforce this demand and the studio capitulated. . . . In the cutting process a great and carefully balanced story was thrown completely out of kilter by the emphasis that was given the role of Juárez."

Primarily because it was based on two separate sources, the picture lacks focus and does in fact emerge as two separate stories. Still, it is full of pomp and pageantry and fine performances (Bette, Aherne, Rains, and John Garfield as Díaz, the best soldier in Mexico). For all his stature, however, Paul Muni is ridiculously bad as Juárez, described in the picture as "an ugly little man." Amusingly, after seeing the makeup test of Muni, Jack Warner reportedly quipped, "Why are we paying Muni all this money? I can't *find* him!"

Juarez premiered at the Hollywood Theatre in New York on April 25, 1939. It was touted as Warner's "greatest motion picture achievement," which of course it was not. Still, both the reviews and the box office were favorable enough to further propel Bette's rising stature at the studio.

"THE JUDGE AND JAKE WYLER"

Bette starred as a retired and hypochondriac judge (a role originally written for a male) in this pilot for Universal television. It was produced by Richard Levinson and William Link, directed by David Lowell Rich, written by Levinson, Link, and David Shaw, and photographed by William Margulies. It costarred Doug McClure, Eric Braeden, Joan Van Ark, Gary Conway, Lou Jacobi, and James McEachin. Also appearing in the cast were Lisabeth Hush, Kent Smith, Barbara Rhoades, John Randolph, Milt Kamen, John Lupton, Rosanna Huffman, Eddie Quillan, and Virginia Capers.

Although the pilot was not picked up as a series, "The Judge and Jake Wyler" aired as an NBC made-for-television movie on December 2, 1972.

JUNE BRIDE ★★½

Warner Brothers
1948   97 minutes   bw
Directed by: Bretaigne Windust
Produced by: Henry Blanke
Screenplay by: Ranald MacDougall, based on the play by Eileen Tighe and
    Graeme Lorimer
Cinematography by: Ted McCord
Cast: Bette Davis, Robert Montgomery, Fay Bainter, Betty Lynn, Tom
    Tully, Barbara Bates, Jerome Cowan, Mary Wickes, James Burke,
    Raymond Roe, Marjorie Bennett, Ray Montgomery, George O'Hanlon,
    Sandra Gould, Esther Howard, Jessie Adams, Raymond Bond, Alice
    Kelley, Patricia Northrop

June Bride reteamed Bette with director Bretaigne Windust directly following their disastrous collaboration on *Winter Meeting*. After a series of dreary melodramas, many, including Bette, thought a comedy would revive her sagging status at the box office.

Rights to the unpublished play *Feature for June* by magazine editors

Eileen Tighe and Graeme Lorimer were initially purchased by Paramount for $50,000. In June 1945, Paramount contracted writers Harold Buchman and Lou Solomon to fashion a screenplay based on the material. The script never materialized to Paramount's satisfaction, and in July 1947 the studio sold its rights in the property to Warner Brothers for $25,000.

The property was brought to Warners' attention by studio writers Ellingwood Kay and Ranald MacDougall as a possible vehicle for rising star Janis Paige or Betty Hutton.

The plot had Casey Jackson, a foreign correspondent for a news magazine, demoted to working as an assistant to an editor of *Home Life*, a woman's magazine. Bette was signed to play Linda Gilman, editor of the magazine. To complicate the scenario, Jackson had been romantically involved with, and had walked out on, Gilman four years before. His first assignment in his new position is to travel with Gilman to a small Indiana town to cover a wedding for the magazine's June feature story.

Cary Grant and Fred Astaire were top contenders for the part of Casey Jackson, but both eventually backed out. Bette's next choice was Robert Montgomery, who was eventually retained by Warners at a considerable price. Montgomery was accorded equal billing with Bette and the then-astronomical fee of $17,500 per week with a 10-week minimum guarantee. He also demanded and got a contractual stipulation that he was not to work after 6:00 P.M.

Bette showed up for hair and makeup tests on Monday, March 15, 1948. She underwent several wardrobe tests with some trepidation because the studio had been unable to acquire the services of Orry-Kelly, her usual designer. Instead she was introduced to Edith Head, whose work she came to admire greatly. In later years Bette would specifically request Head as her designer.

Budgeted at $1,589,000, *June Bride* started shooting without Bette on Monday, May 3, 1948. On the second day of shooting Montgomery called in sick and the company shut down. He reported back to work the following day. Bette did not start shooting until Monday, May 10. On Tuesday, June 1, Bette did not report to work because of the funeral of her uncle, Paul Favor.

On June 7, Bette phoned in sick. Actually she was just staging another of her protests over some injustice, real or imagined, and she reported back to work the following day. Reports emanating from the set claimed that Bette was being difficult when in fact the set was happier than for most Davis pictures. Davis did, however, come to greatly dislike Robert Montgomery for his conservative politics and air of superiority. In later years she accused Montgomery of having attempted to sabotage her performance and steal the picture. He would, in fact, receive the best reviews.

When the love scene between Davis and Montgomery was to be shot, Bette insisted on a closed set. However, ingenue Mary Frances Reynolds, who had a small part in the picture, persuaded one of the lighting men to allow her to sneak up onto the catwalk, 20 feet above the set, to watch the shooting. At one point she slipped, nearly fell, and made a noise. She later recalled:

Davis stopped the kiss. She threw Montgomery off and sat up ramrod straight.

"What's that?!" She looked skyward. So did everyone else below.

"Someone's up thah! Who's up thah? Someone's watching! This is supposed to be a closed set!" . . .

My heart was pounding. She was furious. I thought she was going to kill me. I was going to be fired, machine-gunned, destroyed, and hung on the wall. That commanding voice of hers frightened the hell out of me.

Mary Frances Reynolds survived, of course, changed her name to Debbie, and became a star in her own right.

Although both Bette and Montgomery missed relatively few days of work, they very rarely worked past 5:00 P.M. That and a few other problems put the company far behind schedule. In one case actress Marjorie Bennett was unable to produce a scream to director Windust's satisfaction, and Bette was recruited to unleash an offstage yell that was substituted in postproduction.

Another minor problem was the script's reference to President Harry Truman, which could have been embarrassing if Vice President Truman had not won the election that year. To solve the problem, Windust shot the line using the names of *all* of the major presidential candidates, knowing that he could eliminate the losing names in editing.

Finally, much to the relief of the Warner front office, Robert Montgomery finished shooting on Wednesday, July 21. He had worked on the picture for 12 weeks and ended up costing the studio $210,000. The rest of the company, Bette included, did not finish work until August 4, when the picture closed 30 days behind schedule.

The film, which had promised "a new Bette Davis" with her Edith Head costumes and her bouffant wig, had its first preview at the Huntington Park Theatre outside L.A. on August 26, 1948. The following day studio executive Steve Trilling wired Bette, vacationing in New Hampshire, and enthused, "Sneaked the bride last night and it was worth all the tears, sweat and blood. Excellent all respects. Hilariously funny." He sent the same wire, verbatim, to Robert Montgomery.

After seeing the picture in a theater with a paying audience, Jack Warner wired Bretaigne Windust in New York. "Picture went over even better than previews they had last week. This makes me very happy and proud and want to thank you again for all your good work. Every good wish."

Upon its release *June Bride* received mostly highly favorable reviews. Some went so far as to call it the comedy of the year. Nevertheless, it ended up being a disappointment at the box office, reinforcing the opinion at Warners and among industry analysts that Bette Davis's career, phenomenal as it had been, was near its end.

They would, of course, be wrong.

ORRY-KELLY

Bette Davis's foremost costume designer, Orry-Kelly designed her costumes for virtually all of her pictures, beginning with *The Rich Are Always With Us* (1932) and ending with *A Stolen Life* (1946).

Orry-Kelly (1897–1964) started his career using his real name, Jack Kelly. He went on to win Oscars for his costume designs for *An American in Paris* (1951) and *Some Like It Hot* (1959). He also designed Bette's gowns for the 1959–1960 stage show *The World of Carl Sandburg*.

THE KENNEDY CENTER HONORS

On December 6, 1987, Bette was presented the prestigious Kennedy Center Honors award. Upon learning that she was to receive the award Bette expressed her disappointment that it had taken so long in coming. "I always had a hunch that my never being given the award had to do with my being

such a strong Democrat, and with Mr. Reagan's being in the White House. The Kennedy Center used to send out a brochure asking whom you suggested to receive the awards, and one year I put down 'Me.' "

Also honored that night were Perry Como, violinist Nathan Milstein, choreographer/dancer Alwin Nikolais, and Sammy Davis, Jr. Jessica Tandy and Hume Cronyn, previous winners of the award, were the presenters; Ronald Reagan was in attendance. The ceremony was aired by CBS on December 30, 1987.

KID GALAHAD ★★½

Warner Brothers
1937   101 minutes   bw
Directed by: Michael Curtiz
Produced by: Hal B. Wallis, in association with Samuel Bischoff
Screenplay by: Seton I. Miller, based on the novel by Francis Wallace
Cinematography by: Tony Gaudio
Cast: Edward G. Robinson, Bette Davis, Humphrey Bogart, Wayne Morris, Jane Bryan, Harry Carey, William Haade, George Blake, Soledad Jiminez, Joe Cunningham, Veda Ann Borg, Ben Welden, Joseph Crehan, Harlan Tucker, Frank Faylen, Joyce Compton, Horace MacMahon

One of Bette's last, pre-*Jezebel* outings as a decorative set piece. Here she plays "Fluff" Phillips, torch singer and mistress of boxing promoter Nick Donati (Edward G. Robinson). The story, which focuses on Kid Galahad (Wayne Morris), Donati's young bellhop turned boxing protégé, was adapted from the novel of the same name by Francis Wallace. Rights to the story, which had run as a serial in the *Saturday Evening Post*, were purchased by Warner in an agrement dated June 4, 1936, for the sum of $7,000.

Bette, still at least superficially repentant after her recent court loss to the studio, accepted her assigned cardboard character with minimal protest and played the part with minimal effort. Actually, before assigning it to Bette, Warners almost gave the part to newcomer Sarah Jane Faulks, who would later become known to film audiences as Jane Wyman.

At one point in preproduction, after reviewing one of the early drafts of the script, the Breen Office, the industry censor, stepped in and expressed disfavor with the proposed picture's content. This so enraged Hal Wallis that he considered producing and releasing the film without the Breen Office's consent, a rare if not unprecedented move for a major studio in the Hollywood of 1936. "If after years of contact with their office," Wallis raved to his producer Sam Bischoff, "they still are unconvinced that we know the difference between right and wrong in putting a play on the screen, then I am going to stop talking to them, because it is just a lot of wasted effort."

Wallis, however, resolved his differences (which, fuss aside, turned out to be only petty) with the Breen Office, and *Kid Galahad*, gambling on newcomer Wayne Morris in the title role, went into production on January 25, 1937. The picture was budgeted at $416,000, with Robinson receiving $50,000 for his work. Not surprisingly, although she shared costar billing, Bette would be paid considerably less: $18,400. Poor Wayne Morris would be paid the almost criminally low salary of $66 a week, a total of $396 for the entire picture.

Arthur Edeson was initially assigned to shoot the picture. Early into the production, however, he became ill and was replaced by Tony Gaudio. Edward G. Robinson broke a tooth during a take shot on February 5. Bette called in sick on February 18 and 19, and director Curtiz, never one to appreciate her talent, gladly shot around her. Another mishap occurred during a fight sequence: Morris actually knocked out William Haade, who played prizefight champion Chuck McGraw.

Except for the scenes shot in the ring, *Kid Galahad* completed production with Bette on March 6, 1937. The picture was previewed on April 28, 1937, at Warner's Beverly Hills Theatre with much success. It subsequently opened to highly favorable reviews, with many critics hailing Wayne Morris as a big new star, a promise that was never fulfilled.

Kid Galahad was remade in 1941 as *The Wagons Roll at Night* with Humphrey Bogart in the Robinson role and again in 1962 as the musical *Kid Galahad* with Elvis Presley in the title role. To allay confusion for television airings, the original 1937 *Kid Galahad* was retitled *Battling Bellhop*.

L

THE LADY FROM THE SEA

Play by Henrik Ibsen that Bette, in the part of Boletta, toured with in 1929. Bette was cast in the production after Cecil Clovelly saw her in a performance of *The Earth Between*. He then invited Bette to join the Ibsen Repertory Company in its productions of *The Lady from the Sea* and *The Wild Duck*. Bette was to replace actress Linda Watkins in the company for the final week's run of *The Lady from the Sea*. However, after landing the part Bette contracted the measles and was able to appear in only the final few performances of the play, which was then staged at the Bijou Theatre in New York.

CARL LAEMMLE, JR.

His father, Carl "Papa" Laemmle, may have owned it, but it was Carl "Junior" Laemmle (1908–1979) who was running Universal in 1930. His father had presented him with the studio as a 21st birthday present. Of his contract player Bette Davis, Laemmle is infamous for having said, "I can't imagine any guy giving her a tumble" and "She has about as much sex appeal as Slim Summerville." It was also Laemmle who chose *not* to pick up Bette's option in 1931.

HOPE LANGE

In August 1959 Bette Davis said of young actress Hope Lange, "She's the next great potential star in this town; if she'd come along in my time she could have had *Of Human Bondage*. If she's lucky she may get two good picture parts a year, but continuity of career is what counts. The young players have a tough time today." Not long after expressing those words Bette costarred with Lange in the picture *Pocketful of Miracles* (1961). She became incensed when Lange, who was having an affair with the film's star and associate producer, Glenn Ford, asked to have the *star* dressing room.

Hope Lange, born in 1931, has appeared in other pictures, including *Bus Stop* (1956), *Peyton Place* (1957), and *Blue Velvet* (1986).

ANGELA LANSBURY

Lansbury costarred with Bette in the motion picture *Death on the Nile* (1978) and in the television miniseries "Little Gloria . . . Happy at Last" (1982). The two actresses got along well enough and seemed to have some things in common. As Lansbury relates, "She once said to me, 'The thing about us, we're character actresses.' She wasn't a great beauty, and she knew that. She was a tremendous role model for me. She simply encouraged my aspirations as not [being] a great beauty."

Born in 1925, Angela Lansbury, star of stage and television, has appeared in numerous films, including *Gaslight* (1944), *The Dark at the Top of the Stairs* (1960), *The Manchurian Candidate* (1962), and *Bedknobs and Broomsticks* (1971). She is best known to television audiences as Jessica Fletcher in the popular series "Murder, She Wrote," which began airing in 1984.

"LATE NIGHT WITH DAVID LETTERMAN"

Bette guested on the popular television show "Late Night with David Letterman" in April 1989. Upon her introduction the audience roared with applause. Bette quipped, "No, no, no, no. You've given me more than enough applause. *I want you to look at my dress.*"

VIVIEN LEIGH

Despite the overwhelming reviews (the best of her career) she received for the 1939 picture *Dark Victory,* Bette lost the Best Actress Oscar that year to Vivien Leigh for her performance in *Gone With the Wind.* Bette also lost out to Leigh on the chance to play Blanche DuBois in the film version of *A Streetcar Named Desire* (1951). Years later, when director Robert Aldrich was thinking about replacing Joan Crawford with Vivien Leigh in *Hush . . . Hush, Sweet Charlotte,* Bette objected strenuously, saying that Leigh, who had emotional problems, would be as temperamental as Crawford had been. Nevertheless, Aldrich offered the part to Leigh, who declined, much to Bette's relief.

MARGARET LEIGHTON

Respected Broadway and British stage actress Margaret Leighton was cast opposite Bette in the 1961 play *The Night of the Iguana.* For Bette, Leighton represented a threat. She thus treated her with disdain, even blatant rudeness, and attempted to have her replaced in the show. She was, however, unsuccessful, and Maggie Leighton went on to win the best reviews in the show, to Bette's great resentment, and was eventually awarded a Best Actress Tony for her performance.

Margaret Leighton (1922-1976) appeared in pictures including *Under Capricorn* (1949), *The Madwoman of Chaillot* (1969), and *The Go-Between* (Best Supporting Actress Oscar nomination, 1971).

MERVYN LEROY

LeRoy directed Bette early in her career in the 1932 picture *Three on a Match.* Bette complained that LeRoy was indifferent to her and that he favored costar Joan Blondell. Behind his back Bette denigrated the director, saying that he was in a position of power at the studio only because he was married to Harry Warner's daughter, Doris. LeRoy, in turn, reportedly told his friends in Hollywood that Bette Davis would never have much of a career in pictures. As LeRoy said later, "They gave me three unknown girls in that one—Joan Blondell, Bette Davis, and Ann Dvorak. I made a mistake when the picture was finished. I told an interviewer that I thought Joan Blondell was going to be a big star, that Ann Dvorak had definite possibilities, but that I didn't think Bette Davis would make it. She's been cool to me ever since."

Mervyn LeRoy (1900–1987) got his start in pictures by being the cousin of Jesse Lasky, one of the pioneers in the movie industry. With *Little Caesar* (1930) he became a director of note. His subsequent pictures include *I Am a Fugitive from a Chain Gang* (1932), *Anthony Adverse* (1936), *The Wizard of Oz* (producer, 1939), *Random Harvest* (1942), and *Mister Roberts* (shared credit, 1955). Among LeRoy's talent discoveries were Clark Gable, Lana Turner, and Loretta Young. He was also the man who introduced Nancy Davis to Ronald Reagan.

THE LETTER ★★★½
Warner Brothers
1940   95 minutes   bw
Directed by: William Wyler
Produced by: Hal B. Wallis, in association with Robert Lord
Screenplay by: Howard Koch, based on the play by W. Somerset Maugham
Cinematography by: Tony Gaudio
Cast: Bette Davis, Herbert Marshall, James Stephenson, Frieda Inescort, Gale Sondergaard, Bruce Lester, Elizabeth Earl, Cecil Kellaway, Sen Yung, Willie Fung, Tetsu Komai, Doris Lloyd, Roland Got, Otto Hahn, Pete Kotehernaro, David Newell, Ottola Nesmith, Lillian Kemble-Cooper

W. Somerset Maugham's *The Letter* ran for 107 performances on Broadway during the fall and winter of 1927–1928 with Katherine Cornell in the starring role. Gladys Cooper had previously played the role in London in the spring of 1927. Paramount purchased the screen rights for Jeanne Eagels and released it as a talking picture in April 1929.

Warners purchased the rights to remake the picture in December 1939 for the sum of $25,000. Hal Wallis assigned Bob Lord to produce. The initial director on the project, fresh from the considerable success of *Dark Victory*, was Eddie Goulding, who met with Lord in December 1939 to discuss the project. It was Goulding who had repeatedly pestered Warner to buy the project as a starring vehicle for Bette Davis. Nonetheless, Lord later reported to Wallis that he thought Goulding's ideas for the project were "a trifle radical."

Wallis assigned Howard Koch, still working on scenes for *Virginia City*, an Errol Flynn picture, to write the script. The first matter to deal with was the title. Both the play and the 1929 Paramount picture were named *The Letter*. Upon purchasing the project, however, Warner changed the title to *The Sentence*. This left many disgruntled, and on April 12, 1940, the studio reverted to the original title.

Bette was to play Leslie Crosby, who kills the man she loves, David

"With all my heart, I still love the man I killed."

Newell. The first scene has her wearing a scowl on her face and brandishing a pistol in her well-manicured hand. Bette would later say of the unsympathetic role, "It's a great part, a very wonderful part, but I saw Katherine Cornell do it on the stage. She did it in New York in 1927. I was so fascinated by her acting and genius that I saw the play twice, and I can recall every vivid detail of her performance. But, you see, I'm not at all like Kitty Cornell. I had to make this part mine, all mine, my very own. It was the hardest thing I ever tried, because I kept remembering Cornell in the part." Still, Bette walked into the project with a good deal of confidence. She had, after all, had some success playing a Maugham antiheroine. It was his *Of Human Bondage* (1934) that had brought her the first flush of real acclaim.

Others who were considered for the part of Leslie Crosby as of April 22, 1940 (in the event that Bette backed out of the project), were Merle Oberon, Barbara Stanwyck, Claudette Colbert, Joan Crawford, Vivien Leigh, Marlene Dietrich, Katharine Hepburn, Frances Farmer, and Greer Garson.

Those considered for the role of Robert Crosby, husband of the adulterous Leslie, were Ian Hunter, James Stephenson, Herbert Marshall, Walter Pidgeon, George Sanders, and George Brent, among others. For a while, before the start of the filming, it looked as though George Brent would be awarded the part, but Herbert Marshall was finally cast. Interestingly, Marshall had also appeared in the earlier Paramount film, not as Leslie's husband but in the role of her murdered lover.

As director Bette wanted William Wyler, who had a 16-week break from Samuel Goldwyn Productions and was available. Still, it was questionable whether he would accept the project. Wyler had a reputation for being very selective and had caused a minor scandal by refusing to be loaned out to RKO to make *Kitty Foyle* with Ginger Rogers. In his agreement with Warners to do the picture, dated April 9, 1940, Wyler had a lengthy clause inserted that if, for any reason, Bette dropped out of the picture, Wyler also had the option of leaving the picture. He was to be paid $75,000 for his work on the film.

Wyler wanted a full week of rehearsals prior to shooting and a full eight-week shooting schedule. He also wanted Gregg Toland to be borrowed from Goldwyn as his cameraman. Wyler's requests were denied, however, by an enraged Hal Wallis in a May 1, 1940, memo headed "Dear Willy!" What Wallis eventually conceded was two days of rehearsal, Friday and Saturday, May 24 and May 25, 1940, and a seven-week schedule. As his cameraman Wyler got not Toland but the also talented Tony Gaudio.

Production of *The Letter* started on Monday, May 27. The picture was budgeted at $696,000, with approximately $60,000 allotted for Bette.

An early problem during shooting was the deciphering of the dialect of Herbert Marshall and James Stephenson. Hal Wallis complained about "the way these English actors mumble. . . ." Another problem was the clashing of temperaments between Wyler and Stephenson, with Bette, of all people, acting as some sort of referee. She encouraged Stephenson to tolerate Wyler, promising him that the director's emphatic demands would be worth it in the long run.

Bette would later hail Wyler's opening sequence in the picture as the greatest opening shot ever made on film. "We actually started with the first shot in the script," Wyler later related. "It said something like, 'We hear a shot and see Leslie Crosby coming out and shooting a man.' I felt this opening shot should shock you. To get the full impact of the revolver being fired, I thought everything should be very quiet at first. I also wanted to show where we were, give a feeling of the dark, humid jungle atmosphere of rubber plantation country. We had a nice set. The day before we started, I laid out the shot. The camera started in the jungle, went on to the natives sleeping, showed the rubber trees dripping and ended on a parrot awakened by the shot and flying away, all in one camera movement that took more than two minutes. This was the first day of shooting and since none of this really was in the script, we would end up with a quarter of a page in the can. You were supposed to do three or four pages a day. On the first day of shooting, I had one quarter of a page. Jesus, the whole studio was in an uproar, but it became a famous opening scene."

On *The Letter*, Willie Wyler insisted on letting a scene run for several minutes at a time without a single cut. For one important scene, the confrontation between Leslie and her attorney, Wyler made one shot and let it play for a remarkable eight minutes without a cut. Later he relented a bit and inserted a single close-up shot of James Stephenson. Still, the shot lasted for four minutes without interruption.

For another important scene, the confrontation between Leslie and the "Eurasian woman" (played by Gale Sondergaard), Wyler had difficulty deciding how to convey the Eurasian woman's contempt for Leslie. Since the Eurasian woman did not speak English, Wyler decided to let the scene play without dialogue. He accomplished this, and conveyed the necessary contempt, by having the Eurasian woman drop the all-important letter to the floor so that Leslie would have to bend down at her feet to retrieve it. Wyler further decided to let the scene play without a trace of Max Steiner's music. Instead he opted for the sound of a wind chime, which was used to chilling effect.

Early into the production Tony Gaudio missed a couple of days of work due to illness. On Wednesday, June 5, 1940, Bette called in sick. Reportedly she had had an abortion, possibly of Wyler's child.

Amazingly, given his reputation for perfectionism and his usually deliberate pace, Wyler completed the picture on July 19, 1940, a mere three days behind schedule and an astonishing $55,000 *under* budget.

Upon completion of her work Bette fled to her New Hampshire home for a vacation. She returned to the set, reluctantly, in October for retakes. Wyler wanted to shoot additional scenes to make Leslie appear more sympathetic to an audience. Bette balked but acquiesced. She also fought with Wyler over how the now famous line "I still love the man I killed!" should be delivered. Wyler wanted Bette to deliver the line while looking directly at her husband. Bette argued that Leslie would never be able to look at her husband while saying such a thing. Wyler persevered, however, and Bette again acquiesced.

As scripted, *The Letter* ended with the freed Leslie returning to her husband, even though she had killed the man she really loved. However, the film censor declared that Leslie must pay for her crime with a violent death of her own. Bette and Wyler argued that the original ending of Leslie returning to her husband was punishment enough. They lost, and Leslie was sentenced to die at the film's conclusion.

The Letter was marketed with ads featuring Bette toting a gun and pronouncing, "With All My Heart I Still Love the Man I Killed," and "I Wish I Could Say I Was Sorry." The picture opened to good reviews, with some critics citing James Stephenson for stealing it from Bette.

The Letter was remade as *The Unfaithful* in 1947 and as a 1982 made-for-television movie entitled "The Letter."

LIFE MAGAZINE

Bette appeared on the cover of the January 23, 1939, issue of *Life*. The following year the magazine named her "Queen of the Movies" (with Mickey Rooney as her unlikely king). Fifty years later, in its spring 1989 issue, the magazine published a 50th-anniversary issue commemorating Hollywood's landmark year, 1939. A highlight of the issue were photographs that paired the old Hollywood with the new. Upon approaching Bette, editors of the magazine were informed that the contemporary star she wanted to be paired with was Debra Winger. Winger, however, declined, as did Bette's second

choice, William Hurt. Bette eventually settled for James Woods. In the text accompanying the published photograph Bette said, "James and I have something in common. I didn't delight in the way I looked. I don't think he's insane about the way he looks either." Other inspired pairings in the edition: Ginger Rogers and Patrick Swayze, Kevin Costner and Joel McCrea, and Jimmy Stewart and Tom Hanks.

MARY TODD LINCOLN
One of Bette's career-long ambitions was to star in a biopic of first lady Mary Todd Lincoln. In the midforties Bette sent Jack Warner a letter that read, in part, "I am so terribly anxious for you to buy the Mary Lincoln story. . . . to

me this is a story of so many women—not just a figure out of history—it is the story of any woman who believes in her husband and pushes him ahead— the story of the woman being the power behind the throne—this theme is apt to be box office—also the character has a wonderful combination of Scarlet [sic] O'Hara—a mother faced with giving her son to war—and even the *Back Street* type of woman—the discarded woman. . . . I hope so much—you will decide to let me do it. . . ."

Shortly prior to her leaving in 1949, the studio seriously considered starring Bette in a picture about Mary Lincoln, with Irving Rapper as director. Far from keen on the project, and with his dissatisfaction with Bette growing, Jack Warner eventually canned it.

Almost 15 years later, after appearing in a television drama about Mary Lincoln titled "Recall," Bette was still trying to get a feature film produced about the troubled first lady. At one point, producers Josh Baldwin and Maurice Weiss announced that Bette would star in a picture loosely based on the book *Mr. Lincoln's Wife* by Polly Ann Colver Harris. The film was to be shot, from a screenplay by Eugene Barber, in Springfield, Illinois, in the summer of 1964. This project, however, also failed to reach the production stage.

As late as 1969 Bette was still expressing an interest in playing Mrs. Lincoln. She encouraged screenwriter Alvah Bessie to work on the screenplay, promising to work on getting the interest of Hollywood producers. When Bessie expressed concern that Bette was too old to play the part, she extolled the virtues of makeup and soft-focus lenses. Bessie's fears were allayed, and the two corresponded for a while, each updating the other. Finally, however, Bette lamented to Bessie, "Nobody seems to *want* a film about Mary Lincoln . . . or maybe it is Bette Davis they do not want."

Bette also pursued the idea of a play on the first lady. On July 30, 1946, she entered into an oral agreement to star in a Broadway play by Ramon Romero entitled *Mrs. Lincoln.* Although the two never signed a written contract, Bette did write in a letter to Romero, "For years I have sought a play about Mary Todd and in your play I have found the one I have wanted to do. *No one must do this but me.*

Even the details were worked out. Bette was to receive $5,000 a week plus 10 percent of the box office gross. She was to have done the play in 1949, following the termination of her contract with Warner Brothers. Instead she opted to work on RKO's *Payment on Demand.* Stranded and without other recourse, Romero filed a lawsuit against Bette. Then, on March 23, 1950, he abruptly dropped the charges without explanation.

THE LITTLE FOXES ★★★★
Samuel Goldwyn Productions
Released by RKO
1941   116 minutes   bw
Directed by: William Wyler

Produced by: Samuel Goldwyn
Screenplay by: Lillian Hellman, with additional scenes and dialogue by
    Arthur Kober, Dorothy Parker, and Alan Campbell, based on the play
    by Lillian Hellman
Cinematography by: Gregg Toland
Cast: Bette Davis, Herbert Marshall, Teresa Wright, Richard Carlson, Dan
    Duryea, Patricia Collinge, Charles Dingle, Carl Benton Reid, Jessie
    Grayson, John Marriott, Russell Hicks, Lucien Littlefield, Virginia
    Brissac

The Little Foxes by Lillian Hellman was a major Broadway hit in 1939. At
the time Hellman was under contract to Samuel Goldwyn, who purchased
the rights to the play and then assigned Hellman to adapt it for the screen.

Early drafts of the play, interestingly, had Horace Giddens stricken with
syphilis. His illness was later modified to the more acceptable "heart condition." Set in the South in 1900, the story has Regina's two brothers come up
with a scheme to make a quick and substantial buck by taking over a cotton
mill that they can run on cheap labor. Regina decides to become a third
partner in the operation, but she must first persuade her sickly husband,
Horace, to give her the money to cover her portion of the purchase price.
Horace refuses, citing moral grounds, and Regina becomes furious. But, the
drama has us wonder, is she evil enough to *kill* her husband to get the
$75,000 she so desperately wants?

Nineteen forty had not been a good year for Sam Goldwyn and his
company. Both *The Westerner* and *Raffles* had failed him at the box office.
Still, to his credit, Goldwyn wanted only the best for *The Little Foxes*. No
expense was to be spared. He wanted William Wyler to direct since Wyler
had previously directed the film adaptation of Hellman's *These Three* with
much success.

Both Goldwyn and Wyler wanted Bette Davis for the part of Regina,
which had been originated by Tallulah Bankhead on Broadway. Getting her,
however, was not easy. Bette was then riding a phenomenal crest of critical
acclaim and box office popularity, and Warner Brothers was not about to
lend her out to another studio. In fact, the last time the studio had lent her
out had been for 1934's *Of Human Bondage*, and Jack Warner was embar-
rassed that it had taken RKO to show him how to utilize Bette's talent.

However, as fate would have it, Goldwyn had something that Warner
wanted. Warner and director Howard Hawks both wanted Gary Cooper and
only Gary Cooper, who was under contract to Sam Goldwyn, to star in
Sergeant York. A phone call between Goldwyn and Warner followed, and
though Warner was reluctant to let go of his biggest star, he eventually
acquiesced. Bette complicated things by throwing in a few demands of her
own, not the least of which was the then-astronomical asking price of
$150,000 (not the $385,000 she would later claim). In a letter dated July 31,
1940, Warner wrote to Goldwyn, "If we could make a deal whereby we
furnish Bette Davis for *The Little Foxes* and we pay her, and you, in turn,

furnish Gary Cooper and pay him for his services in *Sergeant York*, we can consummate this deal immediately." It was a deal that Goldwyn, Cooper, and Bette all agreed to. At that time Bette's usual salary was in the $5,000-a-week range, or approximately $60,000 for a picture (on a 12-week shooting schedule).

Despite later protests that she had wanted Bankhead to get the part, Bette was eager to play Regina and even agreed to make one more picture for Warners than the three a year her contract stipulated.

Although Bankhead was not cast to reprise her stage role, other members of the play's cast were. Dan Duryea, Patricia Collinge (as Aunt Birdie), Charles Dingle, Carl Benton Reid, and John Marriott were all signed by Goldwyn.

In preproduction there was some silliness about Bette's also playing Horace and Regina's 17-year-old daughter, Alexandra. Fortunately the idea was dropped when Goldwyn "discovered" young actress Teresa Wright after seeing a performance of the Broadway play *Life with Father*. After the show Goldwyn went backstage and offered Wright a contract on the spot.

Meanwhile, Goldwyn had Lillian Hellman come up with a dozen different drafts of the screenplay, opening the play up, trying to humanize the character of Regina, adding a love interest for daughter Alexandra, etc. She was sick of it. Hellman recommended that the screenplay be turned over for fine-tuning, which it was, to Arthur Kober, her former husband, and Alan Campbell and his wife, Dorothy Parker.

Bette's loan to Goldwyn commenced on April 14, 1941, and extended for 12 weeks. It was to be a tempestuous and unhappy production. Bette got Goldwyn to borrow the services of Perc Westmore and Orry-Kelly to do her makeup and costumes, respectively, but she got little else. She and Wyler fought constantly, with Wyler winning all of the battles. They fought over her costumes. She thought they were too new, too opulent. She thought that the Giddens family should not appear to have so much money—otherwise, she argued, why would it be so difficult for her to raise the $75,000? She argued about the sets for the same reason.

Mostly, she argued about her interpretation of Regina. Wyler, she felt, wanted the character softened, humanized. Bette insisted on playing the part as a monster. "Wyler," Bette would later say, "was very rude about the way I played her, extremely rude. He hated it." At one point, during the shooting of a dinner scene, Wyler snapped in front of the company that it was the lousiest dinner scene he had ever witnessed and that Goldwyn had better try to get Bankhead for the part. Bette, hysterical, stormed off the set.

Wyler argued that Bette was playing the part as a character part, that she was playing Regina too old, too rigid, too unattractive, too humorless, and too sexless. He accused Bette of playing the role lazily and without shading. Wyler argued that if Regina was indeed the witch that Bette was portraying her as, Horace would be a fool to have fallen in love with her and a bigger fool to have stayed with her.

At one point Bette collapsed on the set. Physical exhaustion was cited as the cause by her doctors, who prescribed 10 days of rest at home. Bette complained that her "condition" had been caused by her heavy costumes and her schedule, which had her waking up at 5:30 A.M. daily and working until 7:00 P.M. Bette refused to return to work, shutting down the production for a reported 21 days. Hedda Hopper said on her May 21, 1941, radio broadcast, "Some say she isn't ill, and she's definitely out of *Little Foxes* because she's rowing with director Willie Wyler. . . . Others claim she's going to have a baby, and still more say she's having trouble with her husband." Finally, the insurance company's doctor examined Bette and, determining that there was nothing wrong with her physically, ordered her to return to the set, which she did. She continued, however, to play the part of Regina as she deemed fit. The picture was completed, but Bette's relationship with Wyler never fully recovered.

Even comparing it to her Mildred in *Of Human Bondage* and her Baby Jane Hudson in *What Ever Happened to Baby Jane?*, her Regina may have been Bette's most villainous, unsympathetic, truly *evil* characterization. As Regina she wears her hair in a tight Gibson girl coiffure. Her face is a mask of white makeup. Her lips are painted a garish red. She seethes with inner hatred. Her Regina is not a bitch, but a witch. All she needs is a broom.

The Little Foxes opened to rave reviews and a slew of Oscar nominations, including those for best picture, best director, and best actress. In later years Bette always said that she was unhappy with the film, that even though she had played the role as she saw it, her performance had been tainted by Wyler's direction. Actually, in *The Little Foxes*, Wyler elicited from Bette one of the finest performances she ever gave. Certainly the picture is one of the best she ever made.

"LITTLE GLORIA . . . HAPPY AT LAST"

Excellent 1982 television miniseries directed by Waris Hussein from a teleplay by William Hanley that was adapted from the book by Barbara Goldsmith. It was Hussein who suggested Bette for the part of matriarch Alice Gwynne Vanderbilt. The producers did not think she would consider a part that consisted of only 18 pages in a 200-page script, but Hussein pursued her anyway. Upon arriving at her New York hotel he found Bette standing at the end of a long corridor, completely done up in the hair and makeup of the character as she envisioned it. There was no "Hello," no "Pleased to meet you." Instead Bette drilled Waris: "What do you think?" He replied by boldly telling Bette that her hair was all wrong. She excused herself and walked over to the other side of the room, where her hairdresser was waiting. When she returned with a revised hairdo, Hussein was aware that he had passed the first in a series of Bette Davis tests.

During shooting Bette was extremely agreeable. She approved of the cast and had no desire to change the script. Her only demand was that she not work after 6:00 P.M. One afternoon she approached Hussein and warned him that, at the rate he was shooting, he would not finish with her by 6:00. He told her not to worry about it. At 5:59 Bette again approached him, reminded him of the time, and told him that he would not finish with her until 10:00 P.M. Hussein replied that she was exaggerating, that he would finish with her far before 10:00, and he thanked her for her patience. Shooting finished at one minute to 10:00. Bette marched up to Hussein and said, simply, "I did it for you." Then she walked away.

Bette enjoyed her experience on "Little Gloria," and her performance would win her an Emmy nomination as the year's best supporting actress.

Edgar Scherick and Scott Rudin were executive producers of "Little Gloria . . . Happy at Last." It was produced by David Nicksay and Justine Heroux and shot by Tony Imi. In addition to Bette, the cast featured Lucy Gutteridge, Glynis Johns, Angela Lansbury, Michael Gross, Martin Balsam, John Hillerman, Barnard Hughes, Christopher Plummer, Maureen Stapleton, Rosalyn Landor, Joseph Maher, Leueen Willoughby, and Jennifer Dundas.

ANATOLE LITVAK

Litvak directed Bette in the pictures *The Sisters* (1938) and *All This, and Heaven Too* (1940). At the time he made the latter, Litvak had just become estranged from his wife (and Bette adversary) Miriam Hopkins and engaged in a brief affair with Bette. The affair came to an abrupt end, reportedly when Bette learned that Litvak had dined with Paulette Goddard at Ciro's Restaurant and had spent a good deal of the evening under the table and under Goddard's skirt.

Despite their affair off camera, Bette was never particularly fond of Litvak's style behind the camera. Litvak, known as Tola to almost everyone, planned every shot in detail and then worked his actors around his blueprint. Bette did not relish taking second place to another actor, much less to an inanimate camera. She had many run-ins with Litvak and labeled him "a very stubborn director."

Anatole Litvak (Mikahil Anatol Litvak, 1902–1974) made other pictures, including *Mayerling* (1936), *Confessions of a Nazi Spy* (1939), *City for Conquest* (1940), *The Snake Pit* (1948), and *Anastasia* (1956).

JOHN LODER

John Loder appeared in the 1942 picture *Now, Voyager* and reportedly engaged in an off-camera affair with Bette. He also costarred in the 1943 picture *Old Acquaintance*, after which he married actress Hedy Lamarr.

As an actor he built a reputation in Hollywood for playing the guy who always loses the girl. Explained Loder, "Maybe it's because I have that waiting-at-the-church look in my eyes."

John Loder (born John Lowe in 1898) appeared in other pictures, including *How Green Was My Valley* (1941), *Gentleman Jim* (1942), and *Dishonored Lady* (1947).

JOSHUA LOGAN

Director, coauthor, and coproducer of the ill-fated 1974 stage musical *Miss*

Moffat, an adaptation of the play *The Corn Is Green* by Emlyn Williams. Before commencing to direct Bette in the production, Logan attended one of her one-woman shows and was struck that, in his words, "She had become an amalgam of all her screen roles plus all her impersonators."

Bette backed out of *Miss Moffat* before it got to Broadway and left Logan's production in shambles. He later wrote about the experience in his 1978 autobiography, *Movie Stars, Real People, and Me*, in which he detailed what he characterized to be Bette's neurosis. When she got wind of the book, Bette attempted to block its publication, claiming that it contained "false, malicious material" and could "cause serious damage" to her career. Retorted Logan, "How can what I wrote damage her career? She's been that way for 50 years. Why would it damage her now?"

Joshua Logan, born in 1908, directed pictures including *Picnic*, (1955), *Bus Stop* (1956), *Sayonara* (1957), and *South Pacific* (1958).

THE LONELY LIFE

Bette's 1962 autobiography, which was written with the assistance of Sanford Dody. The book, published by G. P. Putnam's Sons, is an entertaining though largely slanted book in which facts and dates are sometimes confused.

JACK LONG

Bette received her very first movie fan letter from 15-year-old Jack Long of Kansas City, Missouri. Long developed a teenage crush on Bette after seeing the picture *Seed* and continued to correspond with her long afterward. During the making of *Deception* (1946), Long, then a 30-year-old advertising man, visited Bette on the set at her invitation.

JOAN LORRING

During the shooting of the 1945 picture *The Corn Is Green*, Bette took her young costar, Joan Lorring, under her wing. When asked why Bette liked her when she had disliked so many others, Lorring responded, "My insecurity. My feeling myself to be so homely. I believe that she related to that. One day we were in the projection room and there were huge close-ups of me on the screen. I thought I was so ugly, and I kept sliding down in the chair until I finally wound up on the floor. And I heard her voice coming at me from a seat behind. 'You know,' she said, 'when I first started there was a very beautiful actress named Anita Louise. And when we were in the projection room her mother used to say, "Oh, there's my beautiful baby!" when a big close-up of Anita Louise came on. And when my close-ups came, nobody would say anything. Because I wasn't beautiful the way she was. But you know what? *I'm still here.*' " Says Lorring today, "I love that woman. I will love her until I die. I may love her after that, I don't know." For her performance in *The Corn Is Green*, Lorring received a Best Supporting Actress Oscar nomination.

Joan Lorring (born Magdalen Ellis in 1926) appeared in other pictures, including *The Bridge of San Luis Rey* (1944), *The Verdict* (1946), and *Stranger on the Prowl* (1953).

LOWELL, MASSACHUSETTS

Bette Davis was born on April 5, 1908, at 22 Chester Street in Lowell, Massachusetts.

"Thank God my family took me out of there."
Bette Davis on Lowell

"MADAME SIN"

"Madame Sin," produced in 1972 and shot in Glasgow, Scotland, was Bette's foray into the land of made-for-television movies. The ABC telefilm was financed by Sir Lew Grade, with Robert Wagner as executive producer and costar. Julian Wintle and Lou Morheim produced, and David Greene directed from a script he cowrote with Barry Oringer. It was shot by Tony Richmond. The rather far-fetched plot had dominating Bette scheming to take over the world. In addition to Bette and Wagner, the cast included Denholm Elliott, Gordon Jackson, Dudley Sutton, Catherine Schell, Paul Maxwell, Pik-sen Lin, David Healy, Alan Dobie, Roy Kinnear, Al Mancini, Frank Middlemass, and Burt Kwouk.

THE MAN WHO CAME TO DINNER ★★★

Warner Brothers
1942   112 minutes   bw
Directed by: William Keighley
Produced by: Hal B. Wallis, in association with Jerry Wald, Sam Harris,
    and Jack Saper
Screenplay by: Julius J. and Philip G. Epstein, based on the play by
    George S. Kaufman and Moss Hart
Cinematography by: Tony Gaudio
Cast: Bette Davis, Ann Sheridan, Monty Woolley, Richard Travis, Jimmy
    Durante, Billie Burke, Reginald Gardiner, Elisabeth Fraser, Grant
    Mitchell, George Barbier, Russell Arms, Mary Wickes, Ruth Vivian,
    Beverly Carleton, Edwin Stanley, Charles Drake, Nanette Vallon, John
    Ridgely

The primary reason Bette agreed to do *The Man Who Came to Dinner*, in
which she would have a relatively small and inconsequential part, was that
she wanted to work with John Barrymore or Charles Laughton, both of
whom were top contenders for the leading male role.

The story had Bette as Maggie Cutler, supersecretary and indispensable
assistant to the craggy and scathingly witty VIP columnist Sheridan Whiteside, reportedly modeled on Alexander Woollcott. Whiteside breaks his hip
on one of his speaking tours and proceeds to create havoc in the midwestern
home in which he convalesces. Maggie, meanwhile, despite being something
of a worldly woman, falls in love with a small-town newspaper man.

Kaufman and Hart sold the rights to their play in an agreement dated
August 15, 1940. The agreement, later amended, paid them a whopping flat
fee of $275,000. As is custom in Hollywood, no matter how good the original
material, screenwriters were brought in, in this case the Epstein brothers, to
prepare it for the screen. Kaufman was later sent a copy of the script as
revised by the Epsteins. In his March 3, 1941, response Kaufman, understandably perturbed that his play was being tampered with, wrote that the
revision had a lot of "highly amusing" situations but that some of it was
"overly direct and abrupt writing." Kaufman added in his letter, "Is it to be
Laughton?"

Charles Laughton initially tested for the part on February 24, 1941. As
of March 17, 1941, also considered possibilities for the role were Clifton
Webb, Jack Benny, Bob Hope, and Douglas Fairbanks, Jr.

Later Orson Welles was also seriously considered for the role. A meeting
between Welles and Jack Warner took place on the evening of March 28, 1941,
at Warner's home. Welles agreed to play the part on several conditions. He
wanted $100,000 to act in the picture. If he was also to direct, he wanted
$150,000. For Maggie Cutler he wanted either Barbara Stanwyck, Paulette
Goddard, or Carole Lombard. He considered Olivia de Havilland as another
possibility. He did *not* want Bette Davis. If he was not to direct, Welles's first
choice was Leo McCarey. His second was Howard Hawks. He later changed

his mind and made Hawks his first choice. Jack Warner agreed to all of Welles's demands, but negotiations still fell through, probably due to some problem with RKO, with whom Welles was then linked.

The focus then switched to Cary Grant. Warners was to borrow Grant from Columbia. In return Warners would allow Columbia to borrow George Raft, John Garfield, or Geraldine Fitzgerald. Grant, who also wanted Hawks to direct, was to receive no financial compensation for the picture. Instead he wanted Warners to pay $125,000 to the British War Relief. Kaufman agreed to the casting of Grant, and for a while it seemed that Grant would indeed play the part. The one stipulation if Grant played the part was that the script be revised to include a romance between Whiteside and Maggie. Negotiations with Cary Grant, however, also fell through.

On May 9, 1941, John Barrymore tested for the part. The test made it apparent to Hal Wallis that Barrymore was either too sick or too far gone into alcohol to play the part. His May 19, 1941, memo read, simply, "We will forget about John Barrymore."

Fredric March tested for the part on May 27, 1941. His test was well received by director William Keighley. Shortly thereafter, Monty Woolley, who was playing the part on Broadway at the time, was also given a test. "I saw the Monty Woolley test," Jack Warner wrote to Wallis in a June 6, 1941, memo, "and it is excellent." Warner further recommended that if Woolley was to be cast, a test should be made with his "original blondish beard" because "he has become an old grayhaired man since the [opening night] of the play." Keighley, however, opted for March. "I ran the Woolley test," Keighley wrote to Hal Wallis, "and much to my surprise, I didn't like him as well as March."

Finally Warner and Wallis agreed to cast Woolley in the lead, but only after they had, on June 26, cast Bette Davis, whose box office presence they felt would make up for the less certain appeal of Woolley, who was little known to movie audiences.

Early in the process the wish list for Maggie Cutler had included Rosalind Russell, Jean Arthur, Claudette Colbert, Katharine Hepburn, and Joan Crawford. On June 13, 1941, Edith Atwater, who had played the part onstage, also tested for the part. In the meantime Bette Davis had entered the casting picture in May.

For her desirable box office presence Bette, in what was tantamount to a supporting role, would get approximately $70,000. Woolley would receive only $17,500.

Sought for the role of Bert Jefferson, Maggie's newspaper man love interest, were Ronald Reagan, George Brent, Jimmy Stewart, and Henry Fonda, among others. Considered for the part of actress Lorraine Sheldon, reportedly modeled on Gertrude Lawrence, were Olivia de Havilland, Paulette Goddard, Rita Hayworth, Greer Garson, Mary Astor, Lucille Ball, and Betty Grable. Those parts went, respectively, to Richard Travis and Ann Sheridan.

With a budget of $1,051,000, *The Man Who Came to Dinner* started shooting on July 21, 1941. Shooting proceeded without incident until September 13, when Bette's nose was bitten by one of her dogs. For the next several days Keighley shot around her. She returned to work on September 17 but was shot only with her back to the camera. Production was then suspended on the following day to allow time for her nose to heal.

It was not only her nose that needed healing. Bette was also having emotional problems. During her lengthy recuperation she vacationed at her home in Franconia, New Hampshire. While there, she sent a letter to Hal Wallis that read, in part, "Guess this should be a warning that I've been working too hard for a long time. When I cry all day long something is really wrong." Meanwhile, Wallis pressed Bette as to when she would be returning to work. "If I thought it possible to work on Monday," Bette wrote in an October 2, 1941, letter, "I would of my own volition be there. Scab not off yet and nose still very red."

Production of the picture did not resume until October 10, 1941. Because of the delay, Bette agreed to go into her next picture *In This Our Life*, without a break. It was an agreement that Bette would not keep. On October 18, 1941, 16 shooting days behind schedule, *The Man Who Came to Dinner* finally completed production.

Over the years Bette frequently denigrated *The Man*. Her viewpoint is curious. Perhaps she was displeased by just how minor her part really was because the picture is, in fact, highly entertaining with classic comedic lines. At one point Whiteside barks a summons to his homely nurse. When she doesn't show up promptly, he calls after her, "What have you got in there— a *sailor?*" Another time he abuses her with "Go in and read the life of Florence Nightingale and learn how unfitted you are for your chosen profession." Another scene has Whiteside introducing Maggie to the man she will fall in love with by saying, "This aging debutante, Mr. Jefferson, I retain in my employ only because she is the sole support of her two-headed brother." And finally, Jimmy Durante, in a colorful featured role, reportedly inspired by Groucho Marx, says to Whiteside's nurse upon introduction, "I can feel the hot blood pounding through your varicose veins."

It's that kind of picture.

THE MAN WHO PLAYED GOD ★★
Warner Brothers
1932 81 minutes bw
Directed by: John G. Adolfi
Produced by: Darryl F. Zanuck
Screenplay by: Julien Josephson and Maude T. Howell, based on a story by
    Gouverneur Morris and a play by Jules Eckert Goodman
Cinematography by: James Van Trees
Cast: George Arliss, Violet Heming, Ivan Simpson, Bette Davis, Louise
    Closser Hale, Donald Cook, Ray Milland, Oscar Apfel, Murray

Kinnel, Hedda Hopper, Paul Porcasi, William Janney, Grace Durkin, Dorothy Libaire, Andre Luget, Charles Evans, Wade Boteler, Alexander Ikonikoff

Bette Davis's first picture for Warner Brothers, *The Man Who Played God*, was based on the play *The Silent Voice* by Jules Eckert Goodman and the short story "The Man Who Played God" by Gouverneur Morris, the latter of which was published in the January 1912 edition of *Cosmopolitan*.

The fairy-tale plot has George Arliss as Montgomery Royale, a concert pianist. At a royal command performance before the king a bomb explodes, deafening the pianist and destroying his career. He then dedicates his life to helping others, whom he watches through binoculars from his penthouse window.

The film was mounted, of course, as a vehicle for Arliss, who was then perhaps the most powerful actor on the Warners lot. Arliss was also known in Hollywood as something of a mentor to young actresses, with his most famous discovery up to that point being Jeanne Eagels. For *The Man Who Played God* he wanted a Broadway actress with good diction. He found her in Bette Davis.

Defeated after being rejected by Universal, Bette had packed her suitcases and was on the verge of returning to New York, tail between her legs, when the telephone rang. It was Arliss, asking if she was interested in meeting him to discuss his new picture.

Bette, subsequently signed to Warners at $300 a week, was billed fourth behind Arliss, Violet Heming and Ivan Simpson. As Grace, the young blond girl who falls in love with Arliss's much older Montgomery Royale, Bette would have such unabashedly gushing lines in the picture as "I can learn more from you in five minutes than from anyone else in five years. I love you! I love you!"

Bette started shooting on November 19, 1931. Arliss was particularly nurturing to Bette, and she would never forget his kindness. He was certainly not as warm to other actresses in the company. Hedda Hopper, also cast in the picture, would later say that Arliss had treated *her* so coldly and so intimidated her that she was unable to give a good performance. As George Eells wrote in his 1972 biography *Hedda and Louella*, "Hedda claimed that the dour Arliss was kindness itself to Bette Davis, and Miss Davis flowered. When it came to Hedda, she said he coldly demanded to see what she could do and so terrified her that she was unable to relax enough to act. She never forgave him."

Warner Brothers marketed the picture with ads touting, "With an All-Star Broadway Cast." The studio hyped it as an important picture, with ads proclaiming, "The Competition for the Best Picture of 1932 Will End Tonight." Of course the picture was only fair and failed to live up to its hype. A few reviews mentioned Bette Davis, but some complained of her odd penchant for speaking rapidly.

The Man Who Played God was remade as *Sincerely Yours*, a 1955 vehicle for Liberace.

JOSEPH L. MANKIEWICZ

Mankiewicz directed Bette, from his own script, in what was arguably her finest picture, *All About Eve* (1950). For his work on the film Mankiewicz won Oscars for both his direction and his screenplay. Years later he appeared as a presenter at the 1989 Film Society of Lincoln Center's tribute to Bette.

Joseph Mankiewicz (1909–1993) wrote and directed other pictures, including *A Letter to Three Wives* (Best Screenplay Oscar winner, 1949), *Julius Caesar* (1953), *The Barefoot Contessa* (1954), *Guys and Dolls* (1955), *Suddenly Last Summer* (direction only, 1959), *Cleopatra* (1963), and *Sleuth* (direction only, 1972).

> "I felt the urge to direct because I couldn't stomach what was being done with what I wrote."
>
> *Joseph L. Mankiewicz*

NICKI MARCELLINO

Nicki Marcellino was the first marine in World War II to receive the Purple Heart twice. Bette met him at the Hollywood Canteen and invited him to visit her at the studio. While he was there, Bette introduced him to Perc Westmore, head of the studio's makeup department. At Bette's prodding Westmore hired Marcellino, who became one of the studio's makeup artists. He also became Bette's personal makeup artist. His first picture was *Deception* (1946); he also worked on *Winter Meeting* (1948) and *June Bride* (1948).

MARKED WOMAN ★★

Warner Brothers
1937   96 minutes   bw
Directed by: Lloyd Bacon
Produced by: Hal B. Wallis, in association with Lou Edelman
Screenplay by: Robert Rossen and Abem Finkel, with additional dialogue by Seton I. Miller
Cinematography by: George Barnes
Cast: Bette Davis, Humphrey Bogart, Lola Lane, Isabel Jewell, Eduardo Ciannelli, Rosalind Marquis, Mayo Methot, Jane Bryan, Allen Jenkins, Henry O'Neill, Ben Welden, John Litel, Damian O'Flynn, Robert Strange, Raymond Hatton, William B. Davidson, Frank Faylen, Jack Norton, Kenneth Harlan

Marked Woman marked Bette's return to Warner Brothers and her return to the screen after her much publicized walkout that had culminated in a British courtroom. Despite the disclaimer at the beginning of the picture, and Warners' repeated contention that it was not, *Marked Woman* was based on the New York trial of Lucky Luciano. Studio files indicate that there was much concern in preproduction that the script be given some distinction from the trial so as not to arouse too much suspicion. In fact, while the script was being developed, producer Lou Edelman was desperately attempting to get a copy of the court transcript of the Luciano trial. The picture featured Bette as Mary Dwight, a smart, mouthy "hostess" at the Club Intimate, a high-class clip joint. "Hostess" was about as much as the movies could get away with in 1937. She was actually a prostitute, but the word could not be used. The plot had Bogart as David Graham, a district attorney after Bette's boss, the Luciano figure, here dubbed Johnny Vanning (Ciannelli). Graham approaches Mary and asks her to testify against her boss—she laughs in his face. Later, when her kid sister (played by Jane Bryan) is killed by Vanning, Mary agrees to testify against him.

One scene called for Vanning to order his goons to scar Mary's face with a knife wound in the shape of a cross, Vanning's personal signature, hence the picture's title. Controversy erupted during the shooting of the scene. Hollywood policy at the time called for actresses to be nothing but glamorous on the screen. Aware of how important the picture would be to her career, Bette went to a doctor and explained, "I am a girl who has been beaten within an inch of her life. How would you bandage me?" She then walked onto the set with her face made up to look badly beaten and wrapped in a bandage. "Well," she asked the crew, "how do you like this makeup?"

Hal Wallis, for one, did not. On January 13, 1937, he issued an angry memo to Perc Westmore, head of the makeup department. "The last makeup test with Bette Davis with the bandages on and with eyes made up is absolutely out of the question. It is too horrible, and we are not making a comedy. . . . Let's stop trying to make her too horrible looking. We just don't want it that way. Also, the bandage on her cheek, which is supposed to cover the scar, is too big and that should be cut down a little." Despite her frequent contention in later years that she had played the scene *her* way, it was another battle lost for Bette Davis.

Bette and the rest of the cast had not even seen a finished script by the day before shooting started. Shooting commenced, with an estimated budget of $295,000, on December 9, 1936. It was to be a rapid shoot, with delays caused by Bette's illnesses on December 28–30 and January 4–5, which either halted or rerouted shooting. Ciannelli was also sick for a few days, as was director Bacon. Interestingly, rather than shutting down production when Bacon was ill, the studio called in another director, Michael Curtiz to fill in for him. Also delaying the shooting was a song and dance number by Lola Lane, the retakes of which alone took an entire afternoon.

Hal Wallis gave the picture a good deal of attention. In the early scenes shot of Bette, Wallis complained to Bacon that her delivery was "a little too high-pitched and a little too sing-songee." He was also concerned about her appearance and, in a December 7, 1936, memo to cinematographer George Barnes and director Bacon, Wallis warned, "the circles under her eyes are very prominent."

Wallis's objection to the casting of one of the picture's bit parts provided an amusing behind-the-scenes scenario. Wallis issued a scathing memo on January 23, 1937, to casting director Max Arnow. "Who is that monkey you got to play Joe Donnera in *Marked Woman*? Why the hell didn't you get some menacing looking character—somebody with a kick. He looks like those God damn five dollar extra men. Did you ever see this man before he was cast or do you just call names or what is it? And if you saw him couldn't you know that he wasn't right for the part? Do I have to see everybody?" Arnow responded with an understated but powerful memo of his own. "This bit was played by one Hymie Marks," Arnow wrote, "who was formerly a gangster and henchman of Lucky Luciano whom Bacon asked to specifically play this one line bit and which I understand was okayed by [producer] Edelman."

Wallis also oversaw the editing in postproduction, during which he made numerous cuts and changes. His extra effort paid off, particularly with his boss, Jack Warner. In a February 22, 1937, memo from Warner to Wallis, Warner enthused, "I ran *Marked Woman* last night. This is one of the best pictures of this type we ever made. There is really a sock in every foot. After seeing it I arranged to have it previewed Monday night at Warner's Hollywood. Am sure we have nothing to worry about other than trying to make ten a year like this. We can be very proud of this production, especially being Bette Davis's first picture since her return which will vindicate any 'ifs' 'ands' or 'buts' that we are going to give her the run-around. Anyone having anything to do with this picture deserves tremendous commendation."

With a marketing ad that touted "Bette's Back!" *Marked Woman* opened to mostly good reviews. The picture was thought to be distinguished at the time. Actually, however, it's just another mildly involving potboiler.

MARRIAGE

In her later years Bette would alternate among being disenchanted, bored, and melancholy on the subject of marriage. Sometimes she would say that she would never want to marry again and that the whole idea of marriage was overrated. At other times she would seem to be sad that she had never had a successful marriage. Sometimes she would opine that her marriage to Arthur Farnsworth would have lasted if he hadn't died. Typically she would blame her husbands for the failure of her marriages. The men she married were not strong enough, not "man enough" to handle her. Her fame was too much for them. They didn't give as much as they took. . . .

> "It's hell to be married to a star. It's hell for the woman, and it's hell for the man."
>
> *Bette Davis after her divorce from Gary Merrill*

> "I just don't think it can work—not for a career woman. God knows I've tried. It's too bad that it won't work, because I like men. I just can't stay married to them."
>
> *Bette Davis*

"I have been married four times. Three of my husbands were what I would call decent human beings. The other was not."

Bette Davis

I know now that my marriages—all of them—were a farce.

Bette Davis

Bette Davis's Marriages
Harmon Oscar Nelson, Jr.: 8/32 to 12/38
Arthur Farnsworth, Jr.: 12/40 to 8/43
William Grant Sherry: 11/45 to 7/50
Gary Merrill: 7/50 to 7/60

W. SOMERSET MAUGHAM
It was in the film adaptation of Maugham's novel *Of Human Bondage* that Bette Davis had her first taste of great acclaim. She later starred in an adaptation of his play *The Letter*. At the time of the latter Bette expressed interest in playing in Maugham's *Cakes and Ale* and as Sadie Thompson in his *Rain*.

She met Maugham on the set of *The Little Foxes* in 1941 and was surprised by his stuttering. She would later say of the meeting, "When he gave Phillip a club foot in *Of Human Bondage*, that was the equivalent of his stuttering. He would go on sometimes for five minutes and you'd just sit and look at him and pray to God he didn't think you'd noticed it. But he said one of the most brilliant things that was ever said about Hollywood. He said, 'If your scripts were as great as your sets, what a town this would be.' "

W. Somerset Maugham died in 1965 at the age of 91.

HATTIE MCDANIEL

Following her success as Mammy in *Gone With the Wind* (1939), Hattie McDaniel was cast in the 1941 picture *The Great Lie*. Her contract, however, stipulated that Warner Brothers could make no mention of *GWTW* or of Mammy in its marketing of the picture. Also working on the picture was Hattie's brother, Sam. Later McDaniel appeared in the pictures *In This Our Life* (1942) and *Thank Your Lucky Stars* (1943).

Hattie McDaniel (1895–1952), the first African-American actor to win an Academy Award (Best Supporting Actress, *GWTW*), appeared in other pictures, including *Showboat* (1936) and *Margie* (1946).

MEN

Bette Davis liked her men, in a word, *masculine*. Later in life she liked them young.

> "I've *always* liked men much better than women. From high school onward, all my friends were boys. I like the male mind better. Men aren't as pretty as women, but they're more interesting. I miss their company."
>
> *Bette Davis, 1983*

> "Another pitfall for the high-powered woman is a tendency to choose weak men. The successful Hollywood actress often is attracted to rather neutral characters from outside her profession."
>
> *Bette Davis, 1955*

> "I don't dislike actors. It's simply that I would not marry one. It isn't anything they can help. It's just that I dislike the job of acting as it affects a man. The things they have to do and be, happen to be the very things I most dislike in a man. I never have been one for very handsome men. Actors are, for the most part, very handsome men. I dislike men who think about looks. I dislike men who talk about themselves. Actors do. They have to. I wouldn't marry an actor because 1) I couldn't expect fidelity. 2) Because I would feel completely unnecessary to his life, and 3) because while it's natural for a woman to be an actress, it isn't in the nature of man to be an actor. And anything against Nature does funny things. I never will marry an actor—I hope. I can't think of any worse hell."
>
> *Bette Davis, 1940. Ten years later Bette married an actor.*

THE MENACE ★
Columbia
1932   64 minutes   bw
Directed by: Roy William Neill
Produced by: Sam Nelson

A low-budget and embarrassing menace.

Screenplay by: Dorothy Howell, Charles Logue, and Roy Chanslor, based
    on the novel by Edgar Wallace
Cinematography by: L. William O'Connell
Cast: Walter Byron, H. B. Warner, Bette Davis, Natalie Moorhead, William
    B. Davidson, Murray Kinnell, Crauford Kent, Halliwell Hobbes,
    Charles Gerrard

Essentially washing its hands of her, Universal lent Bette to Columbia to
make this low-budget quickie. Based on the book *The Feathered Serpent* by
Edgar Wallace, the picture was initially titled *The Feathered Serpent*, then
The Squeaker, and finally *The Menace*. The plot, essentially, deals with an
escaped convict who undergoes plastic surgery to evade the police. About her
role, Bette was fond of saying in later years, "All I did was pull corpses out
of closets."

JOHNNY MERCER

Bette met lyricist and composer Johnny Mercer at the Hollywood Canteen in
the 1940s, and the two had a passionate affair, which they managed to keep
secret from the Hollywood press.

Johnny Mercer (1909–1976) wrote, among many others, the classic song
"Blues in the Night." He also wrote songs for pictures including "On the

Atchison, Topeka and Santa Fe" from *The Harvey Girls* (1946) and "In the Cool, Cool, Cool of the Evening" from *Here Comes the Groom* (1951), both of which won him Oscars for best song.

GARY MERRILL

"I saw him in *Twelve O'Clock High* and I said, 'I like that man's looks—he's for me."

Bette Davis

Behind the smiles, there were charges of alcoholism and physical abuse.

"We only played two love scenes before I said, 'Will you marry me?' "

Gary Merrill

Bette first saw Gary Merrill in a screening of the movie *Twelve O'Clock High* on December 31, 1949. She made the mistake of commenting that she found Merrill attractive, which allegedly provoked a jealous tirade from her husband, William Grant Sherry.

At the time they started shooting *All About Eve* in San Francisco in April 1950, Merrill had been married to Barbara Leeds for eight years. Bette was still married to Sherry. They met for the first time in Hollywood to do a photo test for *All About Eve*. Director Joe Mankiewicz wanted to make certain that Bette looked sufficiently older than Gary, as called for in the script, which she did. He also wanted to make certain that they looked believable together, which they did.

On the set on the first day of shooting in San Francisco, Bette whipped out a cigarette and waited for it to be lit by Merrill. Instead, however, he fixed her with a gaze and said, evenly, "Bill Sampson would not light Margo Channing's cigarette." It is quite possible that Bette fell in love with Merrill at that moment. During the course of the shooting, as she came to know him, Bette was stricken by Merrill's strength, his seeming steadiness, his defiant independence. She also came to respect him as an actor and entertained dreams of their becoming an acting team à la Alfred Lunt and Lynn Fontanne. As for Merrill, he later wrote in his autobiography, "I was irresistibly drawn to her. My first feeling of compassion for this misunderstood, talented woman was quickly replaced by a robust attraction. . . . From simple compassion, my feelings shifted to an almost uncontrollable lust. I walked around with an erection for three days."

Upon her return to Los Angeles following her Mexican divorce from William Grant Sherry on July 4, 1950, Bette was questioned by the press regarding her relationship with Merrill. "They *always* say an actress is going to marry someone right away [after a divorce]," Bette said, dismissing the question. "You can say I am *not* romantically interested in Gary," she lied. "This is just part of the folklore of Hollywood." After making that statement, Bette sped off in a taxicab. A quarter of a mile from Los Angeles International Airport, Bette ordered the cabdriver to stop. She then got into a waiting yellow convertible. Driving the car was Gary Merrill, the man she was "not" romantically interested in. Three weeks later, on July 28, the day Merrill obtained a Mexican divorce from Leeds, Gary and Bette became husband and wife.

The press made much of the fact that Merrill, then 34, was eight years younger than Bette. Reporters constantly referred to Bette as an "aging" actress and compared her marriage to Merrill to the marriages of Norma Shearer and Martin Arrouge, who were 42 and 28, respectively, when they married; to Ginger Rogers, who was nine years older than her husband Jack Briggs; and to Madeleine Carroll, who was ten years older than her husband, Sterling Hayden.

About six months into their marriage Bette was offered the starring role in *Another Man's Poison*, which was to be shot in England. As a part of her deal Bette requested that Merrill be cast in the male lead and that their family, which by then included the adopted Michael and Margot Merrill, along with Bette's daughter, B. D. Sherry, be flown to England with all expenses paid. The film's producer, Douglas Fairbanks, Jr., agreed, and the Merrills embarked on a paid family honeymoon. The film, however, flopped upon its release in 1952.

Back in Hollywood, Merrill was cast as the lead in *Phone Call from a Stranger* (1952). Perhaps to bolster the box office potential of her husband's picture, perhaps just to be close to the set, Bette volunteered to play a glorified cameo in the picture. It was the last picture the two would make together.

At the time of their marriage Gary Merrill was under contract to 20th Century-Fox and his career looked promising. However, one of the major problems in their relationship would turn out to be that Gary simply did not have Bette's drive. As they settled into a life of domesticity in Maine, three years into their marriage Bette found herself losing respect for Merrill. She admired his ability as an actor, but not his lack of ambition and discipline. On the other hand, Bette would also say that Gary (who dubbed her "Mother Merrill") did not want her to be domestic either, that he wanted her to remain Margo Channing. He would later say that the downfall of the marriage had been Bette's stubborn insistence on perfection. "She would empty the ashtray before the cigarette was out," he said, "and [she] had the bed made before my feet hit the ground."

It was a turbulent marriage. Merrill, Bette would later claim, was an alcoholic who physically abused her. Bette was abusive to Gary in other ways. She taunted him, verbally lashed out at him, and was known to humiliate him in front of others. To make matters worse, Gary was dropped by Fox, and the couple began having financial problems. In June 1957 Bette filed a "separate maintenance" lawsuit against Merrill. "A divorce is a bridge," her attorney told reporters, "she hasn't come to *yet*." The fact is that Bette was too frightened to get a divorce and the two reconciled. In Gary Merrill she saw her last chance at happiness with a man, her last chance at love.

In April 1959 the Merrills were approached by producer Norman Corwin with the proposition of taking *The World of Carl Sandburg* on a cross-country tour. By the time rehearsals started in August, their marriage was all but over. Clark Allen, who embarked on the tour with Bette and Gary, was stricken by Bette's abuse of Merrill. "She was quite unfair to Gary. He never, that I noticed, started a fight with her. He was rather dignified. . . . I wondered, 'God, what's she trying to get rid of this guy for?' He appealed to me as a nice guy. To me, he certainly didn't deserve the treatment he got. She treated him very cavalierly. Everybody knew it. She treated him badly. He just quietly did his job."

With their show Broadway-bound and receiving critical raves, Bette and Gary returned to San Francisco in April 1960 for a run of *Sandburg*. Despite their staying at the same hotel that had been the setting for their romance 10 years before, the only thing rekindled was the memory of what had been.

Bette filed for divorce in May 1960 in Cumberland County, Maine. Her suit asked Merrill to support Bette and their three children. At the time of the filing Bette was living in Laguna Beach, while Merrill was at Universal-International, shooting *The Great Impostor*. In her complaint Bette charged abusive treatment and extreme cruelty. On July 7, 1960, she was granted an uncontested divorce.

Over the next several years Bette and Gary feuded in and out of court over the custody of Michael. Infuriated by Merrill's affair with Rita Hayworth, Bette tried repeatedly to get an amendment to their divorce judgment that forbade him visitation rights. She was ultimately unsuccessful. At one point, shortly after the release of *What Ever Happened to Baby Jane?*, Bette told Hedda Hopper, "At the time of the divorce, I was polite. If he takes me into court, it's going to be the dirtiest case on record and when it's over he will never see the children again. With my head high, I will crucify him!

The thing that's bugging Merrill is that I have a successful picture. He spent 11 years hoping I'd never work again."

Later in his life, Merrill turned to politics. He protested American involvement in the Vietnam War and in 1968 ran for Congress but lost. He got work doing voice-overs for television commercials and landed an occasional acting job. In 1980 he appeared on Broadway in the play *Morning's at Seven*.

Upon the publication of B. D. Hyman's book *My Mother's Keeper* in 1985, Gary, outraged, took to protesting on the streets. He picketed a Falmouth, Maine, bookstore, holding a sign that read, simply, "Please Boycott My Mother's Keeper." He also took out an ad (at considerable expense) in the *New York Times*. "No Mother Deserves This. Anything for a buck," the ad read. "Greed was B. D. Hyman's guide when she wrote *My Mother's Keeper*, the scurrilous new book about B. D.'s mother, actress Bette Davis. And anything for a buck is what William Morrow & Co. must have said when they published it. Support your local library . . . don't fork over almost 20 bucks for this book. Visit your library, or buy one copy and pass it along. And support Bette. Write her c/o Harold Schiff, 455 East 57th St., New York, 10022, and wish her well. Tell her you are boycotting the book. You'll both feel better. A message from Gary Merrill, Bette's friend and former husband."

Certainly Merrill had reason to be upset about the book. In it Hyman accuses him of drinking morning martinis, parading around the house naked, swearing profusely, and physically abusing her and her mother. Once, according to Hyman, Merrill tried to choke Bette, and the police had to be called to restrain him. "Suddenly, Gary let go of Mother and she fell halfway down the stairs," she wrote. "I wanted to run to help her, but Gary spun around, hit me and flattened me against the wall."

The last time Bette and Gary saw one another was when they were both on the same plane to Maine. Bette was going there to shoot the 1987 picture *The Whales of August*; Gary was returning home. They had not seen one another for years. According to Bette, she approached him. She tried to start a conversation, but Merrill continued to read the book he was reading, so Bette returned to her seat. It was a quiet finale to what had been a stormy union.

Gary Merrill died of lung cancer at the age of 74 in Falmouth, Maine. In addition to those already mentioned, his pictures include *Winged Victory* (1944), *Decision Before Dawn* (1951), *The Pleasure of His Company* (1961), and *Huckleberry Finn* (1974).

> "I've spent my life doing as little as possible. . . . And I intend to keep doing exactly the same thing."
>
> *Gary Merrill, 1981*

MARGOT MERRILL

Margot Mosher Merrill was born on January 6, 1951, and was adopted by Bette and Gary Merrill one week later. She was named, of course, after the character Bette had played in *All About Eve* (with a *t* added to the spelling), the picture that brought Bette and Gary together in storybook fashion.

Over the next few years Bette and Gary became increasingly alarmed by Margot's behavior. She cried constantly, became cruel, threw tantrums. It seemed, as Bette would later say, "as if she was possessed by a demon." They took her to one doctor after another for a series of tests. Finally, in 1954, at the age of three, Margot was diagnosed as being mentally retarded. After much despair and deliberation, Bette and Gary decided to send her to the Lochland School in Geneva, New York, where she would live, on and off, for many years. Of his daughter Gary wrote in his 1988 autobiography, "Margot will never progress beyond the mental capabilities of a seven or eight-year-old, though she is now almost forty. Miss Stewart [director of Lochland] once said that she was the most pathetic child at the school because she was just bright enough to know what she was missing."

MICHAEL MERRILL

Michael Woodman Merrill was born on February 5, 1952. He was adopted by Bette and Gary Merrill in a matter of days and moved into their home directly from the hospital. Bette enthused to reporters, "We shall call him Woody."

At the age of five Michael went to his first day of school in Maine. Bette dressed him in shorts. One of the boys called him a "sissy" and beat him up. Michael went home crying, and that night Bette Davis taught her son how to fight.

When Bette was living at One Crooked Mile in Westport, Connecticut, Michael was attending school in Chapel Hill, North Carolina, and would visit Bette on holidays. It was while visiting Bette that he met a girl who lived down the road, Chou-Chou—suffice it to say that he started visiting Bette on weekends as well. Michael and Chou-Chou were married on May 19, 1973.

After graduation from college Michael attended Boston University Law School. He passed the bar exam and got a job as a lawyer with the military. He and his wife lived in Munich, Germany, for three years. Upon his return to the United States, Michael opened his own law firm in Chestnut Hill, Massachusetts.

Still, despite his many accomplishments, one of the most remarkable in the life of Michael Merrill may be that he also managed, given the turmoil of his parents' marriage, to develop into a sound and well-adjusted man, husband, and father. Moreover, he also managed to remain, over the years, close to both of his parents. He named his first son Matthew Davis Merrill in honor of his mother. Following her death in 1989, Michael was bequeathed half of Bette's estate.

METRO-GOLDWYN-MAYER

During her long tenure at the more economical Warner Brothers in the thirties and forties, Bette longed to be transferred across town to the Culver City lot of MGM, where stars were lavished with the full-fledged glamour treatment. Ironically, it was not until she starred in *The Catered Affair*

(1956), in which she played a frumpish housewife from the Bronx, that Bette would star in an MGM picture. During the shooting of the picture Bette was loaned the dressing room belonging to Lana Turner.

BETTE MIDLER
Actress/singer/comedian Bette Midler was named after Bette Davis because her mother had been a big Bette Davis fan. Upon learning this, Bette—Davis that is—was not pleased. At the time the two met in the 1970s, Midler was performing her outrageous "Divine Miss M" camp act, something that Davis wanted no association with.

A MIDSUMMER NIGHT'S DREAM
Bette's first professional appearance occurred on July 23, 1925, when she, then 17, portrayed a dancing fairy in a production of *A Midsummer Night's Dream*. The production, staged by the Mariarden School of Dance, starred Alan Mowbray, May Ediss, Frank Arundel, Lucy Currier, Cecil Clovelly, Richard Whorf, and Frank Conroy. Conroy directed, Whorf designed the sets and costumes, and Roshanara choreographed the ballet.

"THE MIKE DOUGLAS SHOW"
Bette cohosted this Philadelphia-based television talk show for a week in April 1966, celebrating her 58th birthday on the air. Later, in the 1970s, Bette again appeared on the show. She became enraged, however, when she was forced to pay for her own hotel room.

MILDRED PIERCE

Producer Jerry Wald did not develop the 1945 film noir classic *Mildred Pierce* with Joan Crawford in mind. Bette Davis topped a list that included Claudette Colbert, Barbara Stanwyck, and Rosalind Russell. Opting instead to do what she thought was the more prestigious vehicle, *The Corn Is Green*, Bette made the mistake of turning it down. Joan Crawford did not. The film provided Crawford with her comeback vehicle and, to Bette's chagrin, her Oscar.

ALLEN MINER

Miner directed Bette in "The Ella Lindstrom Story," an episode of the television series "Wagon Train," which he also wrote. Miner also directed Bette in "Madame's Place," a failed pilot that he wrote for a series that also aired as an episode of "Wagon Train," and in "Stranded," a May 1957 episode of the series "Telephone Time." At the time Bette hailed Miner as one of the most talented men working in television.

MISS BETTE DAVIS SINGS

Bette recorded, in a husky-singing-talking voice, this EMI album in England, in the 1970s. Released by Celebrity Records in the United States in 1983, it was produced by Norman Newell. See Records.

MISS MOFFAT

In the 1974 biography *Mother Goddam,* Bette commented that she would like to have another crack at playing Miss Moffat from the Emlyn Williams play *The Corn Is Green.* Since she was older and closer to the age as originally written than when she had played it for the 1945 film, she theorized that she could do a better job with it. Stage and film director Joshua Logan also wanted a shot at the property. He wrote Emlyn Williams about his interest, and Williams responded that he had written an unproduced version of *The Corn Is Green.* Williams had relocated his story from a mining town in Wales to a sugarcane field in the southern United States. Morgan Evans, Miss Moffat's prize pupil, had become a black field hand.

Williams sent the manuscript to Logan, and Logan loved the revision. Curiously, however, Bette was *not* his first choice to play Miss Moffat. Along with Williams (who was a friend of Bette's), Logan pitched it to Mary Martin, who expressed interest. Logan enlisted composer Albert Hague to write the score. Hague had written two big hits, *Play and Fancy* and *Redhead.* The three of them flew to Brazil to meet with Mary Martin and her husband, Richard Halliday. Later Martin agreed to star in the production. Two weeks after she agreed, however, her husband died, and the project went into limbo. After a consultation, Logan, Williams, and Hague agreed that the only other stars with the stature and ability to play the part were Katharine Hepburn and Bette Davis. Hepburn turned them down, and they were left with Bette.

By that time Bette had a reputation in theater circles for being undependable and demanding. Still, Logan pursued her. Logan and Hague drove out to her Connecticut home and played the score for her. Bette loved it and signed for the part. Logan could not believe his good fortune.

Rehearsals went well, though Bette and Logan had a different idea about how Bette was to approach the songs. Logan wanted Bette to primarily *speak* the lyrics, half-singing, half-acting. Bette wanted to prove to the world that she could sing. Said Logan, "Although on key, her tones were shaky and not very musical." When Logan approached her and asked her if she was nervous about the songs, she raved, "Nervous? About music? I'm a musician! I understand everything there is to know about music! And I'm very, very good at it, so don't say such things."

The first run-through of the show for backers was a disaster. Bette insisted on carrying her script on stage. Then she began limping, saying that it was caused by a bad back. Bette was subsequently hospitalized. Logan was told by her doctors that she would be out anywhere from three to eight weeks. Logan, along with coproducer Eugene Wolsk, went to her hospital room. At that point, Wolsk asked Bette straightforwardly, "Bette, please be frank. Do you want to continue with this or not?" Bette replied, "Of course! I love it. I'm passionately in love with it. I must do it. If you can wait for me, fine. If you can't, then I'll understand."

The company continued to rehearse for a week without Bette. The cast was then laid off for two weeks before the company went to Philadelphia. Bette was to join the company in Philadelphia on a Sunday. The show was to open a week from Monday. On Sunday, Bette's attorney showed up at the theater and told Logan that she had reinjured herself but that she would report for rehearsals the following morning. Bette reported, and the show was previewed on Friday night in front of its first audience to enormous ovations. *Miss Moffat* loomed as a blockbuster hit.

On Monday, opening night, critics were in attendance. Bette was stricken, according to Logan, by stage fright. She forgot or repeated lyrics; she spoke too softly; she broke out of character and addressed the audience as Bette Davis; and the show went 17 minutes longer than it was supposed to. The performance was a disappointment if not a flop.

Afterward, Bette blamed Logan for her mistakes, charging that his daily changes in the show had confused and exasperated her. She sent him an ultimatum through her attorney that no more changes were to made with the show for a full week—nor would Logan be able to hold rehearsals with the other actors. To placate Bette, Logan held no rehearsals for a week. Meanwhile, the show continued to play in Philadelphia, with critics panning the show but praising Bette's performance.

Eight days passed before Bette returned to rehearsals. For performances Bette's work improved. She assured Logan that she loved the play, would tour with it, and then play a hopefully lengthy engagement on Broadway. The game plan then included the two of them producing the film version.

"Thank God for this play," Bette told Logan. "It's going to save me from those flea-bitten films. The last one I read, they had me hanging in a closet. *Miss Moffat* has saved me—*saved* me."

The next morning Logan found Bette in her suite lying on her bed. She then released the bomb: "Has the doctor phoned you? The doctor in New York. Hasn't he told you that I can't play *it* anymore?" With that Bette proceeded to tell the stunned Logan that she would no longer star in his play because of some mysterious back ailment. The show closed after 15 performances, despite all indications that it would be a big hit.

A year later Bette gave an interview to Rex Reed in the *New York Daily News*. "It was a mistake," she said of the play. "The audience stood up cheering and screaming every night, but I knew it wasn't what they wanted. They wanted me to be a bitch, not a middle-aged schoolteacher. The songs were wonderful. I sang them all and I was good at it, but it was nothing but hell. I had to carry the burden of the rewrites, and I spent three weeks in a hospital traction from the nerves and tension. The monkey on your back when you're carrying a show is wicked. Joshua Logan finished me off in two weeks. He was terrified of the critics and started changing things on opening night in Philly. . . . They wanted me to learn forty pages in four days. . . . I had to get my health back before I could concentrate on that kind of work. So we closed it down. I will never go near the stage again as long as I live."

Miss Moffat, produced by Eugene V. Wolsk, Joshua Logan, and Slade Brown, had a book by Emlyn Williams and Logan. The music was composed by Albert Hague, the lyrics by Emlyn Williams. Musical numbers were staged by Donald Saddler. Scenery and lighting were designed by Joe Mielziner. Costumes were by Robert Mackintosh. In addition to Bette, the cast featured Dorian Harewood as Morgan Evans. Also included were, in order of appearance, Rudolf Lowe, Jaison Walker, Nat Jones, Gian Carlo Esposito, Kevin Dearinger, Randy Martin, Michael Calkins, Lee Goodman, Anne Francine, Dody Goodman, David Sabin, Marion Ramsey, Avon Long, and Gil Robbins.

Miss Moffat premiered at the Shubert Theatre in Philadelphia on October 7, 1974. It closed on October 18, 1974.

MR. SKEFFINGTON ★★★
Warner Brothers
1944   127 minutes   bw
Directed by: Vincent Sherman
Produced by: Julius J. and Philip G. Epstein
Screenplay by: Julius J. and Philip G. Epstein, based on the novel by "Elizabeth"
Cinematography by: Ernest Haller
Cast: Bette Davis, Claude Rains, Walter Abel, George Coulouris, Richard Waring, Marjorie Riordan, Robert Shayne, John Alexander, Jerome Cowan, Johnny Mitchell, Dorothy Peterson, Peter Whitney, Bill

Attempting to play the most beautiful
woman in town.

Kennedy, Dolores Gray, Tom Stevenson, Halliwell Hobbes, Bunny
Sunshine, Gigi Perreau, Walter Kingsford, Molly Lamont

Warner Brothers purchased the novel by Mary Annette Beauchamp Russell,
who used the pseudonym "Elizabeth," in an agreement dated May 11, 1940.
The book had been published on January 9, 1940, but was originally printed
as a series of articles in late 1939 in *Good Housekeeping*. Warners dished out
the sum of $50,000 for the rights.

After she made *Old Acquaintance*, Bette took an extended vacation in
Mexico. She demanded from Warner a revision of her contract that would
give her a raise and limit the number of films she made per year. When
Warner refused, she walked out. When her demands were met, she returned
to the studio to make *Mr. Skeffington*, even though she wasn't thrilled with
the story. It would be her first picture in eight months, then considered a long
time for a star to go without work.

Set in Gramercy Park, New York, from 1914 to 1940, the picture takes us
through World War I, the stock market collapse, and FDR's election. It casts
Bette as Fanny, the belle of New York City, who has a future of infinite
possibilities until her brother, Trippy (Richard Waring), mismanages the
family wealth and swindles money from his boss, Job Skeffington (Claude
Rains). Fanny decides to marry Job to keep him from pressing charges
against her brother. In the latter part of the picture, Fanny is stricken by
diphtheria, ages drastically, and loses her looks.

Bette initially turned down the role after Warners purchased it. Also turning down the role were Tallulah Bankhead, Ruth Chatterton, Claudette Colbert, and Greta Garbo. Bankhead was actually rejected after she demanded $50,000 for the part. There was some talk in 1940 that John Huston was writing the screenplay for the picture and that Eddie Goulding was going to direct it with Irene Dunne starring. Dunne, however, also declined.

Certainly even Bette was reticent about the part. While making the picture she told a reporter, "Fanny Skeffington is the type of useless woman I've hated all my life. After this role I'll be more tolerant of them."

From the start, and throughout the production, there was trepidation about the title *Mr. Skeffington* because the film was a Bette Davis vehicle. Consideration was given to retitling the pic *Mrs. Skeffington*, but Bette, to her credit, insisted that the original title be retained.

Vincent Sherman, who was eventually signed to direct, was also concerned from the outset that the picture would arouse cries that the film had anti-British sentiments because he, along with the Epsteins, had changed the setting from England to New York and had made Bette's character, Lady Fanny in the novel, an American. He was also concerned about the controversy the film might arouse because it featured a marriage between a Jew and a Gentile.

One of the major problems in preproduction was Bette's appearance. While makeup and wardrobe tests for the picture were being shot, Bette's husband, Arthur Farnsworth, fell onto Hollywood Boulevard and died a mysterious death. Instead of postponing the picture, however, Bette elected to go on working. Still, her appearance suffered, and Fanny Skeffington was supposed to be the beauty of the day, the most desirable woman in town. Bette knew that physically she was miscast. Maggie Donovan gave her a new hairdo, and Orry-Kelly designed some spectacular costumes for her. In fact Bette would later say that she thought Kelly's costumes for this picture were the best he had ever designed for her.

Bette had initial hairdress tests on Monday, March 1, 1943. More extensive wardrobe and makeup tests were held on Thursday, August 19, 1943. She showed up for more tests on Wednesday, September 22. The testing process took longer than on most pictures because Bette had 26 wardrobe changes scheduled for the film. More tests were shot on Thursday, September 23, and again on September 30.

In addition to her new look, Bette decided to adopt a new voice for the film. In a word, the voice she affected for the role was shrill. On a musical scale the voice was about six tones higher than her normal voice.

There was some discussion, led by Bette, that the film be made in Technicolor. The budget on the picture, however, was already quite high, and Jack Warner balked at the added expense of color.

Warner must have sensed that there would be trouble on this picture. On the opening day of shooting, October 11, 1943, he wrote Sherman a note stating he was certain the picture would be completed not a single day behind schedule because there was no rewriting to be done. Warner also noted that the script was well written and that the assembled cast was, in his estimation, the best in the history of the studio. He closed by telling (threat-ening?) Sherman that he wanted the picture to be brought in *under* schedule and budget.

Bette did not start shooting until Wednesday, October 13. She set the pace for things to come, however, with her arrival on the set. She surveyed what was supposed to be Fanny Skeffington's house and promptly rearranged the flower arrangements from table to table. She also dismissed a clock that had been chosen for the house by the film's set decorator. "Who," Bette demanded to know, "would live with a thing like *that* in her home?"

Something of a scene was caused on the set on Bette's second day of shooting. In the film there is an important oil painting that hangs in the living room of the Skeffington mansion. The painting is a portrait of Bette as Fanny Skeffington at her most beautiful. The artist commissioned to do the piece wanted $750 for the portrait—the studio wanted to pay only $500. But that wasn't what the commotion was about. When she arrived on the set that day, Bette demanded to see the portrait to determine for herself whether or not it was suitable for the picture (that is, flattering to her). The matter was put off, with an agreement that it would be decided on the following day. However, by November 4 the matter of the portrait was still unresolved. Bette summoned her entourage, which included cinematographer Ernie Haller, costume designer Orry-Kelly, makeup artist Perc Westmore, and director Vince Sherman, along with several Warners publicity men, and elicited their opinions. By that time a second portrait had been commissioned and com-pleted, and Bette didn't like either one. She requested that yet *another* portrait be commissioned. However, this request went unheeded, and the choice between the two existing portraits was made two days later.

Early into the shooting, J. L. Warner wrote Sherman a flurry of angry notes complaining about his slowness. On October 27, 1943, Warner wrote what he said would be his final note since both men were "intelligent people" who knew what needed to be done.

Within a week after she started shooting Bette refused to work after 5:00 P.M. because, she complained, she had to wear a rubber face mask that took hours to peel off after the day's shooting was completed. Then, after only four days of shooting, Bette called in sick to make her point.

The same day, Monday, October 18, while Bette was at home pouting, a storm erupted on the *Skeffington* set. The producers of the film, Julius and Phil Epstein, who, by the way, also wrote the screenplay, arrived on the set with Jack Warner and studio executive Steve Trilling to confront director Vince Sherman about script changes the director was making at Bette's request. The producers ranted that Sherman was not to alter the script without the studio's approval. Sherman yelled back that *Miss* Bette Davis would not be pleased with the Epsteins' demands that their script be adhered to. The producers, however, won the argument—for the time being.

Meanwhile, shooting proceeded slowly, and Warner was more than upset about Sherman's slow pace. Later, in a memo dated October 26, 1943, Frank Mattison, the unit manager of the film, reported back to his bosses at the studio that he now understood why Bette liked being directed by Sherman. Sherman, according to Mattison, let Bette do as she pleased and in essence allowed her to function as the *real* director on the set. A few days later Mattison groused to the studio that before each scene was shot Sherman sat down with Bette to rehearse and rewrite. He also complained that Sherman was allowing Bette a say even in the scenes in which she didn't appear.

What Mattison didn't mention in his report, or what he didn't know, was that the real reason Bette liked being directed by Sherman was that she was having an affair with him. Bette, Sherman would later contend, actually threatened to shut down the picture unless he made love to her!

On November 4, Mattison again complained about the slowness of the shooting and commented that nothing could be done about the slow progress on the film as long as Bette Davis was the director.

On November 9 Mattison shrewdly proposed to his superiors that the next Bette Davis picture might be sped up by making it a "Bette Davis Production" so that she would understand the delays and escalating production costs. Again Mattison noted that Bette, on this picture, was "the whole band—the music and all the instruments, including the bazooka."

Meanwhile, more dissension brewed on the set. The Epsteins, complaining that Bette was no longer just the star of the film but also the director and producer, walked off the set and refused to have anything more to do with the picture—or Bette Davis.

A less serious problem arose for Claude Rains, who, one day on his way to work, was injured when the car in front of him sped down the highway and shot back a speck of gravel that landed and lodged in his left eye. The incident caused Rains a great deal of discomfort and distress.

Things were no better for Bette. While shooting the film's pivotal sailboat scene, she had to endure two hours of being doused with cold water from half a dozen fire hoses. During one take she slipped on the wet deck. At the scene's climax she was to collapse and fall. Actor Johnny Mitchell was to rush to her aid. However, during one take *he* slipped and fell on *top* of her with the full impact of his 180 pounds. For a moment the crew held its collective breath. It was fortunate for everyone involved, none more so than Mitchell that the wind was the only thing that got knocked out of Bette.

More delays were caused by problems with Bette's voice. On some days her voice was too husky for her to work. At other times, because of the shrill voice she adopted for the role, her voice would suddenly break or shift into a falsetto and the scene would have to be reshot. Obviously the fluctuation of her voice gave the sound man, Bob Lee, fits of frustration.

Another delay occurred when Bette suffered an abrasion over one of her eyes. She took three days off. She then returned to the set, but her eye continued to bother her, so she went to see a specialist. She then took off Thursday and Friday, December 9 and 10. Shooting was suspended entirely on Saturday because of Bette's eye problem. Meanwhile, Mattison reported back to his bosses that Bette was suffering from not an eye problem but her usual "monthly trouble."

When she returned to the set on Monday, December 13, Bette was in much better spirits. On Thursday, December 23, she was stricken with the flu, and the company again shut down. She *did* show up for work on Christmas Eve and even hosted a party in her dressing room.

With the new year, shooting sped up somewhat. Apparently one of the Warners executives reprimanded Sherman to good effect, because according to Mattison's January 13, 1944, report, he suggested that if someone had the guts to "sit down on him" more often Sherman would work more quickly.

As shooting began to wind down and as she filmed the aging scenes, Bette became more irritable, attributing it to the heavy rubber mask makeup. During the final days of shooting she spent an average of four hours daily in makeup, followed by a full shooting day, followed by the stripping of the makeup at day's end. Then Bette would go over to the Hollywood Canteen, where she entertained and mingled with the visiting servicemen, some of whom she invited to visit the *Skeffington* set.

More than 40 years later Vincent Sherman would say of the film, "It was a less successful job than *Old Acquaintance*. I didn't achieve all the things that I had originally set out to achieve. I felt that Bette Davis's characterization was not what I wanted it to be. . . . the use of her voice in the kind of falsetto quality I thought was wrong. It may be that the character was so far away from Bette that she may have felt she had to use this silly falsetto voice to achieve the characterization. But it was a very good script by the Epstein brothers."

The production finished, finally, on Thursday, February 17, 1944, after 107 shooting days. The film officially finished 59 days behind schedule. Still, however, Bette's work was not done. She was held to shoot a montage sequence for the film and finished work on Monday, February 21.

After the incredibly long shooting schedule, Bette was still not satisfied with the picture and demanded additional retakes. Jack Warner understandably refused. On March 2 an irate Bette sent a rather wordy telegram to J. L., threatening that, unless her demands were met, she wanted a release from her new contract. The wire read:

> Now that it has been settled that you are not willing to redo anything of mine in *Mr. Skeffington*, particularly on the sound track to replace two days work when I was hardly able to talk due to a bad cold and went ahead because I was assured I could dub it in at the end of the picture, and with the prospect of this lack of cooperation now that our new deal is about to start, I would like a release. I am not only tired of this constant haggling but see no necessity for it. It would be impossible to produce my pictures for you with your apparent lack of confidence in me and apparent lack of desire to make a picture as perfect as possible. The entire procedure during the last three weeks of *Skeffington* caused me unnecessary mental torture. I will never be able to understand such lack of consideration for someone who for

our mutual benefit was striving only for one thing, as perfect a
picture as possible. . . . So I think a release is the solution for both of
us.

Despite her dissatisfaction with the picture, Bette saw a screening of it
with Perc Westmore on July 11, 1944, and had to admit that it wasn't as bad
as she thought. The following day Westmore scribbled a note to Jack Warner,
hailing him as the best cutter in the industry. Warner's final cut of the
picture, according to Westmore, saved the film and Westmore's reputation as
a makeup artist. Westmore also noted to Warner that Bette too was happy
with the completed picture.

Mr. Skeffington would receive mixed reviews upon its release and would
win Bette yet another Best Actress Oscar nomination. Today, in retrospect,
the picture emerges as a highly entertaining soap opera. One of its highlights
has Claude Rains quipping to his disinterested wife, Bette Davis, after she
accuses him of having an affair with his secretary: "Well, you mustn't think
too harshly of my secretaries. They were very kind and understanding when
I came to the office after a hard day at home."

WILSON MIZNER

Playwright and screenwriter who advised Bette, after she was dropped by
Universal in 1931, to bleach her hair to a honey blond. She did and was then
selected by George Arliss, seeking a blond, to play opposite him in *The Man
Who Played God* (1932). Mizner reportedly had known that Arliss was
looking for a blond and helped to arrange their meeting. Later Mizner also
gave Bette a copy of W. Somerset Maugham's book *Of Human Bondage* to
read. He told her that she would be good for the part of Mildred.

Wilson Mizner also cowrote the screenplays for the pictures *Dark Horse*
(1932) and *20,000 Years in Sing Sing* (1933).

MODERN SCREEN MAGAZINE

In October 1961, Bette filed a $1 million lawsuit against *Modern Screen*. The
magazine, according to Bette's suit, charged that she was "washed up" as a
performer in its May 1961 issue. The case was subsequently settled out of
court.

MARILYN MONROE

"Marilyn Monroe was a *real* sex symbol and so was the great Garbo.
They didn't need to say things, they just were. They *photographed*.
Name me a really true sex symbol in today's movies. She doesn't exist.
Fakes, all of them."

Bette Davis, 1965

Marilyn Monroe was featured as Miss Caswell, graduate of the Copacabana
School of Dramatic Art, in the 1950 picture *All About Eve*. "Interestingly

Back in 1950, who would have thought it possible that Monroe's star would rival Bette's?

enough," said Bette of Monroe, "not Gary, not Hugh Marlowe, not any one of the men in the cast thought she was attractive at all. And I told everybody, 'Wait. She's gonna make it.' "

ROBERT MONTGOMERY

At the time Bette Davis was an aspiring actress and usher at the Cape Playhouse in Dennis, Massachusetts, Robert Montgomery was acting in the theater's production of *Clarence* with his wife, Elizabeth Allen. Montgomery later joked "Bette was surely a better usher than I an actor."

In a laudatory editorial about Montgomery, her costar in *June Bride* (1948), that appeared in the October 11, 1948, edition of *The Hollywood Reporter*, Bette said, "It is quite impossible not to react to Bob's charm." She also enthused that *June Bride* was one of the happiest sets she had ever worked on. In fact, however, Bette did not like Montgomery, hated his conservative politics, loathed what she perceived to be his air of cool superiority, and accused him of attempting to steal their scenes together in the picture. "It was upstaging in its most diabolical form," she would say. Bette gave Montgomery a present at the end of the shooting: a pig.

Robert Montgomery (Henry Montgomery, 1904–1981), father of Elizabeth, appeared in numerous pictures, including *Night Must Fall* (1937) and *Here Comes Mr. Jordan* (1941), both of which earned him Best Actor Oscar nominations.

AGNES MOOREHEAD

Early into the shooting of the 1964 picture *Hush . . . Hush, Sweet Charlotte*, costar Agnes Moorehead was the *rope* in a tug-of-war between Bette Davis and Joan Crawford. At one point, after shooting a scene with Moorehead, Crawford, as an intended slap in Bette's face, gushed to reporters, "One of the greatest professional thrills I've had is working with Agnes Moorehead. We did the scene in one take." For her work on the picture, Moorehead would win a Best Supporting Actress Oscar nomination.

Agnes Moorehead (1906–1974) appeared in other pictures including *Citizen Kane* (1941), *The Magnificent Ambersons* (1942), and *Johnny Belinda* (1948). She is best known, however, as Endora, the not-so-wicked witch of a mother-in-law in television's "Bewitched" (1964–1972).

"MORGAN & MCBRIDE"
In 1963 Bette starred in a one-hour pilot for a television series called "Morgan & McBride." The drama was created by Fay Kanin, who coscripted with Bob Dozier, and was produced by Jack Webb for Warner Brothers Television. The show featured Bette as a lawyer with a young assistant played by William Shatner. The show was rejected as a proposed series by ABC on July 26, 1963.

WAYNE MORRIS
Wayne Morris was a virtual unknown when he costarred in the 1937 picture *Kid Galahad*. With the release of the picture, he was hailed all over Hollywood as a promising new star, and he seemed to have all the characteristics: masculinity, good looks, and perceptible natural talent. Even his costar Bette is said to have developed something of a crush on him. The promise, however, went curiously unfulfilled as Morris appeared in a few mediocre pictures before becoming a World War II naval hero. In 1959, at the age of 45, he died of a heart attack. His other pictures include *Brother Rat* (1938), *Brother Rat and a Baby* (1939), *The Time of Your Life* (1947), and *Paths of Glory* (1958).

ROY MOSELEY
Former friend of Bette's who penned the 1989 biography *Bette Davis: An Intimate Memoir,* which was published by Donald I. Fine. According to Moseley, a theatrical agent, as his friendship with Bette developed he was sent a letter by Violla Rubber, Bette's manager, that outlined the rules and regulations of being Bette's friend. One of the rules was, according to Moseley, "You shall not introduce Miss Davis to homosexuals." And, again according to Moseley, although he never had sex with Bette, she once proposed marriage to him. Roy Moseley coauthored the books *Princess Merle* (1983) and *Cary Grant: The Lonely Heart* (1989), both in collaboration with Charles Higham.

MOTHER
Ruth Favor Davis

MOTHER GODDAM
Superlative career biography by Whitney Stine (Hawthorn Books, 1974) with entertaining running commentary by Bette. Obviously her recollections are biased in her favor. Still, the book is perhaps the best biography ever published about Bette.

THE MOVIES
The Ingenue Years

1931: *Bad Sister*
      Seed
      Waterloo Bridge
1932: *Way Back Home*
      The Menace
      Hell's House
      The Man Who Played God
      So Big
      The Rich Are Always With Us
      Dark Horse
      Cabin in the Cotton
      Three on a Match

1933: *20,000 Years in Sing Sing*
      Parachute Jumper
      The Working Man
      Ex-Lady
      Bureau of Missing Persons
1934: *Fashions of 1934*
      The Big Shakedown
      Jimmy the Gent
      Fog Over Frisco

Acclaim: Rising Star

1934: *Of Human Bondage*
      Housewife
1935: *Bordertown*
      The Girl From Tenth Avenue
      Front Page Woman
      Special Agent
      Dangerous

1936: *The Petrified Forest*
      The Golden Arrow
      Satan Met a Lady
1937: *Marked Woman*
      Kid Galahad
      That Certain Woman
      It's Love I'm After

Stardom: The Halcyon Years

1938: *Jezebel*
      The Sisters
1939: *Dark Victory*
      Juarez
      The Old Maid
      The Private Lives of Elizabeth and Essex
1940: *All This, and Heaven Too*
      The Letter
1941: *The Great Lie*
      The Bride Came C.O.D.
      The Little Foxes

1942: *The Man Who Came to Dinner*
      In This Our Life
      Now, Voyager
1943: *Watch on the Rhine*
      Thank Your Lucky Stars
      Old Acquaintance
1944: *Mr. Skeffington*
      Hollywood Canteen

The Warner Brothers Decline

1945: *The Corn Is Green*
1946: *A Stolen Life*
     Deception
1948: *Winter Meeting*
     June Bride
1949: *Beyond the Forest*

On Her Own

1950: *All About Eve*
1951: *Payment on Demand*
1952: *Another Man's Poison*
     Phone Call from a Stranger
     The Star
1955: *The Virgin Queen*
1956: *The Catered Affair*
     Storm Center
1959: *John Paul Jones*
     The Scapegoat
1961: *Pocketful of Miracles*
1962: *What Ever Happened to Baby Jane?*
1964: *Dead Ringer*
     The Empty Canvas
     Where Love Has Gone
     Hush . . . Hush, Sweet Charlotte

1965: *The Nanny*
1968: *The Anniversary*
1971: *Bunny O'Hare*
1972: *Connecting Rooms* (produced in 1969)
     The Scientific Cardplayer
1976: *Burnt Offerings*
1978: *Death on the Nile*
     Return from Witch Mountain
1980: *The Watcher in the Woods*
1987: *The Whales of August*
1989: *The Wicked Stepmother*

The Television Movies

1972: "Madame Sin"
     "The Judge and Jake Wyler"
1973: "Scream, Pretty Peggy"
1976: "The Disappearance of Aimee"
1978: "The Dark Secret of Harvest Home"
1979: "Strangers: The Story of a Mother
      and Daughter"
1980: "White Mama"
     "Skyward"

1981: "Family Reunion"
1982: "A Piano for Mrs. Cimino"
     "Little Gloria . . . Happy at Last"
1983: "Right of Way"
1985: "Murder with Mirrors"
1986: "As Summers Die"

The Movies That Bette Wanted to Make But Didn't

Affair No. 5
The African Queen
Alice in Wonderland
All Our Tomorrows
All Passions Spent
The Angel Manager
Anna and the King of Siam
Anna Christie
Anthony Adverse
Burning Bridges
Caged
Calamity Jane
The Chalk Garden
Congai
Congresswoman
Dear Mr., the Sky Is Falling

The Deep Blue Sea
The Devil to Pay
Driving Miss Daisy
Ethan Frome
An Evening with Bette Davis
Faster, Faster
Fielding's Folly
Finally
Follies
The Furies
The Gambler
The Glass Menagerie
Gone With the Wind
The Greatest Mother of Them All
Hedda Gabler
Helena

Holiday
A House Divided
I'll Take the Low Road
It Happened One Night
Jealousy
The Killing of Sister George
The King and I
The King's General
Kings Row
Lady Windermere's Fan
The Life of Emile Zola
The Life of Sarah Bernhardt
Life with Father
Lilies of the Field
A Little Night Music
Macbeth

Mame   Stage Door Canteen   Up at the Villa
Mary of Scotland   Steel Magnolias   Valley of the Dolls
The Night of the Iguana A Streetcar Named Desire   The Visit
Raffles   Strictly Dishonorable   Who's Afraid of Virginia
Request for Love   The Stubborn Wood   Woolf?
The Return of the Soldier Suddenly, Last Summer   The Woman Brown
The Sea Gull   This Land Is Mine   Wuthering Heights
The Shanghai Gesture   The Two Worlds of Johnny Truro

Bette also wanted, desperately, to star in a film biography of Mary Todd Lincoln.

The Movies That She Turned Down

And Presumed Dead   Garden of the Moon   The Mind Reader
The Case of the Howling Dog The Gay Sisters   The Miracle
Come Back, Little Sheba   God's Country and the Woman Mountain Justice
Comet over Broadway   The Hard Way   Sour Mountain
Cool Hand Luke   Hollywood Bandwagon   The Unforgiven
Danger Signal   Hollywood Hotel   Waterloo Bridge
Danton   Humoresque
Four For Texas   Mildred Pierce

PAUL MUNI

Star of the pictures *Bordertown* (1935) and *Juarez* (1939), Paul Muni was the biggest star at Warner Brothers for most of the 1930s. He scored major hits at the studio with *Scarface* (1932) and *I Am a Fugitive from a Chain Gang* (1932). He was making $50,000 per film and was given story approval, script approval, sole star billing, and permission to star in stage plays at his discretion. He was also a revered actor, though he developed a reputation for taking his work too seriously. For example, when he was scheduled to play a *Chinese* man in the 1937 picture *The Good Earth*, Muni, an *Austrian*, reportedly bade his wife farewell and moved into Chinatown.

Paul Muni (Muni Weisenfreund, 1896–1967) appeared in other pictures, including *The Story of Louis Pasteur* (Best Actor Oscar winner, 1936), *Stage Door Canteen* (1943), and *A Song to Remember* (1944).

"MURDER WITH MIRRORS"

Also known as "Agatha Christie's Murder with Mirrors," this 1985 CBS made-for-television movie was shot in Hertfordshire, England, in the countryside north of London. It was Bette's first job since her 1983 mastectomy and stroke, and she was afraid she might not be able to stand the rigors of a filmmaking schedule. Once shooting started, she woke up every morning at 5:30, drove for an hour from her London hotel to the set, spent an hour in makeup, and acted from 10:00 A.M. to 5:00 P.M. "That first day on the set," she later confessed, "was pure terror for me. I wondered whether I would have trouble with my lines and have the strength to last." With the successful completion of the shooting Bette exulted, "I can go on working for a long time—till I drop dead."

Still, Bette made it a difficult shoot for the entire company. As Helen Hayes related, "She was feisty, always poised to do battle for what she believed was her due. We knew it, but we all wanted to get along with her. Bette made that virtually impossible. She couldn't stand anyone she considered a rival, though no one was trying to compete with her. Her physical condition made her hypersensitive to any potential charges that she was no longer capable of playing the role or any other role. . . . Bette drove herself mercilessly. She was her own worst enemy, at least during this production."

"Murder with Mirrors" was produced for Warner Brothers Television by Neil Hartley, with George Eckstein as executive producer. It was directed by Dick Lowry from a teleplay by George Eckstein, which was of course adapted from a novel by Agatha Christie. It was shot by Brian West. In addition to Bette, the cast included Helen Hayes, John Mills, Leo McKern, Liane Langland, John Laughlin, Dorothy Tutin, Anton Rodgers, Frances De La Tour, John Woodvine, and James Coombes.

MY MOTHER'S KEEPER
Following the publication of Christina Crawford's scandalous tell-all-and-

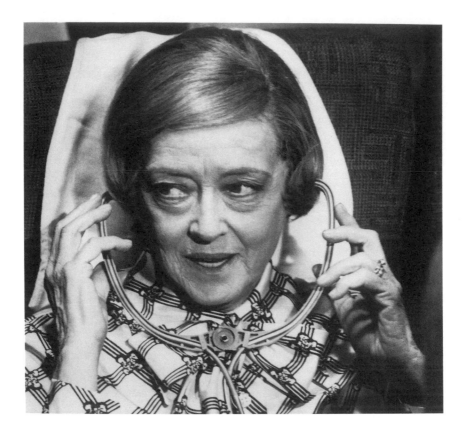

more autobiography, *Mommie Dearest*, Bette Davis told an interviewer for *Playboy*, "I don't blame the daughter, don't blame her at all. . . . One area of life Joan should never have gone into was children."

What goes around comes around, and those words would come back to haunt Bette Davis. Published by William Morrow and Company, Inc., in 1985, *My Mother's Keeper*, written by Bette's daughter B. D. Hyman, is a *Mommie Dearest* wannabe that has much to recommend it—for anyone wanting a superficial glimpse of Bette Davis at her worst. The book is marred by Hyman's relentless, thinly veiled attacks on her mother, which get extremely petty and ultimately tired and even include her complaints about her mother's menu planning and cooking. Still, there's undoubtedly a good deal of truth in Hyman's words. What is true, what is exaggerated, and what is false are judgments that only the readers can make. What cannot be questioned, however, is the devastating impact its publication had on the final five years of Bette Davis's life. Understandably viewed by Bette as an unforgivable act of betrayal, the book caused an irreparable rift between mother and daughter. *"That book,"* Bette would relate, "was literally as catastrophic to me as the stroke. It was heartbreaking and certainly something that I will never get over." She then added, "I *worshipped* that girl."

N

THE NANNY ★★½
Seven Arts–Hammer (England)
Released by 20th Century–Fox
1965   93 minutes   bw
Directed by: Seth Holt
Produced by: Jimmy Sangster
Screenplay by: Jimmy Sangster, based on the novel by Evelyn Piper
Cinematography by: Harry Waxman
Cast: Bette Davis, Jill Bennett, William Dix, James Villiers, Wendy Craig,
    Pamela Franklin, Maurice Denham, Alfred Burke, Nora Gordon,
    Sandra Power, Harry Fowler

Unable to get what she considered to be a decent script in Hollywood, Bette swallowed her pride and accepted an offer from England to star in *The Nanny,* which she adamantly contended was *not* a horror film. Any reporter who made the mistake of referring to it as such would promptly be tongue-lashed, Davis style.

The plot of the picture has child actor William Dix (whose skill astonished Bette) as Joey Fane, a troubled 10-year-old who is placed in the care of Bette, a severe and snarling and even murderous nanny. As *Time* magazine succinctly put it, the film is an "antidote to those who found *Mary Poppins* too sweet to stomach."

Upon its release *The Nanny* was greeted with poor to fair reviews and lackluster box office. It deserved better, particularly because of a strong performance by Bette.

HARMON NELSON, JR.

> "I'm intelligent enough to comprehend that having become a movie
> personality, I'm on the traditional ride. Success on the screen has a
> price. But there is one thing Hollywood cannot do to me. It
> cannot, arbitrarily, make me a divorcée just because that's the
> customary sequel to a Hollywood marriage."
>
> *Bette Davis*

Bette's romance with her first husband, Harmon Oscar Nelson, Jr., began when both were students at Cushing Academy high school in Ashburnham, Massachusetts. "Ham," as she affectionately called him, was a senior; Bette, or "Spuds," as he called her, was a junior. He was an aspiring musician who played the piano and trumpet. She dabbled in drama and developed a crush on him. Ham, as Bette would later say, was "an indifferent louse." She went home and vowed to her mother, "I'm going to get him if it's the last thing I ever do."

At Cushing, Ham was coordinating the school's music and minstrel show, and since they sang in the glee club together, Ham asked Bette if she would be interested in singing in the show. She was, and in time the two began to date. Ham graduated from high school and enrolled in a Massachusetts agricultural college. A year later he attended Bette's high school graduation party, and the two parted ways.

During the summer of 1930, after having success on Broadway in *Broken Dishes*, Bette returned to Dennis, Massachusetts, where she was a member of the Cape Players. One night Bette ran into Ham at a movie theater. He was a member of the Amherst Band, which was performing across the cape at the Old Mill Tavern. They resumed their romance, swimming, driving, talking. At summer's end Bette returned to New York and Ham resumed studies at Amherst.

Hollywood, 1932. Bette, signed to a contract with Warner Brothers, appeared to have a promising future as a film actress. Ham, a trumpet player with the Olympic Band, traveled to Los Angeles to perform at that summer's Olympics. The timing, however, was somewhat unfortunate. Warner Brothers decided to send Bette on a lengthy promotional tour back east. When she returned to Los Angeles, the Olympics, fortunately, were still going on, and Bette and Ham renewed their love and married, with the prodding of Bette's mother, Ruthie, in Yuma, Arizona, on August 18, 1932.

Signs of trouble occurred early in the marriage. A frequent daily routine would have Ham drive Bette to the studio every morning at 5:00 A.M. He would then sit in her dressing room all day, waiting to drive her home.

Press reports of the day referred to Ham as "tall, black-haired, modest, personable." Others called him a "man's man." Perhaps. But he was no match for Bette Davis. Ham got work as a musician, an orchestra leader, and a radio singer. But he lacked the ambition to please his very ambitious wife. He also lacked the money to quiet his own insecurity about being the head of his household, the provider for his family.

The press made quite an issue of the fact that Nelson earned much less money than his wife, and as she became more famous, the gap in their salaries widened. Early into the marriage Ham moved to Daly City, California, where he lived in an "auto camp" so that he could be near the Villa Mateo restaurant, where he had found work. Bette would work all week at Warners, then drive to Daly City on Saturday nights to be with Ham.

In September 1934 the *Los Angeles Examiner* created quite a stir in Hollywood by chronicling the Nelsons' finances. "Here Comes the Percentage Marriage," the article was headlined. It proceeded to inform readers that Bette was then making $1,000 a week at Warner Brothers, while Ham was earning the comparably paltry sum of $100 a week. Bette was being chauffeur-driven around town in a black Packard, while Ham was seen driving around in a Ford roadster, for which he paid $19.50.

In the article Bette and Ham described how they each contributed the same ratio of their earnings to household expenses. "So far it has worked out beautifully," Bette related to reporter Muriel Babcock, "and [it has] enabled each [of us] to keep our self-respect and the respect of the other. It seemed the only way, unless I wanted to retire from work and be just a wife, which I don't. I love acting and I love the movies. . . . Harmon in the role of gigolo to movie wife? It was unthinkable, although I have seen many a man in Hollywood who seemed content in that part. Harmon couldn't. . . . It takes much more intestinal fortitude upon the part of Harmon to carry on under this agreement than I. So far, he has been swell about it, although when things come up like an item in a morning paper two Sundays ago which told of my going downtown and buying a suit of clothes [for him], which I never did! It makes it difficult for him. You can imagine our Sunday morning breakfast table conversation. . . . We happen both to be professional people with an understanding of the demands of a profession. . . ." The article ended with a quip: "Perhaps if there were more 'percentage marriages' in Hollywood there would be a smaller percentage of divorces."

One thing that definitely was *not* working in their marriage was the inconvenience of Ham's working near San Francisco. And so he sought and obtained several jobs at Los Angeles night spots, including one performing in the Blossom Room of the Hollywood Roosevelt Hotel. By mid-1938, however, with Bette on a tremendous wave of acclaim and stardom for her performance in *Jezebel*, Ham decided to give up on his career as a performer. Instead he got a job as an executive with the talent firm of Rockwell-O'Keefe, where he represented musicians and orchestras.

By then, however, Nelson's marriage to Bette was in serious trouble, and the press began speculating about that when Bette was seen around town with a variety of men while Ham was back east on a business trip. More rumors flew when, in August 1938, Bette vacationed without Ham in Glen Brook, Nevada. Hollywood speculated that she had gone there for the six-week residency requirement before obtaining a divorce. When confronted with the rumors, Bette spat out, "Absolutely nothing to it!" In fact, however, she had been having a torrid affair with director William Wyler and another one with Howard Hughes.

Rumors of discord became even more rampant when, in early September 1938, Bette vacationed in Lake Tahoe with her sister, Bobby, while Ham remained in New York. Finally, on September 19, Bette confessed to the press, "I hope there won't be any separation and right now I don't think there will be. There's no use denying that we are having difficulties. I am not the coy type that tried to hide what is true. But I sincerely hope there won't be any separation. . . ."

On September 27, however, the couple agreed to what they termed a "marital vacation." By then they had already moved into separate living quarters. Ham was living at the home of a co-worker, while Bette remained at their Coldwater Canyon home. When divorce was decided on, Bette wired the press: "Ham and I have definitely decided to take a vacation from each other. Signed Bette Davis." When fan magazine writer Mayme Ober Peak called Bette and pressed for more information, Bette replied, "I will not talk. Even if I should go into court, I shall not tell under any circumstances what has happened between Ham and me. It is our own personal affair." Then, 12 hours before Ham filed for divorce on November 22, Bette released a terse statement to the press: "There will not be any reconciliation. Harmon will apply for a divorce."

Upon filing for divorce, Nelson explained, "I think this is the best way out of our difficulties. I think Bette is a pretty grand actress—the best on the screen, but she has become the best to the detriment of her home life."

Nelson's divorce complaint read, "Defendant had become so engrossed in her profession that she had neglected and failed to perform her duties as a wife and has been inattentive, casual and distant to Plaintiff to the point of rudeness and embarrassment." In court Ham also testified that, while at home, Bette read too much. He said that she even read while guests were in the house. "Yes," he said, "on innumerable occasions, she absented herself from the room to pursue the everlasting reading."

Harmon Nelson obtained his uncontested divorce decree on the conventional charge of cruelty on December 6, 1938. Bette, over the years, would attribute the failure of her marriage to Ham's weakness and his inability to make as much money as she did. What she wouldn't say, however, is that what actually caused the final breakup was Ham's discovery of her relationship with Hughes. Allegedly Ham went so far as to document Bette's lovemaking with Hughes by leaving a tape recorder under their bed. The story goes that Ham then used the recording to blackmail Hughes for a substantial sum of money.

Nevertheless, over the years there was constant talk of a reconciliation between Bette and Ham, high school sweethearts. In fact two nights before Bette's elopement with Arthur Farnsworth on New Year's Eve, 1940, Bette went out to dinner with Ham.

After Bette married for a third time in 1945, to William Grant Sherry, Harmon Nelson became involved with a woman by the name of Anne Roberts, whom he later married.

NEW YORK FILM CRITICS

This critics' group was never particularly fond of Bette. It cited only three of her performances in a near 50-year span (compared to Bette's 10 Oscar nominations). In 1935, when Bette won the Oscar for *Dangerous*, the NYFC gave its award to Greta Garbo for *Anna Karenina* and named Katharine Hepburn as runner-up for *Alice Adams*.

In 1939 the award, like every other award that year, went to Vivien Leigh for her performance as Scarlett O'Hara in *Gone With the Wind*. The group cited Bette as a runner-up for her performance in *Dark Victory*.

In 1950 the group finally awarded Bette for her performance in *All About Eve*. On the first ballot she was tied with Judy Holliday for *Born Yesterday*, but Bette won on the sixth ballot, with Holliday and Gloria Swanson as the runners-up.

NEWTON HIGH SCHOOL

For part of her freshman year and all of her sophomore year in high school, Bette attended Newton High School in Newton, Massachusetts. In school Bette was considered quite popular. She even organized a girl's football team that was dubbed the "Coffee-Colored Angels," for which she played right tackle.

THE NIGHT OF THE IGUANA

Tennessee William's *The Night of the Iguana* premiered on Broadway at the Royal Theatre on December 28, 1961. The play was directed by Frank Corsaro and produced by Charles Bowden and Violla Rubber. Additional credits included: sets, Oliver Smith; lighting, Jean Rosenthal; and costumes,

Noel Taylor. The cast starred Bette Davis, Margaret Leighton, Patrick O'Neal, and Alan Webb and included Patricia Roe, Christopher Jones, James Farentino, Bruce Glover, Laryssa Lauret, Heinz Hohenwald, Lucy Landau, Theseus George, Lane Bradbury, and Louis Guss.

Trouble erupted for the play in rehearsals and pre-Broadway tryouts in Rochester, Detroit, and then Chicago. A good deal of the problem was based in Bette's playing Maxine Faulk, essentially a tertiary character. She would be offstage a good deal of the time and had to stand in the shadows while Margaret Leighton, in the starring role of Hannah Jelkes, basked in the spotlight and, worse, in the reviews. Interestingly, both Bette and Tennessee Williams had wanted Katharine Hepburn in the role, but Hepburn had turned it down.

Another part of the problem was Bette's discomfort with the teachings of the Actors Studio. With Frank Corsaro as director and Patrick O'Neal as costar (in addition to quite a few other members of the cast), *The Night of the Iguana* was clearly entrenched in The Method. As Corsaro explained, "Bette would make digging remarks about some of the actors who were pausing and taking time in ways that she thought were not propitious. She would throw a tantrum and walk off over the slightest problem that would arise onstage. She did so, as a matter of fact, several times so that her understudy had to fill in for her. Mr. Williams and Charles Bowden had to go as far as Westport, where she was staying, with roses in hand, on their knees, saying, 'Please, come back.' I'm not kidding! The noose was tightening. Always when she came back she seemed to be friendly toward me and was willing to listen to me. If she challenged me in any way, I would always deal with her very clearly and very simply. I was never antagonistic to her, but there was obviously a lot of hostility building up between herself and the company. It was an exercise of power. You know, 'Regardless of whether I am playing the third character, *I am the most important person here!*' "

Bette reportedly attempted, unsuccessfully, to get both Maggie Leighton and Patrick O'Neal fired from the play. Ultimately O'Neal's tolerance of Bette's relentless and derisive hounding during rehearsals (after she had failed in her alleged attempt to seduce him) was exhausted. "Finally, a moment came," recalled Corsaro, when Patrick O'Neal, not being able to stand it anymore, literally went after her. *Physically*. We had to hold him back. She just stood there on the stage, smiling, loving every minute of it. It was unbelievable, her demonstration. Every four-letter expletive. And then she just *stood* there."

Bette's antagonism was certainly not limited to O'Neal. Eventually, she threatened to walk out on the show unless Corsaro was fired. Not only did she see to it that he was fired; she also had him banned from the theater and, even more incredibly, from the city of Chicago, where the play was still in tryouts. Corsaro would, however, retain his credit as the show's director.

Producer Charles Bowden blames Corsaro, whom he did not like or get along with, for the problems. "The main situation you need in a director is communication between the director and the actor. Any good director has a different, varying form of communication for each individual in the company." Corsaro, according to Bowden, did not have a line of communication with Bette. "I knew after about a week of rehearsals, 'Oh-Oh.' There was no communication. He was busy improvising with the two walk-ons, both talented young men, James Farentino and Chris Jones, who became, quote unquote, 'Hollywood stars,' if you will. Corsaro was busy improvising with them and with Patrick O'Neal."

Bowden also defends Bette by saying, "This was a very complicated lady. She had fought all her life for her *position*. And if anybody seemed to be jeopardizing it, she was on the defense again, like a mother over her chicks."

The Broadway reviews of *Iguana* were mixed at best, and to Bette's horror it was Leighton who received the best notices. Leighton would also win the Best Actress Tony award that year. As for Patrick O'Neal, he had, in the view of director Corsaro, "allowed *her* to get to him. His performance considerably deteriorated on the road, and, what was a singularly beautiful performance became a shadow of itself in New York." The play, despite the horrors of its backstage drama, would win a Tony nomination as the year's best play and would also win the New York Drama Critics Circle Award for Best Play.

After performing the show for only three months in New York, Bette Davis served her notice, and on April 4, 1962, she left the show that perhaps she should never have entered. She was replaced by Shelley Winters. As Bette related at the time to columnist Irv Kupcinet, "I couldn't *stand* the people in the cast. It was plain murder for me, going to the theatre every night and I had to get out or lose my mind."

Nevertheless, when a film version of the play was produced in 1964 by Ray Stark, directed by John Huston, Bette was greatly disappointed when she was not asked to star. Instead Ava Gardner played Maxine, with Richard Burton and Deborah Kerr co-starring. When it was being cast, Bette confided to Hedda Hopper, "Let's *pray* [I get to do it]. I hope I'm allowed to play it. Everything Tennessee Williams writes is better on screen than stage."

NOW, VOYAGER ★★★½
Warner Brothers
1942   117 minutes   bw
Directed by: Irving Rapper
Produced by: Hal B. Wallis
Screenplay by: Casey Robinson, based on the novel by Olive Higgins
        Prouty
Cinematography by: Sol Polito
Cast: Bette Davis, Paul Henreid, Claude Rains, Gladys Cooper, Bonita
        Granville, John Loder, Ilka Chase, Lee Patrick, Franklin Pangborn,
        Katherine Alexander, James Rennie, Mary Wickes, Charles Drake,
        Janis Wilson, Frank Puglia, Michael Ames, David Clyde

Olive Higgins Prouty continued her tale of the Vales, a wealthy Boston family, with the novel *Now, Voyager.* Her previous books about the family

"The perfect Charlotte Vale" looking pensive on the set.

had included *White Fawn, Lisa Vale,* and *Home Port.* Prouty sold the rights of *Voyager* to Warner Brothers for $40,000 in an agreement dated November 28, 1941.

The plot had Bette as Charlotte Vale, the family's bookworm ugly duckling whose witch of a mother suppresses her for her own selfish reasons. Cinderellalike, the ugly duckling turns into a beautiful (and fashionably dressed) woman who engages in a shipboard romance with the suave and married Jerry Durrance. Much of the subsequent drama concerns whether or not Charlotte will return to her old ugly self to appease her mother, who is irate at the change in her daughter. The plot is soap opera, sure, but the performances, the score, and the costumes are perfect. And what wonderful lines have been spun out of Casey Robinson's typewriter.

In February 1942, those up for the role of Jerry Durrance were George Brent, Walter Pidgeon, Ronald Colman, Fredric March, Henry Fonda, Joel McCrea, Franchot Tone, and Herbert Marshall, among others. Initially Bette was opposed to the idea of Paul Henreid, or any other European actor, in the role. Upon seeing Henreid's initial test Bette balked, telling everyone who would listen that Henreid would ruin the film. Subsequently Wallis retested Henreid and Americanized him to Bette's eventual satisfaction. Henreid, then 34, was cast as Jerry Durrance at $4,062.50 a week in a contract dated April 1, 1942.

Those up for the part of Dr. Jacquith, Charlotte's Svengalilike psychiatrist, included Raymond Massey and Charles Coburn. To Bette's delight, however, it would be Claude Rains who was eventually cast. For his work Rains would be paid the sum of $4,000 a week.

Surprisingly, since it would become one of the great roles of her career, Jack Warner did not initially want Bette in the part of Charlotte Vale. Instead those he was considering were Irene Dunne, Norma Shearer, and Ginger Rogers. In a February 16, 1942, casting sheet others mentioned included Greer Garson, Joan Crawford, Claudette Colbert, Helen Hayes, Katharine Hepburn, Jean Arthur, and Miriam Hopkins. At one point Louella Parsons reported that Irene Dunne was to be loaned to Warners for the part. When Bette got wind of this, she blew into Wallis's office with a question: "*Why* are you going outside the studio to cast *Now, Voyager* when you have the perfect Charlotte Vale signed to a contract?" Wallis and Warner acquiesced, and Bette was signed for the part.

In other casting, up for the part of Lisa, Charlotte's sister-in-law, were Geraldine Fitzgerald, Mary Astor, and Fay Wray. Ilka Chase was eventually cast. For the part of Tina, Jerry Durrance's young daughter whom Charlotte befriends, Bette wanted Mary Anderson and even went so far as to do a test with her. The part had yet to be cast even when the film went into production, and many tests of prospective Tinas were considered. Hal Wallis eventually settled on Janis Wilson for the part.

In late 1941 Wallis, in his first venture after relinquishing his post as Warners' executive producer, assigned director Eddie Goulding to the project. Reportedly every producer at the studio wanted the property and every studio had tried to buy it. Goulding went to work on the script and came up with several drafts. He wanted to structure the film without flashbacks. He wanted to start with the story of Charlotte as a young girl and have the film proceed in a straight chronological line.

Meanwhile, the script had problems with the Breen Office, which objected to any suggestion that Charlotte and Jerry have an adulterous affair. Consequently in the film the two fall in love without a real love scene and, at the end of the picture, have to settle for "stars" ("Oh, Jerry, don't let's ask for the moon—when we have the stars") instead of each other. Bette had a problem with the ending, and during the filming she would confide to a reporter, "We struggled with that ending and even though [we kept it] I still think the man is nice enough to have got the girl."

After meeting with him, Wallis was uncertain about Goulding's approach to the property. He held other meetings with directors Lewis Milestone and Irving Rapper and then reported to Jack Warner that Rapper was by far the best choice for the material.

Wallis was also concerned about Bette's appearance for the film. He expressed his concern to Warner that Bette had not looked good in the few pictures prior to *Voyager* and in a February 20, 1942, memo to Warner, Wallis urged him to assign Sol Polito to the picture. Polito had already been assigned to shoot a Jack Benny picture, but Wallis wanted him to be reassigned to photograph Bette. In his memo Wallis noted that photographing Bette was more of a job than photographing Benny in a comedy. Wallis suggested that Tony Gaudio be given the Benny picture and Polito be given *Now, Voyager*. His wish was granted. Thanks to Polito, Bette Davis would look more beautiful in *Now, Voyager* than in any picture she ever made.

Initially Warner thought the title *Now, Voyager* was too abstract and sought to change it to something more obvious. However, the book's author, certainly aware that the film would help sell her book, campaigned vigorously to retain the title. Eventually she won.

Bette was set to return to Hollywood from the East Coast on March 16, 1942, for extensive wardrobe and makeup tests. She was to play the role at three ages, 20, 28, and 29, which required a good deal of testing. She was also to wear 30 Orry-Kelly costumes in the picture. In addition, the character was to undergo a dramatic appearance change. Charlotte was to lose 25 pounds during the course of the story. Said Bette on the set, "I've gone the limit now. Here I am, fat and dowdy. And look at my face! It's plumped out like a melon. Ouch!" To achieve the desired effect, Bette wore padding, heavy fake eyebrows, and a pair of eyeglasses.

Now, Voyager, with a budget of $761,000, started shooting on Tuesday, April 7, 1942. It was allotted 42 shooting days with an estimated finish of May 25. For its first day the company shot on location at Laguna Beach. The following day, April 8, shooting at Laguna was canceled due to bad weather. Instead shooting was held back at Warners on Stage 22.

On Monday, April 13, Bette wasn't feeling well, and shooting was shut down early. The following morning she could barely talk, and Rapper shot around her. On Wednesday, Bette was still sick, and shooting was canceled altogether. On Friday, April 17, Bette reported back to work. Obviously the company was moving at a slow pace. After 18 days of shooting the production was already 6½ days behind schedule. On Friday, May 1, Bette showed up at 9:40 A.M. for a 9:00 call. Her excuse was that her maid had failed to awaken her. The production was also slowed because Gladys Cooper, playing Bette's mother, kept forgetting her lines and mangling her dialogue. Still, Bette was thrilled to be working with Cooper, for whom she had great respect.

On May 18, Jack Warner sent Rapper a letter that read, in part: "I can't understand why you are so slow. You have competent artists, the script is certainly set in everybody's mind, but you are 9 days behind on a 62 day schedule. I cannot sit idly by and permit this, and therefore, if you cannot do any better I must see you personally today. . . . I want to impress upon you that unless there is a marked improvement, I must seriously consider the pictures you will do in the future."

Rapper responded to Warner the following day: "I was terribly disturbed to receive your note; I can only assure you that I have never worked more conscientiously on any picture. . . . Above all, Miss Davis is a very slow and analytical lady whose behaviour has to be treated with directorial care and delicacy. Believe me, that in itself is a full day's work. . . ."

As an example of Rapper's work, a scene called for Bette and Claude Rains to sit down and review blueprints of a proposed hospital, snacking on hot dogs while they worked. Bette objected to the idea that she and Claude Rains would be eating hot dogs for dinner. Nevertheless, Rapper won the argument, and the scene was filmed with Bette and Rains snacking on hot dogs and potato chips.

Another scene called for Bette to write a letter. Rapper planned to shoot the scene with a hand double, but, stubborn trouper that she was, Bette insisted on shooting the scene herself. For the close-up insert her hand was beautified with makeup. However, when it came time to shoot the scene, Bette had a mysterious stroke of camera fright. The scene had to be shot several times because, according to cameraman Pinky Weiss, "She was shaking like a leaf. Nothing but her hand was being photographed, but it seemed to frighten her."

For another scene, a love scene between Bette and Paul Henreid, they did 33 kisses in rehearsal. The actual shooting took three kisses, with one reportedly lasting quite a bit past Rapper's command to "cut."

As for the famous cigarette trick in the film, in which Henreid gallantly places two cigarettes in his mouth at the same time and lights one for himself and one for Bette, it was actually a copy of a scene from *Flesh and the Devil* in which John Gilbert did the same for Greta Garbo. The trick was not in the original script, which called for Bette to light a cigarette held by Henreid, for Henreid to hand the lit cigarette back to Bette, and for Bette to hand the still-lit matchstick to Henreid so that he could light his own cigarette. Years later Henreid recalled, "I suggested it [the cigarette trick] to Bette who loved it and we worked it out together. Then we went to our director who shall be nameless. And I said '*Irving*, how about if we did it like this?' Well, in the course of the great tradition of directors, he wasn't sure about it so he said, 'No.' However, our marvelous producer Hal Wallis liked it and that's how it happened."

Many on the set were aware that Bette was bullying Rapper. As Ilka Chase recalled in one of her autobiographies: "Miss Davis is a fine, hard-working woman, friendly with members of her cast, forthright and courteous to technicians on her picture, and her director's heaviest cross. She will argue every move in every scene until the poor man is reduced to quivering pulp." Since Chase made only one film with Bette, it is easy to discern that the "poor man" she was referring to was Rapper.

Additional location work was done at Lake Arrowhead in late May. Shot on location was the scene showing Tina and Charlotte on vacation. During shooting Janis Wilson almost drowned and was saved from possible death by former lifeguard Bette Davis.

On June 1, a Monday, Claude Rains finished his part and went directly into *Casablanca*. Paul Henreid was also rushed through *Voyager* so that he could join the *Casablanca* company.

Bette failed to report due to illness again on Tuesday, June 9, with the production 12 days behind. She was sick again on June 10, as was Henreid, so shooting was canceled altogether. On Friday, June 12, Bette reported back to work, but Henreid was still sick. On Saturday neither one showed up for work. Both returned on Monday, June 15, with the production 15 days behind. Both Henreid and Bette finished work on Wednesday, June 24. Both returned to the set to do retakes on Friday, July 3.

Irving Rapper was back in Jack Warner's good graces with the release of the picture. On August 3, 1942, Harry Warner sent brother Jack a memo lauding *Voyager* as "a very fine picture. It has about as good a story and is as beautifully done as any picture could be." Harry did complain, however, that the film was too long and suggested cutting the sequence in which Charlotte takes Tina for a trip. "This scene," offered Harry, "is silly and just spoils a good picture." Some of the scene was subsequently cut.

Now, Voyager was accorded out-and-out raves, with some critics predicting that Bette would win her third Oscar for the picture (she would be nominated but wouldn't win). It remains one of her finest achievements.

NUDITY

In 1983, then in her 70s, Bette was asked if she would have done a nude scene when she was younger: "Me? *Never*. Not for a million dollars! I did a lot of things in my time—privately. I was naughty, but I never did it before a camera."

Actually Bette *did* once pose nude. It was for a statue, and she was a Boston teenager at the time.

O

OBITUARIES

Bette Davis, the two-time Oscar winner whose toughness, huge eyes, and haughty, cigarette-smoking style made her a movie industry legend, has died at 81.

Associated Press, October 1989

Bette Davis, 81, preeminent film actress whose Hollywood career is unsurpassed in its number and range of quality performances, died Friday of cancer.

Variety, October 9, 1989

Bette Davis, who won two Academy Awards and cut a swath through Hollywood trailing cigarette smoke and delivering drop-dead barbs, died of breast cancer Friday night.

New York Times, October 8, 1989

Bette Davis, who died in a Paris hospital on October 6, at the age of 81, was one of the most durable of all Hollywood film stars, and—what does not necessarily follow—one of those most unmistakably gifted with an acting talent.

London Times, October 9, 1989

Colleagues, friends, and film fans Saturday mourned the death of Bette Davis, who began her career playing nasty, driven women and died more than a half-century later, as one of the world's most beloved film stars.

Japan Times, October 9, 1989

OF HUMAN BONDAGE ★★★

RKO
1934   83 minutes   bw
Directed by: John Cromwell
Produced by: Pandro S. Berman
Screenplay by: Lester Cohen, based on the play by W. Somerset Maugham
Cinematography by: Henry W. Gerrard
Cast: Leslie Howard, Bette Davis, Frances Dee, Reginald Owen, Reginald Denny, Kay Johnson, Alan Hale, Reginald Sheffield, Desmond Roberts

A seminal, landmark picture in the career of Bette Davis. Reportedly she campaigned for months, waiting outside Jack Warner's door every day, until he agreed to loan her out to RKO for this picture. She knew instinctively that this was a potential career-making vehicle.

Once cast, to prepare for the role Bette hired a British wardrobe mistress to live with her so that she could study and perfect her Cockney accent.

When the film went into production on February 12, 1934, it became obvious to Bette that Leslie Howard regarded her with disdain. As she later

Acclaim: Mildred as alley cat.

related, "Of course, he was a very fine actor, [but] he did not like films. He looked down on films. Films were just a way to make money. He preferred theater. In the beginning of *Bondage* he was so horrified that an American girl was playing it that when he had [to say] his lines offstage when I was on camera in a closeup, he would read. He would stand there and mutter the lines into a book. Yes. He did not help me at all. And one day he was crossing the RKO lot where we were working and this man said to him, 'Mr. Howard, you'd better get with it. This picture's being taken right away from you.' So he behaved much better from then on."

Years later Bette would cite Mildred as having been her most difficult assignment. Not only did she have to affect a Cockney accent; she also had to play with a cast of British actors. She felt a great deal of pressure to "measure up."

Bette responded with a bravura performance that was impossible to overlook. She played Mildred as an alley cat and unleashed the full force of her unparalleled histrionic powers.

Upon the release of *Of Human Bondage*, a quake reverberated throughout Hollywood. Nowhere was it felt more than at Warner Brothers. While the rest of the industry wondered, "*Who* is this girl?" Warners had to bow its head and glumly ask itself, "*Why* haven't *we* done anything with this girl?"

As late as December 1948, *Life* magazine was still calling Bette's performance in *Of Human Bondage* "perhaps the finest performance ever given on the screen."

Of Human Bondage was remade in 1946 with Paul Henreid and Eleanor Parker and in 1964 with Laurence Harvey and Kim Novak. It was never more successful, however, than in its 1934 version.

OLD ACQUAINTANCE ★★½

Warner Brothers
1943   110 minutes   bw
Directed by: Vincent Sherman
Produced by: Henry Blanke
Screenplay by: John Van Druten and Lenore Coffee, from the play by John Van Druten
Cinematography by: Sol Polito
Cast: Bette Davis, Miriam Hopkins, Gig Young, Philip Reed, Roscoe Karns, Anne Revere, Esther Dale, John Loder, Dolores Moran, Ann Codee, Joseph Crehan, Pierre Watkin, Marjorie Hoshelle, George Lessey, Ann Doran, Leona Maricle, Francine Rufo

Warner Brothers paid John Van Druten $75,000 for his Broadway play *Old Acquaintance* per an agreement dated January 16, 1941. Bette, who had been planning to go on a war bond tour, decided against it, so *Old Acquaintance* was prepped for her to begin following her vacation. Edmund Goulding had directed Bette and Miriam in *The Old Maid* and had been driven to distraction by their incessant feuding. As the start date of *Old Acquaintance* approached, Goulding suddenly backed out. Hal Wallis called Vincent Sherman and told him that Goulding had had a heart attack and couldn't do the film. Other stories circulated that Goulding just couldn't stomach the idea of working with Bette and Miriam again. Sherman also turned it down. It was then presented to Irving Rapper, who also turned it down, opting to go into the navy instead. So it was presented again to Sherman, who finally accepted.

The picture would have Bette Davis and Miriam Hopkins square off and duel in designer gowns as Kit Marlowe and Millie Drake, former schoolgirl friends turned popular (and competing) novelists in roles that Jane Cowl and Peggy Wood had done on Broadway.

Naturally Bette had reservations about appearing again with Hopkins, but Warner wanted to pair another big-name star opposite her. On May 20, 1942, Jack Warner voiced the opinion that they were wasting their time trying to get another big star opposite Bette and felt that they should go ahead and sign Mary Astor for the part. But, he noted, "We can still make a test of Miriam Hopkins." Later Warner also suggested Constance Bennett for the part. But it would be Miriam Hopkins who was eventually signed, in an agreement dated September 21, 1942, at a salary of $5,000 per week.

The picture started shooting without Bette on Wednesday, November 11, 1942. Warner had wanted shooting to start by mid-October, a schedule he grudgingly kept postponing. Bette, who had been vacationing in Palm Springs, arrived on the set on November 18, whereupon she informed Sherman that she was interested in seeing the footage of Miriam that had already been shot. An hour later she telephoned Sherman, raving over what he had accomplished with Miriam. *"How* did you get her to be so good?" Bette asked in astonishment. She then added to Sherman's relief, "When do you want me to report?"

Over the next two months Miriam reported sick on a dozen different days. When she *did* work, she had short days, at least when compared to the hours Bette put in.

While making the film, Bette was also coordinating the Hollywood Canteen, making phone calls during breaks in her dressing room. The war and its ravages would have a trivial effect on the picture. One scene in the script called for Bette to order a steak from the menu. Sensitive to the hardships caused by the war, Bette had the steak changed to an omelet.

Meanwhile, the feud between Davis and Hopkins escalated, caused primarily by Hopkins, who was insecure because Warners was Bette's studio and she felt she would be shunned in Bette's favor. Learning that Bette and Sherman were engaged in an affair made her even more insecure. So she overcompensated by creating little bits of business to detract from Bette's performance. One shot, for instance, called for Sol Polito to shoot Bette over Miriam's shoulder. When the camera started rolling, Miriam took a drag on her cigarette and placed it right across Bette's face.

During the course of the shooting Vince Sherman would have to play musical dressing rooms—going into one dressing room to console Miriam, then into the other one to console Bette, or vice versa. It got to the point where the two actresses weren't speaking. It was a constant and petty battle of upstaging. Bette was particularly incensed that as the two women got older she would be in appropriate makeup but Miriam would try to look younger and more beautiful. They had had the same problem on *The Old Maid.* "That bitch," Bette fumed to Sherman. "That bitch. She keeps getting younger while I keep getting older!"

And then it came time to shoot the big fight scene, which was so anxiously anticipated that *Life* magazine wanted to come onto the set and shoot it. Jack Warner, however, refused, feeling that publicity about two women fighting would not be good for the studio. The scene called for Bette to shake Miriam vigorously, and they rehearsed the scene as scripted. But when it came time to shoot, Miriam simply went limp. She did not put up the struggle called for in the script. Miriam had learned that the best way to weather a shaking was to just let her body go slack. Bette stalked off the set in a fit. Sherman went to Miriam, then coaxed Bette out of her dressing room, and the scene was shot to Sherman's satisfaction.

A lot of rewriting was being done as the film was shot—mostly due to demands made by Bette, which naturally caused much delay. Jack Warner, understandably, was irate. On January 29 he sent a memo to producer Henry Blanke, insisting that the picture be completed by February 6, saying, "I will not permit this picture to go on any longer."

He *did*, of course, allow it to go on. On Saturday, February 13, *Old*

Acquaintance finally called it a wrap. The picture had been budgeted at 42 days but took nearly double that, 78.

   Old Acquaintance was remade as *Rich and Famous* (1981) with Candice Bergen and Jacqueline Bisset. It was notable mainly as George Cukor's final picture.

THE OLD MAID ★★★
Warner Brothers
1939   95 minutes   bw
Directed by: Edmund Goulding
Produced by: Hal B. Wallis, in association with Henry Blanke
Screenplay by: Casey Robinson, based on the play by Zoe Akins and the
   novel by Edith Wharton
Cinematography by: Tony Gaudio
Cast: Bette Davis, Miriam Hopkins, George Brent, Donald Crisp, Jane
   Bryan, Louise Fazenda, James Stephenson, Jerome Cowan, William
   Lundigan, Cecilia Loftus, Rand Brooks, Janet Shaw, DeWolf Hopper

In January 1939 writer Casey Robinson told Hal Wallis that he didn't think *The Old Maid* would be a good vehicle for Bette Davis because she needed to have the opportunity to be "sparking" and "electric." Nonetheless, Warners purchased the story from Paramount for $65,000 in an agreement dated February 24, 1939. Paramount had previously purchased the rights from Edith Wharton and Zoe Akins for $25,000 less. First appearing in *Redbook* in 1922, the story was published as a novel in 1924 and then produced as a play in 1935. The play starred Helen Menken and Judith Anderson and won the Pulitzer Prize.

   Upon purchasing the rights, Warners totally discarded the 1935 Paramount screenplay by Wanda Tuchock and Virginia Van Upp and assigned Casey Robinson to rewrite it. Later Tuchock, in pursuit of an on-screen co-writer credit, initiated a case with the Writer's Adjustment Committee. The committee, however, found in favor of Robinson and deemed that he should receive sole screen credit.

   The plot had Delia Lovell marrying Jim Ralston in a wealthy, Philadelphia society marriage. As Delia dresses for the ceremony, she is fussed over by her young, pretty cousin, Charlotte Lovell. Drama sparks just before the wedding when Delia's old love, Clem, shows up to break up the proceedings. Delia shoos him away, however, and Charlotte ends up consoling Clem, whom she has always had a crush on. The night of consolation, however, ends up with Charlotte pregnant. Clem ends up being killed in the Civil War, and Charlotte goes away to Arizona and secretly has her baby. When Charlotte returns to Philadelphia, she opens an orphanage, not telling anyone that one of the parentless little girls, Tina, is actually her own child. Charlotte deteriorates into a tight-lipped old maid and loses her daughter's love to the richer, prettier, happier Delia.

   From the start Bette was the only actress considered for the role of

Charlotte Lovell. A few actresses were initially considered for the role of Delia, including Rosalind Russell and Geraldine Fitzgerald, but it was Miriam Hopkins who landed the part.

Interestingly, according to a February 21, 1939, casting sheet, both Lana Turner and Gene Tierney were considered for the roles of Tina and Dee, Charlotte and Delia's respective daughters (in the later scenes). For the latter, Bette requested that her longtime stand-in, Sally Sage, be tested, but the part went to Joan Shaw. The part of Tina went to Bette's discovery, Jane Bryan.

For Clem, the lover of both women, Hal Wallis reported that he wanted a George Brent or David Niven type. It is curious, then, that it was Humphrey Bogart who was cast.

Obtaining costumes and props for the picture proved to be a challenge. Apparently David Selznick was making a picture of a story from a similar era, *Gone With the Wind*, and had hoarded most of the available costumes and props.

Evidently aware that the two women had little affinity for one another, producer Henry Blanke was careful to schedule makeup and wardrobe tests of Bette and Miriam at different times. Adding to the tension between the two was the fact that although Bette had the more substantial role, she was to be paid $35,000 for the film. Miriam, on the other hand, was to get *$50,000*, a fact she flaunted and reveled in.

With a budget of $778,000, *The Old Maid* started shooting on Wednesday, March 15, 1939, with both Bette and Miriam. At the time the picture started, Goulding had an incomplete script of only 88 pages.

From the first day of shooting there were minor signs of temperament and impending trouble. A few days into the shooting a 45-minute delay was caused by Bette's dress having to be let out. Apparently Bette had gained some weight around the waist since her last fitting, much to the amusement of Miriam.

Bogart started work on Monday, March 20. Both Goulding and Bette had wanted Alan Marshall for the part, and Goulding was immediately displeased with Bogart's work. The actor was given the day off on Tuesday while Goulding had Wallis and Blanke look at the footage shot of him the previous day. The trio then decided that Bogart was not the romantic type and fired him from the picture. Years later Bette mused: "One of the funniest miscastings I remember was Humphrey Bogart playing a nineteenth-century romantic lover with me in *The Old Maid*. In the opening scene, he appeared in a flowing black cloak, running through a railroad station trying to catch up with me. As he pursued me along the platform he looked so sinister that he seemed for all the world like a thug trying to kidnap me—rather than a hero trying to express his devotion. The entire cast became hysterical with laughter, and when we finally subsided, Bogey said to director Edmund Goulding, 'I guess you'll have to get yourself another lover boy.' And he did." George Brent started work in Bogart's place on Saturday, March 25.

Meanwhile, Miriam and Bette fought for their scenes, each trying to get an advantage over the other. The tricks they had been learning and storing for years were hurled across the set with bitchy bravado. One would cough during an important scene for the other and then apologize profusely. They would keep each other waiting on the set. One device Miriam used frequently was to show up at, say, 9:20 A.M. for a 9:00 A.M. call—not too late to get in trouble but late enough to have Bette Davis waiting on *her*; late enough to make an *entrance*.

Once Miriam claimed to have something in her eye, and while she was examined by a first-aid attendant Bette impatiently tapped her high-heeled foot on the set in frustration. The delay lasted 2½ hours.

At one point, in a lighter moment, the two actresses each donned a pair of boxing gloves, while still photographer Bert Six snapped a series of action shots.

Then, of course, there were the illnesses, feigned and otherwise. Miriam called in sick on Saturday, April 1, and then returned on Monday. Soon after, Bette also fell ill but continued to show up for work to make a point of her professionalism. Later, on April 17, Bette fainted on the set. It's uncertain whether she actually passed out or was merely exasperated with her costar and seeking the nearest escape hatch. The following day, a Tuesday, Bette did not report to work. Accordingly Goulding planned to shoot around Bette and focus the day's activities on Miriam. However, while on the set, Miriam suddenly contracted a mysterious illness of her own, and shooting was suspended entirely. Miriam returned to work on Thursday, and not wanting her costar to have the limelight to herself, Bette returned to work the following day.

Naturally the film fell behind schedule. It actually *started* behind schedule because the Bogart recasting necessitated that Goulding shoot five days of retakes. Additional pressure fell on Goulding because delays on the picture caused the start of Bette's next picture, then titled *The Knight and the Lady*, to be pushed back. To complicate matters, before going into *The Old Maid*, Bette had insisted that she be granted a vacation between the two pictures.

As shooting proceeded, and the characters played by the two actresses aged, Bette began to notice that, contrary to the script, Miriam was looking younger and prettier. The matter came to a head on Friday, April 28, when Goulding, accompanied by Al Alleborn, the unit manager on the picture, confronted Miriam on the set. They accused her of changing her makeup from a woman maturing in years to that of a younger woman. Hal Wallis, the executive on the production who had approved the makeup, hair, and wardrobe tests prior to the start of the film, was livid at Miriam's cosmetic creativity. Perc Westmore, the head of the studio's makeup department, was called to the set and was ordered to personally supervise Miriam's makeup from that point forward. The day after the makeup debacle, a Saturday, Miriam reported for work but, probably unhappy with her aging makeup, left the set claiming illness. She called in sick again the following Monday. It was the final week of shooting, and everyone was anxious to call it a wrap.

Miriam finally reported back to work on Tuesday, and the company, after 46 shooting days, finished work on Saturday, May 6.

The Old Maid was marketed with ads that proclaimed, "What Decent Man Would Have Her Now?" and "She Did the One Thing No Man Can Forgive!" The film would receive exceptionally favorable reviews and would be the biggest box office hit ever of a Bette Davis picture.

PATRICK O'NEAL

Early into the 1961 production of Tennessee William's *The Night of the Iguana*, Bette reportedly developed something of a crush on her costar, Patrick O'Neal, cast as the Reverend T. Lawrence Shannon. When O'Neal spurned her advances, she allegedly took every opportunity to lash out at him. Reportedly she tried to get him fired from the show, and she publicly derided his abilities as an actor. "It's actors of his ilk who was are destroying the theater," Bette said in reference to O'Neal's utilization of The Method. "He even took three days to figure out why he should wear a pair of shoes." Tennessee William's refusal to replace O'Neal in the show contributed to Bette's decision to leave the show in April 1962.

Patrick O'Neal, born in 1927, appeared in pictures including *The Cardinal* (1963), *Assignment to Kill* (1967), *The Way We Were* (1973), and *The Stepford Wives* (1975).

ROBERT OSBORNE

One of Bette's best friends and companions during the later part of her life, Robert Osborne is a columnist with the industry trade paper *The Hollywood Reporter*. Over the years Osborne penned numerous pieces on Bette. In November 1986 he campaigned in his "Rambling Reporter" column for the Academy of Motion Picture Arts and Sciences to present a special Oscar to Bette at its 1987 ceremonies. Wrote Osborne, "The Academy's Board of Directors doesn't meet to consider Special Oscars until next January, but some food for thought: when that meeting occurs, one person before all others should be seriously discussed for one of those honorary statues. Namely, Bette Davis. For a myriad of reasons . . . the Davis films (a catalog second to none), her durability (she's still delivering, the latest being the just-wrapped *The Whales of August*. . . ." Osborne also cited Bette's efforts with the Hollywood Canteen. He concluded his plea with "Sometimes we take our Legends too much for granted; it's time Bette Davis got some recognition for her career *since* 1938 [the last time she was awarded an Oscar]." Osborne was, of course, right. Nonetheless, the academy failed to take notice.

A few days after Bette's death in October 1989, Osborne eulogized her in his column: "It's no news that she could be a hellion on two legs. . . . But it's equally true Bette had a deep capacity for friendship and loyalty. She'd put you to the test—in spades!—but once she'd made up her mind you were OK, Yankee material, she was your friend for life. . . ."

THE OSCARS

"Nothing can be greater than the Academy Awards."

Bette Davis, 1988

Bette Davis was one of three people to claim credit for nicknaming the Academy Award "Oscar." Until the day of her death Bette would say that, upon being presented with the award for her 1935 performance in *Dangerous*, she returned to her table and joked that the backside of the statuette reminded her of the rear end belonging to her husband, Harmon *Oscar* Nelson; hence the sobriquet. Others who claimed to have come up with the name were columnist Sidney Skolsky and academy executive Margaret Herrick. The dispute has never been resolved, though Bette did suggest in 1955 that "If the other claimants became very insistent we [should] settle the whole thing with a duel."

The following years indicate when the films were *released*, not when the ceremony took place (the ceremonies are held annually the following year). The lists indicate the nominees in the category of Best Actress.

1934

> Claudette Colbert, *It Happened One Night*
> Grace Moore, *One Night of Love*
> Norma Shearer, *The Barretts of Wimpole Street*

Sidney Skolsky's bold prediction in his column in the January 30, 1935, issue of the *Hollywood Citizen-News*: Bette "will win the Academy Award for the best female performance of the year for her work in *Of Human Bondage* if the votes are cast with the same sincerity that they were last year." Unfortunately, Bette was not even nominated. A write-in campaign resulted in Bette's obtaining the second highest number of votes, losing only to Colbert. Still, the official academy word was that Bette was not nominated.

1935

> Elisabeth Bergner, *Escape Me Never*
> Claudette Colbert, *Private Worlds*
> Bette Davis, *Dangerous*
> Katharine Hepburn, *Alice Adams*
> Miriam Hopkins, *Becky Sharp*
> Merle Oberon, *The Dark Angel*

Because of the controversy caused by Bette the previous year, Price-Waterhouse took over the counting of the ballots. Tension pervaded the ceremony. Both the Screen Actors Guild and the Writers Guild called for an Oscar boycott due to labor feuds. Many stayed away in protest. The president of the academy, Frank Capra, attempted to lure attendees by presenting an honorary award to pioneer D. W. Griffith. Bette attended the ceremony but attempted to make a statement by not dressing up for the occasion. A reporter later called her "a little girl wearing a blue and white print frock with severe lapels and no jewels. The pretty but simple kind of costume a co-ed might wear dancing on a Friday night." The ceremony was held at the Biltmore Hotel, and Bette attended with her husband, Ham Nelson, and her mother. D. W. Griffith presented the award to the winner, Bette Davis. In the succeeding years Bette would say repeatedly that the award had actually been presented to her because she had not won the previous year. Katharine Hepburn, said Bette, deserved to win the 1935 Oscar.

1938

Fay Bainter, *White Banners*
Bette Davis, *Jezebel*
Wendy Hiller, *Pygmalion*
Norma Shearer, *Marie Antoinette*
Margaret Sullavan, *Three Comrades*

Bette's second Oscar was awarded for her performance in *Jezebel*. Said she at the time, "I won't quit until I have a third!"

1939

Bette Davis, *Dark Victory*
Irene Dunne, *Love Affair*
Greta Garbo, *Ninotchka*
Greer Garson, *Goodbye, Mr. Chips*
Vivien Leigh, *Gone With the Wind*

Despite getting the reviews of her career for *Dark Victory*, Bette was no competition for the onslaught that was *Gone With the Wind*. Bette, certain of her fate, did not want to attend the ceremony, but, prodded by her mother, she did.

1940

Bette Davis, *The Letter*
Joan Fontaine, *Rebecca*
Katharine Hepburn, *The Philadelphia Story*
Ginger Rogers, *Kitty Foyle*
Martha Scott, *Our Town*

The race was among Fontaine, Hepburn, and Rogers. The winner? Ginger Rogers.

1941

Bette Davis, *The Little Foxes*
Joan Fontaine, *Suspicion*
Greer Garson, *Blossoms in the Dust*
Olivia de Havilland, *Hold Back the Dawn*
Barbara Stanwyck, *Ball of Fire*

Bette gave one of the best performances of her career in *Foxes*, but the drama that year focused on feuding sisters de Havilland and Fontaine, both of whom were nominated. It was Fontaine who won.

1942

Bette Davis, *Now, Voyager*
Greer Garson, *Mrs. Miniver*
Katharine Hepburn, *Woman of the Year*

Rosalind Russell, *My Sister Eileen*
Teresa Wright, *The Pride of the Yankees*

The race was between Bette and Greer Garson. *Now, Voyager* was one of Bette's most popular performances. Timing, however, was against Bette. With World War II stirring patriotic fervor, *Mrs. Miniver* won most of the major awards that year, including one for Garson.

1944

Ingrid Bergman, *Gaslight*
Claudette Colbert, *Since You Went Away*
Bette Davis, *Mr. Skeffington*
Greer Garson, *Mrs. Parkington*
Barbara Stanwyck, *Double Indemnity*

A tough race between Bergman and Stanwyck, with Bergman the eventual winner.

1950

Anne Baxter, *All About Eve*
Bette Davis, *All About Eve*
Judy Holliday, *Born Yesterday*
Eleanor Parker, *Caged*
Gloria Swanson, *Sunset Boulevard*

One of the most fascinating Oscar contests in history, which pitted the motion picture legends Davis and Swanson. Sentiment was on Swanson's side. She was at the end of her career and had never received an Academy Award. Most critics, however, agreed that the award should go to Bette, which it probably would have if not for one factor: also nominated in the same category was Bette's costar, Anne Baxter. Baxter, who had already received a supporting Oscar years before, insisted on competing in the Best Actress category instead. This, of course, split some of the votes cast by *All About Eve* fans. The beneficiary of all this drama was relative newcomer Judy Holliday, the surprising winner.

1952

Shirley Booth, *Come Back, Little Sheba*
Joan Crawford, *Sudden Fear*
Bette Davis, *The Star*
Julie Harris, *The Member of the Wedding*
Susan Hayward, *With a Song in My Heart*

Hands down, Shirley Booth—in a role that Bette turned down.

1962

Anne Bancroft, *The Miracle Worker*
Bette Davis, *What Ever Happened to Baby Jane?*
Katharine Hepburn, *Long Day's Journey into Night*

Geraldine Page, *Sweet Bird of Youth*
Lee Remick, *Days of Wine and Roses*

A wide-open race, with sentiment on the side of Bette and Katharine Hepburn. Bette was certain that she would win. She wanted this Oscar *desperately*. She wanted to be the first to win three Best Actress Oscars—and sensed that this could be her last opportunity. She also wanted to solidify her recent comeback. She arrived at the ceremony with her children and sat backstage in Frank Sinatra's dressing room, holding hands with Olivia de Havilland. Bette went out onstage to present the award for best original screenplay. Later, Maximilian Schell announced the names of the five nominees. When he announced the winner, "Anne Bancroft," Bette sat, stunned, in silence. She then became livid as Joan Crawford, her *Baby Jane* costar, strutted out onto the stage and accepted the award in the absent Bancroft's behalf. Said Bette, "I was shattered. This was the one I wanted above all." And "I was *positive* I would get it. So was everybody in town. I almost dropped dead when I didn't win."

Bette had one final brush with Oscar, and it wasn't a pleasant one. She was presenting the Best Actor Oscar of 1986. On the live telecast Bette hesitated before announcing the name of the first nominee, Bob Hoskins, and the accompanying film clips jumped ahead of her. Not only was she speaking too slowly; she was also offering her own unscripted comments, which further messed up the timing. In response the show's director, Marty Pasetta, made the snap decision to cut off her microphone. Consequently, confused television audiences saw Bette Davis standing at the podium, looking rather foolish. Bette proceeded to name the winner of the award, Paul Newman. Newman was absent, and the award was accepted by Robert Wise. Bette then interrupted Wise's acceptance speech to offer her own congratulations to Newman and to introduce Wise properly. However, Pasetta again cut off her mike and turned his camera on the surprised cohosts, Chevy Case and Goldie Hawn.

It was an inelegant and unfitting farewell to the woman who may or may not have named Oscar.

Other Oscar Notes

☆ *All About Eve* is the most nominated film of all time with 14.

☆ *The Little Foxes* is the third most nominated film that didn't win a single Oscar—with nine. *The Turning Point* and *The Color Purple* both had 11.

☆ Katharine Hepburn has won the most Best Actress Oscars with four; tied for second with two are Bette, Luise Rainer, Vivien Leigh, Olivia de Havilland, Ingrid Bergman, Elizabeth Taylor, Glenda Jackson, Jane Fonda, Sally Field, and Jodie Foster.

☆ Katharine Hepburn has the most Best Actress nominations with 12. Bette is next with 10.

☆ Tied for the most consecutive Best Actress nominations with five are Bette and Greer Garson.

P

GERALDINE PAGE

Consummate actress though she was, Geraldine Page had difficulty getting a grasp of the character she was playing in *Sweet Bird of Youth* (1962). Specifically, she had difficulty walking and *moving* like the movie star she was playing. The film's director, Richard Brooks, told her to go and watch a certain movie and study the movements of the actress who starred in it. The film was *A Stolen Life*, and the actress was Bette Davis. After screening the movie Page returned to the set and said to Brooks, "Don't say *anything*. That bitch can walk *away* from the camera and look like a star."

PARACHUTE JUMPER ★ ½

Warner Brothers
1933   70 minutes   bw
Directed by: Alfred E. Green
Produced by: Ray Griffith
Screenplay by: John Francis Larkin, based on the story by Rian James
Cinematography by: James Van Trees
Cast: Douglas Fairbanks, Jr., Leo Carrillo, Bette Davis, Frank McHugh, Claire Dodd, Sheila Terry, Harold Huber, Thomas E. Jackson, George Pat Collins, Harold Healy, Frederick Munier, Pat O'Malley, Ferdinand Munley, Walter Miller

Routine programmer with Bette as Alabama (naturally she speaks with an exaggerated southern accent), mistress of a racketeer, based on the story "Some Call It Love" by Rian James. Warner Brothers purchased the rights to the story on March 29, 1932, for $8,500.

Production started on September 20, 1932, and was overseen by Darryl Zanuck. It was allotted the standard 24 shooting days, with a budget of approximately $200,000.

Upon its release *Parachute Jumper* was marketed with the ad copy "A Man a Minute Blonde—and a Mile a Minute Daredevil!" The reviews were poor, but some critics praised the aviation sequences, which were considered advanced for the time. The critics who mentioned Bette mostly complained about the severity of her attempted southern accent.

Robert Aldrich would mock *Parachute Jumper* some 30 years later when he included a clip of it in *What Ever Happened to Baby Jane?* as an example of one of Jane's film failures.

PARIS, FRANCE

Bette toured Paris for the first time in October 1936, before she lost her legal battle with Warner Brothers in a London courtroom. Over the succeeding years Bette became enamored with the city and made frequent return trips there. Certainly she was well appreciated by the French people.

On June 11, 1952, the French minister of commerce and industry, Jean-Marie Louvel, presented Bette with an award as the best actress of the year for her performance in *All About Eve*. On February 22, 1986, Bette was presented with the César, the French Oscar, for lifetime achievement. In accepting the Legion of Honor by the French government in 1987, presented by Culture Minister François Léotard, Bette responded, "Maintenant, I am française" (Now, I am French).

It was at the American Hospital in Paris where Bette passed away on October 6, 1989.

LOUELLA PARSONS

After seeing Bette in one of her earliest appearances, in the 1931 picture *Seed*, columnist Louella Parsons commented that Bette might have a chance of making it in the movies *if*: "Little Bette Davis, blonde, young and with ability," Parsons wrote. "Bette has a great chance if she will put herself in the hands of a capable make-up man. She gave a good performance in *Seed*, and I was not disturbed by over-beaded eyelashes and an over-rouged mouth. . . . Keep an eye on Bette Davis; that girl has something worth developing."

Parsons became an early and important supporter of Bette's. A few years later Parsons wavered in her support, but she boarded the bandwagon in 1934 after the release of *Of Human Bondage*.

The following are excerpts from Louella's syndicated column:

The role of Lynn, I feel, might have been entrusted to better hands than Bette Davis'. To me, Miss Davis is never convincing, and she is far overshadowed by Veree Teasdale.
On *Fashions of 1934*, 1934

An astounding revelation of human nature. . . . Surprising is Bette Davis' remarkable portrayal of the tawdry little waitress with the cruel streak in her nature. . . . Personally, I didn't think she had it in her.
On *Of Human Bondage*, 1934

Bette Davis does extremely well in a role which is not the type of thing she usually plays on the screen. This little Davis girl is going places, for again and again she demonstrates that no matter what role is tossed her way she rises superbly and gives a grand account of herself.
On *Special Agent*, 1935

When you see Bette Davis you will be reminded again why she carried off the Academy Award in 1935 and you will realize that she is one of the finest dramatic actresses on the screen.
On *Marked Woman*, 1937

Bette Davis surpasses even herself!
On *Dark Victory*, 1939

Bette was not unaware of the debt she owed Louella Parsons, and upon her remarkable comeback in 1950 with *All About Eve*, it was to Louella that she granted a radio interview; it was one of the first interviews conducted with the newly married Mr. and Mrs. Gary Merrill and went something like this:

LOUELLA: My guests this evening are Mr. and Mrs. Gary Merrill making their very first radio appearance together. Mrs. Merrill is also known as Bette Davis.

GARY: Yes, indeed, she is.

LOUELLA: Gary, the way you say that sounds as though you don't mind two careers in one family.

GARY: Mind? Why? I'd mind if she had no talent . . . but if she had no talent, I'd have no love for her. . . .

BETTE: Louella, I warn you, if you're trying to start a discussion with Gary, it's no go. He's too relaxed to argue. Confidentially, I started falling in love with him when I observed how he could relax in bed all day long for two solid weeks. . . .

LOUELLA: Bette, you're sure this story can go on the air?

BETTE: Yes, safely, because that bed was for a scene in *All About Eve*, but it was so comfortable that, between shots, the whole cast stretched out on it. The rest of us were always popping up, however, for cigarettes or something. Not Gary. He just lay there, completely at ease, until his scenes were called. Then he was just at ease.

LOUELLA: Bette, you told me he first caught your eye in *Twelve O'Clock High*.

BETTE: That's right.

LOUELLA: But, Gary, I don't believe you ever told me which was the first picture of Bette's that caught *your* eye. Which picture was it, Gary?

BETTE: I don't know the answer to that one myself, Louella. Which picture was it, Gary?

GARY: None. I never saw you before we went to work on *All About Eve*.

PAYMENT ON DEMAND ★★½

RKO

1951 90 minutes bw

Directed by: Curtis Bernhardt

Produced by: Bruce Manning and Jack H. Skirball

Screenplay by: Curtis Bernhardt and Bruce Manning

Cinematography by: Leo Tover

Cast: Bette Davis, Barry Sullivan, Jane Cowl, Betty Lynn, Kent Taylor, John Sutton, Frances Dee, Peggie Castle, Otto Kruger, Walter Sande, Brett King, Richard Anderson, Natalie Schafer, Katherine Emery, Lisa Golm, Moroni Olsen

It was *not All About Eve* but *Payment on Demand* that was the first film Bette landed after her dramatic exit from Warner Brothers in 1949. *Eve*, however was *released* first. Curtis Bernhardt, who had directed Bette in the 1946 picture *A Stolen Life*, was the first to pursue Bette after her release from Warners. He coauthored the script, which he even tailored to Bette's talents. The story cast Bette as Joyce Ramsey, who is divorced by her husband (in love with another woman) of 20 years. Ironically, at the time the picture was being made, Bette's own marriage, to William Grant Sherry, was in the process of breaking up.

Originally and more aptly titled *The Story of a Divorce*, the picture was in production in February 1950 at RKO, Bette's first picture there since *Of Human Bondage* (1934). It was budgeted at $1.8 million. Despite the turmoil in her personal life, Bette was on her best behavior, and the shooting of the picture was one of her more pleasant working experiences. So pleasant that Bette allegedly had an affair with her costar Barry Sullivan, which prompted a jealous on-the-lot tirade by Sherry.

On a lighter note, Bette celebrated her 42nd birthday on the set. She was presented with a huge ostrich egg by the cast and crew for having been a "good egg" during the production. It was during this period that Bette was offered the part of Margo Channing in *Eve*, which she would start within days of completing *Payment*.

Payment on Demand—retitled as such by Howard Hughes and with a marketing campaign that titillated filmgoers with "I Made Him . . . Now I'll Break Him!" and "The One Sin No Woman Ever Forgives! He Strayed . . . and He Paid!"—was withheld from release to capitalize on the success of *All About Eve*. Just days before its opening on February 15, 1951, Hughes summoned Bette, Barry, and Bernhardt back to the studio because he wanted to change the ending. Bette, distraught over the new ending and title change, grudgingly complied. Hughes shipped the new ending to New York just in time for the scheduled opening. The picture was met with highly favorable reviews, although it performed disappointingly at the box office.

Note: Look for Bette's daughter, billed as "B. D. Merrill," in her film debut.

PEOPLE MAGAZINE

Bette Davis was the oldest person in the history of *People* magazine to grace its cover. It was the May 1985 issue, and she was 77 years old.

"PERRY MASON"

After starring in *Of Human Bondage* (1934) for RKO, but before its release, Bette returned to her home studio and was assigned to play secretary Della Street in the Perry Mason picture *The Case of the Howling Dog*. Bette balked and was suspended.

Bette *did* appear in "The Case of Constant Doyle," a January 31, 1963, episode of the hit CBS television series "Perry Mason." Starring in the show in place of Raymond Burr, Bette played a lawyer who defends a youth accused of murder. Also in the cast were Peggy Ann Garner, Les Tremayne, and Frances Reid, along with regulars Barbara Hale as Della Street and William Hopper as Paul Drake. The episode was produced by Gail Patrick Jackson.

"PERSON TO PERSON"

Bette and Gary Merrill were interviewed for this television show by its host, Edward R. Murrow, at their home in Maine in late September 1956. *Time* magazine reported in its October 1, 1956 issue, "Oscar winner Bette Davis couldn't resist some real-life emoting on Ed Murrow's 'Person to Person' (CBS), on which she volunteered a friend's suggestion for her tombstone ('She did it the hard way'), while Gary Merrill suggested that, if Bette had not become an actress, she would have been president of Lord & Taylor. Best bit: Bette reading from Robert Frost's 'Fire and Ice' ('I hold with those who favor fire')."

THE PETRIFIED FOREST ★★

1936   83 minutes   bw
Warner Brothers
Directed by: Archie L. Mayo
Produced by: Henry Blanke
Screenplay by: Charles Kenyon and Delmer Daves, based on the play by
    Robert E. Sherwood
Cinematography by: Sol Polito
Cast: Leslie Howard, Bette Davis, Genevieve Tobin, Dick Foran, Humphrey
    Bogart, Joseph Sawyer, Porter Hall, Charley Grapewin, Paul Harvey,
    Eddie Acuff, Adrian Morris, Nina Campana, Slim Thompson, John
    Alexander

Warner Brothers purchased the rights to the Broadway play by Robert Emmet Sherwood in an agreement dated July 2, 1935, for the large sum of $110,000.

Scheduling of the picture was worked around Leslie Howard, who starred in and coproduced the Broadway play. Howard agreed to return to Hollywood from New York on October 8, 1935, to start work on the picture. Budgeted at $427,000, with $62,500 of that going to Howard and $9,000 to Bette, the film started shooting on October 14. Production had to be swift to accommodate Howard, who informed producer Blanke that he had to appear back on Broadway upon the shooting's wrap.

At the emphatic demand of Leslie Howard, Humphrey Bogart was signed by Warner to reprise his stage role as Duke Mantee. Bogart would be paid $750 a week or approximately $3,750, for his work on the picture.

Unlike their experience on *Of Human Bondage* (1934), their previous pairing together, Howard and Bette loved working together on *The Petrified Forest*. She would later describe him as "one of the most charming men I have ever known." During a gunfight sequence, Howard tried to elicit a

Early Bogart (in a breakthrough role) brandishing a gun.

laugh from Bette (no easy task) by biting her. "I emerged from the scene," said Bette, "with nibble marks on my arms and shoulders which I found difficult to explain for days to come."

Bette, cast as waitress Gabby Maple, in a role played by Peggy Conklin onstage, sprained her ankle and was unable to work on November 22, 1935, but was generally present and punctual. Toward the completion of shooting Howard started arriving late on the set, which caused considerable delays, a curious matter considering his previous demand that the picture be completed expeditiously. On October 30, Hal Wallis issued a memo to producer Blanke complaining that Howard was arriving on the set between 9:30 and 10:30 in the morning and leaving at 5:30 in the afternoon. Wallis groused to Blanke that the picture was costing a fortune and instructed that he try to get Howard to work until at least 6:00 or 6:30 P.M. Wallis ended his memo, however, by sending Blanke a mixed signal: "Naturally," said Wallis, "we don't want to offend Leslie."

The Petrified Forest was shot with two endings, one happy and one not. Leslie Howard, who had a say in the matter, opted for the unhappy ending, and so it was. The picture completed shooting on November 30, 10 days behind schedule.

Interestingly, Warners could not release its picture until the stage version starring Leslie Howard completed its road tour. When it *was* released, *The Petrified Forest* was accorded generally favorable reviews, with Humphrey

Bogart singled out. Today the picture is notable primarily as Bogart's first breakthrough performance.

The Petrified Forest was remade in 1944 as *Escape in the Desert*.

PHONE CALL FROM A STRANGER ★★

20th Century–Fox
1952   96 minutes   bw
Directed by: Jean Negulesco
Produced by: Nunnally Johnson
Screenplay by: Nunnally Johnson, based on a story by Ida Alexa Ross
    Wylie
Cinematography by: Milton Krasner
Cast: Shelley Winters, Gary Merrill, Michael Rennie, Keenan Wynn, Evelyn
    Varden, Warren Stevens, Beatrice Straight, Ted Donaldson, Craig
    Stevens, Helen Westcott, Bette Davis, Sydney Perkins, Hugh Beaumont,
    Thomas Jackson, Harry Cheshire, Tom Powers, Freeman Lusk,
    George Eldredge, Nestor Paiva, Perdita Chandler, Genevieve Bell

Dusty Negulesco was sitting in a beauty parlor engrossed in a story in the current issue of *McCall's* magazine. She took the story home to her husband, and the film version of *Phone Call from a Stranger* was born.

After Gary Merrill was cast in a starring role in the film, Bette volunteered, to producer Nunnally Johnson, to play the small part of Mrs. Hoke. "They laughed," Bette related, "when I sat down to play a bit role in *Phone Call from a Stranger*. 'What,' they asked, 'does Bette Davis mean by taking a subordinate part in a picture?' So I told them. Although the role calls for me to be on the screen less than one-fourth of the film, it probably is the most dynamic part I ever have played. It has character and guts. As a bedridden paralytic, I am afforded some of the most dramatic moments of my career."

In the starring female role, producer Johnson wanted his friend Lauren Bacall. She was out of town, however, on location with her husband, Humphrey Bogart, and Johnson settled for Shelley Winters, hot in Hollywood after her performance in *A Place in the Sun* (1951).

Phone Call from a Stranger was produced at Fox in October 1951. After viewing the first two days of footage, Johnson approached Jean Negulesco, the director, and expressed concern about the voice that Bette was employing for the role. "Is Bette doing something with her voice?" Johnson asked. "It seems to me that it's not the way I think of it. Has she added some gimmick?" Both Johnson and Negulesco decided that something must be done about Bette's voice. Apprehensively, Johnson approached Bette's dressing room and expressed his concern. Bette was livid. "You certainly *don't* expect me to use the same voice or manner of Margo Channing, do you?" she erupted. In the heat of argument, however, Johnson could not recall who this Margo Channing was. He went home to his wife, who said, "Wasn't that the name of the woman she played in *All About Eve*?" to which Johnson sighed and responded, "Oh, how can a man be so stupid. Of course! She was talking about her last big hit *part!*"

Meanwhile, back at the Merrills' home, a screaming match erupted between Bette and Gary after Gary made the mistake of defending Johnson. To punish her producer, Bette did not show up for work the next day, and when she did return, her voice was hoarse from screaming. Johnson was pleased. The vocal effect was just what he had originally wanted for the character. Nevertheless, Bette had Johnson banned from the set—the only time in his lengthy career that he would be banned from one of his own sets.

Upon its release, *Phone Call from a Stranger* was met with tepid critical response and disappointing box office. It mattered little to Bette, however, who walked away with $35,000—for three days' work.

"A PIANO FOR MRS. CIMINO"

When she was first sent John Gay's script of "A Piano for Mrs. Cimino," adapted from the book by Robert Oliphant, Bette was less than enthusiastic. She went ahead with the project because it was to be produced and directed by George Schaefer, and she was glad she did. For her performance Bette would receive some of the best reviews of the latter part of her career, along with the Monte Carlo Award as the year's best actress. Keenan Wynn was cast as her leading man at Bette's suggestion.

"A Piano for Mrs. Cimino" (1982), shot in Vancouver, Canada, was produced for EMI Television by Schaefer and Christopher N. Seitz. Roger Gimble and Tony Converse were the executive producers; and Edward R. Brown was the cinematographer.

JACK PIERCE

Jack Pierce, famous for having transformed Boris Karloff into Frankenstein's monster in the 1932 horror classic of the same name, was the Universal makeup man on the pictures *Bad Sister* (1931), *Seed* (1931), and *Waterloo Bridge* (1931). His evaluation of Bette was that her eyelashes were too short, her mouth was too short, her neck was too long, her face was too fat, and the color of her hair was too nondescript.

THE PLAYS

"The theatre is out. *Never* again!"
Bette Davis, 1954

"The New York theatre is sick, sick, sick. Through terrible
management. The people who really love the theatre can't afford to
go—just the expense account people. Those audiences, bah! I'll take
a crew of 80 men working on a movie set for an audience anytime.
They're more intelligent and more perceptive. They really know what
you're doing."
Bette Davis, 1962

"In Hollywood, [acting] was like any other job. If you were sick and couldn't come to the set, you'd let someone know, and the shooting schedule would be adjusted around you. When you're working on the stage, the body must appear day after day, no matter how you feel."

Bette Davis, 1962

The following is a selective chronological listing of the stage plays in which Bette Davis appeared:

At Cushing Academy
Seventeen

At the Robert Milton-John Murray Anderson School of the Theatre
The Famous Mrs. Fair
The Nightingale and the Rose
Sister Beatrice

Their Anniversary
The Wonder! A Woman Keeps a Secret

As a Member of the Cukor-Kondolf Repertory Company
Broadway
Excess Baggage
Cradle Snatchers
Laff That Off

The Squall
The Man Who Came Back
Yellow

As a Member of the Cape Players
The Charm School
Mr. Pim Passes By
The Constant Wife

The Patsy
You Never Can Tell
The Silver Chord

Off Broadway
The Earth Between (Provincetown Players)

As a Member of the Ibsen Repertory Company
The Lady from the Sea
The Wild Duck

On Broadway
Broken Dishes (1929)
Solid South (1930)
Two's Company (1952)
The World of Carl Sandburg (1960)
The Night of the Iguana (1961)
Miss Moffat (1974; closed in pre-Broadway tryout)

The Broadway Plays That Bette Wanted to Do but Didn't
Follies
Hedda Gabler

Look Homeward, Angel
Saucersand

All was *not* sweetness and smiles behind the scenes.

For years after *Pocketful*, Bette followed the career of Ann-Margret with pride.

POCKETFUL OF MIRACLES ★★½

Franton Productions
Released by United Artists
1961   136 minutes   Technicolor
Directed by: Frank Capra
Produced by: Frank Capra, in association with Glenn Ford and Joseph Sistrom
Screenplay by: Hal Kanter and Harry Tugend, based on a screenplay by Robert Riskin and a story by Damon Runyon

Cinematography by: Robert Bronner
Cast: Glenn Ford, Bette Davis, Hope Lange, Arthur O'Connell, Peter Falk,
    Thomas Mitchell, Edward Everett Horton, Mickey Shaughnessy, David
    Brian, Sheldon Leonard, Peter Mann, Ann-Margret, Ellen Corby,
    Barton MacLane, Jerome Cowan, Fritz Feld, Snub Pollard, John Litel,
    Jay Novello, Willis Bouchey, George E. Stone, Mike Mazurki, Jack
    Elam, Frank Ferguson, Gavin Gordon, Benny Rubin, Hayden Rorke,
    Doodles Weaver, Paul E. Burns

Pocketful of Miracles was based on Damon Runyon's short story "Madame La Gimp," which was adapted into the 1933 film *Lady for a Day*, directed by Frank Capra, with May Robson in the starring role. For his 1961 remake, Capra partnered with Glenn Ford's Newton Productions and made Ford an associate producer on the picture. Capra hired Harry Tugend and Hal Kanter to rework and update the screenplay by Robert Riskin.

For his Apple Annie, the apple vendor/bag lady who provides "lucky" apples to gangster Dave the Dude and is transformed into E. Worthington Manville, Capra wanted Helen Hayes, who accepted but then backed out of the picture.

Bette was not exactly enthusiastic about the project, though she *was* certainly happy to be working on a soundstage again, even a Paramount soundstage, where the picture was being shot. To a visiting reporter on the set in May 1961 she said, "I saw Frank Capra's original *Lady for a Day* with May Robson as Apple Annie. I don't know *why* he just doesn't release it again." At the time Bette was engrossed in plans to do *The Night of the Iguana* on Broadway, unaware of the horrors it would bring.

At Paramount, Bette had to endure three hours of makeup a day. As she told a visitor on the set, "My big job with this picture is to get the appearance. I've never had qualms about appearance on the screen or stage, but *this* is the ugliest, the most appalling, I've ever had."

Meanwhile, romance brewed on the set between Glenn Ford and Hope Lange. Trouble erupted when Bette was asked to move out of the star dressing room, next door to Ford's, so that Lange could be in close proximity. Bette, indignant, suppressed her temper but seethed. As Sheila Graham reported in her May 15, 1961, column, "You could have heard a pin drop when Hope Lange on the set . . . asked to have the dressing room next to Glenn Ford's— because the lady in that room was Bette Davis! Hope and Glenn have been 'going together,' as you probably know. But to push the tempestuous Bette Davis from her rightful place! *Well!* Everyone expected the studio to cave in. Instead, Miss Davis said, 'You can put my dressing room at the end of the row if you like; I couldn't care less.' "

Glenn Ford made another mistake. He relayed to the press that it was he who had approached Bette with the part. He wanted to repay her a favor, he said, for having cast him in the 1946 picture *A Stolen Life*. For Bette this was deeply insulting. The idea that she had been cast in a picture as a *favor* was unthinkable. She was, after all, *the* Bette Davis. The atmosphere on the set was tense and strained, the temperature chilly. It was made colder and infinitely sadder when Bette's mother, friend, and champion, Ruth Favor Davis, died during the production.

United Artists released *Pocketful of Miracles* during the Christmas season of 1961 to mixed reviews. Today the picture seems too long, too dated, and too full of Capraesque schmaltz. Still, it is always fun to watch Bette Davis camp it up. Furthermore, the film is distinguished by two notable passages—the final picture of Frank Capra and the introduction of Ann-Margret.

POLITICS

Bette was an unabashed Democrat, with her political heroes being Franklin Delano Roosevelt and John F. Kennedy. Later she supported Edmund Muskie and Jimmy Carter. Curiously, although Bette did not hesitate to publicly support FDR and others, she was reticent to become more politically involved. For example, when in the 1940s Vincent Sherman and Alvah Bessie asked her to sign a petition protesting New York governor Thomas Dewey's rigging of the state's election laws so that servicemen who were out of state at election time lost their vote, Bette refused to sign it. She agreed with their arguments but still refused to sign, saying that she had once signed a petition to members of Congress and it had caused her grief. Bette was the president of the Tailwaggers Foundation of America at the time, and the petition she claimed caused her trouble was an opposition to vivisection.

Bette also declined to become politically involved in the civil rights movement of the 1960s or the women's liberation and gay rights movements of the 1970s, despite professing her belief in equal rights for all people. Her position (or lack of a more public one) can perhaps be traced back to a comment she made in 1946. "I say not 50% of what I believe politically," she stated, "lest my words be exaggerated or misinterpreted beyond all reason." When she *did* become involved with a political group, it was usually in name only.

Nevertheless, for years Bette entertained the idea of following in Ronald Reagan's footsteps and entering the political arena. "Every politician," she said in 1964, "is an actor, and maybe someday I'll turn the tables. I feel I could contribute in politics. Of course, I have a lot to learn, but I've had a lot of exposure to politics." And "Actually, I'd rather go into politics [than continue making movies]. Of course the whole political scene has changed because of television. Someone trained in my profession would have a great advantage. It wouldn't be an impossibility for me in a few more years. It's the only thing that would challenge me. It would be a new battle to win."

SOL POLITO

Certainly one of Bette's finest cinematographers, known more as an expert technician than as a cosmetician, Sol Polito may have done his best work with Bette on the 1942 picture *Now, Voyager*. His other pictures with Davis are *Dark Horse* (1932), *Three on a Match* (1932), *The Working Man* (1933), *The Petrified Forest* (1936), *The Private Lives of Elizabeth and Essex* (1939), *Old Acquaintance* (1943), *The Corn Is Green* (1945), and *A Stolen Life* (1946).

On the last picture, after several months of work, Polito was pulled out and replaced by Ernie Haller, although Polito would receive sole credit.

Sol Polito (1892–1960) shot other pictures, including *I Am A Fugitive from a Chain Gang* (1932), *Forty-Second Street* (1933), *G Men* (1935), *The Charge of the Light Brigade* (1936), *The Adventures of Robin Hood* (1938), *Confessions of a Nazi Spy* (1939), *The Sea Hawk* (1940), and *Sorry, Wrong Number* (1948).

PRESS CONFERENCES

Over the years Bette held numerous press conferences for a variety of reasons. The following is a small sampling.

☆ When she returned to Hollywood to make *The Virgin Queen* in 1955, Bette, out of the public eye for three years, surprised reporters with her heavy, aged appearance. "I would like to return here [to Hollywood] about once a year for a film," Bette announced from the Bel Air Hotel in February 1955. "But I wouldn't want to give all my energies to motion pictures in the future and I doubt whether I would want to return to the stage or become actively identified with television."

☆ On July 19, 1962, J. L. Warner hosted a luncheon/press conference in honor of Bette Davis and Joan Crawford to announce the production of *What Ever Happened to Baby Jane?* Typically, Bette showed up on time. Crawford was half an hour late.

☆ The following is an excerpt from the 1982 press conference hosted by Bette and producer/director George Schaefer to announce the production of the television movie "Right of Way."

> BETTE: (to photographers) "No more pictures! The pictures are over!"
>
> SCHAEFER: "I guess I should have reminded people that this is a question-and-answer session only."
>
> BETTE: "You already *did* remind them, George!"

☆ During the September 1989 San Sebastian Film Festival, her final public appearance, Bette, frail and dressed in a black suit, a black hat, and clutching a single red rose, held a press conference at the Hotel Maria Christina. She appeared for an hour before 400 journalists who gave her a standing ovation. "I love my work. I love it. I want to always, always be acting." A few weeks later she was dead.

THE PRIVATE LIVES OF ELIZABETH AND ESSEX ★★

Warner Brothers
1939   106 minutes   Technicolor
Directed by: Michael Curtiz
Produced by: Hal B. Wallis, in association with Robert Lord
Screenplay by: Norman Reilly Raine and Aeneas Mackenzie, from the play
    by Maxwell Anderson
Cinematography by: Sol Polito and W. Howard Greene
Cast: Bette Davis, Errol Flynn, Olivia de Havilland, Donald Crisp, Alan
    Hale, Vincent Price, Henry Stephenson, Henry Daniell, Leo G.
    Carroll, Nanette Fabray, Robert Warwick, John Sutton, James
    Stephenson, Rosella Towne, Maris Wrixon, Ralph Forbes, Guy Bellis,
    Doris Lloyd, Forrester Harvey

Warner Brothers purchased Maxwell Anderson's Broadway play *Elizabeth the Queen* for $30,000 in an agreement dated February 8, 1939. The play had been a hit on Broadway in 1930 with Lynn Fontanne and Alfred Lunt.

Warners bought the property with Bette in mind, but others were given some consideration, including Margaret Sullavan, Barbara Stanwyck, Miriam Hopkins, Norma Shearer, Irene Dunne, Helen Hayes, Katharine Hepburn, Tallulah Bankhead, and Geraldine Fitzgerald, the last even doing a screen test.

For the role of Essex, Bette wanted none other than Laurence Olivier, who was indeed under consideration. Others on the list of possibilities were Fredric March, Cary Grant, Ray Milland, Henry Fonda, Joel McCrea, Douglas Fairbanks, Jr., Ronald Colman, and Vincent Price.

Much to Bette's chagrin, Jack Warner cast Errol Flynn in the role of Essex and initially insisted on the title *The Knight and the Lady*. Bette could not do anything about the casting of Flynn, but she wasn't about to give up on the matter of the title. She was outraged that Warner would refer to a queen as "lady." Furthermore, she didn't take kindly to the idea of either herself—or Queen Elizabeth—receiving second billing. The battle between Bette and Warner over the title extended into the shooting. On June 30, 1939, Bette wired Warner with a threat. "I find myself so upset mentally and ill physically by the prospect of this title that unless this matter is settled in writing I cannot without serious impairment of my health finish the picture. You have the choice of *Elizabeth and Essex*, *Elizabeth the Queen*, or *The Love of Elizabeth and Essex*." Warner finally acquiesced, though with a variation, *The Private Lives of Elizabeth and Essex*.

In preparation for the role Bette learned to pitch her voice lower than usual. She also had to age and don artificial eyebrows, a curly red wig, and costumes that weighed nearly 65 pounds each. She even had to have her hairline shaved back two inches to achieve the Elizabethan high forehead.

Bette's appearance was of considerable concern to Hal Wallis, who memoed producer Robert Lord on May 4, 1939, after viewing her hair and makeup tests. He complained to Perc Westmore, the studio's makeup chief, that the greenish tint of Bette's face and the narrowing of the eyes had made her look unattractive. Said Wallis, "We don't want to make Davis up as a female Frankenstein."

Producer Robert Lord, meanwhile, was worried about Bette's health. He even suggested to Wallis that the studio take out an additional insurance policy on Bette. She had been ushered from one picture to the next without much rest and was near collapse. "I have been studying the lady," related Lord, "and in my opinion she is in a rather serious condition of nerves. At best, she is frail and is going into a very tough picture when she is a long way from her 'best.' "

After various delays and with a budget of $1,075,327 the picture started shooting, still under the title *The Knight and the Lady*, on Thursday, May 11, 1939. It was allotted 48 shooting days with an expected finish of July 7, 1939. Bette went through the usual tests on opening day but did not actually start shooting until Wednesday, May 24. While filming a love scene with Errol Flynn she got sick and did not report to work on Wednesday, May 31.

Bette never really forgave Flynn for playing Essex. While shooting, she would later confess, she fantasized that it was Olivier and not Flynn who was playing opposite her. Her frustration culminated in the scene in which Elizabeth slaps Essex across the face. In shooting the scene, Bette gave Flynn more than he was expecting. As he related in his autobiography, "I felt as if I had been hit by a railroad locomotive. She had lifted one of her hands, heavy with those Elizabethan rings, and Joe Louis himself couldn't give a right hook better than Bette hooked me with. My jaw went out. I felt a click behind my ear and I saw all these comets, shooting stars, all in one flash. . . . I felt as if I were deaf."

On Saturday, June 10, Olivia de Havilland, in a meaningless supporting role as Lady Penelope Gray, threw a tantrum after being asked to work after 6:00 P.M. Michael Curtiz pulled her aside and threatened that unless she stayed and finished shooting the sequence with Nanette Fabray, it would be cut from the picture. Olivia, before the entire company, exploded in a fit, and shooting was halted at 6:15 without the sequence being shot.

Meanwhile, producer Lord, in an effort to reduce the payroll, wanted scenes to be shot that would finish the work of Henry Daniell and John Sutton, non-Warner Brothers cast members. Bette, who wanted the film shot with as much continuity as possible, refused to shoot in this manner, and the actors stood on the set and did little beyond collect their paychecks until it was time to shoot their scenes.

More delays were caused when Flynn called in sick on Friday, June 16, and Saturday, June 17. When he reported back to work on Monday, June 19, Bette called in sick, claiming laryngitis. The picture was temporarily shut down, and when shooting resumed On Monday, June 26, it proceeded fairly quickly, although Errol Flynn slowed the process by repeatedly blowing his lines.

The Private Lives of Elizabeth and Essex completed production with Bette on Thursday, July 6. Despite the delays, it came in one day ahead of schedule and significantly under budget.

Upon its release critics generally hailed *Elizabeth and Essex* as a magnificent spectacle, although Flynn's performance was frequently singled out as the picture's primary flaw.

PRODUCERS
The Stage Plays

Producer	Play	Year
Charles Bowden	*The Night of the Iguana*	1961
Slade Brown	*Miss Moffat*	1974
Armand Deutsch	*The World of Carl Sandburg*	1960
Michael Ellis	*Two's Company*	1952
M. Eleanor Fitzgerald	*The Earth Between*	1929
James Light	*The Earth Between*	1929
Joshua Logan	*Miss Moffat*	1974
Alexander McKaig	*Solid South*	1930
Violla Rubber	*The Night of the Iguana*	1961
James Russo	*Two's Company*	1952
Oscar Serlin	*Broken Dishes*	1929
Eugene V. Wolsk	*Miss Moffat*	1974

The Movies

Producer	Picture	Year
Robert Aldrich	*What Ever Happened to Baby Jane?*	1962
Robert Aldrich	*Hush . . . Hush, Sweet Charlotte*	1964
Daniel Angel	*Another Man's Poison*	1952
Michael Balcon	*The Scapegoat*	1959
Pandro S. Berman	*Way Back Home*	1932
Pandro S. Berman	*Of Human Bondage*	1934
Sam Bischoff	*The Big Shakedown*	1934
Sam Bischoff	*Front Page Woman*	1935
Sam Bischoff	*The Golden Arrow*	1936
*Sam Bischoff	*Kid Galahad*	1937
Henry Blanke	*Bureau of Missing Persons*	1933
Henry Blanke	*Fashions of 1934*	1934
Henry Blanke	*Fog Over Frisco*	1934
Henry Blanke	*The Girl from Tenth Avenue*	1935
Henry Blanke	*The Petrified Forest*	1936
Henry Blanke	*Satan Met a Lady*	1936
*Henry Blanke	*Jezebel*	1938
*Henry Blanke	*Juarez*	1939
*Henry Blanke	*The Old Maid*	1939
*Henry Blanke	*The Great Lie*	1941
Henry Blanke	*Old Acquaintance*	1943
Henry Blanke	*Deception*	1946
Henry Blanke	*Winter Meeting*	1948
Henry Blanke	*June Bride*	1948
Henry Blanke	*Beyond the Forest*	1949
Julian Blaustein	*Storm Center*	1956
Charles Brackett	*The Virgin Queen*	1955
John Bradbourne	*Death on the Nile*	1978
Samuel Bronston	*John Paul Jones*	1959
Harry Joe Brown	*Dangerous*	1935
*Harry Joe Brown	*It's Love I'm After*	1937
*William Cagney	*The Bride Came C.O.D.*	1941
Frank Capra	*Pocketful of Miracles*	1961
Jack Chertok	*The Corn Is Green*	1945
Arthur Cooper	*Connecting Rooms*	1972
Jerome Courtland	*Return from Witch Mountain*	1978
Dan Curtis	*Burnt Offerings*	1976
Bette Davis	*A Stolen Life*	1946
Dino de Laurentiis	*The Scientific Cardplayer*	1972
*Lou Edelman	*Marked Woman*	1937
Julius & Philip Epstein	*Mr. Skeffington*	1944
Douglas Fairbanks, Jr.	*Another Man's Poison*	1952
Harry Field	*Connecting Rooms*	1972
Bert Friedlob	*The Star*	1952

Producer	Picture	Year
Samuel Goldwyn	*The Little Foxes*	1941
Richard Goodwin	*Death on the Nile*	1978
Alex Gottlieb	*Hollywood Canteen*	1944
Ray Griffith	*The Rich Are Always With Us*	1932
Ray Griffith	*Dark Horse*	1932
Ray Griffith	*Three on a Match*	1932
Ray Griffith	*20,000 Years in Sing Sing*	1933
Ray Griffith	*Parachute Jumper*	1933
*Sam Harris	*The Man Who Came to Dinner*	1942
Mark Hellinger	*Thank Your Lucky Stars*	1943
Norman T. Herman	*Bunny O'Hare*	1971
Lucien Hubbard	*So Big*	1932
Lucien Hubbard	*The Working Man*	1933
Lucien Hubbard	*Ex-Lady*	1933
Nunnally Johnson	*Phone Call from a Stranger*	1952
Mike Kaplan	*The Whales of August*	1987
Carl Laemmle, Jr.	*Bad Sister*	1931
Carl Laemmle, Jr.	*Waterloo Bridge*	1931
Joseph E. Levine	*Where Love Has Gone*	1964
*David Lewis	*The Sisters*	1938
*David Lewis	*Dark Victory*	1939
*David Lewis	*All This, and Heaven Too*	1940
*David Lewis	*In This Our Life*	1942
Robert Lord	*Jimmy the Gent*	1933
Robert Lord	*Housewife*	1934
Robert Lord	*Bordertown*	1935
*Robert Lord	*That Certain Woman*	1937
*Robert Lord	*The Private Lives of Elizabeth and Essex*	1939
*Robert Lord	*The Letter*	1940
Bruce Manning	*Payment on Demand*	1951
Ron Miller	*Return from Witch Mountain*	1978
Ron Miller	*The Watcher in the Woods*	1980
Martin Mooney	*Special Agent*	1935
Sam Nelson	*The Menace*	1932
Gerd Oswald	*Bunny O'Hare*	1971
Carolyn Pfeiffer	*The Whales of August*	1987
Carlo Ponti	*The Empty Canvas*	1964
Jimmy Sangster	*The Nanny*	1965
Jimmy Sangster	*The Anniversary*	1968
*Jack Saper	*The Man Who Came to Dinner*	1942
Jack H. Skirball	*Payment on Demand*	1951
John M. Stahl	*Seed*	1931
*Jerry Wald	*The Man Who Came to Dinner*	1942
Hal Wallis	*Cabin in the Cotton*	1932
**Hal Wallis	*Marked Woman*	1937

Producer	Picture	Year
**Hal Wallis	*Kid Galahad*	1937
**Hal Wallis	*That Certain Woman*	1937
**Hal Wallis	*It's Love I'm After*	1937
**Hal Wallis	*Jezebel*	1938
**Hal Wallis	*The Sisters*	1938
**Hal Wallis	*Dark Victory*	1939
**Hal Wallis	*Juarez*	1939
**Hal Wallis	*The Old Maid*	1939
**Hal Wallis	*The Private Lives of Elizabeth and Essex*	1939
**Hal Wallis	*All This, and Heaven Too*	1940
**Hal Wallis	*The Letter*	1940
**Hal Wallis	*The Great Lie*	1941
**Hal Wallis	*The Bride Came C.O.D.*	1941
**Hal Wallis	*The Man Who Came to Dinner*	1942
**Hal Wallis	*In This Our Life*	1942
Hal Wallis	*Now, Voyager*	1942
Hal Wallis	*Watch on the Rhine*	1943
**Jack L. Warner	*All This, and Heaven Too*	1940
William H. Wright	*Dead Ringer*	1964
William Wyler	*The Letter*	1940
Darryl F. Zanuck	*The Man Who Played God*	1932
Darryl F. Zanuck	*All About Eve*	1950
Sam Zimbalist	*The Catered Affair*	1956

*Credited as being "Associate Producer" under Hal Wallis—but, in effect, worked as co-producer.

**Produced in a more hands-on executive capacity, with an "Associate Producer" working under him.

Note: Jack L. Warner started taking a "J. L. Warner in Charge of Production" credit beginning with *Thank Your Lucky Stars* (1943) and ending with *Beyond the Forest* (1949). In effect, however, Warner was executive producer on all of Bette's pictures for Warner Brothers.

The Made-for-Television Movies

Producer	Program	Year
Bob Christiansen	"Strangers: The Story of a Mother and Daughter"	1979
Bob Christiansen	"As Summers Die"	1986
Jean Moore Edwards	"White Mama"	1980
Neil Hartley	"Murder with Mirrors"	1985
Justine Heroux	"Little Gloria . . . Happy at Last"	1983
Lucy Jarvis	"Family Reunion"	1981
John A. Kuri	"Skyward"	1980
Jack Laird	"The Dark Secret of Harvest Home"	1978
Paul Leaf	"The Disappearance of Aimee"	1976
Richard Levinson	"The Judge and Jake Wyler"	1972
William Link	"The Judge and Jake Wyler"	1972
Lou Morheim	"Madame Sin"	1972

Producer	Program	Year
Lou Morheim	"Scream, Pretty Peggy"	1973
David Nicksay	"Little Gloria . . . Happy at Last"	1982
Philip Parslow	"Right of Way"	1983
Rick Rosenberg	"Strangers: The Story of a Mother and Daughter"	1979
Rick Rosenberg	"As Summers Die"	1986
George Schaefer	"A Piano for Mrs. Cimino"	1982
George Schaefer	"Right of Way"	1983
Christopher N. Seitz	"A Piano for Mrs. Cimino"	1982
Julian Wintle	"Madame Sin"	1972

PUBLICISTS

Bette was one star who was keenly aware of the importance of publicity and hence the job of the publicist. Over the years she worked with innumerable press agents. Following is a selective alphabetized list.

Rupert Allan
Max Bercutt
David Chandler
Jay Chapman
Carl Combs
Frank Daugherty
Charles Einfeld
Alex Evelove
Bob Fender

Harry Friedman
Frank Heacock
John LeRoy Johnston
Carlisle Jones
Harry Mines
Bob Rhodes
Bill Rice
Nancy Seltzer
Cameron Shipp

Stanley Smith
Mort Stein
Robert Taplinger
Ted Todd
Edna Tromans
Linn Unkefer
Ken Whitmore

Q

QUEEN ELIZABETH

Of the many roles she played, Bette's favorite was probably Queen Elizabeth. She played it twice. Some thought that she liked the role so much that she sometimes played it *off screen* as well. In fact, at the end of a business meeting she would sometimes dismiss others with "Gentlemen . . . the audience is at an end." When confronted with this habit of hers by screenwriter Alvah Bessie in 1960, Bette responded by admitting that when she could not win an argument she would sometimes *become* Queen Elizabeth.

According to her daughter, B.D., after playing Queen Elizabeth the second time Bette fantasized about "having the power to behead people. Just the thought of it could put her in a good mood for days."

Bette was to meet Queen Elizabeth II at a dinner reception in the queen's honor during her 10-day tour of the United States in March 1983. Nancy Reagan assigned Frank Sinatra to be in charge of organizing the event, held at 20th Century–Fox. The dinner and subsequent entertainment were, according to several reports, a fiasco because of poor organization. Bette, who attended along with other prominent Hollywood royalty, was not even granted an introduction to the queen.

QUOTING BETTE

"One of the reasons Ham and I are so happy together is that we never have breakfast together."
Bette giving a reporter her recipe for a happy marriage, 1936

"I shiver each time I see an auction of a star's personal belongings advertised in the papers. I don't want that to happen to me. I don't want to own anything in Hollywood . . . that can't be packed in a trunk."
Bette at the beginning of stardom, 1938

"I have reached the conclusion that probably I am a very disagreeable person."
Bette, 1941

"I'm no Pollyanna. I like to play gutty girls and attractive wenches."
Bette on finding her niche, 1938

"Eventually I realized that I was constantly studying people who interested me, and filing away their personality in my memory, so I could bring it out later in building a screen characterization. . . . Naturally, you study more people than you ever have a chance to play. And by the time you use a particular personality you've forgotten whomever it was who inspired the characterization. You merely realize, when you read a soundly written part, that this is someone you have met before."
Bette, 1953

"I've often thought how simple a day on the set would be as compared to my home day with three children."
Bette, tiring of retirement in Maine, 1954

"Since *Baby Jane* opened, you should hear the phone ring."
Bette, 1962

There's a legend that I'm murder to work with. The only people I've ever been murder to are idiots. With an idiot director it's a matter of self-preservation.

Bette, 1962

"Some of the parts I've been offered! Any child would read them and know that they stink. They're terrible!"
Bette, 1962

"It's an enormous satisfaction to me that I'm considered a good business investment. If you aren't this, you might as well shut your little makeup box and go home."

Bette striving for a comeback, 1962

I had lost my self confidence. Nobody would hire me for a movie unless it was for a little picture like this [*What Ever Happened to Baby Jane?*]. The fact that the picture was a success is a miracle in my life. It's not to be believed. Perhaps it was the great law of compensation after ten hellish years. I sold everything I had to keep going during the past few years. Now at least we'll know we have food in the ice box again. All I want now is a chance to prove my talent is still there for the big, million dollar pictures. I'm all pro. And I think something good will come from *Baby Jane*. Someday I may have to go into supporting roles, but I'm not ready for that yet. I can always find work as an actress, but I don't want to play grandmas and maiden aunts.

Bette, back in the saddle, 1963

"I love to rip the guts out of fish. I like to feel the goo and blood and think of all the people who've done me dirt. Christ! Would I like to do this to a few people I could name!"

Bette as quoted by her daughter, B. D. Hyman

"What I should have said was yes, if I can write just one line. The line would have been when I opened a door, looked at her and said, 'My Mildred, how you've changed.' "

Bette after turning down a cameo in a remake of Of Human Bondage, *1965*

"To work. . . . I'm not the type for bridge clubs. . . . If you don't work, what the hell do you do? Sit around and rot!

Bette on why she moved back to L.A. from the East Coast in 1978, 1983

"Old age ain't no place for sissies."
One of Bette's favorite sayings,
which was embroidered on
one of her pillows

"Just one more good script. Next year I've got to have a good script."
Bette on what she wanted to do with the rest of her life, 1987

"I will never appear in a picture with my name under the title until I die."

Bette, 1971

"I spent a lifetime apologizing for being too bright."
Bette, 1971

"Every now and then there is a part that I say, 'Oh, I *wish* I were 30 or 40 years younger, would I love to play *that* part!"

Bette at 80

"Three things I hate about this business—learning lines, putting on makeup, and taking off makeup."

Bette, 1981

"It's going to be a great world when I pass on. Because I think I've been a difficult, difficult woman. I've been difficult for lots of people."

Bette, 1982

"When I first started acting, they used to spend hours trying to make me look older. Now they spend hours trying to make me look better."
Bette, 1977

"They're my wrinkles, I earned them."
Bette, 1965

"Well, if they hire me, and don't know I can be difficult, it's too bad."
Bette, 1986

"That was never for me, being nice and easy."
Bette, 1988

R

RADIO

In the thirties and forties it was common practice, even prestigious, for top movie stars to perform on radio shows to keep their name in the public consciousness or to promote their current films. Bette was always asking Warners to let her do radio shows, but Jack Warner viewed radio as a threat to the picture business and denied her requests more often than he granted them. Still, Bette appeared on numerous shows, including "Academy Award Theatre," "The Electric Autolite Program," "Silver Theatre Broadcast," "Ford Theatre," "Hollywood Players," "Lux Radio Theatre," "Screen Actors Guild Theatre," "Screen Directors Playhouse," and "Theatre Guild on the Air."

Among her radio play costars were Clark Gable, Ronald Colman, Fredric March, Jimmy Stewart, George Brent, and Tyrone Power.

Bette appeared on the Edgar Bergen–Charlie McCarthy radio program on April 17, 1938, to promote *Jezebel*, in which she was the cause of a duel. On the Bergen–McCarthy show, Bette provoked a similar rivalry between the wooden McCarthy and series regular Jonnie Carter. Bette delivered, with an exaggerated southern accent, lines like "Anytime Ah see anyone so chivalrous, it reminds me of the old South. You know years ago, real gentlemen would settle this on the field of honor. . . . Oh, far be it for me to be the cause of all this trouble. I never thought that a little innocent remark from me could start you great big, brave men fighting. . . ." She concluded her performance with "Oh, there's nothing so thrilling as a duel at dawn!"

In 1958 Bette worked as hostess of a radio soap opera entitled "Whispering Streets" that was directed by Gordon Hughes.

CLAUDE RAINS

In later years Bette would sometimes name Claude Rains as her favorite among the actors with whom she had worked. The two appeared in the pictures *Juarez* (1939), *Now, Voyager* (1942), *Mr. Skeffington* (1944), and *Deception* (1946) and also became friends.

Their relationship started uneasily when they met on the set of *Juarez*. The scene they were working on called for Bette as Empress Carlota to reprimand Rains's Napoleon III. The scene was shot with the camera over Rains's shoulder so that his reaction to Bette's tirade could not be seen. Nevertheless, as Bette delivered her lines, Rains pouted and glowered so convincingly that Bette thought he was expressing disapproval of her emoting. Consequently, when she finished the scene, Bette stalked off the set and sulked in her dressing room. It was not until they met again a few years later that they discussed what had transpired that day. Rains, Bette learned, had simply been trying to inspire *her* performance.

Rains, stealing *Deception* from his friend Bette.

Claude Rains (1889–1967), viewed in Hollywood as a consummate actor, appeared in numerous pictures, including *The Invisible Man* (1933), *The Adventures of Robin Hood* (1938), *Mr. Smith Goes to Washington* (1939), *Here Comes Mr. Jordan* (1941), *Kings Row* (1941), *Casablanca* (1943), *Notorious* (1946), *Lawrence of Arabia* (1962), and *The Greatest Story Ever Told* (1965).

IRVING RAPPER
It was Bette Davis who gave Irving Rapper his start as a film director. After he served as dialogue director on her pictures *Kid Galahad* (1937), *The Sisters* (1938), *Juarez* (1939), and *All This, and Heaven Too* (1940), Bette suggested to Hal Wallis that Rapper would make a good film director. Shortly thereafter, he directed Bette in one of the biggest hits of her career, *Now, Voyager* (1942). Rapper later directed Bette in the pictures *The Corn Is Green* (1945), *Deception* (1946), and *Another Man's Poison* (1952), but none would be nearly as successful as the first. Over the years Bette and Rapper developed a sort of love-hate relationship. Some felt that the only reason she enjoyed being directed by Rapper was that she could dominate him and thus have her way on a production. They had something of a falling out when Bette was not cast in the 1950 film version of *The Glass Menagerie*, a picture Rapper directed.

Irving Rapper, born in 1898, directed other pictures, including *Shining Victory* (1941), *The Gay Sisters* (1942), *Rhapsody in Blue* (1945), *Marjorie Morningstar* (1958), and *The Christine Jorgenson Story* (1970).

Bette with Geraldine Fitzgerald and "Little Ronnie Reagan" in *Dark Victory*.

RONALD REAGAN

Reagan costarred in the 1939 picture *Dark Victory*, for which he received an estimated salary of $1,258, a paltry sum compared to the $35,000 Bette received. Reagan was later a top contender for the part of Craig Fleming in *In This Our Life* (1942) but lost out to George Brent.

Over the years Bette frequently called the governor of California and later the president of the United States "Little Ronnie Reagan." The two didn't like each other much—personally, professionally, or politically.

In the 1960s Bette was incensed that at the farewell tribute to Jack Warner, Reagan chose *not* to sit on the dais with the other Warners stars. Instead he chose to make a special entrance as the governor of California. Not only did this entrance upstage Warner on *his* night; it also prompted a mandatory standing ovation from Reagan's former peers. Bette would later say that she and other stars felt silly standing for Reagan, whose talents as an actor had always been considered inferior.

Bette was also fond of accusing Reagan of being a liberal Democrat—until the day he was hired to host a television series sponsored by the conservative General Electric.

Still, when Bette was honored by the Kennedy Center Honors for lifetime achievement in 1987, Reagan said to her, not entirely joking, "Bette Davis, if I'd gotten roles as good as yours and been able to do them as good as you, I might never have left Hollywood."

Bette's hard stance on Reagan softened publicly in later years. Although she nixed him as a presenter for the 1989 Film Society of Lincoln Center tribute in her honor, she did say of Reagan shortly before her death, "He was not a very talented actor, *but* he gave a very good job as a president. He made us all very patriotic. I miss him."

"RECALL"

Bette's longtime desire to play Mary Todd Lincoln in a feature film was never fulfilled, but she did get to play Mrs. Lincoln in "Recall," a 1963 drama that aired on KTTV in Los Angeles. For her performance Bette was presented with a special, miniature Emmy award.

RECORDS

In 1945 Decca Records wanted to sign Bette to a recording contract. Jack Warner, however, objected. Bette was to have narrated "The Star-Spangled Banner" and "other such selections" according to Decca's press release. Bette's deal with Decca was to pay her 10 percent of all retail sales.

It was not until 1976 that Bette recorded an album. *Miss Bette Davis Sings* was produced in England by Norman Newell for EMI Records. It was not released in the United States, however, until Celebrity Records issued it in 1983. Included on the album were these songs:

"They're Either Too Young or Too Old"   "Loneliness"
"I've Written a Letter to Daddy"   "Growing Older, Feeling Younger"
"Hush . . . Hush, Sweet Charlotte"   "Until It's Time for You to Go"
"It Can't Be Wrong"   "I Wish You Love"
"Life Is a Lonely Thing"   "Mother of the Bride"

Bette had previously recorded a few 45 rpm records, including "Single" by Joe Sherman and George David Weiss and "I've Written a Letter to Daddy," with a flip side featuring a twist version of "What Ever Happened to Baby Jane?" recorded with Debbie Burton.

RELIGION

Bette's family's religious background was Baptist. Her grandfather (on her father's side) was the deacon of the Baptist Church in Augusta, Maine. Still, Bette's father, Harlow Davis, was an atheist. Bette's maternal grandmother was deeply religious, involved in the First Baptist Church in Lowell, Massachusetts. Her uncle, Paul Favor, was an Episcopalian minister. To appease the mother of one of her would-be husbands, Bette decided to become a Catholic. She went so far as to meet with a priest to discuss the specifics of the conversion. However, when the relationship ended, so did Bette's plans to become a Catholic. During another period, she also dabbled in the teachings of Christian Science, introduced to her by her mother, Ruthie.

In 1985, following her stroke, a reporter asked Bette if she was religious. She acknowledged that she was, but not in the traditional sense. She wasn't much of a churchgoer, and she did not believe in life after death or in heaven and hell. "All my life," she said, "morality has been more important to me than religion; honesty, integrity, character—old-fashioned virtues preached by people like Emerson, Thoreau, and my New England grandmother."

When asked, months before her death, if she believed in God, Bette replied, "Oh, of course! Of course! My religious beliefs can be capsulized in two ways. One is 'To thine own self be true' and 'God helps those who help themselves.' Another is 'You get back what you give'—not always true."

RETURN FROM WITCH MOUNTAIN ★★

Walt Disney
1978   93 minutes   Technicolor
Directed by: John Hough
Produced by: Ron Miller, Jerome Courtland
Screenplay by: Malcolm Marmorstein
Cinematography by: Frank Phillips
Cast: Bette Davis, Christopher Lee, Kim Richards, Ike Eisenmann, Jack
     Soo, Anthony James, Dick Bakalyan, Ward Costello, Christian Juttner,
     Poindexter, Brad Savage, Jeffrey Jacquet

A sequel to the popular film *Escape from Witch Mountain*, *Return from Witch Mountain* started shooting on April 11, 1977. It cast Bette as Letha Wedge, Christopher Lee's partner in villainy. Unfortunately it didn't give her much to do other than be unpleasant, which she handled with typical aplomb.

DEBBIE REYNOLDS

While still using the name Mary Frances Reynolds, Debbie Reynolds was a Warner Brothers contract player who was used in a bit as a bridesmaid in the 1948 picture *June Bride*. Reynolds later costarred in the 1956 picture *The Catered Affair*, and her performance won her a good deal of acclaim. Still, shooting the picture was a difficult experience for her. Director Richard Brooks wanted her to cry on cue for a scene. When she couldn't, Brooks ridiculed her in front of everyone. Bette pulled Debbie aside, took her into her trailer, and consoled her. "Debbie, don't let anyone bah-thah you," Reynolds recalled Bette saying to her. "You're quite good. Just do the scene. And don't cry if you can't."

Years later Reynolds hosted a Valentino awards ceremony for the Thalians Charity fund-raising group in Beverly Hills. That year the awards were to go to Burt Reynolds and Bette Davis. Bette became miffed because she felt that Debbie had overstepped her bounds as the evening's hostess by attempting to turn the proceedings into a showcase for herself.

Debbie Reynolds, born in 1932, got her start by working as a morning disc jockey, introducing records on a radio station owned by Warner Brothers. She later appeared in pictures including *Singin' in the Rain* (1952), *Susan Slept Here* (1954), *Tammy and the Bachelor* (1957), and *The Unsinkable Molly Brown* (Best Actress Oscar nomination, 1964).

THE RICH ARE ALWAYS WITH US ★★½

Warner Brothers
1932   73 minutes   bw
Directed by: Alfred E. Green
Produced by: Ray Griffith
Screenplay by: Austin Parker, based on the novel by E. Pettit
Cinematography by: Ernest Haller
Cast: Ruth Chatterton, George Brent, John Miljan, Adrienne Dore, Bette
     Davis, Mae Madison, John Wray, Robert Warwick, Virginia
     Hammond, Walter Walker, Eula Gray, Edith Allen, Ethel Kenyon,
     Ruth Lee, Berton Churchill

Upon her arrival at Warner Brothers, Ruth Chatterton, the new queen of the
studio, had her pick of properties. What she chose was *The Rich Are Always
With Us*, an adaptation of the comic novel of the same name by E. Pettit. In
this story everyone is rich and terribly sophisticated. Bette would be cast as
Malbro, a Park Avenue debutante in love with George Brent, and she would
look more attractive than she had yet been on a movie screen. Her hair was
dyed a lighter shade of blond, and she paraded around (as did the other
women in the picture) in sumptuous gowns by Orry-Kelly.

Shooting started on January 22, 1932, with Bette and finished on February 22. During the making of the picture both Bette and Chatterton fell in
love with George Brent. Chatterton was married at the time, to actor Ralph
Forbes, but that didn't prevent her from engaging in an affair with Brent.
Shortly after the completion of the picture, they would get married.

MARIAN RICHARDS

Marian Richards was Bette's daughter's governess. She later became Bette's husband's wife. Said William Grant Sherry after his divorce from Bette and his engagement to Richards, "After all the recent divorce unpleasantness was over, I suddenly realized that here is a girl who could make my life happy. She is beautiful and calm and spiritual and wants the really worthwhile things in life." Then, in a dig targeted at his ex, Sherry quipped, "She has no complexes."

"RIGHT OF WAY"

Just as she had with "A Piano for Mrs. Cimino" (1982), Bette declined, upon first reading it, the script for "Right of Way," a story about an elderly couple and their desire for euthanasia. "[But] when George Schaefer read the script and liked it," said Bette, "I knew there must have been more to it than I originally suspected. I later learned that when the writer Richard Lees wrote *Right of Way* originally as a play and later as a film, he had both Jimmy [Stewart] and me in mind for the roles."

After five days of rehearsal "Right of Way" shot for 21 days in late 1982 with a budget of $2.8 million. The telefilm was produced by Schaefer-Karpf Productions for Home Box Office cable. For Bette it was a highly pleasurable filming experience. After so many years of stardom on rival lots, she delighted in working with Stewart. "I've never had a more delightful experience," Bette enthused to reporter Richard Hack. "We were both in practically every scene, and if we hadn't liked each other, we would have made it, but it wouldn't have been nearly as special an occasion. I just found him *heaven*."

CORPORAL LEWIS A. RILEY

Corporal Lewis A. Riley engaged in a secret romance with Bette when the two met in Los Angeles (perhaps at the Hollywood Canteen) in 1944. Riley, a former New York real estate agent, was stationed at Fort Benning, Georgia. After making *Mr. Skeffington*, Bette spent the summer and fall of 1944 vacationing in Phenix City, Alabama, near where Riley was stationed. The two renewed their affair, and Bette threw a birthday party for him in Atlanta in October 1944. Bette denied rumors that she was about to get married, saying, "I am 36-years-old and I have reached the age where it is childish to beat around the bush about something like that." The affair ended when Riley was sent overseas on an assignment. The following year, Bette married William Grant Sherry.

RKO RADIO PICTURES, INC.

It was *not* Warner Brothers but RKO Radio Pictures, Inc., that launched Bette to acclaim with the 1934 picture *Of Human Bondage*. The studio later released the 1941 Samuel Goldwyn picture *The Little Foxes*. Bette's other RKO pictures were *Way Back Home* (1931) and, with Howard Hughes at the head of the studio, *Payment on Demand* (1951).

ROBERT MILTON-JOHN MURRAY ANDERSON SCHOOL OF THE THEATRE

Weeks after being rejected by Eva Le Gallienne in September 1927, 19-year-old Bette was practically dragged by her mother, Ruthie, onto a train from Connecticut to New York City. They then cabbed to 58th Street between Lexington and Park avenues to the Robert Milton–John Murray Anderson School of the Theatre. Ruthie deposited Bette in front of the desk of Hugh Anderson, the school's administrator, and announced, "This is my daughter, Bette. She wants to be an actress." Ruth proceeded to tell Anderson that she could not quite afford to pay Bette's tuition but that she would somehow raise it. They worked out a deal in which Ruthie would pay for Bette's acting lessons on the installment plan. Bette was put up at the school's boarding-house, located next door, and Ruthie went to look for work.

It was at the school, under the creative direction of John Murray Anderson, that Bette first learned her craft. Her teachers included Anderson, drama; George Currie, drama; and Martha Graham, dance. Visiting speakers, including George Arliss, also counseled and coached the students.

To Ruthie's relief, Bette won one of the school's three scholarships with her performance in *The Famous Mrs. Fair* in January 1928. Nevertheless, when Bette had the opportunity to become a member of the Cukor-Kondolf Repertory Company later that year, she seized it and dropped out of school. Still, she would frequently say over the years that she had learned a good deal of her technique from the Robert Milton–John Murray Anderson School of the Theatre.

ROBINHOOD ISLAND, MAINE

Following their July 1950 marriage, Bette and Gary Merrill spent the summer vacationing on Robinhood Island, Maine. "We had a wonderful summer," Bette recalled. "Robinhood is a small island. There is no electricity, no gas or conveniences. Life is as primitive as it was in our ancestors' time. I never realized how important running water is for baths and other conveniences. We had to heat every drop of water we used." Merrill enthused, "Bette was superb. . . . Every morning some of the natives would call with fresh lobsters and Bette knew just how they should be prepared."

CASEY ROBINSON

Considered Warner Brother's preeminent screenwriter of the period, Robinson scripted the pictures *It's Love I'm After* (1937), *Dark Victory* (1939), *The Old Maid* (1939), *All This, and Heaven Too* (1940), *Now, Voyager* (1942), and *The Corn Is Green* (shared credit, 1945).

Casey Robinson (1903–1979) wrote screenplays for other pictures, including *Captain Blood* (1935), *Kings Row* (1942), and *The Macomber Affair* (1947).

Robinson was perturbed that in his deathbed scene he was upstaged by upstart Bette.

EDWARD G. ROBINSON

Edward G. Robinson costarred with Bette in *Kid Galahad* (1937). During the shooting of his death scene at the end of the picture, Bette bent over Robinson's body and wept. Robinson, not wanting *his* death scene to be upstaged by anyone, called a halt to the proceedings and complained to the director, "Don't you think Bette is crying too much?" Unlike many others at the studio, Robinson was unimpressed by Bette's acting skills, contending that she would have been better had she had more stage training. In his autobiography Robinson wrote, "Miss Davis was and is every inch a lady—polite, mannerly, gracious, even self-effacing. But by today's standards she could never have gotten a job in a high school production of 'East Lynn.' I know it's goatish of me to say it, but Miss Davis was, when I played with her, not a very gifted amateur and employed any number of jarring mannerisms that she used to form an image. In her early period Miss Davis played the image, and not herself, and certainly not the character provided by the author."

Edward G. Robinson (1893–1973) appeared in a plethora of pictures, including *Little Caesar* (1930), *Double Indemnity* (1944), and *The Cincinnati Kid* (1965).

JAY ROBINSON

In 1958 Jay Robinson, who had appeared in the 1955 picture *The Virgin*

Queen and then, at Bette's behest, in *Bunny O'Hare* (1971), was arrested on a narcotics charge. Bette later wrote a letter in his defense to the *Los Angeles Times*, calling him one of Hollywood's best actors: "I first met Jay Robinson in 1955 and not again until we worked on *Bunny O'Hare*. His drug involvement was over in 1960. He is one of our very fine actors. I have only admiration for his having overcome his problems. He is in a fine position to encourage others. Jay never talked about what happened to him. I know he's been through his own private hell. I think we should forget about it; I believe his life experiences have enhanced his talent, and I believe that, given the opportunity, he can go on to much greater things."

Jay Robinson, born in 1930, appeared in other pictures, including *The Robe* (1953) and *Shampoo* (1975).

FRANKLIN D. ROOSEVELT

Bette was a great admirer of Franklin Delano Roosevelt. She first saw the president and met members of his family, including his mother, Sarah Delano, on the Washington, D.C., stop of the *Forty-Second Street* tour of 1933. Roosevelt had been in office for only a few months.

In the succeeding years Bette continued to support Roosevelt in his repeated and successful reelection campaigns. During the summer of 1944 she wrote to the White House and asked for an appointment with Roosevelt. She was subsequently invited to attend an official White House function. That evening Bette stood in a reception line as the president greeted his guests. When he came upon Bette, Roosevelt, surprised, asked her what *she* was doing there. Bette told him that she simply wanted to meet him. She further told him that she was vacationing in Phenix City, Alabama. Roosevelt then invited her to a dinner he was hosting for polio patients in Warm Springs, Georgia. She accepted. On the night of the dinner, Bette was thrilled to be seated next to the president. She also attended a function in Roosevelt's honor at the Biltmore Hotel in Atlanta and a rally at Madison Square Garden.

In November 1944, just before the election, Bette told the press, "I quite naturally think Roosevelt will win." When asked *why* she was supporting him, Bette retorted impatiently, "To sum it up, I am voting for Mr. Roosevelt because I believe in his way of thinking."

ROSHANARA

Roshanara, real name Jane Cradduck, was Bette's dance teacher at the Mariarden School of Dance in New Hampshire. Bette attended the school during the summer of 1925, at the age of 17. Roshanara coached Bette in the school's production of *A Midsummer Night's Dream*, which she also choreographed. Roshanara reportedly died later the same year.

> "[She] would have been recognized as the greatest dancer of the age had she lived."
>
> *Bette Davis, 1941*

Bette on Billy: "That child is *uncanny*."

BILLY ROY

Roy appeared in the 1945 picture *The Corn Is Green* and had a bit part in *Deception* (1946). In 1945 Billy Roy was an 18-year-old Bette Davis fan who had been collecting Davis memorabilia and photographs since he was 11. By the time he made *Corn* he claimed to have 1,800 photographs.

During the making of the picture he became friendly with his idol. One experience was particularly memorable to him. "We had a read-through of the script in her bungalow," relates Roy, today a well-respected arranger and musical director (for famed New York cabaret singer Julie Wilson, among others). "And there was a great discussion with Irving Rapper and Jack Chertok about whether Miss Moffat was really in love with the John Dall character. And they couldn't come to any agreement. And finally, I couldn't wait any longer. I had read the script and memorized it. I spoke up and said, 'No, no, no, on page 72 she says . . . so obviously, she wasn't in love with him.' Bette turned to the assistant director and said, 'That child is *uncanny*. He knows more about this film than any of us!' " Roy also entertained the *Corn* company with his impersonation of Bette. Recalls costar Joan Lorring, "Bette Davis literally fell off the chair laughing at Billy's impersonation of her. He was waving the cigarette and thumping his thigh. . . . She was charmed by him."

VIOLLA RUBBER

Bette's secretary-companion turned manager in the 1960s and early 1970s. It was Rubber who reportedly suggested to Tennessee Williams that Bette play Maxine Faulk in the 1961 Broadway play *The Night of the Iguana*. Rubber also served as one of the producers of the play.

S

ANWAR EL-SADAT

Bette hosted a function inducting a chair from the television series "All in the Family" into the Smithsonian Institution. That day Anwar el-Sadat, the president of Egypt, was visiting the White House. When he learned that Bette Davis was nearby, Sadat paid her a visit. She later wrote, "Sadat emerged, crossed the hall, hugged and kissed me. He was very dark, not tall, a man who seemed coiled with energy and warmth toward his fellow man. I saw him then as one of the great hopes of this century."

SALLY SAGE

Bette's longtime stand-in, Sally Sage, aka Sally Hutchinson, worked on numerous Davis pictures from 1934 to 1945. She was initially hired by Warner Brothers because she was the same height and had the same shade of blond hair as Bette. Sage related, "I'll never forget *Bordertown*. Through most of that picture I had a terrific cold. Not bad enough to go to bed—just enough of the sniffles to make it miserable working. Bette sensed this and insisted that I rest in her dressing room while she did her own standing in. I think she did as much standing-in work during that film as I did."

Sage started standing in for Bette with the 1934 picture *The Big Shakedown*. At Bette's request Sage was given her chance at an acting career of her own when she was tested for a supporting part in *The Old Maid* (1939). The part, however, went to Joan Shaw. In 1941, Sage retired from the screen to devote herself full-time to being Mrs. Clifford Hutchinson. After Hutchinson went into the army, Sally came out of retirement to work as Bette's stand-in on the 1943 picture *Thank Your Lucky Stars*. A few years later Sage was hired as Bette's "acting double" in *A Stolen Life* (1946). She portrayed one of the twins (though her face was not seen) while Bette portrayed the other. For the picture her salary was increased to $150 per week. She also got another acting job, in a non-Davis film, *The Two Mrs. Carrolls* (1947).

SALARY

"I'd be willing to be frightfully unhappy on $5,000 a week. It's getting a paltry fraction of that that ires me. I can assure you if I were paid $2,500 a week or even $2,000, it would be a considerable raise for me. I really couldn't tell you how much I am getting. I'm too ashamed of it."

Bette, in response to a Warner Brothers charge that she was going on strike despite making $3,000 a week in 1936. Actually, she was making $1,600.

The following is a sampling of the salaries Bette was paid at various times and for various projects.

Salary at Universal: $300 a week
The Man Who Played God: $300 a week
Of Human Bondage: $750 a week
Dangerous: $1,350 a week
Salary at time of 1936 strike: $1,600 a week
Jezebel: $2,250 a week
Dark Victory: $3,000 a week
The Little Foxes: $150,000 for the picture
Mr. Skeffington: $115,000 for the picture
1945–1946: $7,000 per week
Winter Meeting: $150,500 for the picture
Beyond the Forest: $200,000 for the picture
Phone Call from a Stranger: $35,000 for three days' work
John Paul Jones: $25,000 for four days' work
Baby Jane: $60,000 plus a percentage of the profits
Dead Ringer: $100,000 plus percentage
Where Love Has Gone: $150,000
Hush . . . Hush, Sweet Charlotte: $200,000
The Wicked Stepmother: $250,000

SAN SEBASTIAN FILM FESTIVAL

Bette made her final public appearance at the San Sebastian Film Festival, held at the Victoria Eugenia Theatre, on September 22, 1989. Wearing a purple sequined gown, Bette was honored with the Donostia Award for Lifetime Achievement. The award was presented by the mayor of San Sebastian, Xavier Albistur. The audience gave Bette a standing ovation, to which she responded with open arms, *"Muchos gracias! Muchos gracias!"* To reporters she joked sarcastically, "If they had waited a little longer, I would not have been able to be here to receive it." Two weeks later her comment would not seem at all amusing.

While in San Sebastian, Bette and her companion, Kathryn Sermak, stayed at the Hotel Maria Christina. The night after she was presented with her award, Bette presented the festival's top prize to Andrei Konchalovsky for his film *Homer and Eddie*. Accepting his prize, Konchalovsky got down on his knees and paid homage to Bette. For the next few days Bette stayed at the hotel, giving press interviews and working on the update of her autobiography. She was also sick with what she thought was the flu. However, by Tuesday, October 3, Bette was so sick that she had to be flown via air ambulance to the American Hospital in Paris, where she died the following Friday.

> "I hope this will prove to the world I'm not dying."
> *Bette to Robert Osborne upon leaving*
> *for San Sebastian, September 1989*

CARL SANDBURG

In 1959 and 1960 Bette toured the country performing readings of Carl Sandburg's poetry in a stage show entitled *The World of Carl Sandburg*. At the time she signed to do the show Bette told a reporter, "I didn't know anything about Sandburg except that he had written about Lincoln and was the handsomest man I'd ever seen on television." They met for the first time in Los Angeles. Says the show's producer, Norman Corwin, "It was very loving. Bette was fond of the old man. He, of course, always loved women."

SANTA CLAUS

At the age of 10 Bette was costumed as Santa Claus at the Crestalban boarding school. When one of the candles on the Christmas tree burned out, young Bette struck a match and relit it, catching the cotton of her costume with a flicker of fire. The flames scorched her face before they were eventually put out. The teachers and students at the school stood around her in panic and in fear. Bette Davis basked in the limelight. She had her first audience.

THE SARAH SIDDONS AWARD

The Sarah Siddons Award was a fictional prize presented to Eve Harrington in the 1950 picture *All About Eve*. Years later a theatrical organization founded the Sarah Siddons Society in Chicago, which bestowed an annual Sarah Siddons Award. On May 14, 1973, the award was presented, fittingly, by Anne Baxter (who had played Eve) to Bette for lifetime achievement.

SATAN MET A LADY ★
Warner Brothers
1936   74 minutes   bw
Directed by: William Dieterle
Produced by: Henry Blanke
Screenplay by: Brown Holmes, based on the novel by Dashiell Hammett
Cinematography by: Arthur Edeson

Cast: Bette Davis, Warren William, Alison Skipworth, Arthur Treacher, Winifred Shaw, Marie Wilson, Porter Hall, Maynard Holmes, Olin Howard, Charles Wilson, Joseph King, Barbara Blane, William B. Davidson

Satan Met a Lady was known at various times during production as *Money Man* and *The Man with the Black Hat*, both of which were dropped because Warner wanted the title to slant in Bette's favor to capitalize on her recent Oscar win. Other titles considered were *Men on Her Mind* (the title under which it was shot) and *Hard Luck Dame*. It was a Warners office boy who eventually came up with the winning title, *Satan Met a Lady*. His name was Howard Clausen, and he was earning $20 a week at the time. For his achievement Clausen was presented with a $25 bonus.

Initially Bette refused the part of Valerie Purvis. On November 30, 1935, she sent Warner a wire that read, in part, "After working over six weeks on *Petrified Forest* under most trying conditions . . . my physical condition is such that it is impossible for me to report for another picture without at least getting two or three weeks rest and my doctor advises unless I get this rest, I am likely to become seriously ill."

On December 2, 1935, Warner demanded that Bette be given a physical exam by the studio physician, Dr. Conn. Conn went to Bette's home at 6:00 P.M. as arranged, but was told that Bette was not at home. The following day the studio suspended her. Bowing to the pressure, Bette showed up for work on December 6.

If Bette did *not* accept the part, Hal Wallis wanted Tallulah Bankhead, but Tallulah declined the part after reading the script, saying that it was not of sufficient *importance* for her to play it.

Wallis wanted William Powell for the male lead. Spencer Tracy was another top consideration. When both turned the part down, Wallis settled for Warren William.

Satan Met a Lady was allotted 20 shooting days and an estimated budget of $183,000. Of this William was to receive $18,800, while Bette was to get $8,549. This despite the fact that she had won the Best Actress Oscar the previous March. Warners would give Bette the consolation of top billing to capitalize on her escalating popularity.

The picture started shooting on December 2, 1935, with an expected finish of Christmas Eve. Bette didn't start work until Monday, December 9. During shooting Wallis was concerned about Wini Shaw's double chin and advised Dieterle not shoot her in profile. Other than that, the picture proceeded smoothly and finished only slightly behind schedule on December 28.

Ads for the picture proclaimed, "The Screen's Most '*Dangerous*' Woman Meets the Screen's Most Amorous Sleuth!"—the latter in reference to William's work in a series of Perry Mason pictures. Also, "He Was a Devil With the Ladies . . . 'Til He Met This Blonde From Hades!"

Satan Met A Lady was generally panned upon its release. Its failure and the fact that she was virtually forced to do it had much to do with Bette's 1936 strike against the studio.

THE SCAPEGOAT ★★
du Maurier/Guinness Productions
Released by Metro-Goldwyn-Mayer
1959   92 minutes   bw
Directed by: Robert Hamer
Produced by: Michael Balcon
Screenplay by: Gore Vidal and Robert Hamer, based on the novel by
    Daphne du Maurier
Cinematography by: Paul Beeson
Cast: Alec Guinness, Bette Davis, Irene Worth, Nicole Maurey, Pamela
    Brown, Geoffrey Keen, Annabel Bartlett, Noel Howlett, Peter Bull,
    Leslie French, Alan Webb, Maria Britneva, Eddie Byrne, Alexander
    Archdale, Peter Sallis

In selling the rights to her book, Daphne du Maurier's foremost concern was
who was to play her protagonist. She wanted Alec Guinness, who partnered
with her as executive producer, and would not consider any offers that did
not include Guinness in the leading and dual role of John Barret and Jacques
de Gue. Bette was cast as the Dowager Countess De Gue, Alec Guinness's
drug-addicted mother, who played most of her scenes in bed.

The Scapegoat was filmed at MGM Studios in England. For Bette it was
a very unpleasant experience. She viewed Guinness as an egomaniac and was
uncomfortable playing a subordinate though colorful role. She would later
say that she had never worked on an unhappier set and would accuse Guinness of cutting her part to shreds in the editing room.

Upon its release the picture was generally panned.

GEORGE SCHAEFER
It was largely because of George Schaefer's reputation—he was renowned for
his direction for "The Hallmark Hall of Fame" specials on television—that
Bette starred in two made-for-television movies for him: "A Piano for Mrs.
Cimino" (1982) and "Right of Way" (1983). The two got along well, and after
Bette's death Schaefer staged the November 1989 tribute in her honor at
Burbank Studios.

Born in 1920, George Schaefer directed numerous television movies and
features including *Macbeth* (1961) and *An Enemy of the People* (1977).

"SCHLITZ PLAYHOUSE"
Bette starred in "For Better or Worse," a March 22, 1957, filmed episode of the
television series "Schlitz Playhouse." The program was produced by Frank P.
Rosenberg.

"Schlitz Playhouse" aired on CBS from October 1951 until March 1959.
During its first five seasons its name was "Schlitz Playhouse of Stars."

SCHOOLS
The following is a chronological list of the schools that Bette Davis attended.

Elementary School: Wingate Private Kindergarten, Massachusetts
    Crestalban School, Massachusetts (private)
Junior High School: Public School No. 186, New York
High School: East Orange High School, New Jersey (9)
Newton High School, Massachusetts (9,10)
Northfield Seminary, Massachusetts (private, 11)
Cushing Academy, Massachusetts (private, 11, 12)

THE SCIENTIFIC CARDPLAYER ★★
Dino de Laurentiis
Released by C.I.C. Productions
1972 113 minutes EastmanColor
Directed by: Luigi Comencini
Produced by: Dino de Laurentiis
Screenplay by: Rodolfo Sonego
Cinematography by: Giuseppe Ruzzolini
Cast: Alberto Sordi, Bette Davis, Silvana Mangano, Joseph Cotten,
    Domenico Modugno, Maria Carotenuto

Bette was sent the script of *Lo Scopone Scientifico* by Dino de Laurentiis. She flew to Rome in March 1972, hailing the script as the best one she had seen in years. The picture cast her as a nameless American billionairess who is wheelchair-bound and has a passion for cardplaying.

Production was difficult for Bette, primarily because the film was being shot in Italian. An interpreter had to relay director Comencini's instructions to her. To make matters worse, Bette was livid with the picture's star, Alberto Sordi, who she referred to as "Mr. Sordid" and who she claimed refused to speak English to her even though he could.

Also called *The Game, The Scientific Cardplayer* was released in Rome in October 1972. It was never picked up for an American release.

"SCREAM, PRETTY PEGGY"
An attempted take on the Hitchcock classic *Psycho* about a boy, a girl, and his mother, "Scream, Pretty Peggy" starred Bette as Ted Bessell's mother in one of her earlier and more unfortunate television movies. The telefilm was produced by Lou Morheim and directed by Gordon Hessler from a script by Jimmy Sangster and Arthur Hoffe. It was shot by Leonard J. South. Also in the cast were Sian-Barbara Allen, Charles Drake, Allan Arbus, Tovah Feldshuh, Johnnie Collins III, Jessica Rains, and Christiane Schmidtner. On working with Bette, director Gordon Hessler had the following to say.

"She really wasn't doing TV films at that time. I think she may have been in sort of a black spot in her career. It was a period where it was very hard for her to get work; I remember that. I mean, can you imagine Bette Davis accepting a television role after all the roles she's played?

"I was a very young director at the time. What I did was ask for a rehearsal period, which was unusual for a movie of the week. Everything was so quick. I've been in situations with movies of the week where you're filming on Monday and you haven't even got a cast on Sunday. Anyway, Bette Davis agreed to the rehearsal period. We went to her place and brought the principal actors. She was sort of an empress in her home. She sort of reigned there. She sat very imperially in that higher chair, and everybody was placed around her at her feet. She was obviously the queen.

"We read through the script at her house and talked over the picture. Of course I was nervous because of her background and reputation. Everybody was a bit nervous about her. But she was very charming. She was absolutely wonderful.

"At that first meeting we had disagreements about how she should play the part. I was amazed because there was a very stony silence by Bette Davis. And then she said, 'Do you really see the part this way? I didn't see it that way at all.' I was stunned. But I continued on, and I made my point. Of course I was a little worried. And funny enough, she decided to follow the way I had suggested. I was quite surprised. I had no problems with her at all. . . .

"When we had the final party, she gave about a 15-minute speech about me. She castigated the producer in front of everybody. Even the producer was there. And I was ready to crawl under the table. I don't know why; I don't know what she had against this man. . . . But she was a wonderful lady. And she is of course an extraordinary artist."

On "Scream, Pretty Peggy," Hessler added, "It was a second-rate thriller based on cliché ideas. All you can do with something like this is have the panache to make it as visually exciting as you can."

SCREEN ACTORS GUILD

The Screen Actors Guild went on strike in March 1960 over television residuals. Apparently film producers had promised in 1948 to discuss television residuals in 1960. When the time came, however, the producers allegedly tried to back out of the agreement. Bette, whose old pictures were repeatedly shown on television (without compensation to her), endorsed the strike. She was one of 25 major stars who signed a full-page advertisement that appeared in the Hollywood trade papers. The ad backed the action of the guild. "Everyone blames TV for the fix Hollywood has gotten into," Bette said at the time, "but the town was in trouble long before TV. This actors and writers strike is going to separate the men from the boys. It has to end up doing good for the business and those left in it."

SCREEN TESTS
The Samuel Goldwyn Test

While she was appearing on Broadway in the 1929 Broadway play, *Broken Dishes*, Bette was summoned by Arthur Hornblow, Jr., to appear in a screen test for Goldwyn. The test was made at the Paramount Theatre in New York. At the time Bette was being considered for parts in two Goldwyn pictures with Ronald Colman, *The Devil to Pay* and *Raffles*. For Bette the test was a

failure. Said she, "I was *ghastly*. Actors with no knowledge of the screen are shoved in front of a lens and told to act. No thought is given to makeup. I suppose they reason that if the result is remotely favorable you will be a real sensation when they finally go to work on you. I had a crooked tooth of which I was aware, but I had no idea it would stand out like a locomotive. I was badly dressed for the camera, the lighting was awful."

The Universal Test

Universal talent scout David Werner discovered Bette in the 1930 Broadway play *Solid South* and decided to test her. At the time the studio was thinking of casting her in the film version of *Strictly Dishonorable*. By this time Bette's teeth had been straightened, she was better dressed, and she was much more relaxed in front of the camera. Studio head Carl Laemmle, Jr., reportedly approved the test with the condition that another test be made of Bette's legs.

The first test had not shown her legs, and Laemmle apparently wanted to make certain that she had no physical deformity below the waist. Bette ended up not being cast in *Strictly Dishonorable*, but the test did result in her studio contract with Universal.

SECRETARIES

The following is a selective alphabetical list of the people who served as Bette's secretary/personal assistant over the years.

Gerette Allegra	Vik Greenfield	Olive St. John
Robin Brown	Bridget Price	Kathryn Sermak
Helen Darville	Violla Rubber	

SEED ★★

Universal
1931   96 minutes   bw
Directed by: John M. Stahl
Produced by: John M. Stahl
Screenplay by: Gladys Lehman, based on the novel by Charles G. Norris
Cinematography by: Jackson Rose
Cast: John Boles, Lois Wilson, Genevieve Tobin, Zasu Pitts, Raymond Hackett, Bette Davis, Dickie Moore, Helen Parrish, Richard Tucker, Jack Willis, Don Cox, Dick Winslow, Kenneth Selling, Terry Cox

Seed is officially Bette Davis's second picture, even though it was the *first* picture she started shooting and it was later in production concurrently with *Bad Sister*.

Seed shot for 27 days starting on January 12, 1931, with a budget of $283,000. The story cast Bette as Margaret Carter, one of five children of Bart and Peggy Carter, played by John Boles and Lois Wilson. Bart leaves the family for other pursuits, including other women, and then returns 10 years later. The picture completed production on March 4, 1931.

Upon its release Louella Parsons predicted, "Keep an eye on Bette Davis; that girl has something worth developing." Unfortunately for Bette, no one at Universal noticed.

KATHRYN SERMAK

Bette interviewed Kathryn Sermak on June 13, 1979, because she needed someone to accompany her to London for the shooting of *The Watcher in the Woods*. These were questions Bette posed to Sermak during their first interview: What was her astrological sign? Could she boil an egg? Bette also seemed impressed that Sermak knew nothing of the film industry. She was 22 years old, and her life would never be the same again.

Following the film, and upon their return to the United States, Sermak moved into Bette's West Hollywood apartment. She would live there for nearly seven years. She became Bette's assistant, adviser, and close friend. She planned Bette's public appearances and private engagements. She nursed Bette in the hospital during her 1983 mastectomy and stroke. She stayed in Bette's room night and day for eight weeks. Bette would later credit Sermak with having kept her alive.

Prior to Bette's mastectomy and stroke she and Sermak decided that it was time for Sermak to move into her own apartment. After Bette recuperated, Sermak moved to San Francisco and would fly down to be with Bette on weekends. She eventually moved back to Los Angeles and into her own home. She found Bette a Malibu beach house to rent, and she took a nearby apartment.

In 1988, at Bette's suggestion, Sermak was made the associate producer of the picture *The Wicked Stepmother*. Said Bette at the time, "Miss Sermak is very much on her own. She has now become an associate producer of the next film I'm going to make, so she's off on a whole new, wonderful career, and I couldn't be more thrilled."

Skeptics likened Kathryn Sermak to Eve Harrington from *All About Eve*. Actually, she was more like a surrogate daughter, particularly after the publication of *My Mother's Keeper* in 1985. It would be Sermak, not B. D. Hyman, who was at Bette's bedside in a Paris hospital at the time of her death.

In Bette's will, dated September 2, 1987, she left half of her estate to Kathryn Sermak.

SEX

"During the sexual time [you think] Oh, the person is remarkable.
Then comes a day and you look and you say, *What?*"
Bette Davis, 1988

One of Bette's favorite expressions was "Sex is God's joke on human beings." Late in life she believed it. She wasn't, of course, always so cynical. Nor was she, despite the good upstanding Yankee image she liked to project, prudish.

In her younger years Bette's sexual fantasy had been to make love on a bed of gardenias. Bette, married at the time, had an affair with orchestra leader Johnny Mercer, who was also married. One day Bette walked into her suite at the Waldorf-Astoria Hotel in New York to find the bed covered in a sheet of gardenias, and she and her orchestra leader proceeded to frolic in the flowers.

PEGGY SHANNON

Interestingly, before working for Bette as her personal hairdresser, Peggy Shannon worked for Joan Crawford. She was on the sets of the pictures *What Ever Happened to Baby Jane?* (1962) and *Hush . . . Hush, Sweet Charlotte* (1964). While on the set of the former, Shannon selected a wig for Bette to wear as Jane Hudson—it was a shoddy wig full of curls from the MGM hairdressing department that, ironically, Joan Crawford had worn in 1926. Bette loved it.

After doing Eva Gabor's hair for the television series "Green Acres," Shannon became Bette's hairdresser in the 1970s. Her work extended beyond just doing Bette's hair, as she became something of a personal assistant, traveling companion, and friend. Among the movies Shannon worked on were the television films "Scream, Pretty Peggy" (1973) and "The Dark Secret of Harvest Home" (1978) and the features *Burnt Offerings* (1976) and *Death on the Nile* (1978).

VINCENT SHERMAN

Jack Warner was so impressed by the way Vincent Sherman shot dueling stars Bette Davis and Miriam Hopkins in *Old Acquaintance* (1943) that he decided to make Sherman something of a "woman's director"—sort of Warners' answer to MGM's George Cukor.

At the time he made *Acquaintance*, Sherman was 37 years old. During production he engaged in an affair with his 35-year-old married star, Bette Davis. Years later Sherman would say, "When you're directing an actress, if you're about the same age, if it's a harmonious relationship and you get close to each other, you *have* to [have an affair] because you're dealing with human emotions. Intimacy is very conducive." Sherman, who also had an affair with Joan Crawford, said, when asked to compare the two, "I have great affection for both ladies. They were in my opinion extraordinary women. . . . It was very difficult to resist their charms."

Sherman and Bette did not get along quite as well on their next picture, *Mr. Skeffington* (1944), although their affair continued until the picture concluded. Once on the set, when he was explaining to one of his actors how he wanted a particular line read, Bette stepped in and admonished Sherman by telling him that *he* was an "atrocious" actor and that he should let the actor say the line the way he wanted to. On another occasion on the set Sherman wore a pink shirt that Bette disapproved of. When he stood his ground and refused to take it off, Bette, equipped with a pair of shears, proceeded to clip off the buttons of his shirt.

Nevertheless, there was talk that Sherman would direct Bette again in *A Stolen Life* (1946). However, it was not to be. She claimed that he wanted an actress who would dance at his every command, while he viewed her as overbearing.

Vincent Sherman (born Abram Orovitz in 1906) directed other pictures, including *All Through the Night* (1941), *The Hard Way* (1942), *The New Adventures of Don Juan* (1948), *The Hasty Heart* (1949), and *The Young Philadelphians* (1959).

WILLIAM GRANT SHERRY

William Grant Sherry had the distinction of being Bette's least favorite of her four husbands. *"This,"* she would say, "was the worst mistake of my life. I was unhappy from almost the first day." Bette met Sherry at a party hosted by Laguna Beach ceramics artist Russell Leidy on October 20, 1945. He was a sailor on leave. After his discharge from the navy a few weeks later, Sherry returned to Laguna and looked up Bette. He told her that he was a painter and a physiotherapist and professed to have no idea what *she* did for a living. Shortly thereafter, rumors circulated in Hollywood that Bette was about to get married. The rumors were started when Sherry's mother announced to the press that her son was going to marry *Bette Davis*. In response Bette acknowledged only that she "knew a man by that name."

Nonetheless, Sherry proposed and Bette accepted. She was 37. He was 30. One week before the ceremony Bette still denied any romance when the press asked. When the couple finally did publicly acknowledge their intention to marry, Sherry stated pretentiously (and unintelligibly), "We just professed intelligently toward Friday's culmination." The ceremony was held at the Mission Inn in Riverside, California.

The newlyweds then drove to Mexico City for their honeymoon. On the way the tires on their car blew out. Bette would later claim that Sherry also *bodily* threw her out of the car and that on the first night in Mexico he hurled a steamer trunk at her across the hotel room.

Sherry was frequently described in press reports of the period as an "ex-boxer." In fact Sherry had had only one professional fight before he hung up his boxing gloves. Bette would later contend, however, that he occasionally came out of retirement during their more heated marital squabbles. He worked as an artist, and in later years he became a medical illustrator before deciding on a career as a professional landscape painter.

Bette *was* attracted to Sherry's love of nature and adventure. During their marriage they bought a trailer for vacations in the mountains and an airplane for aerial exploration. They also traveled the country in search of a ranch to purchase.

Bette was attracted as well to Sherry's physique. None of her other husbands would compare to Sherry in terms of physical prowess. Hedda Hopper certainly saw what Bette saw in Sherry when she visited them at their Laguna Beach home. "In a suit you couldn't possibly guess what a handsome Greek God he was," Hopper wrote lustfully. "Now he'd run up fresh from the sea with the water still glistening on his mahogany tanned skin. He was in navy trunks, and with a physique that would do for Atlas, stood before me, muscles rippling evenly under a firm skin, young, strong and handsomely male. He smiled. He has an even, confident, ingratiating smile, kindly but masculine as a left hook."

Upon the birth of their daughter, Barbara Davis Sherry, in May 1947, the press marveled that Bette was now the lady who had everything: money, fame, a beautiful husband, home, and child.

It was not to last, though. The fall of 1949 would be an extremely difficult period in the life of Bette Davis. Days after *Beyond the Forest* opened to terrible reviews, and after having abandoned the security of Warner Brothers, Bette filed for a divorce from Sherry. She would claim that he was a fortune hunter and a wife beater.

Sherry's initial response to the action was to tell a reporter, "Divorce is silly. I adore her and she adores me. I know. I honestly don't think she'll go through with it. I've been no crueler than any husband—words are all we've ever had."

To another reporter he said, "I've told her I'll do anything to preserve our marriage. This suit is idiotic because we both love each other. I asked her to call off the suit so I can go to a psychiatrist in the east whom I can talk to and who really knows about the mind. My temper is hooked up with the war, I think. It's one of those nasty things."

And to yet another reporter, "I believe everything may work out all right. I haven't talked to Bette personally but through her attorney. She has promised that she won't rush into court to get her decree. I am going to consult a psychiatrist—the whole trouble is due to my violent temper. But I adore Bette and I'd be miserable if anything happened to this marriage. In her letter, Bette said there was no hate in her heart for me but she just couldn't go on with the threat of our quarrels hanging over her. I don't blame her for not wanting to live with me. Actually her fear is that some day I will do her bodily harm. . . . Aside from loving her, I felt, when we married, that I could give her stability, and I think I did for a while. But I lost sight of my path. I want to get right back on that path. . . . I'm convinced that Bette and I can be happy together."

Bette would say in later years that Sherry had been too fond of the press.

Although divorce papers were not withdrawn, the couple attempted a reconciliation. In November they had lunch together at Lucey's Restaurant in Hollywood. Curiously, they invited the press to accompany them to document the occasion. Bette's condition for the reconciliation was that Sherry publicly acknowledge his temper and wrongdoing and see a psychiatrist, Dr. Frederick Hacker. Bette's attorney released the statement: "Miss Davis has agreed to postpone further action in her divorce suit in hope of solving her marriage difficulties. She and her husband have agreed to a trial reconciliation." Louella Parsons, who had earlier written that Sherry and Bette were all wrong for one another, changed her mind. "Personally," she said, "I am glad they have reconciled because she always seemed happy with him, and any man who was so contrite and told the world that the fault was 100 percent his is entitled to another chance."

During the making of *Payment on Demand* at RKO in early 1950, however, the rumor was that Bette was having an affair with her costar, Barry Sullivan. One night Sherry showed up at the studio and downed the actor in a one-punch brawl. Bette screamed and summoned the studio police. The following day, April 4, she reinstigated divorce proceedings.

Sherry tried to explain his actions by telling a reporter, "She hadn't told me she was going to a party. When she didn't come home to dinner I called the studio. Everyone else had left the party and there was no answer in her dressing room. . . . The studio gateman let me drive right in. She refused to go home. I was mad. I was jealous. She said I was a fool, that it was my imagination, that nothing happened. I blew my top. Any husband, any red-blooded man would have done the same. The next morning she didn't say anything. She left for work with our 3-year-old daughter, Barbara. I knew then that she wasn't coming back. I wish Bette would stop this nonsense and come back. But I'm afraid she's set on a divorce this time. I think she subconsciously resents me because I'm not working eight hours a day." When he told Bette that he just needed more affection, Sherry claimed that Bette snapped, "Go out and get a girl friend."

When Bette returned to Los Angeles from San Francisco after shooting *All About Eve*, she went into hiding. By then she had fallen in love with her costar Gary Merrill, who was also married at the time. She hid out in the homes of various friends while Sherry waited for her at their home in Laguna.

When Bette's lawyers informed Sherry that she wanted a divorce, he balked. Bette sold their Laguna Beach home as well as his studio apartment. She also closed their joint bank account. Sherry still refused to consent to a divorce. Years later he would claim that Bette had had the house he was living in bugged. He also claimed that Bette had planned to have two men swear that they had had sex with him, falsely claiming that he was homosexual.

On April 6, 1950, Sherry announced his plans to contest the divorce. "She is plenty at fault and I'm tired of being kicked around. She was the breadwinner and I was the housewife. And I've loved doing it. All I asked in return was love and affection. I'm a man who needs a lot of that. But when she'd come home from work she'd always say she was too tired. I wouldn't get as much as a kiss from her. She was too absorbed in her work. I'd always have dinner ready for her when she got home. I'd take off her shoes and bring her slippers and fix her a drink. I pressed her dresses when her maid wasn't there. I'd draw a bath and give her massages. I felt it was a privilege to do things for her. She'd say, 'Well, what do you want? You're adequately fed and clothed.' I didn't want money. I wanted love. But she hasn't time for a husband when she works."

On April 7, 1950, Sherry told another reporter, "My wife is a troubled, mixed-up girl. She has never been really happy. She is not alone in this. All artistic people have great problems. I tried to help her as much as I could, but I can't go any further alone. I am too close to her and I lack the knowledge. If she would join me in consulting my psychiatrist, Dr. Frederick Hacker, I am positive that our marital problems could be worked out. But whether she continues with me or not she ought to have treatment. If she does not, she will be a miserable woman all her life."

The subsequent divorce and child custody proceedings were ugly. They resulted in Bette's getting custody of B.D. and Sherry getting alimony—$250 a month for a minimum of four years.

Just over a week after Bette married Gary Merrill in July 1950, Sherry married Marian Richards, B.D.'s 22-year-old governess. Bette claimed that

Sherry had been having an affair with Richards all along. Sherry denied it. The newlywed couple moved to Paris and remained married for many years, having children and grandchildren of their own.

Years later, six months after B.D.'s 1964 marriage to Jeremy Hyman, Bette and Sherry had a reunion of sorts in B.D.'s New York apartment. According to Bette, Sherry apologized for his behavior during their marriage. She also noted that he was still attractive and had become a devout Jehovah's Witness.

SHINING VICTORY

In Irving Rapper's first picture (1941) as a director, the first scene to be shot called for an extra dressed in a nurse's uniform. To wish Rapper luck, Bette secretly donned the nurse's getup and appeared on the set and filmed the scene. At first Rapper did not recognize that the extra he was directing was Bette Davis.

KONSTANTIN SIMONOV

Russian novelist and playwright Simonov met Bette on the set of the 1946 picture *Deception*. He was visiting the United States and had wanted to meet Bette. The two developed an immediate rapport, and Simonov invited Bette to be a guest aboard his ship, a Soviet war vessel docked in Los Angeles Harbor. Bette accepted. Their friendship would make Bette suspect in the eyes of the FBI and various Communist-watchdog organizations.

SISTER

Barbara (Bobby) Davis, aka Barbara Pelgram, aka Barbara Berry

THE SISTERS ★★½

Warner Brothers
1938   98 minutes   bw
Directed by: Anatole Litvak
Produced by: Hal B. Wallis, in association with David Lewis
Screenplay by: Milton Krims, based on the novel by Myron Brinig
Cinematography by: Tony Gaudio
Cast: Errol Flynn, Bette Davis, Anita Louise, Ian Hunter, Donald Crisp, Beulah Bondi, Jane Bryan, Alan Hale, Dick Foran, Henry Travers, Patric Knowles, Lee Patrick, Laura Hope Crews, Janet Shaw, Harry Davenport, Ruth Garland, Rosella Towne, Irving Bacon, Mayo Methot, John Warburton, Paul Harvey, Arthur Hoyt

Warners purchased *The Sisters* for $25,000 in an agreement dated March 18, 1937. The story is set in the mining town of Silver Bow, Montana, beginning in 1904, and features the lives of Louise, Helen, and Grace Elliott. Louise marries a reporter, Frank Medlin, after knowing him for one week. Medlin disappears on a tramp steamer, leaving her in San Francisco to suffer the ravages of the infamous earthquake alone.

Hal Wallis initially wanted Irene Dunne in the leading role of Louise. After her considerable success in *Jezebel*, however, Wallis switched his sights to Bette.

Bette surviving the San Francisco earthquake.

In April 1938 there was considerable interest in landing Fredric March for the part of Frank Medlin. March responded in writing that "[Frank] is not particularly an interesting character, principally because he is so frightfully weak and sorry for himself throughout. I can see how they might consider me for the part as he is similar in some respects to *A Star Is Born*, but without any of the charm of the latter."

As for the director, Warner initially wanted William Dieterle, but Dieterle demurred, and Warner instructed Hal Wallis that if Dieterle did not direct the picture he was to be promptly laid off.

Whether Bette would accept the part was also in doubt. After her success in *Jezebel* she had turned down several films she had been assigned and was consequently suspended. She returned for *The Sisters* in part because she couldn't afford to keep going without income and it was the best thing that Warner had offered her.

On May 2, 1938, with Bette set, Wallis requested that a test be made of Bette opposite the then-unknown John Garfield. By then William Dieterle had been replaced by Anatole Litvak, who shot the tests. On May 5, 1938, Garfield tested with Bette. He would be cast in the picture, but not as Frank. A few days into the shooting he was fired because of his Bronx accent. He was replaced by Dick Foran. Garfield said later, "When I heard who was doing the part—Dick Foran, for God's sake—I knew I was the flop of the year."

Others who tested for the part of Frank Medlin were George Brent and Jeffrey Lynn. On May 6 Hal Wallis pursued Franchot Tone for the part.

Meanwhile Litvak worked on the script, which had been penned by

Milton Krims with an uncredited assist from Julius J. Epstein. Epstein had some problem writing the initial script because he felt there was so much good material in the book and he didn't want to lose any of it. Subsequently an early draft was expected to run to 350 pages. This version told in full the stories for all three sisters featured in the novel. Ultimately only Louise would be featured, with the stories of the other two sisters merely incidental.

Errol Flynn was finally cast as Frank Medlin, a choice Bette instantly protested. First of all, it would be Flynn's first experience with a straight dramatic role. Even Flynn was leery, joking on the set, "What am I going to do without my sword, my pistol, my lance, my bow and arrow? I don't know but I guess I might as well find out right now."

Second, Jack Warner wanted to bill Flynn *alone* above the title. Bette later recalled, "They were not going to give my name above the title. It was going to read, 'Errol Flynn in *The Sisters*.' *Well!* I went up to Mr. Warner and I said, 'That'll be the dirtiest ad you ever saw in your entire life. You cannot do this.' And Flynn was, at that time, bigger box office than I. So they put both our names, 'Errol Flynn and Bette Davis in *The Sisters*.' But that would have been pretty funny—with his reputation and everything. Everybody would have picked up on it, I'm sure."

With a budget of $781,000, and after much research was done to capture the period, 1904–1910, *The Sisters* started shooting without Bette on Monday, June 6, 1938. Bette started shooting the following day, and Flynn joined the company on June 10.

Bette was putting in good 10- and 12-hour workdays. Flynn, meanwhile, was working approximately five hours a day. On Saturday, June 25, Bette worked a 14-hour day, from 9:00 A.M. to 1:00 A.M., while Flynn reported at 9:00 A.M. and left at 2:00 P.M. By the end of her long day Bette had begun losing her voice. On Monday, June 27, her voice was gone altogether, and she did not report back to work until Wednesday, July 6.

During Bette's illness Anita Louise, cast as "the beautiful sister," also reported sick, really cramping the shooting schedule. She reported back on Tuesday, July 5.

When Bette returned, there was a good deal of concern about matching her voice to scenes already shot since she was still suffering from a slight case of laryngitis. Bette's voice continued to be problematic, and on Saturday, July 9, she did not report to work.

Naturally Anita Louise resumed her illness as well, telling unit manager Jack Sullivan that prior to the start of shooting she had suffered a case of acute appendicitis and she feared that she was suffering a relapse. Sullivan noted in his daily report to his superiors that he didn't know if she was sick or if she was engaging in too much of a social life.

Bette reported back to work on Tuesday, July 12, with the picture five days behind. Upon her return Bette presented Litvak with a note from her doctor with instructions that she was to work *half*-days only. This would last for five days. Meanwhile, with Bette's return Anita Louise also reappeared.

On July 13 Warner wrote a letter to Litvak: "Again you insist on doing just the opposite that common sense and good business dictate. In yesterday's work you had 10 takes of one scene. There was a full take on the 3rd try, which you held, the 5th take was held, and you finally printed the 10th take." Warner went on to inform Litvak that he was having the third take printed just to prove that Litvak's subsequent seven takes were unnecessary and superfluous and costly.

Shooting was also slowed by the continuous procession of visitors curious about the Flynn/Davis pairing and Flynn's first dramatic venture. As a result Flynn was frequently nervous and continually blew his lines, requiring numerous takes. Instructions were eventually sent down from Warner himself that only "extremely important" newspaper people were to be allowed on the set.

After she suffered through the miseries of the earthquake sequence, Errol Flynn approached Bette to congratulate her on her success at portraying fear. "Hell's bells," Bette retorted. "If you think I was acting, you're plain crazy. Feel my heart—it's up to here!" said Bette, grasping her throat. "Someone get me a glass of water, quick! I've got to get my heart back where it belongs." Miraculously, the actual earthquake sequence was shot in a single take. Despite publicity claims that they "hit it off immediately, became close friends, and played their many tender love scenes with conviction and warmth," Flynn and Davis only tolerated one another. Bette in particular disdained Flynn's acting ability.

Then there was the problem of Bette's appearance. On July 29 Wallis memoed Litvak that the circles under Bette's eyes were becoming more pronounced as the shooting progressed. Wallis was particularly displeased with her appearance in the balcony scene with Donald Crisp. Wallis instructed Litvak to have Gaudio take extra care to light Bette.

Errol Flynn finished the picture on Tuesday, August 2. On Friday, August 5, Bette worked from 9:00 A.M. to 3:45 A.M., when the picture finally finished shooting, 15 days behind schedule.

"Warner Brothers present the Most Exciting Star Combination of a Decade," hyped the ads for the movie. And "She Lost Her Heart to a Man Who Had Lost His Soul." And "He Wants Love . . . And His Freedom Too! She Asks for Nothing But His Unrequited Adoration!" Photos of Flynn caressing Bette were accompanied by the caption "The First Touch . . . The First Kiss . . . The First Time in Each Other's Arms."

Upon its release the film and Bette received fairly good reviews. Many critics, however, singled out Errol Flynn's performance as a flaw.

BERT SIX
Warner Brothers still photographer on numerous Bette Davis pictures, from the 1935 picture *Dangerous* to the 1964 picture *Dead Ringer*.

"60 MINUTES"
Bette and her children, Michael Merrill and B. D. Hyman, were interviewed

by Mike Wallace on the January 2, 1980, edition of the popular CBS television series "60 Minutes."

SIDNEY SKOLSKY

Popular Hollywood columnist who reported in January 1935, "Bette Davis is winning recognition as a fine actress by playing mean, despicable women who haven't one redeeming quality."

"SKYWARD"

When Bette learned that her director on the 1980 telefilm was Ron Howard, Opie on "The Andy Griffith Show," she panicked. By the time shooting started, she was wary at best. On the first day of shooting Howard called her "Miss Davis." She responded by calling her director, then 26, "Mr. Howard." "Please call me Ron," he told her. Bette slightly stunned Howard by then proclaiming, "I'll call you 'Mr. Howard' until I decide whether I like you or not." At the end of the first day of shooting Bette told her director, "Good night, *Ron*."

"Skyward" was shot on location in the 100-degree heat of Dallas, Texas, in July 1980. "One day while working at the Rockwall airport outside Dallas, where we shot most of the Bette Davis scenes," executive producer Anson Williams told a reporter for *The Hollywood Reporter*, "we measured the heat and it was 121 degrees off the surface, from the tar to the knees. And 117 degrees elsewhere. She never whimpered. I don't know how she did it; she was in that constant heat for two weeks, all day, every day. Sure, I was surprised. You know, you hear stories. I mean, here it is, the first film you produce and a *legend* is coming to your set, and the whole area is so hot it's practically declared a disaster area. But in about two minutes, you know *why* she's a legend, and why she's still in demand as an actress."

"Skyward" was produced by Major H/Anson Productions for NBC

television. Howard and Williams were executive producers, and the producer was John A. Kuri (who also did the aerial photography). The teleplay was written by Nancy Sackett, from a story by Williams. It was shot by Robert Jessup. The story cast Bette as an airline pilot who teaches a teenage paraplegic (Suzy Gilstrap) how to fly. The cast also included Howard Hesseman, Marion Ross, Clu Gulager, Ben Marley, Lisa Whelchel, Jana Hall, Mark Wheeler, Jessie Lee Fulton, Rance Howard, Clint Howard, Cheryl Howard, and Kate Finlayson.

SO BIG ★★
Warner Brothers
1932 80 minutes bw
Directed by: William A. Wellman
Produced by: Lucien Hubbard
Screenplay by: J. Grubb Alexander and Robert Lord, based on the novel by
    Edna Ferber
Cinematography by: Sid Hickox
Cast: Barbara Stanwyck, Dickie Moore, Bette Davis, Hardie Albright,
    George Brent, Guy Kibbee, Mae Madison, Robert Warwick, Arthur
    Stone, Earl Foxe, Alan Hale, Dorothy Peterson, Dawn O'Day, Dick
    Winslow, Elizabeth Patterson, Rita LeRoy, Blanche Friderici, Lionel
    Bellmore

A remake of the 1925 silent film starring Colleen Moore, *So Big* cast Bette as Dallas O'Mara, a young artist who falls in love with Dirk (Dickie Moore).

So Big started shooting on January 11, 1932, although Bette didn't start until January 23, 1932. She finished with the picture on February 3, 1932.

Interesting note: Still new to the studio, Bette is referred to in the production files as "Betty Davis."

So Big was remade in 1953 with Jane Wyman.

SOLID SOUTH
In the fall of 1930 Bette was touring with the road company of *Broken Dishes* when she was summoned back to New York to costar in *Solid South*, a Broadway play by Lawton Campbell. The play, a comedy, cast Bette as Alabama Follensby, granddaughter of Richard Bennett's Major Follensby. Also in the cast were Elizabeth Patterson, Jessie Royce Landis, Moffat Johnson, Georgette Harvey, Owen Davis, Jr. (as Bette's beau), Richard Huey, and Lou Payton. The play was produced by Alexander McKaig and directed by Rouben Mamoulian.

It was while in *Solid South* that Bette was spotted by a Universal talent agent, which resulted in a screen test and a movie contract. *Solid South* received mixed reviews and played 31 performances in 1930 at the Lyceum Theatre.

SONGS SUNG BY BETTE
The following is a selective list.

At Cushing Academy
"Gee, I'm Mighty Blue for You"

As a Member of the Cape Players
"I Passed by Your Window" from *Mr. Pim Passes By*

On Broadway in *Two's Company*
"Good Little Girls"
"Just Like a Man"
"Just Turn Me Loose on Broadway"
"Loathsome Party"
"Purple Rose"
"Roll Along Sadie"

In *Miss Moffat*
"A Wonderful Game Called Reading"
"How Lucky I was to Get Out of the South"
"The Words Unspoken are the Ones that Matter"
"I Shall Experience It Again"

In Her Movies
"Willie the Weeper," *Cabin in the Cotton*
"The Moon Is in Tears Tonight," *Kid Galahad* (lip-synched)
"They're Either Too Young or Too Old," *Thank Your Lucky Stars*
"I've Written a Letter to Daddy," *What Ever Happened to Baby Jane?*
"Shuffle Off to Buffalo," *Dead Ringer*
"Hush . . . Hush, Sweet Charlotte," *Hush . . . Hush, Sweet Charlotte*
"Rock of Ages," *The Anniversary*

On Television
"Just Turn Me Loose on Broadway," "The Andy Williams Show"
"What Ever Happened to Baby Jane?," "The Andy Williams Show"
Medley: "Michael Row the Boat Ashore"/"I Didn't Know She Swallowed a Fly"/"Raise a
      Ruckus Tonight," "The Andy Williams Show"
"Just Like a Man," "Johnny Carson Presents the Sun City Scandals '72"
"Single," "The Hollywood Palace"

In Personal Appearances
To promote the 1962 picture *What Ever Happened to Baby Jane?*, Bette went
on a personal appearance tour during which she would frequently sing "I've
Written a Letter to Daddy," sometimes accompanied by her daughter, B.D.

Songs: Bette and Ham Nelson—"Their" Songs
"Always"
"I Can't Tell You Why I Love You, But I Do"
"Moonlight and Roses"

Songs About Bette:
"Bette Davis Eyes" by Kim Carnes

Songs That Mention Bette:
"Vogue" by Madonna

SPECIAL AGENT ★★
Warner Brothers
1935   74 minutes   bw
Directed by: William Keighley
Produced by: Samuel Bischoff
Screenplay by: Laird Doyle and Abem Finkel, from a story by Martin
     Mooney
Cinematography by: Sid Hickox
Cast: Bette Davis, George Brent, Ricardo Cortez, Jack LaRue, Henry
     O'Neill, Robert Strange, Joseph Crehan, J. Carroll Naish, Joseph
     Sawyer, William B. Davidson, Robert Barrat, Paul Guilfoyle, Irving
     Pichel, Douglas Wood, James Flavin, Lee Phelps, Louis Natheaux,
     Herbert Skinner, John Alexander

Special Agent was purchased on May 23, 1934, from Martin Mooney for
$1,500. Mooney's story had been published in the *Saturday Evening Post*.

Hal Wallis initially suggested that the story be a vehicle for Paul Muni
or Edward G. Robinson. As for Bette, cast as Julie Gardner, personal secretary to a gangster, Keighley was quoted as saying, "If Julie were intended to
be a girl whom the audience hates, we should never have given Bette Davis
the role. It is impossible to hate Bette Davis." Keighley, of course, missed his
mark by a long shot on that one.

There were a few problems with the script. The picture was designed to
repeat the success of the earlier *G Men*, and it was shot with the cooperation
of the U.S. Department of Justice. But it was expected to start on May 20,
1935, and ended up postponed because of script problems until May 27, then
June 17. It was allotted only 21 days for shooting and an estimated budget of
$197,000.

Bette finished work on July 10, 1934; the picture finished three days
behind schedule on the following day. Bette returned for retakes on July 25,
26, and 27.

Even though during production Ricardo Cortez was the star of the
picture, thanks to Bette's success in *Of Human Bondage* and *Bordertown*, it
was billed upon release as "Bette Davis in *Special Agent*."

Special Agent was remade in 1940 as *Gambling on the High Seas* with
Jane Wyman in the Davis part.

STAND-INS
Bette's principal stand-in during her halcyon years at Warner Brothers was
Sally Sage. Others, listed alphabetically, include

Phyllis Clark
Sue Curtis
Edna Mae Jones
Jannell Lynn

BARBARA STANWYCK

Stanwyck starred in *So Big*, a 1932 Warners picture in which unknown Bette had a supporting role. Ironically, Bette's first starring vehicle, *Ex-Lady* (1933), was a remake of Stanwyck's *Illicit*, made only two years before. Interesting also is that despite the fact that she was a "star" before Bette came along, Stanwyck was considered by some to be "the next Bette Davis" in the 1940s.

In 1939, before the release of *Gone With the Wind*, when critics were hailing Bette as the likely Oscar winner for *Dark Victory*, Bette generously forecast, "I should say that Margaret Sullavan and Barbara Stanwyck [for their performances in *The Shop Around the Corner* and *Golden Boy*, respectively] could very easily win the top award this year, or any year. Both of them are unusually expert. They are so absolutely real and unaffected. There are no artificialities to their performances. They are, to me, grand examples of the new order in Hollywood." When the nominations were announced, however, neither Sullavan nor Stanwyck had joined Bette on the list of contenders.

Also of interest, both *Another Man's Poison* (1952) and *Storm Center* (1956) were offered to Stanwyck before being played by Bette. The two actresses had the opportunity to work together in the 1964 picture *Hush . . . Hush, Sweet Charlotte*. Stanwyck was asked to replace the "ailing" Joan Crawford and declined.

Barbara Stanwyck, born Ruby Stevens in 1907, appeared in numerous other pictures, including *Stella Dallas* (1937), *The Lady Eve* (1941), *Ball of Fire* (1941), *Double Indemnity* (1944), *Hollywood Canteen* (1944), *The Strange Love of Martha Ivers* (1946), and *Sorry, Wrong Number* (1948).

THE STAR ★★½

Bert E. Friedlob Productions
Released by 20th Century–Fox
1952   91 minutes   bw
Directed by: Stuart Heisler
Produced by: Bert E. Friedlob
Screenplay by: Katherine Albert and Dale Eunson
Cinematography by: Ernest Laszlo
Cast: Bette Davis, Sterling Hayden, Natalie Wood, Warner Anderson,
    Minor Watson, June Travis, Fay Baker, David Alpert, Barbara
    Lawrence, Katherine Warren, Kay Riehl, Barbara Woodel, Paul Frees

Katherine Albert and Dale Eunson's original screenplay *The Star*, about Margaret Elliott, a faded movie star who is reduced to auctioning off her personal possessions and working as a department store salesclerk, was modeled in part on their friend Joan Crawford. Upon the film's release Crawford reportedly terminated the friendship.

Shot cheaply in Hollywood and San Pedro, California, on a 24-day schedule, *The Star* was originally intended as a vehicle for Lucille Ball.

However, the studios were not interested in Lucy at the time, so it was offered to Bette, still basking in the glory of *All About Eve*. As for the schedule, Bette shrugged it off. "There's no sense dragging pictures on forever. The tighter the shooting schedules get the better the picture is apt to be. This way, everyone has to know his job. It's a challenge and it's good for everybody. It keeps you up. . . . This story is the most realistic story I have ever read about Hollywood. . . . [a] story that only those who have lived and worked here really understand."

The Star was marketed with the ad "The Orchids, the Furs, the Diamonds That Were the Star's Were All Gone Now . . . and Nothing Remained . . . But the Woman!" and "Only the Star of Stars Could Accept the Challenge of Such a Role . . . the Greatest Triumph of the Twice Winner of the Academy Award."

Reviews for *The Star* were mixed, but Bette would receive a Best Actress Oscar nomination for her performance. She was greatly disappointed in the critical and box office reception accorded the picture, hoping that it would one day be recognized as "the damned good movie" it was, in her judgment. In recent years *The Star has* been rediscovered by movie audiences, but primarily for its camp quality.

MAX STEINER

Legendary film composer Max Steiner scored numerous Bette Davis pictures, including *Way Back Home* (uncredited, 1932), *Of Human Bondage* (uncredited, 1934), *That Certain Woman* (1937), *Jezebel* (1938), *Dark Victory* (1939), *The Old Maid* (1939), *All This, and Heaven Too* (1940), *The Letter* (1940), *The Great Lie* (1941), *The Bride Came C.O.D.* (1941), *In This Our Life* (1942), *Now, Voyager* (1942), *Watch on the Rhine* (1943), *The Corn Is Green* (1945), *A Stolen Life* (1946), *Winter Meeting* (1948), *Beyond the Forest* (1949), and *John Paul Jones* (1959).

Max Steiner (1888–1971) composed other scores, including those for *The Informer* (Oscar winner, 1935), *Gone With the Wind* (1939), *Casablanca*

(1943), *Since You Went Away* (Oscar winner, 1944), and *The Treasure of the Sierra Madre* (1947).

STEPFATHERS
Robert Palmer
Otho W. Budd

JAMES STEWART
Despite performing "June Bride" together on a 1949 radio broadcast, James Stewart and Bette Davis never worked together on screen until they costarred in the 1983 telefilm "Right of Way." For Bette it was worth the wait. She lamented, however, that she hadn't met him earlier. "I'd have given anything to have met when we were younger," she said at age 74. "He didn't marry until late, 41, I think; if we had worked together before that I'd have *leapt* at him. First of all, I would have liked him because he is a very nice man. Then, he is also a wonderful actor."

James Stewart, born in 1908, starred in numerous pictures, including *You Can't Take It With You* (1938), *Mr. Smith Goes to Washington* (1939), *The Philadelphia Story* (Best Actor Oscar winner, 1940), *It's a Wonderful Life* (1946), *Rear Window* (1954), *Vertigo* (1958), and *Anatomy of a Murder* (1959).

WHITNEY STINE
Stine was the author of the excellent 1974 biography *Mother Goddam*, on which Bette collaborated. At one point during their friendship Bette, according to Stine, 22 years her junior, suggested that they get married. It was a proposition Stine says he declined. Stine later authored a subsequent book about Bette, *I'd Love to Kiss You . . .*, which was published after both of their deaths in 1989.

ELSA STOKES
For three years Elsa Stokes was governess to Margot and Michael Merrill at Bette and Gary's home in Maine. She was variably called "Stokesy" and "Coksie" by the Merrill family. Gary would later say of her, "She gave Michael much of the mothering of which he was deprived."

A STOLEN LIFE ★★
Warner Brothers/B. D. Productions
1946   107 minutes   bw
Directed by: Curtis Bernhardt
Produced by: Bette Davis
Screenplay by: Catherine Turney, adapted by Margaret Buell Wilder, from a
    novel by Karel J. Benes
Cinematography by: Sol Polito
Cast: Bette Davis, Glenn Ford, Dane Clark, Walter Brennan, Charlie
    Ruggles, Peggy Knudsen, Esther Dale, Clara Blandick, Bruce Bennett,
    Joan Winfield

Based on the book *Uloupeny Zivot* by Karel J. Benes, *A Stolen Life* was purchased by Warner Brothers for $45,000. It had been previously made in England with Elisabeth Bergner as star. This time out the setting was changed from the south of France to an island off the coast of Massachusetts. The title would undergo a series of changes: *Stormy Point* to *Stolen Life* to *A Stolen Life*. Bette had wanted the title of *Pamela and I*, but she was outnumbered.

The picture launched Bette's new career as producer, under her banner "B. D. Inc." The company was entitled to 35 percent of the gross receipts remaining after various payments were made. Assisting Bette in her producing duties were Jack Chertok and the film's director, Curtis Bernhardt. Despite the promise her new career held at the time, *A Stolen Life* would be the one and only picture made by B. D. Inc.

Specified in Bette's new contract with Warners was that the name of her company appear on the screen. However, Bette made the mistake of giving Warners the right to decide the size and position of the screen credit. Consequently "A B.D. Inc., Production" *did* show up on the screen, but it showed up so that it could barely be read—at 5 percent of the size of the title of the film.

If the truth were to be told, Bette had a ball searching for a leading man. Publicly she moaned, "I had no idea that casting of a picture could be so difficult. We could take an unknown for the role, but I had the idea that I'd like to have for a change a man with some stature at the box office."

As publicity would have it, Bette conducted a nationwide search for her leading man. She *did* nix Dennis Morgan. And she did cast Robert Alda in the role, but he was abruptly replaced by Glenn Ford. Ford, fresh out of the Marines, was signed to Columbia. To get him Warners had to pay Columbia *twice* Ford's usual salary. Further, to do the film Ford had to grant Columbia an extension on his contract. Columbia wanted an additional three years; it eventually settled for one year and eight months. As for Ford's salary, he was getting only $450 a week at Columbia at the time, so Warners had to pay $900. However, in the last weeks of shooting Columbia would raise Ford's salary to $1,000 a week, thus forcing Warners to double his salary accordingly to $2,000 a week. That mattered little, though, compared to the $2,500 a week Warners would dish out for Walter Brennan in what was virtually a nothing role. But Bette wanted Brennan, and it was Brennan she got.

The picture was designed with the intention of making Bette wear pretty clothes and look as attractive as possible "for a change." As producer she certainly had a hand in selecting her costumes and the costumes for Ford. Bette was quoted at the time as saying, "These Hollywood men with shoulders out to here and those pulled-in waists! Everything so fancy as though the man thought about his clothes all day. A real guy buys a suit that fits him, if he can, then forgets about clothes." She added, in an attempt at diplomacy, "As producer I do have something to say about story, about choice of director and casting. But mostly now I defer to my director, Curt Bernhardt. We're kind of partners—we work together."

Bette was to play the dual roles of Kate and Pat Bosworth. When Bette was Kate, she played to one of her "acting doubles" on the picture, Sally Sage as Pat. When Bette was Pat, she played to her other acting double, Elizabeth Wright as Kate. Kate was the good sister, Pat the bad sister. Fifteen years after her motion picture debut in *Bad Sister*, Bette was getting to play not only the good sister but the bad one as well. Kate begins a tentative romance with Bill Emerson (Glenn Ford), who is then lured away and into marriage by sister Pat. Later Kate and Pat go on a boating expedition that ends in Pat's accidental death. Kate, sensing the opportunity, assumes the role of Pat, aka Mrs. Bill Emerson.

Shooting began with the second unit, under the direction of Roy Davidson, doing some location work in Balboa, California. Then Bette and company traveled to Laguna Beach on Tuesday, February 13. Production started the following day. Bette allotted her film an ample 72 shooting days. It was thought and hoped by the Warners front office that with Bette now producing her own pictures production would move more rapidly. She was, after all, in a sense, spending her own money. Such, however, would not be the case.

On Saturday, March 3, Bette called in sick and the company shut down. On Monday, Bette was still sick. Glenn Ford also phoned in sick. The company shut down and did not resume shooting until more than two *weeks* later, on Monday, March 19, 1945.

Then, on April 10, production again shut down because Bette's face suffered some sort of outbreak of acne. The following day the company did some postrecording dialogue because Bette's face had not yet recovered. That Saturday, April 14, 1945, the entire Warners lot shut down in observance of a national day of mourning for President Franklin Roosevelt.

Production was inexplicably suspended on Friday, May 18. It resumed on Monday, and the company then went on location to the Long Beach Airport on May 23 and 24. Meanwhile, Glenn Ford missed five days of work in May because of a nasty boil that popped up on his left cheek.

Reportedly he was also having some trouble with his leading lady. Allegedly during the making of the picture Bette made amorous advances toward Ford, who declined them. Ford at the time was married to dancer Eleanor Powell, who had just given birth to their son, Peter. Ford's rebuff of Bette caused considerable tension between the two of them.

All of these delays caused problems for Warner and for Ford, who had been given only 10 weeks off from Columbia to make the picture. Columbia was impatiently waiting for him to return so that he could start a new picture, *Gilda*, with Rita Hayworth. That film, of course, would make a huge star out of Hayworth and a leading man out of Ford.

On Saturday, May 26, Sol Polito was abruptly and inexplicably replaced on the film. It is not known why, but Polito never worked on another Bette Davis picture. What is known is that he was replaced with Bette's favorite cameraman, Ernie Haller. Interestingly, though, despite the considerable work he would do on the picture, Haller would not be listed in the film's credits—only the name of Polito appeared on the screen.

After another brief illness Bette resumed shooting her picture, and on Sunday, June 17, Bette, Ford, Curtis Bernhardt, and Ernie Haller drove to Monterey, California, to scout a location. They were joined the following day by the rest of the company, and on Tuesday, June 19, the company returned before the cameras at the Monterey location. They traveled back to the studio on Saturday, June 23.

Bette was sick again on Saturday, June 30. She returned to work on Thursday, July 5. The following day she left work early, and shooting was suspended. She did not return until Monday, July 16. However, typical of the way the production was proceeding, no work was done that day either because Bernhardt was sick. He reported back to work the following day, and shooting finally resumed. Glenn Ford finished working and returned to Columbia, gratefully, on Saturday, July 21. The production officially wrapped the following week, on July 28. It closed after 105 shooting days, 33 days behind schedule.

After viewing the assembled footage, Bette decided that several days of retakes were necessary to complete the film. But Ford was back at Columbia shooting *Gilda* and was unavailable. Then, when he *did* become available, his appearance was unacceptable to Bette. It seems that while doing *Gilda* Ford had been given a haircut so the length of his hair did not match the length in *A Stolen Life*. Bette opted to wait until his hair grew back out, so it was not until Friday, January 18, 1946, that retakes for *A Stolen Life* commenced. They were completed on Wednesday, January 23.

Bette would later acknowledge that Bernhardt had done a good job with at least one aspect of the film. The critics agreed. Bernhardt's execution of the dual-shot scenes (in which both sisters appeared in the same shot), his use of photographic trickery and split screen, were expertly handled and advanced for the day.

In her humbler moments Bette would later acknowledge that she had been producer in name only. Curt Bernhardt agreed. "Despite what she claims in her autobiography," he said, "she did *not* produce the picture."

A Stolen Life was marketed, in a campaign overseen by Bette, with "Bette Davis Is Doubly Wonderful in Her Double Role!" and " 'You May Be My Sister, But You're Not My Kind,' Says Bette Davis to Bette Davis in Her Sensational Double Role!"

STORM CENTER ★★½

Phoenix Productions
Released by Columbia Pictures
1956   87 minutes   bw
Directed by: Daniel Taradash
Produced by: Julian Blaustein
Screenplay by: Daniel Taradash and Elick Moll
Cinematography by: Burnett Guffey
Cast: Bette Davis, Brian Keith, Kim Hunter, Paul Kelly, Joe Mantell, Sallie
    Brophy, Kevin Coughlin, Howard Wierum, Curtis Cooksey, Michael
    Raffetto, Edward Platt, Kathryn Grant, Howard Wendell, Burt Mustin,
    Edith Evanson

Storm Center was written in 1950 by Daniel Taradash and Elick Moll. Originally it was intended for Mary Pickford, with Stanley Kramer producing. Pickford, then 58, was to be paid $50,000 and a percentage of the profits to come out of retirement. Because she wanted to make a comeback á la Gloria Swanson in *Sunset Boulevard,* she agreed. However, she backed out of the picture, then being called *Circle of Fire,* in September 1952. "Since the decision not to make *Circle of Fire* in Technicolor, I have been very unhappy and very much disturbed," said Pickford. "I do feel that after this long absence from the screen my return should be in a Technicolor production."

After Pickford's exit Kramer signed Barbara Stanwyck. Start on the picture was delayed, however, to accommodate the finish of her picture *Titanic.* Stanwyck would start work on December 15, 1952, and then segue directly into *Stopover* also for Kramer. Then Kramer announced that he was going to shelve *Circle* temporarily so that they could do *Stopover* first. After some dispute, Kramer dissolved his relationship with the studio, and Columbia acquired ownership of the picture in full.

Circle of Fire remained shelved until Taradash's success with *From Here to Eternity* (1953). Apparently studio honcho Harry Cohn gave him free rein to do what he wanted, and what he wanted to do was *Storm Center.* Producer Julian Blaustein, who had been a classmate of Taradash's at Harvard in 1929, approached Bette with the part. "I won't be disappointed if you turn it down," he told her. "I will just kill you, literally." Bette sent him a letter in response, which opened with "Dear Mr. Bossman." She proceeded to tell him that a lynching was unnecessary; she would accept the part. The picture would have Bette playing librarian Alicia Hull, who says things like "I have no intention of leaving. I'm going to stay here, and I'm going to help rebuild the library. And if anybody ever again tries to remove a book from it, he'll have to do it over my dead body!"

Given its controversial subject of book burning, the picture was considered quite a gamble for Columbia and for Taradash and Blaustein. As the latter related to the *New York Times*, "We're a fine pair of businessmen. In exchange for Columbia absorbing all the costs against *The Library* [which it was then being called] and giving it to us for a fresh start, we've agreed to make it for nothing. We'll wait for our share until the profits come in."

Variety reported on August 8, 1956, "It's an open secret that some Columbia exec sentiment in N.Y. is against making *The Library*, presumably because of reservations about the box office potential of a pic dealing with a hot issue. Harry Cohn, Columbia president, though, is high on the project. For one thing, he's been impressed with Taradash's and Blaustein's willingness to produce the film, with Taradash to direct, without salary or guarantee of any payoff. It's to be a straight 50-50 profits plus split between Columbia and the Phoenix unit."

As for its controversial subject, which some felt promoted pro-Communist sentiment, Taradash argued, "I think this is more of an *anti*-Communist picture than the usual variety of melodramas about spies and little men. . . . We're telling Russia we can read a book designed to be inimical to democracy and yet not to be damaged by it because we are stronger than Russia." Blaustein added, "Our picture *is* a dangerous picture. It was considered dangerous when it was first written five years ago. Dan Taradash was told it could not get an audience and I'm not prepared to say such a view was wrong at the time. Now, I believe the public is ready for it. I believe it will get a hearing."

With a budget of $750,000, the picture finally started shooting in September 1956 in Santa Rosa, California.

Before its release, there was some debate over the title. Daniel Taradash asked William Wyler his opinion. "Yes, *The Library* is a possible title," replied Wyler with characteristically venomous wit, "or you could put up on the marquee instead, 'Theatre Closed.' The effect would be the same."

Under the title *Storm Center*, and with an ill-advised campaign ("What Book Did They Make Her Burn?"), the movie opened and closed with very few people seeing it. One of the reasons for its premature demise was that the Catholic Legion of Decency deemed it "propagandistic."

"STRANGERS: THE STORY OF A MOTHER AND DAUGHTER"

Producers Bob Christiansen and Rick Rosenberg approached Bette while the script by Michael DeGuzman was in the early stages of development. They

would go back and forth with Bette over the next two years, tailoring the script to her specifications. Bette also had casting approval of her costar. She wanted Jane Fonda or Cloris Leachman. When she couldn't get either, she agreed on Gena Rowlands.

The story of "Strangers" deals with a daughter who tries to regain the love of her mother after many years of separation. Finally the daughter reveals to her mother that she is dying of cancer.

Rowlands was thrilled to be working with Bette, who had inspired her desire to act. Upon completing the picture she said, "I've never worked with anyone I admired more. And the thing that surprised me—amazed me really is how *modern* she is. I knew she's a marvelous actress—we all know that— but I expected her to be somewhat old-fashioned. . . . She has leaped through the decades, and in every one of those decades she's influenced women so much."

The telefilm was shot at Culver City Studios and on location in Mendocino, California. In the movie Mendocino substituted for Rhode Island. The problem was that it was also supposed to take place during the warmth of summer. In fact, however, the temperature during shooting was often a chilly 20 degrees. As Rowlands related, "It was actually so cold at times we'd blow little steam puffs when we'd talk. There's also a cemetery scene where I carry a little bouquet of summer flowers, and I think if you really look closely you can see my fingers were actually *blue* at the time."

Another problem emerged in preproduction. Both Bette and Rowlands were incessant smokers. However, it was thought that both women smoking on camera might look awkward, with both of them blowing smoke at each other. Surprisingly, it was Bette who gave up her cigarettes. She felt that, given the characters, the daughter would be the more likely to smoke.

Upon its airing in 1979 "Strangers: The Story of a Mother and Daughter" was accorded highly favorable reviews. Bette would go on to win a Best Actress Emmy award for her performance. Still, she is sometimes awkward in the telefilm, overplaying scenes that should have been simple and quiet. But in scenes that require power she delivers spectacularly, particularly in the scene in which she has just learned of her daughter's imminent death.

"Strangers: The Story of a Mother and Daughter" was directed by Milton Katselas and shot by James Crabe. The cast also included Ford Rainey, Donald Moffat, Whit Bissell, Royal Dano, Kate Riehl, Krishan Timerblake, Renee McDonell, and Sally Kemp.

THE STROKE

On July 9, 1983, just nine days after undergoing a mastectomy, Bette suffered a stroke at New York Hospital. Actually it was a series of strokes. Initially she was unable to move. The muscles in her arms, legs, and the right side of her face were paralyzed. She later reflected, "Of all human afflictions, a stroke is about the worst. I would not wish it on Adolf Hitler!"

Bette underwent weeks of physical therapy. "The doctors didn't think I would make it," she recalled with the pleasure that comes from proving the "experts" wrong. "I did not move one muscle in five days. Then one day Kath [Sermak] saw my toe move. With her support, I learned to walk again. I would slap my wrists and make my hand form the correct shape. I'd say to it, 'C'mon, you fool!' "

THE STUBBORN WOOD

In the mid-1950s Bette personally purchased the film rights to *The Stubborn Wood*, a novel by Emily Harvin about a woman in a mental institution. Paul Henreid was to direct from a screenplay by Robert Bassing. Bette, however, never found financing for it.

THE STUDIO SYSTEM

Bette would say in her later years that the "old" Hollywood had one major advantage over the "new" Hollywood, and that was the studio system in which stars were contracted to the studios through weekly salaries. The primary advantage of this, in Bette's view, was that the studios put actors in one picture after another, perhaps six or more in one year, so that they could be discovered by an audience.

She was not, however, always a proponent of the system. In fact, in 1946 she complained that the studio system limited an actor's options on material. She also accused the studios of miscasting actors simply because they happened to be on the company payroll—instead of selecting the right actor for the part even if he or she belonged to another studio. "With a stable of stars under contract," Bette said, explaining her view, "studios like to keep them busy. You can't blame them. But whether or not the stars fit the roles, they're likely to be shoved into them. This is bad for the actor, bad for the picture,

bad for the audience—which, after all, is the final payoff. If stars and producers had a free hand in picking their casts and parts, you'd see fewer actors floundering around in parts that fit them about as well as the well-known sack."

SUDDENLY, LAST SUMMER

Bette came *this* close to costarring with Elizabeth Taylor in the 1959 film version of the Tennessee Williams play *Suddenly, Last Summer.* At the time Bette's film career was in a considerable rut, and she certainly could have used the prestige and quality of this project. Unfortunately, negotiations faltered, and Katharine Hepburn was signed for the part. She was later nominated for a Best Actress Oscar for her performance. For Bette this was one of many that got away.

SUGAR HILL, NEW HAMPSHIRE

"There isn't any lawn. Just trees and wild flowers and grass. And nuts. Butter nuts! Twenty years from now when I'm forgotten by Hollywood, you'll probably find me selling butter nuts along one of the roads near my house. I'll tie them individually with pink ribbons. I can just hear me: 'Bette Davis's pretty pink butter nuts. Home-grown.' "

Bette Davis, 1941

After making a series of pictures in a row, finishing with *The Private Lives of Elizabeth and Essex* (1939), Bette packed her bags and returned to New England. For the first time since she attained stardom, Bette returned to the small towns of her childhood. She ended up at Peckett's Inn in Franconia, New Hampshire. While there, she found and fell in love with a plot of land in nearby Sugar Hill. She bought the land, 150 acres of rolling hills on which she intended to build a home.

After making the 1940 picture *All This, and Heaven Too*, Bette returned to Sugar Hill and proceeded with plans to build her home. Once built, she christened it "Butternut." After making *The Great Lie*, Bette married Franconia resident Arthur Farnsworth, Jr., and together they returned to Butternut to work on Bette's dream house, a white cottage with gardens.

For many years afterward, Bette would return to Sugar Hill for respites from Hollywood. As she was fond of telling anyone who would listen, "My *real* home is always Butternut. I only work in Hollywood."

SUICIDE

Tough as she was, Bette was not beyond contemplating suicide. It was during the tail end of her allegedly abusive marriage to William Grant Sherry that Bette contemplated taking her own life. She went so far as to plan the details. The setting was her Warner Brothers dressing room, which also served as her apartment. She picked out the nightgown she would wear. She laid out the sleeping pills on her bedside table. And then, she claims, she broke out laughing.

According to Bette's daughter, B. D. Hyman, Bette staged mock suicides several times over the years. She would lock herself into her bedroom and toss an empty bottle of sleeping pills outside of her bedroom door while young B.D. and Michael cried and pleaded with her that they loved her. At one point, according to B.D., Bette attempted suicide several times a year.

BARRY SULLIVAN

Sullivan was Bette's costar in the 1951 picture *Payment on Demand*. At the time there were rumors that Bette and Barry were costarring off the set as well. Their alleged affair resulted in the dissolution of Bette's marriage to William Grant Sherry. Sherry, it seems, stormed onto the set one night and flattened Sullivan with a single punch, much to Bette's horror. Ironically, *Payment* was then shooting under the title of *The Story of a Divorce*.

Years later, when Gary Merrill backed out of the stage tour of *The World of Carl Sandburg* (1959–1960), he was replaced by Barry Sullivan—who always seemed to be there when Bette's marriages were falling apart.

Barry Sullivan, born Patrick Barry in 1912, has appeared in other pictures, including *Lady in the Dark* (1943), *The Great Gatsby* (1949), and *The Bad and the Beautiful* (1952).

JACK SULLIVAN

Jack Sullivan was an assistant director for Warner Brothers on numerous Bette Davis pictures, including *Fog Over Frisco* (1934), *It's Love I'm After* (1937), *Juarez* (1939), *The Old Maid* (1939), *The Great Lie* (1941), and *In This Our Life* (1942). While the last picture was being shot, Sullivan made the mistake of attempting to hurry Ernie Haller, who was taking his time lighting a scene. According to costar Olivia de Havilland, Bette lashed out at Sullivan. Said de Havilland, "It was like lightning, like the crack of a whip. All of us froze in absolute terror, including Jack Sullivan."

GLORIA SWANSON

When an interviewer asked her in 1950 if she had seen Gloria Swanson's performance as Norma Desmond in *Sunset Boulevard*, which was considered to be her primary competition in that year's Oscar derby, Bette responded, "Gary and I were on our way to Maine when we saw it advertised at a smalltown theatre. We spent the night there just to see the picture. It was a relief to find one actress portrayed on the screen who wasn't starving. Gloria Swanson was loaded with money. Incidentally, I think she gave a heavenly performance."

T

TAILWAGGERS FOUNDATION

Circa 1938–1939 canine lover Bette was president and chairman of the board of this organization, which cared for abandoned and lost dogs. Also on the board of directors were Jean Arthur, Lionel Barrymore, George Brent, Gary Cooper, Joan Crawford, Hedda Hopper, Carole Lombard, Mary Pickford, Spencer Tracy, and Darryl Zanuck. One Tailwaggers event was a dinner party at the Beverly Hills Hotel. It was here that Bette met Howard Hughes. Also in attendance in support of dogs were Errol Flynn, Miriam Hopkins, Jimmy Stewart, Joel McCrea, and Norma Shearer, among others.

ROBERT TAPLINGER

Longtime Warner Brothers director of publicity with whom, it was rumored, Bette had an affair in 1940, when she took a three-week cruise to Hawaii with him on the Matson liner *Mariposa*. Upon returning in May, Bette told the press, "We are not married nor are we engaged. We were on the same ship, but that was a coincidence. They always say things like that about people in Hollywood."

Later in 1940 Bette married Arthur Farnsworth, but she and Taplinger remained friends. In subsequent years he would help Bette with various public relations functions of the Hollywood Canteen.

ELIZABETH TAYLOR

"Elizabeth Taylor is a survivor, and one helluva dame."
Bette Davis

Bette Davis recognized Elizabeth Taylor as a *star*, something rare in Bette's view and something she knew a little about herself. The two women were friendly enough, expressing mutual admiration. In 1966, however, Bette was none too pleased when Elizabeth stepped in and, with husband Richard Burton, took over the film adaptation of Edward Albee's *Who's Afraid of Virginia Woolf?* Bette had wanted the role of Martha for herself and was in fact under consideration for it. Star that she was, Bette still was no competition for Elizabeth Taylor and Richard Burton in the 1960s. The role would go on to win a Best Actress Oscar for Elizabeth, her second. Bette had to content herself with the script's homage to her, in which Elizabeth says, "What a *dump!*"

At Edith Head's funeral in 1981, Bette and Elizabeth sat in the same pew. Coincidentally, Elizabeth was appearing at the time in a stage revival of *The Little Foxes*, which Bette had played on the screen. Around the same time Bette filled in for Rock Hudson in presenting an award to Elizabeth. During the ceremony Bette made an attempt at wit by saying something along the lines of "From one little fox to another."

Although the two never appeared in a picture together, they did have opportunities to do so. Elizabeth tried to get Bette cast in the 1973 picture *The Driver's Seat*, but it was not to be. Then Bette wanted to be cast opposite Elizabeth in *A Little Night Music* (1978), but that too failed to materialize.

Bette did attend Elizabeth's 55th birthday party at Burt Bacharach and Carole Bayer Sager's home in 1987.

At the time of her death, included in Bette's possessions was a Hermès blanket presented to her by Elizabeth Taylor. It was auctioned off for $1,402.50.

TEACHERS

The following is a selective alphabetical list of Bette Davis's teachers.

John Murray Anderson, drama
Lois Cann, drama
George Currie, drama
Emma Dunn, drama
Martha Graham, dance

Arthur Hornblow, Jr., drama
Marie Ware Laughton, dance
Una Merkel, Sunday school
Roshanara, dance

"TELEPHONE TIME"

Bette appeared in "Stranded," a 1957 episode of the dramatic anthology series "Telephone Time." The show was produced by Jerry Stagg. In April 1957 producer Stagg and executive producer Hal Roach, Jr., entered into a deal that called for Bette to take over the hosting duties as well as to appear in several episodes each season.

"Stranded" shot from March 18 to March 21, 1957. It was directed by Allen Miner and written by Herb Ellis and John T. Kelley. The story was based on the real-life story of rural Minnesota schoolteacher Beatrice Enter, who saved the lives of her young students when a blizzard hit. The cast of unknowns included Tiger Fafara, Pamela Beaird, Claudia Bryar, Edward Byrnes, Anna Marie Nanasi, Wendy Winkelman, Phil Phillips, Hope Summers, House Peters, Jr., and Paul Bryar.

Apparently, after the show aired on May 9, 1957, Bette was displeased with the finished result, because a few days later she backed out of the deal to host and star in the show. The show was hosted by John Nesbitt (1956–1957) and Dr. Frank Baxter (1957–1958).

"Telephone Time" aired on CBS and then ABC on Sunday nights at varying times from April 1956 to April 1958.

TELEVISION

"Television is only for the young and the ambitious, those who want to get ahead—but it's not for me because I've lost too much of my old drive. . . . TV is a wonderful medium for the youngsters. It will mean careers for many who otherwise would go through life unnoticed. But it's terribly exacting and taxing. One must be in first-class physical condition to tackle it."

Bette Davis before *doing television*

"I *adore* television. Not only do I want to get into it, I am in it. I've done half a dozen shows. I would be in it up to my ears if it weren't that one of its prime requisites seems to be knowing how to ride a horse."

Bette after *doing television and in reference to the medium's fondness for westerns, 1958*

"I must say, I do enjoy making TV films. They wrap up a show in two or three days. It doesn't really give you an opportunity to begin disliking your fellow actors or the director."

Bette, 1958

"I got so sick of the early professional snobbery toward television films. I guarantee that you will find more great films on television in the past decade than those made for theatrical release."

Bette, 1987

Bette Davis Television Pilots for Series
"Paula" aka "That's Paula" (1958)
"Madame's Palace" (1960)
"Morgan & McBride" (1963)
"Decorator" aka "The Bette Davis Show" (1965)
"Madame Sin" (1972)
"The Judge and Jake Wyler" (1972)
"Hello Mother, Goodbye" (1973)
*"Hotel" (1983)

---

*Picked up as a series

Bette Davis's Episodic Series Guest Spots
"The 20th Century–Fox Hour," "Crack-Up," February 8, 1956*
"General Electric Theater," "With Malice Toward One," March 20, 1957
"Schlitz Playhouse," "For Better or Worse," March 22, 1957
"Ford Theatre," "Footnote on a Doll," April 24, 1957
"Telephone Time," "Stranded," May 9, 1957
"Studio 57," "The Starmaker," 1958
"General Electric Theater," "The Cold Touch," April 13, 1958
"Suspicion," "Fraction of a Second," 1958
"Alfred Hitchcock Presents," "Out There, Darkness," 1959
"Wagon Train," "The Ella Lindstrom Story," 1959
"The DuPont Show with June Allyson," "Dark Morning," 1959
"Wagon Train," "The Elizabeth McQueeney Story," 1960
"Wagon Train," "The Bettina May Story," 1961
"The Virginian," "The Accomplice," December 19, 1962
"Perry Mason," "The Case of Constant Doyle," January 31, 1963
"Gunsmoke," "The Jailer," October 1, 1966
"It Takes a Thief," "Touch of Magic," 1970

---

*Actually the footage of Bette in this TV program was recycled from the feature film *Phone Call from a Stranger*. Therefore, it really doesn't count as her TV dramatic debut as it was hyped at the time.

The Television Movies
See The Movies.

THANK YOUR LUCKY STARS ★★
Warner Brothers
1943   127 minutes   bw
Directed by: David Butler
Produced by: Mark Hellinger
Screenplay by: Norman Panama, Melvin Frank, and James V. Kern, from
    an original story by Everett Freeman and Arthur Schwartz
Cinematography by: Arthur Edeson
Cast: Dennis Morgan, Joan Leslie, Edward Everett Horton, S. Z. Sakall,
    Richard Lane, Ruth Donnelly, Don Wilson, Henry Armetta, Joyce
    Reynolds
With guest stars: Humphrey Bogart, Eddie Cantor, Bette Davis, Olivia de
    Havilland, Errol Flynn, John Garfield, Ida Lupino, Ann Sheridan,
    Dinah Shore, Alexis Smith, Jack Carson, Alan Hale, George Tobias,
    Hattie McDaniel, Willie Best, Spike Jones and His City Slickers

Modeled on MGM's *The Broadway Melody*, *Thank Your Lucky Stars* was to
feature star turns by the upper echelons of Warners players on the premise
that audiences would flock to see Errol Flynn singing, Olivia de Havilland
attempting a vaudevillian routine, and Bette Davis being manhandled and
thrown around in the guise of a dance called the jitterbug.

Bette agreed to appear in the picture if Warners paid $50,000 to the
Hollywood Canteen. The other stars who appeared in the film also donated
their salaries to the canteen.

She was to perform the production number "They're Either Too Young
or Too Old" with music and lyrics by Arthur Schwartz and Frank Loesser.
Bette was extremely nervous about shooting her first major movie production

number, even confessing to friends that she was more nervous about doing this scene than any she had ever done.

She demanded a closed set. Because there was some doubt about her singing voice, Bette was allowed to rehearse for a couple of days at home with the piano player before officially rehearsing on the set. She showed up on the set on Tuesday, February 16, 1943, for tests and rehearsed the number on the set on Thursday, February 18. Additional rehearsals were held on Friday and Saturday.

On Monday, February 22, Bette rehearsed and prerecorded the number. It was then shot the following day. The sequence called for Bette to do an old-fashioned waltz with an old man, which then transformed into an energetic jitterbug. Her partner in the latter was 24-year-old Conrad Wiedell, billed at the time as "The King of the Jitterbug." Upon meeting Bette on the set, Wiedell was frozen with fear. Bette extended her arm with the dictum "Just forget who I am—and *do* it!"

She had previously insisted to director David Butler that the number be shot in one take. She had no intention of being flung repeatedly through the air until Butler was satisfied. On February 24 the number was completed and the entire production wrapped.

THAT CERTAIN WOMAN ★★
Warner Brothers
1937   91 minutes   bw
Directed by: Edmund Goulding
Produced by: Hal B. Wallis, in association with Robert Lord
Screenplay by: Edmund Goulding, based on a screenplay by Edmund
     Goulding
Cinematography by: Ernest Haller
Cast: Bette Davis, Henry Fonda, Ian Hunter, Anita Louise, Donald Crisp,
     Katherine Alexander, Mary Phillips, Minor Watson, Ben Welden,
     Sidney Toler, Charles Trowbridge, Norman Willis, Herbert Rawlinson,
     Rosalind Marquis, Frank Faylen, Willard Parker, Dwane Day, Hugh
     O'Connell

Edmund Goulding had the idea of taking one of his silent pictures, *The Trespasser*, and adapting it for the talking screen. The rights to the picture, however, were not owned by Goulding, but by the film's star, Gloria Swanson. After some negotiation Warners purchased all rights to the property from Swanson for $20,000 in an agreement dated December 23, 1936.

The rather involved story concerned Mary Donnell, played by Bette, a girl from the wrong side of the tracks who is loved by a married man, her boss (Ian Hunter). She marries Henry Fonda, whom *she* is in love with. Fonda's father (Donald Crisp), who does not approve of her, has the marriage annulled. Bette resumes working as Hunter's secretary. Meanwhile, she secretly gives birth to Fonda's child. Fonda marries Anita Louise, who becomes crippled as a result of an accident suffered on her honeymoon. Hunter then dies from a mysterious disease and leaves Bette and her son a good sum of money. Meanwhile, Fonda's father realizes that Bette's son is his grandchild and plots to have the child taken from her. Bette then lets Fonda and his crippled wife adopt her child, and she goes off to Europe. The crippled wife then dies, and Davis and Fonda finally get back together.

Marketed with the ads "I Wouldn't Remarry My Baby's Father" and "I Kissed You Goodbye on Our Wedding Night and You Ask Me To Love You Now!," *That Certain Woman* was met with mixed reviews. Actually it's just overwrought soap opera, but Bette, still developing her craft, is fun to watch nonetheless. Interestingly, Warners had the audacity to promote the picture with the tag "America's Greatest Actress in the Greatest Role of Her Career!"

"THIS IS YOUR LIFE"

In 1971 Bette appeared, albeit reluctantly, on this show. Host Ralph Edwards took Bette by surprise when he appeared at a "Madame Sin" conference among Edith Head, Robert Wagner, and Bette Davis. At first she was obviously perturbed by Edward's intrusion. Later she adjusted to the idea, as Edwards fawned all over her. Guesting in her honor were William Wyler, Bette's sister, Bobby, comedian Benny Baker, Ted Kent (editor of *Bad Sister*), Sally (Sage) Hutchinson (Bette's longtime stand-in), Olivia de Havilland, Paul Henreid, Victor Buono, and actor Jay Robinson, among others.

"After the show was over, I felt as if I had been to my own funeral."
Bette Davis on "This Is Your Life"

THIS 'N THAT

After both William Morrow and E. P. Dutton passed on her *This 'N That*, an autobiographical recounting of her 1983 mastectomy and stroke along with other random thoughts, Bette took out an ad in *Publishers Weekly*, "Actress Needs Publisher." G. P. Putnam's Sons picked up the book and published it in April 1987.

Morrow and Dutton rejected the book reportedly because it wasn't spicy enough. According to Christine Schillig, Bette's editor at Putnam, "I don't know why the others rejected it. I loved it from the word go. She deals with recovering from major surgery, a stroke, going back to work. . . . She's a woman of strong appetites and opinions. It's not bland."

Written in collaboration with Michael Herskowitz, *This 'N That* is a quick, entertaining read, although some of the material is rehashed from *The Lonely Life* and *Mother Goddam*. The emphasis is on B.D. and how she wronged Bette with an attempt at a *Mommie Dearest*-type biography. Bette is frank when she wants to be, coy when she wants to be, all from her own slanted but fascinating perspective.

THREE ON A MATCH ★★½
Warner Brothers
1932   63 minutes   bw
Directed by: Mervyn LeRoy
Produced by: Ray Griffith

Screenplay by: Lucien Hubbard, based on an original story by Kubec
    Glasmon and John Bright
Cinematography by: Sol Polito
Cast: Joan Blondell, Ann Dvorak, Warren William, Bette Davis, Grant
    Mitchell, Lyle Talbot, Humphrey Bogart, Glenda Farrell, Clara
    Blandick, Allen Jenkins, Jack LaRue, Edward Arnold, Buster Phelps,
    Harry Seymour, Hardie Albright, Virginia Davis, Dawn O'Day, Betty
    Carse

With a budget of $163,383, *Three on a Match* started shooting on June 2, 1932.
Bette joined the company on June 10. The picture was allotted 24 shooting
days with an expected finish of June 29. It's interesting to note that Bette was
initially slated to work on the picture for the entire four-week shooting
schedule but ended up shooting for only six days.

After her considerable successes with *The Man Who Played God, So Big,
The Rich Are Always With Us, Dark Horse,* and *Cabin in the Cotton,* Bette
resented being thrown into this picture, in which she was to have not the
first, not the second, but, the *third* female lead. Nor was she pleased that Joan
Blondell was making $100 a week more than she. Consequently she was
miserable on the set, and director LeRoy could or would not see behind her
petulance and pout. He would later say that he had been totally unimpressed
with her talent as an actress and her potential as a star. Meanwhile, LeRoy
was impressed with Blondell, which Bette also resented. She would frequently
repeat over the succeeding years the story that, following the completion of
the picture, LeRoy predicted stardom for Blondell, success for Dvorak, and
unemployment for Bette.

Three on a Match tells the story of three girlfriends. It opens in 1919 with
the Blondell, Dvorak, and Davis characters (played by child actresses) in
school. Dvorak is voted the most popular girl in school, and she makes plans
to attend an exclusive boarding school; Bette is voted the class valedictorian,
and she makes plans to enroll in a business school; Joan Blondell is sent to

the principal's office and voted the girl most likely to end up in a reform school.

LeRoy advances his fast-moving, economical film with a montage of newspaper headlines intercut with quick takes of the now-adult Blondell in reform school, Bette in business school, etc. As the young women graduate from their respective schools, the story really begins when the three reunite over lunch. Blondell strikes up a match and proceeds to light each of their cigarettes, with Dvorak the last to be lit, supposedly a sign of bad things to come.

Sure enough, we learn that Dvorak, rich as she is, is discontented with her married life to attorney husband Warren William. Nor is she particularly fulfilled by her young son (played with ingratiating charm by Buster Phelps, sort of a little-boy Shirley Temple). Still, Blondell and Davis watch as Dvorak climbs into her chauffeur-driven limousine and shake their heads with envy. Soon enough, however, Dvorak gets mixed up in an adulterous affair with Lyle Talbot and ends up addicted to drugs. Blondell, in an attempt to rescue young Buster from his unfit mother, ends up in love with William, and in fact replaces Dvorak as his well-heeled wife.

The bizarre but compelling finale has Buster kidnapped by Talbot, who seeks money from William to pay off his debt to underworld kingpin Edward Arnold. In an effort to save her child from being murdered, the drugged but not entirely villainous Dvorak writes a message on her nightgown with lipstick and flings her body out of a fourth-floor window to alert the police below as to his whereabouts.

Three on a Match was generally panned upon its release in 1932, but it is in fact a good little picture that does credit to the gritty, economical Warners house style of the early thirties. Unfortunately for Bette, however, she is merely on hand as a decorative third wheel. But, as blond and lithe Ruth Westcott, the stenographer turned nursemaid, she is decorative indeed.

Three on a Match was remade in 1938 as *Broadway Musketeers* with Marie Wilson in the part previously played by Bette.

TED TODD

Upon her return to the United States from England following her legal defeat at the hands of the brothers Warner in 1936, Bette was shunned by the studio publicity machinery. However, in Chicago, en route to Hollywood, one studio publicist, Ted Todd, bravely defied the studio's dictum and met Bette at the railroad station. Bette would later say, "I've never forgotten Ted for that—he's remained my friend all these years."

FRANCHOT TONE

Bette's costar, borrowed from MGM, in *Dangerous* (1935) had looks, education, breeding, and was a member of the Group Theater in New York, all of which Bette found appealing. While filming, Bette fell in love with Tone, despite the fact that he was involved at the time with Joan Crawford and she

As Joyce, Heath with Franchot Tone:
"with gin on her breath and a chip on
her shoulders."

was married to Ham Nelson. The two allegedly had an affair that lasted the
duration of the shooting.

In later years Tone was considered for the male lead in *Jezebel* that went
to Henry Fonda. He was also considered for the male leads in *The Sisters*
(1938), and *Old Acquaintance* (1943). In the latter case he even signed for the
part at a salary of $8,500 a week. However, before shooting started he was
replaced by John Loder.

Franchot Tone (Stanislas Pascal Franchot Tone, 1905–1968) appeared in
other pictures, including *Mutiny on the Bounty* (1935), *Phantom Lady* (1944),
and *Advise and Consent* (1962).

"THE TONIGHT SHOW"

Over the years Bette made numerous appearances on "The Tonight Show."
She developed a friendly on-air rapport with Johnny Carson and never failed
to liven up the proceedings with a feisty retort. In her May 1986 appearance,
Bette deadpanned and sent the audience roaring with "I'm kind of audition-
ing for *Joan's* spot." She was, of course, referring to former "Tonight Show"
guest host Joan Rivers, who was then feuding with Carson after attaining a
late-night talk show of her own.

Bette was later brought into the middle of the fray between Rivers and
Carson when she was scheduled to appear on "The Tonight Show" in March
1987. At the last minute Carson canceled the show because of the death of his
friend Buddy Rich. Bette's appearance was rescheduled for a later date. In the
meantime Bette guested on Joan Rivers's "The Late Show." When he learned
of this, an angered Carson canceled Bette's appearance altogether.

Katharine Hepburn, in Bette's view, had it all: looks, talent . . . Tracy.

SPENCER TRACY

Bette idolized Spencer Tracy and was thrilled to work with him in *20,000 Years in Sing Sing* (1933). He was borrowed from Fox for the picture at $2,000 per week. In contrast Bette was probably making about $400 a week.

It was to Bette's great regret that she and Tracy never made another picture together. She wanted him badly for *Dark Victory*, as did screenwriter Casey Robinson, who campaigned vigorously to get him. For a while it looked as though Warners would be able to obtain him from MGM, but it didn't come to pass. Tracy, reportedly on the heels of an affair with Joan Crawford, opted to do an all-male film instead, *Northwest Passage*.

Shortly before her death Bette would hail Tracy as "the greatest actor ever." She added, "I wish I could have made more movies with him."

Spencer Tracy (1900–1967) appeared in a plethora of pictures, including *Captains Courageous* (Best Actor Oscar winner, 1937), *Boys Town* (Best Actor Oscar winner, 1938), *Woman of the Year* (1942), *Adam's Rib* (1949), *Father of the Bride* (1950), *Bad Day at Black Rock* (1955), *Inherit the Wind* (1960), *Judgment at Nuremberg* (1961), and *Guess Who's Coming to Dinner* (1967).

TRAFFIC COURT

In 1941 Bette was pulled over for going through a stop sign at the intersection of Yucca and Argyle in Hollywood. Opting not to appear in traffic court, Bette paid the five-dollar fine. It was not the first time she had been cited for a traffic violation. On December 20, 1934, Bette's limousine driver was rushing her through traffic so that she could do her Christmas shopping. The motorcycle officer pulled the limousine over and, upon recognizing

Bette, stuttered, "You're Bette Davis, the movie star." Bette batted *those* eyes and admitted that she was indeed *that* Bette Davis. At the time Bette was appearing on movie screens as the villainous Mildred Rogers in *Of Human Bondage*. Bette explained her predicament. The officer thought for a moment and then proceeded to write her a ticket. Such were the hazards of playing bitches in the movies.

20TH CENTURY-FOX

Bette's 20th Century-Fox pictures:

All About Eve (1950)
Phone Call from a Stranger (1952)
The Star (1952)*
The Virgin Queen (1955)
Hush . . . Hush, Sweet Charlotte (1964)*
The Nanny (1965)*
The Anniversary (1968)*

---

*Only released by 20th Century-Fox

20,000 YEARS IN SING SING ★★

Warner Brothers
1932   77 minutes   bw
Directed by: Michael Curtiz
Produced by: Ray Griffith
Screenplay by: Wilson Mizner and Brown Holmes, adapted by Courtenay
    Terrett and Robert Lord; based on the book by Lewis E. Lawes
Cinematography by: Barney McGill
Cast: Spencer Tracy, Bette Davis, Lyle Talbot, Sheila Terry, Edward
    McNamara, Warren Hymer, Louis Calhern, Spencer Charters, Arthur
    Byron, Sam Godfrey, Grant Mitchell, Nella Walker, Harold Huber,
    William LeMaire, Arthur Hoyt, George Pat Collins

Warner Brothers purchased the rights to *20,000 Years in Sing Sing*, a book by former Sing Sing prison warden Lewis E. Lawes, for $15,750 in an agreement dated January 28, 1932.

It was initially intended as a vehicle for Jimmy Cagney. When he couldn't or wouldn't do it, Spencer Tracy was brought on. Bette, cast in the picture as a gun moll, idolized Tracy and was thrilled. Warners borrowed Tracy from Fox for the lump sum of $10,400—$2,000 a week for four weeks plus $2,400 upon signing. At the time Bette was earning about $400 a week.

With a budget of $215,000, principal photography started without Bette on August 15, 1932. Bette, busy getting married to and honeymooning with Harmon Nelson, didn't start until August 25. The production was allotted 29 days, a few days beyond the studio's standard, with an expected finish of September 12. In the succeeding weeks of shooting Bette would actually work for only nine days. The production finished with her on September 14.

There was some problem over *who* was to receive the more prominent billing—a battle not over Tracy and Davis but rather over Tracy and Warden Lawes! It ended up a draw.

The picture was marketed with the ad "The Story of a Thousand Men Without Women . . . and of Their Women Who Can't Do Without Men!"

20,000 Years in Sing Sing was remade in 1940 as *Castle on the Hudson* with John Garfield and Ann Sheridan.

TWO'S COMPANY

Scenic designer Ralph Alswang telephoned his friend Gary Merrill and told him that young producers Jimmy Russo and Mike Ellis were looking for a star for their musical revue called *Two's Company*. Merrill relayed that Bette, who was looking for a change of pace, would indeed be interested in such a project. Bette read the script of sketches written by Charles Sherman. Then composer Vernon Duke met with her, played her the score that he had written to Ogden Nash's lyrics (with contributions from Sammy Cahn), and Bette was sold. Her signing was reported on June 18, 1952.

Bette related to the *Los Angeles Times*, "I had been approached to follow Judy Garland into the Palace and I gave it some serious thought. I knew I didn't want to do the usual 'in person' appearance of re-enacting scenes from my movies, nor did I want to do anything heavy and dramatic. . . . Ralph Alswang, the well-known scenic designer long-distanced Gary from New York. They're old pals and they always phone each other at the drop of a toll call. Well, it seems that Ralph shares his office with two young producers named Jimmy Russo and Mike Ellis, who were about to produce a revue called *Two Is Company* [sic] only they needed a star like Bea Lillie, Gertrude Lawrence or Mary Martin, whom they couldn't get. . . . Just as a gag, Jimmy asked Ralph to ask Gary if I would be interested in doing a revue on Broadway. When Gary said 'yes' and they revived Jimmy from the stool he had fallen off, things began to happen. . . . If it's a hit in New York as we all fervently hope, I'll continue the run for as long as it runs, and then tour with it afterward."

Bette delighted in the idea of shocking her fans (and detractors) with an all-new, singing, dancing, self-deprecating Bette Davis. One number, "Roll Along Sadie" called for her to do a takeoff on Sadie Thompson. One called for her to play a hillbilly TV singer who smokes a pipe and is missing a few front teeth. One called for her to imitate Tallulah Bankhead watching Bette Davis imitate Tallulah Bankhead from a theater box. Other songs included "Good Little Girls," "Loathsome Party," "Just Like a Man," and "Purple Rose."

Rehearsals were held in New York in September 1952. Bette, while pleased with the songs, was constantly asking for rewrites on the sketches, which were directed by Jules Dassin. The show was then to try out in Detroit, Pittsburgh, and Boston before opening on Broadway, initially set for November.

Meanwhile, anticipation of Bette's return to Broadway grew within theater circles. In predicting the hits of the upcoming season, Radie Harris wrote in the August 17, 1952, *Los Angeles Times*: "Looking ahead now, I'd like to envision one premiere that will undoubtedly cause more of a hysterical 'I don't care what it costs' demand for opening night seats than any other offering of the year. Can you imagine that November night when Bette Davis returns to Broadway for the first time in 22 years for the musical revue *Two Is Company* [sic]. I'm getting that spine-tingling feeling already."

On opening night in Detroit on October 20, 1952, with her mother, Ruthie, and husband, Gary, in the front row, Bette *collapsed* during her first number, "Good Little Girls." She fell flat on the stage from what was later attributed to a cold, fatigue, and stage fright. After she recovered, Bette got up, marched to the foot of the stage, and quipped to the audience, "Well, you couldn't say I didn't *fall* for you!" The following night Bette canceled the performance. Still, the reviews in Detroit were generally favorable.

Bette, of course, blamed everyone but herself for her fall. The show stayed in Detroit for an extra week of rewriting. Jerome Robbins, who was staging the musical sequences, summoned Josh Logan and writer Paul Osborn from New York and asked for a consultation. Bette, however, refused to meet with them. By the Pittsburgh opening on November 10, the show's second comic, Nathaniel Frey, was replaced by David Burns.

By the time the show opened in Boston, it was in major trouble. John Murray Anderson, Bette's drama coach nearly 25 years before, was hired to repair the show. Male lead Hiram Sherman was out. Paul Hartman was in. Other changes were made. Ed Sullivan even announced in his syndicated column that Martha Raye was about to replace Bette in the production. Rumors ran rampant back in New York that Bette would back out of the production before its Broadway opening. Bette reported in response, "You've got to take chances if you want to get anywhere in the arts. Let the rumors fly about this revue. When it opens in New York at the Alvin, Bette Davis will be onstage with the rest of the cast. You can count on that."

Two's Company was initially scheduled to open on Broadway in November and then on December 4. Just prior to the appointed date, however, Bette got "laryngitis," and the show was again postponed.

Problems with the revue persisted. Peter Devries came in and assisted on the book. Several other uncredited writers were brought in to help with the sketches. Sheldon Harnick wrote new lyrics. Male lead Paul Hartman was out. Hiram Sherman was back in. One bright spot: after the Boston opening a new opening number was added for Bette, "Just Turn Me Loose on Broadway." She loved it.

Two's Company finally hobbled into its Broadway opening on December 15, 1952. It got mixed reviews. One critic said Bette's performance was "on the elementary side." The show cost an estimated $250,000 to produce, and the press reported it could be a "$1 million malady."

Still, the Alvin Theatre box office had more than $700,000 in advance sales, believed to be the third largest advance in Broadway history. If the show could keep playing, it would easily recoup its costs and turn a profit. *If*.

Bette started complaining of fatigue. On March 7, 1953, she went to a dentist, actor Art Carney's brother, to treat an inflamed wisdom tooth. The following day Bette went to see Dr. Stanley Behrman, the head of dental surgery at New York Hospital. He diagnosed osteomyelitis.

Bette entered New York Hospital on Sunday, March 8. She had planned to leave the show on March 28 anyway. But this was disputed by the producers, who claimed to have her under contract until May 30, *1954*. They wanted her to tour with the show for at least 10 weeks, and they announced their intention to take the matter to Equity for arbitration if necessary. The producers said that the only way they would cancel the tour was if Bette forked over $5,000 from her own pocketbook to defray expenses. It is not known whether she complied.

Bette, from the hospital (much like Joan Crawford would do after leaving *Hush . . . Hush, Sweet Charlotte* more than 10 years later), voiced her discontent with the show and with the theater in general. To Radie Harris she stated, "The theatre today is an entirely different theatre than the show business I left 22 years ago. Today with the union set-up making production costs prohibitive; stop clauses that cancel you out of a playhouse if you go below a certain amount; and a $7.20 top [ticket price] (which the true theatre lover can't begin to afford)—the economic pressure is so great that the entire responsibility falls on the star. And what does this responsibility entail? Dedicating one's self to one's job. Well, frankly, I don't feel *that* dedicated, because my personal life with my husband and three children means something to me, too. In any other profession, if you are ill, you stay home until you are well. But in the theatre—oh, no! 'The Show Must Go On'—come pneumonia or the bubonic plague!"

Two's Company closed on Wednesday, March 11, 1953, after 89 performances. Surgery was performed on Bette on March 16. Her early exit reportedly cost the show $320,000 in losses.

U

THE UNFORGIVEN

Bette was offered a costarring part in this 1960 picture. But, as she shrieked to columnist Sheila Graham, "I-Magine! They want me to play Burt Lancaster's *mother*!" After Bette rejected it, the part was played by Lillian Gish.

UNIVERSAL PICTURES

Universal Pictures was a Laemmle and Son operation in 1930. Actually, Carl Jr., 29, had taken over operation of the studio by then. Universal scored a major success with the April 1930 premiere of *All Quiet on the Western Front*, which would go on to win the Oscar for best picture. Still, 1930 was a rough year financially for the studio, which lost some $2.2 million. The loss prompted a change in the studio's house style. Over the next few years the studio's signature genre would be the horror film. *Dracula*, released in late 1931, was followed in 1932 by *Frankenstein*, *The Mummy*, and *The Old Dark House*. It was a highly successful and relatively cheap mode of operations for the studio. In contrast, "women's pictures," as they were then called, were rare and of the standard formula variety.

Bette was signed to the studio in late 1930. It was not, however, an auspicious beginning. When she arrived at the train station in Los Angeles on December 13, no studio representative met her at the station. Upon arriving at her hotel, she called the studio. The person who was to pick her up told her that he *had* been at the station but that he didn't see anyone who looked remotely like an actress. "You should have known I was an actress," Bette shot back to her apologetic would-be escort. "I was carrying a dog."

Bette's first studio picture was to be *Strictly Dishonorable* opposite Paul Lukas. However, after Laemmle, Jr., got a look at her in person, he decided to go instead with the more delectable, in his view, Sidney Fox. Bette was then up for the title character in the picture *Bad Sister*. Laemmle again interjected, and Bette was cast instead as the *second* female lead, the good sister. The star of the film, the one who played the bad sister, was Sidney Fox. Around the same time Bette was "discovered" by producer/director John Stahl in the studio cafeteria, and he cast Bette as one of the daughters in a picture he was about to shoot called *Seed*. This was followed by another small part, the hero's sister, in *Waterloo Bridge*.

When none of her initial appearances registered excitement at the studio or in the marketplace, Universal essentially washed its hands of Bette Davis, wrote her off as a talent scout's mistake, and loaned her out to other studios for low-budget quickies for the duration of her contract.

After nine months, in September 1931, Universal decided to terminate Bette's contract.

V

VALLEY OF THE DOLLS

Bette wanted to play the part of Helen Lawson in the 1967 film adaptation of the bestselling novel by Jacqueline Susann, *Valley of the Dolls*. Susann even met with Bette to discuss the part. Nevertheless, it was Judy Garland and not Bette who was cast. A few days into shooting, however, Garland was replaced by Susan Hayward.

VARIETY

In September 1962 Bette shocked Hollywood and the entertainment industry at large by placing a "help wanted" ad in the daily trade paper *Variety*. The ad was placed after Bette completed shooting *What Ever Happened to Baby Jane?*—but before its release. Thus she had no way of knowing that the picture would be the hit it became. In later years Bette would claim that the ad was meant as a joke. It wasn't. She wanted—and needed—work. Pragmatist that she was, she decided to take out the ad, which read:

> Situation Wanted, Women Artists
> Mother of three—10, 11, 15—divorcee, American. Thirty years experience as an actress in motion pictures. Mobile still and more affable than rumor would have it. Wants steady employment in Hollywood. (Has had Broadway.) Bette Davis, c.o. Martin Baum, G.A.C., References Upon Request.

VIDEO

The following Bette Davis pictures are available on videocassette:

All About Eve
All This, and Heaven Too
Beyond the Forest
The Bride Came C.O.D.
Bureau of Missing Persons
Burnt Offerings
Cabin in the Cotton
The Catered Affair
The Corn Is Green
Dangerous
Dark Victory
Dead Ringer
Death on the Nile
Deception
The Empty Canvas
Ex-Lady
Fashions of 1934
The Great Lie
Hell's House
Hollywood Canteen
Hush . . . Hush, Sweet Charlotte
In This Our Life
Jezebel
Juarez
June Bride
Kid Galahad
The Letter

The Little Foxes
The Man Who Came to Dinner
Marked Woman
Mr. Skeffington
Now, Voyager
Of Human Bondage
The Old Maid
The Petrified Forest
Phone Call from a Stranger
Pocketful of Miracles
The Private Lives of Elizabeth and Essex
Return from Witch Mountain
Satan Met a Lady
The Star
The Sisters
A Stolen Life
Thank Your Lucky Stars
Three on a Match
The Virgin Queen
Watch on the Rhine
The Watcher in the Woods
Way Back Home
The Whales of August
What Ever Happened to Baby Jane?
The Wicked Stepmother
Winter Meeting

Bette's Made-for-Television Movies Available on Videocassette

"As Summers Die"
"The Dark Secret of Harvest Home"
"The Disappearance of Aimee"
"Family Reunion"
"Little Gloria . . . Happy at Last"
"Madame Sin"
"A Piano for Mrs. Cimino"
"Right of Way"
"Strangers: The Story of a Mother and Daughter"
"White Mama"

Video Documentaries and Specials About Bette

All About Bette
The American Film Institute Life Achievement Awards: Bette Davis
Bette Davis: The Bumpy Ride to Stardom
Power Profiles: Legendary Ladies

Video Compilations That Include Bette

Classic Bloopers
Those Crazy Ol' Commercials

KING VIDOR

Vidor directed Bette in the ill-fated 1949 picture *Beyond the Forest*, which resulted in the termination of Bette's longtime contract with Warner Brothers. Bette tried unsuccessfully to have Vidor fired from the film.

One of the premier silent filmmakers, King Vidor (1894–1982) established himself with the 1925 picture *The Big Parade*, which made a star out of John Gilbert. His subsequent talking films include *Street Scene* (1931), *The Champ* (1931), *Stella Dallas* (1937), *The Fountainhead* (1949), and *War and Peace* (1956).

THE VIRGIN QUEEN ★★½

20th Century–Fox
1955   92 minutes   De Luxe   CinemaScope
Directed by: Henry Koster
Produced by: Charles Brackett
Screenplay by: Harry Brown and Mindret Lord
Cinematography by: Charles G. Clarke
Cast: Bette Davis, Richard Todd, Joan Collins, Jay Robinson, Herbert Marshall, Dan O'Herlihy, Robert Douglas, Romney Brent, Marjorie Hellen, Lisa Daniels, Lisa Davis, Barry Bernard, Robert Adler, Noel Drayton, Ian Murray, Margery Weston, Rod Taylor, Davis Thursby, Arthur Gould-Porter

Darryl Zanuck, convinced that no one else could play the part, reportedly waited for Bette for three years before she finally acquiesced and agreed to make this picture. She had not worked in Hollywood for three years since she had undergone oral surgery. She was apprehensive, frightened, and excited.

Still, in January 1955 Bette was displeased with the revisions that were being made in the script, and she threatened not to do the picture. Zanuck retorted by threatening to cast someone else. Apparently the revised script that Bette was sent in Maine in January was *not* the script that she had approved some months before. Zanuck responded by telling her that her character and the lines accorded her had not been altered at all; some of the other characters merely had been built up—namely, the character of Sir Walter Raleigh, which was rewritten to appease the actor who was to play it, Richard Burton. When Burton dropped out of the picture, the script was refashioned to Bette's satisfaction. Furthermore, the title was changed in her favor from *Sir Walter Raleigh* to *The Virgin Queen*.

Bette was lured back to Hollywood with a salary of $35,000 a week for a minimum of three weeks, plus $25,000 a week if the production ran over schedule. For this she got to play her beloved Elizabeth, perhaps her favorite of all her roles. "I played the part previously for Warners," Bette said at the time, "but that was in *Elizabeth and Essex* when the monarch was 60 years of age. In the present picture, I am playing her at about my own age. I don't expect to be playing Elizabeth again, however."

The plot of this Elizabeth movie was set in London in 1581. Captain

Queen Bette holds court.

Walter Raleigh walks into the palace seeking ships from the queen and ends up getting his ships and her heart as well. The film also featured actress Joan Collins (whom Bette came to be less than fond of) in clothes Alexis Carrington Colby Dexter would have been proud of, delivering lines like "If a woman were not bold she would lack from much pleasure." Meanwhile, of course, Bette's queen, all decked out in ruffles and ridges and sporting a shaved head, bellows at and bullies everyone in sight. It was the shaved head that was, for Bette, the worst part of shooting. Every morning Perc Westmore greeted her by taking an electric razor to her head. It seems that a fever had taken Elizabeth's hair 20 years earlier, and it never grew back.

Bette's Elizabeth was a queen who wanted to be a woman but who could not bring herself to act womanly with a man. Nor was she capable of bearing a child. "England," she would say, "was child enough for me." Still, there were some benefits to being queen. As queen she bestows the men whom she favors with a green cushion on which they kneel—at her feet. And there is no man she favors more than Raleigh. She makes him the captain of the Palace Guard, and needless to say he spends a good deal of time on his knees. Reportedly, during shooting, Bette made advances toward Richard Todd, the actor cast in the part after Burton backed out. Todd reportedly declined Bette's invitation and had his wife, British actress Catherine Bogle, fly out to Hollywood to join him on the set.

To Bette's delight the film was shot in CinemaScope, a new experience for her. Early into the production cinematographer Charles Clarke was still in Hong Kong completing *Love Is a Many-Splendored Thing* so Leon Shamroy did the shooting until Clarke returned to Hollywood.

Surprisingly, instead of taking the expected minimum of three weeks to complete her part, Bette finished it in 11 days. "It's fantastic!" she enthused. "Sixty pages of script. I had anticipated it would take three weeks at the minimum; but we shoot 12 pages without batting an eye. This eliminates the boredom from picture making so completely."

The picture wrapped production in May 1955, and it was premiered in rapid succession in July. Reviews were generally favorable if unenthusiastic.

"THE VIRGINIAN"
Bette appeared in a 1962 episode of the popular NBC television western (1962–1971) that starred James Drury, Lee J. Cobb, and Doug McClure. In "The Accomplice" she portrayed Della Miller, a bank teller who attempts to blackmail a criminal who robbed the bank she works in. The episode was written by Howard Browne and William P. McGivern from a story by Winston Miller. It was directed by Maury Geraghty and produced by Miller. The cast for this episode included Gary Clarke, Lin McCarthy, and Gene Evans. It aired on December 19, 1962.

ROBERT WAGNER

Robert Wagner was the coexecutive producer and costar of "Madame Sin," a 1972 made-for-television movie. He had become friendly with Bette when she appeared on his television series "It Takes a Thief" in early 1970. They also appeared together in a print advertisement for Jim Beam. Bette *adored* "R.J." as his friends call him and had something of a crush on him. "He is the sexiest man now on film," she said. The two remained friends in the succeeding years.

Bette had a crush on Wagner.

"WAGON TRAIN"

Bette appeared in three episodes of the hit western television series that ran on NBC from 1957 to 1962 and on ABC from 1962 to 1965. During its run the show starred Ward Bond, John McIntire, Robert Horton, Terry Wilson, and Frank McGrath.

The first of Bette's episodes was "The Ella Lindstrom Story" (1959), in which she portrayed a pioneer widow with seven children. The second, "Madame's Palace," aka "The Elizabeth McQueeney Story," was a 1960 pilot for a television series and cast Bette as a dance hall hostess. The highlight of the show was Bette's performance of the cancan. The third episode was "The Bettina May Story," which aired in 1961.

HAL WALLIS

In 1922, at the age of 23, Hal Wallis was made director of publicity at Warner Brothers. He later moved into production and served as the "production supervisor" of the 1932 picture *Cabin in the Cotton.*

On March 19, 1933, Wallis was given a raise from $900 to $1,100 a week. A couple of months after Darryl Zanuck left the studio in a dispute, on June 14, 1933, Wallis signed a new Warners contract escalating his salary to $1,750 a week. His job was defined at the time as "an executive and/or administrative character in connection with the supervision and general overseeing of production." What that meant, essentially, was that Wallis was to do the same job that Zanuck had done, but without the title or the pay. Zanuck had been earning $5,000 per week.

The first Bette Davis pictures that Wallis oversaw in his new capacity were *Bureau of Missing Persons* (1933) and *Fashions of 1934* (1934). In 1937 Wallis began receiving an "executive producer" credit. For example, on the picture *Marked Woman* Wallis was executive producer "in association with Lou Edelman." Edelman actually functioned largely as the producer, but Wallis oversaw the production and made a lot of the creative decisions. Wallis would work in this capacity on *all* of Bette's subsequent pictures for the studio, through 1941, with *In This Our Life* being the last.

On February 2, 1942, Wallis signed a new contract with Warners calling for him to produce four pictures a year for the studio. He would have his choice of stories, directors, and on-screen talent. He was to get a salary of $4,000 a week plus 10 percent of the gross receipts once his productions returned 125 percent of their production costs. And his productions were to be billed as "A Hal B. Wallis Production." His first picture under this capacity was *Now, Voyager* (1942). The following year, *Watch on the Rhine,* won him a Best Picture Oscar nomination.

One of Wallis's major successes during this period was *Casablanca* in 1943. By this time Wallis was seriously feuding with Jack Warner over a variety of issues. On the night of the Oscars, when *Casablanca* was named the best picture of the year, Jack Warner leaped to his feet and rushed to the podium to accept the award. Wallis was furious with Warner for taking the credit that should, in his view, have belonged to him. Actually much of Hollywood felt that it was Wallis who deserved the glory. Wallis wanted out of his Warners contract, and the matter ended up in the hands of attorneys. They finally settled the matter out of court in December 1944. Wallis was given the profit shares on his films that were owed him, plus the lump sum of $1 million. For Hal Wallis and Warner Brothers it was the end of an era. No one would miss Wallis's presence more at the studio than Bette Davis. It was during his reign that she had become a star. When he left, her career declined perceptibly.

In April 1949 Bette met with Hal Wallis in New York and discussed plans to make a film for him. It never came to pass. Later he wanted her to star in *Come Back, Little Sheba,* which he was producing at Paramount. Bette made the mistake of turning him down.

Hal Wallis (1898–1986) produced numerous pictures and was executive producer of many more. His post–Warner Brothers pictures include *The Strange Love of Martha Ivers* (1946), *Gunfight at the OK Corral* (1957), *Becket* (1964), *True Grit* (1969), *Anne of the Thousand Days* (1969), and *Mary Queen of Scots* (1971).

WARNER BROTHERS

The brothers Warner—Harry, Albert, Sam, and, of course, Jack—were relatively minor players in the picture business compared to MGM and Para-

mount. All that started to change when the upstart company released *The Jazz Singer*, the first all-talking picture, which launched the talking revolution. Harry Warner, along with Wall Street financier Waddill Cathings, masterminded the studio's expansion from New York. Jack, the youngest, was back in Hollywood providing the product. The studio boasted Hal Wallis as its publicity chief and a *dog* as its first major star. His name was Rin Tin Tin. The teaming of Jack Warner and Darryl Zanuck was not unlike a poor man's version of Louis B. Mayer and Irving Thalberg over at MGM. *The Jazz Singer* premiered on October 6, 1927. At the time the studio operated at Sunset Boulevard and Bronson Avenue in Hollywood and at Vitagraph Studios in Brooklyn, which it had acquired.

In October 1928 Warner bought First National Pictures, which had a massive production complex in Burbank. In September 1928 the studio also purchased the Stanley Corporation, a deal that included 250 movie theaters throughout the country. One of the theaters was the prestigious Strand on Broadway, where many a Bette Davis picture would be unveiled in succeeding years.

Not even the stock market crash of October 1929 slowed the brothers Warner. What it *did* do, though, was change the house style of the studio. Instead of trying to compete with MGM's lavish, well-lit, prestigious pictures, Warners adopted a policy of quick, economical films produced with assembly-line efficiency. The films were stark, gritty—a lot of dialogue and action, but light on sets and costumes and elaborate coiffures.

Darryl Zanuck was promoted as commander of all productions in November 1930 when the studio moved from Sunset and Bronson to First National Studios in Burbank. Warners has been there ever since.

The Warners roster of stars circa 1930–1931 included William Powell, Joe E. Brown, Jimmy Cagney, and Edward G. Robinson. Aware of their lack of *femme* stars, Warners raided the talent roster at Paramount in early 1931, obtaining Kay Francis and Ruth Chatterton. At the time Francis was signed at $3,000 per week, Chatterton at a whopping $8,000 per week. The studio also signed starlets Joan Blondell, Ruby Keeler, and Bette Davis. Bette's starting salary? Three hundred dollars a week.

By the time she made her first picture for Warner Brothers, Bette, 23, had been dropped by Universal and was about to return to New York in defeat. She would have, if not for George Arliss. Arliss had recently been signed by the studio and was arguably its biggest star. Upon meeting her Arliss decided that he wanted Bette for his production of *The Man Who Played God*.

Jack Warner, however, recalled the acquisition of Bette Davis a little differently. According to Warner, it was Rufus LeMaire who entered his office one day and told him, "Jack, there's a very talented little girl over at Universal. . . ." According to Warner *he* then summoned Bette to the studio, recognized her potential, and signed her on the spot. Considering the circumstances, however, the former story is far more believable. Whatever the case, Bette Davis signed her first Warner Brothers contract on November 18, 1931.

Her initial contract was for *The Man Who Played God*, only with the studio having the option of extending it. By the time her work on the picture was completed, on December 24, 1931, Warners had picked up the option and signed Bette to a 26-week option contract. Her salary was raised to $400 a week.

It can be argued that Bette eventually became a star in *spite* of, rather than because of, Warner Brothers. Certainly, for the first three years or so, the studio didn't have a clue about what to do with her. After she scored a success in *Cabin in the Cotton* in 1932 playing a new kind of anti-heroine, Warners demoted her to playing the sweet third fiddle to Joan Blondell and Ann Dvorak in *Three on a Match*.

Meanwhile, controversy erupted over the studio's use of violence in its gritty gangster pictures. The studio seriously considered lowering its blood and bullets profile. That all changed, of course, with the November 1932 release of the ultraviolent *I Am a Fugitive from a Chain Gang*. It starred Paul Muni, a recent defector from Broadway, and was helmed by the studio's top director, Mervyn LeRoy. It was a blockbuster success.

The studio followed that success with another, the Depression-era musical *Forty-Second Street*. The picture was released on March 10, 1933, four days after newly elected president Franklin Delano Roosevelt announced a national bank holiday to launch his national recovery policy. The same week, the entire motion picture industry instituted an eight-week pay cut of 50 percent for all employees earning more than $25 a week.

When Harry Warner back in New York refused to reinstate the salaries by the announced date, Darryl Zanuck abruptly left the studio in a huff. It was April 15, 1933. Before leaving, one of Zanuck's final executive decisions was to promote "that Davis girl" to "star" status with *Ex-Lady* (1933). He ordered for her the full-glamour makeover. But while Zanuck's instincts about Bette were accurate, he was wrong about the vehicle that would take her there. When the picture flopped after his departure, Bette was again relegated to secondary roles in mediocre pictures.

When he left Warners to form 20th Century Pictures, Zanuck took with him George Arliss, Constance Bennett, and Loretta Young. That left Warners with Ruth Chatterton (already in decline), William Powell, Kay Francis, Douglas Fairbanks, Jr., Edward G. Robinson, Jimmy Cagney, and Paul Muni.

By late 1933 every Warners picture was assigned a "supervisor" instead of a "producer," with Hal Wallis overseeing everything. Supervisors would prepare a rough cut of their films and present them to Wallis for approval and/or a recut. Jack Warner, meanwhile, was elated that the studio didn't seem to miss Zanuck. After losing $20 million in 1932–1933, the studio lost only $2.5 million in 1934 and expected to turn a profit in 1935. Obviously this had more to do with the recovering economy than Zanuck or Wallis.

Ironically, it would *not* be Warner Brothers but another studio, RKO, that would really launch Bette's career. After weeks of pressuring Jack Warner, Bette was finally given permission to be loaned out to RKO to do the film adaptation of the W. Somerset Maugham book *Of Human Bondage*. Warner couldn't understand why she was so insistent on wanting to play such an unseemly character. Many years later Warner would promote one of Bette's pictures by proclaiming "Nobody's as Good as Bette—When She's Bad." It took a few years, but he finally learned.

After finally sampling a taste in *Bondage* of what it was like to have a really good part, Bette objected when she was assigned by Warners to play a supporting role as Della Street in the Perry Mason picture *The Case of the Howling Dog*. She barked, she balked, she stalked off. Warners responded by suspending her. It would be one of many suspensions by the studio. Two weeks later *Bondage* was released by RKO, and Bette was accorded rave reviews. Warners summoned her back to the studio with open arms and a good part in a good film, *Bordertown* (1935).

After winning the Best Actress Oscar for *Dangerous* (1935), Bette, sensing her escalating worth, thought that her salary should be more commensurate with her newfound stature. She also wanted more control over the projects in which she worked. She hired powerhouse agent Mike Levee, Joan

Crawford's agent, to negotiate a new contract with the studio. If her demands were not met, Bette would not report to the set of *God's Country and the Woman*, the next picture she was assigned to do. Jack Warner, however, initially refused to negotiate. After all, he had Bette signed to a long-term contract, and there was nothing she could do about it.

On June 19, 1936, Dudley Furse, Bette's attorney, sent a letter to Warner outlining Bette's demands. By this time there were 10 points of contention:

1. Term: Five Years
2. Salary: $100,000, first year
   $140,000, second year
   $180,000, third year
   $200,000, fourth year
   $220,000, fifth year
3. Limit of no more than four pictures a year
4. Three consecutive months' vacation
5. The right to do one outside picture a year
6. The right to do at least four radio shows a year
7. Cinematographer approval—only Tony Gaudio, Ernie Haller, or Sol Polito
8. The right to negotiate through an agent or attorney
9. Quitting time of 6:00 P.M.
10. Billing above title; first billing in an all-star cast, second billing only if it was a male-based picture

On June 20, 1936, Bette, with her attorney, met with Jack Warner, Hal Wallis, and two studio attorneys. Warner told Bette that he would raise her salary from $1,600 to $2,000 if she would do the picture. Bette said no. She wanted a minimum of $3,500. When the meeting failed to end in an agreement, Warner suspended Bette.

She responded by writing Warner a letter dated June 21. "I would be willing to take less money," Bette wrote, "if in consideration of this, you would give me my rights. You have asked me to be level headed in this matter. I feel I am extremely and I hope you can agree that I am. I am more than anxious to work for you again but not as things stand. I really would be unable to do justice to my work at all—as I would feel I was coming back—not entitled to the things I sincerely believe I deserve. As a Happy person, I can work like Hell—as an unhappy one, I make myself and everyone around me unhappy."

Warner, however, called what he thought was Bette's bluff and dismissed her plea. She took her case to the press. "I am justified," she insisted to a reporter. "I would hate to tell you how little the studio pays me—much less than many of the new players, especially men. After all, I was on the stage three years and have been in pictures five years, four of them at Warner Brothers. And I have had some very definite successes. There are only a few years left in which I can hope to make money in this business." The latter would be a common refrain of Bette's. Of course, who could have known then that she'd be working for another 50-plus years?

Around this time Bette got an offer by an Italian producer to make two pictures in Europe. She accepted. Her escape out of the country was intricately plotted and highly dramatic. On a Sunday morning, at 12:01 A.M., she secretly fled Los Angeles and flew to Vancouver. She wore, in her own words, "a Garbo-type hat" that covered her eyes and half her face. She crossed Canada by train and sailed from Montreal to Europe by ship.

Jack Warner, however, would not give in without a fight. As he told the press, "It is high time something were done to make people under contract to the studios realize that a contract is not a mere scrap of paper to be thrown aside because they happen to make a good picture or two."

On September 9, 1936, Warners obtained an injunction in England, forbidding her to make any pictures outside the studio. The case went to trial in London on October 14, 1936. Bette, represented by Sir William Jowitt, argued that her contract with the studio was essentially a slave contract. In court Bette wore the same red and blue tweed coat and red beret for several days in a row, presumably to give the judge the impression of poverty. At one point Sir Patrick Hastings, representing Warner, became so enraged at Bette that he whipped off his wig and flung it to the courtroom floor. Jowitt relied on less dramatic tactics. He argued that Bette's face was used in commercial advertisements without her consent; that she was forced to make personal appearances even if they conflicted with her own beliefs; that she could not divorce her husband for three years after marrying him; that a movie poster could depict her practically nude without her consent; that if she became pregnant Warners had the option of terminating her contract; and that her husband could not even take a snapshot of her in their backyard if he wanted to.

Despite Jowitt's many arguments, on December 19 Justice Sir George Branson issued a verdict in favor of the studio. After it was read, Bette told reporters it was "a real sock in the teeth." In addition to her own court costs, the judge ordered her to pay Warners' court costs. Bette characterized the verdict as "a bitter defeat. I had to pay the Warner court costs as well as my own. All in all, my fight for principle cost me $103,000." Actually, the figure was much lower.

Upon returning to Los Angeles on November 18, 1936, Bette put on a humble face and told reporters, "You can't win. I tried and lost—fairly. The die is cast. I'm just a working girl, not a crusader. Work, work, work, and more work is my motto from now on. No, there are no hard feelings . . . I'm trying to be a good loser . . . and I shall try very hard to play the game."

To Jack Warner, Bette wrote on November 20, "I am ready, able and willing to resume the rendition of service pursuant to the terms of the contract." Warner responded by telling her to report to the studio on November 23 to meet with Hal Wallis.

Speculation abounded in Hollywood over whether Warner would punish the wayward and "naughty" Bette, as she was called in court, and ruin her promising career by forcing her into inferior projects. To Warner's credit he did not. In fact it can be argued that Bette lost the battle but won the war. Her poststrike films were certainly better than the tripe she had been given before she took action. If there was any question left after Warner assigned

Bette to do *Marked Woman, Kid Galahad, It's Love I'm After,* and *That Certain Woman,* it was obliterated when he purchased *Jezebel* for her. The production was given the full-scale A treatment by Warners, with no expense being spared. The picture would not only win Bette her second Oscar; it would make her, finally, a *star,* a major star of box office position.

This time Jack Warner voluntarily tore up Bette's old contract and in August 1938 gave her a new one worth considerably more money. He also decided to release Bette from paying the remainder of the studio's court costs stemming from the 1936 trial. The new contract raised her salary to $3,000 per week for the first year and promised annual raises thereafter.

Bette paid him back with one hit after another. For the next seven or eight years she would stay at the top, or near the top, of the box office. After *Jezebel* there came *The Sisters, Dark Victory, Juarez, The Old Maid,* and *The Private Lives of Elizabeth and Essex* in rapid succession. Each was acclaimed by the critics and embraced by the public. Bette had become the biggest female star in the history of the studio. Some called her "the fifth Warner brother."

After completing *Elizabeth and Essex* in July 1939, Bette finally took a much needed vacation. When it became an extended sojourn, Warner summoned her back to the studio. She refused. On August 31, 1939, she sent Warner a wire from New Hampshire that read, in part, "I am sure if I were lying in my coffin you would finally be convinced I am really exhausted and that I can't turn them out like a machine anymore. I know it would be better for you if I could and I'm truly sorry there is such a lack in me. We will have to reach some agreement for your future and mine." What she was referring to was yet another contract, one that would limit the number of films she had to make each year. She also wanted more money.

Bette still hadn't returned to the studio by October. On the 14th, she sent Warner a wire that read, in part, "From what I read in the papers you are having no trouble replacing me, also the Wood brothers [her managers] have been barred from the Warner lot. All this leads me to believe you have no intention of coming to terms with me. If this is true would you let me know, as I would like to make plans for the winter."

Jack Warner settled the dispute by flying to New Hampshire to meet with Bette in person. There he agreed to devise a new contract that would allow her to work only 40 out of 52 weeks a year. It also gave her a salary increase.

In February 1942, Hal Wallis went from overseeing all studio productions to becoming an independent producer with enormous freedom over his own pictures. His first film with this status was *Now, Voyager.* Meanwhile Warner promoted the studio's "associate producers" to "producers."

In the spring of 1943, after completing *Old Acquaintance,* Bette again rebelled against the studio and took an extended vacation in Mexico. This time she wanted something different. She wanted to establish her own production company, B. D. Inc., and become her own producer. In June 1943

Warner again acquiesced, and Bette signed a new nine-picture contract—five for B. D. Inc., four for Warner Brothers—which would give her production company 35 percent of the net profits of the B. D. Inc. films. Additionally, her personal salary was raised to $115,000 for each of the first four pictures (approximately $5,500 per week) and to $150,000 for the remaining pictures. The first film slated to be a "B. D. Inc. Production" was *A Stolen Life*. The contract would later be amended on February 4, 1946, giving her yet another raise to $6,000 for the first 66 weeks, then $7,000 per week for the remainder of the term. The contract was again modified on October 29, 1946, to accommodate an unexpected event—Bette's pregnancy.

"I'll just ease into the producing end this way," Bette told a reporter back in 1944. It'll be little different from what I've done before—and I'll be co-producer on only one of my three films a year. For the past several years the studio has been nice about letting me make suggestions on my films, and as a co-producer I'll do the same thing, only officially. A desk and an office? Heavens no! There's so much we players don't know about pictures. Most of us don't know what a budget looks like, and we've no idea how a film is cut and assembled. I want to learn. I see a day coming when all pictures will be made by small, individualized units rather than big companies, and they'll be better pictures."

A Stolen Life ended up being the only film produced by B. D. Inc., and the company folded in September 1947. Bette signed another contract with the studio on January 27, 1949, and it was indicative of her declining output. The contract called for only four pictures, one per year. Her last two pictures, *Winter Meeting* and *June Bride*, had performed disappointingly at the box office. Nevertheless, the contract gave her more than $10,000 per week, or approximately $200,000 per picture.

Toward the end of shooting *Beyond the Forest* in July 1949 Bette, unhappy with the picture, called Jack Warner and told him, *threatened* him, that if he wanted the picture to be completed he would have to release her from her contract. Likely it was just a ploy on Bette's part to get what it was that she *really* wanted—King Vidor fired as the picture's director, among other concessions. Warner, however, unhappy not only with Bette but also with her declining popularity at the box office, *this* time decided to call her bluff. He released her from her contract. As the *Hollywood Citizen-News* reported, "It has been known for some time that Warner Bros. executives have been none too happy with the box office grosses of her past half dozen films. And it is believed that this is in back of the studio's willingness to grant her contract release."

Bette made an official (though only partially true) public statement. "This professional divorce is the result of my long-standing wish to be free of any contractual obligation in order to have a wider choice of roles. It is with cordial feelings and a sentimental regret that I take this step. I'm glad it's all over at last. Some people kept sniping that I was 'too difficult' and that the studio was getting rid of a headache, but that's not true at all. I'm most appreciative of J. L. Warner for his consideration of my request."

Warner would later blame the break-up on Bette's agent, Lew Wasserman. In his autobiography he wrote:

> Bette began showing up in my office surrounded by the MCA group,
> and every time we talked about a new script she would say sweetly:
> 'Jack, can I have a copy for Lew?'
>   Before long the ten percenters had Bette so confused that it
> affected her story vision, and she was laying bigger eggs than an
> ostrich. I simply couldn't take it. Or them. . . . When they pushed me
> too far, I told Bette I was through. We settled her contract, and I was
> relieved to see her go elsewhere with her cortege.

After 18 years Bette Davis was a free agent. At the time she was considered one of the highest-paid women in America. In the fiscal year ending in 1947, she had been paid $328,000 by Warner Brothers.

Before leaving, she had to complete *Beyond the Forest*. It was an unfortunate ending to a spectacular and historical partnership.

Many years later Bette made amends of sorts with the studio when it released a small independent picture that turned out to be a surprise hit, *What Ever Happened to Baby Jane?* (1962). Its success resulted in Bette's returning to the studio, at Jack Warner's request, to make the 1964 picture *Dead Ringer*. Bette *really* left Warner Brothers, though, that day in August 1949, when she recorded her final line of dialogue for *Beyond the Forest*: "I can't *stand* it here anymore!"

> "They just said hello and, 'My, it's good to have you back.' "
>   *Bette Davis, on her return to Warners, 1963*

> "The men who ran the studios were tough, but they knew their
> business. They were in touch with the audience. There'll never be
> anything like those 10 years Hal Wallis was in charge of production
> at Warners. They were gamblers; they took chances. You could go to
> them with an idea."
>   *Bette Davis, 1988*

JACK WARNER

Youngest of the Warner brothers, Jack Warner (1892–1978) was the one most directly responsible for the studio's output. Warner was a peculiar man, and his oddities are a part of Hollywood folklore. He was considered a moral man, strange for Hollywood, with no harem of starlets. He would not even allow any of the women on his payroll to show up for work wearing pants. And he had a strange, even vulgar sense of humor. He was known all over town for his bad jokes. Jack Benny once said of him, "Jack Warner would rather make a bad joke than a good picture."

He was also known, while viewing rushes, to talk back to the screen. For instance, he'd see Bette Davis on the screen crying, and he'd encourage her to pour it on. Bette's tears, after all, equated in Warner's view to more dollars at the box office.

Warner and Bette had a father-daughter, love-hate relationship. Unfortunately, during their years together, and despite the phenomenal output of their collaboration, the hate superseded the love.

When Jack Warner finally left the studio he built, a farewell party was thrown in his honor. Bette was invited to sit on the dais along with Mervyn LeRoy, Edward G. Robinson, Rosalind Russell, and Efram Zimbalist, Jr. Frank Sinatra was the emcee. When Bette stood up to speak, she asked for a moment of silence—in honor of the many Warners stars and employees who were no longer alive. She would later say, "The Hollywood that I knew came to an end the night of our tribute to Jack Warner."

> "I miss motion picture executives like Jack Warner. . . . They were gamblers. They gave us all a chance. They gave me a career."
>
> *Bette Davis, 1987*

> "When you're dealing with talented people, I guess you have to expect some trouble and friction. You never hear a peep from the duds."
>
> *Jack Warner*

When asked, late in his life, to define the term *movie star*, Jack Warner responded simply, "Bette Davis."

WATCH ON THE RHINE ★★★★

Warner Brothers
1943   114 minutes   bw
Directed by: Herman Shumlin
Produced by: Hal B. Wallis
Screenplay by: Dashiell Hammett, with additional scenes and dialogue by
  Lillian Hellman, based on the play by Lillian Hellman
Cinematography by: Merritt Gerstad and Hal Mohr
Cast: Paul Lukas, Bette Davis, Geraldine Fitzgerald, Lucile Watson, Beulah
  Bondi, George Coulouris, Donald Woods, Henry Daniell, Eric
  Roberts, Donald Buka, Janis Wilson, Mary Young, Kurt Katch, Erwin
  Kalser, Clyde Fillmore, Robert O. Davis, Frank Wilson, Clarence
  Muse, Anthony Caruso, Howard Hickman, Elvira Curci, Creighton
  Hale, Alan Hale, Jr.

Warner Brothers purchased the rights to the Lillian Hellman play in an agreement dated December 30, 1941. Hellman received $150,000 plus 15 percent of the total gross receipts. She also was given casting approval.

Set in April 1940, *Watch on the Rhine* tells the story of Sarah Mueller and her husband, Kurt, who return to the United States from Europe after 17 years to avoid the Nazi invasion. They stay at her mother's house in Washington, D.C. At the time, unfortunately, Sarah's mother, Fanny, has a houseguest, a Romanian count who is a Nazi sympathizer. This complicates things because Sarah's husband is a member of an underground anti-Nazi group.

Sarah is a 38-year-old wife and mother. She looks like a skinny school-marm. Her children are good-natured but on the pompous side. When Sarah's mother meets her grandchildren for the first time, she asks Sarah, "Are these your children or are they dressed-up midgets?"

The part of Sarah Mueller was played on Broadway by Mady Christians, and Christians was a contender for the film role as well. According to a March 2, 1942, casting sheet, other top contenders were Greer Garson, Irene Dunne, Claudette Colbert, Norma Shearer, Janet Gaynor, and Miriam Hopkins.

For the role of Marthe de Brancovis, wife of the Romanian count, Olivia de Havilland, Geraldine Fitzgerald, and Helen Trenholme were the top contenders, with Fitzgerald winning out.

The most difficult casting assignment for Warners was the star role of Kurt Mueller. Paul Lukas played the role on Broadway and was touring with the road show at the time the film went into preproduction. *Rhine* ended its tour in Chicago in May 1942, and Lukas was available to do the film. Jack Warner, however, stalled in the decision to cast Lukas because he wanted a big-name actor for the picture. As he told Lillian Hellman and Herman Shumlin, he was concentrating his efforts on "some important motion picture star" for the role. Among those considered were Charles Boyer and Paul Henreid.

Meanwhile Lukas became so perturbed by Warner's delay in casting him that at one point he announced he was no longer interested. Casting Sarah was delayed until some decision was made about Kurt.

For a while it looked as though Charles Boyer would be signed for the part, but he finally backed out, claiming that he couldn't portray a German convincingly enough. Hellman and Shumlin, who had a good deal of influence in the matter, wanted Irene Dunne for Sarah. There was also some talk of Helen Hayes in the role.

Finally Warner signed Lukas at $2,500 a week or an estimated $25,000 for the picture. With Lukas in the picture, Warner was intent on a big female box office star, and he found her in Bette Davis. Many were surprised, including Warner, that she would accept so secondary a role. Much to her credit, and against the wishes of the studio brass, Bette refused to take top billing on the picture, insisting that it belonged to Lukas. She *did* accept the higher salary, more than double what Lukas was getting. She also had her part slightly beefed up. In fact she was even given lines that belonged to Lukas in the stage version. Still, the central role in the picture obviously belonged to Lukas.

Also recruited from the Broadway play were Lucille Watson, George Coulouris, Donald Buka, and Eric Roberts.

There were some problems with the script and the censor. The Breen Office had a problem with Kurt Mueller committing the murder of Count de Brancovis, no matter how justified, without being duly punished. Breen was also perturbed by a scripted bathroom scene and reiterated to Warner that the showing of or reference to a toilet was strictly prohibited in Hollywood motion pictures. The toilet was subsequently scrapped. As for the murder, the Breen Office settled the matter by ordering a line of dialogue that said that Kurt would be assassinated if he was reported to the German Embassy; also at the end of the picture, it was clearly established that Kurt had been killed by the Nazis.

With a budget of $879,000 and 48 shooting days, *Watch on the Rhine* started production on June 9, 1942. Bette and Paul, however, did not even show up for makeup tests until June 26, after the film had been in production for 16 days. Bette completed her hair and wardrobe tests on Monday, June 29, and started shooting on June 30.

Herman Shumlin, who directed the stage play, was brought out to do the film even though he was not familiar with the medium. Upon his arrival at the studio Shumlin spent time on the sets of *Yankee Doodle Dandy* and *Now, Voyager*, studying the techniques of Mike Curtiz and Irving Rapper respectively. From the beginning of production, Shumlin had difficulty with cinematographer Merritt Gerstad. Hal Mohr was brought in to replace him. According to Mohr, he also took over the film from Shumlin. "After eight weeks," Mohr recalled, "they were ready to call it off. Shumlin had never made a picture, and he was lost, working at it like a stage play. . . . I simply took hold of the damn picture and made it."

With the production already seven days behind schedule, Bette left early on Friday, July 24, to christen a ship. On Tuesday, July 28, she didn't show up at all. Instead she made an appearance at an army camp. It was during the production of this film, in the summer of 1942, that Bette organized the Hollywood Canteen.

Shumlin was also having problems with Geraldine Fitzgerald, who was displeased with the cuts that were being made in her part. The matter became so serious that Hal Wallis considered replacing her with Margaret Lindsay. That, however, proved to be unnecessary, and the production finished on Saturday, August 22, 14 days behind schedule.

Warner Brothers marketed the picture, naturally, by featuring Bette. One ad proclaimed, "A Love Like Hers, a Man Doesn't Leave Behind. It is Part of His Courage Whatever He Does, Wherever He Goes."

On October 19, 1943, rival David Selznick wired Jack Warner, lauding *Watch on the Rhine* as the best picture of the year. The film would go on to be nominated for a Best Picture Oscar, and Lukas would win an Oscar for best actor. Today the film remains exceptional, exploding with politics and intrigue, told with good acting and better writing.

THE WATCHER IN THE WOODS ★ ½
Walt Disney
1980   100 minutes   Technicolor
Directed by: John Hough
Produced by: Ron Miller
Screenplay by: Brian Clemens, Harry Spaulding, and Rosemary Anne
    Sisson, from the novel by Florence Engel Randall

Cinematography by: Alan Hume
Cast: Bette Davis, Carroll Baker, David McCallum, Lynn-Holly Johnson,
    Kyle Richards, Ian Bannen, Richard Pasco, Frances Cuka, Benedict
    Taylor, Eleanor Summerfield, Georgina Hale, Katherine Levy

The Watcher in the Woods, budgeted at $7.1 million, started shooting at
Pinewood Studios and various locations in and around London in August
1979. Bette, cast in an insignificant supporting part (though she would get
top billing), flew to London with her new assistant, Kathryn Sermak, hired
because Peggy Shannon, Bette's usual assistant and traveling companion,
was unable to do so.

During the six-week shoot in England, Bette actually worked for only
about 10 days and was generally bored. Nothing she saw before the cameras
excited her either. Bette played Mrs. Aylwood, an eccentric recluse who rents
out her home to a vacationing American family. Lynn-Holly Johnson, the
family's eldest daughter, becomes convinced that the house and the surrounding woods are haunted. Bette was unimpressed by Johnson and was vocal in
her concern. The studio, (and Bette) had wanted Diane Lane for the part but
was unable to get her.

Upon its release in April 1980, *The Watcher in the Woods* received mostly
poor reviews. Surprisingly, Disney pulled the film from release for what it
deemed at the time to be "fine tuning." Instead the studio rereleased *Mary
Poppins*. Disney then proceeded to pump another $1 million into the picture
and, after 18 months of rework, rereleased it in October 1981. Again the
reviews were poor. The picture ended up being one of the biggest flops of the
year, with Disney reportedly writing it off as a $6.7 million loss.

WATERLOO BRIDGE ★ ½
Universal
1931   72 minutes   bw
Directed by: James Whale
Produced by: Carl Laemmle, Jr.
Screenplay by: Benn W. Levy and Tom Reed, based on the play by Robert
    E. Sherwood
Cinematography by: Arthur Edeson
Cast: Mae Clark, Kent Douglass, Doris Lloyd, Ethel Griffies, Enid Bennett,
    Frederick Kerr, Bette Davis, Rita Carlisle

An adaptation of the play by Robert E. Sherwood, *Waterloo Bridge*,
Bette's third of three pictures for Universal, was set in World War I, with
Bette the sister of the hero, played by Kent Douglass.

Waterloo Bridge received mixed reviews upon its release, with nary a
mention of Bette's performance. It was remade with better results in 1940
with Vivien Leigh and Robert Taylor and again as *Gaby* in 1956 with Leslie
Caron and John Kerr.

WAY BACK HOME ★★

RKO

1932 81 minutes bw

Directed by: William A. Seiter

Produced by: Pandro S. Berman

Screenplay by: Jane Murfin, based on radio characters created by Phillips
    Lord

Cinematography by: J. Roy Hunt

Cast: Phillips Lord, Bette Davis, Frank Albertson, Effie Palmer, Bennett
    Kilpack, Mrs. Phillips Lord, Raymond Hunter, Oscar Apfel, Stanley
    Fields, Dorothy Peterson, Frankie Darro

Bette was loaned from Universal to RKO to make *Way Back Home*, originally
titled *Other People's Business*, which was based on the Phillips Lord radio
serial "Seth Parker." The picture, shot in Santa Cruz, California, was
budgeted at $400,000, which was quite high for the standard picture of the
period.

Bette, for one, liked the film and for the first time in her fledgling film
career was happy with the way she *looked* on screen. *Variety*, however, didn't
care for it all, saying, "As entertainment, the film is unbelievably bad."

THE WEDDINGS
Harmon Nelson, Jr.

In August 1932 Bette, Ham, Ruthie, Bobby, and an aunt and a cousin drove
to Yuma, Arizona, with two poodles and two cars. In Yuma the temperature
raged to 107 degrees while the ceremony took place on August 18. Bette wore
a beige two-piece dress with gardenias pinned to her bosom and listed "no
occupation" on her marriage application.

Arthur Farnsworth, Jr.

Bette surprised many in Hollywood with her sudden marriage to Arthur
Farnsworth, Jr., of Vermont. On December 30, 1940, she drove from Los
Angeles to Rimrock, Arizona, to the 15,000-acre ranch home belonging to
Justin Dart and his wife, former Davis costar Jane Bryan. Accompanying her
on the trip were her mother, Ruthie, Margaret Donovan, Perc Westmore,
Lester Linsk, John Favor, Ruth Garland, and Bette's dog, Tibby. They were
met in Arizona by Bette's sister, Bobby, and her husband and by Arthur
Farnsworth, who flew in from the east.

The following day Bette, dressed in a white jersey wedding dress designed by Bernard Newman, and Farney were married at the ranch by
Reverend Robert Price, a Methodist parson from Clarksdale, Arizona.

William Grant Sherry

Bette and William Grant Sherry obtained their marriage license at the
Orange County, California, Courthouse in November 1945. They planned to

marry in a formal Episcopalian ceremony with Bette's uncle, the retired Reverend Paul Gordon Favor, conducting the ceremony. However, because she had previously been divorced, Bette was denied a church wedding by Reverend W. Bertrand Stevens, bishop of the Los Angeles Episcopal Diocese. Instead the wedding took place at the St. Francis Chapel of Mission Inn in Riverside, California, on November 29, 1945. The 3:30 P.M. ceremony was conducted by Reverend Francis Ellis. Bette wore a faintly checked powder blue suit and a blue hat made of goose feathers. Her matron of honor and only attendant was her sister, Bobby Pelgram. Following the service Bette asked, "*Who* will give me a cigarette and a glass of champagne?"

Gary Merrill
Bette and Gary Merrill eloped to Juarez, Mexico, on July 28, 1950. The ceremony was performed at the home of attorney Jose Amador y Trias by Judge Raul Orozco. Bette wore a navy blue dress with white gloves. Merrill wore a gabardine suit with a maroon tie. The service was performed in Spanish. After the ceremony Bette refused to pose for a photograph kissing her new husband. She had done it before and said that it was bad luck.

DAVID WERNER
In 1930 David Werner was a New York talent scout for Universal Pictures. After seeing Bette in the Broadway play *Solid South*, Werner gave her a screen test and signed her to a studio contract. "I just don't know why I've done this," he told Bette at the time. "You are the greatest gamble I have ever sent to California. It is quite obvious that you are not the kind of person who is usually a success in pictures. You don't look like any actress I have ever seen on the screen. And yet, for some reason I cannot analyze, I think I am right."

WEST HOLLYWOOD, CALIFORNIA
For the last 12 years of her life Bette lived, for the most part, in a condominium in West Hollywood, California. Located at 1416 N. Havenhurst Drive, the building was known as Colonial House. Bette was proud of the fact that her building was built by Paul Williams, whom she referred to as "the first negro architect." Bette's condo was approximately 2,500 square feet and featured a large living room with a fireplace, a den, a master bedroom suite, and a terrace with city views.

Over the years Bette lived, worked, and played in West Hollywood. One of her first homes in California in the early 1930s was, ironically, a rented apartment, one of the La Ronda apartments, located at 1414 N. Havenhurst—next door to her final home.

PERC WESTMORE
During Bette's 18-year tenure at Warner Brothers (1932-1949) Perc (pronounced "purse") Westmore (1904-1970) was the head of the studio's makeup department. He designed the makeup and oversaw its application on virtu-

ally all of her studio productions during that time. He also became her good friend. After Bette's contract at Warner ended in 1949, Westmore continued to do Bette's makeup for pictures, including *The Virgin Queen* (1955) and *Storm Center* (1956).

THE WHALES OF AUGUST ★★½

Circle/Nelson
1987   90 minutes   TVC color
Directed by: Lindsay Anderson
Produced by: Carolyn Pfeiffer, Mike Kaplan
Screenplay by: David Berry from his own play
Cinematography by: Mike Fash
Cast: Bette Davis, Lillian Gish, Vincent Price, Ann Sothern, Harry Carey, Jr., Frank Grimes, Margaret Ladd, Tisha Sterling, Mary Steenburgen, Frank Pitkin, Mike Bush

Originally an off-Broadway play by David Berry, *The Whales of August* provided Bette with her first picture in eight years. She played Libby Strong, a blind and defiant elderly woman who lives in the Maine house of her sister (Lillian Gish) because her daughter doesn't want her and she has nowhere else to go. The thin plot revolves around the installation of a picture window in the sister's home: Lillian wants one so that she can watch the whales that appear annually in August; Bette tells her that they are too old, too settled to want anything new. Bette would later complain about the plot, "I would have liked the sisters to have a little bigger problem than whether they changed the window. A little bigger issue, yes."

Director Lindsay Anderson recently related: "*The Whales of August* was designed from the start as a film for Lillian Gish, for whom our producer and my friend Mike Kaplan had been determined to make a film with a good, extensive part. Mike had seen the play and taken Miss Gish to see it with him some years before. Miss Gish had agreed to play the part if Mike could find finance for the project.

"Over a period of years Mike got a script written, invited me to direct it, and finally got financing for the project. Bette Davis was invited to play Libby because she seemed to be the ideal actress for the role. This was on the strength of the play—before the script was written and also before she had had her operation. She turned it down.

"Mike Kaplan came back to Bette *after* the script had been written and after she had had her operation. She thought again. Mike and I visited Bette at her flat in Los Angeles, had a friendly meeting, at which Bette gave her opinion about various directors she'd worked with. [She was] complimentary about Wyler and Edmund Goulding and extremely dismissive of Irving Rapper. And Bette agreed to play the part. She was quite aware, of course, of the casting of Lillian Gish, and she made no criticism of the film's script. Nor did either of us mention our previous get-together on *People Are Living There* [the Athol Fugard play that Anderson was going to direct Bette in until she inexplicably removed herself from the project], except that Bette rather hurriedly dismissed it by saying she hadn't played the part because she 'couldn't manage the accent.'

"Bette had nothing to do with the casting of *The Whales of August*, except that I remember she expressed herself very violently on the subject of Danny Kaye when the possibility came up of him playing Maranov, because she had taken a dislike to him when she met him in Paris on the occasion of some award or other."

For the part Bette wanted John Gielgud. She settled for Vincent Price. She demanded her own makeup artist and hairdresser and insisted that the noted (and expensive) theatrical wig maker Paul Huntley do her wig for the picture. She also insisted on her own costume designer, Julie Weiss. All of this was a lot to ask given the modest $3 million budget. It was the issue of Bette's costumes that caused Bette to rebuff Jocelyn Herbert, the picture's production designer. Lindsay Anderson recalls: "It [the matter of costumes] also led to Bette being violently offensive, both personally and professionally, when she met Jocelyn Herbert, the production designer, who came with me from London. Bette thought, I suppose, she was defending herself, but in the end her behavior was terribly and quite unnecessarily self-destructive. Jocelyn and I called on Bette at her hotel in New York, not realizing that she had worked with *her* designer in Hollywood. Jocelyn most certainly wasn't attempting to take over this assignment but simply wanted to be able to be free to discuss and make suggestions (which would have been to Bette's advantage). Bette was very rude to Jocelyn the moment we met at her hotel, and Jocelyn was certainly not going to enter into any sort of argument. Within five minutes or so she had left the hotel, and I don't think that she and Bette ever had much communication again. Bette obviously was, or thought she was, defending herself from any sort of guidance or advice from anyone."

At the time production started, Gish was 90, Bette 78; Ann Sothern 78, Vincent Price 76. Shooting started in the late fall of 1986 on Cliff Island in Casco Bay, not far from Portland, Maine, Bette's residence when she was Mrs. Gary Merrill. Filming at the location would be bittersweet for Bette. She would later recall, "I would look across the bay, and there was the land where Gary and I brought up our family. It made me very homesick for all my children when they were very young."

But if there was sentiment on Bette's part, Lindsay Anderson never saw evidence of it: "The film was not shot in Maine through any expressed desire by Bette, nor did she seem in the least interested in the locality or the people. Anyway, of course, we never shot on the mainland, but on Cliff Island in Casco Bay. I don't think that Bette had made herself at all popular when she was living up there with Gary Merrill, and she made no effort to get in touch with friends from the past (if there were any)."

For one of the few times in her career Bette watched the nightly screening of rushes. Lindsay Anderson continues: "Yes, Bette did come to rushes regularly in the evenings. She seemed to enjoy them, frequently complimented the cameraman Mike Fash on his work, and seemed always to enjoy the experience. She never made any criticisms that I can remember."

Bette was *not* fond of director Anderson. She would refer to him as "very opinionated, disagreeable, macho." Bette was upset, she claimed, because Anderson cut lines vital to her character. He disagrees: "Bette's comments about our relationship and about the script of *The Whales of August* were mostly nonsensical, I'm afraid. I went through the script with her before shooting started, and she had no criticisms to make about the lack of 'conflict.' There were a few comments from her about particular lines, which we agreed about and would change, not very fundamentally, according to her wishes. I had myself sharpened the conflict between herself and her sister, particularly over the 'picture window,' and she accepted this without demur."

For the part Bette insisted on using her sense of touch to compensate for her character's lack of sight. "Interestingly enough," she later said, "my director fought me every inch of the way on that. But I just said forward, march, and did it."

Off camera Bette insisted on smoking, much to Lillian Gish's dismay and despite the fact that smoking had been banned in the wooden lodge in which most of the shooting was done. Lillian would later say, "I never smoke. Smoking makes your hair smell."

Meanwhile, as was typical of her, Bette engaged in something of a geriatric acting Olympics with her costar. She demanded and got top billing even though Gish clearly had seniority. Said Lillian, "Oh dear, I just can't deal with that sort of thing. I don't care what they do with *my* name. If they leave it off, so much the better. It's the work I love, not the glory."

To Bette it was clear that Anderson and producer Mike Kaplan favored Gish. Kaplan enthused to a reporter about Gish's strength, "Inside the lace glove there's a hand of steel. It's not for nothing that they called her the Iron Horse of Hollywood."

Bette treated Gish with disdain, virtually ignoring her off camera. Gish retaliated, Bette charged, by feigning deafness when Bette delivered her lines. Gish would then turn to Anderson and ask *him* to deliver Bette's lines off camera. On Bette's treatment of her costar, Lindsay Anderson relates: "Bette certainly resented Lillian Gish from the start and made no effort to get on with her—until the last days of the picture, when her attitude changed. She took possession, implacably, of the bedroom which had been built onto the house for Libby, which she occupied with her hair people, makeup people, etc. She did *not* invite Miss Gish to relax there. Although every effort was made to treat Bette with respect, care, consideration, etc., I got the feeling that she was determined to treat the world as an enemy. . . .

"Bette did not want to share, or wasn't able to share, stage or screen with another leading actress. However, she did not behave badly towards, for instance, Ann Sothern, who is a very professional and very experienced actress. It was quite clear that Ann would not stand any nonsense, and it's possible that Bette was a bit frightened of her.

"Lillian was quite aware of the hostility in Bette's attitude, though I don't think she was exactly clear that it was based on resentment. She asked me, in fact, more than once, why Bette seemed to behave in a hostile way, to which, of course, Lillian was entirely unused. I suggested that Bette was unhappy and had been ill. Lillian was sympathetic, but of course she never sought to retaliate. And toward the end of shooting Bette definitely did try to be more friendly to Lillian."

Still, Anderson says, "It's clear from Bette's career that she finds it difficult to share. Her triumphs have been her own." Lillian also tried to rationalize Bette's behavior as a result of her stroke: "That face! Have you ever seen such a tragic face? Poor woman! How she must be suffering! I don't think it's right to judge a person like that. We must bear and forbear."

On Bette's health, Anderson adds: "Of course Bette's health and physical condition must have affected her and affected her behavior. She behaved badly at the wrap-party by being extremely rude to the woman who had been her stand-in and who made the mistake of coming to sit down next to Bette and make polite conversation. Bette informed her sharply that the empty chair was not for her and told her to get up and go away. This reduced the poor woman to tears, and I had to go out and calm her down. She was going to write to the newspapers, she said, but I assured her that there was nothing out of the ordinary about Bette's behavior and no one would find it in the least surprising.

"Bette's attitude to me varied. At first she was friendly, then hostile, and finally she was friendly again for the last part of the picture. I only had one real bust-up with her, when she started to try to lay down the law about a scene, which I didn't like much anyway, and to describe how it should be staged and, particularly, how Lillian Gish should play to her. This is where I found myself driven to tell her that she wasn't 'taking over the picture.' Bette got very angry and walked off the set. However, she returned in an hour or so, and shooting proceeded. During the cutting I lost the scene in question, without any difficulty.

"We didn't really have any violent disagreements during the shooting, though unfortunately Bette always seemed happier to conflict than collaborate, with the exception, I might add, of any scenes in which she was acting *alone*. [It was then that] our relationship was always friendly and quite harmonious."

Ann Sothern, who would win a Best Supporting Actress Oscar nomination for her performance, would later say: "You'd just have to call her a gritty lady. There wasn't anything that she wouldn't attempt. . . . [She was also] an impossible person at times. She was very strong-willed and always wanted her own way—but usually she was right."

Lindsay Anderson adds in conclusion: "I should add that I (and everyone else) had the greatest respect for Bette, and she could hardly have been treated better. Unfortunately, by the time she came to make *Whales* she was no longer the perfect mistress of her technique. Of course she knew this, but she could never bring herself to admit it—perhaps not even to herself.

"However, I think that in the end she gave an extremely good performance, and I have absolutely no regrets about her casting and her work.

"In spite of all difficulties of temperament, Bette was respected by everyone for her past and her ability. It was really a pity that she felt the need to be spurred on by aggression and by finding members of the unit to whom she could be nasty. As I told her, she wasted her time and her energy by fighting unnecessary battles. But then perhaps those battles were exactly what she needed to give her dynamic.

"It was probably a pity that her 'Kath' wasn't able to be with her during shooting. To get an assistant-companion for her whom she would tolerate for more than two or three days was practically impossible. Still, as Bette announced at the end-of-the-picture party (at which, I'm afraid, she behaved characteristically badly), *'We made it!'* "

Bette did not attend the New York premiere of *The Whales of August,* which was held on Lillian Gish's birthday; nor did she attend the Los Angeles premiere. She was reportedly outraged that the party was to be held on a soundstage. "A soundstage!" she roared. "There is so little taste left in the world."

WHAT EVER HAPPENED TO BABY JANE? ★★★

A Seven Arts Associates and Aldrich Production
Released by Warner Brothers
1962   132 minutes   bw
Directed by: Robert Aldrich
Produced by: Robert Aldrich
Screenplay by: Lukas Heller, based on the novel by Henry Farrell
Cinematography by: Ernest Haller
Cast: Bette Davis, Joan Crawford, Victor Buono, Anna Lee, Julie Allred, Gina Gillespie, Marjorie Bennett, Maidie Norman, Barbara Merrill, Dave Willock, Ann Barton

> "If Joan and I are going to be in a picture together, who's going to be brave enough to direct it?"
>
> *Bette Davis, 1948*

Bette claimed to Hedda Hopper that she had been sent the book by Bill Frye in 1960. Frye tried to buy the rights to the property without success. Upon finishing the book, Bette sent it to Alfred Hitchcock, who nixed the project.

Joan Crawford, of course, claimed that it was *she* who first discovered the property. According to Joan she sent the book to Robert Aldrich as a project for her and Bette. One night while Bette was doing *The Night of the Iguana* on Broadway in late 1961, a fur-clad Joan Crawford paid her a backstage visit and told her that she had found a novel with prize-winning parts for both of them. She told Bette that she had already sent the novel to Robert Aldrich, who was in Italy finishing a film.

Aldrich told a different story. He claimed that he had received a copy of

the novel from its author, Henry Farrell, and was told that the movie rights were available for $10,000. He then sent the novel to Crawford, who had for years encouraged him to find a story for her and Bette to do together. Crawford was immediately interested, but by the time Aldrich was ready to move on the project the price for rights had escalated to $61,000. Aldrich, partnered with Joe Levine, purchased the rights and hired Lukas Heller to write the script. Actually a script had already been done by Harry Essex, but it was all but nixed by Aldrich. Essex later tried to get a screen credit from the Screenwriter's Guild, which ruled that the sole credit should go to Heller.

The partnership between Levine and Aldrich soured shortly thereafter, and Aldrich bought Levine's interest in the film; Levine asked for and got $85,000. "My immediate problem," Aldrich told a reporter for the *New York Times*, "was to get Bette Davis and Joan Crawford to make *Baby Jane* for what I could pay them, a figure far below their going salaries. From my rapidly narrowing slice of the pie I offered each actress a piece of the picture plus some salary."

Aldrich sent Bette the script from Rome with an attached note that read, "If this script doesn't present you with the best part you have ever been offered, there is no point in our talking. But if it does, I'll fly to New York." The letter was signed by Robert Aldrich, whom Bette did not know. Said Bette: "I knew it was a marvelous part. At the same time it was a dare and a gamble." A month later Bette cabled Aldrich: "[I'll be] happy to see you in New York."

Aldrich flew to New York and met with Bette at her town house on 78th Street. Bette asked Aldrich two questions: what part she would be playing and whether he had ever slept with Joan Crawford.

Bette got top billing and more money up front, plus a piece of the profits. Crawford settled for less money and a bigger percentage of the profits and ended up getting the better deal.

Four major companies refused to read the script. Three that read the script nixed the project, Warner Brothers included. Then Aldrich found Eliot Hyman of Seven Arts Productions, who read the script and agreed to finance the film.

Although Jack Warner refused to finance the picture, he agreed to distribute it. On July 19, 1962, Bette and Joan returned to Warner Brothers—to the Trophy Room that displayed awards the two actresses had won for the studio—for a luncheon hosted by Warner himself. The sentiment of their return to the studio was overshadowed by the speculation by the public and the press as to whether or not Bette and Joan would feud during the making of the picture. Hazel Flynn reported in the July 20, 1962, *Hollywood Citizen-News*, "I talked to Ernest Haller [set to shoot the picture, another nod to nostalgia], the noted cinematographer. He had made fourteen movies with Bette Davis. . . . He also had made several with Joan. . . . He admitted the whole thing may develop into a battle royal."

Bette had a hard time getting a grip on her character. Certainly Jane

Hudson was unlike anyone she had ever played before. In rehearsal she tried out different voices, different *looks*, different mannerisms. Nothing worked. Nothing felt inherently right—until she got dressed in *those* clothes, *that* wig (scavenged from the MGM makeup department—it was ironically, an old Joan Crawford wig), and *that* makeup. Bette wanted Jane to look and feel as if she never washed her face. It was Bette's theory that Jane simply applied another layer of makeup to her face every day. Perc Westmore created the base makeup for Bette. It was a special, flat, dead-white base to which Bette then applied her own layers of makeup. Initially Aldrich objected to the white caked-on look. He thought it was *too* much, too grotesque. After much persistence by Bette, however, he acquiesced.

While Bette had her makeup and costumes to work with, Joan Crawford had her wheelchair. "I have the greatest prop in the world—a wheelchair," she told reporters. "The more she [Bette] screams, the more I hold my screams in."

The story opens in 1913 with Julie Allred playing Baby Jane, age six. Billed as "The Diminutive Dancing Duse from Duluth," Baby Jane was a star. She raked in the money while her 13-year-old sister, Blanche (Gina Gillespie), watched from the wings. The film then cuts to the early 1930s, with Blanche a big movie star. She tries to get has-been, no-talent Jane some acting work, but to no avail. Aldrich shows clips from *Parachute Jumper* and *Ex-Lady* to establish that Jane was not much of a talent or success as an adult actress. She is also always drunk. We learn that on her last picture she had gone through six cases of booze and had slugged two studio cops.

With a budget of $825,000, *What Ever Happened to Baby Jane?* started shooting at the Producers Studio on Melrose Avenue on Monday, July 23, 1962. Both Bette and Joan were on their best behavior, each trying to be more professional than the other. Joan was forever flanked on the set by an entourage that included maids, secretaries, agents, and the like. Bette, in contrast, was always alone.

Robert Aldrich immediately asserted his authority on the set. Despite having two more-than-formidable stars to contend with, he made it clear who was boss and earned the respect of Bette. "Director Bob Aldrich is a man of authority who knows how to run a set," Bette said to Hedda Hopper. "Nowadays, everybody's so polite and sweet, it was refreshing to know that someone was in charge."

The infamous rat scene was, Bette would contend, inspired by a scene out of her own childhood. Once, while her parents were having Sunday breakfast with their neighbors, the Browns, young Bette showed up at the table, pleased as punch, with a dead rat on a platter.

While they feigned camaraderie for the press, Bette and Joan despised each other, pulling out from their closets all the upstaging tricks their experience could summon. Bette was contemptuous of her costar's legendary Crawfordisms. Joan, it seems, hesitated to sacrifice her glamour in the name of art, even low-budget art. Bette scoffed at her attempts to look beautiful, given that her character was an invalid who had been a virtual prisoner for

20 years. During wardrobe tests for the film Crawford approached Bette and said, "I *do* hope my color scheme won't interfere with yours." Bette roared. "Color scheme? The picture is going to be shot in black and white for Chrissake!"

Another battle concerned Crawford's nail polish. She wanted it; Aldrich didn't. Bette would also later charge that Crawford wore three different sizes of strapped-on bosoms and that for the scene on the beach in which she lay flat on her back she wore the largest pair. While shooting the scene Bette fell on top of Crawford and, as she would later say, nearly had the breath knocked out of her. Bette compared the experience to falling on two footballs.

Bette also charged Joan with spiking her omnipresent Pepsi with vodka.

And then there was Joan's fanaticism for cleanliness. One scene called for Bette to hand Joan two pills. During rehearsal Bette handed the pills to her. Joan refused to actually swallow them. Bette, sensing that Joan did not want to put anything in her mouth that had been touched by the hands of someone else, responded by asking if Joan would prefer it if she just brought her the *bottle* of pills. She did.

For the kicking scene Joan insisted that a mannequin be used. For the scene in which she is slapped by Bette, Joan insisted on a double. Both times she was afraid that Bette would deliberately try to do her bodily harm.

On the set the two women referred to themselves as the "Gish sisters" and continued to contend to the press that they were "above" engaging in anything so petty as a catfight. Still, Bette couldn't help quipping to Mike Connolly, columnist of *The Hollywood Reporter*: "Of course there's no feud, although you DO understand that *I* am playing the title role."

Toward the end of shooting, on Friday, August 24, while en route to the Malibu beach location, Bette and her daughter, B.D., were shaken up in an auto accident. She was not seriously injured, though, and Bette proceeded to continue shooting. However, a few days before the film was to wrap, on September 8, Bette walked off the set. Dorothy Kilgallen reported in her column, "Bette Davis has been struck with a mysterious ailment and is out of the movie, *What Ever Happened to Baby Jane?* She will be undergoing a series of tests this weekend in Hollywood." Actually Bette was perfectly healthy and was simply rebelling over some action or inaction by Aldrich. Bette was well aware that nothing irked a producer more than to have a film held up when it was only days from completion.

The beach finale took a few days to shoot. After each take Joan would get up and go to her limousine to avoid the sun. Back at the studio, after the beach scene was completed, Joan complained to Aldrich that the lighting in *her* big beach scene was inferior to Bette's final dancing scene, and she insisted on retakes. Subsequently, a set was built at the studio with tons of sand brought in for the occasion. The retakes cost an additional $60,000.

With a final price tag of $980,000, and after 36 days of shooting, *What Ever Happened to Baby Jane?* completed production on September 12, 1962. Amazingly, the first sneak preview was held a mere month later.

The picture was marketed creatively with a typical ad reading, "Sister,

Sister, Oh So Fair, Why is There Blood All Over Your Hair?" Ads also included a list of warnings: (1) You are urged to see it from the beginning. (2) Be prepared for the macabre and the terrifying. (3) We ask your pledge to keep the shocking climax a secret. (4) When the tension begins to build, please try not to scream.

Certainly not much was expected of the film. It had has-been stars and a low budget. In fact the general consensus in Hollywood was *"How* could Davis and Crawford reduce themselves to *that?"* Then the film opened. While the reviews were mixed, the box office was spectacular. The film was the unexpected hit of the year.

The first sign that they were on to something big happened in previews. On October 23, J.L. wired Bette from New York: "Dear Bette, attended the preview last night here in New York of *What Ever Happened to Baby Jane?* The audience was thrilled and spellbound by you. Feel positive that you will receive another Academy Award for this extraordinary performance." At other previews audiences screamed and broke out into spontaneous applause.

The picture was such a success that it propelled Bette into a comeback of sorts. As she said shortly afterward, "Before *Baby Jane*, I was a Hollywood outcast. Within a few weeks after its first screenings, I began to get offers. . . ."

WHERE LOVE HAS GONE ★ ½

Joseph E. Levine Productions
Released by Paramount
1964   114 minutes   Techniscope
Directed by: Edward Dmytryk
Produced by: Joseph E. Levine
Screenplay by: John Michael Hayes, based on the novel by Harold Robbins
Cinematography by: Joe MacDonald
Cast: Susan Hayward, Bette Davis, Mike Connors, Joey Heatherton, Jane
    Greer, George Macready, DeForest Kelley, Anne Seymour, Willis
    Bouchey, Walter Reed, Ann Doran, Bartlett Robinson, Whit Bissell,
    Anthony Caruso, Jack Greening, Olga Sutcliffe, Howard Wendell,
    Colin Kenny

Where Love Has Gone was based on the bestselling novel by Harold Robbins, which was inspired by the Lana Turner/Johnny Stompanato affair and eventual murder.

During the shooting, part of it done in San Francisco, the company was fraught with tension. Bette almost instantly disliked Susan Hayward. Although she was only 10 years older than Hayward, Bette was playing her mother in the picture, a fact she undoubtedly resented. She was also irritated that Hayward's last picture before *Where Love Has Gone* had been *Stolen Hours*, a remake of one of Bette's greatest triumphs, *Dark Victory*. The director, Edward Dmytryk, later recalled, "Most female stars come on pretty strong—it comes with the territory—but Bette was undoubtedly the champ. . . . A diplomat she is not. It began when I had been shooting for some days, rewriting as I went along. Early one morning, I came on the set with a handful of new pages and found Miss Davis in her dressing room, ready for work. . . . I sat down with her and went over the changes, with which she heartily concurred. . . . Susan heard that *Bette Davis* was rewriting her scenes. Unlike her opponent, Susan was an insecure actress, and suspicions immediately flooded her mind."

Production closed in the spring of 1964, and Bette began preparations for her next picture, *Hush . . . Hush, Sweet Charlotte*. Meanwhile, she got word that Paramount wanted her to return to the set for an additional scene. The 1½-minute scene called for Bette, as Mrs. Gerald Hayden, to go insane. Bette refused to shoot the scene on the grounds that it was incongruous with her character. On June 12, 1964, while Bette was wrapping location shooting of *Hush* in Louisiana, a Los Angeles court forebade her from making *Hush* or any other picture until she shot the added scene for Paramount. Because of this and other matters (namely, Joan Crawford), *Hush* would shut down. Bette, meanwhile, continued to refuse to shoot the added scene, and Paramount eventually conceded, releasing the picture as it was.

Where Love Has Gone was generally panned upon release. Worse, it failed to duplicate the box office success of the previous Harold Robbins picture, *The Carpetbaggers* (1964).

"WHITE MAMA"

"White Mama" was a 1980 made-for-television movie about the friendship between an elderly white woman and a young black boy from the ghetto, the latter played by Ernest Harden, Jr. It was shot on location in East Los Angeles and was directed by Jackie Cooper, former child actor.

The production went smoothly, with the only real debate being over the title. CBS executives argued that it sounded like some Angie Dickinson exploitation picture. Bette retorted that unless the title was retained, she would walk off the picture. In retrospect the network was right.

Thomas W. Moore was executive producer, and Jean Moore Edwards was producer. It was written by Robert C. S. Downs and shot by William K. Jurgensen. In addition to Bette and Harden, the cast included Eileen Heckart, Virginia Capers, Anne Ramsey, Lurene Tuttle, Peg Shirley, Ernie Hudson, Dan Mason, Vincent Schiavelli, Cheryl Harvey, John Hancock, and Eddie Quillan.

WHO'S AFRAID OF VIRGINIA WOOLF?

Bette badly wanted the part of the blowzy, bitchy, battling Martha in the 1966 film adaptation of the Edward Albee play *Who's Afraid of Virginia Woolf?* There was some talk that Bette would star in the picture opposite James Mason as George. However, when Elizabeth Taylor and Richard Burton expressed interest in playing the parts, thoughts of Bette as Martha were discarded. Elizabeth Taylor would win a Best Actress Oscar for her performance. Still, in her impersonation of Bette, Taylor paid homage of sorts to Davis with the picture's opening scene:

MARTHA: What a dump. Hey, what's that from? What a *dump!*
  GEORGE: How would I know what . . .
MARTHA: Aw, come on! What's it from? You know! It's from some
             goddamn Bette Davis picture. Some Warner Brothers
             epic . . .

The line, of course, was from Bette's 1949 picture *Beyond the Forest*.

THE WICKED STEPMOTHER ★ ½

MGM/Largo Productions
1989
Directed by: Larry Cohen
Produced by: Robert Littman
Screenplay by: Larry Cohen
Cinematography by: Bryan England
Cast: Bette Davis, Colleen Camp, Lionel Stander, David Rasche, Shawn
    Donahue, Tom Bosley, Richard Moll, Seymour Cassel, Evelyn Keyes,
    Laurene Landon, Barbara Carrera

Backed by arguably the most spectacular acting career in motion picture
history, with 58 years of movies behind her, Bette embarked with enthusiasm
on a new project. It was called *The Wicked Stepmother*. She had started out
in pictures playing the good sister in *Bad Sister* (1931) and ended up playing
The Wicked Stepmother.

It was not a fitting finale for a queen.

Still, the preproduction and shooting of the picture provide a fascinating, telling look at Bette Davis at the end of her life. The following is derived
primarily from an extensive interview conducted with the picture's writer
and director, Larry Cohen.

"I wrote the script especially for her," related Cohen when asked
how the project developed. "I was over in Hawaii and picked up this
book she had written, *This 'N That*, and I was reading it and thinking,
'You know, everybody gives her awards and dinners and lauds her abilities,
but there are no jobs for this woman.' I had seen her on talk shows. She
seemed to be all right. She was still limping, badly, but she had done the
picture with Lillian Gish, and she finished that. I had the feeling she was
appearing on a lot of programs because she wanted to be visible in hopes
that someone would think of her for a part, which her business manager and
lawyer later affirmed.

"So I wrote the script and gave the script to her agents. Her agents
eventually called me back and said she wasn't interested. I wasn't 100 percent
sure she had seen the material because sometimes agents turn down material
without actually presenting it to the artist. So eventually, through columnist
Robert Osborne, I got her phone number and her address, and sent the script
with a letter. I said, 'I've written this script especially for you, and we're
prepared to make the picture, and we have the financing to do it if you want
to do it, and we're ready to start right away.' A couple weeks later the phone
rang, and I was in the kitchen and picked up the phone, and a voice said,

Impending disaster: on the set with Larry Cohen and Lionel Stander.

'Mr. Cohen,' and I said, 'Yeah,' and she said, 'This is Bette Davis.' I recognized her voice right away. She said, 'I read the script last night, and I had quite a few laughs, and I think we should get together. Why don't you come and see me at my apartment?'

"I was a little bit shocked when I saw her condition. She was very, very tiny. And she limped badly. And seemed to be in some degree of pain, just getting along. But she was all fixed up, pearls, all made up and everything. She seemed to like me, and we spent about an hour and a half up there chatting. She liked the script; she thought it was perfect for her. 'Let's try and do this,' she said.

"She had Kathryn [Sermak] open a bottle of white wine, and we had a little toast, and she said, 'I always toast, "Let's hope we like each other as much at the end as we do at the beginning." '

"Subsequently I had a number of meetings with her, and she was very professional. When I went to her house to go over the script, she had two or three copies of the script all laid out on the dining room table, and she had marked everything with a pen, and she put on her eyeglasses and sat down at the table and went over the script meticulously, every line. She asked me questions about every single line in the piece. She didn't change everything—she changed very little—but she wanted to discuss every scene and every line. Ninety percent of the lines were OK. She thought it was very funny. She said that the material had been submitted to her before, but she hadn't read it because she thought it was a horror movie.

"I thought I had handled all of her infirmities and made them a plus instead of a minus—that she was this horrible old woman who marries into this family, and what could be worse than coming home after a holiday and finding out that your father has married Bette Davis and she has moved into your house and you can't get rid of her? That was the idea.

"I knew that I would have to shoot it in a certain way to move her from one place to another in a graceful manner. It would be painful to watch her try to drag her foot across the room. So I figured I'd have to cut to the next angle and have her walk into the shot or perhaps use a double. But her manager said she wouldn't allow a double to be used—that would be too embarrassing to her—so I figured I'd have to set up each angle so that she wouldn't have to do much walking. She would do her crosses and her moves on cuts to other people, and when you cut back to her she'd just be taking her next position.

"My agent, who had gone with me to the meeting, said I was crazy trying to make a picture with this woman. 'She's too far gone,' he said. I said, 'Yeah, but, she's still Bette Davis. And once she starts to talk, she's Okay.' When you first see her, you get over it after about five or 10 minutes. When she starts talking, you see all the Bette Davis mannerisms and the pep, and the voice was all right, and the mind was very quick. There was nothing slow about her; she was on top of everything. And the humor was there. It also fit the story: the worse she is, in a way, the better it is, because she was supposed to be a horrible old witch. I psyched myself up to believe what I wanted to: obviously, that she could do it.

"MGM liked the idea of Bette Davis, the wicked stepmother, and that I would surround her with a cast of well-known players. But mainly they felt that this was a movie that would do some business on home video, and they had a big home video deal. They didn't think there was any theatrical audience for Bette Davis. But they knew that every video store had a Bette Davis section, and they figured that every video store would take a couple of cassettes. So if they sold 100,000 cassettes at $35–40 apiece, they'd get back $4 million on that, and the picture was going to cost only $2.5 million. So they figured they were safe just on the video sale. And then the cable TV and the foreign and the free television would all be profits. So it seemed like a pretty good investment for them. And in fact I'm sure that MGM has made its money back and has made profits on the picture.

"She had approval on some of the key casting of the picture. So when she said, 'Let's get Lionel Stander for the husband,' I said, 'That's a very good idea.' We had a casting session here at the house. She turned down a lot of people. She turned down Julia Duffy from 'Newhart.' She turned down the girl who's the lead in 'Night Court,' Markie Post. Markie Post was dying to do the thing—she came up twice—but Bette didn't want her. Finally, Colleen Camp came up, and she liked her right away and said, 'That's our girl.' Then she picked Barbara Carrera from watching the James Bond picture *Never Say Never Again*.

"I never found her unreasonable about any of these things, nor did I find her unreasonable about any of the rewrites. She was very precise. She agreed to read with people. She was a good sport.

"She had recommended John Shea [for the part that went to David Rasche], whom she had worked with before. I called John Shea, and he said he liked Bette, but he was doing something else, which was all right with me because I didn't think he was much of a comedian, whereas David Rasche had a lot of comedy experience. She accepted David Rasche on my say-so, but then she called David Rasche up on the telephone to welcome him to the production, and she got what she considered to be a very asinine message on his answering machine. You know, some people put funny messages on their answering machine. She called me up and said that she had called him up and there was a ridiculous message on his answering machine, and she didn't think he was a serious person and she didn't think he should be in the picture.

"And I said, 'Bette, we're gonna fire the guy because he has a message you didn't like on his answering machine?' And she said, 'Well, I don't think him to be a very serious actor, and I don't think I want to work with this person.'

"So I sent over his résumé of all the things that he had done, and she saw that he had a lot of Broadway stage experience and she changed her mind.

"We had in the original script a scene where her ex-husband manifests himself as a ghost. I thought, 'Well, we'll get Vincent Price maybe. In the course of thinking about it, I suggested we get Paul Henreid, because their careers are very well associated. So I said, 'How about Paul Henreid for that part?' 'Oh,' she said, 'Have you seen him lately? He's so old. We couldn't possibly put him on the screen in his condition.' And here she is tottering, but Paul Henreid was too old to be in the picture.

"When we finally had the cast all assembled, we had a reading of the entire picture here, and she didn't read well. At that point I had a feeling that maybe I should terminate the whole thing, that she wasn't going to be up to it. But she was humorous. She came to me after the reading and took me aside and, pointing to Lionel Stander, said, 'You know, I think he is deaf.' Which was partly true; he was hard of hearing. She was pointing out everyone else's infirmities but not her own.

"Then we hired the cameraman. She didn't know the cameraman, but he was quite experienced. I went to New York to meet with Harold Schiff [Bette's attorney]. And I got a phone call from the cameraman saying that Bette had called him up at home and asked him to come to her apartment. He said to me, 'I'm not going to do this picture. I'm not going to work for this horrible old woman. She was so rude to me. She had me come over to her house, and then she threatened me. She said, 'If I don't like the way I look in the picture, you're going to be fired.' He said, 'I don't need to work under these conditions. I'm not going to do the picture.'

"So I called Bette up and said, 'I heard you had a meeting with my cameraman.' She said, 'Oh, yes, wonderful fellow. I'm so looking forward to working with him.' So I called him back and said, 'I just had Bette on the phone, and she said you're a wonderful person and she can't wait to work with you.' And he said, 'Well, that doesn't make any sense to me because she was so nasty to me.' I said, 'Well, let's just leave it at that.'

"Kathryn Sermak was with her all the time. Bette had her own makeup person, her own hair person. She had a beautiful dressing room. I particularly rented the house to shoot in Hancock Park because it had a big pool behind the main house, which I could convert into a huge dressing room for her, similar to what a star would have had in Hollywood in the old days.

"At the very beginning Bette told me she wanted Kathryn to have a chance to get into production. And I found that Kathryn was a very serious and efficient person. I said, 'All right, Kathryn, you can either do the work or you can have the credit. But if you want to do the work, I certainly can use you.' And she said she wanted to do the work, so I put her to work immediately. She went out and did all the things she was supposed to do in terms of locations and wardrobe and liaison—mainly things that were somehow associated with Bette. But she was very efficient as an associate producer and did the work. She could certainly do it on any picture. . . .

"Bette asked me to hire Julie Weiss, who had done her costumes for *The Whales of August*. She was extremely expensive, but I hired her just to do Bette's costumes. So we spent about $25,000 on the costumes and about $7,500 on the alterations, if you can believe that anybody can spend $7,500 to alter clothes. But the alterations were tremendous because nothing fit her because she was so small.

"Bette came out with all these clothes, and unfortunately everything looked exactly like everything else. She said, 'What do you think?' I said, 'Well, I think that we need to add a collar on this one, a handkerchief on this one.' She was angry. Her head flew back, and I saw those Bette Davis eyes flash at me. And she said, 'In that case we'll throw everything out and we'll start all over from scratch.' I said, 'No we won't. We're gonna do what I said. We're gonna put some color, we're gonna put a belt on here, a scarf with this.

We're gonna add some things to it, which Julie Weiss can do, and we're gonna make these things work.' And she looked at me with such anger. And I said, 'Bette, you asked me to come here because you wanted my opinion, didn't you?' And she said, 'Yes.' And I said, 'Well, I'm giving you my opinion.' And that was the end of it. I saw that if you just held your ground and were reasonable that you could prevail in a discussion with her.

"Bette had ears like some kind of creature from the forest. She could hear things from around the corner. Nothing got by this woman. Someone could turn and whisper with their back to her, and she would hear them. She was able to hear everything.

"Towards the beginning I was trying to make Kathryn feel like she was part of the production; very often I would talk to Kathryn, explaining things to her that were her business, her areas. And Bette got angry and said, 'Why don't you ever look at *me* when you're talking?' And I said, 'Well, because Kathryn's the associate producer, and these things concern her. . . . I'm not slighting you.' And she said, 'Well, I thought you weren't looking at me because you were afraid of me.' I said, 'I'm not afraid of you, Bette.' She said, 'I don't want you to be afraid of me, because I think you're a great guy and we're going to get along fine.'

"We had a limousine bring her in every morning and a limousine take her home every night. That was another thing in the contract. She'd be the first one to get there in the morning. She came to me and said, 'I got here at seven o'clock, and no one was here.' I said, 'Bette, the call was for eight o'clock. The crew comes at eight o'clock. That's the call on the call sheet. If you come tomorrow at seven o'clock, no one's gonna be here.'

"She didn't eat any breakfast. When she came to work, she was basically undernourished. She'd eat lunch, and she'd be better in the afternoon, performance wise. In the morning when she came in, she'd be tired and cranky, but after she ate she was always better.

"The grips and the gaffers were all setting up the lights. There'd be guys hanging poles from the ceiling, there would be wires hanging down, there'd be huge light elements being fastened up there with screws and wrenches. The crew would be putting down dolly track and moving the cameras, and in the midst of all this she would have her chair placed in the center of everything and sit down. There'd be all these people moving around her— 'Excuse me, Miss Davis,' 'Beg pardon, Miss Davis.' Ladders over her head, wires hanging down over her face. I used to say, 'Bette what are you doing in the middle of all this? You're gonna get killed if something falls off the ceiling.' She said, 'I like to see what's going on.' There she was, in the midst of all this chaos. It was a sight to behold.

"Her smoking was another matter. It was unbelievable. She smoked Vantage cigarettes. About 5 packs a day, about 100 cigarettes a day. They were all taken out of their packages by Kathryn Sermak in the morning and placed in little cups, which were then placed in her dressing room and around the set. So she would not have to open a package of cigarettes; they would always be available so she could go from one cigarette to the next, which she smoked continually, all day long. She left a big burn on my dining room table. Every time she came here she'd leave a burn someplace.

"Back to her appearance, she insisted on wearing this red wig. She had these blond wigs—at first she wanted this blond wig. I said, 'Bette, you go out and get the wigs that you want to wear in the picture, and I'll pay for them.' So she says, 'I want to model them for you.' So I went to her house and she put on these blond wigs, and they looked very nice on her. The blond hair kind of softened her, took the wrinkles out. She gave me a bill. It was $90. I said, 'How could it be only $90?' She said, 'Oh, they give me the wholesale prices.' I said, 'That's wonderful.' So, I left a hundred-dollar bill on the mantelpiece. She called me up at home and said, 'I found the hundred-dollar bill on the mantelpiece. You left me too much money. I feel like a kept woman.' Then she sent them out to be styled, and I got a bill for $150 from the stylist to style the two $45 wigs. And then she decided she didn't want to wear the blond wigs because they looked too much like her real hair. She wanted to make a *character* out of this; she wanted to wear this bizarre red wig that she had from a previous picture that was never used. She insisted on wearing it, but that made her look awful because the red hair brought out every wrinkle in her face. Then she said, 'Now, we can't just make this picture with one wig; we need a duplicate wig. So we call up the guy in New York who made the wig—he charged $1,700 to make a duplicate!

"In the test she didn't look as bad as she did in the picture. But a couple of weeks intervened between the time of the tests and the time we shot the picture in which there was some kind of deterioration. Something happened in between. What I have since heard happened was that her bridge broke. Instead of going to the dentist to have it repaired, she sent her maid over with the bridge in a paper bag. And the dentist said, 'We can't fix this unless you come into the dentist's office. We can't fix this by proxy. And she got angry at the dentist and said she wouldn't see anybody but her dentist in New York. Anyway, they managed to put the bridge back together again, I guess, because she had it in her mouth when she came to work, but all of a sudden she wasn't speaking very well. She'd stop right in the middle of a speech in a very odd way, and then she'd pick up the dialogue again. And she was very distracted. And I think what happened was the bridge broke and she didn't want to admit it, and she didn't want to come to me and say, 'Larry, I have dental problems and we have to postpone the picture.' If she had done that, then we would have postponed the picture, she would have gotten her teeth fixed, and maybe the disaster that followed wouldn't have occurred. But she tried to fake it and tried to get through it. . . . Sometimes when she'd stop the script girl would start to give her the line, and she'd get angry and say, 'I know my lines. I'm famous for never forgetting my lines. How dare you give me my lines!' "

With a five-week schedule, *The Wicked Stepmother* started shooting on April 25, 1988. Almost immediately there were problems. Director Cohen continues the story:

"She had a series of accidents on the set the first week. She had a very nasty fall. She tripped over some cables on the way from her bungalow to the house in the backyard. She fell down and was lying on the ground for about 20 minutes. I saw what happened, and I was going to go over to her, but then I figured it might be too embarrassing to her, so I went back inside and got all the crew people and all the actors not to go out in the backyard. And her own people—Kathryn, her makeup person, and her wardrobe person—got her up and got her back to her dressing room. Later on, someone came and told me that she was upset that I had seen her and had not come to her aid. I thought that was the end of the day's work, but she went back to work.

"Then, on another day, she was supposed to do a scene where there's a cigarette in her hand that lights by itself. The special effects guy came in and rigged the wires going up her arm and under her clothing and to the bed, and he'd be on the floor behind the bed to push the buttons and make the cigarette light by itself. We shot the scene, I said, 'Action,' he pushed the button, and she began to scream. She was getting a terrible electric shock. I apologized profusely, and the guy found out what was wrong. I said, 'Bette, maybe we shouldn't do this.' She said, 'Oh, no, we must get the shot.' So we went on. The next time he pushed the button the cigarette exploded in her hand and something hit her in the eye and she was doubled up on the bed in pain for about five minutes. And I said, 'We can't do this, Bette.' And she said, 'Oh, no, we must get the shot!' So we did it a third time, and we finally got the shot. It was a terrible experience seeing this poor woman hurt.

"One day Bette asked to see me in the house, and I went into one of the bedrooms that was being used as a dressing room. She was sitting on the bed, and she started to cry. She said she was so depressed and unhappy and she didn't know why I wouldn't let her see the dailies. And I told her that the dailies weren't ready, because it takes the editor on these kinds of pictures a couple of days to get the picture back from the lab and then to synch up the sound, and she didn't want to see the dailies silent. So I told her she could see them on Saturday. And she stopped crying and straightened out. But I couldn't believe that I had brought Bette Davis to tears. I think that, frankly, she didn't know how else to deal with me. Instead of trying to be demanding or fighting with me, she just tried to play on my sympathy. I think it was an act, frankly.

"It was really a mistake to show her the dailies. I should have looked at them myself and weeded out the scenes in which she was particularly bad. Because there were many scenes and takes where she couldn't finish a speech or she forgot her lines. So, when she saw herself in the dailies on Saturday, she was terrible. And when she saw how terrible she was, she realized that she couldn't get away with this broken bridge, that she had to do something about it.

"She called me up on the phone on Saturday night and said, 'I've made a terrible mistake, and I can't go on with the picture. I'm terribly sorry. Goodbye.' And she hung up.

"Bette was not used to seeing mistakes on the screen. She was not used to seeing herself forgetting her lines. She was not used to seeing herself slurring her words. You couldn't understand her sometimes because of her teeth. It must have been a horrible thing for her to see herself up on the screen not only looking bad but not really being able to perform. I think it was her performance that really upset her.

"Monday, Harold Schiff and her agent, Michael Black, called up and said they wanted to have a meeting, and Bette wanted to have a meeting, but she wouldn't have a meeting on the set. Harold Schiff and Michael Black showed up for the meeting, but Bette didn't. They said she felt that she had been mistreated. She also didn't like the footage from the first couple days of shooting. I agreed to reshoot the first couple days, and they said, 'Ok.' But they said that Bette would need a week off for dental work in New York. I also agreed to replace the cameraman.

"Then we continued to shoot for the rest of the week with the other actors. Toward the end of the week I got a call from Harold Schiff saying that they had discovered severe jaw deterioration and they were gonna have to pull additional teeth and make a brand-new bridge, and she probably wouldn't be able to come back for two or three more weeks. So, based on that, I went to the MGM people and said, 'Look, we don't have anything else to shoot after this week, so we can't wait two or three weeks more. So what do you want to do?' They agreed that we should close the picture down and decide what to do about it. In the meantime, they looked at the dailies too, and they thought that everybody else was good but that Bette Davis was terrible. So they said they would go ahead and make the picture and we could get rid of Bette Davis and hire Lucille Ball. I called up about Lucille Ball, and they said, 'She died.'

"The insurance company came back and said, 'We want to examine Bette Davis.' And Bette refused to be examined. This went on for two or three weeks, during which time the production was closed down. We were paying rent on the house, we were keeping the actors on salary, we were keeping key crew members on salary, so hundreds of thousands of dollars were being spent. Finally, under threats of some kind, Harold Schiff advised her that she had to see the doctors. So the doctors examined her and found out she was down to 79 pounds; she had lost 15 pounds. I got a letter from one of the doctors, who said, 'The woman is in absolutely no shape to be put in front of the cameras.'

"So I went back to MGM and said, 'There's no question, she's not coming back. We can either take the insurance claim, and that's the end of the picture, or else we can try to salvage the picture.' By that time I had figured out that we could build the Carrera part up and have Bette *turn into* Barbara Carrera. In the original script Barbara Carrera is Bette's daughter who is a cat—Bette turns the cat into Barbara Carrera. Only in this version Bette turns herself into Barbara Carrera. And Barbara Carrera could play out the picture. So, they said, 'All right.' The insurance company absorbed some of the budget of the picture, and the completion bond company absorbed some of the budget of the picture, so MGM got the picture cheaper than the $2.5 million that they were originally supposed to pay. And they allowed us to complete the picture with Bette Davis in about 20 minutes of the picture.

"Long after it was over, I got a call from Kathryn Sermak that Bette wanted to know about her clothes, the wardrobe. So Kathryn came over, and I gave her all the wardrobe that Bette had in the picture—$25,000 worth of clothes I gave to her as a present. Kathryn said, 'Bette says thanks,' I said, 'I'm very sorry about what happened.' And Kathryn said, 'Well, Bette was very upset because she was ready to come back, and you pulled the rug from under her.'

"They had an honorary thing for Bette in New York at Lincoln Center. Coincident to that she started to be interviewed in all the New York papers and all the local talk shows. And that's when she started talking about *Wicked Stepmother*, saying how badly she had been treated and how she had walked off the picture. She said it had nothing to do with illness. It had nothing to do with her inability to work; it had nothing to do with insurability.

"I felt terrible about it because I felt I started out trying to help this woman and wrote a script for her because I admired her, and here it turned around. And now because of this picture, she'd never be able to work again.

"I never spoke to her or saw her again."

Upon its very brief release, *The Wicked Stepmother* was given horrendous reviews. It has since, as predicted by Larry Cohen, become something of a novelty home video rental success. As the final farewell, however dubious, of Bette Davis, it has also earned a spot in Hollywood history.

THE WILD DUCK

When she was a Boston-area teenager, Bette saw a production of *The Wild Duck* at the Jewett Playhouse. The play, and particularly Peg Entwistle's performance as Hedvig, made a profound impact on young Bette's life. It was then that Bette decided to be an actress. To her mother she vowed she would one day play Hedvig on the stage.

In 1929, after he saw her in the off-Broadway production of *The Earth Between*, Cecil Clovelly asked Bette if she was interested in becoming a member of the Ibsen Repertory Company. Actress Linda Watkins, who had been the ingenue in the company, was departing and needed to be replaced. Bette met with the company's director, Blanche Yurka, and was cast in both *The Lady from the Sea* and as Hedvig in *The Wild Duck*. *The Wild Duck* was subsequently performed in New York City and on tour in Long Island, Philadelphia, Washington, D.C., Newark, and, ironically, Boston.

The *Washington Post* said of her performance, "Especially commendable was the selection of Bette Davis, a talented ingenue with a native sweetness and spiritual wholesomeness that blend ideally into a loveable character. Bette Davis is a young woman who is going to advance far in her stage endeavors."

THE WILL
Bette Davis intentionally left her daughters and grandsons out of her will, dated September 2, 1987. "I declare that I have intentionally and with full knowledge omitted to provide herein for my daughter, Margot, and my daughter, Barbara, and for my grandsons, Ashley Hyman and Justin Hyman," the will read. At the time of Bette's death, her estate was estimated at between $600,000 and $1 million. It was divided equally between Bette's son, Michael Merrill, and her longtime personal assistant, Kathryn Sermak. Smaller bequests were also made to Robin Brown (a painting, a portrait of Bette, and a pearl and sapphire watch); to Bette's niece, Fay Forbes (six silver condiment holders); and Michael's wife (clothing).

WILLIAM DOYLE GALLERIES
The William Doyle Galleries in New York City auctioned off items from Bette Davis's estate on April 11, 1990. Sold at the auction were 19th-century American furniture, decorations, paintings, costume jewelry, books, and memorabilia. Bette's engraved blue leather script cover (which she used for all her scripts) sold for $4,400—it was expected to sell for $50 to $100. The canvas chair Bette sat in on the set of her films sold for $1,320. A group of five dolls, three of them depicting Bette in *Jezebel*, brought $5,775. A round coffee table sold for $9,625—it had been estimated at $800 to $1,200. A collection of eight pillows, including one with a needlework cover sewn by Bette, sold for $3,080—it had been estimated at $250 to $450. Embroidered was "God Knows I Bette Did It the Hard Way." The biggest seller, however, was a fashion sketch of the red "Fasten your seat belts" dress Bette wore as Margo Channing in *All About Eve*. It was autographed by Edith Head and sold for $23,100. The lot had been estimated at $55,000, and it brought in more than $221,000.

TENNESSEE WILLIAMS
Bette came close to portraying Williams's heroines Amanda Wingfield and Blanche DuBois in the screen versions of *The Glass Menagerie* and *A Streetcar Named Desire* respectively. She also almost costarred in the 1959 picture *Suddenly, Last Summer*. However, it was not until the 1962 Broadway play *The Night of the Iguana* that Bette played in a Williams drama.

JANIS WILSON
After a considerable testing process, Hal Wallis decided to cast 12-year-old Janis Wilson in the supporting part of Tina in the 1942 picture *Now, Voyager*. It was her first screen role. During location filming in Lake Arrowhead, California, Bette and Janis went canoeing. About 40 yards from shore, the canoe overturned in deep water. Janis, barely able to swim, was rescued by Bette. Upon reaching shore, Bette was kissed in appreciation by Janis's mother. In Bette's next picture, *Watch on the Rhine* (1943), Janis Wilson was cast as her daughter.

WALTER WINCHELL

After Bette walked out on the 1952 Broadway show *Two's Company*, Walter Winchell reported on his radio broadcast that Bette had been operated on for "cancer of the jaw." Bette, furious and afraid that his statement would cause her to lose future work, demanded a retraction. Her telegram read, "Your recent statements about me are utterly without foundation. Have authorized my physician at N.Y. Hospital to answer any questions you may care to put to him, and to examine hospital's and pathologist's reports. I am sure you have no wish to hurt me. Accept my assurance that I do not have cancer. Please retract on broadcast. Bette Davis." Winchell retracted.

The two Davises had reason to fret: their film was an unequivocal failure.

WINTER MEETING ★★

Warner Brothers
1948   104 minutes   bw
Directed by: Bretaigne Windust
Produced by: Henry Blanke
Screenplay by: Catherine Turney, from the novel by Ethel Vance
Cinematography by: Ernest Haller
Cast: Bette Davis, Janis Paige, James Davis, John Hoyt, Florence Bates, Walter Baldwin, Ransom Sherman

Winter Meeting was one of the biggest flops during Bette's tenure (1932–1949) at Warner Brothers and the picture that signaled her fall at the studio. Warners purchased the novel by Grace Zaring Stone, who wrote under the name Ethel Vance, for $25,000 in an agreement dated May 27, 1946.

On April 21, 1947, Henry Blanke noted in a memo to Warner executive Steve Trilling that he had presented the script to Bette. He added that if Bette rejected the role of Susan Grieve, the prim poetess who falls in love with a naval war hero, it would be a suitable vehicle for Joan Crawford or Barbara Stanwyck.

Bette held off on accepting the film primarily because she felt that it was being tampered with and watered down by the studio censor, the Johnston Office. The censor demanded that no suggestion of sex between the unmarried couple take place in the story. What the censor suggested was having the couple marry, which would make their amorous coupling acceptable under the Production Code.

After reading the revised script Bette penned a note to writer Catherine Turney, saying, "I am very rested and very ambitious to do something really outstanding—and I don't feel this, the way it is, answers these requirements. . . ."

Bette, however, had not made a film since the birth of her daughter, B.D., and allowed her anxiety to get back to work supersede her better judgment. She accepted the part.

On August 11, 1947, a writer for the *Los Angeles Times* was the first to suggest that she had made a mistake. "*Winter Meeting*," he wrote, "doesn't sound good enough for Bette Davis." The writer further commented, "Whatever she does she must have better clothes than she has worn in her last two pictures. Roz Russell won't do a picture without Travis Banton, Crawford insists upon Adrian. Just any old thing isn't good enough for Bette if she wants to hold her place as Warner's queen."

Bette should have listened. Not only did she accept the film; she accepted the notion that it could be made without a costume designer. Instead Bette, accompanied by consultant Leah Rhodes, selected her own fashions *off the rack* at the I. Magnin department store. Upon the film's release, critics would single out Bette's costumes as being particularly bad.

Of the script, which had been revised by the studio censor to have the couple get married, Bette boasted, "I sent it back. The marriage had ruined the story. I told them to use a little elbow grease and give me the book. They did. Now we're filming the book, and we get past the censors because we're subtle about it. It took a little time and some work. But now we have a great story."

She sounded almost smug about it at the time. Later, after the film flopped, she would be more honest. "In *Winter Meeting* I had to be shown coming out of my bedroom door," she related, "and my lover out of his. It was ridiculous and juvenile. We never should have made that movie. It should have been the confessions of two people in a bedroom after an affair, but we had to be in front of a living room fireplace."

There *were* things about the film that attracted Bette, not the least of which was the fact that the role reminded her of herself. She went so far as to say that, if she hadn't become an actress, she might have resembled the prim poetess whose love drives a war hero into the priesthood. Furthermore, Bette rationalized her attraction to the part with "This woman is a New Englander, and so am I. She's a perfectionist, she's sensitive, she's not always confident. All those characteristics remind me of me."

As of May 1947, Bette wanted Robert Mitchum as her male lead, Slick Novak. Others who were considered: Burt Lancaster, Glenn Ford, Mel Ferrer, John Hodiak, George Reeves, Barry Sullivan, Robert Preston, Richard Widmark, and Rory Calhoun.

There was also interest in Jim Davis, who had been signed—and let go—by MGM without creating much of a stir. Just prior to and following his MGM stint, Davis was laying cement for a living. Bette, attracted by his face and physique, thought that he would be a suitable leading man for her and, on September 4 she tested with him in the part. He looked good on film except that his teeth needed to be capped. Blanke ordered that the studio's makeup head, Perc Westmore, take care of the arrangements. He also ordered that Jim be retested after the dental work to determine if the caps caused a lisp or some other defect. The test came out well, and Jim Davis was cast in the part at the relatively paltry salary of $500 per week. In contrast John Hoyt, cast in the second male lead, was hired at $1,500 per week.

Stage director Bretaigne Windust was given his first film opportunity with *Winter Meeting*. He was determined from the outset to present an "all-new Bette Davis" and also to run the shoot his way. He held a script reading and rehearsal on Monday, September 15, 1947. For the next seven workdays Windust held additional rehearsals. Typical of moviemaking at the time, rehearsals were usually held only right before a scene was to be shot, if even then.

Budgeted at $1,027,000, the film went into production under the title *Winter Meeting*. Jack Warner changed it to *Strange Meeting* on January 22, 1948, but reverted to *Winter Meeting* on February 12.

The picture started shooting with Bette on Wednesday, September 24, 1947. The production was allotted a generous 60-day shooting schedule, with an expected finish of December 3. Bette divided her time between her house in Laguna Beach and a dressing room suite provided by the studio that had been converted into living quarters. The dressing room's previous occupant had been Humphrey Bogart.

With the exception of the problem that Hoyt was working on another film at the same time, the production started out quite smoothly. It appeared at the outset that Windust's technique of rehearsals prior to production was an expedient one. Bette seemed on good behavior, and instead of indulging in tirades against her director she spent her breaks sitting alone reading poetry. "I figure that the more poetry I read," she explained to a curious onlooker, "the better grasp I'll have of the way a poet's mind works."

Things, however, began to slow down. On Friday, October 24, Bette stayed home, sick with a cold. Her illness forced the company to shut down on

Saturday and Monday. Bette returned to work on Tuesday, October 28, and shooting resumed. Then, on Thursday, October 30, Windust was taken ill and did not report to the set. His illness forced the company to shut down until he returned on Tuesday, November 4.

Still, Windust was making fairly good time on the days that he did work. On November 12, 1947, he wrote a rather boastful memo to Jack Warner that read in part, "I am taking a certain pride in the fact that on my first picture with Bette Davis, I am officially only eight days behind schedule, which they tell me is unusual to the extent that she has not shot a picture this fast in a good many years. . . ."

Then, just a few days before production was to wrap, things fell apart. On Monday, December 15, Bette did not report. When she failed to report the following day, the company shut down. John Hoyt was released to work on a film at Paramount. Bette did not return to work, and shooting did not resume until Monday, December 29. However, on that day Jim Davis called in sick and didn't report to the set. When he hadn't returned by that Friday, January 2, 1948, the company was forced to shut down again. He had been having a difficult time with the part. Bette would later blame Windust's "overanalytical approach." Because of the director, Bette charged, Jim Davis never again showed any signs of the character he had portrayed in the initial test.

On Monday, January 5, Jim Davis reported to the set and was ready to work at 9:00 A.M. Bette, however, was not. She did not arrive at the studio until 11:50, blaming the delay on the L.A. fog. Then she complained of indigestion and said that she was unable to work. Shooting was halted, and when Bette did not report to work the following day the production, after 69 shooting days, shut down.

On Wednesday, February 4, 1948, Bette returned to the set for additional scenes and retakes. Additional retakes were held from February 18 through February 27 before the picture was finally completed. It ended up costing the then-high sum of $1,520,000.

The studio promoted the picture with typical overstatement: "The Most Esteemed Actress on the American Screen in a Performance More Powerful Than Any You've Known." The film was released nationally on April 24, 1948, but by then the critics had killed any chance the film might have had at the box office. It was, in short, lambasted.

Bette would later blame Windust's desire to present an all-new Bette Davis. What he did produce was a totally unemotional Bette Davis. Charged Bette, "He should've left the old one alone."

On March 27, 1948, Hedda Hopper wrote in her column for the *Los Angeles Times*: "*Winter Meeting*" was an unfortunate choice for Bette Davis' return to the screen after a two year absence. The story, direction, her clothes and make-up didn't come within a mile of the Bette we all applauded and loved in *Dark Victory. Winter Meeting* should have been swept into the dust bin instead of being used as a story for one of our top stars. If she doesn't get better advice, Bette may never regain her proper place on our screen."

Hopper's column so infuriated Jack Warner that he considered filing a damage suit against Hopper because she allegedly wrote the piece without having seen the film.

Still, Hopper wasn't alone in condemning the film. Reviews were horrid, and at least one fan took his case straight to Jack Warner. Daniel H. Shields of Baltimore, Maryland, was so irate that he wrote a letter to Jack Warner that read, in part ". . . Since when does the great Bette Davis deserve this kind of treatment . . . ?"

One of the saddest occurrences in the aftermath of the debacle of *Winter Meeting* was the effect it had on Bette's relationship with her longtime cameraman, Ernie Haller. Numerous critics commented on Bette's unattractive appearance in the film, and Bette subsequently accused Haller of not photographing her well. A fight ensued, and Haller vowed never to work with her again.

JONATHAN WINTERS

Jonathan Winters was a guest on a television talk show in 1962. One of the other guests was Bette Davis, hoarse with laryngitis but glowing and gloating over her unexpected success in *What Ever Happened to Baby Jane?* At one point during the show Winters made the mistake of impersonating Bette's throatiness. Bette, taken aback, turned to him and snapped, "Go to hell!"

WOMAN'S HOME COMPANION

This magazine named Bette as the best actress of the year in its May 1953 poll. It was the magazine's ninth annual award. Bette had won the award in 1951 and had been in the Top 10 in every *Companion* poll up until that time. Placing second to Bette in the 1953 poll was Jane Wyman, who had topped the previous year's list. Readers were also asked to name the star they'd most like to meet personally. Tied for first, amusingly, were June Allyson and Joan Crawford. Bette had to content herself with 10th place.

NATALIE WOOD

When Natalie Wood, age 14, appeared in the 1952 picture *The Star* as Bette's daughter, one incident left an indelible impression on her. (Note the prophetic reference to Catalina, where Natalie would drown nearly 30 years later.) "The first day," Natalie recalled, "we were filming on Sterling Hayden's sailboat, and I had to jump off the boat and swim to a faraway raft. And so there I was, faced with the threat of being flung in the ocean or losing the part. And I went into hysterics that must have been heard all the way to Catalina. In any case, Miss Davis came out of her dressing room to find out what all the commotion was. It was the only time that I ever saw the famous Bette Davis temper surface. And it was not on her own behalf. She told the director that she would not stand around while he threw some terrified kid into the ocean and that if he wanted a swimmer he should have gotten Johnny Weismuller."

Bette came to Natalie Wood's rescue during the shooting of *The Star*.

Through the years Bette and Natalie remained friendly and occasionally socialized, sometimes with Natalie's husband, Robert Wagner.

JAMES WOODS

Early in his career James Woods appeared in the 1976 television miniseries "The Disappearance of Aimee." Years earlier, while a struggling young actor, Woods saw a revival of *Now, Voyager* and, in his words, "saw what real acting was. . . . She presented a glimpse into the human soul that I felt I had no right to be seeing." Woods and Bette became friends in subsequent years and appeared together in a special spring 1989 edition of *Life* magazine.

THE WORKING MAN ★★½

Warner Brothers
1933   78 minutes   bw
Directed by: John Adolfi
Produced by: Lucien Hubbard
Screenplay by: Maude T. Howell and Charles Kenyon, based on a story by Edgar Franklin
Cinematography by: Sol Polito
Cast: George Arliss, Bette Davis, Hardie Albright, Gordon Westcott, Theodore Newton, J. Farrell MacDonald, Charles Evans, Frederick Burton, Pat Wing, Edward Van Sloan, Claire McDowell, Harold Minjir, Ruthelma Stevens, Gertrude Sutton, Edward Cooper, Wallis Clark, Douglas Dumbrille

Based on the story "The Adopted Father" by Edgar F. Stearns under the pen name Edgar Franklin, *The Working Man* was purchased for $1,500 in an agreement dated May 11, 1932. A comedy, it reunited Bette with her mentor George Arliss and cast her as the redheaded flapper Jenny Hartland, who is shown the error of her ways by Arliss. In the picture Bette donned a swimsuit, which is somehow incongruous with her later image as *dramatic actress*.

With a budget of $199,000 and a short schedule of 21 days, the picture started shooting on January 12, 1933. Bette started January 14. The picture actually finished ahead of schedule on February 1.

Upon its release *The Working Man* received favorable reviews, with some critics praising Bette's performance.

THE WORLD OF CARL SANDBURG

An evening of Carl Sandburg's poetry was the idea behind Norman Corwin's production of *The World of Carl Sandburg*. He tried the idea out on a Sunday night at UCLA in 1957. The show was a success, and in early 1959 Corwin approached Bette and Gary Merrill with the idea of taking the show on tour and, eventually, to Broadway. They accepted. As Bette said shortly thereafter, "It was the best offer we had at the time, frankly."

Rehearsals were held in Maine (which is where the Merrills were living) during the summer of 1959. The show was modeled somewhat on a series of readings Tyrone Power had done a few years before called *John Brown's Body*. It was actually more than the recitation of Sandburg's poetry, published and unpublished; it was the *enactment* of his poetry, with Bette playing literally dozens of mini-roles. It also featured the singing and guitar playing of Clark Allen. The show was produced by Armand Deutsch and was adapted and directed by Corwin. For the latter, unlike the experience had by other stage directors, working with Bette was pleasurable.

"I was aware at that first meeting," relates Corwin, "at the photo call—you know when somebody is sizing you up. She was sizing me up. For the photo session I picked out props that were apt; they had allusions, metaphorical and realistic. I could see Bette's caution light getting dimmer. She liked the photographic selections that I had made, and she sort of relaxed. And then, when we got into rehearsal and we came across the first problem of interpretation, I worked with Bette on that. The resistance, the caution completely disappeared. She thought, Now, I'm in good hands. From then on, there was an absolutely untroubled relationship."

The show opened at the State Theatre in Portland, Maine, on October 12, 1959. In a curtain-call speech Carl Sandburg not-so-humbly hailed the show as "One of the finest things that has ever happened to culture in Maine, or anywhere." Sandburg then proceeded to salute Bette with a poem he wrote in her honor.

And so the tour began, traveling from town to town, a series of one-night stands, in a caravan of cars. The people heard the poetry of Sandburg when they came, but they came to *see* Bette. They also came to see Bette and Gary—Margo Channing and Bill Sampson—together. Each night Merrill would introduce Bette to the audience as "the mother of my three children." The audience loved their seeming marital bliss. Actually the marriage was all but over. Backstage Bette and Gary bickered constantly, and Bette even put the make on Clark Allen when Gary wasn't looking. But, as Bette would later say of those audiences, what they didn't know wouldn't hurt them—or the box office.

The show was a hit. It was also, except for the constant travel, relatively painless to do. "It's a joy to work for a management," Bette told Radie Harris in early November 1959, "which only considers the best, not the cost. Deutsch has so set up our production that we never have to worry about new lights and mikes in each town. Our own equipment travels right along with us. Gary takes credit for the wonderful sound system. He recommended a young friend of his in Portland, who had no previous pro experience. Deutsch was willing to gamble on him. The result has been perfect."

Gary left the show to start shooting *The Pleasure of His Company* back in Hollywood and was replaced for a while by Barry Sullivan. However, the film was suspended when Hollywood was hit by an actor's strike. Gary returned to the show and, after much trepidation on the part of Bette (who was terrified to appear before the jaded industry crowd), *The World of Carl Sandburg* opened at the Huntington Hartford Theatre in Hollywood on March 1, 1960. Bette's mother, Ruthie, sat in the front row. It would be the last time that she would share in one of her daughter's successes. All of Hollywood, or so it seemed, was there. The following day the *Hollywood Citizen-News* reported, "While the contributions of Merrill and Allen were excellent, this was meant to be Miss Davis's evening, and Hollywood's biggest names turned out in full regalia to make it an event. Miss Davis lived up to the challenge magnificently and the eager—sometimes overeager—audience responded just this side of idolatry. If there were a carriage available, without doubt Miss Davis would have been drawn in triumph up Hollywood Boulevard." According to Norman Corwin, "Bette characterized it as one of the great nights of her life. The audience was very, very receptive. It was a triumphant appearance."

From Los Angeles the show went to San Francisco, where it opened at the Alcazar Theatre on April 5, 1960. Bette would celebrate her 52nd birthday onstage with this show. But it was while the show was in San Francisco that Gary and Bette Merrill were severed irrevocably.

At the time the show had planned to open on Broadway in September that year. Bette called a meeting with Deutsch to discuss the show's future, insisting that Merrill be replaced. Knowing that Gary was perfect in the part, but also aware that it was Bette who drew the audience, Deutsch decided to replace Gary. After weeks of searching Leif Erickson was signed for the part.

On September 14, 1960, after touring in some 67 cities, *The World of Carl Sandburg* opened on Broadway at the Henry Miller Theatre. The reviews in New York, however, were nowhere near as laudatory as they had been around other parts of the country. Box office receipts also dwindled, and the show closed after only four weeks of performances. Bette would later acknowledge that it had been a major mistake to replace Gary. He had been the right actor, and audiences wanted to see the two of them together. Still, Bette would say, "I wouldn't have missed that year for a million dollars. It was old-time trouping that I'd never had before. There's an excitement and challenge playing different places that you can't get in a single theatre."

WORLD WAR II

"In Detroit they were building tanks,
in Hollywood we were making pictures;
both for the same reason."
screenwriter/producer
Julius Epstein, 1991

Clark Gable, Henry Fonda, Douglas Fairbanks, Jr., David Niven, Glenn Ford, Alan Ladd, Tyrone Power, and Jimmy Stewart, among others, enlisted. Dorothy Lamour launched a series of celebrity war bond tours, reportedly selling more than $300 million in American war bonds. Martha Raye was the queen entertainer of the troops, and Bob Hope was the king. Joan Crawford planted a victory garden on her front lawn. And Bette Davis, along with John Garfield, formed the Hollywood Canteen. The canteen was a mammoth production that every night welcomed thousands of servicemen who were passing through Los Angeles. The canteen provided them with food, fun, dancing, entertainment, and the opportunity to brush shoulders with the biggest stars in Hollywood.

Bette's other World War II efforts included selling war bonds, traveling to army camps and hospitals in the Los Angeles area, recording radio broadcast appeals for donations to the National War Chest, and making short films encouraging her fans to buy war bonds. One such film had Bette giving "her" two kids, "Jenny" and "Billy," war bonds for their Christmas presents.

> BILLY: Gee, thanks a lot, Mom, but—
> JENNY: I wanted a bicycle—
> BETTE: I know you did, Jenny. And I know that Billy wanted a railroad. But I feel that you're both old enough to realize that your country is at war and to be willing to make sacrifices. Just think, if Daddy were wounded, one single war stamp might pay for the medicine that would save him from pain, even save his life.

THE WRITERS
Of Plays That Bette Appeared In

Lawton Campbell	*Solid South*	1930
Phil Dunning	*Broadway*	1928
Martin Flavin	*Broken Dishes*	1929
Virgil Geddes	*The Earth Between*	1929
Henrik Ibsen	*The Lady from the Sea*	1929
Henrik Ibsen	*The Wild Duck*	1929
Joshua Logan	*Miss Moffat*	1974
Carl Sandburg	*The World of Carl Sandburg*	1960
Charles Sherman	*Two's Company*	1952
Emlyn Williams	*Miss Moffat*	1974
Tennessee Williams	*The Night of the Iguana*	1961

Of Movies That Bette Appeared In

Katherine Albert	*The Star*	1952
J. Grubb Alexander	*So Big*	1932

Albert Beich	Dead Ringer	1964
Curtis Bernhardt	Payment on Demand	1952
David Berry	The Whales of August	1987
David Boehm	Ex-Lady	1933
Harry Brown	The Virgin Queen	1955
Robert Buckner**	Jezebel	1938
Niven Busch	The Big Shakedown	1934
Alan Campbell*	The Little Foxes	1941
Frank Cavett	The Corn Is Green	1945
Roy Chanslor	The Menace	1932
Roy Chanslor	Front Page Woman	1935
Stanley Z. Cherry	Bunny O'Hare	1971
Brian Clemens	The Watcher in the Woods	1980
Lenore Coffee	The Great Lie	1941
Lenore Coffee	Old Acquaintance	1943
Lenore Coffee	Beyond the Forest	1949
Lester Cohen	Of Human Bondage	1934
John Collier	Deception	1946
Dan Curtis	Burnt Offerings	1976
Damiano Damiani	The Empty Canvas	1964
Delmer Daves	The Petrified Forest	1936
Delmer Daves	Hollywood Canteen	1944
Laird Doyle	Bordertown	1935
Laird Doyle	Front Page Woman	1935
Laird Doyle	Special Agent	1935
Laird Doyle	Dangerous	1935
Julius & Philip Epstein	The Bride Came C.O.D.	1941
Julius & Philip Epstein	The Man Who Came to Dinner	1942
Julius & Philip Epstein	Mr. Skeffington	1944
Carl Erickson	Fashions of 1934	1934
Dale Eunson	The Star	1952
Henry Farrell	Hush . . . Hush, Sweet Charlotte	1964
John Farrow	John Paul Jones	1959
Abem Finkel	Special Agent	1935
Abem Finkel	Marked Woman	1937
Abem Finkel	Jezebel	1938
Melvin Frank	Thank Your Lucky Stars	1943
Paul Gangelin	Hell's House	1932
Franklin Gollings	Connecting Rooms	1972
Edmund Goulding	That Certain Woman	1937
Paul Green	Cabin in the Cotton	1932
Tonino Guerra	The Empty Canvas	1964
Val Guest	Another Man's Poison	1952
Robert Hamer	The Scapegoat	1959
Dashiell Hammett	Watch on the Rhine	1943
John Michael Hayes	Where Love Has Gone	1964
Lillie Hayward	Housewife	1934
Lillie Hayward	Front Page Woman	1935
Lukas Heller	What Ever Happened to Baby Jane?	1962
Lukas Heller	Hush . . . Hush, Sweet Charlotte	1964
Lillian Hellman	The Little Foxes	1941
Lillian Hellman*	Watch on the Rhine	1943

F. Hugh Herbert	*Fashions of 1934*	1934
Brown Holmes	*20,000 Years in Sing Sing*	1933
Brown Holmes	*Satan Met a Lady*	1936
Dorothy Howell	*The Menace*	1932
Maude T. Howell	*The Man Who Played God*	1932
Maude T. Howell	*The Working Man*	1933
Lucien Hubbard	*Three on a Match*	1932
John Huston	*Jezebel*	1938
John Huston	*Juarez*	1939
Joseph Jackson	*Dark Horse*	1932
Rian James	*The Big Shakedown*	1934
Coslough Johnson	*Bunny O'Hare*	1971
Nunnally Johnson	*Phone Call from a Stranger*	1952
Julien Josephson	*The Man Who Played God*	1932
Hal Kanter	*Pocketful of Miracles*	1961
Charles Kenyon	*The Working Man*	1933
Charles Kenyon	*The Girl from Tenth Avenue*	1935
Charles Kenyon	*The Petrified Forest*	1936
Charles Kenyon	*The Golden Arrow*	1936
James V. Kern	*Thank Your Lucky Stars*	1943
Edwin Knopf*	*Bad Sister*	1931
Arthur Kober*	*The Little Foxes*	1941
Howard Koch	*The Letter*	1940
Howard Koch	*In This Our Life*	1942
Milton Krims	*The Sisters*	1938
John Francis Larkin	*Parachute Jumper*	1933
Jesse Lasky, Jr.	*John Paul Jones*	1959
Robert N. Lee	*Fog Over Frisco*	1934
Gladys Lehman	*Seed*	1931
Benn W. Levy	*Waterloo Bridge*	1931
Ugo Liberatore	*The Empty Canvas*	1964
Charles Logue	*The Menace*	1932
Mindret Lord	*The Virgin Queen*	1955
Robert Lord	*So Big*	1932
Robert Lord**	*20,000 Years in Sing Sing*	1933
Robert Lord**	*Bordertown*	1935
Ranald MacDougall	*June Bride*	1948
Aeneas Mackenzie	*Juarez*	1939
Aeneas Mackenzie	*The Private Lives of Elizabeth and Essex*	1939
Joseph L. Mankiewicz	*All About Eve*	1950
Bruce Manning	*Payment on Demand*	1951
Gene Markey	*Fashions of 1934*	1934
Malcolm Marmorstein	*Return from Witch Mountain*	1978
Bertram Milhauser	*Jimmy the Gent*	1934
Oscar Millard	*Dead Ringer*	1964
Seton I. Miller*	*Marked Woman*	1937
Seton I. Miller	*Kid Galahad*	1937
Wilson I. Mizner	*Dark Horse*	1932
Wilson I. Mizner	*20,000 Years in Sing Sing*	1933
Elick Moll	*Storm Center*	1956
Jane Murfin	*Way Back Home*	1932
William F. Nolan	*Burnt Offerings*	1976

B. Harrison Orkow	*Hell's House*	1932
Norman Panama	*Thank Your Lucky Stars*	1943
Austin Parker	*The Rich Are Always With Us*	1932
Dorothy Parker*	*The Little Foxes*	1941
Robert Presnell	*Bureau of Missing Persons*	1933
Norman Reilly Raine	*The Private Lives of Elizabeth and Essex*	1939
Tom Reed	*Bad Sister*	1931
Tom Reed	*Waterloo Bridge*	1931
Wolfgang Reinhardt	*Juarez*	1939
Clements Ripley	*Jezebel*	1938
Casey Robinson	*It's Love I'm After*	1937
Casey Robinson	*Dark Victory*	1939
Casey Robinson	*The Old Maid*	1939
Casey Robinson	*All This, and Heaven Too*	1940
Casey Robinson	*Now, Voyager*	1942
Casey Robinson	*The Corn Is Green*	1945
Robert Rossen	*Marked Woman*	1937
Jimmy Sangster	*The Nanny*	1965
Jimmy Sangster	*The Anniversary*	1968
Raymond L. Schrock	*Bad Sister*	1931
Kathryn Scola	*Fashions of 1934*	1934
Manuel Seff	*Housewife*	1934
Anthony Shaffer	*Death on the Nile*	1978
Rosemary Anne Sisson	*The Watcher in the Woods*	1980
Wallace Smith	*Bordertown*	1935
Eugene Solow	*Fog Over Frisco*	1934
Rodolfo Sonego	*The Scientific Cardplayer*	1972
Harry Spaulding	*The Watcher in the Woods*	1980
Daniel Taradash	*Storm Center*	1956
Courtenay Terrett**	*20,000 Years in Sing Sing*	1933
Joseph Than	*Deception*	1946
Harry Tugend	*Pocketful of Miracles*	1961
Catherine Turney	*A Stolen Life*	1946
Catherine Turney	*Winter Meeting*	1948
John Van Druten	*Old Acquaintance*	1943
Gore Vidal	*The Catered Affair*	1956
Gore Vidal	*The Scapegoat*	1959
Margaret Buell Wilder**	*A Stolen Life*	1946

*Contributed "additional scenes and dialogue" only

**Adaptation only

Of Television Movies Bette Appeared In

Jeff Andrus	"As Summers Die"	1986
Michael DeGuzman	"Strangers: The Story of a Mother and Daughter"	1979
Robert C. S. Downs	"White Mama"	1980
George Eckstein	"Murder with Mirrors"	1985
John Gay	"A Piano for Mrs. Cimino"	1982
David Greene	"Madame Sin"	1972
Jack Guss	"The Dark Secret of Harvest Home"	1978

William Hanley	"Little Gloria . . . Happy at Last"	1982
Arthur Hoffe	"Scream, Pretty Peggy"	1973
Charles E. Israel	"The Dark Secret of Harvest Home"	1978
Richard Lees	"Right of Way"	1983
Richard Levinson	"The Judge and Jake Wyler"	1972
William Link	"The Judge and Jake Wyler"	1972
John McGreevey	"The Disappearance of Aimee"	1976
Ed Namzug	"As Summers Die"	1986
Barry Oringer	"Madame Sin"	1972
Nancy Sackett	"Skyward"	1980
Jimmy Sangster	"Scream, Pretty Peggy"	1973
David Shaw	"The Judge and Jake Wyler"	1972
Allan Sloane	"Family Reunion"	1981

WILLIAM WYLER

In her later years Bette would reflect on her life and, perhaps colored by time and "what might have been," would say (though she wouldn't provide his name) that William Wyler had been the love of her life. He was also the best director of her career.

Bette met Wyler when she was an ingenue at Universal in 1931. She auditioned for one of Wyler's films. He looked her over, shook his head, and promptly dismissed her with some unflattering remark.

The two would be paired under different circumstances in the 1938 picture *Jezebel*. By then Bette had won a Best Actress Oscar (for *Dangerous*, in 1935) and was considered a rising talent, as was Wyler, who had *These Three* (1936), *Come and Get It* (shared credit, 1936), *Dodsworth* (1936), and *Dead End* (1937) behind him.

Bette, in typical fashion, was initially resistant to Wyler's direction on *Jezebel*. By the end of the shooting, however, he had her in his palm, something no other director could truly claim, and in his bed (something a few other directors *could* truly claim). While shooting the picture Wyler commanded Bette with authority. He wore her down, demanding take after take. At one point, trying to temper her famous jerky mannerisms, he gave her an ultimatum: "If you don't stop moving your head, I'll put a chain around your neck!"

Bette was attracted to Wyler's obsession with perfectionism and his unabashed virility. At least she had a director who challenged her artistic vision and her strength. With Wyler nothing was to be spared for the sake of the picture.

Shortly before directing *Jezebel*, Wyler had been divorced from actress Margaret Sullavan. Bette was still married to Harmon Nelson. Their subsequent affair was tempestuous, ending when Wyler sent Bette a letter with an ultimatum. Either she agreed to divorce Nelson and marry him, or he would marry someone else the following Wednesday. Better would later claim that she had deliberately not read the letter out of anger at Wyler. The following week she was devastated to hear on the radio that Wyler had married actress

Margaret Tallichet. The irony would not be lost on Bette and Wyler that their next picture together was entitled *The Letter*.

William Wyler directed Bette once again in what was arguably their best collaboration, Lillian Hellman's *The Little Foxes*. During the shooting of that picture the sparks between them changed into daggers, with each hurling insults across the set. They parted ways on the picture's completion and never worked together again. In later years Bette said one of her last remaining dreams was to work with William Wyler again. He did appear at a "This Is Your Life" tribute to Bette in the early 1970s, during which Bette introduced him to the audience by saying, simply, "Ladies and Gentlemen, this is my all-time hero."

William Wyler (1902–1981) directed other pictures, including *The Westerner* (1940), *Mrs. Miniver* (Best Director Oscar winner, 1942), *The Best Years of Our Lives* (Best Director Oscar winner, 1946), *The Heiress* (1949), *Detective Story* (1951), *Carrie* (1952), *Roman Holiday* (1953), *The Desperate Hours* (1955), *The Big Country* (1958), *Ben Hur* (Best Director Oscar winner, 1959), *The Children's Hour* (1962), *The Collector* (1965), and *Funny Girl* (1968).

Y

YORKSHIRE, ENGLAND

The 1952 picture *Another Man's Poison* was shot on location in Yorkshire, England. Bette offended the locals by having her food flown in from the United States. She was eating steaks while the rest of the cast and crew indulged in fish and chips.

FRANCIS YOUNG

The first boy Bette ever kissed was Francis Young of Southwest Harbor, Maine. He was the soda jerk at the local drugstore. One summer day Francis, 16, walked Bette, 13, home from the pharmacy and gave her a kiss. More than 50 years later, Young showed up at Symphony Hall in Boston to see *Bette Davis in Person and on Film*. He called out from the audience, and Bette recognized his voice. After the show the two had a brief reunion backstage. Said Bette, "There stood this little old, old man. . . . In seeing the man, I lost the first boy I ever loved."

GIG YOUNG

Young costarred in the 1943 picture *Old Acquaintance*. During the making of the film Bette and Gig allegedly had an affair. Interestingly, in a bit of Hollywood trivia, Young's real name was Byron Barr. He was so taken, however, by the name of his character in the 1942 picture *The Gay Sisters*, "Gig Young," that he adopted it as his own.

Gig Young (1913-1978) appeared in other pictures, including *Desk Set* (1957), *That Touch of Mink* (1962), and *They Shoot Horses, Don't They?* (for which he won the Best Supporting Actor Oscar, 1969).

LORETTA YOUNG

Loretta Young turned down the opportunity to replace Joan Crawford and star opposite Bette in the 1964 picture *Hush . . . Hush, Sweet Charlotte*.

Z

DARRYL F. ZANUCK

Darryl F. Zanuck signed his first Warner Brothers contract in 1924 as a screenwriter. He was 22 years old. The contract paid him $250 a week. He started by writing a series of Rin Tin Tin pictures and became known for his speed in turning out scripts. Actually he wrote for the studio under four different names: Mark Canfield, Melville Crossman, Gregory Rogers, and Zanuck.

By 1927 Zanuck (1902–1979) had been promoted to supervising the script development of *all* the studio's productions. He also oversaw the production of the studio's standard action pictures and melodramas, while Jack Warner himself oversaw the more important productions.

In 1929 Zanuck was promoted to the position of production chief. By November 1930 he had assumed command of all studio operations, and he was in this position at Warner Brothers when Bette Davis first signed there in late 1931. His early successes for the studio in this capacity included *Little Caesar*, *Public Enemy*, and *Forty-Second Street*.

Of Bette Davis's early pictures for the studio Zanuck produced *The Man Who Played God* (1932) and executive-produced *The Rich Are Always With Us* (1932), *Dark Horse* (1932), *Cabin in the Cotton* (1932), *Three on a Match* (1932), *20,000 Years in Sing Sing* (1933), *Parachute Jumper* (1933), *The Working Man* (1933), and *Ex-Lady* (1933).

Zanuck abruptly turned in his resignation to the studio on April 15, 1933, after feuding with Harry Warner over the reinstatement of full employee salaries (which had been cut back temporarily because of the state of the nation's economy). On April 21, 1933, he left to form 20th Century Pictures, later 20th Century–Fox, with Joseph Schenck and William Goetz.

Years later, when Bette resigned from her post as president of the Academy of Motion Picture Arts and Sciences, Zanuck reportedly threatened her with that old show biz cliché, "You'll never work in this town again."

Years later Zanuck made amends by offering her the script for *All About Eve*. Zanuck produced the picture, which won an Oscar as the best picture of 1950. He later produced her again in *The Virgin Queen* (1955).

ADOLPH ZUKOR

Bette was one of the star guests at the 100th birthday bash at the Beverly Hilton Hotel for film pioneer Adolph Zukor. Others in attendance: Barbara Stanwyck, Dorothy Lamour, Bob Hope, Alfred Hitchcock, Frank Capra, Gregory Peck, Rock Hudson, Gene Kelly, Jimmy Stewart, William Wyler, Jack Warner. The event was emceed by Charlton Heston. Bette announced, as she entered the room, "Same old faces in the same old places!"

BIBLIOGRAPHY

ARTICLES

Babcock, Muriel.   "Bette Davis Sets New Marriage Style for Filmdom's Stars." *Los Angeles Examiner* (September 23, 1934).

Busch, Noel F.   "Bette Davis: She Prefers 'Attractive Wench' Parts in Which Her Acting Is Hollywood's High." *Life* (January 23, 1939).

Crosby, Joan.   "Bette Davis and James Stewart Team for HBO's 'Right of Way.' " *Drama-Logue* (November 25, 1982).

Darrach, Brad.   "Grand Old Lillian Gish Makes a Big Splash in *The Whales of August.*" *People* (December 14, 1987).

Davis, Bette, with Bill Davidson.   "All About Me." *Collier's* (November 25, 1955; December 9, 1955).

Davis, Bette.   "An Actress' Return." *San Francisco Chronicle* (August 3, 1963).

Easton, Nina J.   "Bette Davis Smoking Over *Stepmother.*" *Los Angeles Times* (January 3, 1989).

Hall, Gladys.   "Bette Davis' True Life Story—A girl's rise to stardom through sheer determination."

Haller, Scot.   "Bette Davis Is Back, Thank You, and Will Not Be Going Gentle into Anybody's Damned Good Night." *People* (November 2, 1987).

Jahr, Cliff.   "Bette Davis: Survival of a Superstar." *Ladies Home Journal* (February 1988).

Merina, Victor, and Michaelson, Judith.   "Lavish Tributes Pour in for Film Star Bette Davis." *Los Angeles Times* (October 8, 1989).

O'Toole, Lawrence.   "Bette Davis." *Us* (May 1, 1989).

Poe, Gregory.   "All About Bette." *Exposure.* (December 1988/January 1989).

Quirk, Lawrence J.   "Bette Davis: Her First Quarter Century on the Screen Demonstrates the Power of the Will." *Films in Review* (December 1955).

Rader, Dotson.   "Bette: The Story of a Winner." *Parade* (March 6, 1983).

Rimoldi, Oscar A.   "Interview with Director Vincent Sherman." *Hollywood Studio Magazine* (June 1990).

Schreiberg, Stu.   "Bette Davis, Full of Life and Fighting Back." *USA Today* (March 27, 1987).

Scott, Vernon.   "Bette, Joan—an Uneasy Alliance." *San Francisco Chronicle* (July 23, 1962).

Smalley, Jack.   "One Year with Oscar." *Photoplay* (August 1937).

Speck, Gregory.   "We Hate You Bette Davis." *The Cable Guide* (December 1989).

"Stairs Fall Told in Death of Farnsworth." *Los Angeles Examiner* (August 27, 1943).

Sutherland, Christine. "No Guts, No Glory." *Ladies Home Journal* (April 1985).

Sweeney, Louise. "For Acting Honors . . . it's Bette Davis Ayes." *Chicago Tribune* (December 30, 1987).

Williams, Dick. "Strike Will Separate Men from Boys." *Los Angeles Mirror News* (March 14, 1960).

Others

Ladies Home Journal (July 1941).

People (October 23, 1989).

Playboy (July 1982).

BOOKS

Arliss, George. *My 10 Years in the Studios.* Boston: Little Brown Company, 1940.

Berg, A. Scott. *Goldwyn: A Biography.* New York: Alfred A. Knopf, 1989.

Cagney, James. *Cagney by Cagney.* New York: Doubleday, 1976.

Carey, Gary, With Joseph L. Mankiewicz. *More About All About Eve.* New York: Random House, 1972.

Considine, Shaun. *Bette & Joan: The Divine Feud.* New York: E. P. Dutton, 1989.

Cotten, Joseph. *Vanity Will Get You Somewhere.* San Francisco: Mercury House, 1987.

Crist, Judith. *Take 22: Moviemakers on Moviemaking.* New York: Viking, 1984.

Davis, Bette, with Sanford Dody. *The Lonely Life.* New York: G. P. Putnam's Sons, 1962.

Davis, Bette, with Michael Herskowitz. *This 'N That.* New York: G. P. Putnam's Sons, 1987.

Fonda, Henry, as told to Howard Teichmann. *Fonda: My Life.* New York: New American Library, 1981.

Graham, Sheila. *Confessions of a Hollywood Columnist* New York: William Morrow & Company, 1969.

Henreid, Paul. *Ladies Man: Paul Henreid.* New York: St. Martin's Press, 1984.

Higham, Charles, and Joel Greenbaum. *The Celluloid Muse.* New York: New American Library, 1969.

Higham, Charles. *Bette.* New York: Macmillan, 1981.

Hyman, B. D. *My Mother's Keeper.* New York: William Morrow, 1987.

Kobal, John. *People Will Talk.* New York: Alfred A. Knopf, 1986.

LeRoy, Mervyn. *Mervyn LeRoy: Take One.* New York: Hawthorn Books, 1974.

Logan, Joshua. *Movie Stars, Real People, and Me.* New York: Delacorte Press, 1978.

Merrill, Gary.   *Bette, Rita, and the Rest of My Life*. Augusta, Maine: Lance Tapley, 1988.

Peary, Danny, ed.   *Close-ups*. "Bette Davis: A Lifelong Love Affair" by Alvah Bessie. New York: Workman Publishing Company, 1978.

Quirk, Lawrence J.   *Fasten Your Seat Belts*. New York: William Morrow & Company, 1990.

Reed, Rex.   *Valentines & Vitriol*. New York: Dell Publishing Co., 1977.

Schatz, Thomas.   *The Genius of the System*. New York: Pantheon Books, 1988.

Stine, Whitney, with Bette Davis.   *Mother Goddam*. New York: Hawthorn Books, 1974.

Stine Whitney.   *"I'd Love to Kiss You . . ."* New York: Pocket Books, 1990.

Swindell, Larry.   *Charles Boyer*. Garden City, New York: Doubleday, 1983.

Vidor, King.   *King Vidor on Film Making*. New York: McKay, 1972.

SOURCES

A

"Ms. Abernethy . . .": court documents.

"I believe abortion . . .": *Playboy*, July 1982.

"I think acting should look . . .": "The Dick Cavett Show."

"I am afraid that I am not . . .": "Should Actors Think" by Bette Davis, *Los Angeles Mirror-News*, September 12, 1959.

"I don't draw upon any-thing . . .": *The Cable Guide*, December 1989.

"Please let me know . . .": letter, Warner Brothers Archives.

"I've had most of them . . .": "Larry King Live," 1988.

"These ladies are pros . . .": *Look*, March 9, 1965.

"I was fond of Robert . . .": *This 'N That* by Bette Davis.

"It was one of the worst times . . .": *Fame*, December 1989–January 1990.

"That was the wonderful thing . . .": *Chicago Sunday Tribune*, December 3, 1950.

"Dear *boy* . . .": *More About All About Eve* by Gary Carey with Joseph L. Mankiewicz.

"She will come up on the set . . .": BBC documentary.

"Shouldn't he light it?": *Collier's*, December 9, 1955.

"He haunted my office . . .": *More About All About Eve.*

"I'm sorry . . .": *Los Angeles Herald-Express*, May 20, 1950.

"Barring grand opera . . .": *More About All About Eve.*

"The duchess de Praslin . . .": *Charles Boyer* by Larry Swindell.

"Charles was a happy . . .": *Charles Boyer.*

"Davis is going overboard . . .": memo, Warner Brothers Archives.

"The picture was overproduced . . .": *Charles Boyer.*

"She was one of the first . . .": *American Film*, March 1977.

"[*Pocketful of Miracles*] was Ann-Margret's . . .": *The Lonely Life* by Bette Davis.

"Mr. Rakoff didn't have . . .": *Mother Goddam* by Whitney Stine.

"No, he *definitely* . . .": *Take 22* by Judith Crist.

"I've always wanted to play . . .": *Los Angeles Times*, March 18, 1951.

"lousy, less-than-B picture": *Bette & Joan* by Shaun Considine.

"Learn the right speech . . .": *Collier's*, November 25, 1955.

"Bette, you must go home . . .": *Los Angeles Times*, July 6, 1959.

"I think that only two . . .": *My 10 Years in the Studios* by George Arliss.

"I wouldn't be . . .": *Parade*, March 6, 1983.

"Greedy, greedy . . .": *Palm Beach Post*, April 25, 1989.

B

"I almost died . . .": *By Myself* by Lauren Bacall.

"I was *positive* I would . . .": *Los Angeles Times*, October 11, 1970.

"I have a theory that . . .": *Los Angeles Times*, October 11, 1970.

"I didn't think she had . . .": *Seesaw: A Dual Biography of Anne Bancroft and Mel Brooks* by William Holtzman.

"I'm kind of a second-fiddle . . .": *Variety*, November 13, 1950.

"The only time I came . . .": *Hollywood Citizen-News*, November 18, 1955.

"It bothered Bette Davis . . .": *People Will Talk* by John Kobal.

"Yes. Every morning when I . . .": *Variety*, November 13, 1950.

"There was no . . .": *Variety*, November 13, 1950.

"I made a big mistake . . .": *Los Angeles Times*, November 20, 1988.

"There was a lot of passion . . .": *Fasten Your Seat Belts* by Lawrence J. Quirk.

"She has a lovely . . .": *Los Angeles Examiner*, March 9, 1936.

"I'm not going to *adopt* . . .": *Los Angeles Examiner*, March 3, 1938.

"Silly as it may . . .": *Los Angeles Examiner*, March 9, 1938.

"I've decided recently . . .": *Ladies Home Journal*, February 1988.

"A woman doesn't have to be . . .": press release, Warner Brothers Archives.

"Any of the times . . .": *The Cable Guide*, December 1989.

"My God, how could I . . .": *USA Today*, March 27, 1987.

"I always massage . . .": *Pageant*.

"I'm *dying* to do . . .": telegram, Warner Brothers Archives.

"*What* the hell're . . .": *Close-Ups*, edited by Danny Peary.

"Ahl-vah, what're you . . .": *Close-Ups*.

"She would start off . . .": *Ladies Man: Paul Henreid* by Paul Henreid.

"Don't you hate people . . .": *Parade*, March 6, 1983.

"I like *Beyond the Forest* . . .": *The Hollywood Reporter*, May 25, 1949.

"shiver in the cold . . .": *Brooklyn Eagle*, October 16, 1949.

"[She was] one of the screen's . . .": *King Vidor on Film Making* by King Vidor.

"Unbeknownst to me . . .": *King Vidor on Film Making*.

"Such are the problems . . .": *King Vidor on Film Making*.

"It was so cold . . .": *Los Angeles Examiner*, August 9, 1949.

"A producer of infinite . . .": *Mother Goddam* by Whitney Stine.

"Will you tell Bogart . . .": memo, Warner Brothers Archives.

"Be sure and have Bogart . . .": memo, Warner Brothers Archives.

"it would be difficult . . .": *The Genius of the System* by Thomas Schatz.

"You can't appear on the . . .": *Collier's*, November 25, 1955.

"I don't like the way . . .": memo, Warner Brothers Archives.

"I emphatically disagree with . . .": memo, Warner Brothers Archives.

"It took ten . . .": *Boston Globe*, July 15, 1990.

"I had great respect . . .": interview with the author.

"I felt a strange kinship . . .": *Collier's*.

"I wouldn't hire . . .": *Los Angeles Times*, July 21, 1962.

"During the case I used to . . .": *Hollywood Citizen-News*, October 20, 1936.

"Of the men I didn't . . .": *This 'N That* by Bette Davis.

"The first time I . . .": *Us*, May 1, 1989.

"I am 100 percent with . . .": *Variety*, September 7, 1971.

"It's the final irony . . .": *Valentines & Vitriol* by Rex Reed.

"an intimate story . . .": *International Photographer*, March 1976.

"The relationship between . . .": *Los Angeles Examiner*, September 12, 1975.

"I feel like I've spent . . .": *Valentines & Vitriol*.

C

"Mike Curtiz was a mean . . .": *Fasten Your Seat Belts* by Lawrence J. Quirk.

"At Warner Brothers . . .": *Collier's*, November 25, 1955.

"Thank God it did not . . .": *Ladies Home Journal*, April 1985.

"It was a horrid . . .": *Ladies Home Journal*, April 1985.

"The mastectomy was . . .": *USA Today*, March 27, 1987.

"The basic reason is . . .": *The Hollywood Reporter*, May 4, 1983.

"I must have shocked . . .": *Collier's*, December 9, 1955.

"gave the role grand . . .": *Fasten Your Seat Belts*.

"Who *wrote* it . . .": *New York Daily Mirror*, April 28, 1942.

"America is no longer . . .": San Sebastian Film Festival, September 1989.

"If I did not smoke . . .": "Donahue, 1987."

"Our great cameramen . . .": *Exposure*, December 1988/January 1989.

"There was a young woman . . .": interview with the author.

"In all my years . . .": *Los Angeles Times*, January 3, 1989.

"My attitude is . . .": *Los Angeles Times*.

"It is breaking the heart . . .": San Sebastian Film Festival.

"It was a disgrace . . .": San Sebastian Film Festival.

"I would find well-known . . .": *This 'N That* by Bette Davis.

"I know that when . . .": interview with the author.

"Gosh, it's bad enough . . .": *Hollywood Citizen-News*, July 22, 1944.

"She was wonderful . . .": *Movie Story*, August 1945.

"She'd expect you to . . .": interview with the author.

"I know you have had . . .": memo, Warner Brothers Archives.

"Irving just ragged . . .": interview with the author.

"He wasn't a director . . .": interview with the author.

"She'd come on the set . . .": interview with the author.

"You know, I've done many . . .": *Hollywood Citizen-News*, September 5, 1944.

"I don't think it is . . .": memo, Warner Brothers Archives.

"I didn't know *how* . . .": interview with the author.

"It was a very unhappy situation . . .": interview with the author.

"I will admit to having stumbled . . .": *Vanity Will Get You Somewhere* by Joseph Cotten.

"I have admired Joan's performances . . .": *San Francisco Chronicle*, July 23, 1962.

"It's as though I was not . . .": *Hollywood Citizen-News*, May 20, 1963.

"She said, 'Please . . .' ": "Geraldo."

"Oh, no, I'm not compared . . .": *The Cable Guide*, December 1989.

"I never go . . .": *Halliwell's Filmgoer's Companion*.

"Bette said that, so far as Joan . . .": "Geraldo," 1989.

"enough hope in . . .": *Ladies Home Journal*, July 1941.

D

"I really hated missing . . .": *American Film*, April 1987.

"If Bette Davis is going to wear . . .": memo, Warner Brothers Archives.

"How long before the hair . . .": memo, Warner Brothers Archives.

"Driving home at dusk . . .": *Life*, April 24, 1939.

"She told me . . .": interview with the author.

"I think Bette . . .": reprinted in *Halliwell's Filmgoer's and Video Viewer's Companion* by Leslie Halliwell.

"Nobody but . . .": *A Proper Job* by Brian Aherne.

"You see, she was . . .": interview with the author.

"It may sound . . .": *Hollywood Citizen-News*, September 13, 1946.

"If Bette Davis . . .": *New York Times*, September 18, 1962.

"Bette Davis has . . .": *Movie Stars, Real People, and Me* by Joshua Logan.

"Bette Davis—who . . .": *The Hollywood Reporter*, October 9, 1989.

"It's entirely possible . . .": *The Hollywood Reporter*, October 9, 1989.

"Such a person . . .": *Washington Post*, May 18, 1985.

"To me she is . . .": *Vanity Will Get You Somewhere* by Joseph Cotten.

"She was difficult . . .": *People*, October 23, 1989.

"She made bystanders . . .": *Bette, Rita, and the Rest of My Life* by Gary Merrill.

"Why waste time . . .": *The Lonely Life* by Bette Davis.

"We were sent to Florida . . .": Bette in an interview with Gladys Hall.

"He was one of the . . .": *Women's Wear Daily*, October 15, 1976.

"Cripes, I turned down two . . .": *Valley Times*.

"Her mother, frankly, was . . .": *Bette* by Charles Higham.

"She was *not* . . .": *Parade*, March 6, 1983.

"Married Captain . . .": *Los Angeles Examiner*, April 28, 1950.

"It is his . . .": memo, Warner Brothers Archives.

"Despite all the roles . . .": *San Francisco Chronicle*, August 3, 1963.

"It comes up to my fondest . . .": memo, Warner Brothers Archives.

"I would hate to pass . . .": *People*, November 2, 1987.

"Well, I see . . .": *This 'N That* by Bette Davis.

"What if they start . . .": *Los Angeles Times*, December 11, 1977.

"Surely you could have . . .": *Los Angeles Times*.

"It's a long . . .": *Los Angeles Times*, December 11, 1977.

"Never have I been given . . .": press release, Warner Brothers Archives.

"Bette Davis came in and . . .": memo, Warner Brothers Archives.

"*Deception* was completely ruined . . .": *Los Angeles Daily News*, August 19, 1949.

"I had one top . . .": *Take 22* by Judith Crist.

"Our great directors . . .": *Exposure*, December 1988/January 1989.

"Friendly divorces are . . .": *Photoplay*.

"I have never asked . . .": to Marvin Paige.

"My segment was six . . .": *Inside Oscar* by Mason Wiley and Damien Bona.

"Without doubt the most . . .": *The Lonely Life*.

"In this case, it's . . .": Burbank Studios tribute, 1989.

E

"An exhausted-looking Bette . . .": *Detroit Free Press*, October 10, 1989.

F

"Farney not out of danger . . .": telegram, Warner Brothers Archives.

"Do not intend to leave . . .": telegram, Warner Brothers Archives.

"We were standing . . .": *Los Angeles Examiner*, August 27, 1943.

"I had seen him walk . . .": *Los Angeles Examiner*.

"When I learned . . .": *Los Angeles Examiner*.

"The blood in . . .": *Los Angeles Examiner*.

"The previous accident . . .": *Los Angeles Examiner*.

"Bette and I were walking . . .": "Geraldo."

"I played a fashion . . .": *Collier's*, November 25, 1955.

"There was nothing . . .": *American File*, March 1977.

"More than anything else . . .": *Los Angeles Herald-Examiner*, February 12, 1964.

"They've sort of . . .": *Chicago Tribune*, December 30, 1987.

"I do not regret . . .": *The Lonely Life* by Bette Davis.

"I waited a very long . . .": *Us*, May 1, 1989.

"Bette is, as is well . . .": *Hollywood Citizen-News*, September 13, 1946.

"I've told my mother . . .": *Fonda: My Life* by Henry Fonda.

"Holy shit! . . .": *Fonda: My Life*.

"I went to lunch . . .": *People*, October 23, 1989.

"He's a marine . . .": *Los Angeles Times*, July 21, 1962.

"Tell Mr. Ford . . .": *People*, October 23, 1989.

"I just read . . .": memo, Warner Brothers Archives.

"I have just read . . .": memo, Warner Brothers Archives.

G

"She is a very, very . . .": *Silver Screen*, August 1939.

"Someone like Garbo . . .": *Playboy*, July 1982.

"I was the biggest . . .": BBC documentary.

"Miss Davis, I'm Ava . . .": *People*, October 20, 1980.

"From the way John Garfield . . .": *Silver Screen*.

"Would it be possible . . .": letter, Warner Brothers Archives.

"would have tripped . . .": *The Lonely Life* by Bette Davis.

"When I was in films . . .": *People*, December 14, 1987.

"You may inquire why . . .": *Memo from David O. Selznick* edited by Rudy Behlmer.

"Cukor hired me . . .": *Films in Review*, December 1955.

"Mr. Goulding . . .": *Take 22* edited by Judith Crist.

"She had control . . .": *People*, October 23, 1989.

"It's too bad . . .": *Hollywood Citizen-News*, November 6, 1950.

"This is in no . . .": memo, Warner Brothers Archives.

"Let us have it . . .": memo, Warner Brothers Archives.

"Remember your promise . . .": telegram, Warner Brothers Archives.

"overbearing, egotistical . . .": *My Mother's Keeper* by B. D. Hyman.

"Not only did she . . .": *Bette* by Charles Higham.

"I am in awe . . .": *Los Angeles Herald-Examiner*, July 3, 1966.

"If this wasn't a series . . .": *Los Angeles Herald-Examiner*, July 3, 1966.

H

"Yes it is . . .": *Los Angeles Times*, October 8, 1989.

"When I arrived . . .": *Ladies Home Journal*, July 1941.

" 'Someone is sitting . . .' ": *Detroit Free Press*, October 10, 1989.

"I also consider . . .": *Mother Goddam* by Whitney Stine.

"Rita was so beautiful . . .": *Los Angeles Times West Magazine*, February 7, 1971.

"Every man I . . .": *Halliwell's Filmgoer's and Video Viewer's Companion* by Leslie Halliwell.

"Why, I made a picture . . .": *Drama-Logue*, November 25, 1982.

"There was something about . . .": *Ladies Man: Paul Henreid* by Paul Henreid.

"She would tell . . .": *Ladies Man: Paul Henreid.*

"I always wanted to be . . .": *Take 22* by Judith Crist.

"All my film career . . .": *This 'N That* by Bette Davis.

"a disgusting thing . . .": *Interview*, September 1985.

"I would give anything . . .": *Us*, May 1, 1989.

"If only I would have won . . .": *Miami Herald*, October 14, 1989.

"From the time I . . .": *Look*, August 6, 1946.

"Hollywood has changed . . .": *Los Angeles Mirror News*, June 9, 1958.

"Television should have . . .": *Los Angeles Mirror News*, March 14, 1960.

"I am not going to . . .": "Bette Davis: A Lifelong Love Affair" by Alvah Bessie, *Close-Ups*, edited by Danny Peary.

"three girls . . .": *Los Angeles Examiner*, September 17, 1943.

"It was an unfortunate . . .": press release, Warner Brothers Archives.

"I have worked very hard . . .": letter, Warner Brothers Archives.

"He did not seem . . .": *This 'N That.*

"Miriam was a wonderful . . .": *Playboy*, July 1982.

"I got in a perfectly . . .": *Collier's*, November 25, 1955.

"A total disaster . . .": the San Sebastian Film Festival.

"To this day I . . .": *The Hollywood Reporter*, June 7, 1985.

"You know, my . . .": *USA Today*, March 27, 1987.

"Leslie Howard was . . .": *Playboy.*

"Mr. Howard went . . .": *This 'N That* by Bette Davis.

"I think she was . . .": *Los Angeles Times*, November 18, 1980.

"Bette is so easy . . .": *TV Radio Guide.*

"He brought out . . .": *I'd Love to Kiss You . . .* by Whitney Stine.

"I feel I would like . . .": letter, Warner Brothers Archives.

"Thank you so very much . . .": letter, Warner Brothers Archives.

"I sent some flowers . . .": "Geraldo."

"Be a fanny-spanking . . .": *Look*, December 18, 1962.

"I've wanted her . . .": *Modern Screen*, August 1947.

"Barbara will choose . . .": press release, Warner Brothers Archives.

"I'm convinced . . .": *The Hollywood Reporter.*

"I've often said . . .": *New York Times*, March 12, 1979.

"It can't possibly . . .": *Ladies Home Journal*, April 1985.

"It was as catastrophic . . .": *Us*, May 1, 1989.

"That book was . . .": *Ladies Home Journal*, February 1988.

|

"You don't really . . .": *The Cinema of John Huston* by Gerald Pratley.

"With *In This* . . .": *The Cinema of John Huston.*

"You know I . . .": memo, Warner Brothers Archives.

"Best of luck . . .": memo, Warner Brothers Archives.

"In the future . . .": memo, Warner Brothers Archives.

"It was just an . . .": *Take 22* by Judith Crist.

"I think this is . . .": memo, Warner Brothers Archives.

"Saw English picture . . .": memo, Warner Brothers Archives.

J

"Have now read . . .": memo, Warner Brothers Archives.

"I am thrilled . . .": *The Genius of the System* by Thomas Schatz.

"the picture can . . .": memo, Warner Brothers Archives.

"[For] my first scene . . .": *Variety*, March 17, 1976.

"I do not believe . . .": memo, Warner Brothers Archives.

"Possibly Wyler . . .": *The Genius of the System.*

"Is he absolutely . . .": memo, Warner Brothers Archives.

"Dear Jack . . .": *Memo from David O. Selznick*, edited by Rudy Behlmer.

"My leading lady . . .": *Cagney by Cagney* by James Cagney.

"No one swooped . . .": *Look*, August 6, 1946.

"Everybody tremendously . . .": telegram, Warner Brothers Archives.

"Carlota was one . . .": press release, Warner Brothers Archives.

"When Mr. Muni . . .": "Uncertain Glory" by Bette Davis, *Ladies Home Journal*, July 1941.

"Davis stopped the . . .": *Debbie: My Life* by Debbie Reynolds.

"Sneaked the bride . . .": telegram, Warner Brothers Archives.

"Picture went over . . .": telegram, Warner Brothers Archives.

K

"I always had a . . .": *Ladies Home Journal*, February 1988.

"If after years of . . .": memo, Warner Brothers Archives.

L

"She's the next . . .": *Los Angeles Times*, August 2, 1959.

"She once said . . .": *Los Angeles Times*, October 8, 1989.

"They gave me . . .": *Mervyn LeRoy: Take One* by Mervyn LeRoy.

"It's a great part . . .": press release, Warner Brothers Archives.

"We actually started with . . .": Los Angeles County Museum of Art Tribute to Hal Wallis.

"I am so . . .": letter, Warner Brothers Archives.

"Nobody seems to . . .": *Close-Ups*, edited by Danny Peary.

"If we could . . .": letter, Warner Brothers Archives.

"Wyler was very . . .": *Take 22* by Judith Crist.

"Maybe it's because . . .": *The Cincinnati Post*, July 29, 1942.

"She had become . . .": *Movie Stars, Real People, and Me* by Joshua Logan.

"False, malicious . . .": *People*, November 20, 1978.

"My insecurity . . .": interview with the author.

"Thank God . . .": *Take 22.*

M

"highly amusing . . .": letter, Warner Brothers Archives.

"We will forget . . .": memo, Warner Brothers Archives.

"I saw the Monty . . .": memo, Warner Brothers Archives.

"he has become . . .": memo, Warner Brothers Archives.

"I ran the Woolley . . .": memo, Warner Brothers Archives.

"Guess this should . . .": letter, Warner Brothers Archives.

"If I thought . . .": letter, Warner Brothers Archives.

"I felt the . . .": *Halliwell's Filmgoer's Companion*

"The last makeup test . . .": memo, Warner Brothers Archives.

"a little too . . .": memo, Warner Brothers Archives.

"the circles under her . . .": memo, Warner Brothers Archives.

"Who is that monkey . . .": memo, Warner Brothers Archives.

"This bit was . . .": memo, Warner Brothers Archives.

"I ran *Marked Woman* . . .": memo, Warner Brothers Archives.

"It's hell . . .": *Radie's World* by Radie Harris.

"I just don't think . . .": *Los Angeles Herald-Express*, April 19, 1961.

"I have been married . . .": "Bette Davis: She's Still Going Strong" by Lloyd Shearer, *Parade*, November 8, 1964.

"I know now . . .": *The Lonely Life* by Bette Davis.

"I've *always* liked . . .": *Parade*, March 6, 1983.

"Another pitfall . . .": *Collier's*, December 9, 1955.

"I don't dislike . . .": *Silver Screen*, July 1940.

"I saw him . . .": *Los Angeles Examiner*, January 14, 1951.

"We only played . . .": *Los Angeles Examiner*.

"She would empty . . .": *Bette, Rita, and the Rest of My Life* by Gary Merrill.

"I've spent my life . . .": reprinted in the *Los Angeles Times*, March 6, 1990.

"Although on key . . .": *Movie Stars, Real People and Me* by Joshua Logan.

"Nervous? About . . .": *Movie Stars, Real People and Me*.

"Bette, please be . . .": *Movie Stars, Real People and Me*.

"Thank God . . .": *Movie Stars, Real People and Me*.

"Has the doctor . . .": *Movie Stars, Real People and Me*.

"It was a less . . .": *Hollywood Studio Magazine*, June 1990.

"Now that it . . .": telegram, Warner Brothers Archives.

"Marilyn Monroe . . .": *Washington Post*, November 9, 1965.

"Interestingly enough . . .": "Larry King Live," 1988.

"It was upstaging . . .": *The Lonely Life*.

"One of the greatest . . .": *Los Angeles Herald-Examiner*, August 2, 1964.

"That first day . . .": *Ladies Home Journal*, April 1985.

"I can go on . . .": *Ladies Home Journal*.

"She was feisty . . .": *My Life in Three Acts* by Helen Hayes.

"*That book* . . .": *USA Today*, March 27, 1987.

N

"I'm intelligent enough . . .": Reprinted in *Screenland*, January 1939.

"So far it has . . .": *Los Angeles Examiner*, September 1934.

"I hope there won't . . .": *Los Angeles Herald*, September 19, 1938.

"I will not . . .": *Screenland*.

"There will not . . .": *Los Angeles Herald*, November 22, 1938.

"I think this is . . .": *Los Angeles Daily News*, December 7, 1938.

"This was a very . . .": interview with the author.

"Let's *pray* . . .": *Los Angeles Times*, September 14, 1962.

"We struggled . . .": *Los Angeles Herald and Express*, December 30, 1942.

"I've gone the limit . . .": *Chicago Daily News*, April 9, 1942.

"I can't understand . . .": memo, Warner Brothers Archives.

"I was terribly . . .": memo, Warner Brothers Archives.

"She was shaking . . .": *Seattle Times*, July 12, 1942.

"I suggested it . . .": American Film Institute tribute to Hal Wallis.

"a very fine picture . . .": memo, Warner Brothers Archives.

"Me? *Never* . . .": *Parade*, March 6, 1983.

O

"Of course, he . . .": *Chicago Tribune*, December 30, 1987.

"That bitch . . .": *People Will Talk* by John Kobal.

"I will not . . .": memo, Warner Brothers Archives.

"One of the funniest . . .": *Collier's*, November 25, 1955.

"It's actors of . . .": *Los Angeles Times*, July 19, 1962.

"If the other . . .": *Los Angeles Times*, March 25, 1955.

"I was shattered . . .": *Look*, March 9, 1965.

P

"Don't say *anything* . . .": *Take 22* by Judith Crist.

"One of the most charming . . .": *Collier's*, December 9, 1955.

"I emerged . . .": *Collier's*.

"Naturally we don't . . .": memo, Warner Brothers Archives.

"They laughed . . .": *Hollywood Citizen News*, October 12, 1951.

"Is Bette doing . . .": *Screenwriter Nunnally Johnson* by Tom Stempet.

"The theatre . . .": *Los Angeles Examiner*, January 26, 1954.

"The New York . . .": *Los Angeles Times*, December 27, 1962.

"In Hollywood . . .": *This Month*, June 1962.

"I saw Frank . . .": *Los Angeles Times*, May 18, 1961.

"My big job . . .": *The Hollywood Diary*, August 1, 1961.

"I say not 50% . . .": *Los Angeles Times*, June 9, 1946.

"Every politician . . .": *Los Angeles Herald-Examiner*, February 12, 1964.

"Actually, I'd rather . . .": *Los Angeles Times*, August 2, 1964.

"I would like . . .": *Los Angeles Times*, March 1, 1955.

"I find myself so . . .": telegram, Warner Brothers Archives.

"We don't want . . .": memo, Warner Brothers Archives.

"I have been studying . . .": memo, Warner Brothers Archives.

Q

"having the power to . . .": *My Mother's Keeper* by B. D. Hyman.

"One of the reasons . . .": *Los Angeles Examiner*, March 23, 1936.

"I shiver . . .": *Time*, March 28, 1938.

"I have reached . . .": *Ladies Home Journal*, July 1941.

"I'm no Pollyanna . . .": *Time*.

"Eventually I . . .": *Los Angeles Daily News*, January 6, 1953.

"I've often thought . . .": *Los Angeles Examiner*, January 26, 1954.

"There's a legend . . .": *New York Herald-Tribune*, November 11, 1962.

"Some of the parts . . .": *This Month*, June 1962.

"It's an enormous . . .": *Hollywood Citizen-News*, June 16, 1962.

"I had lost . . .": *Hollywood Citizen-News*, February 11, 1963.

"I love to rip . . .": *My Mother's Keeper*.

"What I should . . .": *Washington Post*, November 9, 1965.

"To work . . .": *Parade*, March 6, 1983.

"Just one more . . .": *People*, November 2, 1987.

"I will never . . .": *Los Angeles Times West Magazine*, February 7, 1971.

"I spent a lifetime . . .": *Los Angeles Times West Magazine*.

"Every now . . .": "Larry King Live," 1988.

"Three things I . . .": *Los Angeles Times*, October 7, 1981.

"It's going to be . . .": *Playboy*, July 1982.

"When I first started . . .": *Los Angeles Times*, December 11, 1977.

"They're my wrinkles . . .": *Look*, March 9, 1965.

"That was never . . .": "Larry King Live," 1988.

R

"He was not a . . .": San Sebastian Film Festival, September 1989.

"All my life . . .": *Ladies Home Journal*, April 1985.

"Oh, of course! . . .": *Us*, May 1, 1989.

"Debbie, don't let . . .": *Debbie: My Life* by Debbie Reynolds.

"After all the . . .": *Los Angeles Herald-Examiner*, July 7, 1950.

"[But] when George Schaefer . . .": *The Hollywood Reporter*, November 15, 1982.

"I've never had . . .": *The Hollywood Reporter*.

"I am 36-years-old . . .": *Hollywood Citizen-News*, September 27, 1944.

"We had a wonderful . . .": *Los Angeles Examiner*, January 14, 1951.

"I first met Jay . . .": *Los Angeles Times*, 1971.

"I quite naturally . . .": press release, Warner Brothers Archives.

"[She] would have . . .": *Ladies Home Journal*, July 1941.

"We had a . . .": interview with the author.

S

"Sadat emerged . . .": *This 'N That* by Bette Davis.

"I'll never forget . . .": press release, Warner Brothers Archives.

"I'd be willing . . .": *Los Angeles Times*, July 13, 1936.

"I hope this will . . .": *The Hollywood Reporter*, October 9, 1989.

"I didn't know . . .": *Los Angeles Times*, September 18, 1960.

"It was very . . .": interview with the author.

"After working . . .": telegram, Warner Brothers Archives.

"She really wasn't . . .": interview with the author.

"Everyone blames TV . . .": *Los Angeles Mirror News*, March 14, 1960.

"I was *ghastly* . . .": *Screen Facts* by Gene Ringgold, 1965.

"Miss Sermak . . .": *Exposure*, December 1988/January 1989.

"During the sexual . . .": "Larry King Live," 1988.

"When you're directing . . .": "Geraldo," 1989.

"*This* was the worst . . .": *Collier's*, December 9, 1955.

"We just professed . . .": *Los Angeles Examiner*, November 19, 1949.

"In a suit . . .": *Modern Screen*, August 1947.

"Divorce is . . .": *Los Angeles Times*, October 22, 1949.

"I've told her . . .": *Los Angeles Daily News*, October 25, 1949.

"I believe everything . . .": *Los Angeles Evening Herald*, October 1949.

"Miss Davis . . .": *Los Angeles Times*, November 10, 1949.

"Personally, I am glad . . .": *Los Angeles Examiner*, November 10, 1949.

"She hadn't told . . .": *Los Angeles Daily News*, April 6, 1950.

"She is plenty . . .": *Los Angeles Herald-Express*, April 6, 1950.

"My wife is . . .": *Los Angeles Herald-Express*, April 7, 1950.

"[Frank] is not . . .": letter, Warner Brothers Archives.

"When I heard . . .": *Body and Soul* by Larry Swindell.

"What am I . . .": press release, Warner Brothers Archives.

"They were not . . .": *Exposure*.

"Again you . . .": memo, Warner Brothers Archives.

"Hell's bells . . .": press release, Warner Brothers Archives.

"Mr. Howard . . .": *Variety*, June 24, 1980.

"If Julie were . . .": memo, Warner Brothers Archives.

"I should say . . .": *Silver Screen*, August 1939.

"There's no sense . . .": *New York Times*, September 7, 1952.

"I'd have given . . .": *Drama-Logue*, November 25, 1982.

"She gave Michael . . .": *Bette, Rita, and the Rest of My Life* by Gary Merrill.

"I had no idea . . .": *Hollywood Citizen-News*, August 30, 1944.

"These Hollywood men . . .": *PM*, July 8, 1945.

"Despite what she . . .": *The Celluloid Muse* by Charles Higham and Joel Greenbaum.

"Since the decision . . .": *Variety*, September 19, 1952.

"I won't be . . .": *New York Times*, June 5, 1955.

"We're a fine pair . . .": *New York Times*, June 5, 1955.

"I think this is . . .": *Variety*, July 6, 1955.

"Our picture *is* a . . .": *Christian Science Monitor*, April 3, 1956.

"Yes, *The Library* . . .": *Christian Science Monitor*.

"I've never worked . . .": *The Hollywood Reporter*, May 11, 1979.

"It was actually . . .": *The Hollywood Reporter*, May 11, 1979.

"Of all human . . .": *Ladies Home Journal*, April 1985.

"With a stable . . .": *Los Angeles Times*, June 9, 1946.

"There isn't any . . .": press release, Warner Brothers Archives.

"It was like lightning . . .": BBC documentary.

"Gary and I . . .": *Chicago Sunday Tribune*, December 3, 1950.

T

"We are not married . . .": *Los Angeles Times*, May 14, 1940.

"I *adore* television . . .": *TV Guide*, May 31, 1958.

"I must say . . .": *Hollywood Citizen-News*, April 2, 1958.

"I got so sick . . .": CBS-TV press biography, 1987.

"After the show . . .": *This 'N That* by Bette Davis.

"I don't know why . . .": *New York Post*, August 5, 1986.

"I've never forgotten . . .": *Collier's*, November 25, 1955.

"The greatest actor . . .": San Sebastian Film Festival, September 1989.

"I had been approached . . .": *Los Angeles Times*, August 17, 1952.

"You've got to . . .": *Cue*, November 29, 1952.

"The theatre today . . .": *Los Angeles Times*, March 15, 1953.

U

"I-Magine! . . .": *Confessions of a Hollywood Columnist* by Sheila Graham.

"You should have . . .": AFI Tribute, 1977.

V

"I played the part . . .": *Los Angeles Times*, March 1, 1955.

"It's fantastic! . . .": *Los Angeles Times*, May 15, 1955.

W

"I would be willing . . .": letter, Warner Brothers Archives.

"I am justified . . .": *Los Angeles Times*, July 13, 1936.

"It is high time . . .": *Los Angeles Herald*, July 3, 1936.

"a bitter defeat . . .": *Collier's*, November 25, 1955.

"You can't win . . .": *Los Angeles Examiner*, November 19, 1936.

"I am ready . . .": letter, Warner Brothers Archives.

"I am sure . . .": telegram, Warner Brothers Archives

"From what I read . . .": telegram, Warner Brothers Archives.

"I'll just ease . . .": *Hollywood Citizen-News*, August 7, 1944.

"They just said . . .": *San Francisco Chronicle*, August 3, 1963.

"The men who . . .": *Los Angeles Times*, March 3, 1988.

"I miss motion . . .": CBS-TV press biography, 1987.

"After eight weeks . . .": *The Real Tinsel* by Bernard Rosenberg and Harry Silverstein.

"I just don't . . .": *Screen Facts* by Gene Ringgold.

"I would have liked . . .": *People*, November 2, 1987.

"I would look across . . .": *People*, November 2, 1987.

"very opinionated . . .": *The Lonely Life* by Bette Davis.

"Interestingly enough . . .": *Chicago Tribune*, December 30, 1987.

"I never smoke . . .": *People*, December 14, 1987.

"Oh dear . . .": *People*, December 14, 1987.

"Inside the lace . . .": *People*, December 14, 1987.

"It's clear from . . .": *People*, November 2, 1987.

"That face! . . .": *People*, December 14, 1987.

"You'd just . . .": *The Hollywood Reporter*, October 9, 1989.

"A soundstage . . .": *People*, November 2, 1987.

"If Joan and I . . .": *New York World-Telegram*, June 7, 1948.

"My immediate problem . . .": *New York Times*, November 4, 1962.

"I have the . . .": press material, Warner Brothers Archives.

"Director Bob . . .": *Los Angeles Times*, September 14, 1962.

"I *do* hope . . .": *This 'N That* by Bette Davis.

"Dear Bette . . .": telegram, Warner Brothers Archives.

"Before *Baby Jane* . . .": *San Francisco Chronicle*, August 3, 1963.

"Most female stars . . .": *It's a Hell of a Life but Not a Bad Living* by Edward Dmytryk.

"I am very . . .": letter, Warner Brothers Archives.

"I sent it . . .": *Los Angeles Daily News*, October 14, 1947.

"In *Winter Meeting* . . .": *Los Angeles Daily News*, August 19, 1949.

"This woman is a . . .": press release, Warner Brothers Archives.

"I figure that the . . .": press release, Warner Brothers Archives.

"I am taking a . . .": memo, Warner Brothers Archives.

"The first day we . . .": AFI Tribute, 1977.

"saw what real . . .": *Variety*, November 6, 1989.

"It was the best . . .": *Los Angeles Times*, September 18, 1960.

"It's a joy . . .": *The Hollywood Reporter*, November 3, 1959.

"While the contributions . . .": *Hollywood Citizen-News*, March 2, 1960.

"I wouldn't have missed . . .": *Los Angeles Times*, September 18, 1960.

"In Detroit . . .": *Los Angeles Times*, December 1, 1991.

Y

"There stood this . . .": *Parade*.

THE PHOTOGRAPHS

Photo research for this project was conducted by Neal Hitchens.

Cinema Collectors
Pages: 2, 7, 18, 28, 54, 59, 62, 64, 75, 85, 104, 105, 115, 119, 145, 146, 162, 165, 180, 183, 200, 207, 231, 235, 239, 292, 294, 295, 300, 310, 324, 330, 337, 347, 351, 368, 369, 393, 421, 454, 471, 503

Larry Edmunds Bookshop
Pages: 21, 39, 41, 45, 68, 73, 79, 96, 139, 173, 215, 227, 253, 262, 273, 295, 304, 312, 358, 372, 375, 401, 410, 416, 419, 431, 475

The Randall Riese Collection
Pages: 8, 44, 119, 124, 126, 129, 176, 209, 218, 233, 251, 276, 284, 337, 354, 428, 435, 461, 480

The William Roy Collection
Pages: 95, 377

Collectors Book Store
Pages: viii, 58, 83, 114, 118, 218, 226, 267, 282, 315, 316, 321, 358, 364, 365, 379, 385, 396, 403, 408, 422, 428, 433, 435, 479, 480

Adieu, Ruth Elizabeth Davis.
You did it brilliantly.

Robert Osborne, *The Hollywood Reporter*,
October 9, 1989